Dictionary of Literary Biography

Dictionary of Literary Biography Documentary Series

Dictionary of Literary Biography Yearbooks

1980 edited by Karen L. Rood, Jean W. Ross, and Richard Ziegfeld (1981)

1981 edited by Karen L. Rood, Jean W. Ross, and Richard Ziegfeld (1982)

1982 edited by Richard Ziegfeld; associate editors: Jean W. Ross and Lynne C. Zeigler (1983)

1983 edited by Mary Bruccoli and Jean W. Ross; associate editor Richard Ziegfeld (1984)

1984 edited by Jean W. Ross (1985)

1985 edited by Jean W. Ross (1986)

1986 edited by J. M. Brook (1987)

1987 edited by J. M. Brook (1988)

1988 edited by J. M. Brook (1989)

1989 edited by J. M. Brook (1990)

1990 edited by James W. Hipp (1991)

1991 edited by James W. Hipp (1992)

1992 edited by James W. Hipp (1993)

1993 edited by James W. Hipp, contributing editor George Garrett (1994)

1994 edited by James W. Hipp, contributing editor George Garrett (1995)

1995 edited by James W. Hipp, contributing editor George Garrett (1996)

1996 edited by Samuel W. Bruce and L. Kay Webster, contributing editor George Garrett (1997)

1997 edited by Matthew J. Bruccoli and George Garrett, with the assistance of L. Kay Webster (1998)

1998 edited by Matthew J. Bruccoli, contributing editor George Garrett, with the assistance of D. W. Thomas (1999)

1999 edited by Matthew J. Bruccoli, contributing editor George Garrett, with the assistance of D. W. Thomas (2000)

2000 edited by Matthew J. Bruccoli, contributing editor George Garrett, with the assistance of George Parker Anderson (2001)

2001 edited by Matthew J. Bruccoli, contributing editor George Garrett, with the assistance of George Parker Anderson (2002)

Concise Series

Concise Dictionary of American Literary Biography, 7 volumes (1988–1999): *The New Consciousness, 1941–1968; Colonization to the American Renaissance, 1640–1865; Realism, Naturalism, and Local Color, 1865–1917; The Twenties, 1917–1929; The Age of Maturity, 1929–1941; Broadening Views, 1968–1988; Supplement: Modern Writers, 1900–1998.*

Concise Dictionary of British Literary Biography, 8 volumes (1991–1992): *Writers of the Middle Ages and Renaissance Before 1660; Writers of the Restoration and Eighteenth Century, 1660–1789; Writers of the Romantic Period, 1789–1832; Victorian Writers, 1832–1890; Late-Victorian and Edwardian Writers, 1890–1914; Modern Writers, 1914–1945; Writers After World War II, 1945–1960; Contemporary Writers, 1960 to Present.*

Concise Dictionary of World Literary Biography, 10 volumes projected (1999–   ): *Ancient Greek and Roman Writers; German Writers; African, Caribbean, and Latin American Writers; South Slavic and Eastern European Writers.*

Twentieth-Century American Nature Writers: Prose

Twentieth-Century American Nature Writers: Prose

Edited by
Roger Thompson
Virginia Military Institute

and

J. Scott Bryson
Mount St. Mary's College

A Bruccoli Clark Layman Book

GALE®

Detroit • New York • San Diego • San Francisco • Cleveland • New Haven, Conn. • Waterville, Maine • London • Munich

THOMSON
★
GALE ™

Dictionary of Literary Biography
Volume 275: Twentieth-Century
American Nature Writers: Prose
Roger Thompson and J. Scott Bryson

Advisory Board
John Baker
William Cagle
Patrick O'Connor
George Garrett
Trudier Harris
Alvin Kernan
Kenny J. Williams

Editorial Directors
Matthew J. Bruccoli and Richard Layman

© 2003 by Gale. Gale is an imprint of
The Gale Group, Inc., a division of
Thomson Learning, Inc.

Gale and Design™ and Thomson Learning™
are trademarks used herein under license.

For more information, contact
The Gale Group, Inc.
27500 Drake Rd.
Farmington Hills, MI 48331-3535
Or you can visit our Internet site at
http://www.gale.com

While every effort has been made to
ensure the reliability of the information
presented in this publication, The Gale
Group, Inc. does not guarantee the accuracy of
the data contained herein. The Gale Group,
Inc. accepts no payment for listing; and inclusion in the publication of any organization,
agency, institution, publication, service, or
individual does not imply endorsement of the
editors or publisher. Errors brought to the
attention of the publisher and verified to the
satisfaction of the publisher will be corrected
in future editions.

LIBRARY OF CONGRESS CATALOGING-IN-PUBLICATION DATA

Twentieth-century American nature writers : prose / edited by Roger Thompson and
J. Scott Bryson.
          p. cm. — (Dictionary of literary biography; v. 275)
"A Bruccoli Clark Layman book."
Includes bibliographical references and index.
    ISBN 0-7876-6019-1
    1. American prose literature—20th century—Bio-bibliography—
Dictionaries. 2. Natural history—United States—Bio-bibliography—
Dictionaries. 3. Authors, American—20th century—Biography—
Dictionaries.
    4. Naturalists—United States—Biography—Dictionaries.
    5. Nature in literature—Dictionaries. I. Thompson, Roger, 1970–
II. Bryson, J. Scott, 1968– III. Series.

PS366.N36T94 2002

Printed in the United States of America
10 9 8 7 6 5 4 3 2 1

For the Endres Family

Contents

Plan of the Series

. . . Almost the most prodigious asset of a country, and perhaps its most precious possession, is its native literary product— when that product is fine and noble and enduring.

Mark Twain*

The advisory board, the editors, and the publisher of the *Dictionary of Literary Biography* are joined in endorsing Mark Twain's declaration. The literature of a nation provides an inexhaustible resource of permanent worth. Our purpose is to make literature and its creators better understood and more accessible to students and the reading public, while satisfying the needs of teachers and researchers.

To meet these requirements, *literary biography* has been construed in terms of the author's achievement. The most important thing about a writer is his writing. Accordingly, the entries in *DLB* are career biographies, tracing the development of the author's canon and the evolution of his reputation.

The purpose of *DLB* is not only to provide reliable information in a usable format but also to place the figures in the larger perspective of literary history and to offer appraisals of their accomplishments by qualified scholars.

The publication plan for *DLB* resulted from two years of preparation. The project was proposed to Bruccoli Clark by Frederick G. Ruffner, president of the Gale Research Company, in November 1975. After specimen entries were prepared and typeset, an advisory board was formed to refine the entry format and develop the series rationale. In meetings held during 1976, the publisher, series editors, and advisory board approved the scheme for a comprehensive biographical dictionary of persons who contributed to literature. Editorial work on the first volume began in January 1977, and it was published in 1978. In order to make *DLB* more than a dictionary and to compile volumes that individually have claim to status as literary history, it was decided to organize volumes by topic, period, or

From an unpublished section of Mark Twain's autobiography, copyright by the Mark Twain Company

genre. Each of these freestanding volumes provides a biographical-bibliographical guide and overview for a particular area of literature. We are convinced that this organization—as opposed to a single alphabet method— constitutes a valuable innovation in the presentation of reference material. The volume plan necessarily requires many decisions for the placement and treatment of authors. Certain figures will be included in separate volumes, but with different entries emphasizing the aspect of his career appropriate to each volume. Ernest Hemingway, for example, is represented in *American Writers in Paris, 1920–1939* by an entry focusing on his expatriate apprenticeship; he is also in *American Novelists, 1910–1945* with an entry surveying his entire career, as well as in *American Short-Story Writers, 1910–1945, Second Series* with an entry concentrating on his short fiction. Each volume includes a cumulative index of the subject authors and articles.

Since 1981 the series has been further augmented by the *DLB Yearbooks,* which update published entries, add new entries to keep the *DLB* current with contemporary activity, and provide articles on literary history. There have also been nineteen *DLB Documentary Series* volumes, which provide illustrations, facsimiles, and biographical and critical source materials for figures, works, or groups judged to have particular interest for students. In 1999 the *Documentary Series* was incorporated into the *DLB* volume numbering system beginning with *DLB 210: Ernest Hemingway.*

We define literature as the *intellectual commerce of a nation:* not merely as belles lettres but as that ample and complex process by which ideas are generated, shaped, and transmitted. *DLB* entries are not limited to "creative writers" but extend to other figures who in their time and in their way influenced the mind of a people. Thus the series encompasses historians, journalists, publishers, book collectors, and screenwriters. By this means readers of *DLB* may be aided to perceive literature not as cult scripture in the keeping of intellectual high priests but firmly positioned at the center of a nation's life.

DLB includes the major writers appropriate to each volume and those standing in the ranks behind them. Scholarly and critical counsel has been sought in deciding which minor figures to include and how full their entries should be. Wherever possible, useful references are made to figures who do not warrant separate entries.

Each *DLB* volume has an expert volume editor responsible for planning the volume, selecting the figures for inclusion, and assigning the entries. Volume editors are also responsible for preparing, where appropriate, appendices surveying the major periodicals and literary and intellectual movements for their volumes, as well as lists of further readings. Work on the series as a whole is coordinated at the Bruccoli Clark Layman editorial center in Columbia, South Carolina, where the editorial staff is responsible for accuracy and utility of the published volumes.

One feature that distinguishes *DLB* is the illustration policy—its concern with the iconography of literature. Just as an author is influenced by his surroundings, so is the reader's understanding of the author enhanced by a knowledge of his environment. Therefore *DLB* volumes include not only drawings, paintings, and photographs of authors, often depicting them at various stages in their careers, but also illustrations of their families and places where they lived. Title pages are regularly reproduced in facsimile along with dust jackets for modern authors. The dust jackets are a special feature of *DLB* because they often document better than anything else the way in which an author's work was perceived in its own time. Specimens of the writers' manuscripts and letters are included when feasible.

Samuel Johnson rightly decreed that "The chief glory of every people arises from its authors." The purpose of the *Dictionary of Literary Biography* is to compile literary history in the surest way available to us—by accurate and comprehensive treatment of the lives and work of those who contributed to it.

The *DLB* Advisory Board

Introduction

The 1995 publication of Lawrence Buell's *The Environmental Imagination* (Cambridge: Belknap Press of Harvard University Press) marked the coming of age of a critical movement that has made *Dictionary of Literary Biography* volumes on American nature writing possible. While Buell was certainly not the first to offer an interpretation of literature in terms of the influence or range of ideas about nature, his work has validated the critical projects of those who preceded him and has given credibility to the emerging field of ecocriticism. *The Environmental Imagination* is in part a reassertion of Leo Marx's insistence that nature is a central theme of literary texts—as outlined in *The Machine in the Garden* (1964)—but it is also a wholesale reconfiguration of some of the basic assumptions governing Marx's work. Buell addresses the questions of how our reading shapes our ethical values and how those in turn concretely affect our environment. To answer these questions, he reenvisions reading with "biota," or the living world, as the central point of reference, a move that results in a "greening" of acts of literacy. His theory is a complete reconfiguration of how the imagination involves real-world actions, a reconfiguration centered on the role of the environment in human action. In lending his recognizable and well-regarded name to such an ambitious movement, Buell has given legitimacy to what has been (and still is, by some) considered a suspect and minor field of literary criticism; he has given legitimacy to a new way of reading literary texts.

The power of recent ecocritical work has proceeded not just from analyses of the traditional field of nature writing but also from an expansion of the field. While Buell's work focuses on some traditional canonical figures in American nature writing, especially Henry David Thoreau, the mode of inquiry that it establishes ensures that certain writers who have been ignored by literary studies will have new importance; if literary criticism involves an understanding of ecologies at stake, then a new range of authors suddenly has become central to understanding the cultural work of literature. Thus, the domain of literary studies must now account for a genre of writing previously relegated to the periphery of intellectual inquiry.

These volumes of the *Dictionary of Literary Biography,* then, might be seen as a result of the expansion of the discipline that follows from Buell's work. The present volume, on twentieth-century American prose nature writers, will be followed by a volume on American nature poets. We conceive of these volumes on twentieth-century American nature writing as a starting point for those who want to explore the field, and the classification of the volumes by prose and poetry reflects the emergence of nature writing as a distinct genre as well as the direction of current ecological criticism. "Nature writing" has traditionally been associated with nonfiction prose that focuses entirely on environmental concerns, so that in the traditional conception of nature writing, any themes that the work addresses are subsumed under and examined in light of the author's conception of nature. In recent years, the categories of nature writing have been expanded to include not only nonfiction prose but fiction as well. Critics have argued that writers of fiction whose works center on the pastoral or the agrarian as a theme have often been involved in cultural projects similar to those of writers of nonfiction, so that the work of Nathaniel Hawthorne, for instance, whose writing examines an idealistic agrarian existence in *The Blithedale Romance* (1852), converges in significant ways with that of Henry David Thoreau in *Walden* (1854). Similarly, nature writing as a category has expanded to include environmental poetry, variously labeled nature poetry or ecopoetry. The examination of poetry as performing environmental cultural work has led to new considerations for how the boundaries of nature writing should be drawn, and it has led us to create a separate volume for the biographies of nature poets.

In selecting which prose nature writers to include in the present volume, we relied primarily on the status of a particular writer within academic discourse about the genre and were more concerned with reflecting the current framework of the field than with providing new directions for future studies. The volume includes many names familiar even outside of the discipline—Edward Abbey, John Muir, Rachel Carson, Annie Dillard, and John Burroughs. The writers who are not as widely recognized have nonetheless received scholarly attention in the humanities. Also, we have limited the selections to writers whose reputations were forged primarily in the United States, because the explosion in recent years of nature writers from Canada, in particular, has required us to limit our choices by geographic boundaries in order to ensure an appropriate depth of coverage for the American writers. Both Canada and the British Isles have a sufficient number of writers to merit their own volumes.

Other distinctions governed the selections—among them choices on how to categorize writers who write extensively in pastoral or agrarian modes but who might not be considered self-consciously concerned with producing "nature writing." The wealth of writers whose purpose is primarily the production of texts that centralize a concept of nature led us to remove from consideration many fiction writers or early travel writers. While we see great value in their work and in the critical scholarship that focuses on their ecological concerns, we feel that consideration of their concerns might better be suited for other venues. (Indeed, many of those authors are covered in other volumes of the *DLB;* Sarah Orne Jewett and Jack London are examples.)

In many ways, the selections reflect one of the primary characteristics of nature writing—highlighting the role of nature in order to effect social and environmental change. Each of the authors covered in this volume has in some way argued for that change: some, such as Edward Abbey, on a national basis; others, such as Sigurd Olson, on a regional basis; and still others within highly specialized fields of study, such as Lewis Thomas, a physician. Other literatures at times involve projects of cultural transformation, but nature writing from its inception has sought to reconfigure cultural standards of the value of nature. Likewise, nature writing is not solely an activist phenomenon. Its adherents are artists as well, and creating literature is almost always a chief aim of a nature writer.

The rise of nature writing in America coincided with the burgeoning of the natural sciences from the late eighteenth through the early twentieth centuries. The status of the Swedish botanist Carl Linnaeus (1707–1778) in establishing a means of scientific categorization is well documented, and his scientific arrangement of such categories as class, genus, and species governed to a greater or lesser degree much of the early nature writing. Indeed, the impetus to categorize the natural world was overwhelming in the eighteenth and nineteenth centuries, and the process of categorization and cataloguing relied on a metaphysic that often held unquestioningly to the centrality of humans. According to this worldview, humankind was at best "namer" and at worst "conqueror" of the natural world, and its domain was the lands newly discovered through the

technological advances in marine exploration. Among the lands were the Americas, where European power sought to control and expand its vision of humanity and the wilderness. The early European explorers brought with them the impetus to control and categorize, and the wilderness became a tablet on which to inscribe a new, infallible way of explaining existence.

As civilization achieved more control over the wilderness in early America, a self-conscious concern with the development of a new American literature appeared. The drive for the United States to assert itself as a distinct literary nation culminated in the middle of the nineteenth century with writers such as Ralph Waldo Emerson, whose "The American Scholar" (1837) was hailed by Oliver Wendell Holmes as "America's intellectual Declaration of Independence." This intellectual independence was often couched in terms of the relationship of America with nature. Emerson claims in *Nature* (1836) that "All science has one aim, namely, to find a theory of nature," and that theory is intimately related to the development of an American ethos. In his lecture "The Method of Nature" (1841), Emerson states explicitly that his purpose is to show that the method of nature is "transferable to literary life," invoking organic metaphors to explain not simply the function of the mind but the function of the spiritual in the American mind. Similarly, Thoreau, in the *Walden* chapter "Sounds," relates the United States expansion westward by the railroad to the expansion of intellectual boundaries, both described in terms of a spiritually charged natural world. For many writers of the American Renaissance, connection with nature implied metaphorical connection with the divine, so that nature and God became inextricably yoked together. While not pantheism, the metaphorical conception spiritualized the power of nature and significantly impacted questions of moral authority and action.

This expansion of the moral sense and character of America was often part of American expansion into the wilderness, so that John D. Godman (1794–1830) could claim early in the nineteenth century that among the virtues of the natural world were not only its usefulness in supplying people with natural resources but also its ability to inspire and teach humankind about the relationships between living things. With the connection came a sense of moral responsibility that, in the case of Godman, encouraged use of natural resources to benefit humans only in light of understanding broad impacts of that use on the availability of wildlife and natural resources. The sense of his works, and other works of the time, was that land was plentiful and its use a verification of God's divine plan for the expansion of a new ideal state. Spirituality, then, became a means to justify the use of land for agricultural, commercial, and industrial purposes, and while humankind was aware of other uses of the forest, the lakes, the seas, and the meadows (uses such as contemplation of God), those uses had to work in concert with material uses, such as production of lumber and agricultural goods. A conception of nature as spiritual guide and beacon, in other words, included a conception of nature as producer of the fuel for the new American state.

With this relationship of nature and spirit in the foreground, a tension between nature as place of divine will and nature as product for an expanding nation-state took center stage by the mid nineteenth century. The rise of the American industrial state came at a time when Americans were confronting the wilderness in a wide range of writings, such as travel literature, Western realist literature, and Southern and Western humorist literature. In all of these, the tension between open space and the control of that space figured as a central theme, and nature writing confronted this concern directly. In works such as *Walden,* the desire to confront use of land and the ethics of that use led authors to negotiate concerns as apparently disparate as the expansion westward, the role of the divine in nature, and the intrusion of society and social mores in natural settings. These concerns are apparent even in works that are less often considered nature writing. For instance, Thomas Bangs Thorpe (1815–1878), the Southwest humorist, began his collection of sketches *The Hive of 'The Bee Hunter'* (1854) with a conscious juxtaposition of loss of land and loss of a certain kind of self: "As a country becomes cleared up and settled, Bee-hunters disappear; consequently they are seldom or ever noticed." While Thorpe's tales are not explicitly concerned with the recovery of natural spaces, his work nonetheless confronts the ways in which the clearing of wilderness affects society: for Thorpe, the "bee-hunters" were men of mythic importance to society and disappeared with the loss of the wild.

The late nineteenth century marked the beginning of nature writing overtly concerned with the preservation of wilderness and a repudiation of the moral propriety that propelled the expansion. Literary naturalism, in its rejection of the romanticism of antebellum writing, not only called into question conceptions of self, but, with its rejection of the transcendentalists' human-centered perspective on existence, called for a complete revision of the dominant perception of the power of nature. In works by Stephen Crane, Bret Harte, and, perhaps the most studied, Jack London, the inexorable power of nature dwarfs humanity. For the literary naturalist, humankind became simply another animal competing in the natural arena for survival.

Even so, just as literary naturalism matured, a greater awareness of the precariousness of the natural world arose. Writers such as John Muir and John Burroughs began to declare that for all of its ability to overwhelm humankind, the natural world was being destroyed in significant ways by humanity. The turn of the nineteenth century, then, was a time of an odd tension between a literary naturalism that demonstrated humankind's failings and a scientific naturalism that demonstrated the limits of the natural world. The publication in 1903 of both London's *Call of the Wild* and Mary Austin's *The Land of Little Rain* illustrates the tension: the two books are in many ways desperately at odds, London's a central text of literary naturalism and Austin's a central text of nature writing, but both share a desire to describe the natural environment in new ways. For London, the North was the place of nature in almost complete control of man, whereas for Austin, the West was a place of inquiry into humanity's relationship with the natural world. While the works might differ in means, both helped bring an awareness to and a revision of people's thinking about the natural world and the place of humankind within it.

The type of awareness that came to a pitch in the early twentieth century first emerged in the late nineteenth century and was the key to the creation of the first national park, Yellowstone, in 1872. Shortly afterward, with the creation of Yosemite National Park in 1890, the possibilities of nature writing changed even more significantly. Yosemite was important because its creation demonstrated the way in which nature writers could effect social and environmental change. John Muir's writings and lifework ultimately led to the creation of the park, and his work continued later with the creation of the Sierra Club, an organization that continues to follow some of Muir's most fundamental ideas.

Following Muir, the creation of parklands or other open spaces often became the goal of nature writers in the twentieth century. In authors as diverse as Theodore Roosevelt and Aldo Leopold, the move toward creation of protected areas became part of the mission of their writing. Early nature writers were aware of the need to protect wilderness, and they often worked toward an environmental consciousness, but after the work of Muir, nature writers became self-consciously aware of their ability to shape national policy governing environmental concerns. Early naturalists, of course, were aware that their writing could have a profound impact on the governance of nature. Louis Agassiz (1807–1873), for example, created a group called the "Scientific Lazzaroni," whose purpose was influencing governmental policy toward science and the environment. The Lazzaroni created the proposal that established the National Academy of Sciences, which

President Abraham Lincoln signed into law in 1863. Agassiz was aware of the persuasive impact of nature writing, but the range of influence for such arguments was limited by contention within the federal government.

As the United States simultaneously centralized its governmental power and expanded westward to claim more land as its own, the way in which nature writers could effect change in policy shifted dramatically. For example, Thoreau's work had been seen as an extended argument for the preservation of a limited domain, but with expansion westward and with the rapidly growing consumption of the wilderness places in the West, Muir conceived of his writing as a way to preserve broad stretches of the environment, and he conceived of a more centralized federal government that had the strength and reach to make sweeping national legislation. Nature writing, in its role, its style, its audience, and its arguments, had to be conceived not only in terms of westward American expansion but also, following the Civil War, in terms of focusing power in the federal government.

The frequency with which many twentieth-century writers alluded to Muir and the founding of national parks is perhaps the best testament to the reconception of nature writing. No longer predominantly a place of spiritual contemplation or of consumption and discovery, nature became the site of mediated politics. Nature writing emerged in the early twentieth century as a politicized space, and it became more self-consciously rhetorical. Of course, the politics of nature varied widely (Roosevelt's concerns were, to say the least, not exactly the same as Leopold's), and these variations reflected significant social considerations of the time. The movement from booming economy to crippling depression, bracketed by two world wars, profoundly changed how nature writers went about their work. For many, the wars and the Great Depression gave new weight to what Buell has called "restorationism," or the demonstration of how natural places matter and why environmental reform is needed. Restoration of wilderness in the early and mid twentieth century meant confronting the loss of natural habitats through a demonstration of their worth to a rapidly expanding industrial state. Nature writers as different as Joseph Wood Krutch and Donald Culross Peattie illustrated the various ways to conceive of environmental change: Krutch focused on natural history and considerations of the relationship between humans and animals, and Peattie on what might be called a rebirth of new naturalized life in post-Depression America. Both, however, employed new variations on the themes of social action and awareness initiated in the writings of Muir.

These variations broadened considerably as the twentieth century advanced, and once again, they must be considered in terms of American social and cultural currents. The exponential rise in both the industrial state and the technology that accompanied it became a central concern of nature writers. In addition, the proliferation of weapons of mass destruction and wars throughout the twentieth century was often the backdrop for the writers, to the degree that some, such as nature poet W. S. Merwin, consciously yoked environmental writing with antiwar poetry. Lewis Thomas, a medical doctor and an expansive writer on concerns of the natural world, approached directly the dangers of nuclear proliferation in terms of human relationship to the environment, including the microscopic environment of human cell life.

The potential destruction of natural spaces, microscopic and macroscopic, however, was not the only context for twentieth-century nature writers. The rise in technology was part of the expansion and specialization of the sciences, and the fields of inquiry that the sciences opened have proven fertile ground for the development of the nature essay. John McPhee relied on extensive knowledge of the most recent understanding of geology in his *Annals of the Former World* (1998), and Lewis Thomas forged connections between the world of nature and the world of science that are possible only from a writer well versed in the medical sciences. The nature essay, then, developed at times into a personalized science essay, the purpose of which was to demonstrate a connection between science and the natural world, not only in terms of content but also in terms of form and style. The scientific nature essay bridged the gap between the specialized domain of scientific discourse and the more democratic domain of American nature writing.

This desire to exploit connections may well be the hallmark of the contemporary nature essay. It invokes a notion of wholeness and interconnectedness to the exclusion of the nineteenth-century predilection for invoking deity. This exclusion of "God" in contemporary nature writing might be read as a repudiation of the Judeo-Christian duality that is often blamed for giving rise to a concept of self and "other" that encourages the destruction of the environment. Many writers, chief among them Lynn White Jr., have remarked on the way in which early representations of nature as a fallen Eden led to a justification of its exploitation. Even so, nature writers have not completely abandoned an idea of spiritual power; instead, spiritual power in nature writing is often yoked to "wholeness" or unity or a comprehensive vision of a holistic social structure that centralizes the role of nature in human life. Humankind, then, is made part of a larger web of relations that are at once independent and interdependent, separate but invariably connected.

To suggest that contemporary nature writers argue for a sense of interconnectedness is to suggest that they are part of broader social concerns that seek similar aims. The concern of contemporary nature writing with forging connections may be read as emerging from a culture of the 1960s from which rose various groups seeking power in the American democracy. The rise of the women's movement, the increase in African nationalism, and the push for sexual freedom all contributed to a fundamental mood of the late twentieth century that sought a reconfiguration of social mores, and nature writers have made many such claims. The first "Earth Day," for example, was celebrated in 1970, shortly after the halting of United States whaling and the same year as many disruptions of the American social fabric. Indeed, the convergence of environmental and social awareness groups has been so strong that popular conceptions of "tree huggers" and "bark munchers" have relied on connecting the image of environmentalists with hippies or, at the very least, "bleeding heart liberals." In some instances, those connections have been couched in terms of latent violence, as in the case of Abbey's fiction, so that environmentalism became associated with radical social reconstruction.

Such convergence, moreover, has taken place not only in the popular consciousness but also as part of the American university. In the late twentieth century a reconfiguration of literary studies included redefinitions of literary critic and literary artist as cultural critic and cultural artist. As territory of cultural critics and artists, the academy has courted the creation of new, specialized domains of knowledge, one of them ecocriticism. The emergence of ecocriticism as a distinct field of inquiry parallels the reemergence of literary critic as cultural activist, and the result for the field of nature writing has been a clear connection between environmental criticism and social action. Ecocriticism has tended to present nature writing in terms of its impact on cultural awareness of the environment and any accompanying social action. In addition, it has forged connections between critical concerns never before considered, such as the connection between race, gender, and the environment. For the ecocritic, any inquiry into literature of the environment brings with it a set of broad concerns about social structure and power, so that to raise questions about the environment is to raise questions about, for instance, race and representations of race in society. The result of this view is a broadening of the field of nature writing: works such as those of Leslie Marmon Silko, for example, which have introduced important questions about what it means to be Native American, are shown by the ecocritic to connect that sense of race with representations of the environment.

Such connections have expanded considerably the field of nature writing. Works previously considered only in light of gender-centered or race-centered criticism have been shown to illustrate significant politics about natural space as well. The significance of nature writing and, perhaps more broadly, writing that confronts environmental concerns is, at root, interdisciplinary. In the humanities, ecocriticism has demonstrated that fluency with nature writing demands fluency with a variety of theoretical perspectives, and it demands at least a working knowledge of some basic scientific principles that inform environmental writing.

Thus, American nature writing (along with the ecocriticism that studies it) has essentially stayed true to its Linnaean, classificatory, scientific roots. An impetus exists to categorize nature itself throughout the canon of American nature writing, as well as in the assessments of nature writing by ecocritics and environmental historians. Thomas J. Lyon's important anthology of nature writing, *This Incomperable Lande: A Book of American Nature Writing* (1989), for instance, sets out in its introduction a "taxonomy" of nature writing, including "natural history essays," "field guides and professional papers," and "rambles," and assigns different authors to each category. While Lyon takes great pains to suggest the fluidity of the boundaries he draws, the chart and subsequent discussions of the categories illustrate in clear detail the way in which even the idea of nature writing as a genre owes considerable debt to Linnaeus's methodology. The assessment of that debt is the work of ecocritics and is not in the scope of this introduction; nonetheless, a clear connection to the rise of the natural sciences in early America must be acknowledged as an important first step in the evolution of the genre of nature writing and its current embodiments and appraisals.

As Peter Fritzell has pointed out in *Nature Writing and America: Essays upon a Cultural Type* (1990), however, this commitment to scientific classification and analysis represents only one of the two fundamental features of American nature writing. Combined with an "allegiance to extended scientific catalogues, descriptions, or explications" that American nature writers display is a significant amount of personal autobiography, and the tension that this juxtaposition creates has fashioned an inherently American genre, nature writing. As Fritzell explains, "nowhere in the world are (or were) disinterested biological or geological science and personal identity (or autobiography)—the two defining components of Thoreauvian nature writing—as closely or deeply related as they are (were and have been) in America." Reading the works of the authors represented in this volume makes clear that despite their many differences, these distinctly American nature writers, from the earliest to the most recent, have consistently sought to convey both their wonder at the natural world and their individual, personal experiences within it.

We would like to thank several people for their help in creating this volume. First, we would like to thank Wes Mott, whose early advice provided much needed reassurance. Penny Hope has been a careful, collegial, and skillful editor throughout the process, and Michael Martin has provided quick assistance when it was needed. Many scholars and colleagues, though not always able to contribute, provided critical insight, resources, and encouragement—among them Emily Miller, David Rachels, Kurt Ayau, Terry Gifford, David Backes, and Jim Warren. Annie Dillard and Bob Richardson were gracious with their time and energy at a crucial moment and deserve our most sincere thanks. The librarians at Virginia Military Institute and Mount St. Mary's College were helpful at various stages, and a summer Grant-in-Aid-of-Research from the Virginia Military Institute funded travel so that we could work together on final editing in May and early June 2002. We also thank some of the early influences in our interest for nature writing, among them the Thompson family, the Endres family, Fred Erisman, Lawrence Buell, Patrick Whalen, and Zach Mills. Lastly, we thank our families, particularly Laura Ter Poorten and Tina Bryson, who have offered unconditional support, encouragement, and, at auspicious moments, enthusiasm.

Acknowledgments

This book was produced by Bruccoli Clark Layman, Inc. Karen L. Rood is senior editor. Penelope M. Hope was the in-house editor.

Production manager is Philip B. Dematteis.

Administrative support was provided by Ann M. Cheschi and Carol A. Cheschi.

Accountant is Ann-Marie Holland.

Copyediting supervisor is Sally R. Evans. The copyediting staff includes Phyllis A. Avant, Caryl Brown, Melissa D. Hinton, Philip I. Jones, Rebecca Mayo, Nancy E. Smith, and Elizabeth Jo Ann Sumner.

Editorial associates are Amelia B. Lacey, Michael S. Martin, Catherine M. Polit, and William Mathes Straney.

In-house prevetting is by Nicole A. La Rocque.

Permissions editor and database manager is Amber L. Coker.

Layout and graphics supervisor is Janet E. Hill. The graphics staff includes Zoe R. Cook and Sydney E. Hammock.

Office manager is Kathy Lawler Merlette.

Photography supervisor is Paul Talbot. Photography editor is Scott Nemzek.

Digital photographic copy work was performed by Joseph M. Bruccoli and Zoe R. Cook.

Systems manager is Marie L. Parker.

Typesetting supervisor is Kathleen M. Flanagan. The typesetting staff includes Patricia Marie Flanagan, Mark J. McEwan, and Pamela D. Norton. Freelance typesetters are Wanda Adams and Rebecca Mayo.

Walter W. Ross did library research. He was assisted by Jo Cottingham and the following other librarians at the Thomas Cooper Library of the University of South Carolina: circulation department head Tucker Taylor; reference department head Virginia W. Weathers; reference department staff Brette Barron, Marilee Birchfield, Paul Cammarata, Gary Geer, Michael Macan, Tom Marcil, Rose Marshall, and Sharon Verba; interlibrary loan department head John Brunswick; and interlibrary loan staff Robert Arndt, Hayden Battle, Alex Byrne, Bill Fetty, Marna Hostetler, and Nelson Rivera.

Twentieth-Century American Nature Writers: Prose

Dictionary of Literary Biography

Edward Abbey

(29 January 1927 – 14 March 1989)

Bryan L. Moore
Arkansas State University

See also the Abbey entry in *DLB 256: Twentieth-Century American Western Writers, Third Series.*

BOOKS: *Jonathan Troy* (New York: Dodd, Mead, 1954);
The Brave Cowboy: An Old Tale in a New Time (New York: Dodd, Mead, 1956);
Fire on the Mountain (New York: Dial, 1962; London: Eyre & Spottiswoode, 1963);
Desert Solitaire: A Season in the Wilderness (New York: McGraw-Hill, 1968);
Appalachian Wilderness: The Great Smoky Mountains, photographs by Eliot Porter, text by Abbey (New York: Dutton, 1970);
Black Sun (New York: Simon & Schuster, 1971); republished as *Sunset Canyon* (London: Talmy, Franklin, 1972);
Slickrock: The Canyon Country of Southeast Utah, photographs by Philip Hyde, text by Abbey (San Francisco: Sierra Club Books, 1971);
Cactus Country (Alexandria, Va.: Time-Life Books, 1973);
The Monkey Wrench Gang (Philadelphia: Lippincott, 1975; Edinburgh: Canongate, 1978);
The Hidden Canyon: A River Journey, text by Abbey, photographs by John Blaustein (New York: Viking, 1977; Harmondsworth, U.K.: Penguin, 1977);
The Journey Home: Some Words in Defense of the American West (New York: Dutton, 1977);
Abbey's Road (New York: Dutton, 1979);
Desert Images: An American Landscape, text by Abbey, photographs by David Muench (New York: Harcourt Brace Jovanovich, 1979);
Good News (New York: Dutton, 1980);
Down the River with Henry David Thoreau and Friends (New York: Dutton, 1982);

Beyond the Wall: Essays from the Outside (New York: Holt, Rinehart & Winston, 1984);
In Praise of Mountain Lions, photographs by John Nichols, text by Abbey (Albuquerque: Albuquerque Sierra Club, 1984);
Confessions of a Barbarian, by Abbey, bound with *Red Knife Valley,* by Jack Curtis (Santa Barbara: Capra Press, 1986);
The Fool's Progress: An Honest Novel (New York: Holt, 1988);
One Life at a Time, Please (New York: Holt, 1988);
Vox Clamantis in Desert: Some Notes from a Secret Journal (Santa Fe: Rydal Press, 1989); republished as *A Voice Crying in the Wilderness (Vox Clamantis in Deserto): Notes from a Secret Journal* (New York: St. Martin's Press, 1990);
Hayduke Lives! (Boston: Little, Brown, 1990);
Confessions of a Barbarian: Selections from the Journals of Edward Abbey 1951–1989, edited by David Petersen (Boston: Little, Brown, 1994);
Journals of Edward Abbey (Boston: Little, Brown, 1994);
Desert Skin, photographs by Thomas Miller, essay by Abbey (Salt Lake City: University of Utah Press, 1994);
Earth Apples=(Pommes des terre): The Poetry of Edward Abbey, edited by Petersen (New York: St. Martin's Press, 1994).
Collections: *Slumgullion Stew: An Edward Abbey Reader,* edited by Abbey (New York: Dutton, 1984); republished as *The Best of Edward Abbey* (San Francisco: Sierra Club Books, 1988);
The Serpents of Paradise: A Reader, edited by John Macrae (New York: Holt, 1995).

PRODUCED SCRIPTS: *Lonely Are the Brave,* motion picture, by Abbey and Dalton Trumbo, Joel Productions, 1962;

3

Edward Abbey on 4 March 1989 at a Tucson Earth Rally, his final public appearance
(photograph © Charles Hedgcock)

Fire on the Mountain, television, by Abbey and John Sacret Young, NBC, 23 November 1981.

RECORDINGS: *Freedom and Wilderness,* read by Abbey, Audio Press, 1987;
Resist Much, Obey Little: The Writer as Social Critic, read by Abbey, New Dimensions Foundation, 1989.

OTHER: *Images from the Great West,* photographs by Marc Gaede, essay and quotations by A. B. Guthrie Jr., tribute by Abbey (La Canada, Cal.: Chaco Press, 1990).

Edward Abbey was one of the most important and most explicitly political American nature writers of the second half of the twentieth century. He, however, disliked the phrase "nature writing"; he preferred to think of himself as a novelist who wrote nonfiction pieces—which he termed "personal histories"—on the side. Few people have written with so much affection for freedom and wilderness, especially as represented by the desert Southwest, and with so much anger for the forces working against freedom and wilderness.

Larry McMurtry, as quoted from the cover of *Beyond the Wall: Essays from the Outside* (1984), has called Abbey "the Thoreau of the American West," and in many ways the title suits Abbey well. He was, similar to Henry David Thoreau, a superb prose stylist and a user of wit to question and counter ready-made ways of thinking. Both Thoreau and Abbey were individualists to the core, and Abbey shared Thoreau's great reverence for wilderness as humankind's ancestral home, the sole source of hope for freedom and humanity—a hope that, as Abbey was in more of an historical position to realize, is swiftly being taken away. Though Abbey rarely minced his words in his works, his outrage seldom outran his sense of humor. He was (again, similar to Thoreau) an inventive creator of aphorisms that subvert and reformulate banal clichés—for example, Abbey, eyes open to the realities of development in Alaska, whose motto is "the last frontier," refigured the state as "the last porkchop." Above all, as he himself frequently stated, Abbey was an entertaining writer. As Ann Ronald writes in *The New West of Edward Abbey* (2000), he "makes the reader laugh, and then think."

In addition to his nonfiction, Abbey wrote eight novels, but even in his fiction, he often wrote essentially about himself. He had an unparalleled talent for self-dramatization, and his writings, much like the writer himself, are full of contradictions. On the one hand, Abbey was a populist, a champion of the powerless against the powerful, a scathing critic of consumer society and greed, and an unparalleled defender of public wilderness. On the other hand, his views toward gender and race may with some accuracy be called ultraconservative; such views are, for some readers, an unresolvable impediment to reading Abbey at all. A longtime member of the National Rifle Association, his anarchism led him to, implicitly at least, espouse violence against corrupt government. Abbey's constant joking blurs the lines of his sociopolitical views, though a literal reading of his work may uncover the mind of a misanthropic modern-day American Luddite. As Edward Hoagland suggested in "Standing Tough in the Desert" (7 May 1989), Abbey "was a political radical but a social conservative."

He was never concerned, however, with making his views palatable for anyone. Not only did he not care if some found him offensive, but he actually seemed to take delight in being a gadfly. In his final collection of nonfiction essays he wrote, "If there's anyone still present whom I've failed to insult, I apologize." Critics have accused Abbey of undermining the environmental movement by not staying in line, by introducing controversial opinions into prose that otherwise eloquently defends the idea of wilderness. But Abbey never connected himself with any political action group except Earth First!, although he never officially allied himself to it. He was, as he said, a writer of personal histories, and Wendell Berry writes in "A Few Words in Favor of Edward Abbey," from the collection *Resist Much, Obey Little* (1985), that if Abbey "is writing as an autobiographer, he cannot be writing as an environmentalist."

Though he often claimed he was born in an old farmhouse near a small Appalachian town called Home, Edward Paul Abbey was in fact born ten miles away on 29 January 1927 in a hospital in Indiana, Pennsylvania. The oldest of five children, Abbey inherited some of his political attitude from his father, Paul Abbey, who was a registered socialist and a Wobbly (International Workers of the World) organizer. Abbey wrote that his father taught him "to hate injustice, to defy the powerful, and to speak for the voiceless." From his mother, Mildred Postlewaite Abbey, an elementary schoolteacher, he learned to love music and gained an appreciation for long walks. His appreciation of nature was derived, in part, from both parents. Until Abbey was well into his teens, the family moved around from place to place; for a period in the early 1930s, home for the Abbey family was the road and a series of campsites. By 1941 the family settled down at a small farm that Abbey dubbed "the Old Lonesome Briar Patch." Abbey's mother was a physically small but energetic woman—a pianist, organist, and choir leader at the local Washington Presbyterian Church—and she made sure that her children received religious instruction. Abbey, however, was skeptical toward religion from early on, and he carried this attitude with him into his adulthood. Later, writing in *The Journey Home: Some Words in Defense of the American West* (1977), he called himself an "earthiest" (rather than an atheist), and though in his works he makes no direct claims for a religious or mystical basis on which to preserve wilderness, he does suggest that nature, as it is perceived empirically, is, in an Emersonian sense, sacred: "Just as the earth itself forms the indispensable ground for the only kind of life we know . . . so does empirical truth constitute the foundation of higher truths."

Abbey exhibited some literary and artistic interests early in life by writing and illustrating cartoons. He learned to appreciate the beauty of the hill country in and around Indiana County, but even as a boy he was fascinated with the American West. In the summer of 1944, after graduating from high school, he saw the West of his imagination by hitchhiking, walking, and riding in boxcars and buses. When Abbey saw the Rocky Mountains for the first time, as he wrote in *The Journey Home,* "like a boy's first sight of an undressed girl, the image of those mountains struck a fundamental chord in my imagination that has sounded ever since." His firsthand view of the Southwest made a deep impression, and he was determined to return there as soon as possible. First, though, Abbey was drafted into the Army in 1945, and for most of two years he served, reluctantly, as an MP in occupied Italy. According to Abbey, the experience made him an anarchist. Though not cut out for a career as a soldier, his military service did enable him to attend college under the GI Bill.

After an honorable discharge, he attended, briefly, the Indiana University of Pennsylvania. In Italy, in 1946, he had begun keeping a journal, and he continued the practice for the rest of his life. The journals, which fill up twenty notebooks and are now housed at the University of Arizona Library, became a catchall writer's depository for Abbey—a diary, a storehouse of opinions and philosophical musings, and a place to record ideas that eventually found their way to publication in different forms. In 1947 Abbey moved to the West and enrolled in the University of New Mexico at Albuquerque. Shortly before receiving an undergraduate degree in philosophy in 1951, Abbey created a stir when, as editor of the school's literary magazine, *The Thunderbird,* he published an essay titled "Some Implica-

Abbey at his home in Indiana, Pennsylvania, 1928 (from James M. Cahalan, Edward Abbey: A Life, *2001)*

tions of Anarchy," which urged students to burn their draft cards. The cover of the journal quotes Voltaire— "MAN WILL NEVER BE FREE UNTIL THE LAST KING IS STRANGLED WITH THE ENTRAILS OF THE LAST PRIEST"—but attributes the phrase to Louisa May Alcott. The college dean seized all the copies, and Abbey was fired.

In 1950 Abbey married his girlfriend, Jean Schmechel, and the next year she accompanied him to Scotland, where he studied at the University of Edinburgh under a Fulbright fellowship. The marriage, the first of five for Abbey, ended shortly after they arrived in Scotland, and in 1951–1952 Abbey traveled in England, France, Spain, and Scandinavia. In 1953 he returned briefly with his new wife, Rita Deanin, first to New Mexico and then to New Jersey. He enrolled at Yale University, but, disappointed with the atmosphere and eager to write novels, he withdrew after two weeks. Now with a child, Joshua (a second, Aaron, arrived in 1959), the family returned to Albuquerque, where Abbey resumed his academic studies at the University of New Mexico. In 1957 he won the Stegner Fellowship and moved with his family to coastal California to study creative writing with Wallace Stegner at Stanford University. After six years of intermittent academic studies,

Abbey received a master of arts degree in philosophy at the University of New Mexico in 1959. His master's thesis, "Anarchism and the Morality of Violence," reflected his lifelong political and philosophical views. From his first novel, *Jonathan Troy* (1954; a portion of which had been published as "Some Implications of Anarchy" in *The Thunderbird*), to his last, *Hayduke Lives!* (published in January 1990), Abbey explored the possibilities of anarchy as an alternative form of government. In the early 1950s, the FBI, uneasy with Abbey's anarchism, began keeping a dossier on him.

He attempted to live and work in the New York area on three separate occasions. His wife Rita was a New Jersey native and wanted to stay close to home. Her wish, combined with Abbey's desire to establish himself in the vibrant New York literary world (as Thoreau had tried, unsuccessfully, to do for a brief period in his life) was motive enough to try (in 1953–1954, 1962–1963, and 1964–1965) to live and work in New York. But, as Garth McCann writes in his 1977 book on Abbey, "Each of his attempts to live and work in New Jersey and New York as a factory worker or social worker ended in bitterness and frustration." By contrast, Abbey found some peace of mind working as a seasonal park ranger and fire lookout in the West: with only a few interruptions, from 1956 to 1971 he was a seasonal employee for the National Park Service at several different national parks and monuments. His first ranger job, two seasons at Arches National Monument in Utah, provided the inspiration and raw material for *Desert Solitaire: A Season in the Wilderness* (1968). Throughout most of the 1950s he wrote and submitted novels, only to receive letters of rejection. *Jonathan Troy,* published in 1954, is, unlike most of Abbey's other books, set in the East—in Indiana, Pennsylvania, thinly disguised in the novel as "Powhatan." Though the novel was, by Abbey's own (and most critics') estimation, unsuccessful, it established many of the themes that occupied Abbey for the next thirty-five years—most important, an anarchic philosophy and a freedom-loving B. Traven–like hero. Abbey despised the novel, but its publication provided him with the encouragement to continue writing.

His second novel, *The Brave Cowboy: An Old Tale in a New Time,* published in 1956, was much more successful. The protagonist, Jack Burns, is both an anachronism and an anarchist, a cowboy from the nineteenth-century American West. Hoping to rescue a longtime, like-minded friend, Paul Bondi, from a New Mexico jail, Burns gets into a barroom fight and is arrested. When the police ask him for his identification, he replies, "Don't have none. Don't need none. I already know who I am." Once in jail, Burns is unable to persuade Bondi, who has vowed to serve his term and then settle into family life, to escape with him. Breaking out of jail alone, Burns is pursued by the local police, who, though equipped with modern technologies, fail to catch him. With his horse, Whisky, Burns eludes the police by taking routes into the rough New Mexico wilderness. As Burns seems to be making a decisive escape, he rides his horse onto a busy highway, where he is hit by a tractor-trailer that is transporting bathroom fixtures. The novel ends with the anarchic hero lying, apparently moribund, on the highway.

Although *The Brave Cowboy* is, like most of Abbey's other novels, partially comic, it is also full of serious themes, ones that characterize much of Abbey's writing. Above all, Abbey defines freedom and wilderness largely in terms of one another. As wilderness vanishes as a result of human development, freedom suffers. Thus, an anarchic freedom-lover such as Burns (who, not dead after all, is a recurring character in some of Abbey's later novels) has little hope in the modern world. Moreover, technology (represented, in part, by the police gadgets) and modern conveniences (represented by the truck carrying bathroom fixtures) are not necessities for life and have the end effect of isolating humans from nature. The final scene of the book is an analogy—although maybe overly obvious—for the literal

clash between freedom and the modernity that Abbey finds so repellent. Wilderness, Abbey has written more than once, is vital to humans' sanity and should be preserved, in part, as a place in which outlaws may hide. *The Brave Cowboy* was filmed as *Lonely Are the Brave* (1961), with a screenplay by Dalton Trumbo and starring Kirk Douglas, who has said that Jack Burns is the favorite of all his movie roles. Abbey was paid $7,500 for book rights, and he served as a location scout for the motion picture and even had a bit part (though his scenes did not make the final cut).

By the late 1950s, Abbey, along with friends possessed of similar anarchic views, began practicing what later became known as "monkeywrenching"–the act of destroying commercial materials and machinery in order to preserve the natural state of wilderness areas. Since the operation was obviously illegal and was thus unpublicized, the sorts of sabotage carried out were not exactly clear, but monkeywrenching, over time, came to include such activities as pulling up survey stakes on property to be developed, sawing down or burning billboards and signs, hammering nails into trees to tear up chainsaws, and pouring syrup into the crankcases of tractors and earthmovers to disable them. In 1966, after thirteen tumultuous years of marriage with Rita, Abbey left her and the couple's two boys in Las Vegas, a move that caused Rita to file for divorce. Abbey came to regret his action deeply. Later that year he married Judy Pepper, but this marriage was also stormy, though it resulted in a daughter, Susannah, in 1968. Judy Abbey died in New York City on 4 July 1970 of acute leukemia. Abbey experienced depression after her death; he wrote an entry dated July 11 in his journal, "What now is the aim of my life? To sit on a rock in the desert and stare at the sun until the sun goes black."

Based on real events in the life of John Prather and his fight with the U.S. government over his ranch, *Fire on the Mountain* was published in 1962 and is, like *The Brave Cowboy,* set in New Mexico. Again, the main character, John Vogelin, is a lover of the freedom represented by wilderness and an unyielding nonconformist. Vogelin is an elderly man who refuses to turn over the legal claim he holds to an undeveloped ranch to the government, which wants to build a missile testing site on it. The officials from the Range Management Bureau sent to talk to Vogelin see no monetary or practical value in the land. Confronted by a faceless, militaristic bureaucracy and legal system that sees wild nature and individual freedom as subservient to progress, Vogelin is unable to persuade the agents of his need for the land on its own, ineffable terms. "Progress," Vogelin says, "I say, Let's turn back the clock. Why does progress have to progress over me and the coyotes?" For Vogelin the compromise that would

*Dust jacket for Abbey's 1968 book, an account of his experiences
as a park ranger at Arches National Monument in Utah
(Ken Lopez catalogue, 2000)*

them essentially first-person narratives. The book is a composite account of his two seasons employed as a park ranger at Utah's Arches National Monument (since 1971, a national park) and almost inevitably invites comparisons with Henry David Thoreau's *Walden* (1854). The two books are composite revisions of personal journals, arranged seasonally, by men who lived in relative solitude in more or less natural settings. Both exalt simplification against the backdrop of a materialistic society and both subjectively apprehend nature as a beneficent teacher. Moreover, Abbey, as with Thoreau, has the rare ability to write fresh, vivid descriptions of nature in one sentence and in the next cut to the heart of a profound point, often conveyed humorously.

After an introduction warning readers and would-be visitors that they should not expect to see much remaining of the wilderness areas he describes in the book, Abbey arrives at Arches and, echoing Thoreau (who went to Walden Pond "to live deliberately, to front only the essential facts of life"), Abbey explains that he has come there "not only to evade for a while the clamor and filth and confusion of the cultural apparatus but also to confront, immediately and directly if it's possible, the bare bones of existence, the elemental and fundamental, the bedrock which sustains us." The first several chapters are foremost an evocation of the wilderness world of Arches. As in all his nonfiction, Abbey intermingles personal narrative, vivid description, and direct commentary in the early part of *Desert Solitaire* in order to establish a value system that is informed by observations of the natural order of the desert: "At first look it all seems like a geologic chaos, but there is a method at work here, method of a fanatic order and perseverance." He praises the beauty of the natural world, demonstrates the kinship of all living things, and exalts the ideals of individual freedom and living simply. At the same time, Abbey characteristically ascribes blame to human development, which, he argues, is destroying much of the natural world, is disturbing the symbiotic relationship of all nature, and is making difficult the possibility for human wilderness experience (which, as in all his work, Abbey equates with the loss of basic personal freedom). The development is executed by a select few, who, working under the guise of utilitarianism and progress, are in reality motivated by greed.

In terms of offering a direct alternative to the excessive development in parks such as Arches, "Polemic: Industrial Tourism and the National Parks" is the most important single chapter in *Desert Solitaire*. Abbey's placement of the directly argumentative "Polemic," after five chapters in which he has established values and built identification with his readers, is

lead to a peaceful resolution is not an option, and so, like *The Brave Cowboy,* the novel ends violently. *Fire on the Mountain* is an uncompromising declaration of resistance to the militarism, industrialism, and commercialism Abbey feels is overrunning wilderness. The tone of the novel is softened somewhat by the twelve-year-old first-person narrator, Vogelin's grandson, Billy, but some critics consider this point of view a major flaw in the book. The novel sold modestly, but it received some favorable reviews, and a television movie starring Buddy Ebsen and Ron Howard was produced in 1981.

The other book Abbey published in the 1960s, *Desert Solitaire,* is his most important contribution to American nature writing. More than once, Abbey said he did not care much for the book, though possibly he was attempting to draw attention away from his most celebrated book to the other, less-read work, especially the novels. Unlike the nonfiction books he published later, *Desert Solitaire,* his first book-length work of nonfiction, is composed of interrelated chapters, most of

Abbey with his first wife, Jean Schmechel, in Albuquerque, circa 1950
(from Cahalan, Edward Abbey: A Life, *2001)*

an outgrowth of the seasonal chronology of the book. With summer, the beginning of the peak tourist season, Abbey is ready to confront the issue of mass tourism and its effect on the wilderness. The wilderness of Arches, its silence and unhurried pace evoked in the preceding chapters, has become its opposite–overcrowded, invaded by human technology of dubious value, and, worst of all, an environment that promotes the worst sorts of consumerism. The campground at Arches at this time of year, he writes, resembles "a suburban village."

Abbey turns to a direct discussion of the original, democratic purposes behind the creation of the national parks. This method leads to an evaluation of the role of the government and developers in circumventing those purposes and culminates in an appeal to his readers to "rear up on their hind legs"–the tyrannical automobile is the villain here–"and make vigorous political gestures demanding implementation of the [Wilderness Preservation] Act," which was enacted to preserve wilderness from excessive development. According to Abbey, readers can take three positions toward development in the national parks: the first states that absolutely all development in the parks is

intrinsically good; the second is that absolutely no more development of any kind should take place in the parks; and the third states that a small amount of development should be allowed in order to make the parks accessible to the public. Abbey writes that the first view is "insane," and that while some readers sympathize with the second view, they also realize that some development is necessary.

Abbey provides a sketch of how park development should take place. First he would ban cars in the national parks. Visitors, of course, may walk, or "ride horses, bicycles, mules, wild pigs–anything–" except motorized vehicles: "We have agreed not to drive our automobiles into cathedrals, concert halls, art museums. . . . We should treat our national parks with the same deference, for they, too, are holy places." The little additional development Abbey condones is the building of emergency shelters, the improving of park trails, and the digging of wells. *Desert Solitaire*–the "Polemic" chapter in particular–voices a growing concern among park authorities and others that limits should be set on the commercialism and development of the parks. Abbey's agenda for the road-building policies in the parks served as the basis for the recommendations of the Conservation Foundation in its 1972 report, *National Parks for the Future,* and Yosemite National Park banned cars from a large part of the valley in 1970. Accused by some in the late 1960s and early 1970s as impractical, undemocratic, and elitist, the proposals to limit cars set forth in *Desert Solitaire* continue to serve as a basis for policies as the parks grow more crowded with automobiles every year.

All of *Desert Solitaire* extols the precious value (as opposed to the valuables) of wilderness and of personal liberty, but it is a varied work; it is—among other things—a tour guide, a set of narratives, an autobiography, a philosophy of anarchy, and a political diatribe. "Rocks" follows Abbey's "polemic" on development in the parks; it is largely an adventure story with the desert as a backdrop to explicate human greed. "Cowboys and Indians" and "The Dead Man at Grandview Point" are narrative reflections on mortality. "Cowboys and Indians Part II" is, in part, a rather bleak deliberation on the impoverished present and anticipated state of the Navajos in the desert Southwest. "Water" is a discussion of a precious, rare desert substance essential for life: "There is no lack of water here, unless you try to establish a city where no city should be." In "Terra Incognita: Into the Maze," Abbey and a friend hike into the giant labyrinth of stone known as the Maze (a part of Canyonlands National Park). In this part, as elsewhere in the book, Abbey realizes that words fail to describe the beautiful strangeness of such a place.

The longest chapter in the book, "Down the River," is a narrative account of a 1959 floating trip that Abbey and a friend, Ralph Newcomb, took down the Colorado River through Glen Canyon. The Glen Canyon Dam, under construction at the time, was soon going to flood and destroy the canyon in creating Lake Powell. Setting off in their small rubber boats, they are, Abbey writes, "Cutting the bloody cord, that's what we feel, the delirious exhilaration of independence, a rebirth backward in time and into primeval liberty. . . ." Abbey's tranquil narrative gives way at various points to ruminations on the meaning and use of wilderness. As on several other occasions and in various ways in *Desert Solitaire* and dozens of other essays, Abbey is an unabashed apologist for wild nature as an absolute right: "No, wilderness is not a luxury but a necessity of the human spirit, and as vital to our lives as water and good bread. A civilization which destroys what little remains of the wild, the spare, the original, is cutting itself off from its origins and betraying the principle of civilization itself."

"Down the River," which moves comfortably from narration to commentary and back to narration, provides the rough form for most of Abbey's subsequent travel essays in the later collections. In real life,

the trip, combined with the completion of the dam, caused Abbey to focus more on preservationist themes in his writing. He often used the ruining of Glen Canyon, a canyon that, though different, was every bit as beautiful and important as the Grand Canyon, as a symbol for the worst excesses of industrialism. *Desert Solitaire* received some good reviews, one from Edwin Way Teale in *The New York Review of Books* (28 January 1968), but it did not sell particularly well, and it quickly went out of print. It was republished in an inexpensive Ballantine paperback edition in 1971, and, largely through word of mouth, it developed a wide readership. Its success enabled Abbey to make a living as a writer.

His next book, the novel *Black Sun* (1971), is a love story about an Abbey-like forest ranger—an iconoclast, a loner, and a lover of the wilds—named Will Gatlin, who falls for an alluring nineteen-year-old, Sandy MacKenzie, who is engaged to another (younger) man. Gatlin engages her in sexual experimentation and shows her some of the hidden treasures of the forests, canyons, and mountains; she, in turn, awakens him to love. When she, unable to resolve the conflicts in her life, disappears into the wilderness, he is unable to find her, and he is thrown into a deep gloom. Abbey, throughout his oeuvre, consciously romanticizes the desert world, but he never loses sight of the reality that wilderness can be dangerous and inhospitable—a place of loss and a place where one may perish without trace. The ending of *Black Sun* is a poignant realization of this idea; the novel concludes with Gatlin, unresponsive to the conversation going on around him, staring into the forest. The lean novel is by critical consent, and in his own opinion, one of Abbey's finest.

In 1974, four years after Judy Abbey's death (years marked by several short-term relationships), Abbey married eighteen-year-old Renee Downing. He worked as a park ranger up until the early 1970s and occasionally thereafter, including a relatively long tenure in the late 1970s as a fire lookout at Aztec Peak in Arizona. Abbey also continued intermittently to teach creative writing at various universities, including Western Carolina University, the University of Utah, and the University of Arizona, where he established his deepest academic relationship and eventually became a full professor of English. The 1970s were Abbey's most productive years as a writer. In this decade, among other works, he wrote the text for a number of oversized photography books: *Appalachian Wilderness: The Great Smoky Mountains* (with Eliot Porter, 1970), *Slickrock* (with Philip Hyde, 1971), *Cactus Country* (with Time-Life, 1973), *The Hidden Canyon: A River Journey* (with John Blaustein, 1977), and *Desert Images: An American Landscape* (with David Muench, 1979). Designated as "coffee table" books, these works were ones Abbey said that

Abbey with his second wife, Rita Deanin, and children, Aaron and Josh, in Taos, New Mexico, 1959
(from Jack Loeffler, Adventures with Ed: A Portrait of Abbey, *2002)*

his enemies could afford to buy, but few of his friends could. Some of the prose from these books is collected in *Beyond the Wall.* Although these books tended to be expensive and were enriched by the work of some of the most celebrated nature photographers of the day, Abbey did not soften the prose for a perceived mon-eyed, genteel audience. These books include an unusual amount of direct commentary for their type. In *Appalachian Wilderness,* for example, Abbey, barely into a narrative account of a trip to the Great Smoky Mountains, writes, "Vast crimes are being committed in this region, whole hillsides raped and robbed. . . ." And in *Cactus Country,* while describing a trip into the Superstition Mountains in Arizona, in one paragraph he notes the beauty of the flora in the area—"the scarlet hedgehog and the brilliant yellow cups of the prickly pear"—but in the next paragraph he shifts his tone:

Flowers; also garbage: we were only 40 miles from the great metropolitan miasma of Phoenix. Looking westward we could see, against the light, the 50-mile-wide pall across the sky. Is it possible that Phoenix may someday rise from her ashes? She lives in soot and smoke, dust and confusion and crime, half pickled in sulphuric acid, a city dying from too much gluttonous success.

All of Abbey's nonfiction, the large photograph books included, may be characterized as a literary journalism that blends personal narrative with sharp invective against industrialism, militarism, and misguided government, but it is also characterized by a keen understanding of natural history, and he skillfully, comfortably works both poetic and scientific descriptions into his prose of the flora, fauna, and geology of an area. He begins his book *The Journey Home* by writing, in typical jocular manner, that he is not a naturalist: "the only birds I can recognize without hesitation are the turkey vulture, the fried chicken, and the rosy-bottomed skinny dipper." The careful reader, however, recognizing that Abbey is quite knowledgeable about natural history in general, will not take such admissions seriously. His knowledge of natural history and ecology was not confined to what he had read and written about in books. Abbey's friend Ken Sleight writes in "Abbey & Me" that one day he was cutting and slashing the rabbitbrush from a fence on property that he and Abbey co-owned. Abbey, not pleased, asked Sleight why he was chopping away the rabbitbrush. Sleight replied that it was merely weed and a fire hazard. Sleight writes, Abbey "pointed out to me that the rabbitbrush was shelter and haven for wildlife—rabbits, birds, and such. And not only should we leave a cover for them, he said, we ought to grow additional thickets of brush for their protection." Arriving at a compromise, Sleight and Abbey agreed to trim away only the branches actually interfering with the fence itself and leave the rabbitbrush standing for the animals.

The Monkey Wrench Gang (1975) is, if not Abbey's best novel, certainly his most commercially successful one, and it has had a profound effect on environmentalism in the late twentieth and early twenty-first centuries. This comic novel is concerned with the adventures of four extremely different people who commit acts of sabotage on development in the Southwest. Part of the charm of the novel lies in the development of the four main characters, elements of whom are recognizable in their creator and in some of Abbey's real-life friends. Doc Sarvis—a large, forty-nine-year-old surgeon, financial supporter, philosophical leader of the gang, and sometime hands-on participant—constantly chomps his cigar, spouting extreme distaste for industrialism. Doc's independent-minded female companion is twenty-eight-year-old Bonnie Abbzug, a long-legged, long-haired beauty who is thrilled with the adventure. Strong-willed and insistent on being addressed as "Mizz," she is, nevertheless, the weakest main character in the novel, arguably little more than a cardboard sexual stereotype. George Washington Hayduke, one of the best-known and most intriguing of all Abbey's characters, is a twenty-five-year-old beer-guzzling Green Beret veteran of the Vietnam War. Hayduke, inspired by Abbey's close friend Douglas Peacock, is short but muscular ("built like a wrestler"), antisocial, prone to violence, foulmouthed, but also deeply disturbed by the overdevelopment of the West. The fourth member, Seldom Seen Smith (legally, Joseph Fielding Smith), is so called because he seldom sees any of his three wives, even though they live within a day's drive of one another. "Born by chance" a Mormon, Smith works as a wilderness guide, boatman, and outfitter. Lanky, lean, and thirty-five, Smith is (like Abbey) especially offended by Glen Canyon Dam, which he prays God will strike with a "pre-cision earthquake," and is based loosely on Abbey's friend Ken Sleight.

The gang's goal of blowing up Glen Canyon Dam proves to be unfeasible, so it settles for smaller targets, including road construction sites, countless bulldozers, a railroad to a coal mine, and several bridges. Although at various points Hayduke seems disposed otherwise, the group avoids committing violence against other human beings. Abbey goes into minute, expert detail on an array of "monkeywrenching" activities:

> Hayduke climbed down from the operator's seat. They worked on the patient [a D-8 bulldozer], sifting handfuls of fine Triassic sand into the crankcase, cutting up the wiring, the fuel lines, the hydraulic hoses to fore and aft attachments, dumping Karo into the fuel tanks. Why Karo instead of plain sugar? Smith wanted to know. Pours better, Hayduke explained; mixes easier with the diesel, doesn't jam up in strainers.

The novel is full of episodes of the gang's near escapes from various authorities, which include a group of businessmen vigilantes calling themselves the San Juan County Search & Rescue Team, which is headed by Bishop J. Dudley Love. In addition to being a bishop in the Mormon church, Love is a profit-minded land developer who aspires to be governor of Utah. In the last chapters of the novel, the gang makes a long, risky escape from Love and his men into the inhospitable canyons of the Fins in eastern Utah. Sarvis, Abbzug, and Smith are arrested and, through plea bargaining, are convicted of relatively minor offenses. Hayduke, making his way into the Maze canyons, is cornered, trapped, and apparently falls into the canyon below as he is shot by a barrage of police firepower.

Abbey's deep loathing for what happened at Glen Canyon caused him to write The Monkey Wrench Gang in the early 1970s. He had written in Desert Solitaire, "I am convinced that the desert has no heart," but years later, in Beyond the Wall, he wrote that, in fact, Glen Canyon was the heart of the desert. In effect, in the ultimate affront by industrialization, that symbolic heart was drowned after the erection of the dam. Though Abbey claimed he wrote the novel as entertainment, it proved to be revolutionary, ushering in a new, or at least more publicized, form of hands-on environmental activism, directly influencing the formation of groups such as Earth First! and its offshoots, which were devoted to conducting acts of ecodefense similar to those described in such excruciating, informative detail in the novel. Rarely has a piece of fiction caused such a committed call to action in real life. Similar to Upton Sinclair's The Jungle (1906), which created an awareness of the exploitation of workers in the meatpacking industry and exposed the unsanitary conditions in which they were forced to work, and Harriet Beecher Stowe's Uncle Tom's Cabin (1851–1852), which caused Northern evangelicals to unite against the institution of slavery, The Monkey Wrench Gang precipitated an awareness of and a viable solution to a problem that had previously gone largely ignored. The novel almost single-handedly created the ecodefense movement in the United States. Ecodefense is a controversial and illegal activity, but it has had the effect of establishing a true radical environmentalism, as opposed to the staid, conventional political stance of groups such as the Sierra Club and the Audubon Society.

Though *The Monkey Wrench Gang* never made it onto a national best-seller list, it has sold more than seven hundred thousand copies, and it made Abbey a cult figure. A motion-picture project has been discussed by various moviemakers. The book caused an increasing demand for Abbey as a speaker, especially in the West. Though he was, for much of his life, embittered that his work was seldom reviewed in New York magazines or taken seriously by intellectuals in the eastern United States, he was established by the mid 1970s as one in a handful of important writers of the West, and writers such as Larry McMurtry, Wendell Berry, Hunter S. Thompson, Joan Didion, Gary Snyder, and Thomas McGuane began publicly to praise Abbey's work. He lent his increased stature to activist causes with caution; he appeared at various rallies, including those held by Earth First! which has changed markedly since Abbey's death. (One of its cofounders, Dave Foreman, left the group in 1990 because he felt it had gone ideologically too far to the left.)

Peter Wild writes in *Pioneer Conservationists of Western America* (1979) that Abbey "has inspired other public figures, such as fellow Utahan Robert Redford, to mount their own campaigns to save wilderness, though using somewhat more restrained methods than Abbey seems to suggest." Abbey's anarchic point of view, rather brash and unfocused in the 1950s, was more developed and accessible by the late 1960s and early 1970s. In his 1966 assessment of Abbey's novels, William T. Pilkington found the works admirable but added that Abbey's anarchism is "ineffectual and confused . . . little more than nonsense." Eight years later Pilkington amended his earlier view, writing that "Abbey's books have progressed over the years . . . to a consideration in his later works of the most complex of philosophical questions." But the rise of the youth culture in the wake of a tumultuous decade of civil rights struggles, an unpopular war in Vietnam, and later Watergate, suggests that Abbey's audience developed and came to *him,* as much as the other way around.

By the 1970s Abbey was publishing articles in a wide variety of periodicals, including not only nature and outdoors magazines, such as *Audubon, Sierra, National Geographic, Backpacker,* and *Outside,* but also those with a wider readership, such as *Rolling Stone, Playboy, Harper's,* and even *Reader's Digest.* Many of these articles are col-

Dust jacket for Abbey's 1975 book, in which he advocates damaging construction machinery at sites he thinks should be preserved (Ken Lopez catalogue, 2000)

lected in the five books of nonfiction that appeared from 1977 to 1988: *The Journey Home, Abbey's Road* (1979), *Down the River with Henry David Thoreau and Friends* (1982), *Beyond the Wall,* and *One Life at a Time, Please* (1988). Most of these articles are rather short, and many of them are records of Abbey's excursions, solo and with companions, into the wilds. All of them are brimming with rich, descriptive prose, anarchic humor, and ornery opinions, and they are, taken together, among the most eloquent defenses for preserving wilderness written in the late twentieth century. Although Abbey badly wanted to be respected foremost as a novelist, his self-dramatization is unleashed most powerfully and directly in his nonfiction. Always essentially antiestablishment in tone, his persona is by turns brash and self-defacing; bawdy and poetic; cultured and sophisticated but also consciously anti-intellectual. The persona that comes through in the nonfiction is often rough and contradictory, but it is also uncompromising and believable.

The first of these collections is Abbey's second book of nonfiction, *The Journey Home.* Among the twenty-three short essays is "Hallelujah on the Bum," which relates Abbey's first trip to the West in 1944.

Living hand to mouth, traveling by thumb and boxcar, the first-person narrator Abbey in this selection is a naive young man forced to wise up quickly in order to survive. "The Great American Desert" (a portion of which appears as the introduction to Peggy Larson's Sierra Club guidebook *The Deserts of the Southwest* [1977]) is a good example of the hyperrealism that often characterizes Abbey's romanticism: the desert, Abbey writes, is a miserable place, teeming with rattlesnakes, scorpions, stinging bugs, maliciously barbed flora, a burning sun, arid climate, and no water. Why, then, go into the desert? Typically, Abbey answers the question with a story. Exploring a desert mountain, he comes upon a sign made of arrows and tries to discover at what the sign is meant to point:

> But there was nothing out there. Nothing at all. Nothing but the desert.
> Nothing but the silent world.
> That's why.

"Fire Lookout: Numa Ridge" is a journal of the author's seasonal work at Glacier National Park; in the piece he discusses such subjects as the problem of grizzly bears in the national parks ("Really a human problem," he interjects); ranger duties, including spotting, but not always reporting, forest fires (since ninety percent of them are caused by lightning, he writes, Smokey the Bear "lies" when he says, "Only you can prevent forest fires"); marriage; road building in the parks; the democratic rifle versus the authoritarian B-52 (a recurring statement in Abbey's work); solitude; and meaningful living and work. "Manhattan Twilight. Hoboken Night" is a rare, predictably negative view of New York City and vicinity, where Abbey lived and worked for brief periods in the 1950s and 1960s. "The Second Rape of the West" is a representative piece of Abbey's subjective journalism, which shows how industrial growth is destroying the West. Abbey discovers that, compared to the salaries of a mere $300 per month for conservation activists who report on strip mining, air pollution, clear-cutting, water diversion, and other potentially harmful operations in the West, the energy industry is exorbitantly financed, paying thousands of dollars for single ad campaigns meant to persuade locals that they are a beneficent force in the community. Not for the last time, Abbey questions the prudence of growth and industry with one of his strongest aphorisms: "Growth for the sake of growth is the ideology of the cancer cell."

Two years later, in 1979, *Abbey's Road,* another collection of articles from various periodicals, appeared. The introduction to the book, one of the best from a writer known for strong, often spicy introductions, discusses the author's written correspondence with other writers, influences on him, and his own persona:

> The writer puts the best of himself, not the whole, into the work; the author as seen in the pages of his own book is largely a fictional creation. Often the author's best creation. The "Edward Abbey" of my own books, for example, bears only the dimmest resemblance to the shy, timid, reclusive, rather dapper little gentleman who, always correctly attired for his labors in coat and tie and starched detachable cuffs, sits down each night for precisely four hours to type out the further adventures of that arrogant blustering macho fraud who counterfeits his name. You can bet on it: No writer is ever willing–or even able–to portray himself as seen by others or as he really is.

In the first half of *Abbey's Road* the author is out of the United States, first in the Australian outback and then on a small island off the coast of Mexico and the Sierra Madre in Chihuahua. Driving out of Brisbane into rural Queensland, Abbey is astonished to find a desert ambience resembling the American Southwest of forty years prior, but he concludes, "The forces that are fouling up America are hard at work in Australia too." Abbey explores the Great Barrier Reef, which is threatened by both natural and man-made elements; he visits the cattle ranch of Dick Nunn, a man with whom (ideologically) he has little in common but whom he comes to respect nonetheless. He visits the Outback, the land of the Aborigines ("Their lands taken away, their mythic culture lost, they exist in the limbo between a vanished past and a new world in which there is no place for them"), and, peppering the narrative with humorous exchanges with locals, he hikes to the top of Ayers Rock, climbs the desert mountains in the West, and abandoning his broken-down Ford, walks to Kalgoorlie in the southwest part of the continent.

The remainder of *Abbey's Road* is composed of shorter travel essays and editorials. Of the former are "On the River Again," about a floating trip down the Rio Grande; "Down There in the Rocks," which describes a camping trip in Escalante Canyon that followed a boat trip across the despised Lake Powell; and "Fire Lookout," a recollection of life as a fire lookout at the North Rim of the Grand Canyon. "A Walk in the Park," a reference to a hike Abbey and his daughter Suzie (a name he spells differently from work to work) took through a section of Canyonlands National Park, begins with a discussion of the political debate over the proposed building of a confluence road with accompanying bridge in Canyonlands. Abbey discovers that, as usual, most members of the conservative business community favor building the road, while others, typed by their opposition as "radical environmentalists" and

Abbey in El Gran Desierto, Mexico, May 1982 (from Cahalan, Edward Abbey: A Life, *2001)*

"welfare backpackers," successfully argue that the park should be left in its relatively primitive condition.

Among the editorial pieces in *Abbey's Road* is "Science with a Human Face," which denounces both a strict dependence on science and technology and their opposite, pure mysticism, to determine truth. Ultimately, both set agendas that are unimaginative, confining to the human spirit, brainy but mindless, and ominous for the planet. "The Right to Arms" explains Abbey's position on gun ownership: "I'm a liberal—and proud of it. Nevertheless, I am opposed, absolutely, to every move the state makes to restrict my right to buy, own, possess, and carry a firearm." Citing the gun bans in Nazi Germany and the Soviet Union, Abbey claims that gun ownership is the only safeguard against a totalitarian government; characteristically, the piece concludes with a popular aphorism turned on its head: "If guns are outlawed, only the government will have guns." "In Defense of the Redneck" is an account of a drunken afternoon spent in an unfriendly bar in Globe, Arizona. Along the way, Abbey provides a lively group portrait of a stock American type. Though he defends few of those in the piece, Abbey concludes it with an appreciation for their ability to persevere.

Though his 1980 futuristic novel *Good News* is a change of pace for Abbey, it realizes an idea that he had been discussing for several years: taking his cue, in part, from Robinson Jeffers, whose poetry posits a time in which America will perish because of its incestuous greed and an arrogant isolation from nature, Abbey envisions an apocalypse that will enable a return to a simple, loose-knit, anarchic, agricultural mode of living. Although the novel is not altogether pleasant, Abbey claimed that the title was meant literally, not ironically. In a later essay, "Theory of Anarchy," he writes that the disappearance of the military-industrial state (which he predicts will occur "within a century") is "the basis of my inherent optimism"—a return "of a higher civilization: scattered human populations modest in number that live by fishing, hunting, food gathering." Set in the near-future United States, society has collapsed, not because of a nuclear holocaust but because of the implosion of an unbridled industrialization. As a group of whites and American Indians establish an agrarian community in the Southwest, a megalomaniacal military leader, called simply "the Chief," and his men attempt to reimpose the old order. Through a grand, sweeping military operation code-named "Coronado" (an allusion to the gold-seeking sixteenth-century Spanish conquistador of the American Southwest), the Chief and his men seek to make America "once again the world's foremost industrial, military, and . . . spiritual power." Standing up against this return to a militaristic past are Hopi Indian Sam Bayaca and others, including an older version of the brave cowboy, Jack Burns.

By early 1980 Abbey's marriage with Renee was over. He married Clarke Cartwright (his fifth and final wife) in 1982; they had two children, Rebecca and Benjamin. The children reinvigorated Abbey mentally, and he settled down into a relatively stable life of raising a young family, teaching writing at the University of Arizona, going on excursions, giving public readings, and writing in his little cabin behind his house outside of Tucson. Later in 1982, at the age of fifty-five, he was informed he had terminal pancreatic cancer and only six months to live, but the diagnosis proved to be wrong. Abbey wrote in his journal that the illness was "Gallstones, an 'angry pancreas.' Nothing more, apparently." The painful bout with pancreatitis became a condition that caused internal bleeding in his esophagus. By the mid 1980s Abbey was becoming aware of the growing seriousness of his health problems and of his own mortality, but he continued to write in good humor and to travel, at peace with himself. In 1987 he was offered an award by the American Academy of Arts and Letters, but he declined, preferring instead to go on a float trip down the Salmon River in Idaho.

Down the River with Henry David Thoreau and Friends (1982) is another collection of articles, once again ranging in type, from travel to editorial. Abbey included three book reviews—one, on Paul Horgan's *Josiah Gregg* (1941), is favorable; another, allegedly written by "Dave Harleyson," ridicules Robert Pirsig's *Zen and the Art of Motorcycle Maintenance* (1974); and the third is a "gentle" refutation of René Dubos's *The Wooing of Earth* (1980). "My Friend Debris" is an insider's portrait of the author's close friendship with the Southwestern artist John De Puy. In "MX" (shorthand for the military's Missile Experimental Mobile Defense System) Abbey considers the missile buildup in the Cold War and the fraudulent government claims of improving local business in Utah and Nevada, in whose deserts the government has proposed to build and store the MX. Abbey notes that "the design [of the MX] appears to contain one serious flaw: there is no place . . . for the scientists, generals, and corporation executives who should be allowed—should be honored—should be compelled, at gunpoint if necessary, to ride this thing to its designated designation." With a friend, Abbey visits the desert where the MX is proposed, and he speculates as to how the area will be affected if the system is deployed there. In "Of Protest" Abbey visits Rocky Flats, Colorado, where nonviolent protesters attempt to block a railway leading to Rockwell International, which has contracted with the government to make the plutonium triggers for thermonuclear devices. He follows the protesters' arrest

and trial, in which distinguished experts for the defense confirm the hazard of the project for nearby townspeople. Abbey finds a deep admiration for those who crusade selflessly without pay for such environmental matters. Such people, he writes, are "liberated by their own volition from the tedious routine and passive acquiescence in which most of us endure our brief, half-lived, half-lives. One single act of defiance against power, against the State that seems omnipotent but is not, transforms and transfigures the human personality."

The theme of this collection, however, is rivers and river-running. A dozen years earlier, in *Desert Solitaire,* Abbey had written, "We need wilderness whether or not we ever set foot in it. . . . I may never in my life get to Alaska, for example, but I am grateful that it's there." "Notes from a Cold River" records the realization of a wish, as Abbey and several others float down the Tatshenshini River in eastern Alaska. Though Abbey admires the lofty mountains and holds great respect for, not to mention anxiety about, the local grizzlies (which he does not encounter), in comparison to his home turf in the Southwest, "Alaska seems, well, sort of . . . *banal*. But not bad, not bad." In "River Rats," attendance at a meeting of the Western River Guides' Association provides a context for thoughts on the politics of commercial boating, which is being overtaken by large outfitters and subject to harassment by government agencies. "Floating" is part narrative, part commentary and centers on a float trip down another river condemned to damming, the Rio Delores of southwest Colorado. "Running the San Juan" is concerned with a trip Abbey took floating the river in Utah with his daughter Susie and several other people.

The title essay records a floating trip down the Green River that Abbey, with five friends and a copy of *Walden,* began on 4 November 1980—the day Ronald Reagan won the presidency, and the wilderness was consequently sold "down the river." Throughout the essay, Abbey quotes Thoreau and examines the relevance of Thoreau's ideas for the late twentieth century. Such a meeting of kindred minds provides a means for Abbey's own critique of contemporary America. Abbey writes that whereas, in Thoreau's day, one-sixth of the U.S. population was composed of slaves, today all are slaves to progress and the industrial state.

Beyond the Wall, published in 1984, is another collection of articles previously published in periodicals and in the large, expensive photography books. The periodical articles are spread over four distinct locales—the Sonoran desert, the Guadalupe high country in west Texas, the hated Glen Canyon Dam, and a river in Alaska. In the preface of the book, Abbey, a populist by nature, counters the charge that is often made by various staunch proponents of land development that he and "other natural conservatives" are elitists who want to preserve wilderness areas for selfish motives. On the contrary, Abbey argues, it is inexpensive for anyone to buy a backpack, a sleeping bag, and a bus ticket to enjoy wilderness by foot. "But only the affluent—the financial elite—can afford the heavy expenses of ATCs, ATVs, RVs and ORVs. Machines are domineering, exclusive, destructive and costly; it is they and their operators who would deny the enjoyment of the back country to the rest of us." One of the main, albeit simplest, motifs running through virtually all of Abbey's nonfiction is the idea that those who truly want to enjoy nature must leave their automobiles behind and use their own two legs.

The first and longest essay in *Beyond the Wall* is "A Walk in the Desert Hills," an account of a 115-mile solo walk in Cabeza Prieta National Wildlife Refuge in southern Arizona, near the Mexico border. Using almost no dialogue, Abbey comments on the world at large by finding metaphors in the most mundane of occurrences. For example, while walking along, he finds that his cheap boots "are beginning to pinch my little toes. . . . As always, as everywhere in life, it is the little ones who suffer most." And when a Huey military helicopter hovers nearby (Cabeza Prieta is a military bombing range as well as a wildlife preserve), Abbey instinctively hides under a tree and scribbles "seditious thoughts" in his little notebook. In this essay, as elsewhere, Abbey espouses an ecocentric view of the world, which states, in part, that natural systems and their individual parts possess intrinsic value, independent of human utility, and that humankind is an element within natural systems. Coming to the end of the long, grueling walk, Abbey gets a ride to a nearby town. In words reminiscent of the English Romantic poet William Wordsworth, who fondly recalls his experiences in the natural world while back in civilization, he underscores another value in going into the wilds: "Within minutes my 115-mile walk through the desert hills becomes a thing apart. . . . But it's still there in my heart and soul" and "will grow larger, sweeter."

One Life at a Time, Please is the last essay collection published in Abbey's lifetime and the last to date. The title is appropriated from Thoreau, who, lying on his deathbed in 1862, was asked about the afterlife. "One world at a time," he replied. As the title suggests and his journal entries around this time indicate, Abbey had come to understand that his own life might be approaching its end, but one would never know from the subject matter of the pieces collected, which are among the most controversial of his career. He writes in the "Preliminary Remarks" that his favorite piece in the book is "Immigration and Liberal Taboos," which he claims was rejected for publication by *The New York Times* (even though the newspaper had com-

Abbey with his fifth wife, Clarke Cartwright, and baby, Rebecca, at their home near Tuscon, 1984 (from Cahalan, Edward Abbey: A Life, *2001)*

missioned it) and refused by a host of other periodicals. The piece, which argues for a closed Mexican border, does, as he seems to know, open Abbey up to charges of racism and xenophobia. Liberals approve of open borders, stating that there is room for all, while conservatives approve of cheap immigrant labor, but the "majority of Americans," he writes (ignoring the millions of Americans of a Latino heritage), desire the democracy that immigration works against: "The alternative, in the squalor, cruelty, and corruption of Latin America, is plain for all to see." "Free Speech: The Cowboy and His Cow" is also controversial, though in a much more specialized (and generally acceptable) way. A written version of a speech originally delivered at the University of Montana to an audience sympathetic to ranching in the West, Abbey's essay eases into a diatribe against government-subsidized grazing on public lands, overgrazing, and Western ranching in general. "Eco-Defense," originally published as the introductory piece to a book by Dave Foreman of Earth First! is a call to arms for hands-on activities for protection

Abbey, circa 1986, in his writing cabin outside Tucson (from Loeffler,
Adventures with Ed: A Portrait of Abbey, *2002)*

of the wilderness. Abbey argues by analogy that if an intruder batters down the door of one's home, the owner has the right and duty to protect himself and his family by any means necessary; the wilderness, humans' ancestral home, is being assaulted in the same way and should, therefore, be defended, if necessary, by hands-on activism.

With challenging excursions into the wilderness somewhat curtailed because of health reasons, the book includes few of Abbey's characteristic travel (hiking and floating) essays. The lengthy "A San Francisco Journal," written by commission of *The San Francisco Examiner,* and the comically titled "Lake Powell by Houseboat" are unusually domestic for Abbey. The collection does include, though, a few of the more conventional travel essays. "River Solitaire: A Daybook" records a weeklong solo winter float trip down a stretch of the Colorado River in a small rowboat. In "River of No Return," Abbey describes floating, along with some twenty-four others, down Idaho's Salmon River, which runs through nine million acres of a mountainous, roadless area. In "Big Bend" Abbey describes a trip he and friend Jack Loeffler made, an exploration of the

Texas national park by truck and foot. "Round River Rendezvous: The Rio Grande" more or less follows the great river from Brownsville, Texas, back to its source in the Colorado mountains, into New Mexico, the Chihuahuan Desert, and through Big Bend National Park to the Gulf of Mexico. "Forty Years as A Canyoneer" recounts the author's close relationship with the Grand Canyon, which he first saw in 1944. He had worked as a firefighter and lookout at the canyon's North Rim in 1961 and 1968–1970; he and his wife Rita conceived their first child there; and Abbey even bought some land overlooking a stretch of the canyon, a sign of his growing affluence.

Some of the nontravel essays in *One Life at a Time, Please* crystallize important aspects of Abbey's own positions as a writer. "Mr. Krutch" combines commentary on the work of Joseph Wood Krutch, a literary critic and defender of the desert Southwest, with parts of an interview Abbey had conducted with Krutch some twenty years earlier. Abbey writes that he is aware of his own "self-defeating tendencies as a propagandist," and he contrasts his style with that of Krutch: "Rational thought. Calm, reasonable, gentle persuasion. It was this quality of moderation in his writing that most impressed me, for my own inclinations always tended toward the opposite, toward the impatient, the radical, the violent. A book, I often thought, was best employed as a kind of paper club to beat people over the head with." In "A Writer's Credo," originally a lecture delivered at Harvard, Abbey argues that the freelance writer's duty is to "speak the truth–especially unpopular truth. Especially truth that offends the powerful." That unpopular truth appears in "Theory of Anarchy," in which Abbey attempts directly and concisely to address the problem of "how to keep power decentralized." In this essay he describes the value of anarchy and is careful to draw distinctions between anarchy and a ruleless society. On the specifics of the implementation of an anarchic society, Abbey offers little in this essay. On the other hand, the entirety of Abbey's written work may be seen as a self-dramatized working out of this problem.

Abbey had intended for his 1988 *The Fool's Progress: An Honest Novel* (a portion of which was published in 1986 by Capra Press as *Confessions of a Barbarian*) to be his crowning achievement, his "fat masterpiece." He had conceived of the book long before, in the 1950s, and worked on it intermittently over many years. While it falls below the lofty goals he had set for it, it is an entertaining novel. It is picaresque and more than a little autobiographical: the main character, Henry Lightcap, splits up with his third wife, writes her a good-bye note, shoots his refrigerator, and embarks on a 3,500-mile odyssey with his old dog from his home in Tucson to West Virginia, where he was born and raised. Encountering old friends, places, and memories along the way, Lightcap, by the end of the novel is clearly, like his old dog, dying. By the late 1980s illness and family life kept Abbey close to home, but he did manage a cross-country promotional tour for *The Fool's Progress,* and he suffered through one last excursion into the wilds, a solo camping trip into Cabeza Prieta.

Early in 1989 veins in Abbey's throat ruptured because of a complication with hepatic hypertension. Abbey had always been hostile to the idea of dying in a hospital while hooked up to life-support systems. Witnessing the agonizing death of his third wife, Judy, in a New York hospital years before surely had only intensified that feeling. He was, nevertheless, in and out of the hospital during the last few months of his life. In March he began hemorrhaging in his esophagus and fainting, and when blood transfusions and a portal shunt did little to improve his condition, a few friends and family members transported him into the Arizona desert to await death. Unexpectedly, Abbey grew stronger and was, at his request, taken back home and into his writing cabin in the backyard of his Tucson home. After several hours of falling in and out of consciousness, he died around sunrise on 14 March of internal bleeding. As prearranged before his passing, and in complete disregard of the state's burial laws, his body was placed inside his favorite sleeping bag, transported in the back of Loeffler's truck to a secret place in the desert, and covered with rocks. Abbey wrote before he died that he wanted his body "to help fertilize the growth of a cactus or cliff rose or sagebrush or tree." At the unknown burial site, an inscription is crudely carved into a rock:

> Edward Paul Abbey
> 1927 – 1989
> No Comment

A wake was held in Tucson a few days after Abbey's death. In May, a more formal ceremony was held at an undeveloped area near Arches National Park with around a thousand fans, many of Abbey's friends, and fellow writers such as Barry Lopez, Terry Tempest Williams, Wendell Berry, and Ann Zwinger in attendance.

Abbey's final novel, *Hayduke Lives!,* was published posthumously in 1990. A sequel to *The Monkey Wrench Gang, Hayduke Lives!* continues the subversive theme of a radical, hands-on defense of the environment, but the plot is more episodic than that of its predecessor, and it widens the variety of the gang's foes in the form of business executives, FBI infiltrators, government bureaucrats, industrialists, and greedy developers, including the gang's old nemesis, Bishop Love. Abbey, writing what he knew was probably his last novel, maintains his characteristic scorn for the incessant thirst for development and exploitation of the earth at the expense of wilderness and freedom, but the novel is overall an affirmative book, born out of the hope that kindred spirits such as those he portrays in the book will arise and stand up to stop the industrial machine that is invading the Southwest. There is no mistaking the celebratory tone of the novel, which is full of good and bad jokes (including inside ones), puns, reformulated clichés and common sayings, sexual bravado, cranky opinions, potshots at 1980s pop culture, and many of the Abbeyisms readers would recognize from thirty-six years of the writer's published work, including his near misanthropy. For instance, over a poker game, Seldom Seen casually says,

> People are no damn good. . . . Take 'em one at a time, they're all right. Even families. But bunch 'em up, herd 'em together, get 'em organized and well fed and branded and ear-notched and moving out, then they're the meanest ugliest greediest stupidest dangerest breed of beast in the whole goldang solar system far as I know.

Abbey's gravestone in the Cabeza Prieta Wildlife Refuge of Arizona (photograph by Cahalan)

This time around, the gang works with other radical defenders of the earth, including Jack Burns and members of Earth First! (Real members are portrayed in the novel.) Drinking a beer with Hayduke, Doc Sarvis delivers the "code of the eco-warrior," which states that "The ecology warrior hurts no living thing, absolutely never, and he avoids capture, passing all costs on to them, the Enemy. The point of his work is to increase *their* costs, nudge them toward net loss, bankruptcy, forcing them to withdraw and retreat from their invasion of our public lands, our wilderness, our native and primordial home." True to the code, and counterpointing Hayduke's solo acts of ecodefense, Earth First! members engage in nonviolent protest, disable bulldozers, and hammer nails (intended to tear up chainsaws) into trees marked for clear-cutting. Presumed dead, Hayduke assumes a variety of disguises, sometimes even cross-dressing, under which he maintains anonymity and commits acts of sabotage against industry and development. After coaxing, he persuades Doc Sarvis, Bonnie Abbzug-Sarvis (now married, with a child, and with another on the way), and Seldom Seen Smith—all under surveillance by authorities—to assist him and the Earth First! activists in one last act, commandeering a massive $37 million dragline excavator, code-named GOLIATH, which is chewing up the

desert, and driving it over a cliff 2,500 feet into Lost Eden Canyon.

In addition to *Hayduke Lives!*, three additional books of original work were published posthumously. In 1990 *Vox Clamantis in Desert: Some Notes from a Secret Journal* (1989) was republished as *A Voice Crying in the Wilderness (Vox Clamantis in Deserto): Notes from a Secret Journal* with an introduction dated only ten days before Abbey's death. This thin volume is arranged by subjects as varied as "Philosophy, Religion, and So Forth," "Good Manners," "Sport," "Music," and "Money, Et Cetera," and though it does not add significantly to the corpus of Abbey's work, it does underscore that Abbey, in all his writing, is, like Samuel Langhorne Clemens (Mark Twain), Friedrich Nietzsche, and Thoreau, an aphorist of the highest quality. A collection of entries from Abbey's twenty-one-volume journal, *Confessions of a Barbarian: Selections from the Journals of Edward Abbey 1951–1989*, was published in 1994. Edited by Abbey's close friend David Petersen, the book offers a fascinating glance into the writer's life and work. The collection is a firsthand picture of Abbey in all of his unadorned personae—confident in his writing abilities (especially in the early entries), always humorous (even when writing about his own death), an uncontrolled lover of pretty women, insecure about his stature as a writer (especially among Eastern literati), skeptical toward anything resembling a fad, and, of course, a lover of freedom and wilderness and a hater of industrialism. *Earth Apples=(Pommes des terre): The Poetry of Edward Abbey* (1994) is a slight volume collecting light verse written by Abbey over the years. He had read many of these previously unpublished poems aloud at various public readings. Much of the volume is erotic, playful, unserious; almost all of it is forgettable. Many of Abbey's essays, reviews, and journalistic works have, to date, gone uncollected.

Biographies:

James Bishop, *Epitaph for a Desert Anarchist: The Life and Legacy of Edward Abbey* (New York: Touchstone, 1995);

James M. Cahalan, *Edward Abbey: A Life* (Tucson: University of Arizona Press, 2001);

Jack Loeffler, *Adventures with Ed: A Portrait of Abbey* (Albuquerque: University of New Mexico Press, 2002).

References:

Abbeyweb <http://www.abbeyweb.net/abbey.html>;

James Hepworth and Gregory McNammee, eds., *Resist Much, Obey Little* (Salt Lake City: Dream Garden, 1985);

Edward Hoagland, "Standing Tough in the Desert," *New York Times Book Review,* 7 May 1989, p. 44;

Charles E. Little, "Books for the Wilderness," *Wilderness* (Summer 1988): 56, 59;

Russell Martin, *A Story That Stands like a Dam: Glen Canyon and the Struggle for the Soul of the West* (New York: Holt, 1989);

Garth McCann, *Edward Abbey* (Boise: Boise State University Press, 1977);

Roderick Nash, *Wilderness and the American Mind,* third edition (New Haven: Yale University Press, 1982);

Doug Peacock, "Chasing Abbey," *Outside Online* <http://web.outsideonline.com/magazine/0897/9708abbey.html>;

William T. Pilkington, "Edward Abbey: Southwestern Anarchist," *Western Review* (Winter 1966): 58–62;

Pilkington, "Edward Abbey: Western Philosopher, or How to Be a 'Happy Hopi Hippie,'" *Western American Literature* (9 May 1974): 17–31;

"The Plowboy Interview: Edward Abbey: Slowing the Industrialization of Planet Earth," *Mother Earth News* (May–June 1984): 17+;

Peter Quigley, ed., *Coyote in the Maze: Tracking Edward Abbey in a World of Words* (Salt Lake City: University of Utah Press, 1998);

Ann Ronald, *The New West of Edward Abbey,* second edition (Reno: University of Nevada Press, 2000);

Ken Sleight, "Abbey & Me" <http://www.canyoncountryzephyr.com/archives/abbey-me.html> ;

Henry David Thoreau, *Walden* (Princeton: Princeton University Press, 1973);

Jon Tuska and Vicki Piekarski, eds., *Encyclopedia of Frontier and Western Fiction* (New York: McGraw-Hill, 1983);

Peter Wild, *Pioneer Conservationists of Western America* (Missoula, Mont.: Mountain Press, 1979).

Papers:

The major collection of Edward Abbey's manuscripts is held at the Special Collections Library of the University of Arizona. A smaller collection is housed at the Center for Southwest Research at the University of New Mexico.

Mary Hunter Austin

(9 September 1868 – 13 August 1934)

Benay Blend

See also the Austin entries in *DLB 9: American Novelists, 1910–1945; DLB 78: American Short-Story Writers, 1880–1910; DLB 206: Twentieth-Century American Western Writers, First Series;* and *DLB 221: American Women Prose Writers, 1870–1920.*

BOOKS: *The Land of Little Rain* (Boston & New York: Houghton, Mifflin, 1903);

The Basket Woman: A Book of Fanciful Tales for Children (Boston & New York: Houghton, Mifflin, 1904);

Isidro (Boston & New York: Houghton, Mifflin, 1905);

The Flock, illustrated by E. Boyd Smith (Boston & New York: Houghton, Mifflin, 1906; London: Constable, 1906);

Santa Lucia: A Common Story (New York & London: Harper, 1908);

Lost Borders (New York & London: Harper, 1909);

Outland, as Gordon Stairs (London: Murray, 1910); as Mary Austin (New York: Boni & Liveright, 1919);

The Arrow-Maker: A Drama in Three Acts (New York: Duffield, 1911; revised edition, Boston: Houghton Mifflin, 1915);

Christ in Italy: Being the Adventures of a Maverick among Masterpieces (New York: Duffield, 1912);

A Woman of Genius (Garden City, N.Y.: Doubleday, Page, 1912; revised edition, Boston: Houghton Mifflin, 1917);

The Green Bough: A Tale of the Resurrection (Garden City, N.Y.: Doubleday, Page, 1913);

The Lovely Lady (Garden City, N.Y.: Doubleday, Page, 1913);

California: The Land of the Sun, text by Austin, paintings by Sutton Palmer (London: Black, 1914; New York: Macmillan, 1914); revised as *The Lands of the Sun* (Boston & New York: Houghton Mifflin, 1927);

Love and the Soul Maker (New York & London: Appleton, 1914);

The Man Jesus: Being a Brief Account of the Life and Teaching of the Prophet of Nazareth (New York & London: Harper, 1915); revised as *A Small Town Man* (New York & London: Harper, 1925);

Mary Hunter Austin, 1906

The Ford, illustrated by E. Boyd Smith (Boston & New York: Houghton Mifflin, 1917);

The Trail Book (Boston & New York: Houghton Mifflin, 1918);

The Young Woman Citizen (New York: Woman's Press, 1918);

No. 26 Jayne Street (Boston & New York: Houghton Mifflin, 1920);

The American Rhythm (New York: Harcourt, Brace, 1923; enlarged as *The American Rhythm: Studies and Reexpressions of Amerindian Songs* (Boston & New York: Houghton Mifflin, 1930);

The Land of Journey's Ending (New York & London: Century, 1924; London: Allen & Unwin, 1925);

Everyman's Genius (Indianapolis: Bobbs-Merrill, 1925; London: Bobbs-Merrill, 1926);

The Children Sing in the Far West (Boston & New York: Houghton Mifflin, 1928);

Taos Pueblo, text by Austin, photographs by Ansel Adams (San Francisco: Grabhorn Press, 1930);

Experiences Facing Death (Indianapolis: Bobbs-Merrill, 1931; London: Rider, 1931);

Starry Adventure (Boston & New York: Houghton Mifflin, 1931);

Earth Horizon: Autobiography (Boston & New York: Houghton Mifflin, 1932);

Can Prayer Be Answered? (New York: Farrar & Rinehart, 1934);

Indian Pottery of the Rio Grande (Pasadena, Cal.: Esto, 1934);

One-Smoke Stories (Boston & New York: Houghton Mifflin, 1934);

When I Am Dead (Santa Fe, N.Mex.: Privately printed by Rydal Press, 1935);

The Mother of Felipe and Other Early Stories, edited by Franklin Walker (San Francisco: Book Club of California, 1950);

One Hundred Miles on Horseback, edited by Donald P. Ringler (Los Angeles: Book Club of California, 1950);

Stories from the Country of Lost Borders, edited by Marjorie Pryse (New Brunswick, N.J.: Rutgers University Press, 1987);

Western Trails: A Collection of Short Stories, edited by Melody Graulich (Reno: University of Nevada Press, 1987);

Cactus Thorn, a Novella (Reno: University of Nevada Press, 1988);

Beyond Borders: The Selected Essays of Mary Austin, edited by Reuben J. Ellis (Carbondale: Southern Illinois University Press, 1996);

A Mary Austin Reader, edited by Esther Lanigan (Tucson: University of Arizona Press, 1996).

PLAY PRODUCTIONS: *The Arrow-Maker,* New York, New Theatre, 27 February 1911;

Fire, Carmel, California, Forest Theatre, 1912;

The Man Who Didn't Believe in Christmas, New York, Cohan and Harris Theatre, 1916.

OTHER: "The Tremblor," in *The California Earthquake of 1906,* edited by David Starr Jordan (San Francisco: Robertson, 1907);

Path on the Rainbow: An Anthology of Songs and Chants from the Indians of North America, edited by George W. Cronyn, introduction by Austin (New York: Boni & Liveright, 1918);

"My First Publication," in *My Maiden Effort: Being the Personal Confessions of Well-Known American Authors as to Their Literary Beginnings,* edited by Gelett Burgess (Garden City, N.Y. & Toronto: Doubleday, Page, 1921);

"The American Form of the Novel," in *The Novel of Tomorrow and the Scope of Fiction, by Twelve American Novelists* (Indianapolis: Bobbs-Merrill, 1922);

"Aboriginal American Literature," in *American Writers on American Literature,* edited by John Macy (New York: Liveright, 1934).

"We are most of us only half-breeds, you know, mestizos between the old culture and the new—inheritors of no tradition and not yet like true sons of the soil, able to make our own." Written four years before her death in 1934 to the editor of the *Saturday Review of Literature,* Mary Austin's words accurately sum up a life spent living at the margins of her own culture; a multicultural perspective allowed her to redefine American attitudes toward nature as she found value in the untouched landscape and those who had for centuries adapted to its ways. More than forty years before Rachel Carson's *Silent Spring* (1962), Mary Austin was serving as an important force in protecting regions from overdevelopment and promoting their importance. One of her major themes is women's subordination by men in her society; even her nature works *The Land of Little Rain* (1903), *Lost Borders* (1909), and *Cactus Thorn* (1988) explore ways in which Western patriarchal culture subjects women and nature to both male domination and exploitation. Her more obviously political work received little attention until reprints of her novel *A Woman of Genius* (originally published in 1912, revised in 1917, and reprinted in 1985) brought her new readers and acclaim.

Writing in the tradition of such early-nineteenth-century nature essayists as Susan Fenimore Cooper, Austin records details of the flora and fauna around her homes in California and New Mexico. *The Land of Little Rain,* her first and most famous collection of short sketches, shares with Henry David Thoreau's *Walden* (1854) a preference for rural living, an antimaterialist stance, and a strong sense of respect due to all forms of nature, animate and inanimate. Austin's intimate connection to land also places her alongside Mary Wilkins Freeman and Sarah Orne Jewett, two late-nineteenth-century women who wrote in the genre of literary regionalism.

But Austin's writing also speaks to an ongoing debate among feminist theorists over how to assert gender difference without adopting a determinist understanding either of biological differences or of socially constructed gender roles. Mary Austin's homage to the innate superiority of womanhood, premised on women's capacity for various forms of relationships and caring,

*Mary and Stanford Wallace Austin at
the time of their marriage, 1891*

century female nature writers and those who write within
the modern feminist and ecological traditions.

Austin's literary ambitions vied with socially sanctioned stereotypes of women's roles. Born on 9 September 1868 in Carlinville, Illinois, Mary Hunter was the
second child and first daughter of George Hunter, a
young lawyer noted for his love of books, and Susannah
Graham Hunter, daughter of a drugstore keeper. Mary's
father, who had encouraged her interest in reading, died
when she was ten. Although her mother actively took
part in various social and cultural organizations, she disparaged her child's active imagination. As Austin herself
described—and as such biographers as Augusta Fink,
Dudley Wynn, and T. M. Pearce have amply noted—she
had a traumatic and unhappy childhood. She found refuge in nearby orchards; there, beneath a walnut tree, at
the age of five, she had her first contact with what she
later called the Presence, an inner sense of power that
lasted throughout her life. As Fink notes in *I-Mary: A Biography of Mary Austin* (1983), Mary came to know herself as
two persons: I-Mary, her creative imagination, who provided inspiration for the outer Mary-by-herself, and
Mary-by-herself, who developed a crust of abrasive
self-protection to survive in an often inhospitable world.

In her youth, however, Hunter refused to con-
form to popular female stereotypes, and she continued
this stance when she moved to Southern California in
1888 with her mother and brother, Jim, who planned to
support the family with a homestead. Hunter could not
support herself with her writing, however, and eventually resigned herself to marriage. When Stanford Wallace Austin, a scholarly but luckless gentleman farmer,
showed an interest in her, she married him on 18 May
1891. On 30 October 1892 they had a daughter, Ruth,
who was mentally challenged. Eleven years later she
published *The Land of Little Rain,* a paean to the desert
that had become central to her life. An immediate success, this work provided her an ideal role model in the
figure of Seyavi, the basketmaker. In writing about
Paiute women, in particular the female artisans of that
tribe, Austin sought to negate misogynist images of
women as passive earth mothers while affirming their
connection to the land. Austin's sketches about Indian
life in the California desert found a wide reading audience, and of all her work, *The Land of Little Rain*
endures. As Esther Lanigan notes in *Mary Austin: Song of
a Maverick* (1989), Austin's depiction of a seemingly
unencumbered, preindustrial world sparked the interest
of an alienated public. This market lasted until the
1930s, when a demand for modern art replaced that for
a nostalgic and romantic Western past.

Into *The Land of Little Rain* Austin poured not only
her love of the land but also the aching loneliness and
frustration that she had known in her twelve years of liv-

Outland, published under the pseudonym Gordon Stairs
in 1910 in London and republished under Austin's own
name in 1919 in New York, has been challenged by later
feminist critics, including Ynestra King and Caroline Merchant, who argue that women's nature is to do more than
nurture. A prey to the cultural assumptions of her time,
Austin can sometimes sound like an unwitting proponent
for the argument that women have an essential nature
that transcends culture and socialization. Striving for an
identity as a woman artist in a male profession, Austin
found herself identifying with socially constructed notions
of "femininity" even as she criticized those "feminine" values as hampering women's ambition. While Austin identified herself as "feminine," she chose a life that turned
away from responsibilities (such as marriage and motherhood) traditionally assigned to women. As Vera Norwood notes in *Made from This Earth: American Women and
Nature* (1993), Austin's exploration of the ways in which
Western patriarchal culture subjects women even as it
exploits nature was a forerunner of ecofeminists—theorists
who draw on insights of ecology, feminism, and socialism
in order to analyze connections between the domination
of women and the domination of nature—who picked up
this issue much later in the century. An environmental
ethic that overrides traditional ethics based on rights,
rules, and public good, with considerations of intuition,
caring, and web-like human relationships, this major
theme in Austin's work forms a bridge between nineteenth-

ing in Southern California. The future of this region, destined as it was to become a satellite of its metropolitan neighbor, included an environment no longer compatible with Austin's needs. In her autobiography, Austin stated that she left Inyo County because of the demands of her career and the instability of her health. In 1905 she placed her daughter in an institution for the mentally challenged. Her marriage having ended, though not legally until 1914, she also wanted to leave the area before the desert, too, was destroyed.

In 1906, at age thirty-eight, Austin was enjoying good reviews of *The Land of Little Rain* and in the process of leaving her incompatible marriage in order to pursue a writer's life at Carmel, where the poet George Sterling had persuaded a small group of artists to make their homes. While she was still at Carmel, in 1906, Austin began work on the last two books of the trilogy (including *The Land of Little Rain*) that was perhaps the best writing of her career—*The Flock* (1906) and *Lost Borders*. In *The Flock* she recounts the history of Mexican, Basque, and French herdsmen who had developed the sheep business in the San Joaquin Valley of California's Sierra Nevada during the last two centuries. *Lost Borders*, taken from stories Austin had collected, focuses on accounts of women who, like herself, challenge the patriarchal powers that they question. As David Wyatt notes in *The Fall into Eden: Landscape and Imagination in California* (1986), Austin chose the desert as background because it was "empty, unclaimed, unstoried," an undecipherable text that allowed her freedom of creation. Among all its characters, the Walking Woman best epitomizes the desert spirit in human form that Austin claimed for her own. Unlike men, who wander in the desert in search of some external treasure, this woman guided Austin in her quest to become healed and whole inside. Modeled on the local legend of a mysterious "Mrs. Walker," this final and most important story in *Lost Borders* centers on the woman Austin claimed to have met toward the latter 1880s. In Mrs. Walker she found a kindred spirit—dispossessed of "man-made" human qualities, ageless and nameless. The other woman seemed to have found an alternate identity not defined by patriarchal strictures, an identity that Austin wanted for her own.

During the years until 1924, when Austin sold her house in Carmel and moved to Santa Fe, she traveled for four years in Italy and England, then returned in 1912 to New York, where she lived for some time. But she returned often to California for the next twelve years. During that time she frequented the Greenwich Village salon of Mabel Dodge, a wealthy patron of the arts. Dodge later moved to Taos, along with artists and writers, including Austin, who followed in her wake.

In New York, Austin's contact with such avant-garde theorists as Emma Goldman, along with a disappointing love affair with the muckraker Lincoln

Austin's daughter, Ruth, circa 1900

Steffens, inspired her to turn to writing social commentary. Several of her most feminist novels come from this period, including *A Woman of Genius* (1912), written ten years before her move to another arid landscape, where her attention turned once more to nature writing. In this book she focused on personal concerns, in particular her desire to transcend those oppositions between public and private, gender and vocation, affection and ambition that she believed had hindered gifted women. Olivia Lattimore, her heroine in this novel, mirrors Austin's growing confidence in her abilities as an authoritative writer with a vision.

In this account of a woman's awakening, told in the form of memoirs, Austin reverses the typical pattern of female development. Rather than leading to inner withdrawal, Olivia's dissatisfaction with social norms leads her to follow the path commonly associated with male heroes, that of devotion to a career (in art) as a means toward spiritual growth. Although her success comes at the price of destroying her marriage and intimidating another lover, she is contented at the end of the novel. Olivia, like Mrs. Walker, is a trailblazer; her goal is nothing less than to be a "great lady, good comrade and lover," all roles that were difficult alone for a woman, much less in combination.

*Binding for Austin's 1903 collection of sketches about
Paiute women and their connection to the earth
(Ken Lopez catalogue, 2000)*

In 1924 Austin returned permanently to the West. Settling in Santa Fe, New Mexico, she built Casa Querida, her "beloved house," in which she spent her time collecting Southwestern Native American art and indulging in her love for cooking and gardening. The move West gave her new literary inspiration; she turned much of her attention to nonfiction, examining the relationship between landscape and culture in *The American Rhythm* (1923) and *The Land of Journey's Ending* (1924). With the latter, Austin left behind the lush California terrain for a harsh yet instructive environment, replete with lessons for this lonely woman in how to survive with minimal nurturance. Although her early life had been lonely, the words that Austin used to express her feelings about the desert became a rich reward that she could absorb with appreciation. Significantly, in *The Land of Journey's Ending,* she chose the cactus to represent ultimate adaptation to the desert. Austin felt an affinity with these plants that adapted so well to their environment. Through such associations, she learned not to be overwhelmed by the vastness of the landscape but instead to learn from its plants and animals how to achieve self-nurturance in an apparently arid life.

Austin's only published novel during this period was *Starry Adventure* (1931), which reiterates two of her major themes—the use of indigenous cultures to explore her own complex and contradictory feelings about her position as a woman and the land as a shaping precedent in her story. Financial responsibilities, however, forced her to publish a consistent flow of magazine articles and short pieces, and she soon began work on an autobiography that consumed her time and energy for several years. As she began to look back upon her life, seeing unhappiness at the core of it, she rejected that pervasive gloom. As a writer of autobiography, she became her own mother, the creator in *Earth Horizon: Autobiography* (1932) of her family history and the controlling adult in that literary bonding. Consequently, Austin added to the circle of writers who had already built upon a distinct tradition of writing a female life.

Unburdened as a result of an examination of her past, Austin accepted the reality of her life, not with misgivings but, as Melody Graulich notes, with pleasure. Anecdotes of this period are many and bolster the contention that Austin had stopped "walking" many years before. She had put down substantial roots in Santa Fe—too late, perhaps, to have much influence on her writing—but soon enough to allow her to take pleasure in her lovely garden, her kindly neighbors, and the Hispanic and Indian peoples whose culture she sought to preserve. On 13 August 1934 Austin suffered a brain hemorrhage and died painlessly in her sleep.

Mary Hunter Austin found strength and inspiration in the dry Southwestern desert. Involved in national and local movements of her day, she took her place with men in defining the place of the region in American culture. Perhaps the most important contribution of Austin's nature writing is that she claimed "all places were beautiful and interesting so long as they were outdoors." This insight awakened her sensitivity to the desert, where she found previously ignored beauty and spiritual possibilities. She left a credo that includes an appreciation of everything in nature, a biocentric rather than an anthropocentric ethic; it also posits an end to such dualisms as male/female, thought/action, and spirit/natural. Today, her desires have found company with environmentalists around the world who are searching for an alternate way of living on the earth, one that emphasizes the values of cultural pluralism and fosters regard for limited natural resources. Austin's texts speak of the common desire for a different kind of society, one based on cooperation and community and on the intrinsic value of all people. Longings such as these correspond closely to the ecofeminist concept of a partnership-based society that promotes communication and mutual respect, pursues the development of life-enhancing, rather than life-destroying, technologies, and emphasizes web-like

The Ploughed Lands.

What I like most about the speech of the campody is that there are no confidences. When they talk there of the essential performances of life it is because they _are_ the essential and therefore worth talking about. Only Heaven who made my heart knows why it should have become a pit, bottomless and insatiable for the husks

Page from the first draft of one of the stories in Austin's Lost Borders, *published in 1909*
(Mary Austin Papers, The Huntington Library, San Marino, California)

Austin, circa 1930

relationships rather than hierarchies, circular linking rather than pyramidal ranking.

Letters:
T. M. Pearce, *Literary America, 1903–1934: The Mary Austin Letters* (Westport, Conn.: Greenwood Press, 1979).

Biographies:
Helen Doyle, *Mary Austin: Woman of Genius* (New York: Gotham House, 1939);

Augusta Fink, *I-Mary: A Biography of Mary Austin* (Tucson: University of Arizona Press, 1983);

Esther Lanigan, *Mary Austin: Song of a Maverick* (New Haven: Yale University Press, 1989);

Peggy Pond Church, *Wind's Trail: The Early Life of Mary Austin,* edited by Shelley Armitage (Albuquerque: Museum of New Mexico Press, 1990).

References:
Benay Blend, "Building a 'House of Earth': Mary Austin, Environment Activist and Writer," *Critical Matrix: The Princeton Journal of Women, Gender, and Culture,* 30 (Fall 1996): 73–90;

Blend, "Mary Austin and the Western Conservation Movement," *Journal of the Southwest,* 30 (Spring 1988): 12–35;

Melody Graulich and Elizabeth Klimasmith, eds., *Exploring Lost Borders: Critical Essays on Mary Austin* (Reno: University of Nevada Press, 1999);

Vera Norwood, *Made from This Earth: American Women and Nature* (Chapel Hill: University of North Carolina Press, 1993);

T. M. Pearce, *Mary Hunter Austin* (New York: Twayne, 1956);

David Wyatt, *The Fall into Eden: Landscape and Imagination in California* (New York: Cambridge University Press, 1986);

Dudley Wynn, *A Critical Study of the Writings of Mary Hunter Austin, 1868–1934* (New York: Graduate School of Arts and Sciences, 1941).

Papers:
The principle collection of unpublished Mary Hunter Austin material is in the Huntington Library, San Marino, California. Other significant documents are housed at the Bancroft Library of the University of California at Berkeley. A smaller collection is housed in the library of the University of New Mexico.

Rick Bass

(7 March 1958 –   )

Richard Hunt
Kirkwood Community College

See also the Bass entry in *DLB 212: Twentieth-Century American Western Writers, Second Series.*

BOOKS: *The Deer Pasture*, illustrated by Hughes [Bass] (College Station: Texas A & M University Press, 1985);

Wild to the Heart, illustrated by Elizabeth Hughes [Bass] (Harrisburg, Pa.: Stackpole Books, 1987);

The Watch: Stories (New York: Norton, 1989);

Oil Notes, illustrated by Hughes [Bass] (Boston: Houghton Mifflin, 1989; London: Collins, 1989);

Winter: Notes from Montana, illustrated by Hughes [Bass] (Boston: Houghton Mifflin/Seymour Lawrence, 1991);

The Ninemile Wolves (Livingston, Mont.: Clark City, 1992);

Platte River (Boston: Houghton Mifflin/Seymour Lawrence, 1994);

In the Loyal Mountains (Boston: Houghton Mifflin/Seymour Lawrence, 1995);

The Lost Grizzlies: A Search for Survivors in the Wilderness of Colorado (Boston: Houghton Mifflin/Seymour Lawrence, 1995; London: Constable, 1996);

The Book of Yaak (Boston: Houghton Mifflin/Seymour Lawrence, 1996);

The Sky, the Stars, the Wilderness (Boston: Houghton Mifflin/Seymour Lawrence, 1997);

Fiber, illustrated by Hughes Bass (Athens: University of Georgia Press, 1998);

The New Wolves: The Return of the Mexican Wolf to the American Southwest, illustrated by Hughes Bass (New York: Lyons Press, 1998);

Where the Sea Used to Be (Boston: Houghton Mifflin/Seymour Lawrence, 1998);

Brown Dog of the Yaak: Essays on Art and Activism, edited by Scott Slovic, Credo Series (Minneapolis: Milkweed Editions, 1999);

Colter: The True Story of the Best Dog I Ever Had (Boston: Houghton Mifflin, 2000);

The Hermit's Story: Stories (Boston: Houghton Mifflin, 2002).

Rick Bass (photograph by Nancy Crampton; from the dust jacket for The Ninemile Wolves, *1992)*

OTHER: "The Afterlife" and "Valley of the Crows," in *On Nature's Terms: Contemporary Voices*, edited by Thomas J. Lyon and Peter Stine (College Station: Texas A & M University Press, 1992), pp. 55–82, 166–174;

"The Nantahala," in *Being in the World: An Environmental Reader for Writers*, edited by Scott Slovic and Terrell F. Dixon (New York: Macmillan, 1993), pp. 289–295;

29

"The Fringe," in *American Nature Writing 1994,* edited by John Murray (San Francisco: Sierra Club Books, 1994), pp. 36–44;

"Creatures of the Dictator," in *American Nature Writing 1995,* edited by Murray (San Francisco: Sierra Club Books, 1995), pp. 123–144;

"Getting It Right," in *Headwaters: Montana Writers on Water and Wilderness,* edited by Annick Smith (Missoula, Mont.: Hellgate Writers, 1996), pp. 5–7;

"Untouched Country," in *Testimony: Writers of the West Speak on Behalf of Utah Wilderness,* edited by Stephen Trimble and Terry Tempest Williams (Minneapolis: Milkweed Editions, 1996), pp. 36–38;

"On Willow Creek," in *Literature and the Environment,* edited by Lorraine Anderson, Slovic, and John P. O'Grady (New York: Longman, 1998), pp. 249–258;

The Roadless Yaak: Reflections about One of Our Last Great Wild Places, edited by Bass (Guilford, Conn.: Lyons Press, 2002).

SELECTED PERIODICAL PUBLICATIONS–
UNCOLLECTED: "A Dog in the Hand," *Esquire,* 112 (October 1989): 150–154;

"Why I Hunt," *Esquire,* 114 (October 1990): 116–118;

"Crossing Over," *Petroglyph,* 4 (1992): 17–23;

"The Literature of Loss," *Manōa,* 4 (Fall 1992): 75–76;

"20515 House, 20510 Senate," *American Nature Writing Newsletter,* 5 (Spring 1993): 3–5;

"Paradise Rising," *Conde Nast Traveler,* 28 (June 1993): 120–128;

"Slowing Down in Logan Canyon," *Audubon,* 96 (November/December 1993): 42–50;

"Out on the Wild Fringe," *Audubon,* 96 (January/February 1994): 84–90;

"The Earth Divers," *Weber Studies,* 11 (Fall 1994): 7–10;

"Almost Like Hibernation," *House Beautiful,* 137 (February 1995): 14–16;

"The Perfect Day," *Sierra,* 80 (May/June 1995): 68–78;

"The Woodland Caribou: They're Still Out There," *Audubon,* 97 (May/June 1995): 76–84, 114–115;

"The War on the West," *Harper's,* 292 (February 1996): 13–15;

"Through Rosalind's Eyes," *Audubon,* 98 (July/August 1996): 90–95;

"The Heart of a Forest," *Audubon,* 99 (January/February 1997): 39–49, 96–98;

"Round River," *Orion,* 16 (Summer 1997): 34–39;

"Hold Nothing Back," *Sierra,* 82 (September/October 1997): 32–33;

"The Kootenai Five," *Whole Terrain,* 7 (1997–1998): 62–65;

"Eating Montana: Last Stand of the Wilderness," *Amicus Journal,* 20 (Summer 1998): 33–38;

"The Raccoons of Yaak," *Orion,* 18 (Spring 1999): 18–27;

"Roaring Through the Wilderness," *New York Times,* 7 August 1999, p. A7;

"The Glacier Principle," *Audubon,* 101 (November/December 1999): 50–57;

"A Winter's Tale," *Atlantic Monthly,* 285 (January 2000): 22–26;

"Why So Many Nature Writers?" *Orion,* 19 (Autumn 2000): 68–73;

"Why I Hunt," *Sierra,* 86 (July/August 2001): 58–61;

"Double-Talk," *Audubon,* 103 (November/December 2001): 17–20;

"The Thirty-Years War," *New York Times,* 7 August 2002, p. A17;

"Gold Hill," *Paris Review,* 162 (Summer 2002): 232–236;

"Once Upon a Time," *On Earth: Environmental Politics People,* 24, no. 2 (Summer 2002): 22–27.

Among the nature writers of the late twentieth and early twenty-first centuries, Rick Bass is perhaps the most ardent, the most outspoken, and the most visible environmental activist and defender of wildness. Critical perceptions of Bass's work are scant, owing perhaps to both the usual time lag between an artist's work and the publication of substantial criticism and to a perception of the nonfiction form that makes up the bulk of his work as somehow less than literary. Yet, each of the books Bass has published since *The Deer Pasture* first appeared in 1985 has been widely reviewed in venues ranging from *Mother Jones* to *The New York Times.*

Bass began his literary career while working as a petroleum geologist in Jackson, Mississippi, but found his true voice and calling only after his 1987 move to the Yaak Valley in northwestern Montana. Born on 7 March 1958 in Fort Worth, Texas, one of three sons of C. R. Bass, an oil geologist, and Mary Lucy Robson Bass, a schoolteacher, and raised primarily in Houston, Bass spent much of his youth in the wildlands of the Texas hill country. While in high school, Bass traveled to Utah State University for a scholarship test and afterward found himself increasingly drawn to the mountain West he discovered there. He returned to Utah State for college, majoring in geology and playing football, but perhaps his most significant discovery there was the work of Edward Abbey. Bass took a course called Advanced Expository Writing from Thomas J. Lyon, the longtime editor of *Western American Literature* and editor of many anthologies of American nature writing. Abbey's *The Monkey Wrench Gang* (1975), which Bass read his first year in college, had a major impact on him; he writes in "Crossing Over" (*Petroglyph,* 1992) that he "didn't understand the book then as an article of faith [on] the religion of action," but Abbey's anger and excitement stayed with him, reappearing more forcefully after he found his own place worthy of an avid defending.

Bass writes of these early years in his first book, *The Deer Pasture.* In part a book of praise for an almost archetypal place, one dear to Bass's memory, the essays in the book detail his relationship with a Texas hill country pasture his family had leased for nearly half a century and where he hunted deer. That pasture served as a touchstone for Bass in his first year working as a geologist in Mississippi; pictures of the pasture and surrounding territory decorated his office cubicle, and a map of the territory rested in a desk drawer. In recollecting the times he spent there, Bass initiated many of the themes that resurface in his later work, including the necessity of high-order predators to a healthy ecosystem. But unlike more-radical environmentalists, who are wont to regard any incursion—and especially one intended for hunting—as an affront to nature, Bass never suggests that all humans abandon their presence in these wild areas (though he often suggests that only so many humans can fit in these places without harming them). Bass is careful to argue for responsibility in dealing with the natural world, and in no area is this responsibility more critical than in hunting. Such themes evolved over the next decade and a half into the environmental jeremiads of *The Book of Yaak* (1996) and *Fiber* (1998).

Following his graduation from Utah State University, Bass took a job in Mississippi. But the West continued to call to him; in his second book, *Wild to the Heart* (1987), he writes of weekend road trips into the mountains of Utah and New Mexico. The last of Bass's pre-Yaak books, the thirteen essays of *Wild to the Heart* show him at the end of his time spent as a geologist in Mississippi and trace his fascination with the idea of Western wilderness as a place to live. In this work, as in *The Deer Pasture,* Bass blends detailed sensorial experience with the more-abstract elements of that fascination. The first essay opens by describing a strawberry milkshake he buys in Louisiana on his way west. The shake comes from a drive-in on his route from the Mississippi job to the mountains, where he spends as much time as possible. He writes that "you have to tag the bottom and then come up a good inch or so if you want to get anything." Over the course of these essays, Bass tells of his growing obsession with the mountains. He typically took off immediately after work on Fridays and drove eighteen hours into the New Mexico mountains, carefully accounting for each hour in the wilderness before he had to return to his job. The distinction

between the two places—Mississippi and the mountains—is crucial to Bass, who writes, "Everything before [arriving in the mountains] is Getting There; everything afterward is There Itself." Much of this book foreshadows ideas he explores in more depth in later years, including his continuing insistence that readers need not visit the places he asks them to value. He says much the same thing about the Yaak, fearing that the exposure his writing gives the place may lead to its ruination, much as Abbey feared for Arches in *Desert Solitaire* (1968). Reading the early essays now, one is struck by the extremes of Bass's restlessness. Such energy clearly could not long be constrained by office cubicles. Shortly after publishing these thoughts, in 1987 Bass quit his job, packed everything he owned into an aging Datsun pickup, and with his girlfriend, artist Elizabeth Hughes, and their two dogs, headed northwest in search of a place where they could practice their art.

Oil Notes, published in 1989, both celebrated Bass's career in the oil business and initiated the next phase of his life. On the first page Bass writes, "I don't know if I can even write well enough to explain why oil is found in some places and not in others." And while he is a petroleum geologist (he continued to work in the oil business for a time even after moving to Montana), the oil mentioned in this book appears more metaphoric than metamorphic. Oil is value; oil in the ground makes the ground valuable. But Bass—even this early in his stay in Montana—recognized that value need not always be equated with money. The "wealth" of the Yaak Valley is in its wildness; in *Oil Notes,* though the book is ostensibly about the oil business as he understands it (one back-cover blurb from *Oil Notes* equates Bass's accomplishment with oil to Isaac Walton's with fishing), he is clear that the book is also an act of dissembling, admitting that "Not all [the notes that became this book] are going to be about oil." *Oil Notes* also, for instance, introduces readers to Hughes, whose graceful drawings illustrate many of Bass's books.

Bass also published *The Watch* in 1989, the same year as *Oil Notes.* A collection of short stories set in varied landscapes, *The Watch* offers an early glimpse of Bass's range and interests as a fiction writer. His first book of fiction, *The Watch* offers a rather harsher vision of wildness than does his nonfiction. Its stories can be grouped into three categories: the relationship between old men and wildness; the ills of urban life; and stories of the West. In the title story, Buzbee—who may be a prototype for Old Dudley in his novel *Where the Sea Used to Be* (1998)—is an eccentric seventy-year-old who becomes a wild man of the Mississippi swamps, where he forms a community with societal discards and

Dust jacket for the 1989 book in which Bass describes the value of the wildness in the Yaak Valley of Montana (Richland County Public Library)

rejects. In a battle of wills with his son, Buzbee comes out second-best; as the story ends, he is chained to a house, plotting escape. "Mexico" and "Redfish" use fishing as a metaphor for the intrusion of urban sensibilities into wildness. In "Mexico" Kirby is newly oil-rich. He buys a mansion and turns the swimming pool into a bass pond full of junk. In "Redfish" the same character's big plans for his fishing trip to the Gulf Coast are forestalled by a freak snowstorm. The Yaak Valley is the setting for "Choteau" and allows Bass to reflect in fiction on the danger to wild places that is posed by human indifference and greed.

Bass and Hughes married in 1991, and later two daughters were born to them, Mary Katherine in 1992, and Lowry Elizabeth in 1995. The journey that Bass and Hughes made to the Northwest occupies the opening sections of *Winter: Notes from Montana* (1991), arguably Bass's most important book. The most crucial of all his works, *Winter* marks a distinct turning point in both Bass's life and his artistry. He and Hughes had sought only "a place of ultimate wildness, with the first yardstick of privacy: a place where you could walk around naked if you wanted to." Bass found that place in northwestern Montana's Yaak Valley, where he fell into a caretaker's job and began his new life. In the process of coming to terms with the demands of a life in the woods, Bass also came to love his adopted home; with the passion of the newly converted, he spent the next decade and a half working to preserve its wild character. His passionate environmental activism had not yet become fully formed in *Winter:* he often appears more concerned with fitting into the Yaak's community of humans than into its natural community. Yet, even at this early stage of his career his preoccupation with the wonder of wildness is clearly established; he writes in *Winter,* for instance, that "the valley shakes with mystery, with beauty, with secrets." Though winter seemed far away, Bass understood that he would have to survive it in order to become truly a part of the valley. Most of *Winter* is devoted to his efforts to become acclimatized in this new place; and the bulk of his literary efforts in the following decade and a half draw on the relationship he established with the valley.

Written Thoreau-like in journal form, *Winter* also shows readers the process by which the titular season takes over the lives of all who live in the valley. Bass romanticizes that "Anything I'm guilty of is forgiven when the snow falls"; the sins of which he speaks are those of the newcomer, of one who does not (yet) know how to get along in these woods. He is still an outsider in *Winter,* more spiritually than physically. Yet, even this early in his residency, Bass recognizes with an eerie prescience that his connection to the Yaak will develop into something approximating an obsession: "I can picture getting so addicted to this valley, so dependent on it for my peace, that I become hostage to it." Bass's connection to the valley becomes established in the concluding scene of *Winter.* He has been fishing with his father, returning the fish he catches to the river; but he tosses the last one to a weasel that has been watching the two men. The gesture is, perhaps, merely a random act of kindness; but it is also an act of community, a demonstration of the connection to place that marks Bass's later writing as thoroughly as a connection to place has ever marked an American author. Though isolated in a corner of Montana, the Yaak Valley was—and is—beset by many of the human-created forces affecting the natural environment, such as logging, development, and pollution. Bass did not come to the Yaak to protect it, but he quickly found himself drawn into a life of activism in defense of the valley and its wild creatures. That activism came to overshadow, largely against his will, the artist he wished to become.

The Ninemile Wolves (1992) is a journalistic account of the efforts of a pack of wolves to reinhabit the Ninemile Valley in northern Montana. They came on their own, rather than as part of an officially sanctioned reintroduction effort, but their progress was carefully monitored by agents of the U.S. Fish and Wildlife Service. Bass's primary thesis is that these wolves belong in the Ninemile Valley, and by extension anywhere they can live as wild wolves. In any natural history (this is the first of Bass's three forays into that genre) there is always the problem of anthropomorphicity—that of turning the animals into representations of humans and assigning them human motivations and perceptions. Bass faces this problem head-on: the wolves, he writes, "remind us of ourselves on our better days, our best days."

Between 1991 and 1994, Bass continued to write obsessively about the need to protect and defend his adopted home in the Yaak Valley. During this period, he published more than twenty stories and articles in journals and magazines, and his work appeared in another twenty anthologies of both fiction and non-fiction. Significant among these articles is "The Literature of Loss," published in *Manoa* in 1992, in which Bass argues that damage to the natural world is "a crippling blow to the notion of literature" because it leads to "a reduction of the senses." During this time he also engaged in an extensive letter-writing campaign on behalf of the Yaak. In December 1993 he sent out a mass mailing to the membership list of the Association for the Study of Literature and Environment (ASLE), an academic organization founded the year before to promote and give critical context to the literary study of nature writing. In these letters Bass chronicled the astonishing fecundity of the Yaak Valley, listing the hundreds of species found there. Still ensconced in his scientific background, Bass wanted to rely upon science to argue for the preservation of the Yaak. But the mailing, an agonized cry for help in protecting an endangered place, received only partial support from the ASLE members, some of whom ignored the pleas and instead argued that the organization should not have allowed its address list to be used in such a manner. Though Bass was and is both well-respected and widely read in the circles of literary environmentalism, and though he was a featured speaker at the 1997 ASLE conference in Missoula, Montana, he has not used its membership list for further mailings.

In 1994 Bass ventured into fiction again with *Platte River,* a trio of novellas that consider the problems men face as they work through critical parts of their lives. In "Mahatma Joe," an evangelist comes to an Alaskan valley suspiciously like Yaak. He wants to reform the residents of the valley, who hold an annual "Naked Days" celebration every summer. But though he is ultimately successful, the novella closes with his

wondering what, if anything, he has accomplished. The second novella, "Field Events," set in upstate New York, where Bass had visited while attending the Bread Loaf writers workshop in 1983, is a celebration of physical strength, in which a discus thrower transcends his discipline to become an artist of the body. In the title story, Harley, a former pro-football player, comes to the wild Pacific Northwest. Like Ernest Hemingway's Nick Adams, Harley uses fishing as a means of self-discovery and recovery.

Bass's second collection of short stories, *In the Loyal Mountains,* appeared in 1995. Among the noteworthy stories in the volume are "Four Eyes," "Fires," and "The Valley." In the former, Bass considers the condition of a young boy who wears glasses. As is usually the case, his classmates tease and torment him about his glasses, but Bass wonders whether the boy "could see things with them, invisible things that they could not." The glasses are, then, presented as a passport into forbidden knowledge—and though the story poses as a treatise on the anti-intellectualism of the tormentors, it is also a further exploration into the nature of hidden knowledge, of what lives beneath surface appearances. In "Fires," Bass employs fire as his central metaphor in examining the nature of one's relationship to place. The fictional setting allows Bass to use the cut-and-burn slash piles of the timber industry, objects of great anger in his nonfiction, in a new manner. The move contributes to the dream effect of the story; but in real life Bass was angered because of the clear-cutting those piles represent. "The Valley" shows Bass in a highly narrative mode in a thinly veiled autobiographical account of life in the Yaak Valley.

After *In the Loyal Mountains,* Bass returned to his defense of wildness with *The Lost Grizzlies: A Search for Survivors in the Wilderness of Colorado* (1995). The second of Bass's natural histories, *The Lost Grizzlies* recounts his experiences while searching for remnant grizzly bears in the San Juan Mountains of southern Colorado. Along with Doug Peacock and students from the Round River conservation-studies field education school, Bass explores places where grizzlies have been reported since their officially declared extinction in the area. He does so more with hope than with certainty; yet, such a certainty is not necessary for him: "I wouldn't travel this far," he writes, "if there wasn't that spot, that place in my heart, that vacancy waiting to fill up with belief."

At this point in his career, Bass had not yet given himself over completely to seeking mystery; but though the scientific mind-set gained through his training in geology remained, he shows in this book the beginnings of a mystical sensibility that becomes increasingly prominent in later works. He writes, for instance, that finding the bears is "not quite like trying to prove God's

RICK BASS

THE NEW WOLVES

The Return of the Mexican Wolf
to the American Southwest

Dust jacket for Bass's 1998 book, about the efforts of a pack of Mexican wolves to reinhabit the Ninemile Valley in northern Montana (Richland County Public Library)

cles centered on the theme of saving his adopted home. In this first of his three "Yaak-tivist" books (the word comes from Michael P. Branch), Bass compiles articles and essays that have appeared elsewhere to present what he calls "a sourcebook, a handbook, a weapon to the heart" in the service of wilderness preservation. As he did with the Utah valley in *Wild to the Heart,* Bass asks readers to love the Yaak but not to enter it. Always, for Bass, the reason is the same: too much human encroachment will destroy a wild place, will drive out the animals that make it wild. Where previously he had been relatively circumspect, though, now he becomes explicit about the need for wilderness. "I am convinced," he writes, "that . . . we need wilderness to buffer this dark lost-gyroscopic tumble that democracy, top-heavy with business and leaning precariously over rot, has entered." In *Winter* Bass had written that he wanted only a quiet place to write when he came to Montana. A decade later, he writes that he "had no choice but to react against" the environmental devastation all around him in the valley. He also acknowledges in *The Book of Yaak* that his need to engage in activism started to overtake him as he began to feel he fit into the landscape. He writes with a sense of new urgency: "It's possible art could protect the last roadless areas of Yaak Valley. But I just don't think there's time for it." Throughout the essays in *The Book of Yaak* Bass returns to the themes of his natural histories, especially the idea that the wilderness is a source of magic or mystery, which for Bass (as for the medieval mystics whose spiritual focus Bass's work sometimes resembles) are equivalent terms.

Less "literary" perhaps than his previous nonfiction works, *The Book of Yaak* has a sense of urgency that overpowers other considerations. The forces of destruction are in a hurry, he contends; the forces opposing that destruction cannot be less so. If his art must suffer the sins of haste, so be it. His priorities are as they have always been—wild nature first; everything else after. *The Book of Yaak* is, then, important less for its literary qualities than for its uncompromising vision and clear articulation of purpose. *The Book of Yaak* also includes a more clearly distinguishable sense of anger, situating Bass in the line of environmental jeremiad established by Abbey. Although *The Book of Yaak* lacks the self-deprecating humor for which Abbey is justly famed, Bass's passion is a ready match for Abbey's.

Widely anticipated by his readers, *The Book of Yaak* did not meet with universal approval; the essays are often harsh demands for protection, calls for action by readers, and denouncements of the forces arrayed against environmental protection and preservation. But with that outpouring of emotion, Bass perhaps bought himself some breathing space in which to write the sto-

existence . . . [but] it's almost the same." Bass is operating on faith; the bears, like the wolves of the Ninemile Valley, are important to him not so much for their physical as for their mystical value, both to humans and to the wild areas their presence validates. In this sense, Bass echoes Aldo Leopold's recognition that the predators at the top of a food chain are crucial to its overall health. By extension, then, Bass suggests that the bears are also essential to the health of humankind, for "it is more than metaphor to say that we may as well be looking for ourselves." Ultimately, he argues in closing the book, humans have a duty to take "care of one another, as well as the land." Bass thus continues to strengthen the connection he feels between human and land—between the human and the natural worlds. The explorations suggested by this recurring theme become increasingly obsessive in later writings as Bass frantically increases his efforts on behalf of the Yaak Valley.

The following year, 1996, the fruits of that obsession were printed in *The Book of Yaak,* a collection of arti-

ries that became *The Sky, the Stars, the Wilderness* (1997). Each of the three novellas in the book offers an exploration of the intimacy involved in the relations of humans and the natural world. "The Myth of Bears" recalls some Native American tales about humans transformed into wolves or bears. Bass uses those echoes to describe the mysteries of a relationship between a man and a woman living in the Yukon wilds. In "Where the Sea Used to Be," two oilmen fight over the right to a suspected oil field in the Appalachians. The young man opposed by the older man and the young woman somewhere in the middle are elements that Bass uses again in his novel. The title story takes readers back to Bass's Texas roots. Less fantastical than the first two novellas in this book, it is a woman's account of a long life spent on a Texas ranch.

Bass's long-awaited and long-delayed first novel, *Where the Sea Used to Be,* appeared in 1998. His only novel to date, *Where the Sea Used to Be* is the culmination of a decade of work. It draws in part on *Oil Notes* for its portrayal of the oil industry and on *Winter* for its portrait of a young man's initiation into the fictional Swan Valley. The Swan is, of course, a slightly fictionalized rendition of the Yaak Valley, and many of the background characters in the novel are familiar from *Winter* and Bass's other writings about the people of the Yaak. In the novel Old Dudley sends Wallis, his latest protégé, to the Swan Valley at the start of the winter season. Wallis, a petroleum geologist, is to map the valley for possible oil deposits. The portrait of Dudley that emerges is less than kind; the oil business, with its exploitative and manipulative philosophy and its destructive habits, is no longer something Bass supports, especially in the pristine Swan (or Yaak) Valley.

Wallis comes to Swan as an outsider, as Bass did to the Yaak. He is welcomed by the people of the town and eventually overcomes the initial reservations of Mel, in whose home he is assigned to stay. Mel is a biologist of sorts who has spent her adult life tracking and recording the wolf population of the valley. She looks askance at the prospect of oil drilling in the valley. But for most of the novel she is not concerned that there will be any such drilling; her erstwhile lover, Matthew, another of Dudley's protégés and a native of the town, has already tried and failed to find oil in the valley.

Much of the novel becomes a commentary on maps: those of what exists upon the ground and those of what lies hidden beneath it. Mel has two decades of maps showing the range and behavior of the wolves she studies. Matthew and Dudley before him have already mapped the geology of the valley before Wallis arrives. Wallis, though trained in the science of mapping oil deposits, cannot even see the land under its

coat of snow. His first maps are rejected by Dudley as preposterous. But ultimately, as he becomes acclimatized to the valley, Wallis's map convinces Dudley that there is indeed oil in the area. But the resulting drilling is halted by a forest fire; in the end they realize that the well is just another dry hole. Along the way both Matthew and Dudley die, each of them, separately, as a result of disregard for the necessities of winter seasons in the valley: they appear in town the first time, for instance, driving a rented limousine and wearing city suits and dress shoes. Wallis, on the other hand, has accommodated himself to the place and thrives in what might otherwise be a hostile environment. The message of the novel is clear: the place, not man's will, is paramount. In the novel Bass has, then, encapsulated the philosophies of his "Yaak-tivist" and natural history nonfiction.

Fiber, also published in 1998, is a curious mixture of fiction, nonfiction, humor, and despairing calls for activism. Introduced to many Bass readers in a reading at the 1997 ASLE conference, *Fiber* seems at first the story of a flawed man, a former thief, who seeks to redeem himself by giving things away anonymously. Foremost among these gifts are hundred-inch hemlock logs, which mysteriously appear in the night. Recipients, he writes, "will think it is a strange dream, when they look out in the morning and see the gift trees, but when they go out to touch them, they will be unable to deny the reality." The gifts of this "log fairy" are implausible, but the implausibility of the log fairy and his gifts suggests what is to come. In the last of the four sections of *Fiber,* the narrator confesses that he has been lying, that this is not fiction at all; he begs his readers to take part in his efforts to save the Yaak.

In his 1997 public reading of *Fiber,* Bass was overcome with emotion before he could finish. His tearful departure led some in the audience—and other Bass critics—to question the sincerity of his emotion. But for Bass that emotion had always been there, sometimes just beneath the surface, other times at the forefront. His emotionality sets much of his work apart from other generations of nature writers, corresponding to Terry Tempest Williams's call to "bypass rhetoric and pierce the heart." Bass had long sought a way to integrate his emotional need for fiction with his equally compelling need to preserve the Yaak. In *Fiber* the two elements that define his work—art and activism—fuse uneasily. Readers responded to *Fiber* much as they had to the reading: its emotionality was deemed suspect; its demand for action inappropriate.

Undeterred, Bass expanded the range of his call for environmental preservation with *The New Wolves: The Return of the Mexican Wolf to the American Southwest* (1998), an account of efforts to return gray wolves to

The true story of the best dog I ever had

C O L T E R

RICK BASS

RICK BASS

Dust jacket for Bass's 2000 book, in which he examines his dual roles as artist and activist (Richland County Public Library)

their ancestral homes in New Mexico. The third of Bass's natural history books, *The New Wolves* chronicles the reintroduction of Mexican gray wolves into the New Mexico wilderness. Bass does not employ the journalistic detachment he used in *The Ninemile Wolves;* instead, in *The New Wolves* he takes an active part in this reintroduction. The wolves in question are the descendants of gray wolves held in captivity for many generations; their successful return to the wild is no certainty, because these particular animals have no direct memory of ever being wild at all. Their success, then, becomes a matter, in part, of ancestral memory. Bass uses that fact as the basis for a long meditation on the nature of wildness; building on the theme of "wonder" he established in *The Lost Grizzlies,* he argues for wildness as both a source of and a site for wonder. Wonder becomes perhaps the essential element for the continued success of humans on the land. Thus, he continues to develop his understanding of the relationship between humans and the rest of the natural world: "Do we happen to the land, or does the land happen to us?" In asking this question he further blurs the distinction that has otherwise marked that relationship.

Ultimately, *The New Wolves* is a book about belief and mystery and the subtle connections between them. *The New Wolves* presents just one instance of the precarious state of wildness everywhere, and since "scientific" efforts have failed to persuade, Bass relies upon belief: "We have to believe in [the wolves'] ability to draw things back together." Recognizing that naturalness, which these reintroduced wolves have come to represent as essential to all beings, Bass concludes that the wolves must return not only to their ancestral land but also to their ancestral wildness: for "if [their] success meant not obeying their identity, these wolves would have no part of it. And what good is ghost landscape, or memory, to those of us stranded in the here and now?"

The following year, Bass published another significant essay, "The Raccoons of Yaak," in the influential nature-writing journal *Orion.* Another in the long series of essays advocating the preservation of wilderness areas in his adopted valley, the essay marks the culmination of the shift in Bass's focus. Whereas his early efforts relied on a listing of species—to highlight both the diversity and vast fecundity of the valley—he now shifts entirely into the magic the valley represents as a reason to protect it. Bass had long used mystery as one factor in his calls for preservation, but now he argues that the "sense stored power" of the old growth forests of the valley is at risk. "Will there be a reduction in the magic?" he asks. "Can we measure [the magic]? Probably not—but by God, we'd better consider it."

At this point in his career, Bass is—for a nature writer—famous. An indication of his growing importance to the field may be seen in his place as the first author featured in the Credo Series of Milkweed Editions. Edited by Scott Slovic, *Brown Dog of the Yaak: Essays on Art and Activism* (1999), a collection of book-length essays, offers writers concerned with the relationship between the human and nonhuman world the opportunity to reflect upon their own work and the convictions that underlie it. The title honors Bass's recently disappeared dog, Colter; but the primary focus of the book (as the subtitle suggests) is the tension Bass has long felt between art and activism in his writing. Bass opens the book by declaring, "I know a dog with a bomb in his heart"; series editor Slovic echoes that assessment by beginning his sketch of Bass in a similar fashion by placing the bomb in the writer's own heart.

The phrase aptly describes Bass at this time in his career: the twin needs of art and activism are twisted together almost untenably. Yet, Bass is clear, albeit reluctantly, about priorities; he notes that "nature writers and activists could be attaching themselves to issues [such as] racial inequalities, gender inequalities, [or] worker-employer inequalities," wondering whether they may be merely "lost children, writing instead about salamanders and ferns and mountain ranges of light and shadow, and about the profound movements our hearts undertake when we enter wild places." Yet, he reasons, activism on the part of wildness is "close to the bedrock . . . of human existence." In this work he echoes what he initiated in *The Lost Grizzlies,* that wildness is essential to the preservation of the future of humanity. He—and with him the rest of humankind—needs wild places, he says; and "it would be wrong, unnatural, for me not to act on my needs."

Rick Bass's book *Colter: The True Story of the Best Dog I Ever Had* (2000) is an elegy to the "brown dog of the Yaak" whose unsettling and sudden disappearance brought Bass to despair. *Colter* marks a significant departure from Bass's previous work. It is not a call for activism, nor is it fiction. This version of Bass is still consumed by emotion, but that emotion has a source unlike that in his previous books. His beloved hunting dog Colter simply disappeared one day, and Bass mourns him greatly. Colter is seen by some critics as a symbol for the Yaak Valley; if this analysis is so, Bass may appear to have given up. The long fight to preserve the Yaak has been lost. But other critics see Colter as symbolizing Bass himself, an interpretation presenting a deeper dilemma for readers: Bass is writing about a self who is lost. Yet, in a sense that is what Bass has been writing about in all his nonfiction—about becoming lost in the Yaak.

In an article published toward the end of 2000, titled "Why So Many Nature Writers?" Bass seeks to define the task he has taken on. The job of a nature writer, he argues, is to "explore and map and discover . . . the hidden places, the subtle or beautiful places—the significant places." "The more fragmented the world becomes," he continues, "the more crucial it is that we try and hold the weave of it together, and the more clearly we will notice that which is still full and whole."

Following the release of *Colter,* Bass took time off from publishing. In 2002, though, he brought out two books: *The Hermit's Story,* a collection of ten short stories, and an edited work, *The Roadless Yaak: Reflections about One of Our Last Great Wild Places.* The stories in *The Hermit's Story* explore themes Bass has used before. Both "The Cave" and "The Prisoners," for instance, examine the idea of lost souls redeemed by wilderness, and might be seen as the mythologizing of Bass's long fight to preserve the Yaak. "The Hermit's Story," "Two Deer," and "Swans" each employ metaphors of the physical senses to show the convergence of body and soul in nature.

The Roadless Yaak marks a departure from Bass's other books in that he serves as editor rather than sole author. Bass has enlisted the help of some three dozen writers, William Kittredge, Annick Smith, David James Duncan, Terry Tempest Williams, and Doug Peacock, to bring to life the valley he has spent over a decade fighting to preserve.

The paucity of critical reception is of little matter to Bass. But critical reception is beginning to adhere to his work, both the nature writing and the fiction. In the spring of 2001, *The Literary Art and Activism of Rick Bass,* edited by O. Alan Weltzien, brought together essays by sixteen ecocritics seeking to address that dearth. The essays in Weltzien's collection range from a recounting of Bass's student days by Thomas J. Lyon, through an interview by Scott Slovic, to Jim Dwyer's contention that Bass uses a new form of magic realism in his novels. Added to Weltzien's collection are Terrell F. Dixon's entry on Bass in the massive two-volume *American Nature Writers,* edited by John Elder, and Weltzien's own book on Bass for the Western Writers Series of Idaho State University, *Rick Bass* (1998). This critical attention suggests that further examination of Bass's writing will be forthcoming.

Rick Bass still lives in the Yaak Valley. The valley remains unprotected by federal statutes and susceptible to the ravages Bass has spent his career revealing. Critics may love him or hate him; the cynical may distrust his emotionality; the developers may wish he would move. Bass remains in the Yaak. He continues the fight to preserve the home he has made there.

Interviews:

John Murray, "Of Winter and Wilderness: A Conversation with Rick Bass," *Bloomsbury Review* (April/May 1991): 1, 14–15;

Kevin Breen, "Rick Bass," *Poets & Writers Magazine* (May/June 1993): 18–25;

Bonnie Lyons and Bill Oliver, "Out of Bounds: An Interview with Rick Bass," *New Letters,* 59, no. 3 (1993): 57–73;

Scott Slovic, "A Paint Brush in One Hand and a Bucket of Water in the Other: Nature Writing and the Politics of Wilderness: An Interview with Rick Bass," *Weber Studies,* 11 (Fall 1994): 11–29;

David Long, "Rick Bass: Lessons from Wilderness," *Publishers Weekly,* 26 June 1995, pp. 83–84;

Judy Crowe and Casey Walker, "Rick Bass," *Wild Duck Review,* 2 (December 1996): 18–19;

Bill Stobb, "The Wild into the Word: An Interview with Rick Bass," *ISLE: Interdisciplinary Studies in Literature and Environment,* 5 (Summer 1998): 97–104;

Alden Mudge, "Rick Bass," *Booksense.com* (6 November 2002) <http://www.booksense.com/people/archive/bassrick.jsp>.

References:

Edward Abbey, *The Monkey-Wrench Gang* (Philadelphia: Lippincott, 1975);

Michael P. Branch, "Jeremiad, Elegy, and the Yaak: Rick Bass and the Aesthetics of Anger and Grief," in *The Literary Art and Activism of Rick Bass,* edited by O. Alan Weltzien (Salt Lake City: University of Utah Press, 2001), pp. 223–247;

Terrell F. Dixon, "Rick Bass," in *American Nature Writers,* edited by John Elder (New York: Scribners, 1996), pp. 75–88;

Aldo Leopold, *A Sand County Almanac with Other Essays from Round River* (New York: Oxford University Press, 1966);

Thomas J. Lyon, "Teaching and Learning: An Appreciation of Rick Bass and His Writing," in *The Literary Art and Activism of Rick Bass,* edited by Weltzien (Salt Lake City: University of Utah Press, 2001), pp. 19–23;

David Ruiter, "Life on the Frontier: Frederick Jackson Turner and Rick Bass," *Journal of the American Studies Association of Texas,* 26 (October 1995): 66–73;

Scott Slovic, "A Portrait of Rick Bass," in Bass's *Brown Dog of the Yaak: Essays in Art and Activism* (Minneapolis: Milkweed Editions, 1999), pp. 123–137;

Weltzien, *Rick Bass,* Boise State University Western Writers Series, no. 134 (Boise, Idaho: Boise State University Press, 1998);

Weltzien, ed., *The Literary Art and Activism of Rick Bass* (Salt Lake City: University of Utah Press, 2001).

Papers:

Rick Bass's collected papers, including manuscripts, galleys, proofs, and other revised copies of his work, along with Bass's working papers from his career as a geologist, holograph notebooks, and research materials gathered by Bass are housed in Southwest Texas State University's Southwest Collection at the Special Collections Library, Lubbock.

William Beebe

(29 July 1877 – 4 June 1962)

Gary Kroll
Plattsburgh State University

BOOKS: *Two Bird-Lovers in Mexico* (Boston: Houghton, Mifflin, 1905; London: Constable, 1905);

The Ostriches and Their Allies (New York: New York Zoological Society, 1905);

The Bird, Its Form and Function (New York: Holt, 1906; Westminster, U.K.: Constable, 1906);

The Log of the Sun (New York: Holt, 1906; London: Hodder & Stoughton, 1927);

Geographic Variation in Birds with Special Reference to the Effects of Humidity (New York: New York Zoological Society, 1907);

Ecology of the Hoatzin: An Ornithological Reconnaissance of Northeastern Venezuela (New York: New York Zoological Society, 1909);

Our Search for a Wilderness: An Account for Two Ornithological Expeditions to Venezuela and to British Guiana, by Beebe and Mary Blair Beebe (New York: Holt, 1910; London: Constable, 1910);

Tropical Wild Life in British Guiana, by Beebe, G. Inness Hartley, and Paul G. Howes (New York: New York Zoological Society, 1917);

Jungle Peace (New York: Holt, 1918; London: Witherby, 1919)—includes "Jungle Night" and "A Yard of Jungle";

A Monograph of the Pheasants, 4 volumes (London: Witherby, 1918–1922; revised edition, New York: Dover, 1990);

Edge of the Jungle (New York: Holt, 1921; London: Witherby, 1922);

Galapagos: World's End, by Beebe, Ruth Rose, and Robert McKay (New York & London: Putnam, 1924);

Jungle Days (New York & London: Putnam, 1925);

The Arcturus Adventure, by Beebe and Rose (New York & London: Putnam, 1926);

Pheasants, Their Lives and Homes (Garden City, N.Y.: Doubleday, Page, 1926);

Pheasant Jungles (New York & London: Putnam, 1927);

Beneath Tropic Seas: A Record of Diving among the Coral Reefs of Haiti, by Beebe and John Tee-Van (New York & London: Putnam, 1928);

William Beebe

The Fishes of Port-au-prince Bay, Haiti, with a Summary of the Known Species of Marine Fish of the Island of Haiti and Santo Domingo, by Beebe and Tee-Van (New York: New York Zoological Society, 1928);

Exploring with Beebe: Selections for Younger Readers from the Writings of William Beebe (New York & London: Putnam, 1932);

Nonsuch: Land of Water (New York: Brewer, Warren & Putnam, 1932; London & New York: Putnam, 1932);

Field Book of the Shore Fishes of Bermuda, by Beebe and Tee-Van (New York & London: Putnam, 1933);

Half Mile Down, by Beebe, Otis Barton, Tee-Van, Jocelyn Crane, and Gloria Hollister (New York: Harcourt, Brace, 1934; London: John Lane, 1935);

Zaca Venture (New York: Harcourt, Brace, 1938);

Book of Bays (New York: Harcourt, Brace, 1942; London: Bodley Head, 1947);

High Jungle (New York: Duell, Sloan & Pearce, 1949; London: Bodley Head, 1950);

Unseen Life of New York: As a Naturalist Sees It (New York: Duell, Sloan & Pearce, 1953); republished as *A Naturalist's Life of New York* (London: Bodley Head, 1954);

Adventuring with Beebe (New York: Duell, Sloan & Pearce, 1955; London: Bodley Head, 1956).

OTHER: *The Book of Naturalists: An Anthology of the Best Natural History,* edited by Beebe (New York: Knopf, 1944; London: Hale, 1944).

In the middle of August 1934 William Beebe put a memorable capstone on roughly ten years of oceanographic research by entering a cast-iron bathysphere that was then lowered to the unprecedented depth of 3,028 feet in the waters south of Bermuda. Though he later disparaged the bathysphere dives as scientifically insignificant, the entire affair was widely chronicled in newspapers and magazines and was even the subject of a real-time "radio expedition" that broadcast Beebe's deep-sea observations to listeners in the United States and England. Throughout the 1920s Beebe was both a famous explorer and a nature writer of international fame. The bathysphere descents only increased his public image as a naturalist and a daring adventurer. Perhaps not surprisingly, the events that earned him untoward attention also brought his abilities and motivations as a writer and a naturalist into question. Reviewing *The Arcturus Adventure* (1926), a book that chronicled the similarly ballyhooed *Arcturus* expedition, writer Lewis Gannett for *The Nation* (8 September 1926), noted that the "poison of self-consciousness threatens to make of him a showman exhibiting himself. . . . Sometimes he writes like a celebrity in a dress suit condescending to a cultured audience which has paid $5 a head to look at him." Such criticism highlights the checkered nature of Beebe's formidable oeuvre; the remarks also give a possible explanation for the almost complete neglect of scholarship on Beebe's contributions as a nature writer. Present-day accounts of Beebe are readily found in popular books on deep-sea exploration. Much rarer are references to his nature writing that opened up Burma forests, the tropical jungles of British Guiana, the Galápagos Islands, and the ocean depths to American audiences throughout the 1920s and 1930s.

Both Beebe's scientific and his popular literature paralleled his work as a naturalist, but the latter brought him the popularity that often funded his scientific endeavors. He has been compared with other great American nature writers such as Henry David Thoreau, John Burroughs, and John Muir–writers who saw in the American landscape a certain promise of spiritual regeneration. Thoreau's "sauntering" resembles Beebe's practice of becoming "a stroller or a creeper"; Burroughs on science provides the model for Beebe's nonreductive view of nature; and Muir's passion for mountain cathedrals saturates virtually every geography that Beebe considers. Contemporary commentators often noted how adept Beebe was at translating science for the lay reader, but his writing has both more and less importance. Writing during a time of dizzying specialization in biology, Beebe produced literature more about nature than about science; even when it is about science, it is about the adventure of exploration. While he certainly introduced his readers to distant places abounding with the wonder of life, his true significance as a nature writer lies in his portrayal of discovery. Readers of most of his literature are keenly aware that they are exploring the world through the senses of what naturalist Charles Kofoid called a "facile, brilliant, and sympathetic interpreter of nature and life," as he described Beebe in his review of *Galapagos: World's End* for *Science* (5 September 1924).

Within the diverse anatomy of the nature-writing genre, Beebe's literature combines the traditions of travel writing and natural history. The travel narrative–through both time and space–provided the architectural form on which Beebe hung his observations and commentaries employing the sensorial tools of the professional naturalist. The two came together in the venerable tradition of the natural-history essay; many of his most formidable books were compilations of essays he had written for magazines such as *Atlantic Monthly* and *Harper's Monthly*. Even the books that chronicled cohesive expeditions–such as *Galapagos: World's End* (1924), *The Arcturus Adventure* (1926), and *Zaca Venture* (1938)–were collections of essays in which each essay stood on its own instead of contributing to the logic of the book.

From a family of modest wealth whose ancestry hailed back to seventeenth-century New England, Charles William Beebe, born on 29 July 1877 in Brooklyn, New York, was the son of Charles Beebe, owner of a paper company, and Henrietta Marie Younglove. The family moved in the late 1880s to the then-rural setting of East Orange, New Jersey, where Beebe was raised and began his career—as is so common in a naturalist's tale—observing and cataloguing the insects, and especially the birds, of his local environs. He was an average student in other areas but excelled in the natural sciences. Upon graduating from high school, he attended several courses at Columbia University, where he studied under Henry Fairfield Osborn, Frank Chapman, and Franz Boas—the luminaries of the Columbia University and American Museum of Natural History network. Osborn quickly befriended Beebe and secured for him a position as honorary curator of birds at the New York Zoological Society (the Bronx Zoo) in 1899, which he held until 1952. Beebe's primary responsibility was to maintain the aviary, so his early exploratory expeditions to Mexico and Venezuela were brief and limited in scope. But in 1909, Anthony Kusar, a wealthy Society trustee, offered to finance a seventeen-month expedition to the Far East to prepare a monograph on the ecology of pheasants—an opportunity that required Beebe to forgo his responsibilities at the zoo, much to the consternation of NYZS director William Hornaday. Beebe spent almost the rest of his life splitting his years between New York and various research expeditions.

Beebe's writing during this period of his life had not yet fully matured. While he excelled in his formal natural history—*A Monograph of the Pheasants* (1918–1922) was his most important ornithological contribution—his popular literature in the *New York Tribune, Outing Magazine, The Ladies' Home Journal,* and *Recreation* has only glimpses of the imaginative flare and simile-rich descriptions that characterize his later work. *The Log of the Sun* (1906), his second popular book, was mostly a compilation of simple birding articles he had published in the *New York Tribune.* He did, however, begin to branch out into the travel narrative. *Two Bird-Lovers in Mexico* (1905) chronicles the adventure and romance of Beebe and his first wife, Mary Blair Rice Beebe, whom he had married 6 October 1902 on the first of several expeditions they enjoyed together. *Our Search for a Wilderness* (1910) describes four summer excursions to Venezuela and British Guiana that the couple undertook. The genre of expedition literature had long been a staple in American popular culture, but Beebe's writing illustrates an important moment in the history of nature writing as Americans began looking for subjects beyond the confines of the North American continent. *Our*

*Beebe during his deep-sea oceanographic research (*The Arcturus Adventure, *1926; Richland County Public Library)*

Search for a Wilderness further reflects the back-to-nature desire to locate wilderness, the "jungles untouched by axe or fire, where guns had not replaced bows and arrows," a sentiment that was rife among the turn-of-the-century urban elite.

Beebe and his wife found their ideal of wilderness in the northern reaches of South American jungles, and while his attention was now and again diverted to other parts of the globe, Beebe always seemed to be drawn back to the South American jungles. The couple divorced in 1913, but Beebe returned to the tropics in 1915, this time to Brazil on a birding expedition for the Zoological Park. Beebe came into his own when out of the jungle silence he heard the guttural voice of a great black frog who "asked as plainly as any honest man could ask, Wh-y?" In this early *Atlantic Monthly* piece, "A Yard of Jungle" (January 1916), he goes on to describe how "every sense came into play" as he concentrated on the fauna of a four-square-foot area of jungle debris and a single cinnamon tree. In what may be the earliest articulation of the concept of biodiversity, Beebe was awed by the myriad life-forms that coexisted in such a limited area. The experience hatched in his mind a plan to develop a permanent tropical research station that stressed *intensive* examinations of specific places instead of *extensive* explorations of specific life-forms.

Beebe sought and received the support of Theodore Roosevelt, whose interest no doubt ensured the approval of the New York Zoological Society. With their support, the Department of Tropical Research (DTR), including Beebe and a small staff of naturalists and artists, set off in 1916 to found a semipermanent research station in the tropical jungles of British Guiana. Between 1916 and 1926, with a few exceptions, Beebe and his staff summered in the tropical jungles of Kalacoon, and later Kartabo, British Guiana. After locating a suitable stretch of tropical wilderness, the staff established their lab in the former home of the Protector of Indians in British Guiana. The house was fitted with modern equipment and converted into a "wilderness laboratory." The purpose of the DTR, as described in an *Atlantic* article "A Jungle Laboratory" (May 1917), was "not to collect [animals] primarily, but to photograph, sketch, and watch them day after day, learning of those characters and habits which cannot be transported to a museum. This had not been done before; hence it took on new fascination." The distant laboratories of the DTR became a favorite research site for naturalists from American universities, but more important, in these jungles of British Guiana, Beebe made his first mark as a nature writer. In 1918 his *Atlantic Monthly* editor noted in a letter,

> There ought to be some way of publishing your essays which should call them to a brand-new audience. The difficulty has been that you are pigeonholed in the public mind with some of your fellow naturalists of the *Auk* variety; whereas you are really nothing but an observer of life and manners among animals and men, who can put poetry into prose.

Such ruminations led to the publication of *Jungle Peace* (1918), a collection of *Atlantic* essays that had appeared several years before Beebe's brief tour as an aviator during World War I. Beebe began experimenting with the American pastoral tradition in a sophisticated manner; though Beebe's was less John Burroughs's pastoral tradition of managed farms and gardens than the urban-based "back to nature" pastoralism common to the northeastern metropolitan culture of the turn of the century. The book nominates the tropical jungles of British Guiana as the environment where "the mind seeks amelioration." While the vicious struggle for existence can readily be observed in such settings, "it is infinitely more wonderful and altogether satisfying to

slip quietly and receptively into the life of the jungle, to accept all things as worthy and reasonable; to sense the beauty, the joy, the majestic serenity of this age-old fraternity of nature, into whose sanctuary man's entrance is unnoticed, his absence unregretted." Beebe's escape into nature—his constant movement from metropolis to wilderness—is not an endeavor in living the "strenuous life," despite his friendship with Theodore Roosevelt. The flight to wilderness is rarely a test of virile conquest but rather a sensorial engagement with life itself.

For instance, "A Jungle Clearing" describes the plant, insect, and bird life of a sandy tropical slope in the back of the new laboratory. Beebe brings the reader on a journey of geographical similes. "In my little cleared glade there was no plant which would be wholly out of place on a New England country hillside." Sumac, the spindling button-weed, the vervain, the yellow-breasted white-throated flycatcher, and a monarch were all organisms familiar to his northeast American audience. The sight of a Papilio butterfly causes Beebe's imagination to head south and "live again among the Virginian butterflies and mockingbirds." Then he looks deeper at the glade and comprehends the "one fundamental reality in wild nature—the universal acceptance of opportunity." The minute inhabitants of a single leaf then lead him to a meditation on "the natural history of galls [so] full of romance and strange realities." Suddenly, the orgiastic color of a dozen great toucans brings him to a heightened state of awareness. "The spatial, the temporal—the hillsides, the passing seconds—the vibrations and material atoms stimulating my five senses, all were tropical, quickened with the unbelievable vitality of equatorial life." Beebe is doing more than introducing his readers to a foreign landscape. He is writing about coming to know the jungle environment—a process that weaves together his extraordinary sensory perception, his speculations on the evolutionary possibilities of life, and the complex ecology of the tropics—what Beebe called the "prodigality of tropical nature."

Beebe excelled in narrating the extraordinary events that parade past the sedentary observer whose senses are keenly attuned. "The Army Ants' Home Town" describes Beebe's two-day investigation of an army-ant colony that had made its nest in the outhouse of the station. Predating the superorganism theories of future ecologists (some of whom worked with Beebe in British Guiana), Beebe likened the entire nesting swarm to "the body of this strange amorphous organism—housing the spirit of the army." Indeed, he views the entire scene in thoroughly militaristic terms—a highly bureaucratized army consisting of "battalions of eager light infantry hastening out to battle." Beebe even mentions that the beautiful efficiency of the superorganism

Beebe collecting rare moths on the roof of Rancho Grande in Venezuela
(High Jungle, *1949; Richland County Public Library*)

provides a commentary on the tyrannies of Bolshevism. Such comparisons between nature and human culture recur throughout most of Beebe's writing. While moving to the Kartabo station, Beebe observes a line of leaf-cutter ants heavily laden with bits of jungle flora and then looks up "to see an anthropomorphic enlargement of the ants,—the convicts winding up the steep bank, each with cot, lamp, table, pitcher, trunk, or aquarium balanced on his head."

An unmistakable humility washes through much of Beebe's nature writing as well, especially in this jungle phase of his life. He finds that representing nature is difficult for human beings because of deficiencies in both the human mind and human language. "A Chain of Jungle Life" begins, "To know and think [of life] is very worth while, to have discovered them is sheer joy, but to write of them is impertinence, so exciting and unreal are they in reality, and so tame and humdrum are any combinations of our twenty-six letters." This maneuver is common in the work of the mature Beebe. He is continuously highlighting the incapacity of his senses in achieving the full image and meaning of

nature, and his work is rife with the admission of an ineffable quality of nature. The problem is compounded by the nature of science—where nature's "beauty and romance are in hiding behind certain select and abstruse technicalities." These problems are partially solved through a reliance on the artistic staff that toils under Beebe's watchful eye to capture a variegated natural world. But the problem of observing and describing an ineffable nature shaped Beebe's distinctive literary style, which attempted to capture both the fleetingness of color and the psychology of behavior with a sense of free play and imagination.

Perhaps more than any other writing strategy, Beebe's attempt to see the world from the organism's point of view distinguishes his nature writing. George Reuben Potter, whose 1929 work remains one of the few critical interpretations of Beebe's writing, suggests that "science and literature both need desperately thinkers who will look into the consciousness of other life besides our own and feel its fascination and beauty without letting that beauty cloud their reason. Beebe does this again and again." The opening essay in *Jungle*

Peace begins from the point of view of a bird flying over New York City–observing the trains as caterpillars and the crowds of people as ants. Later, in a *Harpers* article, "Thoughts on Diving" (April 1933), he tells his readers that to understand the ocean realm, "we must descend beneath the surface and become amphibious." Fish, ants, birds, butterflies, jungle sloths, even microscopic organisms–all become the objects of Beebe's own subjectivity. He was keenly aware of the nature-faker controversy and took the side of Roosevelt and Burroughs in their criticisms of William Long and Jack London. But if Beebe had little patience for the nature fakers' inquiry into animal psychology, his feelings did not weigh so heavily as to prevent him from making persistent anthropomorphizations of nature.

In order to delve into the mind of nature–to ask the vital questions of form and function–Beebe depended on the faculties of wonder and imagination. Lawrence Buell, in his *The Environmental Imagination* (1995), states the relationship between science, literature, and the imagination in a manner helpful for understanding Beebe: "To a greater degree than science, literature releases imagination's free play, though the play is not entirely free, since the imagination is regulated by encounters with the environment." Small wonder that Beebe constantly invokes the fantasies of Lord Dunsany and Lewis Carroll when describing the tropical jungle. Responding to the approbation that he was the world's greatest naturalist, Beebe scoffs and calls himself a lousy naturalist. "When I read Kipling or Dunsany . . . Oh my! Dunsany. I put him above Shakespeare." In Beebe's hands, these fashioners of fantastic wonders provide a point of reference that makes tangible not only the spectacle of nature but also the "sense of wonder" that can be the only mental response when experiencing nature. This use of the imagination explains, in part, why Rachel Carson–an admirer and correspondent of Beebe's–later titled her final book *The Sense of Wonder* (1965). Both Carson and Beebe describe the awe, reverence, and wonderment that the observer feels when encountering nature.

If Beebe's jungle literature can be read as a narrative of wonder, it can just as assuredly be considered as a chronicle of imperialism. Beebe's writing often presents a window into the relationship between the white explorer and the indigenous other in a new imperial contact zone. The depiction of his indigenous servants vacillates between admiration, paternalism, and nostalgia. He portrays the peoples of developing worlds, notably Asia and British Guiana, as expert naturalists of their local environments at the same time that he asserts his hegemony over them in making clear master/servant distinctions. To note Beebe's fondness for Rudyard Kipling's chronicles of British imperialism is

helpful. Beebe clearly adopts the yoke of the "white man's burden," for instance, in paying Nupee, his "little Akawai Indian hunter," for services as a guide in Kartoba. But Nupee's ultimate fate seems certain. Beebe fears that someday he will return to his wilderness jungle and "Nupee may not be there," he writes in "Jungle Night," another essay in *Jungle Peace*. "He will perhaps have slipped into memory, with Drojak and Aladdin [previous servants]. And if I find no one as silently friendly as Nupee, I shall have to watch alone through my jungle night." The premonition proved true enough when Beebe returned the following year. His writings are peppered with similar asymmetrical interactions, in which the indigenous Other becomes both an object of the natural history essay and an index to the imperial infrastructure that makes Beebe's expeditions possible.

The theme struck a responsive chord for Theodore Roosevelt, who wrote a glowing review of *Jungle Peace* in *The New York Times Review of Books* (3 October 1913): "some of his most interesting descriptions are of the wild folk he meets in the wilderness–black or yellow, brown or red." Similarly favorable reviews were written of all Beebe's jungle books. Ben Ray Redman wrote of *Edge of the Jungle* (1921) in *The Nation* (11 January 1922): "In this abandon of his senses to the manifold impacts of nature the author reveals himself as an artist rather than a scientist." Nicholas Roosevelt in his article for the *New York Times Book Review* (5 July 1925) noted that *Jungle Days* (1925) "contains snatches of philosophy, mingled with poetry and leavened with the quality of suspense and mystery which Beebe always manages to put into his jungle passages." When E. O. Wilson recently remarked in *Naturalist* (1994) that Beebe was "everyone's favorite naturalist," he no doubt had Beebe's jungle writing in mind. By the early 1920s Beebe had earned a reputation as one of the great naturalist authors of America–a reputation that opened up new scientific projects as the monied elite of New York saw fit to provide him with the patronage necessary to expand his research interests. In Beebe's own words, "one millionaire gave me a yacht, another millionaire gave me a yacht, and the Governor of Bermuda gave me an island. I spent ten years under water." Beebe was entering a new phase in his career as he began leaving the jungles of South America behind for new wilderness areas.

In 1923 Harrison Williams, a member of the Board of Managers of the Zoological Society, donated his yacht, *Noma,* for a ten-week expedition to the Galápagos Islands. Beebe added several members to the staff and proceeded to follow in Charles Darwin's footsteps in search of clues to the mystery of evolution. Beebe narrated the expedition in *Galapagos: World's End,* which biologist Vernon Kellog described in *The Yale*

Review (14; 1925) as "a book of adventure, poetry, and human association." Beebe's dependable readership ensured a warm reception of *Galapagos,* but the text is more a detailed travel account than a meditative reflection on nature. More than ever before, the quotidian work of Beebe can be seen at the helm of the DTR. Upon his return another Society trustee, industrialist Henry Whiton, offered the steam yacht *Arcturus* for a similar expedition, though with a focus on oceanography. This expedition was Beebe's grandest, costing his patrons about $250,000, mostly to outfit the *Arcturus* with the equipment necessary for deep-sea oceanographic research. Though it marked his first foray into oceanography, his objective was much the same as that of his jungle work—to describe the life histories of as many species as possible in the wilderness. The Sargasso Sea was thought to be the home of countless fishes and crustacea, and the Humboldt Current was already known for its diverse and abundant marine life. Beebe called these regions a "wilderness of water." The expedition was closely followed in the daily press. George Palmer Putnam had arranged to receive reports and articles from Beebe while the expedition was still at sea. These pieces were widely published in the popular press and in 1926 were republished in book form, *The Arcturus Adventure.* Instead of the *Atlantic Monthly,* Beebe's new forum was *The New York Times Magazine,* and his writing style changed accordingly. A reviewer of *The Arcturus Adventure* noted that Burroughs, Muir, and Thoreau wrote "in response to an inner creative necessity—not because editors and publishers had told them their experience would make salable reading." The narrative of Beebe's 1927 expedition to Haiti, *Beneath Tropic Seas* (1928), is another example of such "salable" reading. This period of his life was also important for developments in his always public personal life. On 22 September 1927, aboard Harrison Williams's yacht *Warrior,* Beebe married Elswyth Thane Ricker, who was already well known as a writer of historical romances under the name Elswyth Thane.

In these expedition narratives, Beebe introduces his readers to the entirely new environment of the undersea world. Some of *The Arcturus Adventure* is devoted to detailing the finds of deep-sea dredges: "These incredible creatures, painfully secured from their eerie, horizonless world, would be beyond the inventive power of the wildest imagination." Nevertheless, Beebe was not deterred. He reported finding the living fossil amphioxus; cyclothones, with detachable jaws and luminescent teeth; the hatchet fish, with a strangely telescoped head; the pharynx fish, which has a distended stomach; and hundreds of fish with marvelous appendages and bioluminescent organs. These were Beebe's "grotesques, dragons, and gargoyles.

Even the briefest acquaintance with these organisms made the fairies, hobgoblins and elves of Dunsany, Barry, Blackwood, and Grimm seem like nature fakery." Many readers were equally captivated by Beebe's descriptions of helmet diving. He recalled "trembling with terror, for I had sensed the ghastly isolation" while struggling against a huge swell on the steep slope of Tagus Cove. Beebe's explanation for writing these "personal digressions"—his excuse for playing the role of the daring adventurer—was "to make real and vivid in the mind of the reader, the unearthliness of the depths of the sea."

Beebe's most popular underwater natural history took place in Bermuda waters. In 1929 an offer from the Bermudan government made possible the combination of Beebe's earlier strategy of forming permanent tropical research stations with his newfound fondness for oceanic life. Sir Louis Bois, governor of Bermuda, offered the use of Nonsuch Island off the south coast of the Bermuda mainland for the establishment of an oceanographic and marine biology research facility. Here Beebe continued to explore oceanic fauna, but the Bermuda station made possible an intensive survey of life within a prescribed area. Indeed, just as the stations in British Guiana provided the setting for some of Beebe's most effective jungle writing, the Bermuda station became the setting for his most significant oceanic writing. *Nonsuch: Land of Water* (1932) was the first popular account of Beebe's new Bermuda research station, but the book resembles his earlier jungle books, which compiled distinct essays. *Nonsuch* includes essays previously published in *Atlantic Monthly, The Saturday Evening Post, Harper's Monthly,* and other magazines. The environment of Bermuda comes alive: blue sharks, flounders, periwinkles, crabs, flying fish, and the cedars of Nonsuch are all singled out for individual treatment. "Mount Bermuda" includes Beebe's thoughts while accidentally slipping from a cliff into the ocean on a stormy afternoon. Seizing from the surf a single grape-sized Halicystis, Beebe imagines that he is present on the "Third Day of Creation" and proceeds to narrate the deep-time geological history of Bermuda. A kind of secular sacredness emerges in Beebe's writing from time to time; it consistently invokes a sense of awe and reverence in his reader. One oddity of *Nonsuch* is the complete absence of any mention of the 1930 bathysphere dives.

Otis Barton, a young engineer with a considerable fortune, called on Beebe in 1929 and offered to finance the construction of the bathysphere that became the latest research tool in the department's ocean exploration arsenal. Dives were conducted in 1930, 1932, and 1934, but the bathysphere proved of limited value scientifically. While Beebe cherished the experience of

*Beebe at Portachenio Pass in Venezuela (*High Jungle, *1949; Richland County Public Library)*

getting an in situ peek into ocean depths of up to a half mile, his observations would fall on deaf ears without securing specimens–an essential ingredient in natural history. Most scientific reviewers of *Half Mile Down* (1934), the popular account of the dives, complained along these lines. But the general American public consumed news of these dives with a voracious appetite. In the same tradition as Robert Edwin Peary and Charles Lindbergh, Beebe had put life and limb at risk for the sake of a greater scientific cause, and the details of the events could be found in newspapers and magazines across the nation. Beebe himself had recorded a few of his more spectacular observations in *The New York Times Magazine* and *National Geographic*. He compiled and augmented the accounts in *Half Mile Down,* a return to the expeditionary genre used in *Arcturus Adventure* and *Beneath Tropic Seas: A Record of Diving among the Coral Reefs of Haiti* (1928). Between the lines of Beebe's daring bravado and in his descriptions of the opaque darkness of midocean depths, readers can see the ocean taking on a new form. In the same way that mountain landscapes move in the American literary imagination from howling wilderness to sublime grandeur, so, too, readers see Beebe subliming the ocean. More than a geography of

resources, more than a place of danger, Beebe's ocean is a sublime spectacle.

Half Mile Down received mixed reviews. Naturalists such as Carl Hubbs bristled when reading of Beebe's attempts to name uncatalogued fish seen through the quartz windows of the bathysphere. In a July 1935 *Copeia* review Hubbs was "forced to suggest that what the author saw might have been a phosphorescent coelenterate whose lights were beautified by halation in passing through a misty film breathed onto the quartz window by Mr. Beebe's eagerly appressed face." Others were more captivated. In a 1934 letter to Beebe, Kipling wrote that he had "been reading that amazing Fourth Dimensional book of yours that you so kindly sent me–Half Mile Down–and I find I haven't any scale for its measurement. It looks like the first opening up of a new world . . . like Columbus throwing fits on the discovery of the Western Tropics." Rachel Carson informed Beebe that she had read the text four times. As a chronicle of deep-sea adventure the book has stood the test of time, but the student of nature writing will find only disparate lyrics reminiscent of Beebe's jungle writing.

Beebe continued to work from Bermuda following the bathysphere dives, but time and again he took advantage of other research opportunities. In 1936 he and the staff of the DTR spent two months aboard Templeton Crocker's schooner, *Zaca,* on a tour around the Baja Peninsula. *Zaca Venture* and *Book of Bays* (1942) narrate the work of the cruisers as they investigated the marine life of the peninsula; the texts are punctuated with essays on pelicans, the Gray Friars, the cedars of Ceros, and even an encounter with a whale shark. These books represent Beebe's final writing on oceanic themes. The staff left Nonsuch during World War II when the island became the site of a military airstrip, and Beebe brought them, once again, to the jungles of northern South America–this time to the previously established research station of Rancho Grande, Venezuela, which was the setting of *High Jungle* (1949). Always more at home in tropical climes, Beebe established his final research station on Trinidad in 1949. He retired from his position with the New York Zoological Society in 1952 and spent his remaining years as a student of Trinidad's environment. William Beebe died at his estate in Trinidad, Simla, on 4 June 1962 and is buried in Trinidad.

If William Beebe's books, notes, and correspondences paint an accurate portrait of his life, then he rarely participated in the various conservation movements that swept through the early twentieth century. In a 1948 speech at the New York Zoological Society annual dinner he noted that while working "with Birds, Beasts, and Butterflies, all we ask is to be completely divorced from Humans, although we are grateful to the Conservationists for trying to keep Wild Creatures alive for a few more years, so we can study them." But if he did not become an activist in practice, his writings went a long way in fostering a biocentric outlook toward the world. Beebe's writings delivered an at times ambiguous critique of modern civilization. As opposed to many of the participants in the back-to-nature movement, he rarely went to the wilderness for retreat; he went there as a student of nature. He disliked cities and development for destroying these natural places. Behind this development was a self-confidence in the human ability to control and manage nature for utilitarian ends.

This attitude fostered a biocentrism in his writings that did more than offer a nonutilitarian view of nature. He vested nature with an inherent value that was in no way contingent on humans. Viewing nature, for Beebe and his readers, had an inherent aesthetic pleasure. A reviewer of one of Beebe's Bermuda books noted in the *New York Evening News* (23 August 1932) that for most Americans, fish are simply the potential ingredients for a "nourishing bouillabaisse," but in Beebe's hands, these routine observations are "the elements of tremendous dramas, high adventures." These adventures were not solely the province of men of science; they were activities that could be enjoyed by all. He often recommended that his reader put on a diving helmet to "become an active member of the 'Society of Wonders Under-Sea.'" Those who did not follow his advice might have experienced enough of the wonder and awe of jungle and ocean through Beebe's nature writing.

Bibliography:

Tim M. Berra, *William Beebe: An Annotated Bibliography* (Hamden, Conn.: Archon Books, 1977).

Biography:

Robert Welker, *Natural Man: The Life of William Beebe* (Bloomington: Indiana University Press, 1977).

References:

Lawrence Buell, *The Environmental Imagination* (Cambridge: Harvard University Press, 1995);

George Reuben Potter, "William Beebe: His Significance to Literature," in *Essays in Criticism* (Berkeley: University of California Press, 1929), pp. 203–228.

Papers:

The majority of William Beebe's personal papers are held at the Firestone Library at Princeton University. The collection includes correspondences, field notes, and the working drafts of his many publications. Material directly related to the operations and development of the Department of Tropical Research is held at the Library of the New York Zoological Society.

Wendell Berry

(5 August 1934 –)

George Hart
California State University, Long Beach

See also the Berry entries in *DLB 5: American Poets Since World War II; DLB 6: American Novelists Since World War II, Second Series;* and *DLB 234: American Short-Story Writers Since World War II, Third Series.*

BOOKS: *Nathan Coulter* (Boston: Houghton Mifflin, 1960; revised edition, San Francisco: North Point, 1983);

The Broken Ground (New York: Harcourt, Brace & World, 1964; London: Cape, 1966);

November Twenty-Six, Nineteen Hundred Sixty-Three (New York: Braziller, 1964);

A Place on Earth (New York: Harcourt, Brace & World, 1967; revised edition, San Francisco: North Point, 1983);

Openings (New York: Harcourt, Brace & World, 1968);

The Rise (Lexington: University of Kentucky Library Press, 1968);

Findings (Iowa City: Prairie, 1969);

The Long-Legged House (New York: Harcourt, Brace & World, 1969);

Farming: A Hand Book (New York: Harcourt Brace Jovanovich, 1970);

The Hidden Wound (Boston: Houghton Mifflin, 1970);

The Unforeseen Wilderness: An Essay on Kentucky's Red River Gorge, with photographs by Ralph Eugene Meatyard (Lexington: University Press of Kentucky, 1971; revised and expanded edition, San Francisco: North Point, 1991);

A Continuous Harmony: Essays Cultural and Agricultural (New York: Harcourt Brace Jovanovich, 1972);

The Country of Marriage (New York & London: Harcourt Brace Jovanovich, 1973);

An Eastward Look (Berkeley, Cal.: Sand Dollar, 1974);

The Memory of Old Jack (New York: Harcourt Brace Jovanovich, 1974);

Horses (Monterey, Ky.: Larkspur, 1975);

Sayings and Doings (Frankfort, Ky.: Gnomon, 1975); expanded as *Sayings & Doings; and, An Eastward Look* (Frankfort, Ky.: Gnomon, 1990);

To What Listens (Crete, Nebr.: Best Cellar, 1975);

Wendell Berry (photograph by Dan Carraco)

The Kentucky River: Two Poems (Monterey, Ky.: Larkspur, 1976);

There Is Singing around Me (Austin, Tex.: Cold Mountain, 1976);

The Agricultural Crisis: A Crisis of Culture (New York: Myrin Institute, 1977);

Clearing (New York: Harcourt Brace Jovanovich, 1977);

Three Memorial Poems (Berkeley, Cal.: Sand Dollar, 1977)–includes "Elegy," "Requiem," and "Rising";

The Unsettling of America: Culture and Agriculture (San Francisco: Sierra Club Books, 1977);

The Gift of Gravity (Old Deerfield, Mass.: Deerfield Press, 1979; Dublin: Gallery, 1979)–comprises "The Gift of Gravity" and "Grief";

A Part (San Francisco: North Point, 1980);

The Salad (Berkeley, Cal.: North Point, 1980);

The Gift of Good Land: Further Essays, Cultural and Agricultural (San Francisco: North Point, 1981);

Recollected Essays, 1965–1980 (San Francisco: North Point, 1981);

The Wheel (San Francisco: North Point, 1982);

Standing by Words (San Francisco: North Point, 1983);

Collected Poems, 1957–1982 (San Francisco: North Point, 1985);

The Wild Birds: Six Stories of the Port William Membership (San Francisco: North Point, 1986);

The Landscape of Harmony: Two Essays on Wilderness and Community (Madley, U.K.: Five Seasons, 1987);

Home Economics: Fourteen Essays (San Francisco: North Point, 1987);

Sabbaths (San Francisco: North Point, 1987);

Some Differences (Lewiston, Idaho: Confluence, 1987);

Remembering (San Francisco: North Point, 1988);

Traveling at Home (Lewisburg, Pa.: Bucknell University Press, 1988);

Harlan Hubbard: Life and Work (Lexington: University Press of Kentucky, 1990);

What Are People For? (San Francisco: North Point, 1990);

The Discovery of Kentucky (Frankfort, Ky.: Gnomon, 1991);

Fidelity: Five Stories (New York: Pantheon, 1992);

A Consent (Monterey, Ky.: Larkspur, 1993);

Sex, Economy, Freedom & Community: Eight Essays (New York: Pantheon, 1993);

Entries (New York: Pantheon, 1994);

Watch with Me: And Six Other Stories of the Yet-Remembered Ptolemy Proudfoot and His Wife, Miss Minnie, née Quinch (New York: Pantheon, 1994);

Another Turn of the Crank: Essays (Washington, D.C.: Counterpoint, 1995);

A World Lost (Washington, D.C.: Counterpoint, 1996);

Two More Stories of the Port William Membership (Frankfort, Ky.: Gnomon, 1997);

The Selected Poems of Wendell Berry (Washington, D.C.: Counterpoint, 1998);

A Timbered Choir: The Sabbath Poems, 1979–1997 (Washington, D.C.: Counterpoint, 1998);

Life Is a Miracle: An Essay Against Modern Superstition (Washington, D.C.: Counterpoint, 2000);

Jayber Crow: The Life Story of Jayber Crow, Barber, of the Port William Membership, as Written by Himself (Washington, D.C.: Counterpoint, 2000);

In the Presence of Fear: Three Essays for a Changed World (Great Barrington, Mass.: Orion Society, 2001);

The Art of the Commonplace: The Agrarian Essays of Wendell Berry, edited by Norman Wirzba (Washington, D.C.: Counterpoint, 2002);

The Gift of Gravity: Selected Poems 1968–2000 (Ipswich, U.K.: Golgonooza, 2002);

That Distant Land: The Collected Stories of Wendell Berry (Washington, D.C.: Counterpoint, 2002);

Three Short Novels (Washington, D.C.: Counterpoint, 2002)–includes *Nathan Coulter, Remembering,* and *A World Lost.*

Edition: *The Unsettling of America: Culture and Agriculture,* afterword to third edition by Berry (San Francisco: Sierra Club, 1996).

OTHER: Ralph Eugene Meatyard, *Ralph Eugene Meatyard,* with notes by Berry and Arnold Gasson (Lexington, Ky.: Gnomon, 1970);

Masanobu Fukuoka, *The One-Straw Revolution: An Introduction to Natural Farming,* preface by Berry (Emmaus, Pa.: Rodale, 1978);

William Dunbar, *The Nativity: Rorate Celi Desuper,* adapted and translated by Berry (Great Barrington, Mass.: Penamen, 1981);

Meeting the Expectations of the Land: Essays in Sustainable Agriculture and Stewardship, edited by Berry, Wes Jackson, and Bruce Colman (San Francisco: North Point, 1984);

"Earl Butz versus Wendell Berry," in *News That Stayed News: Ten Years of CoEvolution Quarterly, 1974–1984,* edited by Art Kleiner and Stewart Brand (San Francisco: North Point, 1986), pp. 116–129;

"Higher Education and Home Defense," in *From the Heartlands: Photos and Essays from the Midwest,* Midwest Writers Series 1, edited by Larry Smith (Huron, Ohio: Bottom Dog, 1988);

David Kline, *Great Possessions: An Amish Farmer's Journal,* foreword by Berry (San Francisco: North Point, 1990);

"Remembering Ralph Eugene Meatyard," in *Ralph Eugene Meatyard: An American Visionary,* edited by Barbara Tannenbaum (New York: Rizzoli, 1991), pp. 83–86;

David T. Hanson, *Waste Land: Meditations on a Ravaged Landscape,* preface by Berry (New York: Aperture, 1997);

Theodora C. Stanwell-Fletcher, *Driftwood Valley: A Woman Naturalist in the Northern Wilderness,* introduction by Berry (Corvallis: Oregon State University, 1999);

Gene Logsdon, *Living at Nature's Pace: Farming and the American Dream,* foreword by Berry (White River Junction, Vt.: Chelsea Green, 2000);

Sim Van der Ryn, *The Toilet Papers: Recycling Waste and Conserving Water,* foreword by Berry (Sausalito, Cal.: Ecological Design, 2000).

SELECTED PERIODICAL PUBLICATIONS–
UNCOLLECTED: "The Cool of the Day," *Blair & Ketchum's Country Journal,* 5 (March 1978): 62–67;

"The Air of the Free," *The Progressive,* 60 (July 1996): 32;

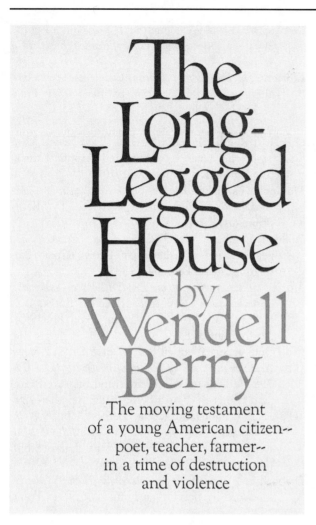

The
Long-
Legged
House
by
Wendell
Berry

The moving testament
of a young American citizen--
poet, teacher, farmer--
in a time of destruction
and violence

*Dust jacket for Berry's 1969 book about his family's wilderness
camp on the Kentucky River, the favorite place of his childhood
and youth (Richland County Public Library)*

"Why We Need the Tobacco Program," by Berry and
John M. Berry Jr., *Progressive,* 62 (October 1998):
28–29;

"Conserving Farm-Raised Children," *Progressive,* 63
(January 1999): 41.

An author of more than thirty books of fiction,
poetry, and essays, Wendell Berry has received high
praise from major nature writers such as Wallace Stegner and Edward Abbey. Stegner, with whom Berry
studied, comments, "It is hard to say whether I like this
writer better as a poet, an essayist, or a novelist. He is
all three at a high level," and Abbey proclaimed Berry
to be "the best essayist now working in America."
Indeed, even within a single genre—nonfiction prose,
the primary form of traditional nature writing—Berry's
work ranges widely, with certainty and force, addressing manifold purposes, audiences, and topics.

The autobiographical, personal essay dominates
Berry's early work, essays such as those collected in *The
Long-Legged House* (1969), *The Hidden Wound* (1970), and
*The Unforeseen Wilderness: An Essay on Kentucky's Red River
Gorge* (1971); a transitional book, *A Continuous Harmony:
Essays Cultural and Agricultural* (1972), includes autobiographical essays mixed with literary and agricultural
pieces. In 1977 Berry published his major work of cultural criticism, *The Unsettling of America: Culture and Agriculture,* a book-length essay intended to be a criticism of
"modern or orthodox agriculture," which is, in actual-
ity, an environmentalist critique of contemporary
American culture from a farmer's perspective. Many of
Berry's "agricultural" essays address a general audience; one of his main criticisms of modern farming is
the dwindling number of farmers and farm families,
and if he were to write only to a "farm audience," his
readership would be small indeed. Nevertheless, he has
often written for smaller, particular audiences on practical issues of farming techniques and technology, publishing articles in such magazines as *Blair and Ketchum's
Country Journal,* Jerome Irving Rodale's *Organic Farming
and Gardening,* and *New Farm,* many of which are collected in *The Gift of Good Land: Further Essays, Cultural and
Agricultural* (1981).

Other types of nonfiction include polemical
essays written to engage debate on issues such as education, consumerism, technology, and feminism.
Essays on such topics are included in *Home Economics:
Fourteen Essays* (1987), *What Are People For?* (1990), *Sex,
Economy, Freedom & Community: Eight Essays* (1993), and
Another Turn of the Crank: Essays (1995). Berry's statements on poetry, community, and language were published in *Standing by Words* (1983), a major collection of
literary essays, and he has written a biography of the
Kentucky artist Harlan Hubbard, *Harlan Hubbard: Life
and Work* (1990). In *Life Is a Miracle: An Essay Against
Modern Superstition* (2000) he returns to the book-length
polemic, entering into a debate on the "two cultures"
of the sciences and the humanities by responding to
Edward O. Wilson's *Consilience: The Unity of Knowledge*
(1998). In 2001 he published a small book, *In the Presence of Fear: Three Essays for a Changed World,* consisting
of three essays that respond to terrorism and the global economy.

Wendell Erdman Berry was born in Kentucky on
5 August 1934, the eldest of the four children of John
M. and Virginia Perry Berry, and grew up in the small
town of New Castle and on farms in the nearby countryside of Henry County. His father was a lawyer and a
farmer who also worked for fifty years with the Burley
Tobacco Growers Cooperative, ultimately serving as its
president. His mother was a housewife who passed on
her love of books and reading to her son, influencing

his decision to become a writer. The Berry family's residence in Kentucky extended back to the early nineteenth century–to Berry's mother's great-great-grandfather and his father's great-grandfather–and all of Berry's grandparents and great-grandparents lived and farmed around Port Royal, in Henry County. In his novels and short stories, the fictional town of Port William represents Port Royal and its community. Berry grew up on farms just before the period of rapid mechanization in the post–World War II era. To him this change made a vast difference because he was trained in old-time farming techniques by his paternal grandfather, especially in the use of draft animals, such as mules and horses. This experience shaped Berry's sense of place in specific and concrete ways. After the eighth grade, he left New Castle to attend the Millersburg Military Institute, and he recalls in the essay "A Native Hill," collected in *The Long-Legged House:*

> I could comfort myself by recalling in intricate detail the fields I had worked and played in, and hunted over, and ridden through on horseback. . . . I could recall even the casual locations of certain small rocks. I could recall the look of a hundred different kinds of daylight on all those places, the look of animals grazing over them, the postures and attitudes and movements of the men who worked in them, the quality of the grass and the crops that had grown on them.

What makes many of Berry's essays fine examples of traditional nature writing is this attachment to and sense of place; in fact, "place" is the dominant theme of his writing in all genres. The other motivations and concerns that he brings to the idea of place, however, are what make his nature writing distinctive. Nearly equal in weight as a motivating principle is the idea and fact of marriage. Farming, the crucial third topic, mediates and complements place and marriage. These three terms are so integral to Berry's worldview and writing that considering one more significant or weighty than another assumes a separation that is false to Berry's vision. Place precedes the others as a theme, but it is incomplete until marriage and farming become a part of it. All of Berry's other concerns radiate from this triad.

If the primary mode of nature writing in American literature is the pastoral, then Berry's major contribution is to recast nature writing in a georgic mode. The pastoral can be summed up as the movement from complex to simple cultural conditions, as a retreat from society to a simple life closer to nature; it is usually seen as an escape from social obligations, and its landscape is wilderness or the frontier. Georgic, the classical genre that emphasizes labor and cultivation of the earth, is practical and didactic, and its

environment is the "middle landscape" between the civilized and the wild. Berry's nonfiction begins in the pastoral mode in the early essay "The Long-Legged House," but even at this early stage it moves beyond the pastoral as marriage and farming emerge as themes. As a georgic, or agrarian, writer, Berry is more concerned with work than play, settlement than escape, and community than the individual.

The "long-legged house" of the title is a cabin built by Berry's great-uncle, Curran Mathews, and during the writer's childhood it was the family's retreat on the Kentucky River, simply referred to as "the Camp." The Camp was Berry's first site of place awareness in a particularly pastoral way. After many family visits to the Camp, Berry writes, "I began to be bound to the place in a relation so rich and profound as to seem almost mystical, as though I knew it before birth and was born for it. . . . It was the family's wilderness place, and lay beyond the claims and disciplines and obligations that motivated my grownups. From the first, I must have associated it with freedom." Berry recounts his relationship with the Camp through his adolescence and young adulthood, and the sense of freedom is exemplified by escape from routine and domestic responsibilities. As he embarked on his career as a writer, the Camp became the site of his literary labor–reading and writing–and after college and graduate school at the University of Kentucky (B.A., 1956; M.A., 1957), Berry and his new wife spent their first summer together there.

Berry married Tanya Amyx on 24 May 1957, and after that summer at the Camp he taught composition and literature at Georgetown College. Their daughter, Mary, was born in May 1958, and that fall the family moved to California, where Berry attended the writing program at Stanford University as a Wallace Stegner Fellow. At Stanford, Berry continued work on his first novel, *Nathan Coulter* (1960), and attended writing workshops taught by Stegner and Richard Scowcroft. Berry began his second novel, *A Place on Earth* (1967), in California and returned to Kentucky in 1960. In 1961 he received a Guggenheim Foundation grant and traveled to Europe, spending most of the time in Florence, Italy, continuing work on *A Place on Earth*. The Berrys returned to Kentucky in July 1962, and their son, Pryor ("Den"), was born in August. Throughout these years, Berry returned to the Camp periodically, cleaning and repairing it, but never staying for more than an extended visit. Nonetheless, his experiences there continued to deepen, and his place awareness became more ecological, encompassing a sense of complexity and community much like Aldo Leopold's famous "land ethic." In 1961, using the Camp as a summer retreat before leaving for Europe, Berry wrote,

Berry in Frankfort, Kentucky, at a 26 April 1975 rally to oppose a dam on the Red River
(photograph by Pam Spalding)

"that summer, I remember, I began to think of myself as living within rather than upon the life of the place. I began to think of my life as one among many, and one kind among many kinds."

Yet, the return to Kentucky after the year in Europe was not permanent. Berry served as the director of freshman English at New York University's Bronx campus, University College, from 1962 to 1964. Eventually, after two years in New York City, Berry and his family returned to Kentucky, where he taught at the University of Kentucky. He rebuilt the dilapidated cabin with the intention of using it as a writing retreat, commuting on weekends from Lexington. Beginning his permanent residence in Kentucky, he further solidified his sense of place at the Camp and finally conceived his mature relation to the land. "By coming back to Kentucky and renewing my devotion to the Camp and the river valley," Berry writes in "The Long-Legged House," "I had, in a sense, made a marriage with the place." In the autumn of 1965 the Berrys purchased a farm, called Lane's Landing, on property downriver from the Camp, and thus he began his life-long task of living fully and consciously in one place.

Three books of essays followed *The Long-Legged House* in quick succession, each motivated by a central purpose or theme. *The Hidden Wound* focuses on race and racial division in the South; *The Unforeseen Wilderness* collects various essays describing camping and canoeing trips in the Red River Gorge; and *A Continuous Harmony* is Berry's first foray into "essays cultural and agricultural," as the subtitle explains. During this time, the late 1960s and early 1970s, Berry proved himself to be a superb essayist after he had already established himself as a novelist and a poet. Along with two novels, Berry produced many collections of poetry in the 1960s, published with small presses as well as major publishers. George Braziller published *November Twenty-Six, Nineteen Hundred Sixty-Three* (1964), Berry's elegy for John F. Kennedy, designed and illustrated by Ben Shahn, and in 1969 Prairie Press published a slim volume, *Findings,* which includes elegies for patriarchs of the Berry family. Berry's first collection, *The Broken Ground,* was published in 1964 by Harcourt, Brace and World, which continued to publish his major books through the 1970s. *Openings,* which came out in 1968, included a long serial poem, "Window Poems," focused on the Camp, and *Farming: A Hand Book* (1970), expanded his poetic repertoire to narrative poems ("The Birth") and verse drama ("The Bringer of Water," in which characters from his novels are the dramatis personae). In 1971 Berry was elected a Distinguished Professor of English at the University of Kentucky and also received a National Institute of Arts and Letters Award. This list of honors and publications for an author not yet forty years old reveals Berry's dedication to the craft of writing and indicates how fully he was integrated into the academic and professional community of writers who taught in university writing programs during the post–World War II decades. However, as Berry began to write essays from the position of a farmer and public intellectual rather than as a member of an academic or cultural elite, his relationship to creative writing as a profession changed.

Berry reprinted the central chapter from *The Hidden Wound,* "Nick and Aunt Georgie," in *Recollected Essays, 1965–1980* (1981). It is a white southerner's account of his dawning awareness of racial difference as a young member of a family that once owned slaves in a society still bound by old prejudices. He describes his friendship with Nick Watkins, a black farmhand who worked for Berry's grandfather, and his family's relationship with Aunt Georgie, Nick's wife. From Aunt Georgie, Berry first learned of civil rights, the significance of Africa to black southerners, and African American folklore; from Nick, he learned about work and friendship, and began to understand the long history of racism intertwined with his family and place. In a moment of childhood ignorance, Berry invited Nick to his ninth or tenth birthday party, and the awkwardness for everyone involved revealed to him the social codes people in a racially divided culture live by: "I had done a thing more powerful than I could have imagined at the time; I had scratched the wound of racism, and all of us, our heads beclouded in the social dream that all was well, were feeling the pain." Scholar and critic Margaret Walker Anderson included *The Hidden Wound* on her list of the most influential books of the 1970s in the journal *Black Scholar* (1981).

The Unforeseen Wilderness is a series of excursion essays describing various hiking and canoeing trips in the Red River Gorge and the Daniel Boone National Forest and is illustrated by the photographs of Ralph Eugene Meatyard. These essays are Berry's most extensive commentary on the significance of wilderness, an idea and a place that the human, domestic economy of his farm required for possibility and renewal. The book was conceived as a response to the plans by the Army Corps of Engineers to dam the Red River in order to control flooding and create a recreational reservoir. Berry was involved as both a writer and an activist in saving the Red River Gorge. Andrew J. Angyal records in *Wendell Berry* (1995) that "As late as April 1975, as chairman of the Cumberland Chapter of the Sierra Club, Berry helped to organize a rally in Frankfort to present to Gov. Julian Carroll a petition with 44,200 signatures opposing the dam." The proposed dam was never built, and, aside from his political activism, Berry's major contribution to the cause was *The Unforeseen Wilderness,* which Angyal considers "a modern masterpiece of nature writing–profound, subtle, metaphysical, and ultimately religious in its sensibility."

The title essay begins, "That the world is stable and its order fixed is perhaps the most persistent human delusion." The Red River disabuses the author of this delusion, the idea that he could "foresee what I was going to do and then do it." By foot and by canoe, Berry, alone and with various companions, explored the river and gorge, trying to experience each as fully as possible. Other humans, and their traces, were a part of the experience, and finding trash and excrement in this wild place sparked an anger in Berry familiar to many environmentalists and wilderness recreationists. Interestingly, Berry reconsidered some sections of "The Unforeseen Wilderness," and in reprinting it in *Recollected Essays,* he omitted a number of paragraphs in which he expressed his disgust at humanity, including references to the Vietnam War, the nuclear arms race, and other contemporary issues. Most significant, he deleted a commentary on the humanistic "hubris" that he saw as the cause of the environmental crisis. In the original publication of this essay, in *The Hudson Review* (Winter 1970–1971), Berry first expressed a key concept of his nonfiction prose–propriety. Without a sense of propriety, excessive pride, or hubris, causes humans to disregard their proper place in Creation.

> Now we face cosmic disaster: the extinction of human life, and of all other life associated with it. For it may be that our species has now implemented its power and pride on such a scale, swelled as far out of its proper place in the ecological order that it can be forced back into its true limits–the limits of creatures and mortals– only by its destruction.

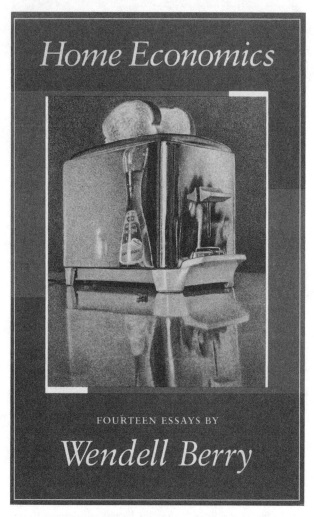

Dust jacket for Berry's 1987 book of essays about the practical aspects of making one's home in one place (Richland County Public Library)

Evidently, Berry thought in revising the essay that since the dam project had been abandoned, such an extreme statement was no longer required, but it reveals the extent to which he was influenced by the environmental rhetoric of the time period and the wilderness ideals of the twentieth century as well. After this statement, he invoked the "pastoral impulse" as the idea behind his wilderness excursions: "A man may cast off from the comforts and securities of civilization as he knows it and enter the wilderness. . . . He may begin with plans, but as soon as he leaves the roads and the beaten paths he is perforce contending at every step with the unforeseen." Wilderness is the cure for hubris, returning humans to a proper sense of their limits. Berry never abandons this idea, invoking it in his agricultural writing as well as in particular essays such as "Preserving Wildness" in *Home Economics,* but he never again states it as forcefully or as emotionally as he did in the article for *The Hudson Review.*

Berry included topical and occasional essays in *The Long-Legged House,* and *A Continuous Harmony* extends that format, but with the explicit acknowledgment that the essays engage topics in two broad categories, culture and agriculture. The collection includes some of his first literary essays—"A Secular Pilgrimage," on contemporary and traditional nature poetry; "An Homage to Dr. Williams," on the work of William Carlos Williams; and "The Regional Motive," on literary regionalism. The agriculture essays begin with "Notes from an Absence and Return," which documents Berry's sense of dislocation when he spends fall 1968 and winter 1969 as a visiting professor at Stanford University, and the homecoming he feels when he and his family return to Lane's Landing. His absence confirms the bond he has begun to establish with his farm: "This place has become the form of my work, its discipline, in the same way the sonnet has been the form and discipline of other poets: if it doesn't fit it's not true." The major essay, "Discipline and Hope" (reprinted in *Recollected Essays*), expands on the idea of discipline and "the failure of discipline" that Berry sees as the cause of the "general cultural disorder" of the time. The Vietnam War is the prime example of that disorder, and this essay is Berry's statement of principle defending his "refusal to be a partisan of *any* side." Berry wants to rediscover the old disciplines that honor good work and responsibility and to redefine discipline to include such concepts as community and faith. By the end of the essay, he can assert that the problem is not the cultural disorder of the times but human character and that returning to the ideals of discipline in one's personal life will make hope possible.

Five years passed between *A Continuous Harmony* and the publication of Berry's next nonfiction book, *The Unsettling of America.* During this time, Harcourt Brace Jovanovich published three major books by Berry—two collections of poetry, *The Country of Marriage* (1973) and *Clearing* (1977), and the novel *The Memory of Old Jack* (1974). Reading Berry as an autobiographer, Janet Goodrich, in *The Unforeseen Self in the Works of Wendell Berry* (2001), finds that he uses the conventions of fiction and poetry to contemplate the cultural and agricultural issues addressed in his nonfiction. For example, the central character of *The Memory of Old Jack,* Jack Beechum, represents the traditional ways of farming that are in decline, and his recollections implicitly critique the present disorder. Goodrich writes, "Berry dramatizes in fictional characters an order in the attitudes that contribute to a cultural crisis in both agriculture and character. His use of fiction personalizes this dilemma and prepares the way for the outrage of *The Unsettling of America.*" This book-length essay is the culmination of Berry's writing about farming, and it is his argument for the centrality of agriculture to human culture and the farm crisis to the environmental crisis. It is the key nonfiction text in Berry's body of work, and perhaps the most important of all his books. Not only did *The Unsettling of America* confirm Berry's status as a cultural critic and agrarian thinker, it also marked a turning point in his commitment to farming as a way of life. The year that *The Unsettling of America* was published, he resigned from the English faculty at the University of Kentucky to write and farm full-time.

The core argument of *The Unsettling of America* emerges in the two central chapters, "The Use of Energy" and "The Body and the Earth"; the latter is one of the longest chapters of the book (excerpted in *Recollected Essays*), and both chapters together constitute his major statement on the biological and cultural importance of farming. Berry's holistic view encompasses technology, ecology, religion, politics, literature, health, and sexuality. Energy, he argues, is the irreducible source that human and natural economies depend on, and he seeks to reestablish the link between the human use of energy as a resource with the other, more profound realm of energy as source. Berry asserts that both qualitative and quantitative differences exist between energy produced by living organisms and energy produced by mechanical technology, and he argues for a moral imperative in the use of energy and technology: "Our technology is the practical aspect of our culture. By it we enact our religion, or our lack of it." Technological energy convinces people that there are such things as unlimited resources, and infinite energy encourages a technological hubris, "the monstrous pride of thinking ourselves somehow entitled to undertake infinite destruction." (Berry's sense of human pride and its limitations is directly influenced by his reading of tragic drama, especially William Shakespeare's *King Lear,* act 4, scene 6; the title *Life Is a Miracle* is drawn from the same scene.) Conceiving of an unlimited source of fuel means committing to its use, Berry believes, and thus humanity is trapped in a cycle of production and consumption. Mechanical energy is a twofold process—energy is used as fuel and expended as waste—and this simplified system creates the illusion that people have no obligation to the source from which the fuel is extracted. This hubris is remedied when humanity's connection with biologically produced energy is maintained: "The moral order appropriate to the use of biological energy . . . requires the addition of a third term: production, consumption, and *return.*" With the advent of industrialized agriculture—"agribusiness" in the technocratic jargon that Berry opposes— "the responsibility of return" was removed from farming, and one of the most intimate connections of culture to the health of the earth (literally, the soil) was dam-

aged. From this argument stems Berry's commitment to organic farming and appropriate technologies that use biological energy, such as draft animals and hand tools.

Nonetheless, the technical solution is never adequate by itself. Berry is practical above all else—everything has an appropriate use and fitting tools are available—but the conditions and circumstances of use are moral. The argument throughout *The Unsettling of America* is that environmental problems are brought on by human behavior, and human behavior is a matter of character. The titles of the chapters leading up to "The Use of Energy" lay out the claim almost syllogistically: "The Ecological Crisis as a Crisis of Character," "The Ecological Crisis as a Crisis of Agriculture," and "The Agricultural Crisis as a Crisis of Culture." In order to make his case for the last claim, Berry posits the moral conditions of energy use described above and argues that the current state of agriculture is corrupted by the devaluation of the responsibility of return. Thus, "If we corrupt agriculture we corrupt culture, for in nature and within certain invariable social necessities we are one body, and what affects the hand will affect the brain." This line of reasoning brings Berry to the cultural criticism of the central chapter in the book, "The Body and the Earth."

In this chapter, Berry extends his argument into the realm of sexuality, gender roles, and domesticity. As a holistic argument, his thesis is undeniable: through our bodies we are connected to nature, and the cultural forms that bring our bodies together, especially marriage, are an integral part of our relation to nature. In detail, however, many of his points are problematic and have been challenged, especially his comments regarding women's ability to control their own reproduction. For example, he writes that "For the care or control of fertility, both that of the earth and that of our bodies, we have allowed a technology of chemicals and devices to replace entirely the cultural means of ceremonial forms, disciplines, and restraints." The holistic argument—appropriate is right, natural is better, traditional culture is closer to nature—applies here, but Berry ignores the meanings of "discipline" and "restraint" when it comes to women's actual experience in a conventional, patriarchal system. To his credit, Berry never shies away from the provocative claims of his critiques: he returns to these issues to clarify and adjust his arguments and responds to readers who take issue with arguments.

Ultimately, the argument of "The Body and the Earth" confirms Berry's sense of the importance of place, in terms of land and local culture, marriage, and farming. He views everything in its proper relationship to everything else. The farm, or domestic economy, must be seen in its relationship to the wilderness, or the economy of nature. The individual must be seen in his or her relationship to the community—and for Berry the communal connection is through marriage. The farm connects the household economy to the wilderness. The household connects the labor of husband and wife: "Marriage and the care of the earth are each other's disciplines."

The last two chapters of *The Unsettling of America* return to particular arguments about agriculture, agricultural policy and research, and specific examples of farm practice. "Jefferson, Morrill, and the Upper Crust" explores Thomas Jefferson's vision of a democracy of yeoman farmers and the institutionalization of that vision in the Morrill Act of 1862, which created the land-grant-college system. Berry acknowledges the importance of the combination of liberal and practical education specified in the Morrill Act and laments the division of such an integrated education in modern schools of agriculture. Divorced from values, practical education becomes dangerously abstract, as Berry sees it, and divorced from practical use, values become "attenuated and aimless." This chapter is an example of Berry's animus toward the expert and the specialist, and he takes particular aim against professors in schools of agriculture, the "academic upper crust that has provided a species of agricultural vandalism with the prestige of its professorships and the justifications of a bogus intellectuality, incomprehensible to any order of thought, . . . decked out in statistics, charts, and graphs to silence unspecialized skepticism and astonish gullibility." In the final chapter, "Margins," he presents counterexamples of healthy agriculture against this agribusiness "orthodoxy"; he offers concrete descriptions of preindustrial farming, modern organic farming, and Amish farming practices—all types of holistic agriculture still flourishing at the margins of the orthodoxy.

The Unsettling of America was published by Sierra Club Books in 1977; portions of it had appeared in such publications as *The Nation*. Writing as a "marginal" farmer, celebrating traditional culture and farming, staking an essentially conservative position in relation to mainstream, liberal society, Berry nonetheless aligned himself with environmentalists, the counterculture, and political dissenters, and his appeal was mainly with these groups. In November of that year, Berry was invited to debate the agricultural crisis with Earl Butz, former U.S. Secretary of Agriculture and current dean emeritus of a school of agriculture—one of the orthodoxy whom Berry criticized in his book. The debate was inconclusive, both men respectfully arguing positions they honestly believed to be the best for farmers. In "Earl Butz versus Wendell Berry" (1986), a transcription of the debate, Berry rephrases the core argument of *The Unsettling of America* and comments that he and Butz

"never meet, because he's arguing from quantities and I'm arguing from values." Those values were the ones Berry had been discovering and refining throughout his novels, poems, and essays, and in his personal experiences on his Lane's Landing farm.

The Unsettling of America was the culmination of Berry's agrarian and conservationist values in the post-1960s milieu of environmental awareness and activism, but the argument of the book remains relevant, because its charges were never countered by the agricultural orthodoxy, the Butz-Berry debate notwithstanding. The Sierra Club issued a new edition of *The Unsettling of America* in 1986 and in 1996 published a third edition with a new afterword by the author. In it Berry reviews the arguments of the book and points out that they have still gone unmet by the agribusiness establishment. Nevertheless, he takes heart in its having found another audience among readers concerned with improving farming and protecting the environment. This audience is a community, Berry believes, and that community has read other books that constitute "a lineage of works, influences, and exemplars." These books and the people who read them are united by the common interest of preserving places and communities. "What we are working for," he writes, "is an authentic settlement and inhabitation of our country." Although *The Unsettling of America* is concerned with particular problems within an historical period of farming, Berry feels that the argument of the book remains as relevant in 1996 as it was in 1977.

As part of the transition from professor to full-time farmer and writer, Berry began writing articles for popular farming, gardening, and environmental magazines, and he served for two years (1977–1979) as a contributing editor for Rodale Press. He continued to publish poetry and fiction, as well as contributing poems and another verse drama to popular magazines, but the nonfiction he wrote in conjunction with *The Unsettling of America* is decidedly practical and aimed at a nonliterary audience. Many of these essays were collected in *The Gift of Good Land: Further Essays, Cultural and Agricultural,* published by North Point Press, his main publisher throughout the 1980s and early 1990s. In the foreword, Berry points out that although these various articles and essays were written for magazines, they nonetheless extend the single argument of *The Unsettling of America*. It is a somewhat random collection, he admits, but it presents more, and more diverse, examples of his interrelated propositions about culture and agriculture. This book represents another transition in Berry's career. Goodrich writes, "Berry's departure from Rodale Press in 1979 grew from his recognition that *The New Farm* and *Organic Gardening* had turned from their original audience of small farmers. . . . *The Gift of Good Land* thus constitutes Berry's assertion of independence from publishers held by commercial interests rather than principle."

The Gift of Good Land is divided into five sections. Section 1 comprises journalistic travel essays: Berry travels to Peru to observe traditional Andean farming methods; visits the Southwest and, in the company of Gary Paul Nabhan, examines Papago and Hopi farms in the Sonora Desert; and travels in the grasslands of his own region in Kentucky and Tennessee. Practical and political essays on agricultural tools and techniques and on farm politics and policy are grouped in section 2. Many essays in this book address the issue of mechanical versus biological energy use raised in *The Unsettling of America*. "Horse-Drawn Tools and the Doctrine of Labor Saving," for example, proposes a distinction between labor-saving tools and labor-replacing tools. Berry argues that "technological determinists," who view all technological change as good and inevitable, want to remove the choice of horse-drawn tools even if they are better designed, more efficient, and more appropriate for the task at hand than modern ones. Making work faster and easier is not the value Berry looks for in a tool, and according to his own experience, a team of horses and a well-designed plow are the fitting and proper tools for the farming he does.

An essay included in section 3 extends Berry's argument about horse-drawn tools. "A Good Scythe," a simple and charming essay, compares a gas-powered scythe that Berry struggled to use and maintain to a human-powered scythe, which works more effectively on his steep and marginal land. After a point-by-point comparison of the two tools, he adds that the considerations are not all practical—that there is an aesthetics to the hand scythe, a pleasure he takes in the work and the weariness of mowing with it. Other essays in this section focus on the personal commitments that inform Berry's life on the farm, such as tracts on subsistence farming and raising children at home, gardening, and protesting against nuclear power. Section 4 looks at other families and their ways of life; it includes profiles of organic farmers, Amish farmers, and Berry's friend Wes Jackson, a plant geneticist who runs the Land Institute in Salinas, Kansas. The title essay constitutes all of section 5.

"The Gift of Good Land" is an attempt at "a Biblical argument for ecological and agricultural responsibility" and also a critique of institutional Christianity as "not *earthly* enough." The first point is a response to Lynn White Jr.'s article "The Historical Roots of Our Ecological Crisis," which asserts that the destruction of the environment in the West is based in the biblical imperative to subdue and dominate nature. Berry counters White's selective use of biblical citations, from

Wendell and Tanya Berry, March 1990
(photograph by Dan Carraco)

Genesis mostly, with extensive quotations from Deuteronomy, Leviticus, and Numbers, as well as Genesis, arguing for a biblical notion of stewardship as the proper role for humans. The land, according to Berry's interpretation of scripture, was given for human use, but undeservedly so, and thus humans are obligated to conserve it and replenish what they take from it. Ultimately, "The Gift of Good Land" is a religious and spiritual defense of the moral and practical farming detailed in the other essays in this volume. Berry writes, "To use knowledge and tools in a particular place with good long term results is not heroic. . . . It is a small action, but more complex and difficult, more skillful and responsible, more whole and enduring, than most grand actions."

Although not nature writing in a proper sense, Berry's next collection of essays, *Standing by Words,* is perhaps second only to *The Unsettling of America* in importance. The literary essays of *Standing by Words,* most regarding poetry, reflect Berry's primary concerns—place, marriage, and agriculture—with the focus on the writer's medium, language. In fact, Berry takes an approach to language and poetry similar to his approach to agricultural and ecological topics: he sets out to diagnose, analyze, and remedy a crisis. He finds the same disease in poetry that he found in agriculture–specialization. The first two essays, "The Specialization of Poetry" and "Standing by Words," attack the problem head-on. To Berry, poetry is a discipline, and he admits that any discipline gains an immediate benefit when it becomes a specialty: "The primary aspect of specialization is practical; the specialist withdraws from responsibility for everything not comprehended by his specialty." For poets, however, the particular danger in specialization is a loss of one's connection to the world through language. Specialized poetic language, which asserts the primacy of poetry above all else, "is a seeking of self in words, the making of word-world in which the word-self may be at home. The poets go to their poems as other people have gone to the world or to God–for a sense of their own reality." This corruption of the referential capacity of language, in Berry's view, is not confined to literary discourse.

"Standing by Words" addresses the specialization of both literary and professional language use, analyzing texts ranging from *Paradise Lost* to an article called "The Evolution and Future of American Animal Agriculture," discussing authors from Shakespeare to R. Buckminster Fuller. Berry proposes a practical, accountable, referential theory of language based in the idea of context:

> no statement is complete or comprehensible in itself . . . in order for a statement to be complete and comprehensible three conditions are required: 1. It must designate its object precisely. 2. Its speaker must stand by it: must believe it, be accountable for it, be willing to act on it. 3. This relation of speaker, word, and object must be conventional; the community must know what it is.

Thus, for Berry, language is always communal, in a literal sense. Words cannot be simply split into signifiers and signifieds in the absence of speaker, because the speaker's presence is always implied. Specialization denies conventional usage, reducing community to a smaller and smaller set of jargon-speaking initiates. Without a larger community to weigh and judge the statement, the speaker cannot "stand by it," and it cannot precisely refer to anything. This breakdown in language results in a breaking apart of moral connections, the accountability that Berry sees as essential. For example, when agribusiness replaces the dairy cow as "family companion animal" with cow as "manufacturing unit . . . for the efficient transformation of unprocessed feed into food for man," then the moral connection between dairy farmer and dairy cow is rendered meaningless and nonexistent.

Two other essays in *Standing by Words* are central to the rest of Berry's writings. "Poetry and Place," the longest essay in the collection, and "Poetry and Marriage" articulate the integral position poetry occupies among his three main themes–place, marriage, and farming. "Poetry and Place" is a sign of Berry's continuing engagement with the British literary tradition. He had always expressed an admiration and fondness for the poetry of Andrew Marvell (as early as "The Long-Legged House"), but he did not find much else in the British tradition until the Romantics, especially William Blake. In "A Secular Pilgrimage" (1970), Berry writes, "Though English poetry is full of nature *imagery,* and though it has had a constant interest in one or another of the *concepts* of nature, it seems to me surprisingly seldom that the immediate and particular manifestations of nature are acknowledged and looked at for their own sake." What is most remarkable about "Poetry and Place," and most significant for the rest of his writing, is that Berry revisits his earlier reading of the Western literary tradition, mostly British but also classical and European literature, in order to formulate his ideals for nature poetry and nature writing. The ideal that emerges distinguishes Berry's sense of literary history from the mainstream literary history of nature writing because he aligns his values with those of John Milton, Dante, and Alexander Pope against those of Romantics such as William Wordsworth and Percy Bysshe Shelley, and modernists such as William Butler Yeats and W. H. Auden. What Berry believes has been lost from poetry is a sense of decorum, the notion that certain forms fit certain occasions, and the concomitant sense that decorum in literary form implies respect for ethical hierarchies that establish order and maintain connections in nature and society. Berry recovers one of those concepts of nature he noted in "A Secular Pilgrimage," 'the great chain of being,' and constructs an elaborate defense for this metaphor, arguing that its hierarchy of beings embodies a sense of the proper place for humanity in the natural order. He writes,

> Implicit in the Chain of Being is the idea that creatures are protected in their various kinds, not by equality, but by difference; and that if humans are responsibly observant of the differences between themselves and the angels above them and the animals below, they will act with respect, restraint, and benevolence toward the subordinate creatures, and it is part of, inseparable from, their duty to the higher creatures and to God.

Whether such a hierarchy requires a belief in angelic orders, or the divinity of monarchs for that matter, does not concern Berry. He is satisfied with the 'chain of being' as a metaphor for decorum, propriety, and order.

In "Poetry and Place" Berry outlines a tradition unified not by schools of style or patterns of influence, for there is no such connection between two of his favorite poets, Pope and Gary Snyder, or even by genre or discipline–as his examples are drawn from poetry, agriculture, and architecture–but by a concept. He finds in this tradition a perennial and changeless truth, a truth that expresses the connection between nature and human nature. He finds this truth in Pope's idea of 'sense':

> Sense is the soul of art, for it governs the relations of parts to one another and to the whole. It is the understanding of what a part is, and how it should behave, as a part. . . . It is the old decorum or propriety, the intelligence of what is fitting or seemly or becoming in the parts of a garden or a poem or in the behavior of a human being. If one knows where one is in the hierarchical, the vertical, order, then one can *see* where one is in the horizontal order, in the world, and one can attain seemly competences of whereabouts.

This relation of part to whole, and the decorum or propriety that defines and maintains the health of that connection, informs all of Berry's writing at this time. The titles of two of his poetry collections are intended to convey this synecdochic relationship: *A Part* was published by North Point Press in 1980, and *The Wheel,* which refers to the endless cycles of growth and decay (as in "the Wheel of Life") followed two years later. Such is the integration that Berry strives for throughout his career as a writer, and it is inseparable from his life as farmer and husband. As he writes in "Poetry and Marriage," the final essay in *Standing by Words:* "The work of poetic form is coherence, joining things that need to be joined, as marriage joins them–in words by which a man or a woman can stand, words confirmable in acts." Without his discipline as a writer, he would not be able to practice the disciplines of marriage and farming, and vice versa.

Berry's next four collections of nonfiction gather polemical, personal, and literary essays that address a variety of topics, such as wilderness preservation, community preservation, feminism, education, and sustainable economies. From the mid 1980s to the mid 1990s, Berry wrote as an advocate for local communities, especially rural and farming communities, often arguing against the globalization of production and the power of multinational corporations. As the title of his 1987 collection, *Home Economics,* is meant to suggest, his essays have turned to the practicalities of making one's home in one place. This endeavor, of course, has been his lifelong project–his second novel was called *A Place on Earth,* after all–but as an essayist he often takes a practical approach to his topics and offers suggestions to readers who share his interest in defending local, domestic economies against the national and global

forces that would destroy that way of life. In the same year that *Home Economics* was published, Berry received the Jean Stein Award from the American Academy of Arts and Letters, and he rejoined the English faculty at the University of Kentucky. Reflecting his opinions expressed in essays such as "The Loss of the University" and "Higher Education and Home Defense," Berry's approach to and interest in teaching had changed in the ten years he had spent outside of academe. "I don't like teaching so-called creative writing anymore," Berry says in an interview during the 1990s with L. Elisabeth Beattie. "I've been teaching, since the fall of '87, a course called Composition for Teachers, for people who are going to teach English in the public schools. Then I've taught, usually, a literature course of some kind." Such courses reflect the importance Berry places on local community and the ability of literature to connect with the world and influence people's values.

One essay in *Home Economics* embodies Berry's abiding interest in religious and spiritual matters, and reveals how he makes connections between these concerns and the seemingly practical and materialistic values of economics. In "Two Economies," Berry distinguishes between "the Great Economy," which is in essence religious (he also calls it the Kingdom of God and the Tao), and the human economy, which participates in and depends upon the Great Economy. The Great Economy creates value and defines limits, and the human economy should attempt to preserve that value and understand those limits or, eventually, face serious consequences. The human economy requires two kinds of knowledge–the knowledge of how to act and how to use the value of the Great Economy, and the knowledge of when not to act and to stop using a resource. Berry writes, "Both kinds of knowledge are necessary because invariably, at some point, the reach of human comprehension becomes too short, and at that point the work of the human economy must end in absolute deference to the working of the Great Economy. This, I take it, is the practical significance of the idea of the Sabbath." To ignore the limitation that the idea of the Sabbath puts on human action–that there is a time for rest, reflection, and inaction–is to violate the relationship between the two economies. In Berry's moral terms, it is an act of hubris.

Combining the Great Economy with the emphasis on propriety and traditional forms that he discusses in *Standing by Words,* Berry's poetry of this time exemplifies these ideas and is an index to the conservative turn in his writing in general. In 1987 he published a collection of formal poems, *Sabbaths* (1987), written in meditation on his days of rest spent at the Camp or walking in the fields and woods. The poems are arranged chrono-

Tanya and Wendell Berry plowing at Lane's Landing, their Kentucky farm, 1990
(photograph by Dan Carraco)

logically, beginning in 1979 and running through 1986; two stanzas from a 1979 poem express the two kinds of knowledge required to keep the Great Economy and the human economy in balance:

> The mind that comes to rest is tended
> In ways that it cannot intend:
> Is borne, preserved, and comprehended
> By what it cannot comprehend.
>
> Your Sabbath, Lord, thus keeps us by
> Your will, not ours. And it is fit
> Our only choice should be to die
> Into that rest, or out of it.

This poetic sequence has become one of Berry's major writing projects, and the collection was expanded to include poems through 1997 in *A Timbered Choir: The Sabbath Poems, 1979–1997* (1998). It is another example of the integrity of Berry's vision in poetry and prose, and a confirmation of his sense of propriety in literary and cultural matters.

Berry has never shied away from controversy when the issue was central to the values he espoused as a nature writer, and essays in *What Are People For?*, *Sex, Economy, Freedom & Community,* and *Another Turn of the Crank* show Berry at his most polemical. "Why I Am Not Going to Buy a Computer," for example, extends Berry's preference for hand tools and biologically powered machinery in farming to his labor as a writer. He says that as an ecologically minded writer he strives to remain independent from power companies, and so he writes manuscripts by hand, and his wife types and edits them. Berry feels that he can write with a cleaner conscience if he continues with this "literary cottage industry" rather than buying a computer, as people have suggested he should. He includes a list of criteria for the technical innovation in the tools he uses; if a computer surpassed his Royal standard typewriter in these criteria, he might consider buying one. The implied comparison between a computer and a manual typewriter recalls the point-by-point comparison of the gas-powered scythe versus the manual scythe. When this essay was reprinted in *Harper's* magazine, many readers wrote to the editor to take issue with it, and some of these letters are included in *What Are People For?*, in which Berry wrote a response to the readers' complaints, many of which took issue with his wife's typing his manuscripts. So important is this "cottage industry" to his domestic economy, Berry wrote another essay clarifying his comments on work and gender, "Feminism, the Body, and the Machine," in which he comments that "It is . . . regrettable that all of the feminist attacks on my essay implicitly deny the validity of two decent and probably necessary possibilities: marriage as a state of mutual help, and the household as an economy." This exchange with his critics leads Berry to write extensively about sexuality and gender, a return to a major topic last addressed in *The Unsettling of America*.

Concurrent with *What Are People For?* the University Press of Kentucky published *Harlan Hubbard*. Originally delivered as the Blazer lectures at the University in 1989, these essays narrate the biography and discuss the paintings of Kentucky artist Harlan Hubbard, who lived by or on the Ohio River for much of his life, writing about it in his journals and portraying it in his paintings and prints. Hubbard and his wife, Anna, lived the attentive, creative, integrated life that Berry admires and emulates, and his lectures pay tribute to the Hubbards as forebears and models. He knew the couple personally, having met them by chance on a canoe trip in 1964 when he and a friend stopped at Payne Hollow, the Hubbards' homestead on the river, to ask for fresh water. Like Berry's transition from pastoral bachelor to georgic husbandman during his time at the Camp, the Hubbards represent the maturation and domestication of Henry David Thoreau's experiment: Harlan and Anna's economy at Payne Hollow "differed from Thoreau's economy radically in some respects, and also advanced and improved upon it. The main differences were that, whereas Thoreau's was a bachelor's economy, the Hubbards' was that of a married couple." All of Hubbard's creations—his house, his paintings, his journals, his music—represent to Berry the integrated economy of disciplines that a marriage rooted in place achieves.

In the title essay of *Sex, Economy, Freedom & Community*, Berry explores the collision of public and private life, beginning with the example of the sexual-harassment charges made by Anita Hill against Clarence Thomas. As an example of "community disintegration," the Thomas confirmation hearings show the impossibility of treating private behavior as a public issue, and Berry argues that community must be a mediating presence between public and private interests, especially when sex and sexual behavior are involved. "For," he writes,

"sexual love is the heart of community life. Sexual love is the force that in our bodily life connects us most intimately to the Creation, to the fertility of the world, to farming and the care of animals. It brings us into the dance that holds the community together and joins it to its place." The essay makes his case for the central role of such community in society, arguing that community is based in the household, whereas the public is based in the individual. A globalized economy, which destroys local communities, relies on this debased idea of the public to gain power. Its version of multiculturalism is a plurality of identities based on ancestry and abstractions. To Berry, real multiculturalism comes from people's being part of a community shaped by a place: "So long as we try to think of ourselves as African Americans or European Americans or Asian Americans, we will never settle anywhere. For an authentic community is made less in reference to who we are than to where we are. I cannot farm my farm as a European American—or as an American, or as a Kentuckian—but only as a person belonging to the place itself."

In "The Problem of Tobacco," Berry addresses another of the controversial issues that have provoked sometimes angry response to his views. As a Kentuckian, he has a nostalgic appreciation of tobacco as a crop, and as a small farmer he supports the tobacco program (federal regulation that limits tobacco production to ensure a decent return on the crop). Since many of his readers are environmentalists who do not live in rural communities, they take offense at Berry's apparent support of tobacco companies and disregard for health issues; this essay, as well as others he has published in magazines, attempts to clarify and defend his position.

The title of his next book, *Another Turn of the Crank*, signals, with a serious humor, Berry's continuing polemical cantankerousness. It is an explicitly political book, and the author warns his readers on all sides, liberal and conservative, Democrat and Republican, not to assume his statements are endorsements of any of their positions. Defining himself as an "agrarian," which means he believes "that good farming is a high and difficult art, that it is indispensable, and that it cannot be accomplished except under certain circumstances," Berry positions himself as a member of a cultural minority, one that the U.S. Census no longer counts—a person who lives on a farm. Thus, for him, the old political distinctions of liberal and conservative no longer obtain; there is a new bipartisan struggle—the global economy versus the local community. Whatever the topic of the individual essay, the approach to it stems from this condition. Berry writes about such issues as forest management, private property, abortion, and the health care crisis, staking essentially conservative positions, but always qualified by his commitment to community. Half of the essays were originally delivered as speeches at conferences, and so the sense of audience is important and immediate, and in keeping with the emphasis on local communities.

Life Is a Miracle is both an obvious outgrowth of Berry's lifelong concerns and a distinctive addition to his body of nonfiction. Like *The Unsettling of America,* it is a unified argument elaborated throughout a single book, and it is also a reaction to and critique of contemporary cultural and social conditions. However, unlike the earlier book, Berry's argument in *Life Is a Miracle* takes the shape of an attack on a single idea represented by one book, Wilson's *Consilience. Life Is a Miracle* certainly does not have the moral scope of *The Unsettling of America,* which supported Berry's personal position with years of experience, reading, and research; for that and other reasons, the more recent book has received mixed acceptance among longtime readers of his work. Writing in *The Hudson Review* (Winter 2001), a journal which has published Berry's work for decades, Harold Fromm detects "an insidious worm"—what he sees as Berry's blind religious faith—"that eats away at the virtues of this book and leads me to believe that Berry's eminence as a cultural guide has peaked." On the other hand, environmental journalist and author Bill McKibben, writing for *The Washington Monthly* (June 2000), concludes that "*Life Is a Miracle* is an indispensable handbook for the new age into which we now stumble." Aside from the somewhat conservative religious faith that Berry espouses, which is in fact nothing new, what seems to bother many critics is that Berry and Wilson, as prominent conservationists, ought to be allies rather than adversaries. What is more, Berry has long argued for the integration of the practical and the fine arts, for the dialogue between disciplines and against their overspecialization, so why now does he oppose "consilience," an idea that Wilson defines as "a 'jumping together' of knowledge by the linking of facts and fact-based theory across disciplines to create a common groundwork of explanation"? *Life Is a Miracle* is the answer to such a question, but the main point is Berry's familiar concern with propriety.

Berry's problem with consilience is that the concept subordinates all the disciplines to the control of a single discipline—science, Wilson's "fact-based theory." In the terms of Berry's earlier essay from *Home Economics,* consilience reduces the Great Economy to a material economy completely comprehensible by human knowledge. In a chapter titled "Propriety," Berry writes, "My general concern is with what I take to be the increasing inability of the scientific, artistic, and religious disciplines to help us address the issue of propriety in our thoughts and acts." In other words, Berry cannot accept that a science that reduces organisms to machines,

knowledge to information, and the whole to a sum of its parts, can offer the basis for making moral decisions and aesthetic judgments. Each discipline has its proper place, according to Berry, and each should inform the other but not violate the decorum that determines which occasion is properly addressed by which discipline. Wilson's book, he charges, "is an exercise in a sort of academic hubris."

Although Fromm accuses Berry of abandoning the rules of intellectual debate by appealing to unprovable religious faith in his argument, the most convincing sections of the book draw on Berry's skills as an essayist to provide concrete, descriptive examples. In it are scenes and moments familiar from the rest of Berry's nature writing. Arguing against the reductionism essential to modern science, he describes his experience writing at the Camp for thirty-seven years, how he has witnessed countless wonders in the world about him as he has looked out the window of the cabin. Seeing the particulars of "deer swimming across [the river], wild turkeys feeding, a pair of newly fledged owls, otters at play, a coyote taking a stroll, a hummingbird feeding her young, a peregrine falcon eating a snake" has helped him to learn "the distinction between reduction and the thing reduced," a distinction that science cannot make. A chapter titled "A Conversation Out of School" describes Berry's friendship with Wes Jackson and explains that their ongoing conversation about soil conservation and plant genetics exemplifies an intercourse between the disciplines that could not take place in the specialized language of academic discourse. For Berry, a set of local, common interests have to be present for a plant geneticist and a farmer-poet to be able to produce a "consilience" of their disciplines; each specialist must be able to leave behind his narrowly focused expertise and be able to discuss common problems, to ask the same questions, and to practice the same solutions, and so they must be able to talk to one another in the same language and understand the limits of their disciplines.

Berry concludes the book with an anecdote about walking on his farm with his son and grandson. The story is intended to show that knowledge cannot be completely transmitted by human language, that knowledge is not information or data, and that knowledge itself is inexplicable sometimes. In one sense, although he takes issue with Wilson's scientific materialism, this belief is Berry's version of materialism. The "generational procession" that he describes is an embodied one—his grandfather had to be bodily connected to the land in order to ground his son, to whom he is bodily connected, in that place. That experience is recalled in Berry's body and memory and is imparted to his son and his grandson. These are all material connections: Berry's memory exists in his mind, which is embodied in his brain and consciousness, and thus dependent upon his body; but these connections transcend his individual materiality by becoming familial and cultural. They cannot simply be reduced to genetic information or cultural constructions. But human culture does sustain and enable this kind of knowledge, and it is the culture that Berry has defended since returning to Kentucky and settling on his farm. Once the small farmer is removed from the land, once farm families no longer live on the land, this knowledge disappears. Berry concludes, "When the procession ends, so does the knowledge." *Life Is a Miracle,* like all of Berry's essays, addresses a specific crisis as he sees it, but it also draws on a unified, experiential view of nature and culture in order to assert its argument.

In the fall of 2001, a crisis more immediate than genetic modification and overreaching science occurred in the United States. Berry responded to the terrorist attacks on Washington, D.C., and New York City with an essay composed of twenty-seven numbered paragraphs, "Thoughts in the Presence of Fear," commissioned and published by *Orion* magazine. The Orion Society subsequently collected two more recent essays, "The Idea of a Local Economy" and "In Distrust of Movements," with the response to September 11 and published them together as *In the Presence of Fear.* The book may be addressed to a changed world, but Berry's arguments are rooted in the cultural and agricultural essays he has been publishing throughout his career. He contends that "free market" capitalism created the opportunity and conditions for such an act of terrorism and that a naive optimism based on prosperity, technology, and a global economy led to a sense of invulnerability among the beneficiaries of that system. To respond to the attacks with real effect, Berry believes, people have two choices: to maintain a global police force to protect the global economy or to promote a local economy. In his view, the global economy–based in values of innovation, disposability, and unlimited growth–requires a constant state of war; a local economy–based in tradition, thrift, and respectful use–can create "peaceableness." The two other essays articulate this idea further, defining what a local economy might be and arguing against piecemeal solutions offered by specialized reform movements. Thus, even in topical, occasional essays, Berry draws on the values that have sustained his nature writing from the beginning–independence and community, work and mindfulness, and propriety and form. As always, he argues for wholeness over fragmentation, humility over hubris, and the local over the corporate, international, and global.

For nearly four decades, Berry has been a preeminent practitioner of the essay, writing in a variety of

Paperback cover for the 1995 book in which Berry explains
his positions on such issues as health care, abortion,
private property, and forest management
(Richland County Public Library)

modes and forms. He avails himself of the major techniques and themes of nature writing, describing encounters with a particular landscape, narrating an ongoing story of a homecoming to a native place, and arguing for ethical and aesthetic principles derived from a holistic vision of the natural and human estates. He has made a distinctive contribution to American nature writing in the second half of the twentieth century by passionately defending the human and natural economies of the place he loves. His and his family's long residence in Kentucky–as it is documented in his essays, poems, and stories–provides readers with an unparalleled example of the possibilities of living consciously, responsibly, and completely in one place.

Interviews:

Mindy Weinreb, "A Question a Day: A Written Conversation with Wendell Berry," in *Wendell Berry,* edited by Paul Merchant (Lewiston, Idaho: Confluence, 1991), pp. 27–43;

Marilyn Berlin Snell, "The Art of Place: An Interview with Wendell Berry," *New Perspectives Quarterly,* 9, no. 2 (1992): 29–34;

Lionel Basney, "A Conversation with Wendell Berry," *Image: A Journal of the Arts and Religion,* 26 (Spring 2000): 45–56.

Bibliographies:

Jack Hicks, "A Wendell Berry Checklist," *Bulletin of Bibliography,* 37 (1980): 127–131;

John B. Griffin, "An Update to the Wendell Berry Checklist, 1979–Present," *Bulletin of Bibliography,* 50 (1993): 173–180.

References:

Andrew J. Angyal, *Wendell Berry* (New York: Twayne, 1995);

Laura Barge, "Changing Forms of the Pastoral in Southern Poetry," *Southern Literary Journal,* 26, no. 1 (Fall 1993): 30–41;

L. Elisabeth Beattie, ed., *Conversations with Kentucky Writers* (Lexington: University Press of Kentucky, 1996);

Lawrence Buell, *Writing for an Endangered World: Literature, Culture, and Environment in the U.S. and Beyond* (Cambridge, Mass.: Harvard University Press, 2001);

Robert Collins, "A More Mingled Music: Wendell Berry's Ambivalent View of Language," *Modern Poetry Studies,* 11 (1982): 35–56;

Nathaniel Dresser, "Cultivating Wilderness: The Place of Land in the Fiction of Ed Abbey and Wendell Berry," *Growth and Change,* 26 (Summer 1995): 350–364;

Peter A. Fritzell, *Nature Writing and America: Essays upon a Cultural Type* (Ames: Iowa State University Press, 1990);

David E. Gamble, "Wendell Berry: The Mad Farmer and Wilderness," *Kentucky Review,* 2 (1988): 40–52;

Janet Goodrich, *The Unforeseen Self in the Works of Wendell Berry* (Columbia: University of Missouri Press, 2001);

John R. Knott, "Into the Woods with Wendell Berry," *Essays in Literature,* 23, no. 1 (Spring 1996): 124–140;

John Lang, "'Close Mystery': Wendell Berry's Poetry of Incarnation," *Renascence,* 35 (1982): 258–268;

Paul Merchant, ed., *Wendell Berry* (Lewiston, Idaho: Confluence, 1991);

Dana Phillips, "Is Nature Necessary?" *Raritan,* 13, no. 3 (Winter 1994): 78–100;

Bernard W. Quetchenbach, *Back from the Far Field: American Nature Poetry in the Late Twentieth Century* (Charlottesville: University Press of Virginia, 2000);

Leonard Scigaj, *Sustainable Poetry: Four American Ecopoets* (Lexington: University Press of Kentucky, 1999);

Scott Slovic, *Seeking Awareness in American Nature Writing: Henry Thoreau, Annie Dillard, Edward Abbey, Wendell Berry, Barry Lopez* (Salt Lake City: University of Utah Press, 1992);

Stephen Whithed, "On Devotion to the 'Communal Order': Wendell Berry's Record of Fidelity, Interdependence, and Love," *Studies in the Literary Imagination,* 27, no. 2 (Fall 1994): 9–28.

Henry Beston
(Henry Beston Sheahan)
(1 June 1888 – 15 April 1968)

Daniel G. Payne
State University of New York at Oneonta

BOOKS: *A Volunteer Poilu,* as Henry Beston Sheahan (Boston & New York: Houghton Mifflin, 1916);

The Firelight Fairy Book, as Henry B. Beston (Boston: Atlantic Monthly Press, 1919);

Full Speed Ahead: Tales from the Log of a Correspondent with Our Navy, as Henry B. Beston (Garden City, N.Y.: Doubleday, Page, 1919);

The Starlight Wonder Book, as Henry B. Beston (Boston: Atlantic Monthly Press, 1923);

The Book of Gallant Vagabonds (New York: Doran, 1925; London: Laurie, 1925);

The Sons of Kai: The Story the Indian Told (New York: Macmillan, 1926);

The Outermost House: A Year of Life on the Great Beach of Cape Cod (Garden City, N.Y.: Doubleday, Doran, 1928; London: Selwyn & Blount, 1928);

Herbs and the Earth (Garden City, N.Y.: Doubleday, Doran, 1935);

Five Bears and Miranda, by Beston and Elizabeth Jane Coatsworth (New York: Macmillan, 1939);

The Tree That Ran Away, by Beston and Coatsworth (New York: Macmillan, 1941);

The St. Lawrence, Rivers of America (New York & Toronto: Farrar & Rinehart, 1942; London: Hodge, 1951);

A Glimpse of the Indian Past (Cohasset, Mass.: South Shore Nature Club, 1946);

Northern Farm: A Chronicle of Maine (New York: Rinehart, 1948);

Fairy Tales (New York: Aladdin, 1952);

Chimney Farm Bedtime Stories, by Beston and Coatsworth (New York, Chicago & San Francisco: Holt, Rinehart & Winston, 1966);

Especially Maine: The Natural World of Henry Beston from Cape Cod to the St. Lawrence, edited by Coatsworth (Brattleboro, Vt.: Stephen Greene, 1970).

OTHER: *American Memory: Being a Mirror of the Stirring and Picturesque Past of Americans and the American*

Henry Beston

Nation, edited by Beston (New York & Toronto: Farrar & Rinehart, 1937);

White Pine and Blue Water: A State of Maine Reader, edited by Beston (New York: Farrar, Strauss, 1950).

SELECTED PERIODICAL PUBLICATIONS–
UNCOLLECTED: "The Wardens of Cape Cod," *World's Work,* 47 (December 1923): 186–194;

"Sound and Life," *Atlantic Monthly,* 151 (January 1933): 124–125;

"Some Birds of a Maine Lake," *Audubon Magazine,* 45 (September 1943): 277–280;

"The Crisis of the Peasant Civilization," *Human Events,*
    3 (21 August 1946): 1–4;

"End of a Farm Summer," *Progressive,* 12 (October
    1948): 27–28;

"Comment on Is America a Civilization?" *Shenandoah,*
    10 (Autumn 1958): 23–26.

Late in the summer of 1926, Henry Beston went
to Cape Cod for a two-week vacation in a small cottage
that overlooked the Atlantic Ocean and that a local carpenter had built for him. Beston was in his late thirties,
a little-known author and editor who had as yet given
no indication that he had any particular interest in writing about nature, despite what in *The Outermost House: A
Year of Life on the Great Beach of Cape Cod* (1928) he called
his "field naturalist's inclination." When the vacation
ended, Beston found that he had become so intrigued
by the beauty and mystery of life on the dunes that he
could not bring himself to leave, and he stayed there for
a year, observing and recording what he experienced.
Beston's account of his year spent living alone on Cape
Cod, *The Outermost House,* was almost immediately recognized as a classic work of American nature writing. In
his introduction, Thomas J. Lyon, editor of *This Incomperable Lande: A Book of American Nature Writing* (1989),
compares *The Outermost House* to Henry David Thoreau's *Walden* (1854) and Edward Abbey's *Desert Solitaire*
(1968), calling it a "talismanic book of solitude."

Beston was born Henry Beston Sheahan in
Quincy, Massachusetts, on 1 June 1888. His father,
Joseph Sheahan, was an Irish American physician who
was studying medicine in France when he met and married Beston's mother. Marie Louise Maurice Sheahan
was born in Paris, and Beston later said that his French
upbringing was one of the greatest influences in his life
and that his bilingual education had been instrumental
in forming his style as a writer. Beston's early years
were primarily spent in the busy Boston suburb setting
of Quincy, with summer vacations often spent with his
mother in the country, boarding at farmhouses. Beston
attended Adams Academy, a private school in Quincy,
and from there went on to Harvard University, where
he majored in English. He received his bachelor's
degree from Harvard in 1909 and a master's degree in
1911. Beston then went to France for a year, where he
taught English at the University of Lyons and spent
much of his free time touring the countryside. This
period was important, Beston later wrote, because rural
France was "the first place where I encountered and
knew and loved the earth." Following his year in
France, Beston returned to the United States to teach
English at Harvard for the next two years.

When war broke out in Europe in 1914, Beston–
like many other young Americans, particularly those

with personal ties to France and England–was anxious
to find a way to assist the Allied war effort. A few
months later he joined the American Field Service, serving as an ambulance driver on the western front in
France until 1916. During his service in France, Beston
also wrote articles as a war correspondent for several
publications, including two pieces, "Verdun" (July
1916) and "Vineyard of Red Wine" (August 1916), for
the *Atlantic Monthly.* A collection of his wartime essays
was published as *A Volunteer Poilu* in 1916 under his
given name of Henry Sheahan. For reasons that are not
entirely clear, he published his next few books under
the name Henry B. Beston and then dropped the middle initial entirely in the early 1920s. When the United
States declared war against Germany in 1917, Beston
signed on as an official observer serving with the U.S.
Submarine Service. The articles he wrote as a naval correspondent were published in many periodicals and
were later compiled for his second book, *Full Speed
Ahead: Tales from the Log of a Correspondent with Our Navy*
(1919). Although Beston's wartime correspondence was
his initiation as a writer, he was not particularly
impressed with his efforts or by their having resulted in
his first published works, referring to them in several
places as mere "journalism." Following the war, Beston
took a position as editor of the magazine *The Living Age.*
Beston edited *The Living Age* until 1923 and also wrote
prolifically for that publication and for other periodicals
throughout the 1920s.

Like many of the young Americans who witnessed the horrifying carnage of World War I, Beston
was disillusioned by what he saw as the dehumanizing
effect of modern industrial society. To Beston, the link
between industrialization and violence was clear, but
unlike many of his literary contemporaries who com-
prised the "Lost Generation" after the war, Beston did
not seek refuge in alcohol or sink into nihilistic despair.
Instead, he found new sources of inspiration and
renewal–nature and writing for children. Beston's first
book of children's stories, *The Firelight Fairy Book* (1919),
was a collection of original fairy tales, as was his second
children's book, *The Starlight Wonder Book* (1923). In
1925 Beston published *The Book of Gallant Vagabonds,* a
set of historical narratives about the lives of unconven-
tional adventurers such as James Bruce, a Scottish
explorer of Africa; Thomas Morton, an English
explorer of the area around what is now Quincy, Massachusetts; and Arthur Rimbaud, an early French sym-
bolist poet. The following year Beston published
another story for young readers, *The Sons of Kai: The
Story the Indian Told* (1926). Beston maintained an interest in children's stories throughout the rest of his life
and later collaborated on several with his wife, Elizabeth Jane Coatsworth, who was herself an

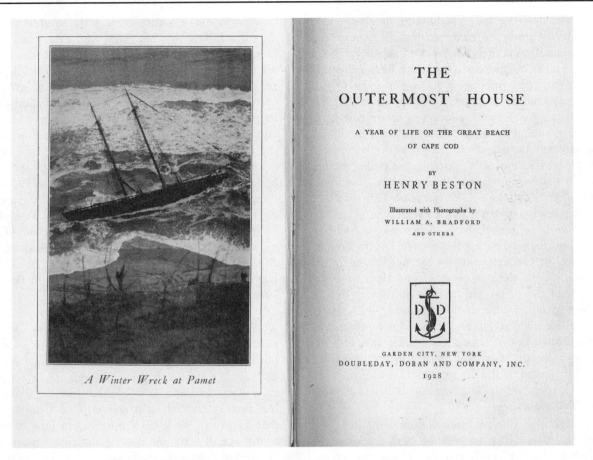

A Winter Wreck at Pamet

THE
OUTERMOST HOUSE

A YEAR OF LIFE ON THE GREAT BEACH
OF CAPE COD

BY
HENRY BESTON

Illustrated with Photographs by
WILLIAM A. BRADFORD
AND OTHERS

GARDEN CITY, NEW YORK
DOUBLEDAY, DORAN AND COMPANY, INC.
1928

*Frontispiece and title page for Beston's account of his solitary twelve-month sojourn
on the Massachusetts coast (Richland County Library)*

award-winning author of children's stories. Although writing children's stories was undoubtedly therapeutic for Beston following the horrors of the war, fairy tales and journalism were not a sufficient literary outlet for a talented writer who thus far had written little that he considered noteworthy. As Coatsworth later wrote of these works in the introduction to *Especially Maine*, "none came up to Henry's demanding standards."

In the early 1920s Beston made several trips to Cape Cod, where he bought a plot of land near Eastham, on the eastern shore of the cape. In 1925 he drew up plans for a cottage and hired a local carpenter to build it for him. The tiny cottage, which he dubbed the "Fo'castle," was just twenty feet by sixteen feet and was divided into two rooms, a bedroom and a kitchen-living room. Reflecting what Beston called his "amateur enthusiasm for windows," the house had ten windows, affording him an excellent (if sometimes glaring) view of the ocean and beach. While Beston framed his reasons for staying at the cottage for a twelve-month period beginning late in the summer of 1926 as a desire to get to know the coast and its "mysterious and elemental life," some critics have suggested

that Beston might also have been experiencing something of a midlife crisis, as he was a middle-aged man at a crossroads in his literary career who was contemplating a late marriage. Whatever underlying personal reasons might have influenced Beston to stay on the cape, no doubt the time spent alone in nature was a welcome change from a modern world that he felt was "sick to its thin blood for lack of elemental things." Life on the great beach of Cape Cod had these elemental presences in abundance, and for Beston the experience was transformative and healing. In the world of the dunes, he experienced a life vastly different from the one the "new synthetic man" was forced to endure in a modern industrial civilization that was a constant affront to the senses. Beston's delight in the sensual pleasures of the natural world he experienced during his year on the cape was a sharp contrast to the horrors of the recent war and the noise and "stench" of modern urban existence.

Much of the charm of *The Outermost House* derives from Beston's remarkably vivid descriptions of the natural world. Although Beston was extremely nearsighted and nearly deaf in one ear, he was apparently able to compensate for these physical handicaps by a remarkable power of concentration. The book has been praised universally for its vivid imagery and the poetic beauty of Beston's style, which he attributed in part to his French upbringing and in part to his writing sentences that were meant to be spoken aloud. He never used a typewriter, choosing instead to write in longhand so that the noise of the typewriter would not interfere with the sound and rhythm of the words as he composed his sentences. Beston's visual descriptions are often stunningly beautiful, as when he describes a moonlit night in June when a tide made luminous by a phosphorescent microorganism suffused the ocean and beach with an eerie light, or when he observed an enormous flight of geese passing overhead on a moonlit night. Beston's descriptions are not limited to the visual, and he devotes most of one chapter to the sounds of the ocean and laments in another that he cannot spend a whole chapter discussing the sense of smell. Beston's descriptions are meant not only to convey an obvious truth about the beauty of nature but also to make the point that modern industrial civilization had served to dull the spirit and the senses; otherwise, he says, "we would never have built a civilization which outrages them."

Beston's concern about the effect of industrial civilization on the senses and the spirit is always just below the surface of *The Outermost House*. Beneath the carefully honed prose and the reassuringly familiar structure and subject matter is an ecological sensibility that quietly questions many of the underlying premises of modern life, including anthropocentrism. As Beston saw it, not only had modern industrial civilization dulled humans' senses and exacerbated their tendency toward violence, but it had also helped to foster the mistaken notion that the human species was somehow separate from and superior to other species and from nature itself. Like a few earlier nature writers, such as John Burroughs and John Muir, Beston challenges the traditional anthropocentric notion that humankind stands at the center of creation, arguing instead that "we need another and a wiser and perhaps a more mystical concept of animals. . . . They are not brethren, they are not underlings; they are other nations, caught with ourselves in the net of life and time, fellow prisoners of the splendour and travail of the earth." Industrialism had also severed humans from the cycles of the seasons and the sun, distancing them from the poetic, spiritual, and life-affirming rhythms that came from living a life as part of the natural world rather than as its master. *The Outermost House* is arranged chronologically, starting with the autumn and progressing through the seasons. While this structure is not particularly original, it is consistent with Beston's belief that humankind must reestablish a connection with the natural cycles of the earth and the seasons. Many of the most important images in the book—such as the sun, the ocean breakers, and the constellation Orion rising over the dunes—are reminders that the passage of time is not just a linear progression along a calendar but a cyclical event that for most of human history had been celebrated and acknowledged. For Beston, this connection with the earth and its rhythms was not simply an abstract issue but one that went to the heart of what it means to be human; as he states in the preface to the 1949 edition, "When the Pleiades and the wind in the grass are no longer a part of the human spirit, a part of very flesh and bone, man becomes, as it were, a kind of cosmic outlaw, having neither the completeness and integrity of the animal nor the birthright of a true humanity." In one form or another, much of Beston's later work built on this theme.

Initial sales of *The Outermost House* were somewhat disappointing following its publication in 1928, partly because of the onset of the Great Depression, but Beston was certain that the book was the best that he had ever written. It drew frequent comparisons to such works as Thoreau's *Cape Cod* (1865) and *Walden,* but Beston disliked such comparisons, complaining that Thoreau's work "lacked heart." In June of 1929, at the age of forty-one, Beston married Coatsworth. Following a honeymoon spent at the Fo'castle, the couple bought a house in Hingham, Massachusetts, an old village overlooking Boston Harbor that was gradually turning into a suburb. The Bestons' first child, Margaret, was born in June 1930, and a second daughter, Catherine, was born in April 1932. After the transformative experience of his year on Cape Cod, however, Beston soon realized that suburban life would not provide what he needed, either spiritually or as a writer. He abandoned plans to write a book about the inner cape, complaining that "the touch of Boston Harbor which lies in front of the house and beyond the cars has absolutely no meaning to me in terms of beauty and the spirit; it is nothing but a glacial spillover surrounding a *tub de mud.*" In 1931 Beston was visiting friends in Damariscotta, Maine, when he heard of a small farm for sale just outside nearby Nobleboro. He almost immediately decided to buy it. As Coatsworth later wrote, "He who might hesitate for hours on the choice of a few words, could make up his mind on the future course of his life in an instant." The Bestons spent summers at "Chimney Farm," as they called it, for the next several years, and in 1944 moved there for good.

In many ways, Beston responded to rural life in Maine as he had to his year on Cape Cod. A sensitivity to the rhythms of the seasons was an integral part of life on the farm, and Beston felt that this type of life-style could reestablish the link between humankind and the earth that had been severed by a modern life-style. In *The Outermost House,* Beston had observed that "A year indoors is a journey along a paper calendar; a year in outer nature is the accomplishment of a tremendous ritual," and although Beston's own labors at Chimney Farm had more to do with his writing than with working the soil, he found the setting consistent with his belief, as he said in *Herbs and the Earth* (1935), that humankind needed to have a direct and "poetic" relation with the earth. At the farm, Beston began an herb garden that proved to be the inspiration for his next major work, *Herbs and the Earth.* The choice of subject matter was deliberate because for Beston the act of working with plants that were among the earliest cultivated by humans symbolized a renewal of humankind's age-old connection with the earth. *Herbs and the Earth* is not really about gardening at all, at least not in the general sense, and Beston barely touches upon what he calls "the elementary side of garden making." In *The Outermost House,* Beston had identified the artificiality of modern life as one of the primary causes of the violence and spiritual emptiness of modern man; in *Herbs and the Earth,* he proposes one possible remedy. Working in a garden or other agricultural pursuit is at once a tangible act of creation and a symbolic one that signifies the human connection to the earth's continuing act of creation. When this bond is intact, suggests Beston, the relationship between humans and the plants they tend is a truly symbiotic one in which, in return for the human care for the garden, "something of the earth's patience and instinct of life, something of the peace of gardens, shall find its way into the flowing of the blood." Beston's clear and graceful prose in *Herbs and the Earth* is as beautiful as that in *The Outermost House,* and Beston himself believed that the final chapter, "Epilogue to Spring," was the finest piece he ever wrote.

Although Beston did not write another major work that could really be considered nature writing until *Northern Farm: A Chronicle of Maine* (1948), his other books still reflect a strong connection with the earth and a sort of wistful nostalgia for life prior to the modern industrial era. In an anthology of Colonial and early American selections edited by Beston and published as *American Memory: Being a Mirror of the Stirring and Picturesque Past of Americans and the American Nation* (1937), he began by citing what he saw as the irreplaceable quality of the Indians, "their religious relation to the beauty and mystery of the American earth." Beston pointedly ends the anthology with a selection from *The Education of Henry Adams* (1905) titled "The Dynamo," in which Adams equates the

Dust jacket for Beston's 1948 book, about the passage of the seasons and the natural rhythms of farm life
(Bruccoli Clark Layman Archives)

transforming effect of the dynamo and steam engine on society in the industrial age with the power of religion in an earlier era. While Beston's focus was more on humankind's spiritual connection to the earth than with any specific religious dogma, both writers felt that industrialism was a force that had spiritually impoverished contemporary society. Although Beston and his family were somewhat insulated financially from the worst effects of the Great Depression, the economic hardships and suffering that he observed during that period further reinforced his belief that modern civilization, with its emphasis on materialism and what he termed its "brutal egotism," was a poor substitute for a way of life with poetic and spiritual ties to the earth. The dispiriting effect of the Great Depression and the chilling events in Europe leading up to the start of World War II in 1939 may explain in part why Beston renewed his interest in writing children's stories such as *Five Bears and Miranda* (1939) and *The*

Tree That Ran Away (1941), both of which were written in collaboration with his wife.

During the 1930s and 1940s the Bestons traveled extensively throughout North America, making trips to the western United States, Mexico, and Canada. Although they still occasionally returned to Cape Cod, Beston was increasingly drawn to the Canadian Maritimes and the St. Lawrence River, which became the focus of his next book, *The St. Lawrence* (1942), written for the "Rivers of America Series." Beston apparently intended to write an ecological history of the St. Lawrence that centered on the river itself rather than on the people who lived there; however, the majority of the book discusses the people of the region and how human activity affects and changes the river and its watershed. Beston divided the book into three parts—the first dealing with the past history of the region, the second describing the present, and the third covering "the almost timeless forces of nature neighboring the river and its coasts." Beston pointedly contrasts both the Indians' and the French Canadians' relationship with the earth with the Anglo-American drive to subjugate the land. Despite his cultural and philosophical affinity with the French Canadians, however, Beston was forced to confess that they, too, had been extraordinarily careless in their dealings with the land, citing the "savage business" of pulpwood logging as one example. In many ways, despite the change of locale, *The St. Lawrence* continues to develop the themes Beston first articulated in *The Outermost House* and *Herbs and the Earth*. Beston once again argues that industrial society has damaged both the earth and our souls, covering "the face of the earth with negative dirt, with wreckage, pollution, and yahoo squalor," and suggests that humankind must look to the past for a sense of the proper relationship between itself and the earth. One such link to the past was the Ursuline community, a French Canadian sect that dated back to the founding of Quebec and, like the herb garden of *Herbs and the Earth,* symbolized a spiritual connection to the earth.

Beston's strong belief in the salutary effect of rural life as an antidote to the spiritual decay and violence of the modern world led him and his family to move to Maine on a full-time basis in 1944. Soon after, he was asked to write a weekly feature on country life in Maine for Robert La Follette's *The Progressive*. These articles formed the basis of *Northern Farm*, Beston's last major work. Thematically and structurally, *Northern Farm* has much in common with *The Outermost House* and *Herbs and the Earth* and is in many ways a companion piece to these works. Like the earlier two works, *Northern Farm* is structured on the passage of the seasons and the natural rhythms of farm life. Beston believed that, as opposed to the linear nature of time in the cities, the passage of time in the country was a cyclical ritual of rebirth and renewal. In this work Beston once again criticizes the trend toward violence and alienation that he saw as an inevitable consequence of modern industrial life and cites World War II as another consequence of such a course. *Northern Farm* is mostly devoted to descriptions of farm life, including excerpts from Beston's farm diary. The strain of nostalgic pastoralism that had long been a part of Beston's writing is more pronounced in *Northern Farm* than in any of his other works, and the recurring phrase "Home. Going home" in the opening chapter signifies both a physical and a spiritual return to Maine, to the countryside, and to a life that is rooted in the earth-based values and practices of the past. In its celebration of the simple, yet deeply spiritual, pleasures of rural life, *Northern Farm* is Beston's final, quietly emphatic statement on what ails modern civilization and what course is needed as a remedy.

Northern Farm proved to be Beston's last major work, in large part because of his slowly declining health as a consequence of atherosclerosis. While he did continue to write, much of his time was spent revising and editing his earlier work. In 1950 he edited an historical anthology of writing from Maine titled *White Pine and Blue Water: A State of Maine Reader*. Two more children's books were also published, *Fairy Tales* (1952), a collection of Beston's favorite original fairy tales, and *Chimney Farm Bedtime Stories* (1966), written in collaboration with Coatsworth. Beston was often invited to give talks on nature writing and was a regular guest lecturer at a class on nature writers given at Dartmouth College. As succeeding generations of readers discovered his work—particularly *The Outermost House*—he was accorded many literary and academic honors, including the Emerson-Thoreau Award in 1960. In 1964 the Fo'castle was designated a National Literary Landmark and was the site of many gatherings to recognize Beston and his work, until a great winter storm in February 1978 destroyed the cottage. For the last four years of his life, Beston's illness made him a virtual invalid; he died on 15 April 1968 at the age of seventy-nine. He was buried behind his farmhouse, in which his wife continued to live until she died in 1986 at the age of ninety-three.

Although *The Outermost House* has been widely acknowledged as one of the classic works of American nature writing, literary scholars have given remarkably little critical attention to Henry Beston and his work. While his three major nature works, *The Outermost House, Herbs and the Earth,* and *Northern Farm*—some critics have included *The St. Lawrence* as a fourth—have found a significant audience, only *The Outermost House* has been examined to any great extent by scholars. This oversight might have occurred because, unlike many contemporary nature writers, Beston is not overtly political, and his worldview is clearly one that seems—and in many ways is—rooted in a nostalgic pastoralism. In some ways, however, Beston is quietly radical, as in his rejection of anthropocentrism and in his espousal of an earth-based spirituality. *The Outermost House*, though, has been acknowledged as a source of inspiration by many readers, including other literary environmentalists such as Rachel Carson, who wrote Beston on 14 May 1954 to tell him, "I hesitate to guess how many times I have read the book . . . but I don't hesitate to say that I can think of few others that have given me such deep and lasting pleasure, or to which I can return with such assurance of a renewal of my original enjoyment."

References:

Elizabeth Coatsworth, *Personal Geography: Almost an Autobiography* (Brattleboro, Vt.: Stephen Greene, 1976);

Donald Federman, "Toward an Ecology of Place: Three Views of Cape Cod," *Colby Library Quarterly*, 13 (1977): 209–222;

Thomas J. Lyon, *This Incomperable Lande: A Book of American Nature Writing* (Boston: Houghton Mifflin, 1989);

Sherman Paul, "Another Journal for Henry Beston," *North Dakota Quarterly*, 59 (Spring 1991): 92–111; essay also included in Paul's *For Love of the World: Essays on Nature Writers* (Iowa City: University of Iowa Press, 1992);

Daniel G. Payne, "Henry Beston," in *American Nature Writers*, 2 volumes, edited by John Elder (New York: Scribners, 1996), I: 107–120;

Maryellen Spencer, "Henry Beston (1888–1968): A Primary Checklist," *Resources for American Literary Study*, 12 (Spring 1982): 1, 49–63;

Nan Waldron, *Journey to Outermost House* (Bethlehem, Conn.: Butterfly & Wheel, 1991);

Peter Wild, "Henry Beston's *The Outermost House*," *North Dakota Quarterly*, 55 (Winter 1987): 188–195.

Papers:

Dartmouth College Library, Hanover, New Hampshire, holds Henry Beston's papers dating from 1933 to 1956. Additional papers are held in the Special Collections at the Bowdoin College Library and at the Widener Library at Harvard University.

John Burroughs

(3 April 1837 – 29 March 1921)

James Perrin Warren
Washington and Lee University

See also the Burroughs entry in *DLB 64: American Literary Critics and Scholars, 1850–1880.*

BOOKS: *Notes on Walt Whitman as Poet and Person* (New York: American News, 1867);

Wake-Robin (New York: Hurd & Houghton, 1871; revised and enlarged, New York: Hurd & Houghton, 1877; Edinburgh: Douglas, 1884);

Winter Sunshine (Boston: Hurd & Houghton, 1875; Edinburgh: Douglas, 1883);

Birds and Poets, with Other Papers (Boston: Hurd & Houghton, 1877; Edinburgh: Douglas, 1884);

Locusts and Wild Honey (Boston: Houghton, Osgood, 1879; Edinburgh: Douglas, 1884);

Pepacton (Boston: Houghton, Mifflin, 1881; London: Sampson Low, 1881);

Fresh Fields (Boston & New York: Houghton, Mifflin, 1884; Edinburgh: Douglas, 1885);

Signs and Seasons (Boston & New York: Houghton, Mifflin, 1886; Edinburgh: Douglas, 1886);

Indoor Studies (Boston & New York: Houghton, Mifflin, 1889);

Henry David Thoreau (Philadelphia: Lippincott, 1892);

Riverby (Boston & New York: Houghton, Mifflin, 1894);

Whitman: A Study (Boston & New York: Houghton, Mifflin, 1896; London: Watt, 1896);

The Light of Day; Religious Discussions and Criticisms from the Naturalist's Point of View (Boston & New York: Houghton, Mifflin, 1900);

Squirrels and Other Fur-Bearers (Boston & New York: Houghton, Mifflin, 1900);

John James Audubon (Boston: Small, Maynard, 1902);

Literary Values and Other Papers (Boston & New York: Houghton, Mifflin, 1902);

Far and Near (Boston & New York: Houghton, Mifflin, 1904; London & Cambridge, Mass.: Constable, 1904);

Ways of Nature (Boston & New York: Houghton, Mifflin, 1905);

John Burroughs, 1881

Bird and Bough (Boston & New York: Houghton, Mifflin, 1906; London & Cambridge, Mass.: Constable, 1906);

Camping with President Roosevelt (Boston & New York: Houghton, Mifflin, 1906); revised and enlarged as *Camping and Tramping with Roosevelt* (Boston: Houghton, Mifflin, 1907);

Leaf and Tendril (Boston & New York: Houghton, Mifflin, 1908; London & Cambridge, Mass.: Constable, 1908);

Time and Change (Boston & New York: Houghton Mifflin, 1912; London & Cambridge, Mass.: Constable, 1912);

The Summit of the Years (Boston & New York: Houghton Mifflin, 1913);

The Breath of Life (Boston & New York: Houghton Mifflin, 1915);

Under the Apple-Trees (Boston & New York: Houghton Mifflin, 1916);

Field and Study (Boston & New York: Houghton Mifflin, 1919);

Accepting the Universe (Boston & New York: Houghton Mifflin, 1920; London: Constable, [1921]);

Under the Maples (Boston & New York: Houghton Mifflin, 1921);

My Boyhood, with a Conclusion by His Son Julian Burroughs (Garden City, N.Y. & Toronto: Doubleday, Page, 1922);

The Last Harvest (Boston & New York: Houghton Mifflin, 1922; London: Cape, 1923);

John Burroughs at Troutbeck; Being Extracts from His Writings, Published and Unpublished (Amenia, N.Y.: Troutbeck Press, 1926);

The Heart of Burroughs's Journals, edited by Clara Barrus (Boston & New York: Houghton Mifflin, 1928).

Collection: *The Writings of John Burroughs,* Riverby Edition, 23 volumes (Boston & New York: Houghton Mifflin, 1904–1922).

OTHER: "Walt Whitman and the Common People" and "Walt Whitman and his Recent Critics," in *In Re Walt Whitman,* edited by Horace Traubel and others (Philadelphia: McKay, 1893), pp. 93–108, 363–365;

"Alaska: Narrative of the Expedition," in *Alaska, The Harriman Expedition, 1899,* 2 volumes in 1, by Burroughs, William Healey Dall, George Bird Grinnell, and John Muir (New York: Doubleday, Page, 1901; London: Doubleday, Page, 1901), I: 1–118;

"Introduction," *Songs of Nature,* edited by Burroughs (New York: McClure Phillips, 1901), pp. v–x;

"Walt Whitman," *Encyclopedia Britannica,* 10th edition (1902), 23: 840–841; 11th edition (1911), 28: 610–611.

SELECTED PERIODICAL PUBLICATIONS–
UNCOLLECTED: "Expression," *Atlantic Monthly,* 6 (November 1860): 572–575;

"Analogy," *Knickerbocker,* 60 (1862): 477–484;

"Walt Whitman and His *Drum-Taps,*" *Galaxy,* 2 (1866): 606–615;

"Mere Egotism," *Lippincott's Monthly Magazine,* 39 (February 1887): 298–306;

"The Poet and the Modern," *Atlantic Monthly,* 78 (October 1896): 565–566;

"Real and Sham Natural History," *Atlantic Monthly,* 91 (1903): 298–309.

One of the best-known and most widely read nature writers of the late nineteenth and early twentieth centuries, John Burroughs is largely unknown and unread today. Prolific and consistent, Burroughs published scores of essays in influential large-circulation magazines between the Civil War and World War I. Such journals as *Appleton's, The Atlantic Monthly, Century, Galaxy,* and *Scribner's Monthly* made his reputation as important as that of Henry David Thoreau, to whom he was often compared. Unlike Thoreau, however, whose reputation grew posthumously, Burroughs earned a reputation by publishing nearly thirty books during his long career. As a celebrity author, he lived to see his essays taught widely in secondary schools in the early twentieth century. A telling instance of Burroughs's celebrity occurred in the spring of 1903, when he accompanied President Theodore Roosevelt to Yellowstone National Park. During the overland trek, the presidential train stopped in many towns and cities so that Roosevelt could make speeches, but the president shared the spotlight with Burroughs on several occasions. In *Camping with President Roosevelt* (1906), Burroughs describes the stop at St. Paul, Minnesota: "I spied in the throng on the curbstone a large silk banner that bore my own name as the title of some society. I presently saw that it was borne by half a dozen anxious and expectant-looking schoolgirls with braids down their backs. As my carriage drew near them, they pressed their way through the throng and threw a large bouquet of flowers into my lap. I think it would be hard to say who blushed the deeper, the girls or myself." The combination of celebrity and modesty is characteristic of Burroughs throughout his life and career.

Burroughs was born in humble circumstances on 3 April 1837. His parents, Chauncey and Amy Kelly Burroughs, owned a three-hundred-acre dairy farm on the slope of Old Clump, a three-thousand-foot mountain near the village of Roxbury in Delaware County, New York. John was the seventh of ten children, the only one to move away from the farming community of Roxbury and occupy a place in a wider world. John was also the only member of the family to pursue more than a rudimentary education. His father had been a schoolteacher for one or two winters, but the family library included no books other than the Bible and the Baptist hymnal.

For the first seventeen years of his life, Burroughs led the existence of a Catskill farm boy. Work began before sunup, summer and winter, and the farm provided a substantial living for the large family. The herd of thirty dairy cattle produced more than two tons of butter each year, and even as a small boy John helped his mother skim cream, churn, and pack the butter into fifty- and one-hundred-pound firkins. The family raised grains for feeding both the herd and the owners—rye, corn, oats, and buckwheat; they kept enough sheep to produce wool for carpets and winter clothing; and they grew flax in a small plot. The younger children helped Amy Burroughs as she spun thread, wove cloth, and sewed her family's clothes. The older children did the twice-daily chores of feeding and milking, and during the day the older boys worked in the fields and wood-lots, hoeing corn, digging potatoes, clearing fields of stone, cleaning stables, cutting wood, burning stumps, plowing fields, spreading manure, sowing, harvesting, and threshing grain. Younger children and girls attended school except for the summer butter-making time, but after the age of twelve John's schooling was limited to winter sessions.

In *The Life and Letters of John Burroughs* (1925), edited by Clara Barrus, Burroughs's own account of his early life and learning on the Catskill dairy farm emphasizes the blend of practical and literary knowledge. Though Burroughs read eagerly, he claimed in a letter to Barrus reprinted in *The Life and Letters of John Burroughs,* that he "could never acquire any of the marks or accomplishments of a scholar" and never mastered "the technical part of literature and science." Instead, he claimed, "My natural-history knowledge is more like that of the hunter and trapper than like that of the real scientist. I know our birds well, but not as the professional ornithologist knows them. I know them through my heart more than through my head." Although in some ways his "farmer ancestry" ruled him, Burroughs realized his need for wider, deeper knowledge, and so in the spring of 1854, just before his seventeenth birthday, he found employment as a teacher at a rural school in Ulster County, New York. Over the next several years Burroughs engaged in a program of self-culture, alternating positions as a country schoolmaster with stints as a summer student at college preparatory schools. Two important events in his life took place during this period. At summer school in Cooperstown during 1856, he first read the essays of Ralph Waldo Emerson. In late July 1857 he married Ursula North, who remained his wife until her death in 1917.

In the late 1850s Burroughs developed a lifelong habit of keeping a journal—recording daily events, meetings, and readings and experimenting with different styles of prose and poetry. As a young man, he developed a voice by adopting more and more modern styles. In the beginning he imitated Samuel Johnson; he then went on to Joseph Addison and Richard Steele; his poetic taste moved from Alexander Pope and Oliver Goldsmith to William Wordsworth. But the encounter with Emerson's essays was the first great galvanizing contact for the young writer. Burroughs published brief essays in the *Saturday Press* in 1859 and 1860, but his first major publication, the essay "Expression," appeared in the November 1860 issue of *The Atlantic Monthly*. The editor of *The Atlantic Monthly,* James Russell Lowell, was so sure the essay was written by Emerson that he looked through all of Emerson's published works before deciding the essay was not plagiarized. Even *Poole's Index* attributes the unsigned article to Emerson.

One of the most telling sentences in "Expression" relates to the problem of the beginning writer: "The difficulty in writing, is to utter the first thought, to break the heavy silence." In breaking the silence and uttering his first thought, Burroughs pays an immense debt to the style and thematic content of Emerson. Because Emerson was his first great mentor and model, Burroughs made such Emersonian pronouncements as "Nature exists to the mind not as an absolute realization, but as a condition, as something constantly becoming" and "Ordinary minds inherit their language and form of expression; but with the poet, or natural sayer, a new step is taken." The thought and the expression are indistinguishable, and Burroughs seems to be trying to perform a perfect imitation of his writing hero. That he succeeds so completely is unfortunate, especially since the subject is original expression, but as a twenty-three-year-old novice, Burroughs's successful imitation is remarkable.

Just as the country was lumbering toward the Civil War, Burroughs wrote essays on such topics as butter making and sugar making for the small magazine the *New York Leader* under the general title "From the Back Country," as well as more Emersonian papers, such as "World Growth," "Theory and Practice," and "Some of the Ways of Power." The "Back Country" papers foretold the kind of pastoral writing Burroughs later made his signature. In addition, they caused Myron Benton, a literary farmer in Leedsville, New York, to write him an admiring letter, beginning a friendship and correspondence that lasted until Benton's death in 1902. A minor poet and essayist, Benton was twenty-eight when he wrote to Burroughs in 1862, and the two shared an admiration for Emerson, Thoreau, and Walt Whitman. Eventually, the two friends met Emerson at West Point in June 1863, seeking out the famous lecturer and essayist at his hotel and spending an hour with him, walking him to his ferry and peppering him with questions about Thoreau, Bronson Alcott, and David Wasson.

During the same period in 1863, Burroughs began the serious study of botany and ornithology, partly by walking in the fields and partly by reading in the library of the U.S. Military Academy at West Point. In a May 1863 letter to Benton, for instance, Burroughs notes that he has "taken an unusual interest in flowers this spring, chiefly, I suppose, because I live so near the woods. I have found some fine specimens, though I suppose they are common enough." In May or June 1863, browsing in the library at the academy, Burroughs found a copy of John James Audubon's *The Birds of America* (1827–1838) and used its illustrations and the mounted birds at the academy for reference. He bought binoculars and an illustrated field guide and began recording his bird identifications along with his notes on wildflowers. In addition, he began taking specimens with a cane gun, afterward mounting the birds in lifelike poses. In an 1865 letter to a young Connecticut admirer, Sarah W. Adams, Burroughs gruffly answered possible objections: "as to shooting the birds, I think a real lover of nature will indulge in no sentimentalism on the subject. Shoot them, of course, and no toying about it." In this same letter he also urged Adams to try her hand at taxidermy, for it trained one in patience, manual skill, imagination, and familiarity with nature. Burroughs made two cases of mounted birds, one for his mother and one for his wife, and he found in his own specimens "little of the stiff artificial look of the work of a professional."

During the summer of 1863 Burroughs made a two-week camping trip to the Adirondacks with his friends Elijah Allen and Myron Benton. The three men shared a wholesale admiration for the poems of Whitman, and Allen was personally acquainted with Whitman, whom he had met in Washington, D.C. The trip abounded in good conversation, good fishing, and good hunting. Perhaps more important, it resulted in one of Burroughs's finest narrative essays, "The Adirondacks," which appeared in his first volume of nature essays, *Wake-Robin* (1871). The trip also prompted Burroughs to seek his fortune in Washington, D.C. He lived in that city for a decade, published his first books there, and became a lifelong friend of Whitman.

Arriving in Washington in October 1863 without a job and with little money, Burroughs for several weeks slept on a cot in the back of Allen's army-supply store and worked for the quartermaster general on

Burroughs in 1857

burial details. Not long after arriving, Burroughs made Whitman's acquaintance at Allen's store, and soon thereafter Burroughs was accompanying Whitman on visits to the army hospitals in the city. The two also went for long walks along Rock Creek, which became Burroughs's favorite haunt in the capital. At their first meeting, Whitman was forty-four years old, Burroughs twenty-six. By January 1864 Burroughs had secured a position as clerk in the Department of the Treasury, earning an annual salary of $1,200. The following month his wife joined him in Washington, and by the spring the couple were renting a small redbrick house on Capitol Hill, where they raised vegetables and kept chickens and a cow. Whitman was a constant visitor and intimate friend to both John and Ursula Burroughs.

Whitman is without doubt the most important influence on Burroughs's career as a writer (Emerson, Thoreau, and Thomas Carlyle following closely behind). Whitman was at first a model and mentor for Burroughs, but Burroughs was not merely a disciple of

Whitman. At the same time that Burroughs was examining Whitman's status as a poet, he was writing some of his best nature essays, a form Whitman never mastered, even in *Specimen Days* (1884). In May 1865 Burroughs published "With the Birds" in *The Atlantic Monthly,* followed by "In the Hemlocks" in the June 1866 *Atlantic.* "A Night-Hunt in the Adirondacks" appeared in *Putnam's Monthly* in August 1868, and from May to July 1869 Burroughs published three essays in the *Atlantic:* "Spring in Washington," "Birds'-Nests," and "Birch Browsings." In addition, he published "Walt Whitman and His 'Drum-Taps'" in the December 1866 issue of *Galaxy,* followed in June 1867 by his first book, *Notes on Walt Whitman as Poet and Person,* which he published at his own expense in February. In a 20 March 1866 letter to Benton, Burroughs set out a view of Whitman's poetry that went largely unchanged for the next fifty years: "the drift or conclusion to be that Walt Whitman is a return to Nature—that 'Leaves of Grass' is an utterance from Nature, and opposite to modern literature, which is an utterance from Art; that W.W. gives the analogies of the earth, and that he is the only modern or democratic man who has yet spoken, and our only hope from utter literary inanition." For Burroughs, Whitman and nature were always intimately related to one another.

Despite these points, Whitman exerted considerable influence—editorial and otherwise—on both *Notes on Walt Whitman as Poet and Person* and *Wake-Robin.* Burroughs was quite candid about that influence in his later years, even attributing to Whitman the entire section of *Notes* called "Standard of the Natural Universal." But this admission does not mean that Burroughs was without ideas and expressions of his own; rather, the two writers collaborated to create a complex union. Indeed, the blending of voices refines the strategy of "Expression," in which Burroughs imitated Emerson's style to perfection. The style is clearly Whitman's in "Standard of the Natural Universal," but otherwise the essay is an early version of Burroughs's own critical writing style. Diction and syntax occasionally recall Whitman, but Burroughs readily admits that in the preface: "My Notes come from personal contact, and doubtless from thoughts brought under that influence. The literary hints in them are experimental, and will show the student of Nature more than the student of books."

In the spring of 1871, Boston publishers Hurd and Houghton brought out Burroughs's second book, *Wake-Robin,* which collected eight essays written in the Washington years. The title, chosen by Whitman from a list of possible titles Burroughs gave him, refers to the nodding trillium, a fit emblem of the "universal awakening and rehabilitation of nature" in spring. The publication of this book began a relationship with

Oscar Houghton that lasted all of Burroughs's life. *Wake-Robin* sold well and was praised by such reviewers as Helen Hunt and William Dean Howells. In a clear echo of his first book, Burroughs prefaced the volume with the disclaimer that "what has interested me most in Ornithology is the pursuit, the chase, the discovery; that part of it which is akin to hunting, fishing, and wild sports, and which I could carry with me in my eye and ear wherever I went."

Burroughs's description of his harvest in *Wake-Robin* emphasizes the direct, experiential quality of the essays and the imagery and tone of discovery. The essays themselves match that description: they impart knowledge of nature through Burroughs's concrete observations. In "The Return of the Birds," for instance, the narrator describes the songs of the birds as they return to his home in New York State, often translating the song into accurate onomatopoeia. Thus, he exactly renders the call of the black-billed cuckoo as "*k-k-k-k-k-kow, kow, kow-ow, kow-ow*" and notes that it "sometimes suggests the voice of the turkey." In another famous instance, he describes the song of the hermit thrush without imitating it, characterizing it as "wild and ethereal," a "pure, serene, hymn-like strain."

In all of the essays in *Wake-Robin,* Burroughs delivers a clear sense of direct, concrete experience, what it feels like to hear a particular birdsong. The hermit thrush plays a prominent role in the second essay, "In the Hemlocks," in which Burroughs remarks that the song "appeals to the sentiment of the beautiful in me, and suggests a serene religious beatitude as no other sound in nature does." In fact, much of the essay came from a visit Burroughs made to the Catskills in the summer of 1865. When he returned to Washington, he gave Whitman his account of the hermit thrush, which the poet turned to significant use in the famous elegy for Lincoln "When Lilacs Last in the Dooryard Bloom'd" (1865–1866). Other essays also stem from Burroughs's past experiences in New York State. Burroughs's camping trip of summer 1863 comes out in "The Adirondacks" and "Birch Browsings," two of his best narratives. "Spring at the Capital" is a present-tense "ramble," taking the reader on a hike through the woods of Rock Creek and its tributaries. In the final essay, "The Invitation," Burroughs praises Audubon above all other ornithologists but notes that "ornithology cannot be satisfactorily learned from the books. The satisfaction is in learning it from nature. One must have an original experience with the birds. The books are only the guide, the invitation." The essays of *Wake-Robin* won an audience because they delivered Burroughs's original experience and functioned admirably as "the guide, the invitation."

In October 1871 the Treasury Department sent Burroughs and two other employees to England to convey $15 million in United States bonds and to superintend the destruction of the old bonds. Burroughs spent two months in England, meeting Thomas Carlyle, William Michael Rossetti, and Moncure Daniel Conway. Four essays of travel narrative, grouped under the title "An October Abroad," came out of the trip and were published in Burroughs's third book, *Winter Sunshine,* in 1875. The eight essays of *Winter Sunshine* are arranged seasonally, beginning with "Winter Sunshine," running to "A March Chronicle" and "Autumn Tides," and ending with the "October Abroad" series. Several employ the ramble or hike as a narrative device, but others–such as "The Fox" and "The Apple"–are descriptive or meditative. The ramble essay "Exhilarations of the Road" develops a telling set of contrasts between the Englishman and the American. Reviewing the volume in *The Nation* (27 January 1876), Henry James called Burroughs "a sort of reduced but also more humorous, more available, and more sociable Thoreau."

In January 1873 Burroughs left his position as clerk for the Treasury Department and accepted a federal appointment as special national bank examiner for districts along the Hudson River and elsewhere in New York and Virginia. For the next twelve years he worked four or five months each year as a bank examiner until he was ousted from office by the Cleveland administration in 1885. Leaving Ursula behind, Burroughs took his first assignment in Middletown, New York, and spent his spare time finding property for a new home. After much searching, he purchased a nine-acre fruit farm on the west shore of the Hudson River at West Park, ninety miles north of New York City, a day's journey from Burroughs's parents in Roxbury and two miles away from the nearest post office, at Esopus. Without consulting Ursula, Burroughs designed and supervised the building of a new stone house, which he named Riverby. He worked with a hired man to plant and tend vineyards, berries, and apple orchards, intending to make the farm profitable. In May 1876 Burroughs began keeping a journal, replacing the smaller notebooks he had been using since 1854. He maintained the habit of nearly daily journal writing until his death in 1921.

The Riverby years were momentous in several respects. The January 1877 issue of *Scribner's Monthly* ran a feature article on Burroughs by Joel Benton, praising his alertness and authenticity as a naturalist and describing his writing style as "racy, full of blood, vascular and bristling with just the words for the description in hand." Later in 1877 Burroughs published his fourth book, *Birds and Poets, with Other Papers,* which fea-

Ursula North, whom Burroughs married in July 1857

tured both nature essays and literary criticism. Clearly Burroughs was attempting to bring his two major types of writing together in one volume so that they could reflect upon one another, and the strategy resulted in one of his best books. In a complex mosaic of seventeen sections, the essay "Touches of Nature" ranges widely and plunges deeply into the relations between the natural and the human, arguing that "it is well to let down our metropolitan pride a little. Man thinks himself at the top, and that the immense display and prodigality of Nature are for him. But they are no more for him than they are for the birds and beasts, and he is no more at the top than they are." Two essays–"Before Genius" and "Before Beauty"–lay out principles of "simple manhood" and power as necessary for real literature, while the essays "Emerson" and "The Flight of the Eagle" focus on the concrete, specific examples in Burroughs's two great masters, Emerson and Whitman. But the maturing essayist shows yet more range, making "Our Rural Divinity" a humorous paean to the cow ("I have owned but three cows and loved but one") and "A Bird Medley" a loose, charming treatment of his trademark topic.

The most important personal event of these years was the birth of Burroughs's son, Julian, in April 1878.

The child's mother, Amanda Henion, had been a housemaid at Riverby; she gave birth to the baby at a home for orphans in New York City. Burroughs arranged to adopt the child, with Ursula's consent, though only eight years later did she learn that the baby's father was her husband. Julian's role in the family became critical, for he provided his father with a companion on his outdoor adventures and kept peace between his warring parents.

During the Riverby years Burroughs developed a growing reputation as the premier nature essayist in the country, largely because of his magazine publications and collections. *The Atlantic* had been his first significant outlet, and he continued to place essays with the magazine in the 1870s and 1880s. But his defense of Whitman rubbed the associate editor, Thomas Wentworth Higginson, the wrong way, and Burroughs's style was not in keeping with the conservative aesthetics of Thomas Bailey Aldrich, editor from 1881 to 1890. In addition, Burroughs found a ready, encouraging editor in Richard Watson Gilder, who served as assistant editor at *Scribner's Monthly* after 1870 and became editor in chief of the successor magazine, *The Century,* in 1881. Burroughs and Gilder enjoyed a close friendship and literary relationship until Gilder's death in 1909. Afterward, Robert Underwood Johnson served as editor of *The Century* until 1913, and while the relationship between Burroughs and Johnson was not intimate, it was still productive. Both *Scribner's Monthly* and *The Century* featured fine illustrations to accompany nature essays, and the combination made the nature essay into an immensely popular form by the end of the century.

In addition to the regular magazine publications, Burroughs continued to publish essay collections every two or three years. In 1879 he published his fifth book, *Locusts and Wild Honey,* and in 1881 he followed with his sixth, *Pepacton.* The former collection featured, as Burroughs wrote in the preface, "the wild and delectable in nature . . . the free and ungarnered harvests which the wilderness everywhere affords to the observing eye and ear." But even Burroughs's idea of wilderness included some pastoral elements. So, such essays as "The Pastoral Bees" and "Strawberries" are included with three narratives of wilderness camping and fishing expeditions—"Speckled Trout," "A Bed of Boughs," and "The Halcyon in Canada." Aaron Johns, as quoted from a manuscript reprinted in Edward J. Renehan Jr.'s *John Burroughs: An American Naturalist* (1992), had accompanied Burroughs on the camping trips and noted Burroughs's "encyclopedic knowledge of birds, flowers, trees, rocks." The essay "Sharp Eyes" details Burroughs's talent for making field observations, and these skills are the solid basis for his reputation as a naturalist.

Pepacton displays Burroughs's interest in experimenting within the genre of the nature essay. The title refers to the east branch of the Delaware River, an Indian name meaning "marriage of the waters," and Burroughs calls his book "also a union of many currents." "Pepacton: A Summer Voyage" is a narrative of Burroughs's trip in his own homemade boat. Burroughs develops other essays by indirect, mosaic compositions, the kind of short sketches he had used in "Touches of Nature" and in his first book on Whitman. Particularly successful examples are "Notes by the Way" and "Winter Pictures." In addition, Burroughs marries his literary criticism to his observations as a naturalist in the essay "Nature and the Poets." Although Higginson found Burroughs's criticisms of the New England poets unfair and overly demanding, the essay in fact praises Emerson nearly as much as Whitman, and criticizes only Longfellow, for a general lack of accuracy. In his critical observations, Burroughs is particular and concrete.

In January 1882 Burroughs began writing in a new, one-room outbuilding he built and named the Bark Study. He wrote his next four books there. In May, he took Ursula and Julian on a trip to England, having arranged to publish seven to ten papers with Gilder's *Century* as well as a book with Houghton, Mifflin. Burroughs made pilgrimages to Carlyle's grave, Wordsworth's home, and the naturalist Gilbert White's grave at Selborne. The family was back at Riverby in early August, and Burroughs went directly into the Bark Study to write articles. Gilder eventually published a half-dozen essays in 1883 and 1884, and Houghton brought out *Fresh Fields* in 1884. The eleven chapters form one of Burroughs's most cohesive, best unified books, framed by the narrative of the family's journey. Burroughs treats characteristic themes of literary appreciation and natural history, often on the same page, and he finds ample space for new discoveries and keen observations. England, he argues, displays in many ways a richer, more fertile landscape than that of America, and the constant comparison between the two lands dominates the book.

As if in deliberate contrast to the unity of *Fresh Fields,* the next book, *Signs and Seasons* (1886), is a loose miscellany of essays. None stands out as particularly noteworthy, though Whitman wrote appreciatively of "A Sharp Lookout," and Sarah Orne Jewett admired the camping narrative "A Taste of Maine Birch." The essay "A Salt Breeze" relates the seashore to American poetry, with Whitman's work at the top of the list; not surprisingly, the narrative frame to the paper is a two-week stay at Ocean Grove, New Jersey, with Whitman himself. The volume suggests that Burroughs was showing signs of creative fatigue. As of 1885 he no longer had the labor of bank examining to take him away from the Bark Study and the farm, but he did not respond to the new time by increasing the number of essays. His journals suggest that he was experiencing a profound and prolonged depression, perhaps brought on by the deaths of his mother and father, in 1880 and 1884, respectively.

Even if the 1880s were a period of retreat, Burroughs remained productive. His last book of the decade, *Indoor Studies*, appeared in 1889, and while he deprecated it as "less satisfying" than his "out-of-door papers," it actually included several important essays of literary criticism from his own particular point of view. The lead essay, "Henry D. Thoreau," reprints the article published in the July 1882 *Century*, and it is a clear-sighted account of Thoreau's tone and style, while it also delivers a strong sense of Thoreau's personality. Two essays treat the relationship between science and literature, while two others respond to Matthew Arnold's 1883–1884 lectures on Emerson and Carlyle. Eight "Brief Essays" range widely, abstractly, and sometimes too generally, but the book ends with a fascinating essay, "An Egotistical Chapter," which recounts Burroughs's love of the "master enchanter" Emerson and his refusal to acknowledge "any great debt to Thoreau." Burroughs notes his method of observation and expression: "People say, 'I do not see what you do when I take a walk.' But for the most part they do, but the fact as it lies there in nature is crude and raw: it needs to be brought out, passed through the heart and mind and presented in appropriate words. This humanizes it and gives it an added charm and significance. This, I take it, is what is meant by idealizing and interpreting nature. We do not add to or falsely color the facts: we disentangle them, and invest them with the magic of written words." He clearly states the emotional quality of his work: "If I had run after the birds only to write about them, I never should have written anything that any one would have cared to read. I must write from sympathy and love, or not at all."

In addition to continuing to produce new work, Burroughs saw a new development in reaching a younger audience. A young Chicago schoolteacher, Mary E. Burt, taught *Pepacton* to a class of thirty-six pupils. The publisher Oscar Houghton visited the school and, seeing the enthusiasm of the children for Burroughs's writing, asked Burt to edit a small volume for schoolchildren. The result was *Birds and Bees* (1887), the first of several school anthologies of Burroughs's works. This book was the beginning of Burroughs's celebrity, which led to the large bouquet of flowers landing in the writer's lap in St. Paul, Minnesota. The new sense of audience rejuvenated his writing, as can be seen in the last volume of the Riverby years, appro-

Binding for Burroughs's 1871 collection of essays, written in Washington, D.C., during the time of his friendship with Walt Whitman (Ken Lopez catalogue, 2000)

priately titled *Riverby* (1894). The author himself felt a chapter closing, for he noted in the preface that *Riverby* was probably his "last collection of out-of-door papers." Instead of closing, however, Burroughs's style opens up or returns afresh. In a narrative essay, "The Heart of the Southern Catskills," he details the ascent of Slide Mountain in a June snowstorm and the surprise of a sudden vision as the clouds lift: "The world opened like a book, and there were the pictures; the spaces were without a film, the forests and mountains looked surprisingly near; in the heart of the northern Catskills a wild valley was seen flooded with sunlight. Then the curtain ran down again, and nothing was left but the gray strip of rock to which we clung, plunging down into the obscurity."

Other essays in *Riverby* appeal to a young audience because of their subject matter. In "A Young Marsh Hawk," for example, Burroughs uses Julian as a figure of the "country boy" to represent the viewpoint of young readers. "Talks with Young Observers" teaches young readers by telling stories of young correspondents and visitors. The nature Burroughs represents is available and near at hand in such essays as "Birds' Eggs," "The Chipmunk," "Glimpses of Wild Life," "A Life of Fear," "Lovers of Nature," "Hasty Observation," and "Bird Life in an Old Apple-Tree." Many essays are only a few pages long, suitable for a young reader, and they often have a clear moral message, as in "Birds' Eggs," "Lovers of Nature," and "The Ways of Sportsmen."

Three important events further suggest that the end of the Riverby period marks new possibilities. First, in 1889 Burroughs met and became friends with Theodore Roosevelt, a successful author and naturalist in his own right and a great admirer of Burroughs's works. For the next thirty years the two men were close friends and consistent correspondents. Second, Burroughs made three separate land purchases as the Riverby period ended: in 1887 he signed a mortgage on his parents' "Old Home" outside Roxbury, leaving his brother Hiram to manage it, and in 1889 he was forced to call in the note and rent the property; in 1890 he purchased nine acres and more than doubled the fruit production of his farm; in 1895 he purchased twenty acres of woods a mile away from Riverby and built a cabin retreat he named Slabsides. Now a prosperous and public man of letters, Burroughs still had plans to write more essays. Finally, at a literary dinner in New York City in 1893, he met John Muir, who proved a fast and infuriating companion over the next twenty years. Muir was one of the earliest visitors to Slabsides, spending a night there in July 1896. On nearer acquaintance Burroughs found Muir "a little prolix" and remarked, "Ask him to tell you his famous dog story . . . and you get the whole theory of glaciation thrown in. He is a poet and almost a Seer."

The poet and seer who occupied Burroughs most thoroughly at the turn of the century was still Walt Whitman. In March 1892 Whitman died in Camden, New Jersey, and Burroughs was one of the pallbearers. From 1892 to 1896 Burroughs published eighteen major essays on Whitman, and in 1896 he published the book *Whitman: A Study*. During the same period, Burroughs wrote few nature essays: *Riverby* included no essay less than three years old. Burroughs's writing retreat at Slabsides and the landscape surrounding it come together in the image of "Whitman Land," which he names the place in the opening paragraph of *Whitman: A Study*:

The writing of this preliminary chapter, and the final survey and revision of my Whitman essay, I am making at a rustic house I have built at a wild place a mile

or more from my home upon the river. I call this place Whitman Land, because in many ways it is typical of my poet,—an amphitheatre of precipitous rock, slightly veiled with a delicate growth of verdure, enclosing a few acres of prairie-like land, once the site of an ancient lake, now a garden of unknown depth and fertility. Elemental ruggedness, savageness, and grandeur, combined with wonderful tenderness, modernness, and geniality.

Repeatedly in *Whitman: A Study,* Burroughs employs figures of boundless, elemental nature in order to make a place for Whitman in the map of American culture. He also repeatedly seeks to correct the conventional standards of literary value in late-nineteenth-century America, which he defines as restrictive, limited, and even trivial: "We make a mistake," he argues, "when we demand of Whitman what the other poets give us,—studies, embroidery, delicate tracings, pleasing artistic effects, rounded and finished specimens. We shall understand him better if we inquire what his own standards are, what kind of a poet he would be. He tells us over and over again that he would emulate the great forces and processes of Nature." Whitman Land stands for *Leaves of Grass* (1855), for Whitman's place in American literature and culture, for Burroughs's place as critic of Whitman, and for his fundamental principle of criticism. Burroughs merges these four identities in one singular passage on beauty:

Is there not in field, wood, or shore something more precious and tonic than any special beauties we may chance to find there,—flowers, perfumes, sunsets,—something that we cannot do without, though we can do without these? Is it health, life, power, or what is it? Whatever it is, it is something analogous to this that we get in Whitman. There is little in his 'Leaves' that one would care to quote for its mere beauty, though this element is there also. One may pluck a flower here and there in his rugged landscape, as in any other; but the flowers are always by the way, and never the main matter. We should not miss them if they were not there. What delights and invigorates us is in the air, and in the look of things. The flowers are like our wild blossoms growing under great trees or amid rocks, never the camellia or tuberose of the garden or hot-house,—something rude and bracing is always present, always a breath of the untamed and aboriginal.

Although Burroughs is best known as a writer of nature near-at-hand and accessible, the nature often called "pastoral," he was also clearly attracted to wild places, as shown by both his frequent camping expeditions and his love of Whitman's untamed writing. In May 1899, at the age of sixty-two, Burroughs translated his attractions into a new experience by joining a two-month scientific expedition to Alaska, organized

Manuscript for a lyric poem first published in the March 1863 issue of The Knickerbocker
(*from Clara Barrus,* The Life and Letters of John Burroughs, *1925*)

and financed by the railroad magnate Edward Henry Harriman. The purpose of the expedition was to map the coast of Alaska, collect natural history specimens and cultural artifacts, and produce a series of scientific reports. The expedition brought together some one hundred and twenty-six members, all told, including twenty-five members of the "scientific party," three visual artists, and two photographers. Many of these professionals were luminaries in their fields. Burroughs was the official historian and wrote "Alaska: Narrative of the Expedition," which began a series of twelve volumes titled *Harriman Alaska Series* (1901–1914). John Muir, listed on the official roster as a "student of glaciers," was perhaps the most experienced explorer of the Alaskan coast in the group, having traversed much of the Inside Passage in a native canoe in 1879 and 1880. William Healey Dall, paleontologist with the U.S. Geological Survey, was a highly respected expert on Alaska; B. E. Fernow was dean of the School of Forestry at Cornell University; Henry Gannett was chief geographer of the U.S. Geological Survey; and C. Hart Merriam was chief of the Biological Survey of the U.S. Department of Agriculture, leader of the scientific party, and eventually the editor of the *Harriman Alaska* series. Two artists became famous after the expedition—Louis Agassiz Fuertes, a painter of birds, and Edward S. Curtis, a young photographer from Seattle who became renowned for his pictures of Native Americans. In addition, George Bird Grinnell, founder of the Audubon Society, cofounder with Roosevelt of the Boone and Crockett Club, and editor of *Forest and Stream* magazine, contributed essays on the natives of the coastal region and the salmon industry.

Harriman assembled most of this group in New York City on 23 May 1899, took his own private train across the country to Seattle, and there met Muir, Curtis, and Charles Keeler, a California poet and naturalist. Harriman had chartered the steamship *George W. Elder* from the Pacific Coast Steamship Company and had it completely refurbished and outfitted for the two-month voyage from Seattle to Siberia and back. Most members had their own private staterooms, and the expedition was luxuriously provisioned. John Muir described the expedition as "a floating University in which I enjoyed the instruction and companionship of a lot of the best fellows imaginable." Certainly Burroughs was both chafed and cheered by two months of constant contact with Muir, who was so thorough an expert on glaciers, said Burroughs, "that he would not allow the rest of the party to have an opinion on the subject. The Indians used to call him the Great Ice Chief," as Burroughs recollected in "In Green Alaska." The expedition landed at thirty-four localities, at three of which the students of glaciers camped for several days. In addition, the scientists analyzed thousands of photographs in order to study changes in the sizes of glaciers.

The Harriman Alaska Expedition gave Burroughs a new vision of nature, and his descriptions employ the rhetoric of elemental forces that he most admired in the poetry of Whitman. They also recall Thoreau's *Walden* (1854), especially the "sand foliage" and "tonic of wildness" passages from the "Spring" chapter. On a particularly sunny day, Burroughs and Charles Keeler climbed Mt. Wright, three thousand feet above the Muir Glacier in Glacier Bay, and Burroughs described the scene below them in terms that recall his great teachers:

> It was indeed a day with the gods, strange gods, the gods of the foreworld, but they had great power over us. The scene we looked upon was for the most part one of desolation—snow, ice, jagged peaks, naked granite, gray moraines—but the bright sun and sky over all, the genial warmth and the novelty of the situation, were ample to invest it with a fascinating interest. . . . But the largeness of the view, the elemental ruggedness, and the solitude as of interstellar space were perhaps what took the deepest hold. It seemed as if the old glacier had been there but yesterday.

Perhaps this largeness of view led Burroughs to write a series of papers on religion in the modern world, which he published in book form as *The Light of Day; Religious Discussions and Criticisms from the Naturalist's Point of View* in 1900. As if to introduce the new century, Burroughs presents the reader with arguments for a rational, skeptical, scientific view of knowledge, while he also maintains the necessary role of the religious sentiment and the aesthetic sense. The "light of day" for Burroughs is the plain light of natural facts, and "the difference between our times and the times of our fathers is mainly in the greater light of our day, the light of exact science." In addition, the essays strike upon the "solitude as of interstellar space" in several passages. For instance, in "The Decadence of Theology," he notes that "the universe is going its own way with no thought of us; to keep in its currents is our life, to cross them is our death. This discovery sends the cosmic chill, with which so many of us are familiar in these days; it makes the religious mind gasp for breath, but we must face it, and still find life sweet under its influence. The world is not yet used to the open air of this thought—the great out of doors of it; we are not hardened to it." Burroughs does not reject religion, nor is he a thorough materialist. He recognizes the truth of the religious sentiment, but "the objects of faith may be real and they may not. They are not truths unless they are verifiable. The world within we re-create daily. The outer world is always the same." In another essay he concludes that spiritual truth "appeals to the soul as distinct from the reason and the intellect, or to our higher and finer sense of the beauty and mystery of the world," and he gives an example: "Emerson's essays are full of spiritual truth, as are all the great poems of the world." Similarly, Burroughs quotes Whitman's poems several times in the final essay, "The Divine Ship," in order to praise the vast, awesome power of the natural universe and its endlessly dynamic renewals. Though at times repetitive and abstract, the essays of *The Light of Day* represent the literary naturalist's sharp view of the great controversies of the time, to which readers have returned on more than one occasion since.

For much of the Riverby period and all of the Slabsides years, Burroughs received visits from admiring readers, who traveled from near and far to meet him, walk and talk with him, and gain a direct impression of the genial naturalist whose work they had read so often. Many of these visitors were women, including hordes of students from nearby Vassar College. In 1901, however, a special visitor came to Slabsides. In September, after a summer of steady correspondence, Clara Barrus arrived at Slabsides to see Burroughs. At the time of her visit, Barrus was thirty-three years old, an unmarried physician at the state psychiatric hospital in Middletown, New York. By December 1901, the young doctor and the sixty-four-year-old writer had embarked upon an affair that remained more friendship than relationship. More important to both of them, certainly, was Barrus's role as literary helpmate. In just a few months after their initial meeting, she was proofreading and copyediting Burroughs's books. He sent her all of his journals through the 1880s, noting to her in a December 1901 cover letter, "I seem to have put all my sunshine into the books and all my gloom into the diaries. Remember they were written for my eye alone—a sort of cemetery where I could turn and mourn over my vanished days, and vanished thoughts." For the rest of the writer's life, Barrus remained his intimate companion and literary partner, typing his essays and even taking dictation from him. She eventually became one of his most important correspondents, after Myron Benton and Julian Burroughs. She was also his literary executor, editing the two posthumous volumes and publishing important books such as the two-volume *The Life and Letters of John Burroughs* (1925), *The Heart of Burroughs's Journals* (1928), and *Whitman and Burroughs: Comrades* (1931). Though she could be proprietary and greedy for literary fame, Barrus undoubtedly helped Burroughs rejuvenate his writing career as he reached old age. As he approached the age of seventy, he published dozens of articles for magazines, five new volumes of essays, a collection of his poems, an anthology

Slabsides, Burroughs's retreat near Riverby, his country home in Upstate New York (from William Sloane Kennedy, The Real John Burroughs, *1924)*

of English and American nature poetry, a biography of Audubon, and, in 1904, an autographed edition of the *Writings of John Burroughs.*

The year 1902 was eventful in many ways. In February, Burroughs and Julian sailed to Jamaica and spent several weeks there, the trip paid for by the Hearst organization in return for an article. Julian announced his plans to marry Emily Mackay and return from Harvard University to live at Riverby, so in the spring his father began working on the new home for his son, a house that Julian himself designed. In addition, Burroughs signed over the deed to the farm to Julian, keeping the stone house and Bark Study for Ursula and Slabsides for himself. Two losses counterbalanced Julian's welcome news: Burroughs's brother Hiram died in May, and in November Burroughs's best friend, Benton, died. Burroughs himself showed marked vitality: he published a short, workmanlike biography of Audubon for the Beacon Biographies of Eminent Americans; the same year, he brought out one of his most important works of criticism, *Literary Values and Other Papers.*

Not surprisingly, Burroughs finds literary values in the same qualities in which he finds human values—the personal, the simple, the acute, the vivid, the passionate, the natural, the genuine, the sincere. His principles of aesthetic judgment are surprisingly classical, emphasizing balance, proportion, and taste. But in this and other essays, Burroughs takes the naturalist's view of literature, just as he had in his many writings on Whitman, for in both cases the experience of the writer's voice is most important.

As both a critic and a nature writer, Burroughs found models in a variety of figures from the past. In "Gilbert White Again," for example, he praises the eighteenth-century naturalist as "a type of the true observer, the man with the detective eye. He did not seek to read his own thoughts and theories into Nature, but submitted his mind to her with absolute frankness and ingenuousness." In "Another Word on Emerson" and "Thoreau's Wildness," Burroughs explores the limits and limitlessness of two predecessors, while Whitman continues to play the role of touchstone in "Nature in Literature," "Suggestiveness," and "On the Re-reading of Books." In addition to these predictable models, however, Burroughs praises the work of Carlyle, Wordsworth, Alfred Tennyson, and Arnold. The essays of the volume bristle with allusions to major novelists, poets, and essayists from English, American, French, and German literature. Much of *Literary Values and Other Papers* is taken up with a summarizing of a lifetime of reading, thinking, and writing. The last two essays turn from retrospection to the present and future, from summarizing to further work. Thus, Burroughs can admit "The Spell of the Past" and yet dispel its power; he calls work "The Secret of Happiness" and is happy to divulge the secret.

In 1904 Burroughs brought out a collection of nature essays, *Far and Near,* the first "outdoor book" since the publication of *Riverby* ten years before. The most sustained work in the book is "In Green Alaska," a slight revision of the "Narrative of the Expedition" for *Alaska, The Harriman Expedition, 1899* (1901). Now that interesting and vivid account was available to Burroughs's many readers. At the other end of the book, he placed "A Lost February," a narrative of the trip he and Julian took to Jamaica in 1902. Unlike the Alaska piece, "A Lost February" had never before been published. Apparently, the Hearst company had never received the promised work from Burroughs. Between the bookends of these two essays were seven essays of the "near," including the excellent "Wild Life About My Cabin" and several other papers that revisit old themes, such as "Bird Life in Winter" and

"Two Birds'-Nests," which would have fit well in one of the early books, such as *Wake-Robin* or *Winter Sunshine.* After a series of literary, religious, and philosophical books, the return to the "out-of-doors" seems fresh. Because of the ever increasing popularity of the nature essay, moreover, the work found a ready audience of eager readers.

Burroughs was one of the prime movers in the "Back to Nature" movement at the turn of the century, largely as a result of his popular essays and books. In the first years of the twentieth century, nature writing and nature study were tremendously popular, and Burroughs felt compelled to defend the need for accuracy in observation. As in the essays of *The Light of Day* and *Literary Values,* Burroughs insisted on the distinction between the observer and the observed, between the subjective and the objective. In "Real and Sham Natural History," published in the March 1903 issue of the *Atlantic,* Burroughs takes to task the writers Ernest Thompson Seton and William J. Long. Seton's *Wild Animals I Have Known* (1898), Burroughs wrote, "is full of such far-fetched anthropomorphic wildlife that it should be retitled 'Wild Animals Only I Have Known.'" In one egregious example, Seton describes a fox that lures a pack of hounds onto a railroad track in time to be killed by a train: "The presumption," wrote Burroughs, "is that the fox had a watch and a timetable." Long's three books for children included *School of the Woods* (1902), in which the author argued that birds taught their young to sing, hunt, nurse injuries, and build nests. Burroughs responds to these representations with withering sarcasm, and his article prompted responses by Long in the May 1903 *North American Review* and in the September 1903 *Outlook.* Even though Burroughs softened his rhetoric, he never changed his basic position.

The most important result of the controversy was the growing friendship between Burroughs and Roosevelt. On 10 March 1903 the youthful president of the United States wrote Burroughs a warm letter commending the "Real and Sham Natural History" article, offering his own criticism of the article and the writers he named "Nature Fakers," and inviting Burroughs to accompany him on a trip to Yellowstone. Burroughs replied humbly and knowledgeably, for he was familiar with Roosevelt's many essays and books on nature. Eventually, the voluble president could not contain himself, issuing public condemnations of Long and others in the June and September 1907 issues of *Everybody's Magazine.* Burroughs kept up the controversy as well, publishing essays in *Harper's, Century, Atlantic,* and *Outing Magazine.* In June 1905 Burroughs's collected essays, excluding "Real and Sham Natural History," were published as *Ways of Nature.* Both

Roosevelt and Muir are cited more than once as examples of real nature writers. Burroughs also consistently holds that reason is a specifically human attribute: he says that Muir in his story "Stickeen" (*The Century*, 1897), "makes his dog act like a human being under the press of great danger; but the action is not the kind that involves reason; it only implies sense perception, and the instinct of self-preservation. Stickeen does as his master bids him, and he is human only in the human emotions of fear, despair, joy, that he shows."

Roosevelt's genuine respect and affection for Burroughs comes out clearly in their correspondence, but one of the best examples is a public letter Roosevelt wrote on 2 October 1905, as a dedication of his new book, *Outdoor Pastimes of an American Hunter* (1905). Roosevelt addresses Burroughs as "Dear Oom John" (Dutch term for "uncle") and praises him: "Every lover of outdoor life must feel a sense of affectionate obligation to you. Your writings appeal to all who care for the life of the woods and the fields, whether their tastes keep them in the homely, pleasant farm country or lead them into the wilderness. It is a good thing for our people that you should have lived; and surely no man can wish to have more said of him." Roosevelt takes the opportunity to state his solidarity with Burroughs in their "warfare against the sham nature-writers" and praises Burroughs's type of essay: "You in your own person have illustrated what can be done by the lover of nature who has trained himself to keen observation, who describes accurately what is thus observed, and who, finally, possesses the additional gift of writing with charm and interest." In chapter 9, Roosevelt recounts their visit to Yellowstone Park in 1903: "No bird escaped John Burroughs's eye; no bird note escaped his ear."

Burroughs's own account of the Western trip with the president was published in two different editions. *Camping with President Roosevelt* was published as a brief pamphlet in 1906; a year later he published a lengthy essay in *Outlook Magazine* titled "President Roosevelt as a Nature-Lover and Observer." Then Burroughs combined the two pieces to make *Camping and Tramping with Roosevelt* (1907). Burroughs returns Roosevelt's compliment concerning Burroughs's gift for identifying birds, finding the president's interest in bird life keen and "his eye and ear remarkably quick." The narrative of the Yellowstone Park trip is both informative and amusing. For instance, Burroughs tells the story of seeing three thousand elk in the Buffalo Plateau area north of Tower Falls:

> I was some distance behind the rest of the party, as usual, when I saw the President wheel his horse off to the left, and, beckoning to me to follow, start at a tear-

Burroughs in his office at Slabsides, circa 1920 (from Clifton Johnson, ed., John Burroughs Talks, *1922)*

> ing pace on the trail of the fleeing elk. . . . Now and then the President, looking back and seeing what slow progress I was making, would beckon to me impatiently, and I could fancy him saying, "If I had a rope around him, he would come faster than that!" Once or twice I lost sight of both him and the elk; the altitude was great, and the horse was laboring like a steam engine on an upgrade. Still I urged him on. Presently, as I broke over a hill, I saw the President pressing the elk up the opposite slope. At the brow of the hill he stopped, and I soon joined him. There on the top, not fifty yards away, stood the elk in a mass, their heads toward us and their tongues hanging out. They could run no farther. The President laughed like a boy.

The self-deprecating narrator was sixty-six at the time of the stampede; the president, a youthful forty-five.

The central fact of Burroughs's career in the twentieth century is his amazing popularity. The retreat at Slabsides was a kind of guest house, with visitors ranging from President and Mrs. Roosevelt to large groups of students from Vassar College and local secondary schools. Burroughs could never say "No" to a request from a potential visitor, and he admitted to

Burroughs with Thomas A. Edison and Harvey S. Firestone at Ausable River, New York, September 1916

enjoying the limelight. He also frequently attended literary dinners in New York City, some hosted by Andrew Carnegie and others by Gilder and the Century Association. Burroughs was invited to college campuses as a speaker for literary societies, and a host of John Burroughs Society chapters sprang up in secondary schools across the country. Much of this activity was orchestrated by the promotional staff of Houghton Mifflin, which outgrew the editorial staff in the first two decades of the century. In addition, Burroughs enjoyed the friendship of Bliss Perry, editor of the *Atlantic* from 1899 to 1909. Both were strong admirers of Emerson, Thoreau, and Whitman. Perry ran Thoreau's *Journals* in the magazine in 1905–1906 and convinced Houghton, Mifflin to publish them in a complete edition. In 1906 Perry published the first modern critical biography of Whitman, having interviewed Burroughs on several occasions for the book. During the first decade of the century, Burroughs was as much a literary celebrity as Mark Twain.

Burroughs closed the first decade with two new books and an important journey. The books have not fared well in the eyes of his readers. *Bird and Bough* (1906) collected thirty-four of Burroughs's poems, none truly distinguished. Burroughs's best poem, in nearly every reader's estimation, is "Waiting," a quiet, conventional lyric published in the *Knickerbocker Magazine* in March 1863. In *Leaf and Tendril* (1908), Burroughs collected nature essays (the "leaf" of the title) and "other papers in which I have groped my way in some of the

great problems, seeking some law or truth to cling to. The tendril is blind, but it is sensitive and outreaching, and aided by the wind, never ceases to feel this way and that for support." The mixing of genres and types, signaled by the double title, recalls such earlier volumes as *Birds and Poets, Locusts and Wild Honey, Signs and Seasons,* and *Far and Near.* Instead of literary criticism, the "indoor" papers continue the "Nature Fakers" controversy from *Ways of Nature* and further explore the relationship between science and religion, an exploration begun in *The Light of Day.* The "outdoor" papers include such genial rambles as "A Breath of April" and "A Walk in the Fields," and at least one essay, "The Art of Seeing Things," balances between outside and inside in several ways.

An important journey took place from February to May 1909. Accompanied by Barrus and Mrs. Maurice C. Ashley, Burroughs took a train across the country to the desert town of Adamana, Arizona. After ten years of separation, Burroughs and Muir were reunited. The company visited the Petrified Forest, the Grand Canyon, and the Mojave Desert. At one point Barrus said to Ashley, "To think of our having the Grand Canyon, and John Burroughs and John Muir thrown in!" To which Burroughs replied, acccording to an article by Barrus in *Century,* "I wish Muir *was* thrown in sometimes, when he gets between me and the Canyon." The two old friends continued their combative relationship, especially concerning the role of glaciers in forming the landscapes of the Southwest. Eventually,

Burroughs and his companions took up residence in Pasadena, California, where Muir often visited them. In April the group was taken for a Sierra Club outing to Yosemite Valley, for more lectures on glaciation and for the redwoods. But after four days, Barrus was ready to continue to Hawaii. The trip to Hawaii, paid for by the Hawaiian Promotion Company, included hikes in the tropical forest, native feasts, swimming and surfing in the sea, and visiting the volcanoes Haleakala and Kilauea. Upon returning to California, the party spent one day at Muir's ranch in Martinez. Many of Burroughs's best descriptions of the journey appear in letters to Julian, striking for their easy tone and extensive descriptions. In letters to Muir dated from late summer 1909, Burroughs expressed his appreciation and good humor: "You contributed greatly to the success of our trip, and I know the 'fun' you had out of me was a very inadequate return. But we shall treasure it all in our hearts, and associate you with some of the great moments of our lives. . . ."

Over the next several months in 1910 and 1911, Burroughs kept up correspondence with Muir, especially arguing with him about the central role Muir attributed to glaciers in the formation of Yosemite and the Sierras. The long perspective taken by the geologist appealed to Burroughs, but Muir continually chastened his friend's theories with superior knowledge and greater experience. Yet, the friendship led to a fine collection of essays, *Time and Change,* published in 1912 as Burroughs turned seventy-five years old. The journey to the western states and to Hawaii resulted in several excellent geological essays: "The Divine Abyss," "The Spell of the Yosemite," "Through the Eyes of the Geologist," and "Holidays in Hawaii." In other essays, Burroughs meditates upon evolution, applying it to nature, to culture, and to religious faith. "The Long Road" leads the collection with the metaphor of evolution, but the essay evolves into a metaphorical journey toward "some vaster being or intelligence." This sense of vastness informs many of the essays, a sense awakened by Burroughs's trip to the Pacific Coast and beyond. In short papers such as "The Old Ice-Flood" and "The Friendly Soil," he applies his geologic sense of time and change to his home landscapes of the Adirondacks, the Catskills, and the Hudson River valley. *Time and Change* is the single volume of Burroughs's essays most influenced by Muir and his geological perspective. Like earlier influences, such as Emerson and Whitman, Muir clearly provoked a deep and powerful response from Burroughs.

The play of multiple perspectives operates in many of Burroughs's old-age writings. From age seventy-five to his death in 1921, just a few days before his eighty-fourth birthday, Burroughs published five more books, many of which are miscellanies of nature writing, literary criticism, philosophy of science, and philosophy of religion. But these last volumes do not show any weakening of energy or interest on the writer's part. As he remarks in the preface to *The Summit of the Years* (1913), "Old age is practically held at bay so long as one can keep the currents of his life moving. The vital currents, like mountain streams, tend to rejuvenate themselves as they flow." The "vital currents" became, in fact, the subject of many essays on materialism and vitalism in philosophy. For Burroughs, science reduced all of life to mechanical forces, but he refused to accept the reduction. The French philosopher Henri Bergson, in his book *Creative Evolution* (1911), gave Burroughs a way of dividing the human subject between the logical, scientific faculties and what Bergson called "that faculty of seeing which is immanent in the faculty of acting." Burroughs wished to escape from the bondage of the mechanistic, materialistic perspective. One of his best late books, *The Breath of Life* (1915) is thoroughly occupied with this philosophical problem, and Bergson repeatedly provides the writer with a means of introducing a spiritual, idealist component to Burroughs's thought. Bergson resurfaces in *Under the Apple-Trees* (1916), a thorough mixture of essays on geology ("The Friendly Rocks"), natural history ("Under the Apple-Trees" and "Nature Leaves"), and philosophy of science ("Literature and Science," "Life and Chance," "Life the Traveler," and "Great Questions in Little"). Indeed, the collection includes an extended treatment of Bergson in the essay "'A Prophet of the Soul,'" which takes its title from Emerson and argues for the transcendentalism of Bergson's philosophy.

The last volumes continue to revisit characteristic themes and concerns. They never offer any sense of a definitive or final statement; instead, Burroughs finds new ideas in earlier ones, calling one collection of seven short nature essays in *Field and Study* (1919), "New Gleanings in Old Fields." In *Accepting the Universe* (1920), Burroughs continues to speculate on the perennial questions, the stakes raised by the mass deaths of World War I, but characteristically he calls one collection of fourteen short essays "Horizon Lines" and another collection of fifteen short essays "Soundings," as if to emphasize the infinite mystery of the cosmos and the necessity of continual explorations. He returns, moreover, one last time to Whitman in the essay "Poet of the Cosmos."

The last two volumes in the Riverby Edition of the *Writings of John Burroughs* are posthumous collections compiled by Barrus. *Under the Maples* (1921) was Burroughs's own title for a loose collection of brief essays on characteristic topics, none especially illuminating. The final volume, *The Last Harvest* (1922), includes two

as his companions, and in meeting such men as Woodrow Wilson or Henri Bergson, he could shake hands as in some ways an equal.

Despite the glow of the final years, there were also many losses. World War I was a depressing tragedy, especially when such friends as Roosevelt's son, Quentin, and the poet Joyce Kilmer were killed. In 1912, the year his seventh-fifth birthday was celebrated by the Museum of Natural History in New York City, Burroughs lost the last two of his siblings, leaving him the sole survivor of his once-large family. Among many deaths noted and mourned in his journals, these three stand out: in 1914, John Muir died, followed by Ursula Burroughs in 1917 and Theodore Roosevelt in 1919. Always elegiac and deeply moved by such losses, Burroughs approached his own death with a sense of homelessness. That was how death found him—on the road. Burroughs and Barrus spent the winters of 1920 and 1921 in southern California, but toward the end he was confined for four weeks to a hospital bed. Finally, in late March he and Barrus took a train back east, heading home. But as the train crossed Ohio after midnight on 29 March 1921, the dying Burroughs awoke and asked, "How far are we from home?" He died twelve hours before the train arrived at West Park.

Lionized in his own day, John Burroughs was largely forgotten in the aftermath of modernism. With the recent interest in nature writing, ecocriticism, and environmentalism, however, the time seems right for a renewed interest in this varied and talented writer. Never a politically active writer, Burroughs appealed to a general readership and was instrumental in the "Back to Nature" movement. He gave voice to the art of simple living and to the beauty of the immediate and near-at-hand. In the 1990s scholars published new biographies, critical studies, and anthologies of his work; perhaps they will initiate further study of this prolific and important writer.

*Burroughs in the Muir Woods, California, 1920
(from Clara Barrus,* The Life and Letters
of John Burroughs, *1925)*

important essays on Emerson—"Emerson and his Journals" and "Flies in Amber"—and one on Thoreau—"Another Word on Thoreau." In "A Critical Glance into Darwin," Burroughs meditates on the uses of evolution as a theory for humankind, while in "Sundown Papers" he returns to Bergson and Whitman but, as he admits, "with little success." Still, the final volumes give a certain closure to his life, for they show how Burroughs was writing near his death. The final statement in the last essay, "Facing the Mystery," could serve as Burroughs's final insight into the complexity of multiple perspectives: "We must look upon death as a legitimate part of the great cycle—an evil only from our temporary and personal point of view, but a good from the point of view of the whole."

In his old age Burroughs was much honored and highly praised. He received honorary degrees from Yale University, Colgate University, and the University of Georgia. He met and became friends with the wealthy, famous, and powerful. Perhaps most famously in his old age, he took motor-camping trips through New England and the South with Henry Ford, Thomas Edison, and Harvey Firestone. Indeed, Ford became a particularly close friend in Burroughs's last decade, giving him several Model-T cars and financing vacations and land purchases. Burroughs was as much a celebrity

Letters:

John Burroughs and Ludella Peck (New York: Vinal, 1925).

Interviews:

Joyce Kilmer, "Interview with John Burroughs," *New York Times,* 21 May 1916;

Clifton Johnson, ed., *John Burroughs Talks: His Reminiscences and Comments* (Boston: Houghton Mifflin, 1922).

Biographies:

Clara Barrus, *Our Friend John Burroughs* (Boston: Houghton Mifflin, 1914);

Barrus, *John Burroughs, Boy and Man* (Boston: Houghton Mifflin, 1921);

Barrus, ed., *The Life and Letters of John Burroughs,* 2 volumes (Boston: Houghton Mifflin, 1925);

Dallas Lore Sharp, *The Boys' Life of John Burroughs* (New York: Century, 1928);

Edward J. Renehan Jr., *John Burroughs: An American Naturalist* (Post Mills, Vt.: Chelsea Green, 1992);

Edward Kanze, *The World of John Burroughs* (San Francisco: Sierra Club, 1996).

References:

Clara Barrus, *Whitman and Burroughs: Comrades* (Boston: Houghton Mifflin, 1931);

Julian Burroughs, *Recollections of John Burroughs* (West Park, N.Y.: Riverby Books, 1991);

Norman Foerster, *Nature in American Literature* (New York: Russell & Russell, 1958);

William H. Goetzmann and Kay Sloan, *Looking Far North: The Harriman Expedition to Alaska 1899* (New York: Viking, 1982);

Elizabeth Burroughs Kelley, *John Burroughs, Naturalist* (New York: Exposition Press, 1959);

Nancy Lord, *Green Alaska: Dreams from the Far Coast* (Washington, D.C.: Counterpoint, 1999);

Ralph H. Lutts, *The Nature Fakers* (Charlottesville, Va.: University Press of Virginia, 2001);

William D. Perkins, *Indexes to the Collected Works of John Burroughs* (New York: John Burroughs Association, 1995);

Theodore Roosevelt, *An Autobiography* (New York: Scribners, 1922);

Roosevelt, *Outdoor Pastimes of an American Hunter* (New York: Scribners, 1905);

Peter J. Schmitt, *Back to Nature: The Arcadian Myth in Urban America* (New York: Oxford University Press, 1969);

Dallas Lore Sharp, *The Seer of Slabsides* (Boston: Houghton Mifflin, 1921);

Charlotte Zoe Walker, ed., *Sharp Eyes: John Burroughs and American Nature Writing* (Syracuse, N.Y.: Syracuse University Press, 2000);

Jim Warren, "Whitman Land: John Burroughs's Pastoral Criticism," *ISLE,* 8, no. 1 (Summer 2001): 83–96;

Perry Westbrook, *John Burroughs* (New York: Twayne, 1974).

Papers:

The best collection of letters and journals by John Burroughs is housed in the Special Collections of Vassar College Library. The Berg Collection at the New York Public Library has important holdings of letters, early journals, and other manuscripts. The Clifton Waller Barrett Collection at the University of Virginia includes significant manuscript essays and letters. The Huntington Library in San Marino, California, has Burroughs's journals from the Harriman Alaska Expedition and other manuscripts. The Charles E. Feinberg Collection at the Library of Congress includes Burroughs's correspondence with Walt Whitman. Materials relating to Burroughs's friendship with Theodore Roosevelt are housed in the Theodore Roosevelt Collection at the Houghton Library, Harvard University.

Rachel Carson

(27 May 1907 – 14 April 1964)

Bernard Quetchenbach
Florida Southern College

BOOKS: *Under the Sea-Wind; A Naturalist's Picture of Ocean Life* (New York: Simon & Schuster, 1941; corrected edition, New York: Oxford University Press, 1952; London: Staples, 1952);

Food from Home Waters . . . Fishes of the Middle West (Washington, D.C.: U.S. Government Printing Office, 1943);

Food from the Sea: Fish and Shellfish of New England, U.S. Fish and Wildlife Service Bulletin, no. 33 (Washington, D.C.: U.S. Government Printing Office, 1943);

Fish and Shellfish of the South Atlantic and Gulf Coasts (Washington, D.C.: U.S. Government Printing Office, 1944);

Chincoteague: A National Wildlife Refuge (Washington, D.C.: U.S. Government Printing Office, 1947);

Mattamuskeet: A National Wildlife Refuge (Washington, D.C.: U.S. Government Printing Office, 1947);

Guarding Our Wildlife Resources, U.S. Fish and Wildlife Service, Conservation in Action, no. 5 (Washington, D.C.: U.S. Government Printing Office, 1948);

Bear River: A National Wildlife Refuge, text by Carson and Vanez T. Wilson, U.S. Fish and Wildlife Service, Conservation in Action, no. 8 (Washington, D.C.: U.S. Government Printing Office, 1950);

The Sea Around Us (New York: Oxford University Press, 1951; London: Staples, 1952; revised and enlarged, New York: Oxford University Press, 1961);

The Edge of the Sea (Boston: Houghton Mifflin, 1955; London: Staples, 1956); chapter "The Rocky Shores" republished separately as *The Rocky Coast,* with photographs by Charles Pratt and illustrations by Robert Hines (New York: McCall, 1971);

Silent Spring (Boston: Houghton Mifflin, 1962; London: Hamilton, 1963);

The Living Ocean: A Special Report (Chicago: Field, 1963);

The Sense of Wonder (New York & Evanston: Harper & Row, 1965);

Rachel Carson (photograph by Stanley Freeman Sr., Freeman Family Collection)

Lost Woods: The Discovered Writings of Rachel Carson, edited by Linda Lear (Boston: Beacon, 1998).

Collection: *The Sea* (London: McGibbon & Kee, 1964)—comprises *Under the Sea-Wind, The Sea Around Us, The Edge of the Sea.*

PRODUCED SCRIPT: "Something About the Sky," television, *Omnibus,* CBS, 11 March 1956.

OTHER: "Odyssey of the Eels," in *The Book of Naturalists,* edited by William Beebe (New York: Knopf, 1944), pp. 478–495;

Claude Debussy, *La Mer,* NBC Symphony, conducted by Arturo Toscanini, jacket notes by Carson, RCA, 1951;

"To Understand Biology," in *Humane Biology Projects* (New York: Animal Welfare Institute, 1960);

Ruth Harrison, *Animal Machines: The New Factory Farming Industry,* foreword by Carson (London: Stuart, 1964).

SELECTED PERIODICAL PUBLICATIONS–
UNCOLLECTED: "It'll be Shad Time Soon," *Baltimore Sunday Sun,* 1 March 1936;

"Undersea," *Atlantic Monthly,* 160 (September 1937): 322–325;

"The Bat Knew It First," *Collier's* (18 November 1944): 24;

"The Birth of an Island," *Yale Review,* 40, no. 1 (September 1950): 112–126;

"Wealth from the Salt Seas," *Science Digest,* 28 (October 1950): 321–329;

"Mr. Day's Dismissal," *Washington Post,* 22 April 1953, p. A26;

"Our Ever-Changing Shore," *Holiday,* 24 (July 1958): 71–120;

"Rachel Carson Answers Her Critics," *Audubon,* 65 (September/October 1963): 262–265, 313–315.

Rachel Carson is known primarily as the author of *Silent Spring,* a 1962 book that introduced readers to the hazards of pesticide abuse, shifting the focus of environmental writing by addressing dangers posed to the natural world by human technology. But before the publication of this seminal work, Carson was well known as a nature writer. Her three best-selling books about the sea earned recognition for their combination of the precise observation of the scientist and the vital language of the poet. Carson also wrote magazine articles and composed and edited a significant body of government publications for the U.S. Bureau of Fisheries, which in 1939 became a part of the new Fish and Wildlife Service. Though Carson's writing for magazines and the government should be considered in developing a thorough and complete understanding of her career, her lasting reputation rests primarily on *Silent Spring* and on her role as a "biographer of the sea."

Rachel Louise Carson was born on 27 May 1907, in Springdale, Pennsylvania, near Pittsburgh in the valley of the Allegheny River. The family lived on a farm, but Carson's father, Robert Warden Carson, made his living as an electrician and an insurance agent. He also speculated, without much success, in real estate, subdividing the family's land into building lots, most of which went unsold. Her mother, Maria McLean Carson, is generally credited as one of the most important influences on Carson. Carson was the youngest of three siblings; her sister, Marian, was the oldest, followed by Robert. Despite her birth order in the family, Rachel Carson eventually assumed responsibility for her mother and for Marian's daughters and grandson as well.

Biographers agree that Carson was a bright student in elementary and high school, though she was often absent because of illness and her mother's concern about contagious diseases in the schools. According to Linda Lear, author of the standard biography, *Rachel Carson: Witness for Nature* (1997), Carson's frequent school absences helped her develop a firm bond with her mother. On these occasions, they often walked about the farmland that Robert had bought, with Maria providing natural-history instruction for her daughter.

After graduating from Parnassas High School, Carson attended Pennsylvania College for Women, which later became Chatham College. Because of the Pittsburgh college's proximity to Springdale, Carson's mother was a frequent visitor to the campus. Among her peers, Carson was thought of as an intelligent student, though a bit distant, perhaps because she continued to identify primarily with her family. Still, she participated in extracurricular activities and became a respected, if not outstanding, member of the school basketball team.

Carson wanted to be a writer from an early age. She began publishing with a series of short stories in *St. Nicholas,* a magazine that had built a reputation for "discovering" adolescent authors, among them William Faulkner and F. Scott Fitzgerald. Her first publication in the magazine (September 1918) was a World War I story, "A Battle in the Clouds," which won a silver award in the St. Nicholas League contest. Later entries also won several prizes from the magazine, including a gold badge for "A Message to the Front" (February 1919). In keeping with her literary ambitions, Carson's first major in college was English. Her familiarity and regard for literature is reflected in her books–for example, in the epigraphs that introduce chapters of *The Sea Around Us* (1951).

If Carson's mother is generally considered to be her first significant influence, the second was her biology teacher, Mary Scott Skinker. Skinker provided Carson with a model of a woman who was also a scientist and revealed to her the possibility of exploring her other great interest, the sea. The source of Carson's fascination with the ocean, however, is difficult to pinpoint. Certainly, her interest was firmly established before she saw saltwater.

Under Skinker's tutelage, Carson's interest in biology grew, and she eventually changed her major to natural science. In 1929 she received a bachelor's degree. With Skinker's encouragement and assistance, she then applied to and was accepted into the Johns Hopkins University graduate program in zoology.

Before starting graduate school, she had the first of several opportunities to conduct research at the Marine Biological Laboratory at Woods Hole, Massachusetts. According to Lear, Carson's first direct experience of the ocean was as a passenger on a boat from New York to Massachusetts.

During her time at Johns Hopkins, Carson's family responsibilities grew. Her father's economic circumstances worsened, and her parents eventually moved to Maryland to be closer to their daughter. The Carson household settled in the Baltimore area, with Carson working on her studies while contributing to the family income through a teaching assistantship at the University of Maryland. Beset by uncertainty about her research topic and problems obtaining necessary specimens, Carson found finishing her thesis difficult and had to request an extension. Eventually, she completed her master's degree in marine biology in 1932; according to Lear, her thesis, "The Development of the Pronephros during the Embryonic and Early Larval Life of the Catfish (*Ictalurus punctatus*)," concerned a stage in the development of an unusual organ known as the "head kidney." Carson stayed on at Johns Hopkins as a doctoral student until 1934, when she was forced to drop out because of financial difficulties. Robert Carson's death in 1935 effectively eliminated any chance of Carson's returning to school and marked the close of her academic life.

During the 1930s, opportunities for female scientists were mostly limited to teaching, and Carson knew from Skinker's experience that the position of women in science was tenuous at best. While Carson taught school, she attempted to publish magazine articles, but with little initial success. In response to her need for steady, dependable employment, she took a series of federal civil service examinations and applied for a position with the United States Bureau of Fisheries. Impressed not only by her scientific background but also by her ability as a writer, District Chief Elmer Higgins hired Carson to edit radio broadcasts, a position that eventually evolved into a steady full-time job writing and editing government publications. In 1937 Carson's sister, Marian, died, leaving Rachel and Maria responsible for Marian's two young daughters. The Carson family relocated closer to Washington, settling in Silver Spring, Maryland, which was Carson's primary residence for the remainder of her life.

Carson's work for the Bureau of Fisheries led to the resumption of her literary career. She wrote a series of nature columns, often addressing fisheries-related topics, for the *Sunday Sun* in Baltimore. More important, when Higgins reviewed her introduction to a fisheries brochure, he found it too literary for a government publication but suggested that she send it to *The Atlantic Monthly*. Carson developed this work into an essay, "The World of Waters." Its September 1937 appearance as "Undersea" in *The Atlantic Monthly* constituted a major publication breakthrough for Carson, uniting her literary and scientific ambitions. "Undersea" is noteworthy for introducing Carson's notion of "material immortality." Spiritual or metaphysical immortality may be beyond the purview of science, but Carson establishes that the materials of life do achieve a kind of immortality as they shift from one temporary owner to another.

"Undersea" caught the attention of Quincy Howe of Simon and Schuster and eventually led to Carson's first book, *Under the Sea-Wind; A Naturalist's Picture of Ocean Life,* which appeared in 1941. In composing *Under the Sea-Wind,* Carson was influenced by the works of such American writers as Henry Beston and by such English nature writers as Richard Jeffries and, especially, Henry Williamson, author of *Tarka the Otter* (1927) and *Salar the Salmon* (1935). As Williamson does, Carson builds her narrative around the representative activities of a typical animal, showing that animal's interactions with its environment. Though the narrative structure of the book, which follows the life history of selected animal characters, may appear to invite anthropomorphism, Carson is careful to portray her characters as representative of their species rather than as individual animals with human personalities. Carson emphasizes the generic nature of her characters by giving them names based on scientific nomenclature. For example, the mackerel, a central figure in the second section, is called Scomber, reflecting its scientific name. In other cases, where English names are necessary, Carson's choices reflect characteristics common to the species. The sanderlings, for example, are named for their field marks. *Under the Sea-Wind* places Carson at the border of nonfiction and fiction, with fictionalized animal biographies used as a vehicle for what is basically a nonfiction account of sea life. In her study *Rachel Carson* (1983) Carol Gartner considers *Under the Sea-Wind* a "nonfiction account of the life of the sea" employing a "fictional approach."

Under the Sea-Wind is divided into three sections—the seashore, the continental shelf, and the open sea. This tendency to subdivide her books into distinct sections is a characteristic structural feature that reflects Carson's methodical approach, the same one she later used to advantage in constructing the progressive argument of *Silent Spring*. The first section follows the story of sanderlings Silverbar and Blackfoot. But these two main characters do not appear until the second chapter. In the first chapter, Carson introduces her readers to the world of the seashore by following Rynchops, the black skimmer, making his rounds on a night at the

*Carson at about age five, reading to her dog, Candy (courtesy of Rachel Carson
History Project / Rachel Carson Council)*

beginning of the seasonal shad run. By setting the scene on a small island inhabited only by fishermen, Carson immediately signals her intention to focus on natural cycles fundamentally unaltered by human activities and to allow the animals to emerge as the central figures of the book. On this natural, untrammeled beach, Silverbar and Blackfoot arrive in the midst of their spring migration. Carson's narrative follows the sanderlings to the Arctic tundra, where they breed. In the process, readers are introduced to crabs and other shore creatures and to tundra dwellers such as snowy owls. Toward the end of summer, Silverbar, long since left by Blackfoot to raise her young, in turn abandons them to complete their maturing process alone. She leaves the Arctic and returns, finally, to the original island. At this point the narrative veers away from the sanderlings to other creatures of the shore environment, including the fishermen, who invade the natural system to net mullet.

In the second section of the book, "The Gull's Way," the scene shifts to the waters of the continental shelf. The central figure in the second section is Scomber the mackerel, and the narrative follows the first year of Scomber's life, during which he migrates northward and inward to a New England harbor and eventually back out to sea again. Carson introduces new organisms, such as tuna and dogfish, but she also links the narrative to the previous section by reintroducing creatures seen earlier, including the fishermen, who at one point capture Scomber in their nets. As in the first section, the focus alters through graceful point-of-view shifts, though the narrative always returns to Scomber.

The third section deals with the open sea, though by focusing on the migration of eels from inland ponds and rivers to the deep ocean, Carson covers new environments and revisits ones previously described. Anguilla, the main character, descends to the sea from "Bittern Pond." This migration gives Carson the opportunity to introduce freshwater ecology, with appropriate animal life, such as herons, ospreys, and raccoons. The eels journey through the environments central to the other two sections, passing through coastal bays and beaches and the waters of the continental shelf on their way to the open Sargasso Sea.

Under the Sea-Wind achieves a unity based on Carson's interweaving of the sections. The interactions of the creatures result in a kind of cross-referencing as they encounter each other and each other's environments. In her 1993 volume on Carson for Twayne's United States Authors series, Mary A. McCay notes this effect in Carson's portrayal of eels. This technique, along with the reiteration of descriptive motifs and ideas, gives the book coherence. And while each part of the book has its own sense of completion, the whole work also has a circular rhythm, following a seasonal pattern. This pattern is emphasized by the main and secondary characters' migrations, which overlap or pass each other. Migration is a central motif in each of the three sections, with the sanderlings' flight to the Arctic and back, the mackerels' journeys along the continental shelf, and the eels' travels from inland waters to the Sargasso Sea. The shad, whose movements appear at the beginning of the book, are encountered by the eels at the end.

Like all of Carson's books, *Under the Sea-Wind* conveys a great deal of information on science and natural history in a literary context. Carson's informative intention is signaled by the presence of a glossary, in which the organisms whose stories comprise the narrative sections of the book appear again in a field-guide format. She later applied the same technique in *The Edge of the Sea* (1955), which began as a seashore guide but developed into a naturalist's exploration of three coastal environments, followed by an extensive appendix.

As McCay points out, *Under the Sea-Wind* continues to advance the idea of "material immortality," first expressed in "Undersea," an eternal quality based on the physical transmutation of the material components of creatures into the bodies of other creatures and the totality of the surrounding environment. For example, the generation of eels that breed in the final section and then disappear into the abyss to "die and become sea again." In this sense, the beginning and ending of life are illusory. However, Carson's idea differs from a transcendental sense of immortality in the scientific objectivity of the book. She posits an immortality of ingredients, with each individual organism seen as a temporary arrangement of constituent parts. For Carson, though, this rearranging of life's parts has both beauty and order and is a source of the "sense of wonder" that she advocates in her later work.

Under the Sea-Wind illustrates Carson's fascination with natural cycles and systems. Her conservationist sense, though perhaps less pronounced than in her later works, is also evident in the disruptive quality of the human appearances in the book. Mostly, though, humans are absent, thus allowing the sanderlings and other nonhuman creatures to emerge as independent entities, not particularly concerned with the human presence and not measured according to any intrusive human system of value.

Contemporaneous and later writers and critics have generally been enthusiastic in appraising *Under the Sea-Wind*. Oceanographer William Beebe selected an excerpt for inclusion in his 1944 anthology *The Book of Naturalists*. In his foreword to *Always, Rachel: The Letters of Rachel Carson and Dorothy Freeman 1952–1964* (1995), Paul Brooks, Carson's early biographer, finds the book notable for its "sense of wonder." In *Under the Sea-Wind,* as elsewhere in her writing, Carson's belief in the primacy of emotion over intellect, her insistence that the emotions must be engaged prior to intellectual interest, pervades her reaction to the natural world. In *The House of Life: Rachel Carson at Work* (1972), Brooks also notes that Carson herself believed that *Under the Sea-Wind* represented one of her most creative efforts. In a *Time* magazine profile of Carson as one of "The 100 Most Influential People of the Century," Peter Matthiessen agrees that *Under the Sea-Wind* was "Carson's favorite among her books." Gartner concludes that "*Silent Spring* is Rachel Carson's most important book," but in "*Under the Sea-Wind,* Carson's gifts as a writer and as a scientist most perfectly come together."

Despite the favorable response, *Under the Sea-Wind* did not sell especially well. The generally accepted explanation, shared by Carson herself, is that the chance for the book to make an impact was lost when the Japanese attacked Pearl Harbor shortly after its publication. Lear, however, notes that Carson was generally unhappy with what she saw as the failure of Simon and Schuster to support the book with an active publicity campaign. *Under the Sea-Wind* eventually was rereleased by her next publisher, Oxford University Press, after Carson's remarkable success with her 1951 book, *The Sea Around Us,* and sold well enough to earn a place on the best-seller list.

Carson did not produce and publish a second book until a decade later. She was, however, active as a writer throughout the 1940s. As she moved up through the ranks as a government biologist, her job, as she describes it in Brooks's *The House of Life,* amounted to the "general direction of the publishing program of the service." Among other documents, she produced a series of bulletins for the Fish and Wildlife Service detailing and promoting the fisheries of various regions. Perhaps the most widely known of her government writings is the series of brochures titled Conservation in Action. Carson wrote all or part of five of these, four of which were portraits of specific federal wildlife refuges and one of which constituted a more general statement of conservation principles. The production of these works provided Carson with one of her few opportunities to travel widely. Her portrait of the Bear River refuge in Utah brought her west of the Rocky Mountains for the first time. For Carson, travel was always complicated by her obligations, especially her responsibility for her aging mother, who lived until 1958, and later by her own failing health.

Carson became a familiar figure in conservation organizations in the Washington area and frequently attended outings and meetings of the Washington Audubon Society, of which she eventually served as a director. She continued her involvement in conservation and land preservation causes throughout the rest of her life, serving briefly on the board of the Bok Tower Gardens/Mountain Lake Sanctuary in Florida and working toward the establishment of a Nature Conservancy branch in Maine. Carson's involvement in Washington conservation circles also serves to underscore that early portrayals of her as a somewhat reclusive "spinster" originated in general stereotypes of unmarried women and did not accurately reflect the circumstances of her life. She worked for the federal government for fifteen years, living with her mother and other relatives. Though she and her acquaintances occasionally expressed frustrations with the constraints that she was under, there is little evidence that she believed her life to be uneventful.

Between the publication of *Under the Sea-Wind* and *The Sea Around Us,* Carson continued to publish magazine articles. Notable among her magazine pieces was "The Bat Knew It First," which, appearing first in *Collier's* (18 November 1944), was reprinted in *The Reader's Digest* (August 1945) and eventually distributed by the U.S. Navy. This article discussing the scientific principle behind sonar as embodied in bat echolocation demonstrates one of Carson's most widely noted skills as a writer, the ability to render complex scientific data in language that is clear and accurate, and at the same time literary. The essay also demonstrates the creative synergy between Carson's government work, the evolving scientific research of the time, and Carson's artistic sensibility—a relationship that was a key to the genesis of her next book, *The Sea Around Us.*

World War II brought changes to Carson's life and work. It resulted in a brief move to Chicago, as the government shifted its offices and resources in conducting the war. Of more lasting importance to Carson was the scientific knowledge that the war generated. Since so much of the war was either fought at sea or depended on naval support, government oceanographers embarked on an ambitious, comprehensive effort to increase knowledge about the sea using modern research methods and technology. As a government scientist, Carson was an indirect recipient of much of the new knowledge resulting from this effort, and her ability to explain this new information in an appropriately powerful lyrical voice made her among the first and certainly the most successful of the early writers who brought this information to the reading public. *The Sea Around Us* grew out of Carson's access to this information and her belief that increasing human demands on land resources would inevitably lead to more human dependence on the oceans.

As was generally the case, Carson's research methods were thorough and deliberate, and her attention to accuracy added to the time spent in developing and preparing the manuscript. She consulted widely with specialists, many of whom she knew as a result of her government work or her association with Woods Hole. One reason that Carson was such a slow worker was the process of peer review to which she subjected her material. In *The Sea Around Us,* Carson supplements her own observations and analysis with frequent references to such leading scientists as R. A. Daly and to such ocean travelers and adventurers as Thor Heyerdahl.

Her research also took on a firsthand character. In Florida, she had her only diving experience. Though her dive, limited and delayed by weather conditions, was brief, she was impressed by the way it affected her feeling for the sea. Lear quotes Carson's 26 August 1949 letter to oceanographer William Beebe, who had urged her to get a fuller sense of the sea by going beneath the surface: "But the difference between having dived—even under those conditions—and having never dived is so tremendous that it formed one of those milestones of life." Carson, accompanied by her literary agent Marie Rodell, also sailed to the Georges Bank aboard the research vessel *Albatross III.* Though Carson was an inveterate explorer of tidal shallows and mud flats, these two adventures were the highlights of her limited open-sea experience.

While *Under the Sea-Wind* evolved from Carson's magazine writings, Carson and Rodell reversed the process with *The Sea Around Us,* attempting to publish chapters first in magazines, thus providing advance publicity for the book and financial remuneration for Carson. Though this effort was not an immediate, unqualified success, one chapter, "The Birth of an Island," was published in *The Yale Review* in 1950 and won the Westinghouse Science Writing Award for the best piece of magazine science writing in 1950.

Carson's efforts to secure magazine publication for chapters of *The Sea Around Us* eventually led to a major career breakthrough when *The New Yorker* editor William Shawn elected to use several chapters as a multi-installation magazine "Profile" (2 June 1951, 9 June 1951, and 16 June 1951). This unusual use of the profile series, which had previously dealt exclusively with human subjects, allowed a substantial sampling of the book to reach a large audience prior to the appearance of the book itself. Because the magazine articles continued across several issues, considerable anticipation developed before the release of the book. The *New Yorker* series was one significant factor in its success.

Like *Under the Sea-Wind, The Sea Around Us* is structured in sections, each consisting of a group of related chapters. The first section is dedicated to the

*Carson during her first summer at Woods Hole Biological Laboratory, 1929
(Rachel Carson History Project / Rachel Carson Council)*

topography of the sea, the second section to the dynamic interaction of forces on the sea, and the final section to human involvement with the sea. In each section, Carson makes use of the new oceanographic knowledge resulting from research during World War II. Carson's first section, "Mother Sea," presents oceanography as a mixture of earth history, geology, geography, and biology. The chapters are arranged topically, beginning, appropriately, with the history of the sea, and moving from the world of the sea surface downward to its bottom, exploring regions such as the continental shelf, the slope with its mysterious canyons, and the deep ocean basins. Chapters covering the "long snowfall" of sediment and organic debris and the development of islands are also included before the section circles back, in a chapter on ancient seas, to the historical focus that characterizes the beginning of the section. The second section, "The Restless Sea," consists of three chapters covering waves, currents, and tides, respectively. These chapters are noteworthy for the clarity with which they present the complex interaction of forces moving the waters. They also provide excellent examples of Carson's drawing from various sources of information. She consults practical sailing guides, such as *The British Islands Pilot,* for descriptions

based on long experience of turbulent ocean regions, while the chapter on currents begins with a reference to Carson's own experience aboard the research vessel *Albatross III.* The third section, "Man and the Sea Around Him," considers the relationship between humanity and the oceans.

Carson finishes *The Sea Around Us* with a substantial annotated bibliography of additional works, arranged topically in categories such as "Sea Life in Relation to Its Surroundings" and "History of Earth and Sea." The recommended texts include the government publications and scientific sources that might be expected in a book on oceanography but expand to embrace examples of sea adventure, such as Gilbert Klingle's *Inagua* (1940), described by Carson as "the personal experiences of a modern castaway on a lonely island." Her final category includes memorable sea literature ranging from Beston's *The Outermost House* (1928) to Joseph Conrad's *The Mirror of the Sea* (1906).

Carson's evolving sophistication as a conservationist is reflected in her first two books. In *Under the Sea-Wind,* humans are only present as occasional intruders temporarily breaking up the rhythms of the main characters' lives. *The Sea Around Us,* though it does not posit the degree of human danger to the sea that a similar book might today (and that, in fact, her own revision of the book did a decade later), recognizes serious if localized disruptions caused by human societies. For example, in "The Birth of an Island," she addresses the role of humans in compromising the fragile ecology of island environments, concluding that humanity has "one of his blackest records as a destroyer on the oceanic islands."

Still, *The Sea Around Us* illustrates both faith in the ultimately unchangeable nature of the sea and trust in the basically benign quality of at least some intensive human uses of the ocean basins. Her discussion of mineral and oil reserves in the sea, for example, gives little warning of environmental problems that later were associated with the quest to obtain these resources. She also notes that French fears that the Panama Canal would alter the climate were unfounded. Carson does, however, exhibit a well-developed sense of human dependence on the environment. Particularly noteworthy is her discussion of climate, in which she recognizes global warming as "a startling alteration of climate" in which "the frigid top of the world is very clearly warming up." Carson sees this change as "now established beyond question." Though she does not recognize this process as human-generated, she devotes considerable space to the way climatic change has shaped human history, including a discussion of the Viking presence in the New World.

Lear's biography details the success of *The Sea Around Us*. A Book-of-the-Month Club alternate selection, the book reached the top of the best-seller list, remained on the list for eighty-six weeks, and was eventually translated into thirty-two languages. The book won the John Burroughs Medal for writing in natural history and the National Book Award for nonfiction. In *Lost Woods: The Discovered Writings of Rachel Carson,* her 1998 collection of Carson writings, Lear notes that in her address at the Burroughs Medal ceremony, Carson focused on the harmful separation of scientific and literary cultures in a manner that resembles the later work of C. P. Snow. In the same speech, Carson urged nature writers to follow her example in writing for the general public rather than for a narrowly focused audience of nature and nature-writing aficionados.

The Sea Around Us was also produced as a motion picture. Though Irwin Allen's movie version won an Academy Award for best documentary, Carson herself considered the motion picture a major disappointment. She believed that it failed to reflect her scrupulous scientific accuracy and care, and editorial suggestions she made to eliminate errors were apparently not followed.

The popularity of *The Sea Around Us* has been ascribed to several causes, among them its poetic flourishes, its new information, and its contemporaneous appearance with other works involving the ocean, such as James Jones's *From Here to Eternity* (1951). In addition to recounting these factors in her biography, Lear adds her belief, which she says was "either missed . . . or denigrated" by most contemporary critics, that Carson's concentration on the large-scale and long-range rhythms and meanings of the experience of life on earth was particularly reassuring for people apprehensive about the dangers of the Cold War.

The Sea Around Us brought Carson fame as the "biographer of the sea." It also brought her a measure of financial security. Her family arrangement continued to be demanding and became more complicated with the birth of her grandnephew, Roger Christie, who eventually became part of the Carson household when his mother, Carson's niece Marjorie Williams, died five years later. Nevertheless, *The Sea Around Us,* followed by the successful rerelease of *Under the Sea-Wind,* allowed Carson to quit her government job after fifteen years of service. Additionally, it provided her with sufficient resources to purchase a plot of Maine coastal land, on which she had a cottage built that became her most direct link to the sea in her later years. The cottage also provided her with the society of new friends, among them neighbor Dorothy Freeman, with whom she eventually exchanged frequent, sometimes daily, letters.

Carson's newfound fame brought a wealth of opportunities as a writer and public speaker. One unusual example was her jacket note for a 1951 recording of Claude Debussy's *La Mer.* Though generally reticent about becoming a public figure, especially during and shortly after her niece's pregnancy, Carson understood that her new status and name recognition carried the potential to influence public opinion. One conservation issue that she responded to was the politicization of the natural resources bureaucracy of the federal government following the 1952 election, concerning which she wrote an editorial letter to *The Washington Post* (22 April 1953) that later appeared in other newspapers. Written in support of one of her former government associates, Fish and Wildlife Service director Albert M. Day, Carson's letter denounces the replacement of experienced wildlife conservation professionals with political appointees having no scientific training or expertise in conservation.

Even before the completion of *The Sea Around Us,* Carson had agreed to produce a guide to seashore life for Paul Brooks of Houghton Mifflin. Brooks's support led to Houghton Mifflin's becoming Carson's primary publisher and developed into a personal friendship. In fact, Brooks and his wife, Susie, became the legal guardians of Roger Christie, Carson's grandnephew, at Carson's death. Brooks's field-guide project evolved into the last of her sea books, *The Edge*

One night the mackerel came upon an abandoned gill net swaying in the water. The net was buoyed at the surface by cork floats; and from the cork line it hung down perpendicularly — It, like a giant tennis net. Its meshes were 2 inches(?) across so that the yearling mackerel could have slipped through, although larger ones would have been gilled in the twine. Tonight no fish would have tried to pass through the net, for all its meshes were hung with tiny warning lamps. ~~the~~

~~Peridinium and Ceratium~~ ... *clung to* ~~the net~~ ... It was as though all the myriad lesser fry of the sea, the animals small as a dust mote, the plants tinier than a _____ drifting ~~endlessly~~ *from birth to death* in oceans, _____ (endlessly fluid) seized upon the meshes of the gill net as the one firm _____ in their fluid world, and clung to it with protoplasmic hair and cilia, with tentacle and _____ . The gill net glowed like a thing alive; its radiance shown out into the black sea, shown down into the darkness below, and *brought* as amphipods and _____ + _____ drawn by the light, and these larger creatures also clung to the meshes. So the net gave _____ — to

Page from the manuscript for Carson's first book, Under the Sea-Wind *(1941), with a sketch of her cat
(from Paul Brooks,* The House of Life, *1972)*

of the Sea. Though conceived as a field guide, complete with illustrations by Carson's friend and Fish and Wildlife Service colleague Robert Hines, *The Edge of the Sea* grew into an ecological portrait of the Atlantic coast, beginning with the rocky shores of New England, continuing through the mid-Atlantic sandy beaches, and concluding with the coral reefs of South Florida. Carson's typically methodical approach again resulted in a long lead time: the book appeared in 1955 after portions had been published in *The New Yorker* (20 August 1955 and 27 August 1955).

If *The Sea Around Us* deals mostly with the physical forces of the ocean, *The Edge of the Sea* returns Carson to the life sciences. Geographically, *The Edge of the Sea* can be seen as a reprise of Carson's first book, but her approach is different. Instead of constructing narratives centered on animals as characters, in *The Edge of the Sea* she offers a close focus on the three major ecological provinces of the Atlantic coast. Thus, she creates another variation on the familiar three-part structure that characterizes each of her sea books.

By relegating taxonomic and other technical information about the creatures she describes to an appendix, Carson frees herself to concentrate on the relationships between the animals and their environments. Carson's motivation in diverging from the standard field-guide format is clear from her preface. "To understand the shore," she asserts, "it is not enough to catalogue its life." Instead, as she says about a shell, "True understanding demands intuitive comprehension of the whole life of the creature that once inhabited the empty shell." Her outlook is clearly ecological, considering each creature as only truly revealed in the context of its relationships with other creatures and with its environment. Much more so than in her previous books, Carson herself appears as part of the ecological community. *The Edge of the Sea* is her clearest example of traditional nature writing, as she builds from her own shore experiences, confident in her long-held belief in the interconnectedness of emotional and intellectual responses, certain that "Underlying the beauty of the spectacle there is meaning and significance."

Carson's introductory chapters revisit territory she had mapped out in *The Sea Around Us,* as she describes the oceanography of the Atlantic Coast. Such important natural features as the Gulf Stream are portrayed. In *The Edge of the Sea,* though, her focus remains on the living creatures of the seashore, and she discusses the reactions of shore life to the monumental forces of currents and tides.

With the extended section on "The Rocky Shores," Carson begins her survey of the seashore environment of the Atlantic coast of North America. Her method is to present a series of worlds—the various levels or zones of the exposed shore, the underwater forests of rockweed and kelp, and the tide pools. Each realm is described in detail, with profiles of characteristic life forms. Much more so than in *Under the Sea-Wind,* humanity, and especially the writer herself, partakes in the scene, whether as a scientist watching tubeworm larvae through a microscope or as a coastal resident discovering favorite places, such as the "hidden pool," an intimate space in which "one feels the rhythm of the greater sea world beyond." The rich detail of the section suggests Carson's increasing intimacy with the Maine coast.

The section devoted to "The Rim of Sand," like its predecessor, begins with a brief consideration of the shore itself—in this case the nature of the sand, its age, and the process by which it came to be deposited on the shore. She follows this discussion with closely-observed intimate portrayals of sand burrowers such as mollusks, crustaceans, and various kinds of worms, again supplementing her own observations with material gathered from the work of other scientists. For example, her discussion of trumpet worms is partly derived from Scottish scientist A. T. Watson's long-term studies of this organism. Though Carson's most obvious personal loyalty is to the coast of Maine, she also visited the sandy banks of Virginia, the Carolinas, Georgia, and Florida, and her personal experience again supplements the expert testimony of her sources.

After establishing the geographical parameters of the coral world, the final major section of the book, "The Coral Coast," focuses on the ecological associations connecting corals, sponges, fishes, and other creatures of the reef. The reef provides Carson with an opportunity to explore the sense of continuous creation that characterizes all of the sea books. In the Florida Keys, the growing of reefs around islands that were once reefs themselves and the spread of mangrove islands are evidence that the sea is constantly remaking itself and its edges. The material immortality of the reef, in which "many thousand thousand beings—plant and animal, living and dead—have entered into its composition," is remarkably evident.

The book ends with a brief coda, "The Enduring Sea," in which the scientist in Carson withdraws in favor of the nature writer in the transcendentalist vein, a seeker of "the ultimate mystery of Life itself." Carson strikes an Emersonian note in her discussion of unity emerging from diversity, but the source of the unity is not beyond nature; the sea itself provides the "unifying touch" linking all of the various regions she has discussed.

Though less obviously than in *The Sea Around Us,* Carson's awareness of new information gathered in the war and postwar years impacts *The Edge of the Sea.* For example, she includes the findings of a Duke University diving project from the 1940s in which the "biologist divers" discovered that rock outcroppings in the sandy bottoms of the Atlantic continental shelf were not coral, as had previously been supposed, but marl rock. Carson's scientific interest and research serve to intensify rather than diminish the sense of wonder, as witnessed by her reaction to the discovery of intact angel wing shells on the beach and the even more surprising bioluminescence of this sand-dwelling animal. Carson is led to question "Why? For whose eyes? For what reason?"

The Edge of the Sea was generally well received critically and commercially, though reviewers found it more limited in scale than *The Sea Around Us*. The book did not match its predecessor in recognition, but it did receive awards from the National Council of Women of the United States and the American Association of University Women. Current criticism is mixed. Gartner is particularly critical, finding that although Carson still exhibits the combination of poetic and scientific language for which she is known, the result is ultimately less satisfying than in earlier works. She concludes that "Carson was working at a lower level in *The Edge of the Sea.* . . . But Carson's lower level is still writing of a higher quality than most guidebooks to the shore or nature books about the sea." McCay is more positive about the book but still expresses a hint of reserve in her comment that "Even in this narrowest of her books, Carson gives the reader a sense of the largeness of the sea and its connection with the land."

The publication of *The Edge of the Sea* marks the completion of Carson's sea books. By the mid 1950s, she was one of America's best-known nonfiction writers and perhaps the most prominent science writer in the country. In the years between the publication of *The Edge of the Sea* and *Silent Spring,* she had many new and ongoing projects in various stages of development. One of these commitments, for a book on evolution, dated to 1953. She was also approached by her original publisher, Simon and Schuster, and asked to participate in an anthology series. Spurred by her own experiences with her grandnephew Roger and by her belief in the crucial importance of interesting children in nature, Carson also wrote and planned to expand on an article, "Help Your Child to Wonder," which appeared in *The Woman's Home Companion* in July 1956. Simon and Schuster developed *The Sea Around Us* into a version for youths, with Carson reviewing the manuscript prior to its publication in 1958. Furthermore, the development of knowledge in oceanography that had been instrumental in the original conception of *The Sea Around Us* had continued, and when a second Oxford edition was released in 1961, it included Carson's updated notes and her preface, notable for a growing awareness of the potential scope of human alteration of the environment.

In *Under the Sea-Wind* and in the 1951 edition of *The Sea Around Us,* Carson presents humans as invaders and explorers, respectively, but expresses confidence in the fundamental resistance of the sea to human influence. A decade after the initial publication of *The Sea Around Us,* alarmed by Cold War atomic waste dumping, she no longer saw the sea as inviolate. Her sense of the scale and danger of human effects on the environment had been growing throughout the 1950s. In a July 1958 article for *Holiday* magazine, "Our Ever-Changing Shore," she expresses concern about habitat destruction, as the coasts were undergoing widespread and rapid development. Lear also notes in *Lost Woods* that in the 1956 television script "Something About the Sky" Carson exhibits a growing awareness of a possible human role in changing the global climate.

While working on these projects and coping with deteriorating health and voluminous correspondence, Carson was consulted by Olga Owens Huckins, a Massachusetts resident concerned about the effects on wildlife resulting from recent and ongoing aerial spraying of pesticides. According to Brooks in *The House of Life,* Huckins thought Carson could help her find appropriate sources of assistance in Washington. Carson eventually decided to write an article on the subject herself and began in 1958 to conduct the research that grew into *Silent Spring.* Published in 1962, *Silent Spring* is the last book that Carson completed.

As Carson notes at the beginning of the acknowledgments page, *Silent Spring* revisits a long-standing concern. Her interest in the possible effects of DDT and other chemical pesticides dates from the end of World War II. She had unsuccessfully queried *The Reader's Digest* about writing an article on the subject in 1945 and had continued to follow developments concerning pesticide use and abuse. Her interest intensified in the late 1950s, when a lawsuit in which one of the plaintiffs was ornithologist Robert Cushman Murphy provided more data and nudged Carson into a more activist frame of mind. Huckins's letter proved to be the catalyst needed to turn Carson's attention from her other projects. Gradually, as her research in this area expanded, pesticide abuse became her primary focus and the subject of her next book.

Silent Spring, as with the earlier books, is arranged in sections. After a literary opening "fable" detailing the effects of pesticides on a fictional community, Carson maps the historical roots of the pesticide problem and describes the chemicals involved. In doing so, she introduces a continuing motif of comparing the unacknowledged danger of pesticides to the danger that was most familiar to Americans at the time, that of radiation and nuclear weapons. Noting the mutagenic effects of certain herbicides, she asks that since "We are rightly appalled by the genetic effects of radiation; how then, can we be indifferent to the same effect in chemicals that we disseminate widely in our environment?"

Carson's next step is to trace the effects of pesticides on various natural systems and environments. She begins with overviews of realms such as water and soil and moves on to discuss chemical damage to plants, wildlife and livestock, birds, and fish and shellfish. Typically, Carson enlists a wide variety of sources, ranging from museum curators to residents of impacted communities to conservation activists, but especially scientists, to support her points. Though most of the material concerns the United States, Carson makes occasional references to international situations, demonstrating the global reach of the pesticide problem. Examples such as the Atlantic salmon of the Miramichi River in Canada and the milkfish farms of Asia broaden the scope of the book and expand its ecological argument. Although Carson's main concern, as usual, is with the eastern United States, she forges connections with other regions and nations and ultimately with the world as a whole.

Carson moves on to consider the documented and potential effects of pesticides on human beings. The placement of this extended treatment of human health is in keeping with Carson's ecological focus. The earlier chapters trace impacts of pesticides in a sequence that generally reflects both the Judeo-Christian concept of hierarchical creation and the more scientific framework of the food chain. In either case the book leads up to humankind in such a way that the links between humanity and the rest of the systems and inhabitants of the earth become apparent. This ecological approach provides Carson with a base from which to connect animal studies and effects covered in previous chapters to similar effects observed or projected in humans, who are revealed as part of the web of life on earth. For example, in her discussion of energy production at the cellular level, Carson considers that "There is no reason to suppose that these disastrous events are confined to birds. ATP is the universal currency of energy, and the metabolic cycles that produce it turn to the same purpose in birds and bacteria, in men and mice."

If the motion of the previous chapters is "up" the scale to humans, the chapters dealing with human health turn inward and "downward" to the microscopic level of the individual cell. This motion culminates in Carson's discussion of cancer. While Carson's suggestion of a link between DDT and cancer in humans has been noted as one of the few factual errors in the book, Carson's purpose is not so much to describe already established connections as to warn that little is known

Carson at the time of The Sea Around Us, *1951 (photograph by Brooks Studio, Rachel Carson History Project / Rachel Carson Council)*

about links between human illnesses and the use of pesticides. The studies she references suggest concerns that she feels should be resolved before a pesticide is approved. Failure to do so creates a situation in which the public acts "as guinea pigs, testing the carcinogen along with the laboratory dogs and rats." Carson relies on establishing the mechanisms by which chemical exposure could lead to cancer. Though her discussion is typically careful and well researched, critics seized on the necessarily speculative nature of her conclusions, noting that many of the links she points to are unproven. It has also been noted, however, that the safety of the chemicals Carson implicates was also unproven. As H. Patricia Hynes in *The Recurring Silent Spring* (1989) and others have pointed out, Carson rejected the elevation of the economic prerogatives of companies over the right of individuals to avoid exposure to potentially harmful materials.

Carson concludes with projections regarding the future of pesticides and insect control, shifting the focus of the argument from the dangers of chemical pesticides to their ultimate ineffectiveness, resulting from undesirable ecological side effects such as the elimination of predators and from the insects' capacity to develop resistance to chemical insecticides. The final chapter surveys alternatives to chemical spraying–including sterilization, lures, and introduction of predators. Carson cautions that these approaches also involve risk. For example, the chemicals used in sterilization, if introduced wholesale into the environment, would be no less dangerous than the current pesticides. However, the conclusion places Carson's ultimate faith in science. Indiscriminate chemical spraying is characterized as retrograde, an example of the idea of "control of nature," which, according to Carson, represents "the Stone Age of science" and ignores rather than embodies scientific progress.

Despite the earlier reluctance of magazines to consider the subject, *The New Yorker* published a three-part series of excerpts from *Silent Spring* (16 June 1962, 23 June 1962, and 30 June 1962) coordinated with the release of the book. *Silent Spring* became a Book-of-the-Month Club main selection and moved up the best-seller lists. Like her previous works, the book generated significant positive responses. A positive review for the Book-of-the-Month Club, for example, was provided by Supreme Court Justice William O. Douglas. Especially gratifying for Carson was her eventual reception of the Schweitzer Medal from the Animal Welfare Institute; she admired Albert Schweitzer's "reverence for life," and she had dedicated *Silent Spring* to him. But unlike her earlier works, *Silent Spring* also resulted in controversy and criticism from scientists, government agencies, and most obviously, industry. One company, Velsicol, tried to intimidate Carson's publisher by threatening lawsuits before the book was released. Robert White-Stevens of American Cyanamid, for whom, Brooks writes in *The House of Life,* "refutation of her book became a full-time job," and other chemical-industry spokespersons declared the book to be unscientific and riddled with unspecified "errors." Industry attempts to discredit Carson did have consequences. Brooks notes that *The Reader's Digest,* for example, withdrew its offer to publish a condensation of *Silent Spring.* Other magazines opted to side with the powerful industry in reviewing the book. Nonetheless, Carson's research generally stood up to the intense analysis to which it was subjected. Though hampered by deteriorating health, Carson proved to be an effective advocate for her positions. CBS News broadcast "The Silent Spring of Rachel Carson," in which Carson appeared calm and reasonable in contrast to White-Stevens, whose appearance struck viewers as emotional and perhaps disingenuous. But Carson received her most important confirmation from a report commissioned by the Kennedy administration, which generally verified Carson's claims.

As has often been pointed out, the content of *Silent Spring* was misrepresented in the uproar that followed its publication. For example, in contrast to her portrayal in the Monsanto parody "The Desolate Year," Carson admits in *Silent Spring* that "it would be unrealistic to suppose that all chemical carcinogens can or will be removed from the modern world." Instead, she concludes that efforts to control carcinogens should focus on those that are "by no means necessities of life" and that "the most determined effort" should be devoted toward eliminating carcinogenic contamination of food, water, and the atmosphere.

One of the most controversial parts of *Silent Spring* is the introductory "A Fable for Tomorrow," in which Carson presents in composite form various effects of pesticide abuse. Critics pointed out that Carson's scenario was in a sense exaggerated, since the combination of effects that she included had never been reported in a single case. The reaction to the fable, reaching its most extreme form in "The Desolate Year," might have been based partly on the perceived incompatibility of literary devices and scientific literalness, but the rhetorical effectiveness of the passage was another factor influencing the intensity of the reaction to it. The "everytown" described was recognized by millions of readers, whom the fable alerted to the widespread use of pesticides in their own towns and suburban neighborhoods. The mobilization of residents of these communities was instrumental in the development of the direct citizen involvement that has since become a hallmark of contemporary environmentalism. In the chapter immediately following the fable, Carson quotes Jean Rostand's assertion of a "right to know." This right has become a point of contention for later generations of environmentalists; the concept has become encoded into various "right to know" statutes, which have provided legal underpinnings for citizen involvement in toxic-contamination cases.

Carson anticipates future environmental activism in questioning the economic connections linking university scientists with corporations that fund their work. That many of these scientists ignore findings that question the effectiveness of pesticides, she concludes, is not surprising. Carson's exposure of the potential for collusion between scientists and industry might have led some scientists to refrain from actively supporting her findings. But her early critique of business- and government-generated misinformation is particularly well informed considering her years of experience in editing government writing. This critique has since been echoed by environmental writers ranging from Barry Commoner to Wendell Berry.

As Gartner says, *Silent Spring* is Carson's most significant book. By general consensus it is recognized as a milestone in the history of environmental writing. Reviewing the book for the *New York Times* on 23 September 1962, Lorus and Margery Milne compare the book to her previous offerings, concluding that "*Silent Spring* is similar in only one regard to Miss Carson's earlier books . . . : in it she deals once more in an accurate, yet popularly written narrative, with the relation of life to environment."

Though the book represents a major shift in content and emphasis from her previous work, it is not inconsistent with themes and concerns established in her earlier writings. The subject matter is notably different from Carson's other books. In her government and magazine work, however, Carson had written about many subjects not directly related to the ocean, and her projects on evolution and childhood nature study after *The Edge of the Sea* demonstrate an expansion in the subject matter she intended to address in book form. Furthermore, Carson's interest in birds, a significant catalyst in the genesis and development of *Silent Spring*, had long been established both in her writing and in her involvement with the Audubon Society. Moreover, the basic method she followed and the skills she employed are similar to those in her other works. Like the sea books, *Silent Spring* is a combination of science presented clearly and accurately for an audience of nonscientists and the poetic, literary flair that Carson's writing is known for. As with the sea books, Carson was scrupulous and methodical in composing *Silent Spring*, submitting chapters to experts in particular fields for review. The research that went into *Silent Spring*, as well as the author's anticipation that the book would generate controversy, are clear in the meticulous, comprehensive List of Principal Sources that concludes the book.

Carson's use of the already acknowledged danger of radiation as a touchstone for comparison places *Silent Spring* firmly in the Cold War context in which it was composed and has been the subject of critical discussion and debate. In an article comparing Carson's techniques to those used in science fiction, M. Jimmie Killingsworth and Jacqueline S. Palmer consider *Silent Spring* a leading work in establishing an apocalyptic tradition in environmental writing. But they also stress that the more hopeful and perhaps ultimately more useful posture in the last chapter of the book offers an essential alternative to the apocalyptic tradition. Ecocritic Cheryll Glotfelty, on the other hand, questions the long-term viability of Carson's Cold War rhetoric, concluding that a less martial rhetorical approach

Carson in a tidal pool, 1956 (photograph by Stanley Freeman Sr., Freeman Family Collection)

than Carson's might prove more productive in a post–Cold War world. Perhaps Frank Graham Jr.'s observation, highlighted in Hynes's *The Recurring Silent Spring*, that Carson "knew that by taking up her pen to write honestly about this problem, she had plunged into a kind of war," sums up Carson's attitude toward her book and its opponents, and the reaction to the book demonstrates that this perception would not have been wrong. But Carson's Cold War references were also a useful rhetorical technique in translating an unseen, unacknowledged danger into terms palpable to a 1962 audience. A measure of the influence and effectiveness of the technique can be seen in ecofeminist Andrée Collard and Joyce Contrucci's 1989 *The Rape of the Wild*, in which Carson's antichemical rhetoric is seen as informing a statement of concern over nuclear contamination, thus reversing the process initiated by Carson. According to Collard and Contrucci, Helen Caldicott's *Nuclear Madness* (1978) was written "in the activist, ecological tradition of Rachel Carson." Moreover, Collard and Contrucci go on to compare the response to *Nuclear*

Madness to the reaction to *Silent Spring,* noting that similar arguments were used to discredit both authors.

After *Silent Spring,* Carson was much in demand for appearances and interviews, and her support and expertise were sought by environmental advocates and even by the United States Congress. Though she devoted much of her time to defending the claims made in *Silent Spring,* Carson's environmental advocacy continued to evolve. The Lear biography notes an increasing involvement in animal-welfare concerns late in Carson's life, citing her contribution to *Humane Biology Projects* (1960), a booklet published by the Animal Welfare Institute, and her foreword to Ruth Harrison's *Animal Machines: The New Factory Farming Industry* (1964). These concerns were not new to Carson, but they were apparently much on her mind in the time between the conception of *Silent Spring* and the end of her life. In *The House of Life,* Brooks quotes journalist Ann Cottrell Free's assertion of Carson's spirited opposition, based on Schweitzer's ideals, to government predator-control programs.

By this time Carson's health was in serious decline, though she successfully kept the nature of her disease private until her death in 1964. In her final appearances, Carson used a cane or wheelchair, which she claimed she needed because of a flare-up of an arthritic condition. In truth, she had been receiving treatment for cancer since 1960, when she had a mastectomy. Her motivations for keeping her disease secret included her generally private approach to sensitive personal matters and her concern that public knowledge of her disease would lead readers to question her objectivity concerning the health effects of pesticides.

Much controversy has surrounded her medical treatment. Until she sought the advice of a physician friend, George Crile, her doctors appear to have consistently understated the nature and seriousness of her condition, withholding information despite her status as a science writer. Carson's doctors followed the governing protocol of the day, which was to direct medical information concerning a woman to her husband. Consequently, single women were often not provided with detailed or conclusive information about their conditions. Perhaps the most remarkable aspect of her situation was the length of time for which she apparently acquiesced to it, trusting her physicians despite the vagueness of their answers. Carson died on 14 April 1964 of a heart attack, a not unexpected complication of several years of cancer and cancer treatment.

The circumstances surrounding her death constitute one factor in making Carson a subject of feminist analysis. Though she did not identify herself as a feminist and generally avoided suggesting that male-dominated power structures were responsible for the environmental problems she addressed, Carson is a compelling figure for feminist analysis because of several factors: her qualified but spectacular success in the male-dominated world of science, her tendency to maintain close and lasting friendships with women and networks of women, and her relationship with close friend Dorothy Freeman, with its apparently lesbian overtones. The correspondence between the two women has been explored for its lesbian content, and Carson has been considered as a lesbian writer based largely on this relationship and the testimony of the letters. However, while Carson and Freeman apparently were themselves aware that their relationship was sexually ambiguous or risky (they took some steps to prevent some of the more private notes, which they enclosed as "apples" in more general letters, from becoming public), those who have worked most closely with the letters refrain from declaring her sexual orientation. Lear, for example, is inconclusive, preferring even as her biographer to respect Carson's essential privacy.

Silent Spring was the last work Carson completed during her lifetime. However, her intention to create a guide for parents based on her 1956 article "Help Your Child to Wonder" was at least partially fulfilled when the article was released as *The Sense of Wonder* in 1965. In this work, based on Carson's own experience with her grandnephew Roger (the book is dedicated to him), Carson recognizes the importance of a childhood awakening to the natural world and also the difficulties that parents, themselves sometimes poorly versed in natural history, face in fostering the relationship between children and nature. Carson's own early experience with her mother is reflected in her appreciation of the importance of informal nature study such as she had enjoyed on the Carsons' Springdale property. *A Sense of Wonder* reiterates long-term Carson themes—the interconnectedness of life and the primary importance of an emotional attachment from which intellectual curiosity develops. "I sincerely believe that for the child, and for the parent seeking to guide him," she concludes, "it is not half so important to *know* as it is to *feel.*" Carson believes that children come to intellectual understanding through their early experiences, since "the emotions and the impressions of the senses are the fertile soil in which the seeds must grow."

Two additional significant posthumous works were published by Beacon Press in the 1990s. *Always, Rachel,* a selection of the Carson-Freeman correspondence, edited by Freeman's granddaughter Martha Freeman with an introduction by Brooks, appeared in 1995. In 1998 *Lost Woods: The Discovered Writings of Rachel Carson,* edited by Lear, was released. *Lost Woods* provides a retrospective of Carson's writing—including articles, letters, government writing, and magazine versions of chapters from Carson's books. It also includes a sampling of Carson's speeches and editorials. The collection demonstrates Carson's growth as a conservationist and her development of a modern environmentalist sensibility.

Carson's final public address, included in *Lost Woods*, was to a symposium sponsored by the Kaiser Foundation Hospitals and Permanente Medical Group. The meeting was held in San Francisco, and Carson was seriously ill, needing a cane to walk and delivering the speech while seated. As Lear points out, this speech is notable in that Carson identifies her well-established interest in interconnected environmental systems with the science of ecology, which was at the time a rather obscure branch of biology.

Carson is often credited with playing a seminal role in the formation of the modern environmental movement. Brooks, for example, in his preface to *The House of Life,* claims that "Carson's last book, *Silent Spring,* may have changed the course of history," a declaration echoed by the Internet site of the United States Environmental Protection Agency. Certainly, her focus on pollution and on the endangered status of the natural world at a relatively early date provides evidence in support of this claim. Also important is Carson's environmental advocacy through private nongovernmental organizations such as the Audubon Society, the Wilderness Society, and the Nature Conservancy. She identified garden clubs as important allies in her campaign against pesticide abuse. To quantify the influence of *Silent Spring* may not be possible, but the book surely must be included in any list of the most influential environmental texts of the twentieth century. This influence was recognized at the time of publication, not only in the positive public reaction to the book but also in the extraordinary efforts of the chemical industry to discredit it.

The regard in which the book and its author are held has not diminished in the years since her death. Craig Waddell, in the introduction to his critical anthology *And No Birds Sing: Rhetorical Analyses of Silent Spring* (2000), assembles an impressive list of testimonies to the importance of *Silent Spring* as the seminal text of modern environmentalism, noting comparisons of the impact of the book to that of Harriet Beecher Stowe's *Uncle Tom's Cabin* (1852). Carson was awarded the Congressional Medal of Freedom by President Jimmy Carter in 1980. She is portrayed in Kaiulani Lee's one-woman theater presentation *A Sense of Wonder,* and was selected as one of the "100 Most Influential People of the Century" by *Time* magazine. Carson's influence may be most obvious in government; Hynes credits her with laying the groundwork on which the United States Environmental Protection Agency was built. As is often

Dust jacket for Carson's best-known book (1962), about pesticide abuse and its effects on the environment (Between the Covers, *catalogue 78)*

noted in works concerning the aftermath of *Silent Spring,* however, Carson's success in changing human attitudes toward the environment, though certainly significant, has not been complete. The banning of DDT in the United States stands as an example of her influence, but the continued reliance on pesticides and agricultural chemicals in general argues that Brooks's claim may at least be premature.

Carson's contributions to traditional nature writing are somewhat overshadowed by *Silent Spring* and the controversy surrounding it. Her biographies of the sea, however, cover a wide range of the nature writer's spectrum. *Under the Sea-Wind* represents the tradition of animal biography Carson admired in writers such as Henry Williamson, an influence she acknowledged, according to Brooks's biography, as primary. *The Sea Around Us,* though primarily science writing, retains the personal, poetic involvement of the nature writer. In *The House of Life,* Brooks quotes Carson as noting that, while working on *The Sea Around Us,* she wrote until late at night and then read from Henry David Thoreau's journals or the essays of Richard Jeffries before sleeping. In *The Edge of the Sea,* Carson transforms a field guide into an ecological portrait of the seashore.

Carson has been the subject of a small but persistent body of biographical and critical studies in the years since her death. Despite the presence of a number of Carson biographies written for children, Brooks's *The House of Life: Rachel Carson at Work,* a combination biography and anthology with relatively little in the way of specific life details, remained the most significant biography until the 1997 publication of Lear's *Rachel Carson: Witness for Nature.* Several works ranging from Graham's *Since Silent Spring* (1970) to Hynes's *The Recurring Silent Spring* have focused on Carson's influence on government policy and social attitudes. Waddell's anthology of essays *And No Birds Sing* is unusual in focusing on Carson's rhetorical techniques. Beginning with Beebe's *The Book of Naturalists* (1944), Carson has usually been included in collections of nature or environmental writing and in profiles of influential environmental scientists.

Taken as a whole, Rachel Carson's writings trace the development of traditional conservation into post–World War II environmentalism. Her significance in the development of a modern environmental sensibility is evidenced by the fact that all of her major books remain in print. She is generally regarded as one of the most significant nature writers of her time, a groundbreaking female science writer, and a founder of modern environmentalism.

Letters:

Always, Rachel: The Letters of Rachel Carson and Dorothy Freeman 1952–1964, edited by Martha Freeman, introduction by Paul Brooks (Boston: Beacon, 1995).

Biographies:

Philip Sterling, *Sea and Earth: The Life of Rachel Carson* (New York: Crowell, 1970);

Paul Brooks, *The House of Life: Rachel Carson at Work* (Boston: Houghton Mifflin, 1972);

Linda Lear, *Rachel Carson: Witness for Nature* (New York: Holt, 1997).

References:

Andrée Collard and Joyce Contrucci, *The Rape of the Wild* (Bloomington & Indianapolis: Indiana University Press, 1989);

Carol Gartner, *Rachel Carson* (New York: Ungar, 1983);

Cheryll Glotfelty, "Cold War, Silent Spring: The Trope of War in Modern Environmentalism," in *And No Birds Sing: Rhetorical Analyses of Silent Spring,* edited by Craig Waddell (Carbondale: Southern Illinois University Press, 2000), pp. 157–173;

Frank Graham Jr., *Since Silent Spring* (Boston: Houghton Mifflin, 1970);

H. Patricia Hynes, *The Recurring Silent Spring* (New York: Permagon, 1989);

M. Jimmie Killingsworth and Jacqueline S. Palmer, "Silent Spring and Science Fiction: An Essay on the History and Rhetoric of Narrative," in *And No Birds Sing: Rhetorical Analyses of Silent Spring,* edited by Waddell (Carbondale: Southern Illinois University Press, 2000);

Mary A. McCay, *Rachel Carson,* Twayne's United States Authors Series (New York: Twayne, 1993);

"Profile," *Time* <http://www.time.com/time/time100/scientist/profile/carson.html>;

United States Environmental Protection Agency, "People and Profiles" <http://www.epa.gov/epapages/epahome/people2_0608.htm>;

Waddell, *And No Birds Sing: Rhetorical Analyses of Silent Spring,* edited by Waddell (Carbondale: Southern Illinois University Press, 2000).

Papers:

Collections of Rachel Carson documents are held by the Rachel Carson Council in Chevy Chase, Maryland, and in the Rachel Carson Collection at Beinicke Library, Yale University, New Haven, Connecticut.

Annie Dillard

(30 April 1945 –   )

Mary L. Warner
Western Carolina University

See also the Dillard entry in *DLB Yearbook: 1980.*

BOOKS: *Tickets for a Prayer Wheel: Poems* (Columbia: University of Missouri Press, 1974);
Pilgrim at Tinker Creek (New York: Harper's Magazine Press, 1974; London: Cape, 1975);
Holy the Firm (New York: Harper & Row, 1977);
The Weasel (Claremont, Cal.: Rara Avis, 1981);
Living by Fiction (New York: Harper & Row, 1982);
Teaching a Stone to Talk: Expeditions and Encounters (New York: Harper & Row, 1982; London: Pan, 1984);
Encounters with Chinese Writers (Middletown, Conn.: Wesleyan University Press, 1984);
An American Childhood (New York: Harper & Row, 1987; London: Picador, 1988);
The Writing Life (New York: Harper & Row, 1989; London: Picador, 1990);
The Living (New York: HarperCollins, 1992);
Mornings like This: Found Poems (New York: HarperCollins, 1995);
For the Time Being (New York: Knopf, 1999).
Collections: *The Annie Dillard Library* (New York: Harper & Row, 1989);
Three by Annie Dillard (New York: Harper & Row, 1990)–comprises *Pilgrim at Tinker Creek, An American Childhood,* and *The Writing Life;*
The Annie Dillard Reader (New York: HarperCollins, 1994).

OTHER: Fred Chappell, *Moments of Light,* introduction by Dillard (Newport Beach, Cal.: New South Press, 1980);
"Writing 'God in the Doorway,'" in Jeffrey L. Duncan, *Writing from Start to Finish* (New York: Harcourt Brace Jovanovich, 1985), p. 279;
"How I Wrote the Moth Essay–and Why," in *The Norton Sampler: Short Essays for Composition,* edited by Thomas Cooley (New York: Norton, 1986);
The Best American Essays, 1988, edited by Dillard and Robert Atwan (New York: Ticknor & Fields, 1988);

Annie Dillard (photograph © Shana Sureck; from the dust jacket for An American Childhood, *1987)*

Irene Zahava, ed., *Through Other Eyes: Animal Stories by Women,* includes a story by Dillard (Freedom, Cal.: Crossing Press, 1988);
"Luke," *Antaeus,* edited by Daniel Halpern (New York: Ecco Press, 1989);
"Seeing," in *Late Harvest: A Gathering of Rural American Writing,* edited by David R. Pichaske and Edward Abbey (New York: Paragon House, 1991);
Modern American Memoirs, edited by Dillard and Cort Conley (New York: HarperCollins, 1995);
"Schedules," in *The Essayist at Work: Profiles of Creative Nonfiction Writers,* edited by Lee Gutkind (Portsmouth, N.H.: Heinemann, 1998);
"This Is the Life," *Image* (Spring 2002).

SELECTED PERIODICAL PUBLICATIONS–
UNCOLLECTED: "The Merchant of the Picturesque: One Pattern in Emily Dickinson's Poetry," *Hollins Symposium,* 3, no. 1 (1967): 33–42;

"The Purification of Poetry–Right Out of the Ballpark," *Parnassus,* 11, no. 2 (Fall/Winter 1984): 13;

"Singing with the Fundamentalists," *Yale Review,* 74 (Winter 1985): 312;

"Making Contact," *Yale Review,* 77 (Summer 1988): 615;

"Write Till You Drop," *New York Times,* 28 May 1989;

"Writing Back," *Harper's* (June 1989): 28+.

Annie Dillard, a contemporary nature writer of major significance, combines the study of nature with readings in theology, philosophy, and the sciences. Dillard writes primarily narrative nonfiction essays, but her literary contributions include a memoir, poems, and a novel. Her most characteristic books, however, are imaginative nonfiction narratives–witnessings or accounts, stories, and speculations. *Pilgrim at Tinker Creek* (1974) won her a Pulitzer Prize for general nonfiction in 1975, and while *Pilgrim at Tinker Creek* is a landmark in Dillard's career, her writing continues to mature.

Dillard, born Meta Ann Doak on 30 April 1945 in Pittsburgh, Pennsylvania, is the oldest of three daughters of Frank and Pam Lambert Doak. The family–of Scotch-Irish, French, and German roots–provided Dillard with a strong sense of intellectualism and adventure. Frank Doak was a minor corporate executive; his passions were Dixieland jazz, taking his boat down the Mississippi, dancing, and telling jokes. Pam Doak loved dancing and practical joking. She also had a strong sense of social justice. "Opposition emboldened Mother, and she would take on anybody on any issue," Dillard asserts in *An American Childhood* (1987), particularly in instances such as cruelty to classmates and neighbors, and Dillard and her sisters were expected to take a stand. Pam Doak also had a passion for the English language that provided her daughter with a keen sense of words.

The Doak sisters–Annie, Amy, and Molly–grew up in Pittsburgh. The family moved from house to house in the general neighborhood of Frick Park. The children spent summers at their grandparents' home on the southern shore of Lake Erie. Dillard went to the Presbyterian church and to the Ellis School in Pittsburgh. Among Dillard's childhood interests were drawing, rock and bug collecting, sledding, bicycling, and playing baseball. Above all, she was an avid reader, particularly of novels. After she got a bird book, she learned to recognize the birds she was seeing in the deep woods of the park. One was, as she writes in *An American Childhood,* "a downy woodpecker working a tree trunk; the woodpecker looked like a jackhammer

man banging Edgerton Avenue to bits. I saw sparrows, robins, cardinals, juncos, chipmunks, squirrels."

The reference to reading indicates her sense of the importance of books. Dillard, as quoted in Grace Suh's essay "Ideas Are Tough; Irony Is Easy" (4 October 1996), advises aspiring writers that by the time they are five years old they have enough experience, but what they need is the library: "What you have to learn is the best of what is being thought and said. If you had a choice between spending a summer in Nepal and spending a summer in the library, go to the library." In her essay "Write Till You Drop" (1989) Dillard further acknowledges that the writer studies literature, not the world. Writers live in the world, and they cannot miss this world; thus, they do not write about experiences such as buying a hamburger or taking an airplane flight. What writers read, however, becomes the substance of what they write, so writers need to be selective in their reading.

By late adolescence, Dillard was rebelling against mandatory church attendance among people she found hypocritical, against various parental expectations, and against school rules, such as those that forbade smoking; she was nearly impossible for her parents to control. Her range of reading mirrored her inner turmoil. She read Alfred Korzybski's early work on semantics, which she hit on by accident. She read Sigmund Freud's standard works, which interested her at first, but in her view they denied reason, and Dillard knew that "denying reason had gotten Rimbaud nowhere," as she recalls in *An American Childhood.* She read works by Henry Miller, Helen Keller, Thomas Hardy, John Updike, John O'Hara, war novels, and popular social criticism–*The Ugly American* (1958), *The Hidden Persuaders* (1957), and *The Status Seekers* (1959). She claims in *An American Childhood* that she was exhuming lost continents and plundering their stores.

She wanted nothing more than to dedicate her life to a monumental task as had Jonas Salk and Louis Pasteur. "I was what they called a live wire. I was shooting out sparks," she says in the same book; one of her teachers described Dillard by saying, "Here, alas, is a child of the twentieth century." Dillard was singularly devoted to coming to consciousness, "a consciousness so heightened by what appears to be an overactive autonomic nervous system that one sometimes fears her nerves will burst through her skin," as Mary Cantwell describes her in a 1992 article titled "A Pilgrim's Progress." Hollins College in Virginia provided the perfect intellectual, theoretical, and physical environment to engender her extensive nature writing.

Dillard's parents and Marian Hamilton, the headmistress of Ellis School for girls, wanted her to attend college in the South to, as she records in her book *An*

American Childhood, "smooth off my rough edges." Dillard's response was characteristic of the nonconformity and intellectual playfulness she inherited from her parents: "I had hopes for my rough edges. I wanted to use them as a can opener, to cut myself a hole in the world's surface, and exit through it. Would I be ground, instead, to a nub? Would they send me home, an ornament to my breed, in a jewelry bag?" She felt she was in no position to comment since she and her family had visited the school and found it a beautiful site at the foot of the Great Valley of Virginia, where the Scotch-Irish settled in the eighteenth century, following the Alleghenies south. Dillard had actually decided on Randolph-Macon Women's College, thinking it seemed less foreboding. Her visit to Hollins, as quoted by Nancy C. Parrish in *Lee Smith, Annie Dillard, and the Hollins Group: A Genesis of Writers* (1998), had given her the sense that the school was "more serious academically than the other schools I visited—terrifyingly so." At that acutely sensitive stage in her life, she was moved to a decision by a dream about Hollins she had one night. The dream was about the beauty of the little stream, Carvin's Creek, that ran behind the library, and it convinced her to apply to the school.

What Dillard found at Hollins was a strong, supportive writing community in both peers and professors. Lee Smith was a classmate and friend. Her classmates offered collaboration, competition, and honest friendship. Her professors modeled the writing life, guided her in literary experimentation, and supported her in understanding "her identity as an observer of the world around her and as a writer," Parrish contends. Several professors influenced her profoundly. One personal influence was Richard H. W. Dillard, a professor and poet, and later the director of the creative-writing program at Hollins, to whom she became engaged by Christmas 1963 of her sophomore year and whom she married on 5 June 1964. In a letter to Anna Logan Lawson, Dillard conveys something of the influence of Richard Dillard: "he was my education. I don't remember life before Richard." According to her, as quoted in Lawson's "Thinker, Poet, Pilgrim" (1974), Richard Dillard "liked a kind of intellectually sophisticated literature, an ironic, self-referential, playful literature that I soaked myself in perfectly happily." The Dillards lived in a quiet suburban development in Roanoke, their backyard sloping to an unremarkable stream, Tinker Creek. During this time Dillard taught herself to read topographical maps and hiked and camped on the Appalachian Trail and along the Blue Ridge Parkway. She finished a B.A. and an M.A. at Hollins and wrote poetry, eventually publishing a book of poems, *Tickets for a Prayer Wheel* (1974). During the late 1960s and early 1970s Dillard began to write prose as well as poetry.

That the literary theory of New Criticism dominated scholarly thought at the time was evident in the Hollins Writing Program. The emphasis of New Criticism on attention to language resonated with Dillard. It "prized concision" and ignored politics, gender, and class. It implied that someone would read the text and discover its structure and internal relationships: "We never read texts because they were written by women or by men; we read them for their intrinsic interest," Dillard recalls in Parrish's book. In addition to New Criticism, other Hollins influences on Dillard's academic life and writing included Louis Rubin Jr., whom Dillard saw as an example of how teachers should treat students. Lex Allen, aware of Dillard's intensity, urged her to work in poetry. Julia Randall Sawyer, according to Parrish, gave Dillard a feminine model of a "woman who has committed her life to her art." John Rees Moore was a major reader of the manuscript of *Pilgrim at Tinker Creek,* and Dillard has remarked on the respect he showed for his students. The professor who had the most substantive influence on the ideas of *Pilgrim at Tinker Creek,* however, was a Methodist minister, George Gordh. Gordh was a kindred spirit; he fascinated Dillard because of the "clarity of his mind," she is quoted as saying in *Lee Smith, Annie Dillard, and the Hollins Group.*

Dillard was also influenced by two writers who were the subjects of her own early scholarship. She wrote her senior thesis on Emily Dickinson, tracing Dickinson's pattern of description and disappearance. Dillard observed Dickinson's habit of describing someone or something good or beautiful but noticed how Dickinson would ultimately "kill off" the beautiful. In this scheme, Dillard explained, any liminal experience—faraway places, sunset, the sea, the sky—is a threshold touching on the eternal. The experience is not, however, the eternal: "The liminal experience . . . occurs on the periphery of cosmic meaning and subverts the usual ways of knowing God. And once this transgressive moment occurs, the liminal is no longer at the margins but becomes part of the center of meaning: once we see beneath the disguise of nature, we discover ourselves facing a divine revelation." The other formative influence was Henry David Thoreau, on whom Dillard wrote her master's thesis, "Walden Pond and Thoreau." She criticized Thoreau for "scarcely noticing the wildlife, only noting creatures in 'glimpses.'" She, however, capitalized on the pond as a liminal place, saying that "It is the source and the milieu of all life, necessary to the survival of the flesh and of the harvest; it is cleansing, refreshing, and sacramental. But water kills in surfeit."

Throughout Dillard's writings, readers see connections to the nineteenth-century Romanticism of Wil-

Dillard as a young girl (photograph from the dust jacket for An American Childhood, *1987)*

liam Wordsworth, to the later Romanticism of Gerard Manley Hopkins, and to Dickinson and Thoreau, as these writers use the concept of the revelation by nature of a divine spirit or of the metaphysical world. Dillard's Romantic characteristics are most akin to those of British Romanticism. She shares with these earlier Romantics the luminous organicism of the mind working upon a natural scene, the defiance of religious-social-political institutions, the analysis of the peculiar detail, the desire for the virgin insights of child or rustic, and the belief that the poet or the literary artisan can be called to her work in order to illuminate the world. Dillard, though, brings twentieth-century science to bear on her sense of Romanticism. With many modern nature writers, Dillard, according to Sarah Humble Johnson, shares a set of qualities that include "a close observation of nature, within an awareness of the modern science of ecology; a journal of the author's own growth by means of the intense relation to nature; a speculation about larger religious and political issues connected with the cause of wilderness preservation." The major difference of this literature from the Transcendentalist literature, particularly the work of Thoreau and Dickinson that preceded it, is its concentration on ecological implications rather than on literary or transcendental musings. Dillard also

diverges, though, from the wilderness literature of John Muir; she always charts the interior landscape of the psyche. She acknowledges that the natural world, albeit beautiful, is not reasonable or predictable and, above all, is not under human control. Her examples of the minute and factual abound, prototypically in those of the Polyphemus moth and the praying mantis, which appear in *Pilgrim at Tinker Creek* and other works. In these examples, Dillard notes the painful and recognizes the imperfect but highlights that they are bound in a kind of ecological unity. The greatest moments of illumination for Dillard come in moments of unification.

In 1971 Dillard experienced a near-fatal attack of pneumonia. After she recovered, she decided she needed to live life more fully. She eventually turned the journal of her experiences from a year at Tinker Creek and of being awake to this particular natural world into the well-crafted *Pilgrim at Tinker Creek*. During the time leading up to the work, Dillard had been writing extensively, both as a columnist for *Living Wilderness,* from 1973 through 1975, and as a personal journal writer. Aside from drawing upon her experiences and journal, *Pilgrim at Tinker Creek* emerges from her college writing career, her senior thesis, and her master's thesis.

Critics struggle to classify Dillard's prose. *Pilgrim at Tinker Creek* crosses boundaries between prose and poetry, nature writing and personal memoir, and religious treatise and scientific tract. Among all these categories, however, Dillard strives for the illuminated moment. She writes of returning from a walk, knowing "I cannot cause light; the most I can do is try to put myself in the path of its beam. It is possible, in deep space, to sail on solar wind. Light, be it particle or wave, has force: you rig a giant sail and go. The secret of seeing is to sail on solar wind. Hone and spread your spirit till you yourself are a sail, whetted, translucent, broadside to the merest puff." This sense of illumination dominates Dillard's life experiences and, not inconsequently, her writing. Many references to it occur in *Pilgrim at Tinker Creek*.

While Dillard lived near Tinker Creek, she was acutely aware of being awake to the natural world. Meticulous observations dominate the book. Dillard is engaged always in an intensity of life as if walking a high wire without a net; her nonfiction repeatedly displays this engagement and requests of her readers a similar engagement. First, she guides the reader through the microscope that is "her eyes, enlarging frogs, bugs, spiders, water snakes—whatever flies, swims or crawls—to monstrous proportions." Then she aims that microscope, only by now it is a telescope, at the heavens, because she believes that to perceive God's creatures is, in a sense, to perceive God, though Dillard recognizes that "in the end, God defeats her (and all of us), being unknowable." Dillard speaks often of the "created" world. To her, woods and fields, streams and oceans, and creepy-crawlies are no happenstance.

Pilgrim at Tinker Creek places many demands on readers, by the multiple levels of meaning, the disparate and often stark imagery, and the metaphors describing the profound mysteries of life. Several images described in *Pilgrim at Tinker Creek* and in Dillard's essays are emblematic of her concern with mystery and metaphor and with her willingness to revisit images to assign new value. The description of the Polyphemus moth in *An American Childhood*, for example, is particularly telling:

> The freshly hatched moth was crippled because its mason jar was too small, particularly for it to spread its wings. The moth had clawed a hole in its hot cocoon and crawled out, as if agonizingly, over the course of an hour, one leg at a time; we children watched around the desk, transfixed. After it emerged, the wet, mashed thing turned around walking on the jar's bottom, then painstakingly climbed the twig with which the jar was furnished. There, at the twig's top, the moth shook its sodden clump of wings. When it spread those wings— those beautiful wings—blood would fill their veins, and the birth fluids on the wing's frail sheets would harden to make them tough as sails.

When rendering the same experience in *Pilgrim at Tinker Creek*, Dillard recalls that the wingspan of up to six inches made the Polyphemus one of the few huge American silk moths. She traces the experience of having the cocoon passed around among the students: "As we held it in our hands, the creature within warmed and squirmed. . . . The pupa began to jerk violently, in heart-stopping knocks." Dillard recalls the slow and painful emergence of the moth from the cocoon; she captures the pain of the creature in the limited space of the mason jar and then its ultimate struggle to live once given its freedom: "He heaved himself down the asphalt driveway by infinite degrees, unwavering. His hideous crumpled wings lay glued and rucked on his back, perfectly still now, like a collapsed tent." She goes on to describe the moth's tortuous crawl back up the driveway. The impact on Dillard of the moth's emergence into life that paradoxically involves death is hard to gauge. The impact was dominant enough, however, for the description to appear in two of her major works, and in *Pilgrim at Tinker Creek* to include the additional description of the moth's plight even after it has been freed.

Another image, one again focusing on an insect, a subject that captivates Dillard, is the praying mantis. In a pivotal description from *Pilgrim at Tinker Creek* Dillard presents minute and excruciatingly factual detail. First, she describes what adult mantises eat, then goes on to

recall an experience from elementary school, when one of the teachers brought in a mantis egg case in a mason jar. Dillard watched newly hatched mantises emerge and shed their skins. Particularly troubling to her, even at this young age, were the moments that followed when the mantises devoured each other. Dillard says she felt as though she herself "should swallow the corpses, shutting my eyes and washing them down like jagged pills, so all that life wouldn't be lost." These images introduce the inevitable reflection on death; Dillard philosophizes frequently on the paradox of life amid death and the sacrifice the living make to cling to life.

In a 1981 interview with Karla Hammond for the *Bennington Review*, Dillard discussed the structure of *Pilgrim at Tinker Creek*, illuminating some of the mystical levels and helping readers make the connection she makes, from the physical, natural world to the metaphysical. Central to the book are two notions from early Christian theology describing the soul's approach to God: the *via positiva* and the *via negativa*. The *via positiva* suggests that the person actively attempts to come closer to God through good works, loving God and God's works. Figuratively, one on the *via positiva* climbs a ladder of good works toward God. The *via negativa*, as Dillard describes it, suggests that the soul approaches God by denying anything that can be said about God: "All propositions about God are untrue. Language deceives; the world deceives. God is not perfectly good, perfectly powerful, perfectly loving; these words apply to beings, and God is not a being."

The soul on the *via negativa* rejects everything that is not God; the person experiences an abyss or dark night and can only hope that God finds him or her outside the senses and outside reason. Dillard explains that the first half of *Pilgrim at Tinker Creek* represents the *via positiva*; the second half, the *via negativa*. Thus, in the first half of the book a growing sense of the good of the world dominates, but in the chapter "Fecundity," the downhill spiral begins. Too much goodness sates the soul, and the mind quarrels with death. In the second half of *Pilgrim at Tinker Creek*, realms of greater and greater emptiness emerge. The soul is emptying for the incursion of God. The first and final chapters of the book provide a frame, with, Dillard hopes, "a year's wisdom in between."

After the publication of *Pilgrim at Tinker Creek* and her receiving the Pulitzer Prize, Dillard's marriage to Richard Dillard ended. Partially to avoid the press and the public after winning the Pulitzer Prize, Dillard moved to an isolated cabin on an island near Puget Sound. During her years in Washington State, while she was scholar in residence at Western Washington University in Bellingham and worked as a contributing editor for *Harper's,* Dillard met Gary Clevidence, a writer, whom she later married. She also wrote the book she has claimed to like best, *Holy the Firm* (1977). The research she did while living in the Bellingham area led to a long piece of fiction, "The Living" (published in *Harper's,* November 1978), which she later expanded into her first novel.

Two essays, "Singing with the Fundamentalists" and "The Deer at Providencia," first published in 1985, present the theme of commitment on a small scale. In the first essay, Dillard is not fascinated by the beliefs or stances that the group of fundamentalist students holds; she is intrigued by their sense of dedication and with their willingness to witness publicly even in the face of ridicule. In "The Deer at Providencia," the sight of a trapped, roped, injured deer, waiting for death and experiencing pain in each passing moment, is the central image Dillard graphically describes. She conveys the animal's struggle with several references to the time that passes and to the comment of the observers, "It [the deer] will have given up; now it will die." Right after one observer comments about the deer's demise, it "would heave." The men of the group all watch Dillard, a woman, calculating her reaction to the animal's agony. Dillard concludes the essay with a parallel story of agony, that of Alan McDonald, who experienced serious burns from gasoline, went through torturous healing processes and surgeries, but then, after having been healed, was burned again. The essay asks, How can living things be asked to experience such pain? There is nothing "fair" about these experiences. As Dillard reads the newspaper clipping that recounts the burn victim's double agony, she remembers the deer. Her question voices what many others cannot articulate: "Will someone please explain to Alan McDonald in his dignity, to the deer at Providencia in his dignity, what is going on?" This movement from an image in nature, the deer, to the burned man is typical of Dillard's work and demonstrates the metaphorical power of the natural in providing insight into the human condition.

As Dillard continued to write, her imagery grew increasingly disparate as she stretched language in the attempt to convey ineffable realities. *Holy the Firm* is nearly noncategorizable in its structure and content. The text opens with a kind of prologue signaling several of the strands of exploration: a moth aflame, the gods of nature, and the environment formed by the mountains and islands of the northern Puget Sound, where Dillard was living alone. Then she moves to a monologue, probing the multiple layers of meaning related to creation and the "firm," which is holy, and then to several images of dedication or total life sacrifice. Dillard first pictures the physical: "A golden female moth, a biggish one with a two-inch wingspan, flapped

into the fire, dropped her abdomen into wet wax, stuck, flamed, frazzled and fried in a second. Her moving wings ignited like tissue paper, enlarging the circle of light in the clearing." Then, moving through the physical reality of what happens to the moth, Dillard explores nature's intolerable and "a-sensitive" demands: "And then this moth essence, this spectacular skeleton, began to act as a wick. She kept burning. The wax rose in the moth's body from her soaking abdomen to her thorax to the jagged hole where her head should be, and widened into flame, a saffron-yellow flame that robed her to the ground like any immolating monk." Dillard's intense description invokes both an acute sense of pain and an acute sense of the divine: it appears "like a hollow saint, like a flame-faced virgin gone to God" while Dillard reads by the light of the flame. The comparisons to a monk or a saint or a virgin "gone to God" cause the reader to imagine the total self-sacrifice to God of these religious figures and invoke the parallel sacrifice demanded by something as unknowing as the moth or other elements of nature.

Holy the Firm is a reflection on suffering, evil, and God's role in the universe. Dillard uses the graphic metaphors of death by flame and of living with disfigurement from burns to examine the commitment demanded by a relationship with God. In a 1978 interview with Philip Yancey about *Holy the Firm,* Dillard compared the challenges for those who believe and those who doubt, merging, as she so frequently does, the natural, scientific, metaphysical, philosophical, and theological worlds. Agnostics who might disparage those who trust in religion "think religion is safety when in fact *they* have the safety. To an agnostic you have to say over and over again that the fear of death doesn't lead you to love of God. Love of God leads you to fear of death. Agnostics often think that people run to God because they are afraid of dying. On the contrary, the biblical religion is not a safe thing." People in the Bible, Dillard acknowledged, "understood the transitory nature—the risk—of life better than most people. . . . Agnostics don't remember all the time that they are going to die. But Christians do remember. All our actions in this life must be affected by God's point of view."

Holy the Firm is in many ways this remembering of flame, and the narrative explores this remembrance through the events of three days spent alone. One event is an airplane crash, which disfigures the face of a young girl, Julie Norwich, whom Dillard knows. Dillard questions, in light of this tragedy, what is holy? Are the earth, the created world, and all creation holy? Is the firm a shortened version of firmament? She explains that the term "firmament" comes from "Esoteric Christianity," which posits a substance lower

Lee Smith and Annie Dillard with writer in residence Colin Wilson at
Hollins College, 1966–1967 (Hollins College)

than metals or minerals on a "spiritual scale" and lower than salts and earths, occurring beneath salts and earths in a waxy deepness of planets, but "never on the surface of planets where men could discern it; and it is in touch with the Absolute, at base. In touch with the Absolute! At base. The name of this substance is: Holy the Firm." Dillard explored this theme five years later in "An Expedition to the Pole": only those who perceive the ambiguities of nature and the perceptions of the natural world are attuned to God; they are seeking the Absolute.

In *Holy the Firm* she also reflects on time and the recurring theme of what it means for humans to be alive. Is the supreme sense of "aliveness" known through total giving? What is real? The indescribable pain that burn patients experience, which in *Holy the Firm*

Norwich knows after "a glob of flung vapor hit her face," is undeniably real. So what of a god who allows such suffering? Dillard answers this eternal question in reminding humankind: "we are created, *created* sojourners in a land we did not make, a land with no meaning we can make for it alone. Who are we to demand explanations of God?" *Holy the Firm* demonstrates Dillard at her best, moving figuratively, metaphorically, and analogically through the essential questions of human existence, building on the observable natural world to make sense of the unknowable supernatural world.

Dillard was twenty-nine when she wrote *Pilgrim at Tinker Creek* and was approaching her mid thirties when she published *Holy the Firm;* her total absorption in writing often involved fifteen to sixteen hours a day, during which she was cut off from society, not even keeping up with the latest world news. In 1979 Dillard and Clevidence moved east, making a home in Middletown, Connecticut. Dillard again held a light teaching position, this time as one of several writers in residence at Wesleyan University. She and Clevidence married on 12 April 1980. "I came to Connecticut because, in the course of my wanderings, it was time to come back east–back to that hardwood forest where the multiple trees and soft plants have their distinctive seasons," Dillard said in a 1984 *Esquire* article, "Why I Live Where I Live." She and Clevidence had a daughter, Cody Rose, born in 1984. The family spent their summers in South Wellfleet on Cape Cod, where Clevidence's daughters, Carin and Shelly, continued to play major roles in Dillard's life, as they had since 1976.

In the years after *Pilgrim at Tinker Creek* and before the later works, such as *The Living* (1992) and *For the Time Being* (1999), Dillard produced two works related to the act of writing: *Living By Fiction* (1982) and *The Writing Life* (1989). Both present insight into Dillard as writer and the standards she demands of herself. She makes clear distinctions about writers who create for readers and those who create for movies or television. Dillard, a "readers' writer," asserts in *The Writing Life* that "the more literary the book–the more purely verbal, crafted sentence by sentence, the more imaginative, reasoned, and deep–the more likely people are to read it. The people who like to read are the people who like literature, after all, whatever that might be."

In *Living by Fiction,* Dillard attempts to define "contemporary modernists" rather than advise would-be writers on how to make a living on fiction. Key to the body of her own works, Dillard asserts that fiction by contemporary modernists is a branch of metaphysics. In such fiction, as opposed to other writing–history, for example–"one may find ideas that give meaning to life in an apparently meaningless world." This confrontation with meaninglessness is often couched in natural terms, so that for Dillard, not unlike the Transcendentalists, contemplation of the natural world can lead to insight into the foundations of existence. Unlike the Transcendentalists, however, for Dillard the existential dilemma is at the center of her writing, so that instead of producing optimism, Dillard's writing works through creating doubt. This doubt is at the center of contemporary modernism, and in her later fiction, such as *The Living,* and in the nonfictional *For the Time Being,* produced at the end of the twentieth century, Dillard has demonstrated her belief that she belongs to this category of contemporary modernists.

Teaching a Stone to Talk: Expeditions and Encounters (1982) includes "Total Eclipse," one of her best-known essays. On 26 February 1979 Dillard and Clevidence had driven five hours inland from the coast of Wash-

ington, where they were living, to be at the best site for the eclipse. The essay conveys a sense of seeing and fully experiencing an occurrence in nature, a comparatively rare experience for many people shielded and prevented from such perceptions because of work, pressures, or daily tedium. When an avalanche blocked passage across the Cascade Mountains, Dillard and her husband drove through a tunnel dug by highway crews who had bulldozed a one-way passage. Others who braved the winter weather and brought telescopes and cameras to capture this strange natural event joined them. Dillard explains that the eclipse "began with no ado. It was odd that such a well-advertised public event should have no starting gun, no overture, no introductory speaker. I should have known right then that I was out of my depth. Without pause or preamble, silent as orbits, a piece of the sun was missing; in its place we saw empty Sky."

The essay, typical of Dillard's work, then moves from what is seen literally to what is experienced figuratively or metaphorically. Reflecting on that blackness in midday, she probes what humans find in "the deeps"–violence and terror. "But if you ride these monsters deeper down, if you drop with them farther over the world's rim, you find what our sciences cannot locate or name, the substrate, the ocean or matrix or ether that buoys the rest, that gives goodness its power for good, and evil its power for evil." Everything depends, though, on humans' being awake to experiences in the natural world. Echoing Thoreau later in the essay, Dillard reminds readers that humans teach their children to wake up, to look, and to participate by word and action with other humans. She claims that adults have mastered this transition from sleep to waking, making it many times a day, but without someone to articulate the experience, they will not achieve perception: "We live half our waking lives and all of our sleeping lives in some private, useless, and insensible waters we never mention or recall. Useless, I say. Valueless, I might add–until someone hauls the wealth up to the surface and into the wide-awake city, in a form that people can use."

Besides "Total Eclipse," *Teaching a Stone to Talk* includes several other essays of interest to the student of nature writing. In "An Expedition to the Pole" Dillard moves amid layers of interpretation by moving between the natural world and human action in and perception of that world. She demonstrates her fluency with the physical and scientific world in the sections titled "The Land," "Assorted Wildlife," and "The Technology," which convey factual knowledge of polar expeditions. In the section "The People" she speaks in the realm of philosophy, religion, and metaphor. Early in the essay, while ruminating on music at a Catholic mass, Dillard establishes a primary theme for the essay: "A taste for the sublime is a greed like any other." A repeated phrase from the sections on "The Land" defines one such sublime: "The Pole of Relative Inaccessibility is 'that imaginary point on the Arctic Ocean farthest from land in any direction.'" In a pun, Dillard says, "I take this as given—[it is] the Pole of Great Price." Dillard uses this geological metaphor as a natural trope for divine action in the world, and the essay includes speculation about the cost of human dedication in achieving the sublime pole of inaccessibility and what humans carry with them on the journey. She engages this speculation through an analogy of an historic arctic exploration. The explorers who were part of Sir John Franklin's 1845 expedition to the Pole carried cut-glass crystal, china, sterling silver knives, forks, and spoons in ornate Victorian design, and a 1,200-volume library, but only a twelve-day supply of coal for a two-to-three-year voyage. None of the 138 members of the expedition survived; the Inuit have for years found frozen remains of the crew: "Accompanying one clump of frozen bodies, for instance, which incidentally showed evidence of cannibalism, were place settings of sterling silver engraved with officers' initials and family crests."

Dillard ponders the humans who would praise the Pole with absolutes such as "eternity and perfection" and acclaim the "land's spare beauty as if it were a moral or a spiritual quality" while they experienced frostbitten toes, diarrhea, bleeding gums, hunger, weakness, mental confusion, and despair. Her essay blends theological musings with these reflections on human antics. She maintains, "God needs nothing, asks nothing, and demands nothing, like the stars. It is a life with God that demands these things." At the same time she ponders, "What are the chances that God finds our failed impersonation of human dignity adorable? Or is he fooled?"

The essay offers ultimately a mediated form of Romanticism: the luminous organicism of the mind working upon a natural scene, along with the modern scientific sense of a natural environment indifferent to human quest. It also employs the *via negativa* Dillard used in *Pilgrim at Tinker Creek*. In describing Franklin's death, Dillard collapses all the metaphors of the essay into a climax: "You quit your house and your country, you quit your ship, and quit your companions in the tent, saying, 'I am just going outside and may be some time.' The light on the far side of the blizzard lures you. You walk, and one day you enter the spread heart of silence, where lands dissolve and seas become vapor and ices sublime under unknown stars." For Franklin and for readers "This is the end of the Via Negativa, the lightless edge where the slopes of knowledge dwindle, and love for its own sake, lacking an object, begins."

Dillard in 1974, after completing Pilgrim at Tinker Creek *(Hollins College)*

The theme of dedication spreads out in many avenues throughout Dillard's work, but essentially it translates into the logic that dedication can make one passionate, but passion brings excess, and excess is never "pure," because it brings with it "extra baggage." In the "extra" or the excess, one can mill around with idea, intellect, and emotion; all of this excess, because it supplies myriad intricacy, is itself a mystery. Such ruminations are at the heart of "Living Like Weasels," probably Dillard's most anthologized essay, collected in *Teaching a Stone to Talk*. In this essay Dillard uses the metaphor of the weasel to convey the idea that one should find one's true passion and cling to it furiously. Dillard uses an animal to model human behavior, showing how the weasel clings to its prey even in death by relating the story of the body of a weasel, long dead, hanging from the throat of an eagle as it flies through the air. The moment of living like a weasel, of blending with the natural world, is a moment when one can passionately cling to one's own true calling, and out of this passionately developed and mysterious excess one can rise, if one is fortunate, to the illuminated moment.

Other essays in *Teaching a Stone to Talk* continue the use of nature as metaphor for human insight into the divine. In "Life on the Rocks: The Galápagos," the Galápagos Islands become representative of a possible new world for humanity, and in "A Field of Silence," a place called "the farm" offers a reflective world where natural space and angels intermingle and provide insight to both narrator and audience. Even "Aces and Eights," the final essay of the collection, uses the natural world to usher in a new understanding of death. In the essay, named after the famous "Dead Man's Hand," the narrator confronts an image of herself as a young child while simultaneously narrating the story of Noah Very, a woodland hermit who once told her stories about Indians in the woods. The essay ends in the narrator's contemplation of death as she senses the arrival of autumn in a gust of wind that "blackens the water where it passes, like a finger closing slats."

An American Childhood, published in 1987, blurs the lines between autobiography and fiction and might be seen more as a reflection on a new life sprung in the wilderness than on imminent death. Dillard says in the prologue that when her mind has lost all of its memories of the contingencies of the world, all that "will be left, I believe, is topology: the dreaming memory of land as it lay this way and that." This concern with land and place is central to the book, so that the work moves from memory to self-insight along the axis of the natural world; her life is remembered in terms of place. Dillard allows readers to see the world as she saw it, in all its intricacies and trivialities, its paradoxes and illuminations. Whether it portrays the actual life of Annie Doak or a persona created by Annie Dillard is not significant. What is clear is that this carefully crafted memoir allows readers to meet Dillard the nature writer through her own words, emotions, and events and to be guided through her childhood into the complex consciousness of the author.

In *An American Childhood,* Dillard describes a time of her life she calls her awakening, and part of that awakening was the discovery of a book, Ann Haven Morgan's *The Field Book of Ponds and Streams* (1930), which at one point Dillard compares to *The Book of Common Prayer.* The comparison foreshadows the blend of nature and mysticism that marks many of Dillard's essays. She read this book year after year, allowing it to lead her into the world of nonfiction and the world of cheesecloth, microscopes, and an intense observation of nature. In a segment from *An American Childhood* that is frequently anthologized as a separate essay titled "Handed My Own Life," Dillard explains how getting a microscope and finally being able to see the elusive amoeba taught her a sense of independence: "I had essentially been handed my own life. . . . My days and nights were my own to fill." The excitement of seeing "paramecia . . . or daphniae, or stentors, or any of the many other creatures I had read about and never seen: volvox, the spherical algal colony; euglena with its one red eye; the elusive glassy diatom; hydra, rotifers, water bears, worms" convinced Dillard that anything was possible. That conviction and her seemingly unquenchable thirst for knowledge of the natural world have driven her writing career.

A central passage from *An American Childhood* demonstrates that drive for knowledge of the natural environment and helps display Dillard's approach to nonfiction. She compares what it feels like to be alive to standing under a waterfall: "You leave the sleeping shore deliberately; you shed your dusty clothes, pick your barefoot way over the high, slippery rocks, hold your breath, choose your footing, and step into the waterfall. The hard water pelts your skull, bangs in bits on your shoulders and arms. The strong water dashes down beside you and you feel it. . . . Can you breathe here?" Under the power of this natural rush, the force of water is greatest, and only the strength of one's neck holds the river out of one's face, but yes, Dillard exclaims, "you can breathe even here. You can learn to live like this. . . ." One has, as it were, "turned on the lights. . . . You did, by waking up: you flipped the switch, started the wind machine, kicked on the flywheel that spins the years. . . . Knowing you are alive is feeling the planet buck under you, rear, kick, and try to throw you; you hang on to the ring." Dillard assures readers and writers that learning to live under this rush is possible.

By 1988 Dillard had divorced Clevidence and married Robert D. Richardson Jr., a professor, scholar, and author of seminal biographies of Thoreau (1987) and Ralph Waldo Emerson (1995). She and Richardson took up residence in Connecticut. In 1989 Dillard published *The Writing Life,* in which she reconfigures writing from an act of production into an act of necessary grace and power. Her descriptions of writing center on a life to be lived rather than on an object to be produced, and she employs nature and place as metaphors for the type of life she encourages. The book moves between different writing retreats, such as a shed on Cape Cod and a cabin on Haro Strait in the Pacific Northwest. In these places a kind of primal power seems possible, and writing becomes a confrontation with space and time. Dillard isolates herself in these places, but at times she also engages the world around her. She converses, for instance, with Paul Glenn, a painter, who relates the dedication of Ferrar Burn, who was nearly dragged out to sea in his fierce determination to row in a log from the sea. The determination is reminiscent of Dillard's weasel, and the description becomes a battle of will among Burn, the log, the sea, and even Glenn's description. Glenn ends his description of Burn with a question for Dillard: how was her writing progressing? The story of the log is a confrontation with Dillard's work.

This confrontation sometimes seems a game, so at times Dillard invokes games to convey the point of the work. A lover of baseball, she uses baseball metaphors throughout her prose, and in *The Writing Life* she invokes those metaphors for writers themselves. In describing the sensation of writing at its best, Dillard asserts that it is like any "unmerited grace" and that if "it were a baseball, you would hit it out of the park. It is that one pitch in a thousand you see in slow motion; its wings beat slowly as a hawk's." In all such cases, however, Dillard invariably returns to both her work and her place in the world, so that the unmerited grace is pitched in terms of a confrontation with a life of writing deeply rooted to place.

This sense of being totally alive through involvement and confrontation with place and the natural environment serves as one of the major motifs of *The Living*. The work has undergone several metamorphoses, beginning as a short story published by *Harper's* in 1978 and eventually evolving into the novel version published in 1992. The version in *The Annie Dillard Reader* (1994) is a third form, a changed short story. With the underlying story, regardless of format, Dillard's intention was to write, as did Ivan Sergeevich Turgenev, about "little-bitty people in a great big landscape." She wanted to tell the story of the Northwest, but the book is largely a reflection on the past in order to renew a sense of wakefulness. Dillard covers the lives of a group of settlers in four linked communities on Bellingham Bay in Washington from 1855 to 1897. She writes about Caucasians, primarily, but also about Chinese and Native Americans, and she describes their experiences in carving out an existence in the wild. She shows that some survive all the wilderness can throw at them, while others die deaths as arbitrary as that of the frog in *Pilgrim at Tinker Creek*.

The novel and the revised short-story version probe the same familiar theme—wakefulness through or despite the natural world. Dillard's key characters symbolize the extremes. Beal Obenchain, named aptly since he and his life are chains of rigidity, functions totally by reason. He is unable to see into the heart of things. He has already killed a Chinese man: "lashing him to a piling under the old wharf one midnight; [they] left him to drown when the tide came in." A careful thinker, Obenchain even leaves a lantern so the Chinaman can watch the tide come in. Obenchain's cruelty is calculated: "he was a stranded mystic, an embodiment of reason's directing will, who alone understood the Chinaman's luck in sacrificing his body for this experiment on his mind." Readers can see Dillard's conception of sacrifice

Dust jacket for Dillard's 1977 book, written while she was living on an isolated island in Puget Sound (Richland County Public Library)

working here. She creates in Obenchain a man of dedication to the intellect, to science, with "access to metagnostical structures, a man of methods conceived in purity, who knew secrets."

The physical setting where Obenchain goes to think is the mudflats, where images of death abound. One emblem of death, an old shark carcass, has ceased changing and looks "like a creosoted log, or a lava tube, or a vein of coal or a sewer pipe." Obenchain, who lives for death, threatens to kill Clare Fishburn, a man who has been his teacher, but Obenchain instead observes how Fishburn lives with the reality of imminent death: "You tell a man his life is in your hands, and, miraculously, his life is in your hands. You own him insofar as he believes you. You own him as God owns a man, to the degree of his faith."

Fishburn represents Obenchain's polar opposite. His name is symbolic: "clare" means clarity; the "fish" is emblematic of Christ; and "burn" refers to fire or flame. Thus, a literal translation of his name is "clear Christ aflame." Fishburn is a family man who would do a favor for anyone; he hates anything fussy or detailed; "he enjoyed enjoyment, he sought deeds and found tasks, he was a giant in joy, racing and thoughtless, suggestible, a bountiful child." Readers follow this man and his wife–since Fishburn confides in her that he is going to be killed–living in the face of death. This contrast of Fishburn's life and imminent death creates a gripping narrative focused on the natural world and the Romantic sense of the inner world. Because Fishburn expects death, he each day observes the natural world with a sense that it will be his last vision of the place. The result of living this way is for Fishburn a new, awakened life.

Fishburn constantly chooses life in the face of death, and Obenchain grows more annoyed and hateful toward this man "in his control." Ultimately, Obenchain exerts his power one more time. He arranges to meet Fishburn and tell him that he is not going to be killed. Fishburn's response is the climactic realization of life in death: even as the earth is plowing the men and horses under, no generation sees it happen, and the broken new fields grow up forgetting. Fishburn, therefore, "was burrowing in the light upstream. All the living were breasting into the crest of the present together. All men and women and children ran up a field as wide as earth, opening time like a path in the grass, and he was borne along with them. No, he said, peeling the light back, walking in the sky toward home; no."

The Living demonstrates Dillard's ability to use the physical, scientific perspective of the nature writer and the visionary eye of the Romantic writer to convey the consummate human journey, toward "the light upstream," toward an intensified sense of life that is Dillard's representation of "perfection." Perfection allows the stuff of life to invade and engorge, and eventually the pleasure of life is made more acute by the knowledge of its transitory nature. Fishburn can burrow in light upstream as Dillard in *Pilgrim at Tinker Creek* faces upstream to the unknown future where the "wave that explodes over my head . . . the live water and light" from "undisclosed sources" brings renewed "world without end."

In *For the Time Being* Dillard continues her epistemological interrogation of the fundamental questions about life, death, and the natural world. In an author's note she comments, "This is a nonfiction first-person narrative, but it is not intimate, and its narratives keep breaking. Its form is unusual, its scenes are remote, its focus wide, and its tone austere. Its pleasures are almost purely mental." Dillard uses several natural subjects that recur throughout, including scenes from a paleontologist's explorations in China, a natural history of sand, individual clouds and their moments in time, and human birth defects. The book is Emersonian in one sense: it

presents a collection of philosophical ruminations that blend with natural metaphors. Unlike Emerson, however, Dillard finds musings in more-recent philosophical considerations, particularly those of Teilhard de Chardin and Hasidic Jews. *For the Time Being* also includes references to journeys, such as the journey in 1982 when Dillard was invited to be part of a cultural delegation of scholars traveling to China. References to Chinese culture recur, particularly to a massive excavation site in China where the first Chinese emperor, Qin, had buried sculptures of thousands of individual soldiers.

Readers encounter, then, reflections on suffering and death, and on inexplicable mysteries such as human deformities and natural elements such as the clouds. Each image, metaphor, aphorism, and encounter allows Dillard to assemble her treatise on nature, life, death, and humans' relation to nature and God, and to raise more questions for readers to consider. These questions are often couched in the confrontation of life and death that is typical of the natural world: "*The Mahabharata* says, 'Of all the world's wonders, which is most wonderful? That no man, though he sees others dying all around him, believes that he himself will die.'" Dillard challenges this human ignorance and pride: "Is it not late? A late time to be living? Are not our generations the crucial ones?" Almost immediately she responds to her own questions: "These times of ours are ordinary times, a slice of life like any other." Dillard, with St. Augustine, notes that while humans of each generation are lost in their own tragedies, triumphs, and earthshaking events, in the face of the mysteries of life, humans must learn that "We are talking about God. What wonder is it that you do not understand? If you do understand, then it is not God."

Sarah Humble Johnson has commented that "Dillard views herself through much of her work as a poet-priestess, a visionary artist intent on receiving the vision, or epiphany, and then transmitting the moment through her exquisite prose." *For the Time Being* is a book that disturbs and confirms en route to epiphany. Readers of *For the Time Being* face an intense experience in existential ruminations that sometimes assault wisdom, as in Dillard's reflection that the God humanity embraces is more likely "to kill by AIDS or kidney failure, heart disease, childhood leukemia, or sudden infant death syndrome–than he is pitching lightning bolts at pedestrians, triggering rock slides, or setting fires." She points out that "the very least likely things for which God might be responsible are what insurers call 'acts of God.'"

Annie Dillard, who holds an adjunct professorship and is a writer in residence at Wesleyan University, writes in a way that defies easy categorization–not surprising considering the eclectic range of professors throughout her

*Dust jacket for Dillard's 1999 book, which she has described as offering the reader
"pleasures" that are "almost purely mental" (Richland County Public Library)*

academic life, her acute sensitivity throughout childhood, the wide range of interests her childhood allowed her to pursue, and her relentless pursuit of ultimate meaning. Johnson has remarked that "Language theory, ecology, art, literary criticism, religion, and history, among other matters, are brilliantly woven into a soft, mystically intriguing collage, which, in one sense, defies genre definition but in a more important sense announces the emergence of a new genre that uses illumination at its core." The bulk of her writing is prose nonfiction, but Dillard's writing includes a potent blend of poetic language and a scientific, perceptive observation of nature. As Johnson explains, Dillard brings into her discussions knowledge from a whole spectrum of thought, "referencing physics, literature, numerous religious traditions, anthropology, medicine and folklore. . . . Through her stories, she transports to the mystical dimension—her stories invoke an understanding of the mystical that goes beyond words. Somehow, you're reading what seems just like another bird story, and it suddenly turns into much more." Readers experience a "writer's writer" capable of rendering the language exquisitely, and "an extremely well-read intellectual . . . who has become as much a metaphor as the creek she once portrayed."

Interviews:

Philip Yancey, "A Face Aflame: An Interview with Annie Dillard," *Christianity Today,* 22 (5 May 1978), pp. 14–19;

Karla Hammond, "Drawing the Curtains: An Interview with Annie Dillard," *Bennington Review* (10 April 1981): 32.

Bibliographies:

William Sheick, "A Bibliography of Writings by Annie Dillard," in *Contemporary Women Writers: Narrative Strategies,* edited by Catherine Rainwater and Sheick (Lexington: University Press of Kentucky, 1985), pp. 64–67;

Dawn Evans Radford, "Annie Dillard: A Bibliographical Survey," *Bulletin of Bibliography,* 52 (June 1994): 181–194.

Biography:

Sandra Stahlman Elliott, "Annie Dillard: Biography" <http://www.well.com/user/elliotts/smse_dillard.html>.

References:

C. D. Albin, "A Ray of Relation: Transcendental Echoes in Annie Dillard's *Pilgrim at Tinker Creek,*" *Jour-*

nal of the American Studies Association of Texas, 23 (October 1992): 17–31;

Vance Bourjaily, "Contemporary Modernists–A Dreadful Mouthful," *New York Times,* 9 May 1982;

Mary Cantwell, "A Pilgrim's Progress," *New York Times,* 26 April 1992;

Marc Chenetier, "Tinkering, Extravagance: Thoreau, Melville, and Annie Dillard," *Critique Studies in Modern Fiction,* 31, no. 3 (Spring 1990): 157–172;

Jim Cheney, "The Waters of Separation: Myth and Ritual in Annie Dillard's *Pilgrim at Tinker Creek,*" *Journal of Feminist Studies in Religion* (Spring 1990);

Suzanne Clark, "Annie Dillard: The Woman in Nature and the Subject of Nonfiction," in *Literary Nonfiction: Theory, Criticism, Pedagogy,* edited by Chris Anderson (Carbondale: Southern Illinois University Press, 1989);

Robert Paul Dunn, "The Artist as Nun: Theme, Tone, and Vision in the Writings of Annie Dillard," *Studia Mystica,* 1, no. 4 (1978): 17–31;

John C. Elder, "John Muir and the Literature of Wilderness," *Massachusetts Review,* 22 (1981): 375–386;

Helen H. Hitchcock, "Annie Dillard: Mystique of Nature," *Communio* (Winter 1978): 388–392;

Sandra Humble Johnson, *The Space Between: Literary Epiphany in the Work of Annie Dillard* (Kent, Ohio: Kent State University Press, 1992);

Anna Logan Lawson, "Thinker, Poet, Pilgrim," *Hollins* (May 1974): 12;

Sara Maitland, "Spend It All, Shoot It, Play It, Lose It," *New York Times,* 17 September 1989;

Beverly Matiko, "Fictionalizing the Audience in Literary Nonfiction: A Study of the Essays of Annie Dillard and Lewis Thomas," dissertation, University of Alberta, 1993;

James I. McClintock, *Nature's Kindred Spirits: Aldo Leopold, Joseph Wood Krutch, Edward Abbey, Annie Dillard, and Gary Snyder* (Madison: University of Wisconsin Press, 1994);

McClintock, "'Pray Without Ceasing': Annie Dillard among the Nature Writers," *Cithara,* 30, no. 1 (November 1990): 44–57;

Mary Davidson McConahay, "Into the Bladelike Arms of God: The Quest for Meaning through Symbolic Language in Thoreau and Annie Dillard," *Denver Quarterly,* 20 (Fall 1985): 103–116;

Gary McIlroy, "*Pilgrim at Tinker Creek* and the Burden of Science," *American Literature,* 59, no. 1 (March 1987);

McIlroy, "The Sparer Climate for Which I Longed: *Pilgrim at Tinker Creek* and the Spiritual Imperatives of Fall," *Thoreau Quarterly,* 16, nos. 3–4 (Summer-Fall 1986);

James A. Papa Jr., "Water-Signs: Place and Metaphor in Dillard and Thoreau," in *Thoreau's Sense of Place: Essays in American Environmental Writing,* edited by Richard J. Schneider (Iowa City: University of Iowa Press, 2000);

Nancy C. Parrish, *Lee Smith, Annie Dillard, and the Hollins Group: A Genesis of Writers* (Baton Rouge: Louisiana State University Press, 1998);

Margaret Loewen Reimer, "The Dialectical Vision of Annie Dillard's *Pilgrim at Tinker Creek,*" *Critique: Studies in Modern Fiction,* 24, no. 3 (1983): 182–191;

Bruce Ronda, "Annie Dillard and the Fire of God," *Christian Century* (18 May 1983): 483–486;

Ronald Schleifer, "Annie Dillard: Narrative Fringe," in *Contemporary American Women Writers: Narrative Strategies,* edited by Catherine Rainwater and William Scheick (Lexington: University Press of Kentucky, 1985);

Scott Slovic, *Seeking Awareness in American Nature Writing: Henry Thoreau, Annie Dillard, Edward Abbey, Wendell Berry, Barry Lopez* (Salt Lake City: University of Utah, 1992);

Linda Smith, *Annie Dillard* (New York: Twayne, 1991);

Grace Suh, "Ideas Are Tough; Irony Is Easy," *Yale Herald,* 4 October 1996;

Steve Wegenstein, "Nature in Annie Dillard's *The Living,*" in *The Image of Nature in Literature, the Media, and Society,* edited by Will Wright and Steven Kaplan (Pueblo, Colo.: Society for the Interdisciplinary Study of Social Imagery, 1993), pp. 88–93.

Gretel Ehrlich

(21 January 1946 –)

Marie Bongiovanni
Lebanon Valley College

See also the Ehrlich entry in *DLB 212: Twentieth-Century American Western Writers, Second Series.*

BOOKS: *Geode/Rock Body* (Santa Barbara: Capricorn, 1970);

To Touch the Water, edited by Tom Trusky (Boise, Idaho: Ahsahta Press, 1981);

The Solace of Open Spaces (New York: Viking, 1985);

Wyoming Stories, published with *City Tales* by Edward Hoagland (Santa Barbara: Capra Press, 1986);

Heart Mountain (New York: Viking, 1988; London: Heinemann, 1989);

Drinking Dry Clouds: Stories from Wyoming (Santa Barbara: Capra Press, 1991);

Islands, the Universe, Home (New York: Viking, 1991);

Arctic Heart: A Poem Cycle (Santa Barbara: Capra Press, 1992);

A Match to the Heart: One Woman's Story of Being Struck by Lightning (New York: Pantheon, 1994; London: Fourth Estate, 1995);

Yellowstone: Land of Fire and Ice, photographs by Willard and Kathy Clay (San Francisco: HarperCollins, 1995);

Questions of Heaven: The Chinese Journey of an American Buddhist (Boston: Beacon, 1997);

The Horse Whisperer: An Illustrated Companion to the Major Motion Picture, text by Erhlich, photographs by Jay Dusard and others (New York: Dell, 1998);

A Blizzard Year: Timmy's Almanac of the Seasons (New York: Hyperion, 1999);

Cowboy Island: Farewell to a Ranching Legacy, text by Ehrlich, edited by Nita Vail (Santa Barbara: Santa Cruz Island Foundation, 2000);

John Muir: Nature's Visionary (Washington, D.C.: National Geographic, 2000);

This Cold Heaven: Seven Seasons in Greenland (New York: Pantheon, 2001).

PRODUCED SCRIPTS: *Autopsy,* television, PBS, 1969;

By Pass, television, PBS, 1972;

Gretel Ehrlich (photograph by William Webb; from the dust jacket for Islands, the Universe, Home, *1991)*

Journey, television, PBS, 1973;

One-Man Sawmill, television, PBS, 1974;

Counting on Breath, television, PBS, 1976;

Lives, television, PBS, 1976.

RECORDINGS: *Ahsahta Cassette Sampler: 14 Western Poets Read from Their Ahsahta Volumes,* read by Ehrlich and others, Boise, Idaho, Ahsahta Press, 1983;

Gretel Ehrlich Reads to Touch the Water, read by Ehrlich, Boise, Idaho, Boise State University, 1983;

The Solace of Open Spaces, read by Ehrlich, Minocqua, Wisconsin, NorthWord Audio Press, 1988;

Thoreau and the American Nature Tradition, read by Ehrlich, Key West Literary Seminar, Key West, Florida, 1996.

OTHER: *Legacy of Light,* contributions by Ehrlich, edited by Constance Sullivan, introduction by Peter Schjeldahl (New York: Knopf, 1987), pp. 17–21;

"Spring," in *On Nature: Nature, Landscape, and Natural History,* compiled by Ehrlich, edited by Daniel Halpern (San Francisco: North Point, 1987), pp. 172–181;

John Muir, *My First Summer in the Sierra,* introduction by Ehrlich (New York: Penguin, 1987);

"River History," in *Montana Spaces: Essays and Photographs in Celebration of Montana,* edited by William Kittredge (New York: Lyons, 1988), pp. 69–72;

"Life at Close Range," in *The Writer on Her Work: Women's Prose and Poetry about Nature,* edited by Janet Sternburg (New York: Norton, 1991), pp. 175–179;

Denise Chávez, Linda Ellerbee, Linda Hogan, Teresa Jordan, Brenda Peterson, and Sherman Apt Russel, *Writing Down the River: Into the Heart of the Grand Canyon,* foreword by Ehrlich (Flagstaff, Ariz.: Northland, 1998);

"Cornwallis Island: Canada," in *Patagonia: Notes from the Field,* edited by Nora Gallagher (San Francisco: Chronicle, 1999).

SELECTED PERIODICAL PUBLICATIONS–
UNCOLLECTED: "In Wyoming: Horse and Rider Learn Together," *Time,* 128 (6 October 1986): 16–17;

"Surrender to the Landscape," *Harper's Bazaar* (September 1987): 24–27;

"The Pond," *Sierra* (May/June 1990): 62–63;

"This Autumn Morning," *Antaeus* (Spring/Autumn 1990): 358–369;

"Time on Ice: Images and Encounters Frozen in the Arctic," *Harper's Bazaar* (March 1992): 68–72;

"A House Born of Storms," *Architectural Digest,* 54, no. 6 (1997): 46–50;

"Ray Hunt: The Cowboy Sage," *Shambhala Sun,* 6 (July 1998): 22–29, 64;

"On the Road with God's Fool," *New York Times Magazine* (6 June 1999): 90–93.

For most of her life, Gretel Ehrlich has been on the move, and her adventures have led her east and west and back again. Aspects of these adventures are revealed in autobiographical details woven throughout her accounts of life in the American West, travels in the Far East, and many trips to the Arctic. Whether she is writing poetry, fiction, or nonfiction about Wyoming, China, or Greenland, her keen observations and descriptions of the natural world evoke a strong sense of place. According to her friend, writer Pico Iyer, "the connection between two different kinds of nature,

within us and without, has always been her subject, and the way the seasons pass inside us and we find in the world a mirroring, or a guide, for our own inner geography." She has been described as a nature writer, a Western writer, and a travel writer, and she often blends elements of autobiography, ethnography, philosophy, and natural history into poetic and lyrical prose.

Ehrlich was born on 21 January 1946 in Santa Barbara, California. Her parents, Grant Ehrlich, a successful businessman, and Gretchen Woerz Ehrlich, raised Gretel in Montecito on the coast of California. She developed an appreciation for nature and the outdoors during her formative years, while learning to sail and ride horses. At the age of six, she knew that someday she wanted to write a novel; at twelve, she aspired to a career in painting, and as a fourteen-year-old student in boarding school, she began to study Zen Buddhism, a practice she has continued through the years. Even in her early years, Ehrlich was fascinated by words and ideas. Her love of language was influenced by seven years of studying Latin, and she still reads poetry every day, including works by Catullus, Horace, and Virgil in Latin.

In the 1960s she enrolled in Bennington College in Vermont to study dance, then abandoned that pursuit and headed west again to study moviemaking at the University of California at Los Angeles. In 1967 she started working as an editor for educational television in New York City, where she attended the New School for Social Research. The following year she returned to California and started to write screenplays and to direct documentaries. Until 1976 Ehrlich worked on various projects for the Public Broadcasting System (PBS). While writing, editing, and producing documentaries for PBS, she explored other forms of writing and created a series of poems. Her first published collection of poems appeared in the chapbook *Geode/Rock Body* (1970). In these early poems, Ehrlich explores Eastern philosophy and Zen Buddhism, and breaks down boundaries between internal and external landscapes. Her poetry investigates relationships between the body, the spirit, and the natural world as well as physical and spiritual aspects of life in the West. In "Poem for a Geologist," for example, Ehrlich writes:

granite for me;
granite and crystal and deep red apples;
learn darkness, for night will come;
learn darkness, and surround it with
granite and berries and poppies;
go to the river that cannot be stepped into twice,
know that it is not a mirror to be looked into,
but to be looked through, to where
the pebbles shift at the bottom;
for there is nothing but granite and light.

Ehrlich's passion for Wyoming, her focus in many works, was triggered in 1976 when she received a grant from PBS to create a documentary movie about sheepherders in the Big Horn Mountains of Wyoming. As she reveals in later essays and poems, she soon became enamored of the Western landscape, characters, and the way of life of the herding and ranching community. She had planned to work on the sheepherding documentary with David Hancock, a moviemaker and the man whom she loved, but at the age of twenty-nine Hancock was diagnosed with cancer. When he became unable to continue work on the project and had to return to New York, Ehrlich stayed in Wyoming to work on the movie *Herders* throughout the summer of 1976. Hancock died in September of that year, not long before the completion of the documentary, and Ehrlich ended her career in educational television.

Overcome by grief, she decided to stay in the West, traveling and "drifting" around for a while. Following the suggestion of John Lewis Hopkin, a sheepherder whom she had befriended while working on *Herders,* she eventually moved onto a ranch in the Big Horn Basin of Wyoming. For the first time in decades, she felt a sense of community, and over the next few years she learned how to herd sheep, rope cattle, and deliver lambs and calves. In 1978 she decided to leave the ranch to spend the winter in solitude in a one-room log cabin on a river that flows out of Yellowstone National Park. She had sought a quiet place to write and had found one, along with a place to endure one of her loneliest winters. While Ehrlich was living in the cabin, she experienced one of the worst winters on record in Wyoming. Beginning in early November, it snowed almost incessantly; at times, during subzero temperatures—about fifty degrees below zero—she was without sufficient wood to heat the cabin. Despite such hardships, she continued to write and, while living in the cabin, created a cycle of poems. These poems were published in *To Touch the Water* (1981), her second book of poetry, in which she describes interactions and intimacies between humans and other facets of the natural world. Throughout the book, she focuses on Wyoming and her experience with its harsh and gentle extremes.

These poems provide readers with a sense of the physical landscape of Wyoming as well as some of the rugged yet gentle characters who appear in Ehrlich's later works. For example, in "A Sheepherder's Binge" she introduces Pinkey, a distinctive character who plays a role in Ehrlich's later fiction. In "A Sheepherder Named John," to whom she dedicated this collection, readers meet a character who appears again in her essays. She also refers to another unnamed character, most likely her deceased lover, in another poem,

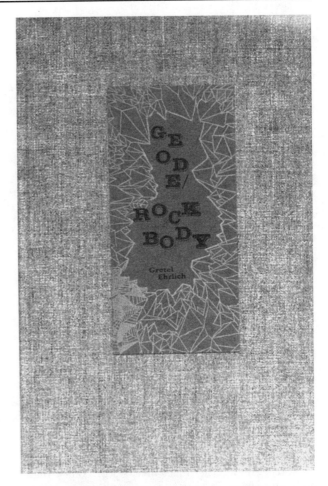

Binding for Ehrlich's first book, a collection of nature poems published in 1970 (Ken Lopez catalogue, 2000)

"Self-Portrait Through Four Ages, Four Phases of the Moon." The continued impact of her lover's death on her life is clearly evident in another poem, "For David," in which she explores the conflation of absence and presence. Her preoccupation with Eastern philosophy is evident in many of her works, in which she often highlights her perception of the illusion of differences in life and death, emptiness and fullness, and other questionable binary oppositions.

In June 1979 Ehrlich left the cabin near Yellowstone Park and moved into the vicinity of Shell, Wyoming, a small, isolated town in which she started to write the collection of essays that became her first nonfiction book. *The Solace of Open Spaces* (1985), which had begun as "a series of raw journal entries sent to a friend," as she describes its origins in the introduction, earned her widespread acclaim. In 1986 she received the Harold D. Vursell Memorial Award from the American Academy and Institute of Arts and Letters, and in 1987 the Writer's Award from the Mrs. Giles Whiting Foundation. "With her first book, *The Solace of Open*

Spaces, Ehrlich proved herself to be a prose poet of impressive talent and breadth," wrote Michael Dorris for *The Los Angeles Times Book Review* (10 July 1994). "Her vivid, intelligent meditations on the land, especially the wide horizons of a Wyoming ranch, invited readers to experience an almost mystical connection to an environment few had ever known directly." This collection recounts Ehrlich's impressions as she learns to herd sheep and cattle and discovers the tightly knit community that bridges wide-open spaces in the West. In essays such as "From a Sheepherder's Notebook: Three Days" she presents detailed descriptions of the land, the sky, the weather, and her response to a radically different way of life she had experienced in the East. Full of vivid metaphor and imagery, this book grew out of Ehrlich's grief after Hancock's death. Her writing, her involvement in the ranching community, and the restorative power of the natural world helped her begin to come to terms with her loss.

In *The Solace of Open Spaces* Ehrlich writes that she had sought a "numbness" in Wyoming but instead was reawakened and inspired by the vitality of the ranching community. She describes Westerners' relationship to land, to animals, and to each other, and in concise yet descriptive profiles, she introduces readers to herders, ranchers, and other men and women in the community. In "About Men" she dispels the myth of the American cowboy, and in other essays she sometimes reinforces and at other times breaks down other Western stereotypes.

She married Press Stephens of Shell, Wyoming, and took up residence on a small sheep ranch; Stephens, consequently, is mentioned several times in *The Solace of Open Spaces,* including in the chapter titled "Just Married." In a review for *Western Humanities Review* (1986) Edward Lueders described *The Solace of Open Spaces* as a "sensitive yet tough-minded narrative [that] follows Ehrlich's own story into the Wyoming settings that it absorbs and reflects so authentically." He ranked Ehrlich among a group that included such writers as Edward Abbey, Annie Dillard, Ivan Doig, Barry Lopez, Ann Zwinger, and Terry Tempest Williams, who are providing "literary redefinition" of the "ethographic diversity" of the United States. Lynn Ross-Bryant, in her 1990 article for the *Journal of the American Academy of Religion,* also compared Ehrlich to "twentieth-century literary naturalists" Annie Dillard and Barry Lopez and examined the way that these authors "turn again to nature and find there the sacred." *The Solace of Open Spaces* received many other favorable reviews, but it also received some mixed reviews. C. L. Rawlins, in *Hungry Mind Review* (Summer 1996), wrote that "*The Solace of Open Spaces . . .* is loathed by Wyoming's agricultural working class (real ranchers and cowboys as opposed to owners of rural properties)." But he also said that "it sells like crazy each summer, when the Golden Horde engulfs poor Jackson Hole." Christopher Merrill described Ehrlich's as "a refreshing, an almost artless approach to the essay," but he suggested that if Ehrlich had spent more time editing the "series of raw journal entries," the book would have been stronger and more coherent.

Ehrlich's first collection of prose fiction, *Wyoming Stories* (1986), was bound with Edward Hoagland's *City Tales.* In the foreword, Ehrlich explains that she wrote these stories in 1985 in the same order in which they appear in the collection. The stories take place in northwest Wyoming near the Heart Mountain Relocation Camp, an internment camp for Japanese and Japanese Americans during World War II. Ehrlich writes that she was confronted with "a cast of characters who would not quiet down." Readers encounter such characters as the rancher McKay, the heavy-drinking Pinkey, Bobby Korematsu, and Kai Nagouchi. The intersection of the lives of characters from the camp with those from the ranch highlights issues of identity, loss, loneliness, and what might be described as love.

Some of these characters and stories appear in Ehrlich's novel, *Heart Mountain,* published in 1988 and described by Gregory Morris as "a work of Western fiction rooted profoundly in the historical, cultural, and emotional contexts of the American World War II experience." The seeds for the novel had been planted during Ehrlich's formative years on the West Coast. She told James Wackett in an interview published in 1990 that while she was growing up, she had had many Japanese American friends who had been born in the camps. For years she had been concerned about the plight of those friends, and since Heart Mountain was relatively close to her ranch, she decided to write about "issues of racism, war, and peace" amid a Western setting. The novel explores the characters' relationships with each other and with the natural world. "At the Big Horn river . . . [Carol] saw a tree with five herons perched in its branches. . . . The bright sky silhouetted them. She pointed out the tree to Willard, and he raised his willow so that it looked like part of the tree, as if the birds had come to rest on its pale branches. 'It's our tree of life,' she whispered." The characters in *Heart Mountain* appear again in *Drinking Dry Clouds: Stories from Wyoming* (1991), a collection of stories that Ehrlich wrote in the winter of 1989–1990. In this collection, the characters tell their stories in the first person, thereby providing insights into their lives that were not revealed in *Wyoming Stories* or *Heart Mountain.* The collection includes four stories that appear in *Wyoming Stories* along with ten other stories that take place after the end of World War II.

Ehrlich returns again to nonfiction in *Islands, the Universe, Home* (1991), a collection of essays that includes interior and exterior journeys through the seasons in her life. The book received favorable reviews, and critics enjoyed impressions of Ehrlich's travels through various regions, including Japan, the Channel Islands off the coast of California, and a tiny island in a lake on her Wyoming ranch. In various essays in this book, as well as in much of her other writing, Ehrlich explores the nature of her journey—physical and spiritual and something more. In "The Bride to Heaven," set in Japan, the author writes, "I have come here to sniff out *Shizen*—the Japanese word for a spontaneous self-renewing, inherently sacred natural world of which humans are an inextricable part. I wanted to see how and where holiness reveals itself, to search for those 'thin spots' on the ground where divinity rises as if religion were a function of geology itself." Despite, or perhaps because of, her peripatetic predisposition, she conveys a sense of longing for a place to call home, a place where she can understand the relationship between spirit, mind, and heart.

In the summer of 1991, after visiting a biologist and friend in the Canadian High Arctic, Ehrlich wrote *Arctic Heart: A Poem Cycle* (1992). Choreographer Siobhan Davies had commissioned these poems to accompany a ballet. Following Ehrlich's stay in a tent on frozen seas with her friend Brendan Kelly, she flew directly from the Northwest Territories to London, where rehearsals for the ballet were under way. An intense collaboration took place between the poet, choreographer, composer, set designer, and the dancers, and the performance included a dramatic backdrop and movements that reflected the rich, sensual imagery in these poems. In her next book, *A Match to the Heart: One Woman's Story of Being Struck by Lightning* (1994), Ehrlich mentions her trip to London for the opening night performance of this ballet. This book vividly describes her near-death encounter with lightning and a lengthy physical, psychological, and spiritual transformation following that experience. Ehrlich had been struck by lightning in August 1991 while living alone on the ranch in Wyoming, separated from her husband, whom she later divorced. Late one afternoon she had gone out for a walk, accompanied only by her two dogs. After the lightning struck, she lost consciousness and awoke to find herself lying in a pool of blood. A resultant brain stem injury led to repeated losses of consciousness; her parents' intervention helped her find proper medical treatment on the West Coast. She describes her journey back and forth between Wyoming and her native California, and, as in other works, she again searches for "home." Her words vividly convey the loss, loneliness, and sense of exile from Wyoming that accompanied her

Dust jacket for Ehrlich's 1991 book, essays in which she explores the nature of physical and spiritual journeys (Richland County Public Library)

lengthy recuperation process. Some critics claimed that Ehrlich did not include enough personal information in this book, while others found it to be one of her most revealing works.

In 1995 Ehrlich published *Yellowstone: Land of Fire and Ice;* she had first visited the Yellowstone region soon after moving to Wyoming, about twenty years prior to the publication of the book. In the introduction, she explains that she was calmed by her awareness that she lived in relatively close proximity to Yellowstone Park. This book, based on many experiences in the park, reveals Ehrlich's deep appreciation of the wilderness and the intricate web of interrelationships that characterize the extensive ecosystem of Yellowstone. The author reveals her astute perceptions as a naturalist and blends them with history and natural history to create an engaging account as well as an excellent introduction to the many facets of the Yellowstone region. "Far inside the deep quiet of the park, I understood that this place is truly a living organism. . . . Everywhere in the park death is replaced by life and life by death, and mountains, lakes, talus slopes, petrified forests, and every community of plants, each herd of animals, every migration of songbirds and shorebirds that soars through is connected." Complemented by the brilliant photography of Willard and Cathy Clay, the narrative opens amid snow squalls in springtime and ends with autumn in the air. The combination of images and text introduces readers to the seasonal rhythms of the dramatic and diverse landscape of Yellowstone Park.

Ehrlich's next book, *Questions of Heaven: The Chinese Journey of an American Buddhist* (1997), is an account of her 1995 trip to China. Her journey was prompted by a desire "to pick up the threads of a once flourishing Buddhist culture," which she hoped she would find "in their sacred mountains." She had initially set out to climb four mountains but revised her plan after encountering obstacles while ascending the first, Emei Shan. Although Mao Tse-tung's regime and the Communist Party had destroyed the social and religious infrastructure of China, Ehrlich had hoped to discover traces of the cultural legacy of the country. Ehrlich seems simultaneously satisfied and disappointed in her quest, especially saddened by the losses prompted by the Cultural Revolution. *Questions of Heaven* received some favorable reviews and was described as superior travel writing, but Alexandra Hall, in *The New York Times Book Review* (18 May 1997), questioned how Ehrlich as a visitor could have discovered "the heart of a lost culture" in such a relatively brief period of time.

In *The Horse Whisperer: An Illustrated Companion to the Major Motion Picture* (1998), Ehrlich describes the context of the creation of the movie and its setting in southwestern Montana. The book opens with a foreword by Robert Redford, who directed and starred in the film. Ehrlich's text follows, and she sets the stage for the movie by describing the impact of the Western landscape on history, values, and the ranchers' way of life. Ehrlich contextualizes the motion picture within the broader physical and social landscape of the West and draws attention to the interaction between ranchers and the land. She highlights the rhythms of ranch life and introduces readers to the seasonal cycles of birthing calves, repairing fences, turning out cattle onto spring range, and moving them to higher elevations. *The Horse Whisperer: An Illustrated Companion to the Major Motion Picture* continues themes found in *The Solace of Open Spaces* and other books, and Ehrlich offers insights into life in the American West, conveying a sense of place that she claims is gained only after an individual has "put in some time." Accompanied by color photographs provided by Jay Dusard and others, the book presents insights into how the movie was put together, including

details on the construction of the set, the ranch house, and a creek house. And, as in much of her writing, Ehrlich explores the concept of finding a home and relationships between internal and external realms. The healing of an injured and troubled horse parallels the healing that takes place in some of the other characters.

Ehrlich's first book for children, *A Blizzard Year: Timmy's Almanac of the Seasons,* was published in 1999. Like much of Ehrlich's writing, this story is structured around seasonal rhythms, and relationships between natural cycles and the lives of ranchers and sheepherders figure prominently throughout the text. Ehrlich's descriptions of expansive vistas and snow-covered landscapes echo those in her previous books, and the book presents a young reader's version of many of Ehrlich's previous essays about the American West. The story is told from the perspective of Timmy, a thirteen-year-old girl who lives with her family in a one-hundred-year-old log cabin in Wyoming. The family, having lost all of its calves and most of its cows during a blizzard, faces the risk of losing the ranch. Amid Ehrlich's portrayal of Timmy's worries and concerns, she presents an engaging description of life on the ranch. "May is the month of apple trees flowering, of meltwater coming down, of Indian paintbrush blooming, of Canada geese and ravens hatching, and blue herons incubating eggs. . . . It is the month when we work the hardest, irrigating, putting in a garden, fixing fences, and riding colts. As snow melts, we continue moving cows and calves, ewes and lambs farther away from the ranch, and higher in the mountains." As in *The Solace of Open Spaces,* a sense of community is dominant, even across vast spaces, and the economic impact of the blizzard prompts the narrator and her young friends to seek a way to save the ranch. Their efforts, in turn, elicit a positive response from an even larger community. In the end, the ranch is saved. Throughout the book, Ehrlich uses imagery and personification to reveal connections between different forms of life, thereby expanding the notion of community to encompass more than humans. "That's how it is on our ranch. Animals, people, land, water, plants, trees, bugs, fish, birds—we all belong to each other."

A community embracing all forms of life is also evident in *John Muir: Nature's Visionary* (2000), published more than a decade after Ehrlich wrote an introduction for the 1987 edition of Muir's book, *My First Summer in the Sierras,* originally published in 1911. *John Muir* presents a biographical overview of the "patron saint of American wilderness" and leads readers on the visionary's journey from Scotland through the wilds of California, Alaska, and other regions of America and its West. This inspiring portrait traces Muir's evolution from naturalist to activist and conveys a sense of his

Dust jacket for Ehrlich's 1994 book, an autobiographical account of a near-death experience while living alone on a ranch in Wyoming (Richland County Public Library)

critical role in the conservation movement. His influence on Ehrlich's perceptions and writing is evident throughout the book, as when she describes how Muir discovered "wonder and solace . . . in the open sky." She also describes his transformative experience in the Sierra Nevada Mountains of California. Dramatic spectrums of light and shadow are displayed in contemporary color photographs that accompany the text, along with Muir's words and sketches, and historical photographs of Muir, his descendants, and the landscapes that inspired him.

Ehrlich's love of landscapes and light is evident in *This Cold Heaven: Seven Seasons in Greenland* (2001), an inspiring and at times riveting account of her fascination with the culture and topography that she first discovered in the summer of 1993.

Part jewel, part eye, part lighthouse, part recumbent monolith, the ice is a bright spot on the upper tier of the globe where the world's purse strings have been pulled tight, nudging the tops of the three continents together. Summers, it burns in the sun, and in the dark it hoards moonlight. I liked how the island was almost uninhabitable, how ice had pushed humans all the way to the edge, where they lived in tight villages on a fili-

gree of rock, how on topo maps the white massifs were marked 'unexplored.'

In the preface she suggests that during her initial trip to Greenland, she was still recovering from the effects on her heart of the lightning strike, which had prevented her from spending time at the altitudes where she felt most "at home." She soon discovered that in Greenland, she felt euphoric above a certain latitude and experienced a feeling that she had previously experienced only above a certain altitude. For seven seasons she traveled to some of these villages by air, by boat, and often by dogsled, taking risks and enduring hardships that she vividly describes in this book. The accounts of her own adventures are interspersed among those of early Arctic explorers such as Knud Rasmussen and his partner, Peter Freuchen. The text is enriched by incorporation of a variety of excerpts from these early explorers' diaries, journals, and books as well as threads of Inuit legend and lore. In fact, Ehrlich had carried volumes of Rasmussen's expedition notes with her while traveling by dogsled, and she stopped at some of the villages along his routes. Ehrlich shares Rasmussen's curiosity and sense of adventure, along with his interest in gathering and recording Inuit stories, customs, dreams, ideas, and beliefs. Her book includes some of the stories Rasmussen had collected and some of her own and reveals ways in which the native culture had been altered by the influx of Danes.

The book received positive reviews for its poetic prose and dramatic imagery, but a few critics focused on the absence of personal information about the author. Elizabeth Royte, for example, in *The New York Times Book Review* (18 November 2001) praised Ehrlich's "stoicism" and the images she used to describe some of her adventures but wondered what the author felt as she endured various hardships. Although Royte clamored for images of what Ehrlich "saw of herself" in the "looking glass" of Greenland, *This Cold Heaven* vividly describes what the author observes in the characters of humans and the landscape, and in the dynamic relationships between humans and the natural world. "It's said that Inuit people have a pronounced paleocortex sharpened by keen powers of observation and memory for landscape," writes Ehrlich. "The shape of each island, inlet, and fjord is engraved in their minds, they can draw them in dirt or snow, scratching a safe route through open water on the palm of other hunters' hands, or outlining the coastline with fingers in the air." She introduces readers to the dominant role of storytelling in the Inuits' lives and ways in which reliance on oral tradition shapes memory, perceptions, and an ability to survive in this land of harsh extremes.

In all of her books Gretel Ehrlich raises readers' awareness of the ways in which landscapes shape human lives and lifestyles affect landscapes. Her continued discussion of parallels between interior and exterior landscapes, and her unique ways of combining elements of the East and West rank hers among notable voices in contemporary American literature. "Arctic beauty resides in gestures of transcience," she writes in *This Cold Heaven.* "Up here, planes of light and darkness are swords that cut away illusions of permanence, they are the feuilles mortes on which we pen our desperate message-in-a-bottle; words of rapture and longing for what we know will disappear." Ehrlich's overall importance and contributions as a writer and recorder of threatened landscapes and cultures, can perhaps best be assessed only in years to come.

Interviews:

Christine Ford, "Gretel Ehrlich in Deeper Spaces," *Bloomsbury Review* (November/December 1988): 18–19, 31;

James Wackett, "An Interview with Gretel Ehrlich," *North Dakota Quarterly,* 58, no. 3 (1990): 121–127;

Gregory L. Morris, ed., *Talking Up a Storm: Voices of the New West* (Lincoln: University of Nebraska Press, 1994), pp. 81–101;

Jonathan White, "A Call from One Kingdom to Another," in *Talking on the Water: Conversations about Nature and Creativity* (San Francisco: Sierra Club, 1994), pp. 1–17.

References:

David Axelrod, "*Arctic Heart,*" *Western American Literature* (Fall 1992): 275–276;

Dan Cryer, "Strength in Oneness with a Montana Ranch," *Newsday* (7 October 1991): 2, 52;

Pico Iyer, "A Waiting Room for Death," in his *Tropical Classical: Essays from Several Directions* (New York: Knopf, 1997), pp. 234–237;

Cassandra Lee Kircher, "Working in Counterpoint: Disjunction and Attachment in *The Solace of Open Spaces,* Women in/on Nature: Mary Austin, Gretel Ehrlich, Terry Tempest Williams, and Ann Zwinger," Ph.D. thesis, University of Iowa, 1995;

Christopher Merrill, "Voyages to the Immediate: Recent Nature Writings," *New England Review and Breadloaf Quarterly,* 10 (1988): 368–378;

Gregory L. Morris, *Gretel Ehrlich,* Western Writers Series (Boise, Idaho: Boise State University, 2001);

Lynn Ross-Bryant, "The Land in American Religious Experience," *Journal of the American Academy of Religion,* 43, no. 3 (1990): 333–355;

Kent Ryden, "Landscape with Figures: Nature, Folk, Culture, and the Human Ecology of American Environmental Writing," *Interdisciplinary Studies in Literature and Environment,* 4, no. 1 (1997): 1–28.

Papers:

A collection of Gretel Ehrlich's work, in the form of complete and partial manuscripts, correspondence, galleys, and proofs from the archives of Capra Press, is housed at the Lilly Library, Indiana University.

Loren Eiseley

(3 September 1907 – 9 July 1977)

Kathleen A. Boardman
University of Nevada, Reno

See also the Eiseley entry in *DLB Documentary Series 17: The House of Scribner, 1931–1984.*

BOOKS: *The Immense Journey* (New York: Random House, 1957; London: Random House, 1957);

Darwin's Century: Evolution and the Men Who Discovered It (Garden City, N.Y.: Doubleday, 1958; London: Gollancz, 1959);

The Firmament of Time (New York: Atheneum, 1960; London: Gollancz, 1961);

Francis Bacon and the Modern Dilemma (Lincoln: University of Nebraska Press, 1962); revised and enlarged as *The Man Who Saw Through Time* (New York: Scribners, 1973);

The Mind as Nature, John Dewey Society lectureship series, no. 5, foreword by Arthur G. Wirth (New York: Harper & Row, 1962);

Man, Time, and Prophecy, University of Kansas centennial address (New York: Harcourt, Brace & World, 1966);

The Unexpected Universe (New York & London: Harcourt, Brace & World, 1969);

The Brown Wasps: A Collection of Three Essays in Autobiography (Mount Horeb, Wis.: Perishable Press, 1969);

The Invisible Pyramid (New York: Scribners, 1970; London: Hart-Davis, 1971);

The Night Country (New York: Scribners, 1971); republished as *The Night Country: Reflections of a Bone-Hunting Man* (London: Garnstone Press, 1974);

Notes of an Alchemist (New York: Scribners, 1972);

The Innocent Assassins (New York: Scribners, 1973);

All the Strange Hours: The Excavation of a Life (New York: Scribners, 1975);

Another Kind of Autumn (New York: Scribners, 1977);

The Star Thrower, edited by Kenneth Heuer, introduction by W. H. Auden (New York: Times Books, 1978; London: Wildwood House, 1978);

Darwin and the Mysterious Mr. X: New Light on the Evolutionists (New York: Dutton, 1979; London: Dent, 1979);

All the Night Wings (New York: Times Books, 1980);

Loren Eiseley, 1966 (photograph by Ross Photography Studio; from Kenneth Heuer, The Last Notebooks of Loren Eiseley, 1987)

The Lost Notebooks of Loren Eiseley, edited by Heuer (Boston: Little, Brown, 1987).

Editions: *The Invisible Pyramid,* Bison Books edition, introduction by Paul Gruchow (Lincoln: University of Nebraska Press, 1997);

The Night Country, introduction by Gale E. Christianson (Lincoln: University of Nebraska Press, 1997);

The Firmament of Time, introduction by Gary Holthaus (Lincoln: University of Nebraska Press, 1999);

All the Strange Hours: The Excavation of a Life, introduction by Kathleen A. Boardman (Lincoln: University of Nebraska Press, 2000);

The Lost Notebooks of Loren Eiseley, edited, with a reminiscence, by Kenneth Heuer (Lincoln: University of Nebraska Press, 2002).

OTHER: Federal Writers' Project of the Works Progress Administration, *Nebraska: A Guide to the Cornhusker State,* compiled, with contributions, by Eiseley and others (New York: Viking, 1939).

SELECTED PERIODICAL PUBLICATION–UNCOLLECTED: "The Folsom Mystery," *Scientific American,* 161 (December 1942): 260–261.

Anthropologist, educator, historian of science, and poet, Loren Eiseley is best known as the essayist who explained the processes and implications of evolution, especially human evolution, to the lay reader. His lyrical prose and his knowledge of paleontology and archaeology allowed him to bridge science and literature in nonfiction works that reflect on the dynamics of scientific discovery, the abuses of technology, and the beauty of the natural world. A superb stylist who made striking use of metaphor, Eiseley drew upon personal anecdote to illustrate complex ideas, and his writing often resonates with haunting childhood memories.

Writing during the mid twentieth century, when many Americans were becoming concerned about the natural world, Eiseley portrayed the intricate relationships among living things. Constantly returning to the theme of time and its passing, he meditated on the importance of the past in the present and showed the inevitability of change. He expressed a deepening concern for the future of a planet where Western scientific knowledge and technological application had outrun humanity's ability to control them or use them beneficially. Eiseley is known for the brooding melancholy of his essays, in which he argues that loneliness is not just a personal problem but rather the condition of Homo sapiens, a species that has separated itself from other life on Earth. Although other writers during and since Eiseley's time have dealt with similar themes, Eiseley remains significant for his elegant style, his powerful vision of time and change, his memorable evocations of personal experience, and his unusual way of combining science and art in his work.

Loren Corey Eiseley was born in Lincoln, Nebraska, on 3 September 1907, the son of Clyde Eiseley and Daisy Corey Eiseley. He spent most of his early years in this midsized capital city on the eastern edge of the Great Plains; in later writing he referred to himself as a son of the middle border, descendant of pioneer immigrants. As a child he spent much of his time alone, and as soon as he was old enough to escape his mother's watchful eye, he spent hours exploring the fields, hedgerows, and wooded creeks at the edge of town or riding his bicycle to the city library to find books to feed his appetite for reading.

Eiseley's childhood was not only solitary but also difficult. The marriage of his parents–his father's third and his mother's second–was neither happy nor peaceful. Clyde Eiseley held many different jobs, often as a hardware salesman; generally he worked long hours or had to be away from home for days at a time. Loren's half brother, Leo, fourteen years his senior, was out of school and working in a different town before Loren reached school age. Daisy Eiseley suffered from degenerative hearing loss and probably from an undiagnosed mental illness as well. After her only child's birth she was almost totally deaf, and an increasing number of violent, irrational episodes led her relatives to worry that she might experience the same sort of mental breakdown that had claimed her grandmother, Permila Shepard.

By his own account, Eiseley's youth was profoundly shaped by the dark silence of the family's drab little house, his anxiety over his mother's outbursts and his parents' quarrels, his fear that he might inherit the disorder of "the mad Shepards," and his sense of alienation from the community. Although in 1918 the Eiseleys moved into a small house in a middle-class professional neighborhood in order to be near Daisy's sister and brother-in-law, they themselves were working-class. Their isolation deepened because of Daisy's difficulties and their own eventual agreement with the neighbors' verdict: that they were a peculiar family. Eiseley's best elementary-school friend was eventually told by his family to end the friendship, as Eiseley found out years later when the former friend sent him a letter. In personal essays written forty and more years later, Eiseley detailed the influence of these early years on his own class consciousness and, more important, on his image of himself as a solitary man, a fugitive, a person more at home at the edges of human society.

At the same time, young Eiseley loved and admired his father and received a good deal of help from other relatives. His Aunt Grace and Uncle Buck Price allowed him to stay with them and helped him financially. Grace Price was Daisy Eiseley's older sister, and her husband, William Buchanan "Buck" Price, was a Lincoln attorney. Uncle Buck took Eiseley on his first visit to the museum on the University of Nebraska campus in Lincoln, where he had his first view of mammoths and other prehistoric skeletons.

Eiseley's maternal grandmother, Malvina Corey, provided a listening ear and a place to visit when he needed to get away from the stress of home. Leo Eiseley inaugurated his young brother's life as a voracious reader when on one visit he brought the boy Daniel Defoe's *Robinson Crusoe* (1719), read him a few chapters, and then returned home. Left alone with his curiosity and this adult book, five-year-old Loren, knowing only the alphabet and a few short words, taught himself to read. After that, books from the library became both resource and refuge. In his autobiography, Eiseley credits the author of one of these books as a "hidden teacher"—Eugene Smith, whose *The Home Aquarium: How to Care for It* (1902) opened for Eiseley a new world of scientific observation and interest in nature. Thus, Eiseley's childhood and youth also set a second pattern important in his life—the presence of helpers and mentors who recognized his talent and his need. He acknowledges some of these helpers on the dedication pages of his books.

Eiseley's early years are especially important because he remembered them so vividly and drew on them so frequently in his later writing. Seeing Halley's Comet with his father, exploring the sewers with his friend "Rat," watching in horror as some older boys killed a turtle with rocks, hiding in a hedgerow and suddenly noticing a flock of quiet little birds in the same bushes, and hearing from his father about some men who had escaped from prison and hoping they would get away—all these early memories, and more, found their way into essays he wrote decades later.

At age fifteen Eiseley began attending Lincoln High School, but he felt at odds with the other students and dropped out, taking odd jobs and avoiding the truant officer. Through the influence of his uncle, he was admitted to Teachers College High School on the University of Nebraska campus, and he agreed to give school another try. In one of his essays for class, he wrote that he wanted to become a nature writer, and indeed this ambition fit his twin interests in the natural world and in books. At his new high school, with its smaller classes and new teaching methods, Eiseley developed his abilities as a writer of essays, short stories, and poetry. In 1925 he graduated from high school—the first member of his family to do so—and enrolled at the University of Nebraska that fall.

For the next eight years Eiseley was in and out of college, a self-described late bloomer who excelled at writing but had difficulty joining "contradictory" interests in literature and science. In 1928 his father died of cancer, and Eiseley began struggling with insomnia as well as grief; his experiences in the "night country" of the insomniac provided material for many an essay in later life. During the same year he devel-

Eiseley and his mother, Daisy Corey Eiseley, during his childhood in Nebraska (from Heuer, The Last Notebooks of Loren Eiseley, *1987)*

oped a serious infection that a doctor diagnosed as tuberculosis. One therapeutic sojourn in Colorado and another in the Mojave Desert cured his lung problems, but as he rode the rails back to Nebraska from California in 1930, he saw the poverty and joblessness of the Great Depression, a period that permanently marked him and his generation. By that time he had been hopping an occasional boxcar for five or six years already. Although just how much time he actually spent riding the rails, or whether he actually had all the adventures he claimed in his autobiography is not clear, his experiences as a hobo provided some important themes and images for his later writing. Indeed, the first third of his autobiography, *All the Strange Hours: The Excavation of a Life* (1975), is labeled "Days of a Drifter."

Eiseley returned to Nebraska in 1930 with the intention of finishing his undergraduate education; he received a B.S. in English and Geology/Anthropology in 1933. During his time at the University of Nebraska, he served as a student editor and wrote poetry and essays for *Prairie Schooner,* the university-associated literary magazine. The founder and editor of the magazine, English faculty member Lowry Charles Wimberly, became for a time one of Eiseley's mentors. Because of the *Prairie Schooner,* Eiseley was a published poet well before becoming a practicing scientist. Pursuing his scientific interest as a member of the Morrill Paleontological Expedition, Eiseley joined the fossil hunters of the "South Party" during the summers of 1931, 1932, and 1933. These expeditions took him to remote areas on the Great Plains of western Nebraska and South Dakota and eastern Wyoming and Colorado. Later, during a break in his graduate study, Eiseley worked four months in Nebraska for the Federal Writers Project; his essays on paleontology and archaeology appeared in *Nebraska: A Guide to the Cornhusker State* (1939).

Moving on to the University of Pennsylvania, where he worked with faculty adviser Frank Gouldsmith Speck, Eiseley received both a master's degree (1935) and a Ph.D. (1937) in anthropology. He began his forty-year university career by accepting a faculty position in the Department of Sociology and Anthropology at the University of Kansas (Lawrence), where he remained from 1937 to 1944. Having received a fellowship from the Social Science Research Council, he did postdoctoral research in physical anthropology at Columbia University and the American Museum of Natural History in New York during the summers and the academic year of 1940–1941. When he returned to Kansas the following autumn, his department added a course in physical anthropology to its curriculum. Eiseley also taught anatomy for the medical school.

On 29 August 1938 Eiseley married Mabel Langdon; the couple had known each other for more than a decade, since the time he was finishing high school and she was studying to become an English teacher. Their marriage lasted until his death; the Eiseleys had no children. Although he used autobiographical material frequently in his essays, Eiseley insisted on the privacy of his family life as an adult. It is apparent, though, that he bore the financial pressures of taking care of his mother and aunt, and also that Mabel Langdon Eiseley did a great deal behind the scenes to support her husband's career and encourage his writing.

In 1941 Eiseley was elected as a fellow of the American Association for the Advancement of Science. He left Kansas in 1944 for a position as head of the Department of Sociology at Oberlin College (Ohio), where he developed a program in anthropol-

ogy. In 1947 he was offered a professorship at the University of Pennsylvania, the institution where he had done his graduate work. Eiseley accepted, and he remained affiliated with the University of Pennsylvania for the rest of his life. He served as Chairman of the Department of Anthropology and Curator of Early Man for the museum at the university. In 1959 he became provost of the university and occupied that administrative position for two years, returning to teaching and writing in 1961. After 1968 he was Benjamin Franklin Professor of Anthropology and History of Science.

In his academic career, Eiseley engaged in scientific and scholarly research that resulted in some monographs and articles written for professional colleagues. His forte apparently lay in his powers of synthesis rather than in original discoveries from the field. He was also an excellent lecturer, although uncomfortable with students, according to some accounts. His public service included the presidency of the American Institute of Human Paleontology (1949), membership on the advisory board for national parks for the U.S. Department of the Interior, and consultant for various museums, foundations, and government agencies. However, after the 1957 publication of his first book, *The Immense Journey,* he became best known for essays and books written for the general public. In fact, some professional colleagues criticized Eiseley for spending too much time researching in libraries and writing for lay audiences and too little time doing fieldwork and technical writing for the scientific community. At the time, combining the scientific and the literary in one's writing was even more suspect than it is today. But the "literary" way of writing about nature and science suited Eiseley's particular talents, inclinations, and background; in addition, he became convinced that it was wrong to continue to separate the "two cultures" of science and humanities and to excise feeling and poetry from scientific prose.

In the early 1940s, Eiseley decided to try his hand at writing about science for a popular magazine, and the positive response was encouraging. "The Folsom Mystery," based on his research on Ice Age hunters and their prey, appeared in the December 1942 *Scientific American;* two additional articles followed in later issues. A few years later, Eiseley began regularly submitting articles to *Harper's Monthly,* and again he found enthusiastic readers. In his autobiography Eiseley notes a turning point, a time when he began to think consciously about what was happening in his writing and decided to push further in the direction of what he called "the concealed essay, in which personal anecdote was allowed gently to bring under observation thoughts of a more purely scientific nature." This "concealed essay," informed by his scientific training as an expert on early man and shaped by his experience as a poet, became his trademark. Editors began to suggest that Eiseley pull some of his magazine articles together into a book on nature and evolution. He agreed with this idea, and after several years of revising previously published essays, establishing connections among them, and writing new material, he finished *The Immense Journey*.

The Immense Journey is a collection of essays on man, nature, and evolution. (As an anthropologist trained in the 1930s and professionally active at midcentury, Eiseley always used the term "man" to refer to humanity in general.) He proceeded on the assumption that educated people knew about Charles Darwin's theory and accepted its validity but did not necessarily understand everything about how it worked or what its implications were. Thus, his purpose was not to defend a theory of evolution but rather to explain and illustrate it in terms that were comprehensible and interesting to the lay reader. In short, he meant to delight as well as instruct. To that end, he drew from the humanities as well as the sciences.

The Immense Journey begins with a personal experience: as a "bone hunter" on a paleontological expedition, Eiseley had once gone down into a "slit" in the rocks and found himself face to face with a skull set in a geological layer older than Homo sapiens. "We stared a little blankly at each other, the skull and I," he remarks, and then reports his next vivid impression—that while excavating this fossil, he pictured himself as a fossil. "The truth is," he adds, "that we are all potential fossils still carrying within our bodies the crudities of former existences, the marks of a world in which living creatures flow with little more consistency than clouds from age to age." The evolutionary process comprises thousands of alternatives and complexities; there is nothing deterministic about it. In addition, Homo sapiens is not the culmination of this process. Humanity stands not at the end or apex but rather somewhere in the middle: the future stretches before us, just as the past lies behind us. In spite of his professional interest in the history of humankind, Eiseley resists the "species egotism" that tends to separate human beings from other life on the planet. He suggests, rather, that the inevitable loneliness that accompanies self-consciousness is quite separation enough.

An extremely influential book, *The Immense Journey* presents a rich variety of life—discussing fish, birds, plants, amphibians, mammals, and primates in vivid language. These three sentences from "How Flowers Changed the World," one of the most highly regarded essays in the book, suggest the lyrical rhythms of Eiseley's prose style and his use of examples:

Eiseley in his teens (from Gale E. Christianson,
Fox at the Wood's Edge, *1990)*

Without the gift of flowers and the infinite diversity of their fruits, man and bird, if they continued to exist at all, would be today unrecognizable. Archaeopteryx, the lizard bird, might be snapping at a beetle on a sequoia limb; man might be a nocturnal insectivore gnawing a roach in the dark. The weight of a petal has changed the world and made it ours.

The passage reinforces major themes of the book—that change is constant in the world and that evolution has many alternative paths it might have taken, and might yet take. In addition, the sentences express wonder in the presence of the natural world as humans experience it. In such ways, Eiseley not only explains evolution as seen through the lens of physical anthropology but also combines his profound sense of the passage of time with his vivid sense of the importance of an individual moment.

Like the classic essays of Michel Eyquem de Montaigne, Eiseley's essays usually begin with or are centered on a personal experience, usually a small everyday happening or observation that suggests a question or concept that the essayist explores in hopes of gaining insight. This exploration proceeds not just through further attention to the experience but also through any kind of research that might bear on the case, such as scholarly study, wide reading, or fieldwork. This technique appealed to a wide audience, who could vicariously join Eiseley on his journey of discovery.

A year after publication of *The Immense Journey*, Eiseley published *Darwin's Century: Evolution and the Men Who Discovered It* (1958), approaching the history of evolution from a different angle. In this book, Eiseley studies the development of the theory of natural selection, sketching the history of evolutionary thought from medieval times and focusing on Darwin and his eighteenth- and nineteenth-century forerunners. Not content to stop with Darwin and his publication of *The Origin of Species* (1859), Eiseley goes on to discuss the revisions of the book—and the modifications of the theory—that were made in response to scientific criticism.

A long book of fairly dense scholarship in the history of science, *Darwin's Century* is nevertheless accessible to the lay reader and written in nontechnical language. In discussing the development of a theory, Eiseley is, in effect, also telling a story about intellectual evolution—which ideas lead along a mainstream to recognized and well-publicized theories, and which ideas lead to dead ends or remain at the margins of scientific discussion. Besides telling an important story in the history of science, Eiseley also encapsulates his own ambivalent view of mankind, a perspective that propelled his later writing as well: "Man is many things—he is protean, elusive, capable of great good and appalling evil. He is what he is—a reservoir of indeterminism. He represents the genuine

triumph of volition, life's near evasion of the forces that have molded it." In 1959 *Darwin's Century* won the first Phi Beta Kappa Science Prize for the best scientific book of the year. Eiseley was now well established as a writer who could artfully combine science with humanism for a lay audience.

During that same year, Eiseley delivered six lectures at the University of Cincinnati in his capacity as visiting professor of the philosophy of science. His aim was to explore the impact of modern science on humanity's vision of itself and nature. These explorations appeared in book form as *The Firmament of Time* (1960). Beginning with "How the World Became Natural," five of the six chapters include the word *natural* in their titles. Eiseley notes that humankind has always had two ways of looking at nature—pragmatic and mystical. Even prehistoric peoples, supposedly mystical and superstitious, were scientists and technologists in their development and use of tools; and even in modern technological societies, humans ask questions such as "Why does the universe exist?" As science moves along, answering questions and providing new technologies, "it often opens vaster mysteries to our gaze," and still humankind is not satisfied. "Indeed," says Eiseley, "so restless is man's intellect that were he to penetrate to the secret of the universe tomorrow, the likelihood is that he would grow bored on the day after."

Writing in the midst of the Cold War, when Americans were simultaneously fearing atomic destruction and poisoning the environment with waste and pesticides, Eiseley in this volume warns a technological society to change its ways. Excess consumption, noise, indiscriminate destruction of the natural world, thoughtless economic exploitation by special-interest groups—all threaten "to extinguish the species," Eiseley warns, adding that humanity's progress in science and technology has dangerously outdistanced its conscience. In spite of the accomplishments of Western science, it has not made humans more responsible; humanity's insatiable curiosity, which has helped the species to flourish, may have become a "Faustian drive" that spells disaster for the planet. Eiseley leavens his deepening pessimism with some hope and a strategy for change: survival depends upon a new attitude toward education, progress, and science. Schools must cultivate conscience and reflection, not just aim at utility. "Science is not enough for man," Eiseley argues. "Progress that pursues only the next invention . . . is not progress at all."

The Firmament of Time was well received by Americans of a wide range of political affiliations. Rachel Carson, for example, who had just completed

Silent Spring (1962), wrote Eiseley an appreciative letter. In 1961 *The Firmament of Time* received the John Burroughs Medal, the highest award for a popular book in the natural sciences. Eiseley also received the Pierre Lecomte du Nouy American Foundation Award for the best work dealing with spiritual life and human destiny.

Shortly thereafter, two more sets of Eiseley lectures, along with many revisions and additions, appeared in print. *Francis Bacon and the Modern Dilemma* (1962) stemmed from speeches delivered at the University of Pennsylvania and the University of Nebraska to celebrate the four-hundredth anniversary of Bacon's birth. Eiseley's lecture-essays are more than a courtesy nod to a renowned Renaissance scientist who happened to be having an important anniversary. Beginning with an examination of Bacon's continuing role as educator, Eiseley defends and extends Bacon's reputation, claiming him as one of the "great synthesizers"—those people who alter the outlook of a whole generation and are sometimes feared or hated for doing so. Himself an early practitioner of the essay genre, Bacon in a sense opened the door to the modern world and to modern scientific method. Eiseley argues that, in spite of some errors in his details, Bacon is the model for what a good scientist should be: he practiced with compassion and understanding, combining natural science with literature in ways that Eiseley found encouraging for his own career. A decade later, in *The Man Who Saw Through Time* (1973), Eiseley combined the 1962 materials with a new introductory essay on Bacon.

A year after speaking on Bacon, Eiseley was invited to give the annual lecture for the John Dewey Society for the Study of Education and Culture. His presentation was published later that year as *The Mind as Nature* (1962). In this work, Eiseley delves into autobiographical material from his lonely childhood and difficult adolescence in order to support his thesis that the teacher serves as both protector and agent of change. Writing at a time when many educators were expounding on the value of individual creativity, Eiseley places that creativity into the context of nature and the "immense journey" of life on the planet: "The reality we know in our limited lifetimes is dwarfed by the unseen potential of the abyss where science stops," he writes, and individual creativity flashes forth "only to subside in death while the waves of energy it has released roll on through unnumbered generations." The creative spirit generally finds itself at some point in conflict with social norms, many of which are necessary for humanity's survival. The challenge for the teacher, then, is to induce the necessary social confor-

Mabel Langdon, whom Eiseley married in 1938 (from Heuer, The Last Notebooks of Loren Eiseley, *1987)*

mities while at the same time allowing for the "free play of the creative spirit."

While still on the faculty at the University of Pennsylvania, Eiseley served for a year (1963–1964) as director of the Richard Prentice Ettinger Program for Creative Writing at the Rockefeller Institute. Part of his responsibility was to attract writers with scientific interests. His opening address for the new program, "The Illusion of Two Cultures," appeared in *The American Scholar* and was later collected in *The Star Thrower* (1978). Deploring the deepening rift in the intellectual community between scientists and nonscientists, Eiseley argues that these two so-called cultures are only an illusion, "a product of unreasoning fear, professionalism, and misunderstanding." He sharply criticizes the scientific discipline for "intolerance of those of its own membership who venture to pursue the way of letters."

In 1966 Eiseley had an opportunity to extend his science teaching to television by becoming host-narrator of a new television series, *Animal Secrets*. Each episode dealt with a different topic and illustrated how wild animals were able to match or surpass humans' achievements in that area. Eiseley stood before the camera each week to introduce the topic and then served as voice-over narrator for scenes that were shot on location. The program received a Thomas Alva Edison Award as the best science series for youth; the last episode aired in 1968.

The Unexpected Universe (1969) was Eiseley's next collection of lectures and essays on natural history. These pieces tell of a scientist's personal encounters with the universe; they are not "objective" science. Returning to the journey motif of his first book, Eiseley arranges this group of writings around the myth of Odysseus—the curious, restless, inventive voyager who longed to return home. Just as in the *Odyssey,* the alternating themes of desolation and renewal permeate Eiseley's meditations on seeds, shells, fossils, lost tombs, city dumps, and their significance in the universe. "The Star Thrower," one of Eiseley's most famous essays, first appeared in this collection. Its central image is a man Eiseley encountered on the shell-strewn beach of Costabel (a fictional name for a real beach). The man is picking up beached starfish, one by one, and saving them by flinging them back into the ocean. When Eiseley asks him if his effort is not a futile activity, considering that there are always so many stranded starfish, the star thrower replies that he can save the animals one by one.

In this collection Eiseley also takes a swipe at "irrational activists" who want to reject a past of which they remain ignorant. A loss of faith in the past, he argues, makes planning for the future impossible, as "the lessons of the past have been found to be a reasonably secure instruction for proceeding against the unknown future." "The Hidden Teacher" compares a technological society, with its network of observatories, electronic microscopes, and radio telescopes, to a spider Eiseley once saw in a web. When he touched the web, the spider ran out, mistakenly thinking that prey had arrived. Pursuing the analogy, Eiseley asks, "What is it that we are a part of that we do not see?"

The Unexpected Universe received enthusiastic reviews and was a finalist for the National Book Award in the category of philosophy and religion. It also received notice from English poet W. H. Auden, who reviewed it enthusiastically in a seven-page article in *The New Yorker*. Eiseley later met Auden personally and dedicated one of his volumes of poetry to Auden.

Eiseley continued to cast a jaundiced eye upon technological development in *The Invisible Pyramid* (1970), a book of seven lectures and essays on the space age. Responding to an invitation to place the American arrival on the Moon into the context of other explorations on planet Earth, Eiseley wrote that he did not think much of the moon landing and did not consider the astronauts to be true adventurers in the spirit of Captain James Cook or Meriwether Lewis and William Clark. The title of the book comes from his comparison of the "space race" to the building of the Great Pyramid of Cheops at Giza: both enterprises required many years of toil and taxation merely to build a monument to a few egos. Continuing the quest to learn from the past, the essays make other connections between civilizations past and present; for example, Eiseley notes that the Maya's development of the concept of "zero" provides the platform for Western science today.

In 1971 Eiseley was elected to membership in the National Institute of Arts and Letters. Late that year, another collection of his essays appeared; these were filled with autobiographical material, the most personal of his personal essays to that point. *The Night Country* (1971) takes as its territory the hedgerows, caves, borderlands, badlands, wastelands, no-man's-lands—all the "marginal" places that many people might overlook and that therefore provide refuge for animals and an occasional human being. Eiseley opens by saying, "I am a fugitive. I was born one." He adds, "The fact that I wear the protective coloration of sedate citizenship is the ruse of the fox—I learned it long ago. The facts of my inner life are quite otherwise." Another no-man's-land that Eiseley explores is the night: humans are not nocturnal creatures, but insomniacs such as Eiseley and his grandmother Malvina Corey, to whom the book is dedicated, are well acquainted with the night.

From his vantage point at the edges of things, this insomniac bone-hunter from the middle border tells stories about the odd, sometimes disturbing things he has seen and heard: his first observation of evil, a house whose cellar leads deep into a cave, a skull in a box in his office, an ancient burial site, the fearsomeness of a herd of cattle in the middle of the night, a recluse who has fallen in love with a rock formation he thinks is a "petrified woman." Eiseley listens, too, when odd individuals make strange comments, and he spins tales that make these stories sound like prophetic utterances. In "The Creature from the Marsh" he also has some fun at his own expense, telling of the time he thought he had discovered the footprint of a creature who might be an evolutionary "missing link." Further investigation revealed that he was looking at his own footprint.

Taken as a whole, essays in *The Night Country* reveal a great deal about Eiseley's inner life. But their importance is not just autobiographical: viewed eco-

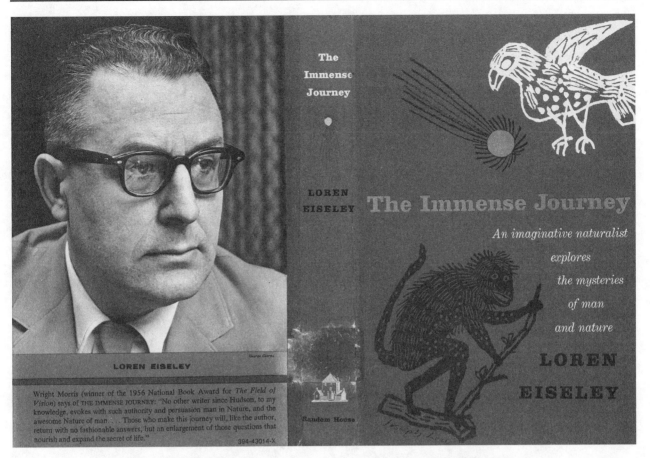

LOREN EISELEY

Wright Morris (winner of the 1956 National Book Award for *The Field of Vision*) says of THE IMMENSE JOURNEY: "No other writer since Hudson, to my knowledge, evokes with such authority and persuasion man in Nature, and the awesome Nature of man . . . . Those who make this journey will, like the author, return with no fashionable answers, but an enlargement of those questions that nourish and expand the secret of life."

394-43014-X

The
Immense
Journey

LOREN
EISELEY

The Immense Journey

An imaginative naturalist

explores

the mysteries

of man

and nature

LOREN
EISELEY

Random House

*Dust jacket for Eiseley's first book (1957), a collection of influential essays in which he explained the workings
and implications of Darwinian evolution (Richland County Public Library)*

logically, they also show the importance of the marginal places, strange creatures, and "fugitive" people whom mainstream society might overlook or even destroy. The work of evolution, of change, takes place along the edges, Eiseley suggests, and many of humankind's insights occur in the night country. In one essay he quotes Bacon: "There is no perfect beauty that hath not some strangeness in the proportion." The volume ends with one of Eiseley's most famous essays, "The Brown Wasps," which deals with the ways humans and animals find of going home again when home is gone. *The Night Country* received positive reviews, some of which claimed it to be Eiseley's best work since *The Immense Journey*.

Decades earlier, Eiseley had begun his writing life as a poet. The poetry he published as an undergraduate in *Prairie Schooner* even earned him the title of University Poet Laureate. Now, forty years later, he assembled his poetry into two volumes that appeared a year apart. *Notes of an Alchemist* (1972) alludes to the medieval scientist-sorcerers who attempted to turn base metals into gold. Eiseley presents himself as a man of science who has trans-

formed his observations into poetic language and imagery. The title poem of *The Innocent Assassins* (1973) focuses on an unusual fossil discovered by the Morrill Paleontological Expedition in 1932, when Eiseley was a member of the party. A saber-toothed tiger's fang was found embedded in the shoulder blade of a second tiger. Twenty-five million years ago, the two huge cats had fought to the death. As might be expected, Eiseley draws the imagery for most of his poems from the natural world: the calls and flights of birds, a beaver pond and how it resembles the mind, the austerity of timberline as a metaphor for life in nature, the silence of the plains now that the buffalo are gone, and autumn and its forebodings of death.

Eiseley wrote primarily in free verse, although a few of his poems are in blank verse. For students of his prose, the poems are interesting for their imagery, tone, and rhythms, which can also be found in Eiseley's essays. The cadences, sounds, and phrasing in his poetry are often quite similar to those in his prose. The vividness of the individual image in Eiseley's prose can also be traced to the poetry.

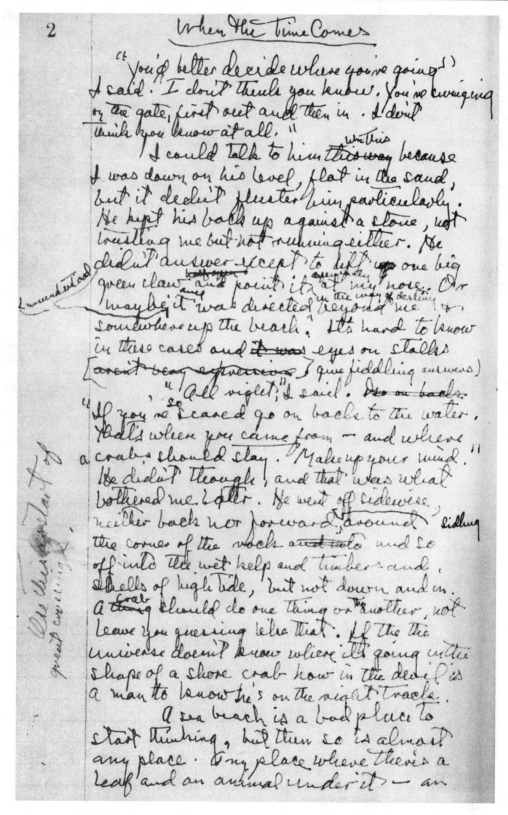

Notebook entry written by Eiseley during a 1968 trip to an island in the Gulf of Mexico
(University of Pennsylvania Archives)

All the Strange Hours, which appeared in 1975, is the long-awaited autobiography of a writer who had used autobiographical material throughout his career. Loosely organized in chronological order, with individual essays gathered under three headings—"Days of a Drifter," "Days of a Thinker," and "Days of a Doubter"—this book nevertheless surprises readers who expect a conventional autobiography, a story of a life that moves in chronological order and names all the important people in the author's life. In contrast, Eiseley's book is, as the subtitle suggests, more of an excavation, with memories becoming exposed like artifacts as the "dig" moves through the layers of a life. Flashbacks are common, as one experience reminds the narrator of another. Eiseley gives readers some sense of what to expect when he opens the book with two metaphors for memories. First, they are like the objects carried back and forth by pack rats, never completely lost, but somewhat rearranged. Second, they are like the shards of a broken mirror, each piece reflecting a child's face. In both cases, Eiseley says, "Nothing is lost, but it can never be again as it was."

Melancholy, some pessimism, and a deepening preoccupation with death are prominent in *All the Strange Hours.* However, the book also includes some good tales, some of them fictionalized: stories about animals—including one about a "talking" cat—and Eiseley's idyllic story about "The Most Perfect Day in the World," when hoboes from all over the country (and perhaps from different eras of time) all relaxed together on a beautiful day, no questions asked. While Eiseley does not name all the important people in his life, he does discuss the development of his ideas, the impact of illnesses and accidents, and the times he struggled with his conscience or with tough decisions. In this sense, *All the Strange Hours* is an intellectual autobiography—an account of the development of the author's thoughts and ideas. The book ends with the reappearance of a key figure—the Player, or gambler. Eiseley shows himself playing against this gambler for his life. The gambler also reintroduces the theme of Chance: chance, Eiseley believes, operates in each individual life as it does in the life of the planet. Each species can be seen, at the beginning, as another roll of the dice, and the ones who survive are the winners. Thus, the last book Eiseley published before he died shows some of the same concerns and themes as his first book.

"The Star Dragon," the first essay in *The Invisible Pyramid,* begins with Eiseley's vivid memory of viewing Halley's Comet, at age four, by his father's side. His father whispers to his young son that, if he lives long enough, he will see the comet return after seventy-five years, and then he will have to look at it for both of them—his father and himself. Eiseley did not live to see his seventieth birthday. Like his father, he developed cancer; he died in Philadelphia on 9 July 1977 and is buried in Bala-Clynwyd, Pennsylvania.

Five books appeared posthumously. Two were volumes of poetry: *Another Kind of Autumn* (1977), which Eiseley had assembled during the last months of his life, and *All the Night Wings* (1980). Before his death Eiseley had also selected the contents of *The Star Thrower,* a collection of previously published prose and poetry, some of which had not been available in book form. This large volume of more than twenty essays and ten poems includes an introduction by Auden.

Most of *Darwin and the Mysterious Mr. X: New Light on the Evolutionists* (1979) had been written years earlier, shortly after *Darwin's Century,* but its publication had been delayed partly because of its controversial nature. This collection of eight essays centers on Eiseley's claim that Edwin Blyth, a colonial farmer and self-taught scientist, had written and published several articles on artificial selection that must have influenced Darwin's thinking on natural selection. Eiseley presents evidence that Darwin was likely to have seen and used the articles without acknowledging them. While in this volume Eiseley claims only one small piece of the puzzle for Blyth, still giving Darwin credit as the person who synthesized the bits and pieces of thoughts on evolution into a coherent theory, his arguments about Blyth continue to be disputed.

The fifth of the posthumous books is actually a collection of notes and letters. A decade after Eiseley's death, his last editor, Kenneth Heuer, received the Eiseley family's permission to compile and publish material from notebooks that Eiseley had kept over the years. *The Lost Notebooks of Loren Eiseley* (1987) also includes Heuer's reminiscences and excerpts from letters Eiseley received from such writers as Auden, Lewis Mumford, Wright Morris, T. H. White, and Archibald MacLeish.

In "The Ghost Continent," the opening essay in *The Unexpected Universe,* Loren Eiseley writes, "Let it be understood that I claim no discoveries. I claim only the events of a life in science as they were transformed inwardly." This inward transformation is what makes his writing noteworthy: he combines scientific knowledge and close observation with personal memories and an unusual ability "to see from an inverted angle," as he says in "The Judgment of the Birds." More important, he expresses this vision in a distinctive prose style. In fact, his style is the magnet that has continued to attract readers to his works. The impact of Eiseley's vivid, rhythmic, sometimes painfully personal writing is clearly substantial. His originality of thought is not always as simple to judge, because many literary naturalists who have written since *The Immense Journey* was published have expressed ideas similar to Eiseley's: the dangers of technology in the absence of an ecological conscience, the importance of joining the forces of sciences and arts in service of the planet, and the limitations of any vision that puts humankind at the center of the universe. However, Eiseley was one of the few mid-century literary naturalists who was also a professional scientist and who wrote from that point of view. Apparently reconciled to a vision of himself as fugitive and drifter, he is notable for his peculiar ability to work in the somewhat inhospitable borderlands between science and art. Also peculiar to Eiseley are his deep awareness of time in all its guises and his vision of humanity's place in the great flow of evolutionary time.

Biography:

Gale E. Christianson, *Fox at the Wood's Edge: A Biography of Loren Eiseley* (New York: Holt, 1990).

References:

Andrew Angyal, *Loren Eiseley* (Boston: Twayne, 1983);

W. H. Auden, "Concerning the Unpredictable," *New Yorker,* 21 February 1970, pp. 118–125;

Caravan: Newsletter of the Friends of Loren Eiseley (1987 –   );

Fred Carlisle, *Loren Eiseley: The Development of a Writer* (Urbana: University of Illinois Press, 1983);

Gale E. Carrithers, *Mumford, Tate, Eiseley: Watchers in the Night* (Baton Rouge: Louisiana State University Press, 1992);

Leslie E. Gerber and Margaret McFadden, *Loren Eiseley* (New York: Ungar, 1983);

Gene V. Glass, "Searching for Loren Eiseley: An Attempt at Reconstruction from a Few Fragments"   <http://glass.ed.asu/gene/papers/eiseley.html>;

Peter Heidtmann, *Loren Eiseley: A Modern Ishmael* (Hamden, Conn.: Archon, 1991);

Loren Eiseley: Essayist, Philosopher, Literary Naturalist <www.eiseley.unomaha.edu>;

Mary Ellen Pitts, *Toward a Dialogue of Understandings: Loren Eiseley and the Critique of Science* (Bethlehem, Pa.: Lehigh University Press, 1995).

Papers:

Much of Loren Eiseley's individual and general correspondence, lectures, awards, articles, reviews, interviews, and introductions to his books are held in the archives of the University of Pennsylvania. In addition, the University of Pennsylvania holds files of Eiseley's published works, with detailed analyses by Caroline E. Werkley.

John Hay

(31 August 1915 –)

Jen Hill
University of Nevada, Reno

BOOKS: *A Private History* (New York: Duell, Sloan & Pearce, 1947);

The Run (Garden City, N.Y.: Doubleday, 1959; revised and enlarged, 1965);

Nature's Year: The Seasons of Cape Cod (Garden City, N.Y.: Doubleday, 1961);

A Sense of Nature, by Hay and Arline Strong (Garden City, N.Y.: Doubleday, 1962);

The Great Beach (Garden City, N.Y.: Doubleday, 1963);

The Atlantic Shore: Human and Natural History from Long Island to Labrador, by Hay and Peter Farb (New York & London: Harper & Row, 1966);

The Sandy Shore (Chatham, Mass.: Chatham, 1968);

In Defense of Nature (Boston: Little, Brown, 1969);

Six Poems (N.p.: Privately printed, 1969);

The Primal Alliance: Earth and Ocean, photographs by Richard Kauffman, edited by Kenneth Brower (San Francisco: Friends of the Earth, 1971);

Spirit of Survival: A Natural and Personal History of Terns (New York: Dutton, 1974);

The Undiscovered Country (New York: Norton, 1982);

The Immortal Wilderness (New York: Norton, 1987);

The Bird of Light (New York: Norton, 1991);

A Beginner's Faith in Things Unseen (Boston: Beacon, 1995);

In the Company of Light (Boston: Beacon, 1998);

The Way to the Salt Marsh: A John Hay Reader (Hanover, N.H.: University Press of New England, 1998).

OTHER: *Thoreau on Birds: Notes on New England Birds from the Journals of Henry David Thoreau,* introduction by Hay, edited by Francis H. Allen (Boston: Beacon, 1993);

The Great House of Birds: Classic Writings about Birds, edited by Hay (San Francisco: Sierra Club Books, 1996).

John Hay (photograph by Gordon S. Smith; from the dust jacket for The Bird of Light, *1991)*

John Hay is recognized by many as a preeminent force and voice in nature writing and regional nonfiction of the twentieth century. He is identified with Cape Cod, where he lives and has written and where he has remained active in environmental politics. Despite his lengthy publication record, which spans more than sixty years, Hay's emphasis on subjects immediate, focused, and local has led to his work at times being overlooked by literary scholars. Still, critics and writers identify his work as being significant in furthering an American tradition that links personal experience to close observation of the natural world. Hay's writing has always found an audience, and he is recognized by Annie Dillard as "of the world's handful of very great nature writers." For many, he is the voice of nature and environmental conscience in the Atlantic Northeast, communicating in his work his deeply personal experience of the land and sea while enacting that experience in a career of public service and philanthropy that reinforces the environmental ethics and practice found in his writing.

Born on 31 August 1915 in Ipswich, Massachusetts, to Clarence Leonard Hay and Alice Appleton Hay, John Hay was named after his famous paternal grandfather, John Milton Hay. The elder Hay had a distinguished career as a poet and journalist and, in addition to being Abraham Lincoln's private secretary during the Civil War, was later assistant secretary of state under President Rutherford B. Hayes and secretary of state under Presidents William McKinley and Theodore Roosevelt. In 1883 the elder John Hay purchased one thousand acres of farmland on the shore of Lake Sunapee, New Hampshire, where he built a summer home he named The Fells. He died ten years before his grandson was born, but the younger John Hay spent summers at The Fells with his family. His father, Clarence, was an amateur botanist who, with his wife, Alice, devoted the years between 1914 and 1940 to developing and cultivating several gardens on the estate, including an alpine garden with 650 species of wildflowers. The landscape of The Fells, with its orchards, shrubberies, rockeries, and water gardens, as well as the surrounding mountains and wilderness, led their son, John, "toward wild things [he] missed in a society that was apart from them to an increasing degree." Hay has said, "I had a tree house and learned a lot about white pines, but it was really just being in all that space that got me." Hay also explored the lake, cruising and fishing its eleven-mile length in a fourteen-foot houseboat he built from plans in Daniel Carter Beard's *The American Boys' Handybook of Camp-Lore and Woodcraft* (1920).

As a youth, Hay received his formal primary education in New York City, where his father was curator of archaeology for the American Museum of Natural History, specializing in Aztec and Mayan civilizations. Hay pursued secondary education at St. Paul's School in Concord, New Hampshire, from which he graduated in 1934, having received the school prize in poetry. He cites Henry Kittredge, a master at St. Paul's, as having a lasting influence on his literary development. He was also influenced by the writing of his grandfather, which, in addition to a multivolume biography of Lincoln, included volumes of poetry and novels. Clarence Hay, too, was a poet. Hay's other youthful influences included Walt Whitman, James Fenimore Cooper, Henry David Thoreau, and Robinson Jeffers, as well as Leo Tolstoy and D. H. Lawrence. He continued his education and further developed his interests in literature and poetry at Harvard University, from which he graduated in 1938.

For a year following his graduation, Hay was the Washington correspondent for the *Charleston* (S.C.) *News and Courier.* He remained interested in poetry, however, and for two months before being called up by the U.S. Army in 1940, he visited Brewster, Massachusetts, in a sort of apprenticeship with Conrad Aiken, who won a Pulitzer Prize for a collection of his poetry and also wrote short stories and novels. Hay alternately wrote and cleared brush, convening with Aiken later in the day to talk about form, aesthetics, and poetry. The combined attention to the physical experience of landscape and its relation to form and language influenced Hay's writing from then on. Aiken encouraged Hay to break from poetic forms of the past and provided a model for a literary life and an introduction to Cape Cod, which became Hay's home for years. Before leaving for military service, Hay had written many poems and had purchased acreage on the cape.

Hay married Kristi Putnam on 14 February 1942, and after his tour as an enlisted man was up—some of which he spent as an associate editor of *Yank,* the army newspaper—they moved to Brewster, then a sleepy town of nine hundred people. The Hays built a house on sixty acres of pine and oak forest called Dry Hill, where they raised their children Susan, Katharine, Rebecca, and Charles. In 1947 Hay's first book, *A Private History,* was published. This collection of poetry is remarkable for its varied stylistic approaches and voices. While Hay abandoned the modernist style in his later work, his early experimentation shows the influence of Aiken. The flexibility of range revealed in subject matter (from vivid stream-of-consciousness war poetry to more-formal poems on nature) reveals a young writer experimenting with his voice. The poems on nature foreshadow the questions and obsessions that have preoccupied Hay as a writer.

During the late 1940s and early 1950s Hay supported himself as a freelance writer and reviewer as he prepared the manuscript for his next book, *The Run,* published in 1959. *The Run* was Hay's first book-length prose work. Recognized as an important work upon its publication and acknowledged today as a classic in nature writing, *The Run* establishes what remained Hay's approach in later books. In it, he explores the lives of alewives that frequent Cape Cod, seasonally glutting the creeks and inlets in their annual spawning. As fish that live in saltwater but return to freshwater to reproduce, the alewives remain a mysterious lens through which to look more closely at natural systems and human presence. They are at once tantalizingly familiar and frustratingly unknowable. Lacking scientific studies to provide answers, Hay relied on close observation in the tradition of natural historians dating to the Englishman Gilbert White and to the American Thoreau. Through his daily walks, Hay understood that observation was always situated, and thus the annual run of the alewives was a means through which to learn about and communicate human as well as natu-

THE RUN

JOHN HAY

THE RUN

JOHN HAY

THE RUN

THOMAS BOUCHARD

JOHN HAY THE RUN

"A delightful and often beautiful book, and incidentally one of the best things on Cape Cod landscape and atmosphere that I have ever seen."
Conrad Aiken

JOHN HAY
A CAPE COD NATURALIST
EXPERIENCES THE BEAUTIES AND THE DANGERS
IN THE CYCLES OF THE MIGRATING ALEWIFE
ILLUSTRATED BY DAVID GROSE

Dust jacket for Hay's 1959 book, about a species of fish that annually returns from saltwater to freshwater to spawn (Richland County Public Library)

ral history and to document the timelessness of the alewives' rituals and the adverse rhythms and impact of the human inhabitants of Cape Cod.

This awareness of the human, both as a way through which to experience the world of nature and as an organism having potentially severe and irreversible impact on the land that Hay loved, led him to become active in conservation and preservationist activities in and around Brewster. In 1958 he helped found the Cape Cod Museum of Natural History. In his twenty-five years as president of the board of trustees for the museum, he helped establish its permanent home and preserved eighty acres of salt marsh for public education. "A constant force and the philosophical focus of the museum," according to its education director, "Hay was able to enact the conservation practices for which his writing called, ensuring that the land and ecology of Cape Cod would be preserved in more than just the pages of his books."

While Hay worked to preserve the natural heritage of Cape Cod against increasing urbanization, in 1960 the Hay family donated 650 acres of the New

Hampshire property to the Society for the Protection of New Hampshire Forests. The following year, 1961, Hay published *Nature's Year: The Seasons of Cape Cod,* a broader account of the landscape and biosystems of his home. The book reflects his increasing awareness of the interrelatedness of all creatures, captured in the short chapters of the book, each of which focuses on a seemingly mundane topic, such as an insect, a bird, or a change in temperature. Hay took up the same themes of interrelation and situatedness in his 1963 account of Cape Cod, *The Great Beach.* In it, he draws attention to the dominant and least understood feature of the cape—the beach—and the dangers that humans present to it. *The Great Beach* won Hay the John Burroughs Medal for excellence in nature writing in 1964 and brought Hay to more prominent national attention. With it Hay joined the ranks of other nature-writing luminaries such as Edwin Way Teale and Roger Tory Peterson. Harvard University also recognized its prominent alumnus Hay in 1963, appointing him Phi Beta Kappa Poet and conferring upon him honorary membership in Phi Beta Kappa.

Dust jacket for Hay's 1974 book, about seabirds related to but smaller than gulls (Richland County Public Library)

In addition to conferring literary honor on Hay, *The Great Beach* served as a segue into Hay's more determinedly environmental works of his midcareer. Coinciding with a shift to more concerted environmental advocacy in his writing was Hay's appointment as chairman of the Brewster Conservation Commission in 1964, a position he held until 1971. While on the Brewster Conservation Commission, Hay spearheaded an effort for the town to acquire more than two hundred acres of salt marshes by right of eminent domain, citing the loss of marshland to development in Connecticut and awareness that similar land loss was sure to follow on Cape Cod. In 1965, in response to the region's growing urbanization and to escape the ever more populous Cape Cod summers, the Hays bought a cottage on Broad Cove near Bremen, Maine, where Hay continues to write in the mornings in an old barn on the property when he is not gardening, boating, or birding. "Cape Cod I am afraid gets more impossible all the time," Hay writes. Despite a professed unease with any defined "environmental movement," Hay's political involvement demonstrates the close connection of his literary interests to his political and ethical practice.

The 1969 publication of his environmental treatise *In Defense of Nature* marked a more concerted political and educational agenda for Hay and reflects his public service in his writing. Compared to his early work, *In Defense of Nature* is less stylistically experimental and personal and is more educational in tone. By moving away from introspective, Thoreau-inflected observation and meditation, he sought a wider audience for his continued call for environmental awareness. He took advantage of his increased reputation and readership to popularize environmental awareness, co-authoring *The Primal Alliance: Earth and Ocean* (1971) with photographer Richard Kauffman. This text, like his 1962 *A Sense of Nature* (co-authored with Arline Strong), was written to educate and introduce environmental awareness to a popular nonliterary audience. The text in turn brought Hay's work to a larger audience and ensured him a place on the national environmental scene as the ecology movement gained momentum. For his ceaseless preservation and public education efforts, Hay was named Conservationist of the Year by the Massachusetts Wildlife Federation in 1970. Throughout the 1970s, as a member of the Standing Committee of the Massachusetts Trustees of Reservations, an organization dedicated to nature preservation and conservation, Hay continued to support and nurture conservation efforts around the state.

Hay's increasing emphasis on education resulted in his affiliation with Dartmouth College, where he was visiting professor of environmental studies for fifteen years (1972–1987). Dartmouth enabled Hay to pursue his interdisciplinary approach to learning about the environment–combining natural history, ecology, and literature in courses such as "Nature Writing" and "Nature and Human Values." During Hay's tenure at Dartmouth, the Hays spent autumns in Hanover and split the rest of the year between their beloved spots on Cape Cod and Broad Cove in Maine. In recognition of his achievements as an educator and author, the Henry David Thoreau School of Wilderness Studies at Eastern Connecticut State College awarded Hay the first Richard D. Perkins Award in 1978, presented to "people who have absorbed the natural and human history of a particular place and found its essence, and expressed it in some form."

Hay's retirement from Dartmouth at age seventy-two also marked his retirement from many of his most time-consuming public service roles. Upon the death of Hay's mother, Alice, in 1987, the remaining acreage of the The Fells at Sunapee Lake–including the main house and gardens, fields, woodlands, and lakeshore–were deeded to the U.S. Department of Fish and Wildlife and were named the John Hay National Wildlife Refuge after Hay's grandfather. Hay ensured that the estate would be used as a land studies center for conferences and study related to the human-land interactions that he values in his life's work and writing.

Hay redirected his energies once again to his writing—writing or editing eight books and collections during the 1980s and 1990s. He found a publishing home at Beacon Press, the publication branch of the Unitarian Universalist Association, whose social agenda fit Hay's own. In 1991, in recognition of his commitment to writing that addresses the relationship between people and nature, environmental education, and conservation, the Orion Society inaugurated the John Hay Award. Hay was its first recipient, and the award has since been given to such writers as Wendell Berry, E. O. Wilson, Ann Zwinger, Gary Snyder, Jane Goodall, Peter Matthiessen, Homero Aridjis, and W. S. Merwin. Vision problems due to macular degeneration have not stopped Hay from producing some of his finest work in the late decades of his life. In *The Bird of Light* (1991) and *In the Company of Light* (1998) Hay once again turns his focus to the mysteries of migration and the seasons. His edited collections, *The Great House of Birds* (1996) and *Thoreau on Birds* (1993), explore and reveal his delight in birdwatching that dates to his early poetry and figures prominently in his writing throughout his career. They also document his literary influences and tastes. *A Beginner's Faith in Things Unseen* (1995) is a series of reminiscences and reflections, and *The Way to the Salt Marsh* (1998), Hay's own selection of the best of his writing, reveals his understanding of his own literary life and progress.

According to Christopher Merrill, John Hay is "the nature writer's nature writer, an elegant stylist and illustrator of the Emersonian notion that the world is emblematic." Yet, Hay is the first to admit the limits of human understanding of nature, when in *The Run* he asks, "Is there any man who knows the length and breadth of anything, let alone a creek?" Thus, he acknowledges the limits of human knowledge and endeavor even as he relentlessly pursues them.

References:

Robert Finch and John Elder, *Nature Writing: The Tradition in English* (New York: Norton, 2002);

Cynthia Huntington, "John Hay," in *American Nature Writers,* edited by Elder (New York: Scribners, 1996);

Thomas J. Lyon, *This Incomperable Lande* (Boston: Houghton Mifflin, 1989);

Christopher Merrill, introduction to John Hay, *The Way to the Salt Marsh* (Hanover, N.H.: University Press of New England, 1998);

Andi Rierden, "Bringing Back Coastal Treasures," *Gulf of Maine Times* (Summer 2001): 1–3;

Stephen Trimble, ed., *Words from the Land: Encounters with Natural History Writing* (Salt Lake City: Peregrine Smith, 1988);

Frederick Turner, *Spirit of Place: The Making of an American Literary Landscape* (San Francisco: Sierra Club Books, 1989).

Joseph Wood Krutch

(25 November 1893 – 22 May 1970)

Paul N. Pavich
Fort Lewis College

See also the Krutch entries in *DLB 63: Modern American Critics, 1920–1955* and *DLB 206: Twentieth-Century American Western Writers, First Series.*

BOOKS: *Comedy and Conscience after the Restoration* (New York: Columbia University Press, 1924; enlarged, 1949);

Edgar Allan Poe: A Study in Genius (New York: Knopf, 1926; London: Knopf, 1926);

The Modern Temper: A Study and a Confession (New York: Harcourt, Brace, 1929; London: Cape, 1930);

Five Masters: A Study in the Mutations of the Novel (New York: Cape & Smith, 1930); republished as *Five Masters: Boccaccio, Cervantes, Richardson, Stendahl, Proust. A Study in the Mutations of the Novel* (London: Cape, 1931);

Living Philosophies, by Krutch and others (New York: Simon & Schuster, 1931);

Experience and Art: Some Aspects of the Esthetics of Literature (New York: Smith & Haas, 1932);

Was Europe a Success? (New York: Farrar & Rinehart, 1934; London: Methuen, 1935);

The American Drama since 1918: An Informal History (New York: Random House, 1939; revised and enlarged edition, New York: Braziller, 1957; London: Thames & Hudson, 1957);

Samuel Johnson (New York: Holt, 1944; London: Cassell, 1948);

Henry David Thoreau (New York: Sloane, 1948; London: Methuen, 1949);

The Twelve Seasons: A Perpetual Calendar for the Country (New York: Sloane, 1949);

The Last Boswell Paper: Printed for the Friends of Philip and Fanny Duschnes (Woodstock, Vt.: Elm Tree Press, 1951);

The Desert Year (New York: Sloane, 1952);

The Best of Two Worlds (New York: Sloane, 1953);

"Modernism" in Modern Drama: A Definition and an Estimate (Ithaca, N.Y.: Cornell University Press, 1953);

Is the Common Man Too Common? An Informal Survey of Our Cultural Resources and What We Are Doing about

Joseph Wood Krutch, late 1960s (from John D. Margolis, Joseph Wood Krutch, 1980)

Them, by Krutch and others (Norman: University of Oklahoma Press, 1954);

The Measure of Man: On Freedom, Human Values, Survival and the Modern Temper (Indianapolis: Bobbs-Merrill, 1954; London: Redman, 1956);

The Voice of the Desert: A Naturalist's Interpretation (New York: Sloane, 1955; London: Redman, 1956);

The Great Chain of Life (Boston: Houghton Mifflin, 1956; London: Eyre & Spottiswood, 1956);

Grand Canyon: Today and All Its Yesterdays (New York: Sloane, 1958);

Human Nature and the Human Condition (New York: Random House, 1959);

The Forgotten Peninsula: A Naturalist in Baja California (New York: Sloane, 1961);

Modern Literature and the Image of Man (San Francisco: Industrial Indemnity, 1962);

More Lives than One (New York: Sloane, 1962);

If You Don't Mind My Saying So . . . : Essays on Man and Nature (New York: Sloane, 1964);

Herbal (New York: Putnam, 1965; London: Phaidon, 1976);

The Most Wonderful Animals That Never Were (Boston: Houghton Mifflin, 1969).

Editions and Collections: *And Even If You Do: Essays on Man, Manners and Machines* (New York: Morrow, 1967);

Baja California and the Geography of Hope, text by Krutch, photographs by Eliot Porter, edited by Kenneth Brower (San Francisco: Sierra Club Books, 1967);

The Best Nature Writing of Joseph Wood Krutch (New York: Morrow, 1969);

A Krutch Omnibus: Forty Years of Social and Literary Criticism (New York: Morrow, 1970);

The Great Chain of Life, preface by Edward Abbey (Boston: Houghton Mifflin, 1977).

RECORDINGS: *The Modern Idea of Man,* read by Krutch, McGraw-Hill, 75838, 1968;

What Does Human Nature Mean? read by Krutch, McGraw-Hill, 75572, 1969.

OTHER: "Modern Love and Modern Fiction," in *Our Changing Morality: A Symposium,* edited by Freda Kirchwey (New York: Boni, 1924), pp. 167–179;

The Comedies of William Congreve, edited by Krutch (New York: Macmillan, 1927);

Eugene O'Neill, *Nine Plays by Eugene O'Neill, Selected by the Author,* introduction by Krutch (New York: Liveright, 1932);

Marcel Proust, *Remembrance of Things Past,* 4 volumes, translated by C. K. Scott Moncrieff, introduction by Krutch (New York: Random House, 1934);

Montrose J. Moses, ed., *Representative American Dramas, National and Local, Edited, with Introductions . . . ,* revised by Krutch (Boston: Little, Brown, 1941);

Great American Nature Writing, edited by Krutch (New York: Sloane, 1950);

Thomas Gray, *The Selected Letters of Thomas Gray,* edited by Krutch (New York: Farrar, Straus & Young, 1952);

The Gardener's World, edited by Krutch (New York: Putnam, 1959);

The World of Animals: A Treasury of Lore, Legend and Literature by Great Writers and Naturalists from 5th Century B.C. to the Present, edited by Krutch (New York: Simon & Schuster, 1961);

Henry David Thoreau, *Thoreau: Walden and Other Writings,* edited by Krutch (New York: Bantam, 1962);

A Treasury of Birdlore, edited by Krutch and Paul S. Eriksson (Garden City, N.Y.: Doubleday, 1962);

Eighteenth Century English Drama, edited by Krutch (New York: Bantam, 1967);

Grand Canyon, photographs by Ernst A. Heiniger, texts by Krutch and others, German texts translated by Ewald Osers (Washington, D.C.: Luce, 1975).

The life of Joseph Wood Krutch is a study in transformation. In the 1920s he was a spokesman for the cynical modernists, who felt that all values had been lost. As part of the New York intellectual circle, he had observed the alienation of many of his contemporaries. His 1929 book, *The Modern Temper: A Study and a Confession,* was hailed as a crucial assessment of the pessimistic spirit of the times. It posited that humanity was separated from any connection to nature and that traditional faiths were irrelevant to modern existence. While he reveled in the attention that this book brought him, he was uneasy with its pervasive sense of detachment and despair. Over the next two decades he struggled to find a creed that would take him beyond the philosophical negativity of the early twentieth century. He discovered such a belief in understanding and experiencing the wonders of the natural world. By the 1950s he had become a vocal critic of the excesses of American materialism and the degradation of the environment, a byproduct of a misguided notion of progress. At the same time, he began to write works that were detailed analyses of the natural world, especially of his new home in the Sonoran Desert. There he became an enthusiastic student of ecology, biology, zoology, and geology in addition to literature and the arts.

Krutch was born to middle-class parents in Knoxville, Tennessee, on 25 November 1893. In his autobiography, *More Lives than One* (1962), he says that his conservative upbringing was typical for a child at that time, although he had a few relatives whose nonconformity rubbed off on him. His primary interests in school were mathematics and science. In 1911 he decided to enroll at the University of Tennessee, where he became more and more interested in the theater and literature. Upon completion of his undergraduate degree in 1915, Krutch moved to New York City to start graduate studies in English at Columbia University. At Columbia he began the scholarly career that spanned the next five decades and brought him into contact with some of the

Krutch, circa 1897, with his older brother's bicycle (from Margolis, Joseph Wood Krutch, *1980)*

intellectual and artistic luminaries of the twentieth century, including Eugene O'Neill, T. S. Eliot, H. L. Mencken, and Sergei Eisenstein. Krutch also took another important step in New York on 10 February 1923 when he married Marcelle Leguia, his beloved companion for the rest of his life. Krutch began his writing profession in earnest in 1924 when he accepted a position as contributor to the liberal magazine *The Nation,* a post he retained for more than a quarter of a century. *Comedy and Conscience after the Restoration,* his first major work, appeared that same year. Two years later, in 1926, he published a controversial biography, *Edgar Allan Poe: A Study in Genius,* which added to his reputation as an important new voice in American letters.

In 1929 he achieved national attention with the publication of *The Modern Temper: A Study and a Confession.* While this book brought him recognition, it also launched him on a quest for some meaning to fill the modernist void he described. Krutch's positions in this work are that the humanistic notion of mankind's importance in the universe has been shattered by the discoveries of science and psychology, that religious belief has become an empty form clung to desperately by those who need reassurance of their centrality and purpose, and that the idea of a connection to nature is a romantic illusion. He is convinced that mankind's role

in the universe is one of total alienation. In his conclusion Krutch voices his deep pessimism about the human condition, which he sees as a "lost cause." His thesis that "there is no place for us in the natural universe" proved to be the crucial issue for him, one that he later rejected as his knowledge of the workings of nature grew.

Within months of the publication of *The Modern Temper,* the stock market crashed and the Great Depression began. The pessimism that characterized Krutch's work threatened to overwhelm all of America. People looked for answers in a variety of systems, among them communism and fascism. Krutch had witnessed first-hand the Soviet system in Moscow when he had gone there on a tour to assess the state of the theater under the Marxist regime in the late 1920s. He was appalled by the control that the state assumed over both the arts and people's lives in general. While many of his colleagues at *The Nation* openly espoused the Marxist cause, Krutch aligned himself with humanism and individualism. He was viewed as a reactionary and was rejected by some of the intellectuals who had formerly supported him. Eventually, Krutch felt so out of step with many of his contemporaries at *The Nation* that he retained only his position as drama critic.

During the 1930s he published *Five Masters: A Study in the Mutations of the Novel* (1930), *Experience and Art: Some Aspects of the Esthetics of Literature* (1932), *Was Europe a Success?* (1934), and *The American Drama since 1918: An Informal History* (1939). While these works were not best-sellers, they further increased Krutch's scholarly prestige. His growing reputation came to the notice of Columbia University, where he became a professor of dramatic literature in 1937. During this same period he made a decision that had a great influence on his later nature writing. He decided to buy a country home in Connecticut, where he began to observe a different drama, that of his environment. This move had a profound effect on the way he viewed both urban culture and nature.

In the 1940s Krutch turned his attention to completing two more biographies, one of Samuel Johnson and the other of Henry David Thoreau. The response to *Samuel Johnson* (1944) was favorable and gave Krutch the incentive to complete *Henry David Thoreau* in 1948. This work was a crucial step in his own development as a nature writer. Thoreau had interested Krutch for more than a decade, but his experience in the Connecticut countryside had created a clearer understanding of Thoreau's message. Krutch shared Thoreau's notion that society needed less complexity and less mechanization in order to find the leisure time to enjoy life. Thoreau questioned the easy optimism of America about progress and Manifest Destiny, suggesting instead that people shape their own destinies. Krutch believed that the twentieth century likewise had problems with systems that took away a sense of individualism. Freudianism, Marxism, Darwinism, and their philosophical offshoots presupposed an environment in which people were playthings of enormous forces over which they had no control. Both writers rejected such a deterministic view in favor of self-reliance and individual moral choice.

In Thoreau's writings Krutch found answers to some of his own profound questions about existence. He was sure that his contemporaries could benefit from Thoreau's belief in sharing in "the wonder and joy of living things." The traits that Thoreau valued were precisely what Krutch was looking for himself–joy, simplicity, delight, originality, and individuality. Moreover, Thoreau's style, a blend of detailed observation of nature and familiar narration, was one that Krutch soon experimented with on his own.

The Twelve Seasons: A Perpetual Calendar for the Country, Krutch's reflections on a year spent at his country home in Connecticut, was published in 1949. Using Thoreau's *Walden* (1854) as a model, Krutch discusses various aspects of the environmental cycle from one spring season to the next. His discourse is not only about interesting facets of natural phenomena but also about contemporary social and philosophical issues. In this book he likewise discusses his growing attraction to the idea of pantheism. When he describes the spring peepers–the small, noisy frogs that populate the area–Krutch says, "we both, equally, belong to something more inclusive than ourselves." He believes that there is an affinity among all life forms, a spiritual democracy. His earlier pessimism of *The Modern Temper* is overcome by his astonishment at the complex relationships he witnesses in nature; Krutch now feels he is a part of something, not alienated and purposeless as he felt in 1929.

The Twelve Seasons is extremely different from much of Krutch's scholarly work. While the sophisticated, analytical academician is still evident, he uses a familiar style in his descriptions, one that seems to include the reader almost as a friend. He also demonstrates an eye for the absurd and a gentle sense of humor about humanity's foibles. One of the more humorous passages in the book is Krutch's account of a visit from one of his New York City friends. The man is unhappy with the prospect of spending so much time in a natural setting, which seems to pose some vague threat. Krutch ponders the reasons why nature makes people so uncomfortable. He connects the fear to those aspects of modernism about which he had written so eloquently twenty years earlier. Many of his urban contemporaries appear to be completely detached from the realm of nature and ultimately from any meaning at all.

Krutch now proposes the idea that overcrowded cities seem to breed disillusionment.

Reaction to the book was positive; critics noted its charm, wisdom, and style. The critical success of the book fueled Krutch's desire to delve more deeply into experiencing the natural world and to record those experiences for what appeared to be an appreciative audience. He immediately took on the task of collecting a wide variety of essays on nature, which he published in 1950 as *Great American Nature Writing.*

He begins the collection with a lengthy commentary that both discusses the evolution of the nature essay and offers valuable insight into his own developing interest in the field. Krutch notes that during the Age of Enlightenment some members of the scientific and intellectual world, while interested in the study of nature, also became emotionally detached from it. To them the cosmos was a vast machine, with the creatures that inhabited it simply smaller machines. He sees a reaction to this idea in the Romantic period with its notions of the sublime unity of all creation. An unfortunate outcome of the tension between the two views is that some Romantics became contemptuous of science and concerned themselves only with a mystical apprehension of their environment. Krutch finds in Thoreau a sense of balance between the two views and both an appreciation of the scientific examination of nature and an awareness of the spiritual interrelatedness of all life. In this collection Krutch includes essays by those writers who share this balanced view and rejects essays by those writers who are either detached scientists or explorers recording only their hopes for exploitation of the land.

In order to do the research necessary for his next book, Krutch requested that Columbia University grant him a sabbatical for 1950–1951. He moved to Tucson and spent more than a year there recording his experiences in the desert. The result was one of his most popular and enduring works, *The Desert Year* (1952). His enjoyment of life in this dry setting is readily apparent. Despite that much of his life had been spent as a New Yorker, he seems completely at home in Arizona. Krutch says that it "almost seemed I had known and loved it in some previous existence." He fell under the spell of the Southwest, as have so many other writers from John Van Dyke and Mary Austin to Edward Abbey and Barbara Kingsolver. Krutch's biographer, John D. Margolis, notes that Krutch "reveled in the society of the plants and animals surrounding his new desert home." He again turns to the familiar essay to discuss everything that catches his attention–bats, frogs, roadrunners, scorpions, saguaro cactus, mountains.

The Krutch country house in Redding, Connecticut, during the 1940s
(*from Margolis,* Joseph Wood Krutch, *1980*)

At the same time, Krutch reiterates his concern with the increasing materialism and spiritual vacuity of mid-century America. Krutch thinks that too many people are passive consumers unable to enjoy the richness of life by actively engaging in and understanding the complex process of nature. He also assails those biologists who refuse to connect with the object of their studies. According to Krutch, many of these scientists are so eager to dissect everything that the real name for their discipline should be *thanatology,* the study of death, rather than *biology,* the study of life. He is even more insistent than in his previous books that humanity learn to treasure the environment and to "share in her joy."

The positive reception of *The Desert Year* launched him on yet another phase of his multifaceted career: interpreter and defender of the desert. Ruthven Todd, in his review in *The Nation* (19 April 1952), said that Krutch had "succeeded in making the desert appear, to one who has never known it, a real and intensely interesting place." Fellow writers Frank Waters and Edwin Way Teale were also enthusiastic in their praise of the book. More accolades came when the American Museum of Natural History honored Krutch with its John Burroughs Medal for *The Desert Year.*

With this success under his belt, Krutch returned to New York City, where he struggled with his realiza-tion that his primary interest was no longer in review-ing for the theater, which he found nearly nihilistic, nor in teaching, which made overwhelming demands on his time. His Thoreauvian existence in the Southwest had produced both a positive effect on his often frail health and a desire to spend more time in writing and enjoying the desert, which he had grown to love. In 1952, to the amazement of some of his friends, he gave up his posi-tion as contributor to *The Nation* as well as his professor-ship at Columbia University and moved permanently to his new home in Tucson.

The next two books that he published demon-strate the intellectual ferment he was undergoing at this point in his life. In *"Modernism" in Modern Drama: A Defi-nition and an Estimate* (1953) he takes a hard-nosed approach to what he believes has been the devaluation of the human spirit in modern literature. The man who was the standard-bearer of modernism in 1929 now totally rejects its premises. He cites the despair and alienation of modernism as a philosophical dead end resulting in mental and spiritual apathy.

For him the antidote to this problem resided in nature, so not surprisingly, in *The Best of Two Worlds* (1953) he again turns to the nature essay. This work is a collection of observations completed while he was still in Connecticut, a type of companion piece to or extension of *The Twelve Seasons*. In *The Best of Two Worlds* he reflects on a wide variety of flora and fauna, including cats, mice, spiders, and the Christmas cactus. One of his major philosophical concerns is the increasing mechanization of humanity and the concurrent diminishing of a sense of organic participation in the cycle of nature. In the midst of considering serious moral problems, he is still able to retain his sense of humor. At the end of the book he jokingly suggests to readers who do not want to be troubled with ethical considerations that they tear out the postscript. With tongue in cheek he concludes, "Most of the preaching can then go into the wastebasket with it."

His next book was yet another pivotal moment in his development. *The Measure of Man: On Freedom, Human Values, Survival and the Modern Temper* (1954) is his insightful rebuttal to the skepticism and disbelief of *The Modern Temper*. Krutch rejects all systems that dehumanize and trivialize existence. *The Measure of Man* added further to Krutch's status when it received the prestigious National Book Award for nonfiction for that year.

Krutch's growing understanding of nature became the basis for the renewal of his sense of purpose, which ultimately led to the contentment he had sought for so long. In the process of putting down new roots in the desert, he felt he was beginning to achieve the sense of awareness and joy that Thoreau had insisted was central to living life fully. He summarized the changes he experienced in *The Voice of the Desert: A Naturalist's Interpretation* (1955). Krutch demonstrates that the few years he has spent living in that arid region have already deepened his comprehension of its mysteries. He insists even more than in his earlier writing that all life is continuous and shares to some extent the same emotions humans have. He appreciates the endurance of the creatures that inhabit the area and their ability to adapt to such difficult conditions. He states, "We tend to admire trees, as well as men, who bear the stamp of their successful struggles with a certain amount of adversity."

In the midst of his metaphysical musings Krutch warns that one cannot be solely "mystical" in encountering nature but also must learn as much as possible in order to achieve a complete appreciation. To those who rhapsodize over natural phenomena, he recommends a full course of studies as well. He believes that "It is not ignorance but knowledge which is the mother of wonder." Krutch suggests that one can retreat to the desert, as did many mystics, to experience a different type of reality. But he thought that the result of such a retreat should be both a fascination with the environment and a desire to know more about it. During this period Krutch practices what he preaches by engaging in a

wide variety of scientific investigations. The outcome of all this study is a different perspective that enables him "to participate with a fresh understanding in the life of other natural communities." The alienation of his earlier years has now been replaced with a sense of harmony and wholeness.

In 1956 Krutch followed *The Voice of the Desert* with an extended discourse on the values to be found in nature, *The Great Chain of Life*. During this investigation of the range of life forms from single-celled creatures to human beings, Krutch takes issue with some aspects of the theory of evolution. He is troubled by those adherents of Darwinism whose vision of the world relegates people to the role of automatons. Again he assails members of both the literary and the scientific worlds who have reduced life to a set of mechanical responses to stimuli. The more he has observed nature, the more he is convinced that there is some drive at work that is beyond mere survival. While he does not deny that there is an evolutionary process at work in the universe, he firmly believes that the inclusion of a moral and spiritual dimension in this process is absolutely essential to a meaningful life.

He begins the book with a discussion of the amazing existence of the single-celled organism the volvox. His reflections on the organism's ability to reproduce sexually lead him to the conclusion that in order for it to participate in procreation it also must die. Wondering if sexuality is worth the steep price, Krutch writes that "Nature's answer . . . has been a pretty steady *Yes*." In his typical fashion he moves from consideration of the volvox to philosophical reflections on larger issues. He wonders why so many people accept the idea that humans have souls but absolutely reject the possibility that other forms of life might also possess them. Repudiating simplistic anthropocentric views, he celebrates the complex lives of wasps and butterflies, birds and bighorn sheep. As he moves into the realm of the "higher beings," Krutch restates his position that evolution is not merely mechanical but that it has as its goal increased consciousness and the development of intelligence. He asserts that everything plays a role in this evolution and hence deserves respect. In the chapter "Reverence for Life" he presses his point by berating those who hunt merely for sport. He is disturbed that often these hunters seem to feel no connection with other beings, because for them the world has become one vast shooting gallery designed solely for their pleasure. Krutch rejects the argument that other creatures cannot share some of the same emotions that humans have, what has been termed the pathetic fallacy. For him this so-called fallacy has become an article of faith.

The conclusion of this book includes some of Krutch's most lyrical writing. He characterizes as real

*Krutch observing nature in the desert near Tucson, Arizona,
1960s (from Margolis,* Joseph Wood
Krutch, *1980)*

the joy of a cardinal that is singing outside his home. In Krutch's judgment the bird's apparent happiness is a quality that remains the missing element in many people's lives. He suggests that if human society were more open to understanding the larger environment, then perhaps it would regain its lost joy. Krutch observes, "Nothing the lesser creatures can teach us is more worth learning than the lesson of gladness." The enthusiastic response to *The Great Chain of Life* demonstrated that such sentiments had struck a responsive chord with readers. Marston Bates, reviewing the book for *The New York Times* (6 January 1957), said it was "the best introduction to natural history that has yet been written." In his mid sixties Krutch undertook a series of expeditions to northern Arizona that culminated in the 1958 publication *Grand Canyon: Today and All Its Yesterdays.* The work is not just a tourist's description of the landscape but also a free-ranging study of many facets of the area from the nearly unbelievable geological formations to the overpopulation of the deer on the rim to a record of the human presence in the area. Krutch celebrates the rejuvenating solitude,

peace, and spaciousness that are available to those who will take the time to saunter off the road and discover that there is much more to enjoy than what is available to the "automobilists" who hover around the rim road. When he hikes the trail to the bottom, he marvels at the changing layers of the rocks as well as the different flora and fauna he experiences as he nears the Colorado River. In awe of all the life zones he has passed through, he remarks that "the five-thousand foot drop to the bottom is equivalent climatically to a journey of some three thousand miles southward." The wondrous spectacle reminds him of the absurdity of humanity's concentrating solely on its own accomplishments in light of the brevity of its tenure on the land.

The beauty he witnesses prompts him to contemplate the importance of wilderness and the pressure put on both the land and other species from what he thinks is euphemistically termed "progress." Krutch's apprehensions about the development of the Southwest reflect Thoreau's concern for New England a hundred years earlier. He is unhappy that so much environmental degradation takes place in order to respond to the demands of the consumer culture of America for those things that are often superfluous. Especially troubling is the extinction of plants and animals in the name of human "improvement." Krutch laments, "The variety of nature grows less and less. The monotony of the chain store begins to dominate more and more completely." His answer is that individuals must find ways to simplify their lives so that the environment may be protected. In the conclusion of the book he requests that his readers bear in mind the significance of cultivating an appreciation of wilderness, since it is "one of the permanent homes of the human spirit."

In his 1959 book *Human Nature and the Human Condition,* Krutch once more returned to his role as social critic before shifting back to the nature essay in what was his last major work in that genre, *The Forgotten Peninsula: A Naturalist in Baja California* (1961). For many years the elderly Krutch had been taking trips into the then nearly roadless Baja Peninsula. He records his undiminished joy in the sparsely settled region, which is filled with so many surprising manifestations of adaptability in both the natural and the human realms. While the going is often difficult, he explains that he has found the patience to endure physical hardship when the goal is to partake in the pleasure of interpreting a new environment.

In this book Krutch emphatically restates his concern over the consequences of overpopulation, already evident in the explosive growth of some cities in Arizona. In musing about the basis of what is termed the greater good, he concludes that "the greater number and the greater good are often not compatible." He mentions that bad roads are a boon to those who enjoy

Joseph Wood Krutch with one of Nature's small wonders

JOSEPH WOOD KRUTCH, a man of many distinguished careers—drama critic, teacher, naturalist, philosopher, man of letters—had his first book published in 1924; and the many that have followed, ranging in subject matter from Restoration comedy to American wildlife to the cinema's New Wave—attest to the extraordinary breadth of his interests. Born in Knoxville, Tennessee, he lived for many years in New York and Connecticut and now resides in Tucson, Arizona. In 1967 he was awarded the Emerson-Thoreau medal of the American Academy of Arts and Sciences.

THE BEST NATURE WRITING OF JOSEPH WOOD KRUTCH

SELECTED AND WITH AN INTRODUCTION BY THE AUTHOR

Dust jacket for a volume of previously collected essays published during the last year of Krutch's life
(Richland County Public Library)

experiencing untrammeled wilderness, since they keep out the crowds of people who really are not interested in the land. He demonstrates prophetic insight in foreseeing that the building of a good road in Baja California will bring with it rows of luxury resorts in which people will demand the same "amenities" they expect in the other California to the north.

Krutch also worries about the impact of industrialization on the wildlife of the area, especially the whales that calve in the lagoons of Baja. His sometimes carefree mood in *The Forgotten Peninsula* changes when he reflects upon this issue. The bleak statement "genocide is a human invention" is offset by his confidence that enlightened people can still learn to treasure all the creatures that make up the chain of life. The cultivation of such respect is the basis of what Krutch believes is truly the good life. He is fully aware that he is a tourist just as are many other visitors to Baja. His hope is that the book will convince like-minded tourists to join him in treading lightly and enjoying the place for what it has to offer rather than trying to force it to become a carbon copy of so many "developed" areas.

The Forgotten Peninsula was followed by his autobiography, *More Lives than One,* and a book of previously published essays, *If You Don't Mind My Saying So . . . : Essays on Man and Nature* (1964). His 1965 book, *Herbal,* profusely illustrated with woodcuts, traces the history of the medicinal uses of scores of herbs. In the introduction Krutch mentions that during the Middle Ages every herb was thought to have a purpose. He lightheartedly berates those skeptical people who scoff at traditional remedies in favor of the drugs found in their pharmacies, since they do not understand that many of those drugs are herb-based. He also points out that while the modern scientist may be unwilling to celebrate the beauty of a plant when describing its usefulness, as an amateur he feels no such reluctance.

In 1967 the Sierra Club published *Baja California and the Geography of Hope,* a book that featured selections from Krutch's earlier works interspersed with photographs by Eliot Porter. In the introduction Krutch honors Porter for creating art that represents a connection with wilderness rather than following the tendency of many contemporary artists to foster alienation. He again reaffirms the notion that spiritual growth and awareness cannot be achieved outside of nature. This work was followed by three more collections of previously published essays—*And Even If You Do: Essays on Man, Manners and Machines* (1967), *The Best Nature Writing of Joseph Wood Krutch* (1969), and *A Krutch Omnibus: Forty Years of Social and Literary Criticism* (1970). Fittingly, one of the last books he completed was the fanciful *The Most Wonderful Animals That Never Were* (1969), an account of creatures such as griffins and unicorns.

On 22 May 1970 Joseph Wood Krutch, attended by his wife, succumbed to the cancer he had been battling. As he was dying, he commented to her that it was not so bad but that he wished he could have had a little more time so that he might have played a larger role in the budding environmental movement. Krutch's career spanned more than four decades and a wide variety of occupations—theater reviewer, university professor, social critic, and nature writer. He was a prolific author whose expertise was recognized in both the arts and the sciences. Hundreds of his essays appeared in leading American journals such as *Harper's Magazine, The Saturday Review of Literature, The Nation,* and *The American Scholar* as well as in popular magazines such as *Life* and *House & Garden.*

One of the accomplishments in which he took special pride was helping to establish the Arizona-Sonora Desert Museum, acknowledged as one of the foremost institutions for the study of natural history in the country. A man of integrity, he was just as unafraid of standing up to unthinking developers who wanted to destroy the landscape of the Southwest in the 1960s as he had been to defying the Marxist intellectuals who conveniently overlooked Stalinist atrocities in the 1930s.

Krutch holds a position of prominence in the field of nature writing. He has been hailed as a twentieth-century Thoreau and cited as one of the founders of the environmental movement. In *Southwest Classics: The Creative Literature of the Arid Lands* (1974), Lawrence Clark Powell notes that Krutch's answer to the question of the meaning of life went beyond human society to include a regard for the entire ecological system. Another of Krutch's admirers, writer and fellow environmentalist Abbey, describes him as an outspoken champion of those values essential to existence. Commenting in the preface to *The Great Chain of Life,* Abbey heartily approves of Krutch's "unwavering insistence,

to the very end of his life, on the primacy of freedom, purpose, will, play, and joy, and on the kinship of the human with all forms of life."

Interview:

Edward Abbey, "On Nature, the Modern Temper and the Southwest: An Interview with Joseph Wood Krutch," *Sage,* 2 (1968): 13–21.

Bibliography:

Anthony L. Lehman, "Joseph Wood Krutch: A Selected Annotated Bibliography of Primary Sources," *Bulletin of Bibliography,* 41 (June 1984): 74–80.

Biography:

John D. Margolis, *Joseph Wood Krutch: A Writer's Life* (Knoxville: University of Tennessee Press, 1980).

References:

Paul Brooks, ed., *Speaking for Nature: How Literary Naturalists from Henry Thoreau to Rachel Carson Have Shaped America* (Boston: Houghton Mifflin, 1980), pp. 192–198;

Patricia Nelson Limerick, *Desert Passages: Encounters with the American Desert* (Albuquerque: University of New Mexico Press, 1985), pp. 127–148;

James I. McClintock, *Nature's Kindred Spirits: Aldo Leopold, Joseph Wood Krutch, Edward Abbey, Annie Dillard and Gary Snyder* (Madison: University of Wisconsin Press, 1994), pp. 46–65;

Fred Y. Osborne, *The Osborne Index of Twelve Books by Joseph Wood Krutch* (Tucson: Arizona-Sonora Desert Museum, 1977);

Lawrence Clark Powell, *Southwest Classics: The Creative Literature of the Arid Lands* (Los Angeles: Ritchie Press, 1974), pp. 331–341;

Peter Wild, *Pioneer Conservationists of Western America* (Missoula, Mont.: Mountain Press, 1979), pp. 131–139.

Papers:

The majority of Joseph Wood Krutch's papers, including some of his journals, lecture notes, and letters, are in the Manuscript Division of the Library of Congress. Some of Krutch's papers also can be found in the libraries of Columbia University, Harvard University, and the University of Arizona.

Ursula K. Le Guin

(21 October 1929 –   )

Charlotte Zoe Walker
State University of New York, Oneonta

See also the Le Guin entries in *DLB 8: Twentieth-Century American Science-Fiction Writers, DLB 52: American Writers for Children Since 1960: Fiction,* and *DLB 256: Twentieth-Century American Western Writers, Third Series.*

BOOKS: *Rocannon's World* (New York: Ace, 1966; London: Tandem, 1972; revised edition, New York: Harper & Row, 1977);

Planet of Exile (New York: Ace, 1966; London: Tandem, 1972);

City of Illusions (New York: Ace, 1967; London: Gollancz, 1971);

A Wizard of Earthsea (Berkeley, Cal.: Parnassus, 1968; London: Gollancz, 1971);

The Left Hand of Darkness (New York: Walker, 1969; London: Macdonald, 1969);

The Lathe of Heaven (New York: Scribners, 1971; London: Gollancz, 1972);

The Tombs of Atuan (New York: Atheneum, 1971; London: Gollancz, 1972);

The Farthest Shore (New York: Atheneum, 1972; London: Gollancz, 1973);

The Word for World Is Forest (New York: Berkley, 1972; London: Gollancz, 1977);

From Elfland to Poughkeepsie (Portland, Ore.: Pendragon, 1973);

The Dispossessed: An Ambiguous Utopia (New York: Harper & Row, 1974; London: Gollancz, 1974);

Dreams Must Explain Themselves (New York: Algol Press, 1975);

Wild Angels (Santa Barbara, Cal.: Capra Press, 1975);

The Wind's Twelve Quarters: Short Stories (New York: Harper & Row, 1975; London: Gollancz, 1976);

Very Far Away from Anywhere Else (New York: Atheneum, 1976); republished as *A Very Long Way from Anywhere Else* (London: Gollancz, 1976);

Walking in Cornwall (N.p., 1976);

Orsinian Tales (New York: Harper & Row, 1976; London: Gollancz, 1977);

The Eye of the Heron (South Yarmouth, Mass.: Curley, 1978; London: Gollancz, 1982);

Ursula K. Le Guin (photograph by Wes Guderian; from the dust jacket for The Lathe of Heaven, *1971)*

The Language of the Night: Essays on Fantasy and Science Fiction, edited by Susan Wood (New York: Putnam, 1979; revised and edited by Le Guin, London: Women's Press, 1989; New York: HarperCollins, 1992);

Leese Webster (New York: Atheneum, 1979; London: Gollancz, 1981);

Malafrena (New York: Berkley, 1979; London: Gollancz, 1980);

Tillae and Tylissos, by Le Guin and Theodora Kroeber (St. Helena, U.K., Berkeley, Cal. & Portland: Red Bull, 1979);

The Beginning Place (New York: Harper & Row, 1980); republished as *Threshold* (London: Gollancz, 1980);

Gwilan's Harp (Northridge, Cal.: Lord John Press, 1981);

Hard Words, and Other Poems (New York: Harper & Row, 1981);

The Adventure of Cobbler's Rune (New Castle, Va.: Cheap Street, 1982);

The Compass Rose: Short Stories (New York: Harper & Row, 1982; London: Gollancz, 1983);

In the Red Zone, by Le Guin and Henk Pander (Northridge, Cal.: Lord John Press, 1983);

Solomon Leviathan's Nine Hundred and Thirty-First Trip around the World (New Castle, Va.: Cheap Street, 1983);

The Visionary: The Life Story of Flicker of the Serpentine of Telina-Na, published with *Wonders Hidden: Audubon's Early Years,* by Scott Russell Saunders (Santa Barbara, Cal.: Capra Press, 1984);

Always Coming Home (New York: Harper & Row, 1985; London: Gollancz, 1986);

King Dog: A Screenplay, published with *Dostoevsky: A Screenplay,* by Raymond Carver and Tess Gallagher (Santa Barbara, Cal.: Capra Press, 1985);

Buffalo Gals and Other Animal Presences (Santa Barbara, Cal.: Capra Press, 1987; London: Gollancz, 1990);

Catwings (New York: Orchard Books, 1988);

A Visit from Dr. Katz (New York: Atheneum, 1988; London: Collins, 1988);

Wild Oats and Fireweed: New Poems (New York: Perennial Library, 1988);

Catwings Return (New York: Orchard Books, 1989);

Dancing at the Edge of the World: Thoughts on Words, Women, Places (New York: Grove, 1989; London: Gollancz, 1989);

Fire and Stone (New York: Atheneum, 1989);

The Way of the Water's Going: Images of the Northern California Coastal Range, text by Le Guin, photographs by Ernest Waugh and Alan Nicholson (New York: Harper & Row, 1989);

Tehanu: The Last Book of Earthsea (New York: Atheneum, 1990; London: Gollancz, 1990);

A Winter Solstice Ritual for the Pacific Northwest, by Le Guin and Vonda N. McIntyre (N.p.: Ygor & Buntho / Make Books Press, 1991);

Searoad: Chronicles of Klatsand (New York: HarperCollins, 1991; London: Gollancz, 1992);

Blue Moon over Thurman Street (Portland, Ore.: NewSage Press, 1992);

Findings (N.p.: Ox Head, 1992);

Fish Soup (New York: Atheneum, 1992);

No Boats (N.p: Ygor & Buntho / Make Books Press, 1992);

A Ride on the Red Mare's Back (New York: Orchard Books, 1992);

Earthsea Revisioned (Cambridge, Mass.: Children's Literature New England / Cambridge, U.K.: Green Bay Publications, 1993);

A Fisherman of the Inland Sea: Science Fiction Stories (New York: HarperPrism, 1994; London: Gollancz, 1996);

Going Out with Peacocks and Other Poems (New York: HarperPerennial, 1994);

Wonderful Alexander and the Catwings (New York: Orchard Books, 1994);

Four Ways to Forgiveness (New York: HarperPrism, 1995; London: Gollancz, 1996);

Unlocking the Air and Other Stories (New York: HarperCollins, 1996);

The Twins, The Dream: Two Voices / Las gemelas, el sueño: dos voces, by Le Guin and Diana Bellessi (Houston: Arte Publico Press, 1996);

Steering the Craft: Exercises and Discussions on Story Writing for the Lone Navigator or the Mutinous Crew (Portland, Ore.: Eighth Mountain Press, 1998);

Sixty-Odd: New Poems (Boston: Shambhala, 1999);

The Telling (New York: Harcourt, 2000);

Tales from Earthsea (New York: Harcourt, 2001);

The Other Wind (New York: Harcourt, 2001);

The Birthday of the World and Other Stories (New York: HarperCollins, 2002).

OTHER: *Nebula Award Stories Eleven,* edited by Le Guin (London: Gollancz, 1976; New York: Harper & Row, 1977);

"The Diary of the Rose," in *Future Power,* edited by Jack Dann and Gardner Dozois (New York: Dutton, 1977);

Interfaces: An Anthology of Speculative Fiction, edited by Le Guin and Virginia Kidd (New York: Ace, 1980);

Edges: Thirteen New Tales from the Borderlands of the Imagination, edited by Le Guin and Kidd (New York: Pocket Books, 1980);

The Norton Book of Science Fiction: North American Fiction, 1960–1990, edited by Le Guin and Brian Attebery with Karen Joy Fowler (New York: Norton, 1993);

Lao Tzu: Tao Te Ching, A Book about the Way and the Power of the Way, translated by Le Guin and J. P. Seaton (Boston: Shambhala, 1997).

Ursula K. Le Guin is best known as a science-fiction writer whose work has been recognized by the mainstream literary establishment, a writer whose work includes not only adult science fiction but also a series of fantasy novels for young adults, children's books, and experimental "speculative fiction" that sometimes takes place in the present time or in recognizable locales (often the West Coast of North America). Only recently has her work also begun to be recognized as significant in its ecological and environmental emphasis; yet, a reader who considers her work in relation to "ecocriticism," the newly emerging field of literary criticism with a nature-oriented emphasis, comes to realize that much of Le Guin's work can be illuminated by such a focus.

In "The Non-Alibi of Alien Scapes: SF and Ecocriticism" (2001), Patrick D. Murphy offers a useful critical basis for reading science fiction ecologically, one that is helpful when considering the works of Le Guin:

> Certainly SF is not nature writing, in the sense of that genre's definition as being scientifically based, personal observation written in nonfiction prose. What it can be, however, is nature-oriented literature, in the sense of its being an aesthetic text that, on the one hand, directs reader attention toward the natural world and human interaction with other aspects of nature within that world, and, on the other hand, makes specific environmental issues part of the plots and themes of various works. SF also at times shares with both nature writing and other forms of nature-oriented literature detailed attention to the natural world found in the present as well as to the scientific disciplines that facilitate such attention. . . .

Murphy makes another statement especially relevant to considering Le Guin's writing from an ecocritical perspective: "While some ecocritics and environmental philosophers doubt that it is possible to be anything but anthropocentric, others argue for the need to become, at least intellectually if not instinctively, ecocentric or biocentric. From that perspective, literary works, then, that are anti- or de-anthropocentric can be understood as environmental literature." Le Guin's writing, while it displays a great fascination with the forms and potentialities of human society, is also strongly committed to ecocentric or biocentric points of view and encourages both an understanding of the interrelatedness of all life and an ethic of communication with all forms of life.

Ursula Kroeber was born on 21 October 1929 in Berkeley, California, to Alfred L. Kroeber, a distinguished anthropologist known for his work on the California Indians, and Theodora Kracaw Kroeber, author of the classic work *Ishi in Two Worlds* (1961). Ursula was the youngest of four children; she had three older brothers: Theodore, Clifton, and Karl. Discussions of Le Guin's science fiction often mention the felicitous

Dust jacket for Le Guin's 1972 novel about human colonizers who are destroying the forests of the planet Athshe and enslaving its gentle inhabitants (Richland County Public Library)

influence of her father's career in anthropology on her interest in culture and social systems, explored so keenly in her science fiction. Her family background might also have helped to form the ethical understanding of the interconnectedness of all life and respect for all life that informs her work. Le Guin has stated, for instance, that her father used to tell Indian tales and legends to the family. She also spent many summers of her childhood at "Kishamish," the family summer home in Napa Valley, where she was free to explore nature and wander through forty acres of country land. Le Guin has stated that she loved reading fairy tales as a girl and also read science fiction at a young age. Another early interest that stayed with her was Lao-tzu's Taoism, a philosophy that Le Guin says is basic to much of her fiction and might well have contributed to the concern for balance—including ecological balance—that she explores in her fiction. Suzanne Elizabeth Reid in *Presenting Ursula K. Le Guin* (1997) writes of Le Guin's childhood: "Ursula learned early from her family and their many acquaintances to look beyond the boundaries of a single viewpoint; to carefully listen, watch, and consider alternate views about human morality, human motivations, and the effects humans have on each other and on their environment. These habits of shifting her viewpoints to raise new questions are evident in her thinking."

Kroeber was inducted into Phi Beta Kappa and received her B.A. degree from Radcliffe College in 1951, and in 1952 she received an M.A. degree from Columbia University in French and Italian literature. She began her doctoral studies, but while on her way to begin residency for a Fulbright scholarship in France, she met Charles Le Guin, a scholar of French history. The two fell in love and were married in France on 22 December 1953. She worked at secretarial and teaching positions while her husband completed his doctorate at Emory University, then began teaching at the University of Idaho in 1956. They had two daughters, Elisabeth (born in 1957) and Caroline (born in 1959), and a son, Theodore (born in 1964). In 1959 the family moved to Portland, Oregon, where Charles Le Guin began teaching at Portland State University, while Le Guin pursued her writing career. Le Guin and her husband continue to live in the house in Portland where their children grew up.

Le Guin began writing early–in childhood, in fact. Her first publications were poetry, beginning in 1959. She published a fantasy story in 1962 and her first science-fiction story in 1963. Her first novels, *Rocannon's World* and *Planet of Exile,* appeared in 1966, followed by *City of Illusions* in 1967. These early novels established the "Hainish" universe that Le Guin has continued to explore throughout her career. Her major Hainish novels are *The Left Hand of Darkness* (1969) and *The Dispossessed: An Ambiguous Utopia* (1974), followed by the brief but significant work *The Word for World Is Forest* (1972), but she was still exploring the same universe as late as 2000 in *The Telling.* James Dwyer notes in "Ursula Le Guin: An Ambiguous Utopia," a chapter from his unpublished book "Where The Wild Books Are: A Guide to Ecofiction," that "The Hainish cycle can be viewed as a complex, continuing sociopolitical allegory with environmental aspects." One of the key concepts of this series is the "Ekumen," a "League of All Worlds," which seeks voluntary membership among the worlds in an ongoing effort at balance and harmony in the universe.

The Left Hand of Darkness was the first of Le Guin's books to receive major critical acclaim, winning both the Hugo Award and the Nebula Award. Although some feminists criticized Le Guin's tendency in her earlier works to write about male protagonists, this novel was appreciated for its examination of the socially imposed aspects of gender, as it explores a world in which all people share the same sexual characteristics and enter into periodic states of sexual readiness in which they vary in assuming either male or female biological roles. Through this "thought experiment," as Le Guin called it, she was able to call into question many of the assumptions of society about gender and sexuality. Inasmuch as sexuality is a part of "nature," it might well be considered an aspect of Le Guin's explorations of nature in her work. In addition, *The Left Hand of Darkness* develops and describes an Ice Age planet called Winter. The descriptions of travel through this frigid environment in an imagined world remind the reader of the great narratives of polar exploration in the real world and comprise memorable "nature writing."

Le Guin has not developed her speculative worlds in a chronological order of publication but has interwoven them with other works. Her much respected "Earthsea" fantasy series, written for young adults but commanding an admiring adult readership as well, began in 1968 with the publication of *A Wizard of Earthsea,* followed in 1971 by *The Tombs of Atuan* and in 1972 by *The Farthest Shore.* These three works stood as a completed trilogy until 1990 when *Tehanu: The Last Book of Earthsea* was added, then in 2001 *Tales from Earthsea* and *The Other Wind.* As with all of Le Guin's work, this fantasy series has a strong ethical concern based on her Taoist philosophy, as well as intensive exploration of social and environmental concerns. The Earthsea setting of an island archipelago (and indeed the name Earthsea) in itself creates a Taoist sense of balance between earth and sea, one of Le Guin's continuing concerns.

Though not writing from a specifically ecocritical perspective, James W. Bittner comments on the connection the Earthsea books make with ancient nature-based religions, noting that the institution of the wizards in the Earthsea books "shares much with Celtic druidism. . . . Becoming a druid meant undergoing a protracted period of oral instruction in subjects like astrology, geography, physical science, and natural theology. The school for wizards on Roke in Earthsea, like the colleges for druids reputed to have existed in Ireland, provides just this kind of training for would-be mages." Bittner's comments on the importance of trees in these novels are instructive for explaining the significance of trees throughout Le Guin's writing: "The vital significance of the Innermost Grove for all of Earthsea is a reflection of the importance of trees for the druids. The Romans knew very well that tree worship was the heart and soul of druidisms. . . . Although Le Guin shrouds the Immanent Grove in mystery, she clearly indicates that it means as much to Earthsea as the sacred grove of

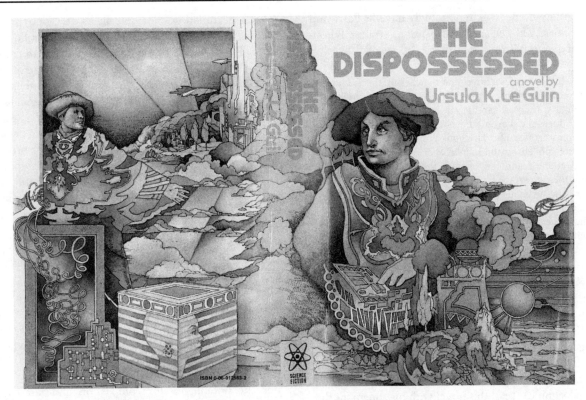

Dust jacket for Le Guin's 1974 novel, which explores the notion that environmental destruction leads to the loss of human freedom (Bruccoli Clark Layman Archives)

oak meant to the druids." A passage from *The Wizard of Earthsea* makes this point clearly:

> What is learned in the Immanent Grove is not much talked about elsewhere. It is said that no spells are worked there, yet the place itself is an enchantment. . . . It is said that the trees themselves are wise. It is said that the Master Patterner learns his supreme imagery there within the Grove, and if ever the trees should die so shall his wisdom die, and in those days the waters will rise and drown the islands of Earthsea.

Bittner discusses the influence of anthropologist Bronislaw Malinowski on Le Guin's ideas about magic. As Malinowski does, Le Guin emphasizes connections between magic and science more than those between magic and religion. Further, Bittner says that "Like Malinowski, Le Guin herself is 'deeply convinced of the mysterious intrinsic power of certain words.'" In corroboration, he quotes Le Guin herself: "As for wizards, to know the name of an island or a character is to know the island or person." Bittner's conclusion from these remarks is relevant not only to the Earthsea fantasies but also to other Le Guin works: magic is "an activity that makes possible a coherent relationship between humanity and nature, between perceiving mind and

perceived object. In this sense, in terms of its purpose, it is no different from art and science." This association is clear in *The Wizard of Earthsea:* "Now he enters the Immanent Grove and apparently experiences that ultimate reality of Being into which all contraries and dualities merge. Perhaps in the Immanent Grove the mage hears the one word Segoy spoke when he created the world, that 'great word that is very slowly spoken by the shining of the stars.'"

In addition to the Hainish novels and the Earthsea young-adult series, Le Guin has also written a series of books and stories set in a future West Coast of North America. The first of these to appear was *The Lathe of Heaven* (1971), a novella set in twenty-first-century Oregon that begins with the image of a drifting jellyfish but centers on the drama of George Orr, a man whose dreams predict and influence reality. The book has both a strong Taoist influence, with Taoist quotes at the beginning of each chapter, and also a strong environmental focus.

In 1974 Le Guin published the next in her series of Hainish novels, *The Dispossessed*—whose title is a reference to Fyodor Dostoevsky's *Besy* (1873; translated as *The Possessed,* 1913) and expresses Le Guin's interest in anarchist philosophy while exploring her understand-

159

ing that any utopia will undoubtedly have its flaws and ambiguities. *The Dispossessed* also has a strong environmental theme. Murphy says of it:

> Le Guin generates a novel that matches up the working out of an anarchist society with conditions of environmental scarcity. Near the end of the novel, Le Guin introduces the Terran ambassador to Urras, who tells the protagonist Shevek about conditions on Earth, a planet spoiled by the human species, who "multiplied and gobbled and fought until there was nothing left, and then [they] died" (279). In response to the devastation, the surviving people had to submit to total centralization and rationalization of all resources. Devastating the planet will lead, Le Guin argues, not only to human self-destruction but also to the loss of human freedom.

Comparing *The Dispossessed* with Pat Frank's *Alas, Babylon* (1959), Murphy remarks that both novels make the point that science fiction "has a strong potential to function as parable addressing the issue of how people become inhabitant and what it means to be indigenous in relation to environmental responsibility and the mutual adaptation between humans and the rest of nature." Murphy further develops the environmental significance of this novel with his statement that Le Guin

> posits the world of Anarres as a place where human beings are working out a sustainable relationship with the rest of nature, where culture and economy are being adapted to environmental constraints. And it is that possibility with which Le Guin wants readers to identify in contrast to the blighted landscape of Earth that the ambassador describes. But in a way, Le Guin might be providing a loophole, in that the Al Anarresti are able to work out this new nature-culture relationship on a planet where there are no other sentient beings to challenge their right to settle and transform the environment even as they adapt to it.

Murphy's summary statement regarding *The Dispossessed* might be applicable to most of Le Guin's work: "Human beings have to act in ethically responsible ways while realizing that they are not ever in control of the overall situation and that what they understand to be ethically justified or technically correct today may prove to be erroneous tomorrow. Such works can turn readers' attention toward the major socioenvironmental issues facing humanity today."

The much briefer *The Word for World Is Forest*, which first appeared in 1972 in Harlan Ellison's *Again, Dangerous Visions* and appeared as a separate volume in 1972, is another of Le Guin's Hainish novels. While many critics saw it as a direct response to the Vietnam War, others have noted that it may also be seen as a warning against war in general and against environ-

mental degradation. Not only in its title, but throughout, this novel also continues Le Guin's symbolic use of trees. The situation of the novel is that human colonizers, whose own forests have been devastated, have been ruthlessly exploiting and exporting lumber from the forest of a planet whose indigenous people are small, gentle beings whose "word for world is forest" (another reminder of Le Guin's association between word and nature). Through making the most brutal of the colonizers one of the characters whose viewpoint is revealed in the novel, Le Guin is able, among other points, to expose connections between the degradation of women and the degradation of the environment. Much of the plot hinges not only on Captain Davidson's destroying the forest of Athshe and enslaving its people but also on his raping one of the indigenous women so brutally that she dies.

Reid observes that this novel shares with *The Lathe of Heaven* "graphic depictions of how destructive misuse of modern technology affects the plants, trees, water, air, and inhabitants of the world." Through the eyes of another character, however—Lyubov, a scientific observer among the colonizers—Le Guin also develops the potentiality for compassion and interspecies communication and respect. Lyubov attempts, in vain, to persuade the authorities to stop destroying the forests, and despite having grown up on a barren, deforested planet Earth, has gradually come to love it:

> His throat had tightened so that his voice came out high and husky. He had counted on Gosse for support. "How many Sitka spruce have you seen in your lifetime, Gosse? Or snowy owl? or wolf? or Eskimo? . . . A forest ecology is a delicate one. If the forest perishes, its fauna may go with it. The Athsean word for *world* is also the word for *forest*. I submit, Commander Yung, that though the colony may not be in imminent danger, the planet is . . . "

In the end, there is a note of optimism despite the deaths of Lyubov and many others, as the higher authority agrees to leave the planet and its people to themselves and not to return.

Always Coming Home (1985) is another of Le Guin's books set in a future West Coast world. Indeed, passages from this novel are interwoven with photographs of northern California in *The Way of the Water's Going: Images of the Northern California Coastal Range,* published in 1989. *Always Coming Home* draws upon Le Guin's anthropological background, presenting itself as an anthropological study of the lives of the Kesh. The scope of this work is vast and visionary and includes a strong environmental consciousness as it purports to explore an entire culture, its history, songs, stories, and environment. "Flicker of the Serpentine," one of the stories in this novel, conveys, through Flicker's mystical vision, the visionary and unifying reach of Le Guin's writing:

> It was the universe of power. It was the network, field, and lines of the energies of all the beings, stars and galaxies of stars, worlds, animals, minds, nerves, dust, the lace and foam of vibration that is being itself, all interconnected, every part of another part and the whole part of each part, so comprehensible to itself only as a whole, boundless and unclosed.

Some of Le Guin's most interesting writing from an environmental point of view can be found in her shorter fiction, her novellas and short stories. Her first story collection, *The Wind's Twelve Quarters,* appeared in 1975 and includes some of her most enduring stories, such as "Vaster than Empires and More Slow" and "The Direction of the Road," which Dwyer describes as "a delightfully radical tale about relativity and relatedness told from the perspective of a giant roadside oak . . . a wry commentary on technologies, particularly the automobile, which separate humans from the rest of nature and enable them to live at an unhealthily frantic pace." This story is also another instance of Le Guin's writings that make symbolic use of trees. In addition, Le Guin's anthropomorphic entry into the point of view of the oak tree is representative of her interest in communication between species:

> For fifty or sixty years, I have upheld the Order of Things, and have done my share in supporting the humans' illusion that they are "going somewhere." And I am not unwilling to do so. . . . I am an oak, no more, no less. I have my duty, and I do it; I have my pleasures, and enjoy them, though they are fewer, since the birds are fewer, and the wind's foul. But, long-lived though I may be, impermanence is my right. Mortality is my privilege. And it has been taken from me.

In a remarkable philosophical twist, Le Guin suggests that the tree and the road have been helping enact illusions of travel and distance for human beings but that an accident, in which a car runs into the tree, has caused the death of one of the humans; the tree is outraged by the affront to its own values:

> This is unendurable. I cannot uphold such an illusion. If the human creatures will not understand Relativity, very well, but they must understand Relatedness. If it is necessary to the Order of Things, I will kill drivers of cars, though killing is not a duty usually required of oaks. But it is unjust to require me to play the part, not of the killer only, but of death. For I am not death. I am life: I am mortal.
>
> If they wish to see death visibly in the world, that is their business, not mine. I will not act Eternity for

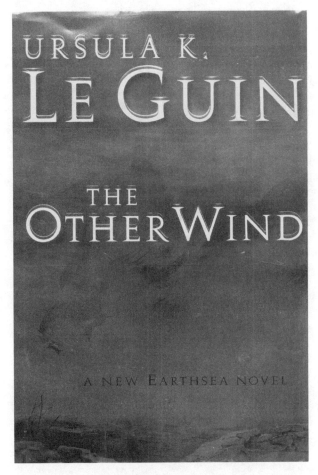

Dust jacket for Le Guin's 2001 novel that was the fifth book of the fantasy series that emphasizes the interdependence of nature and humankind (Richland County Public Library)

them. Let them not turn to the trees for death. If that is what they want to see, let them look into one another's eyes and see it there.

Le Guin's second story collection, *Orsinian Tales* (1976), is somewhat less interesting from an environmental point of view, but the third collection, *The Compass Rose: Short Stories* (1982), includes several stories with environmental interest. One of the most memorable is the amusing feminist fable "Sur," an imagined polar exploration narrative in which a group of women explorers cover their tracks so as not to disappoint Roald Amundsen with the knowledge that they reached the pole before he did.

Buffalo Gals and Other Animal Presences (1987) has inspired, in the form of an essay by Karla Armbruster, one of the fullest ecocritical and ecofeminist readings of Le Guin's work to appear to date. In an excellent model of environmental literary criticism, Armbruster singles out the title story for an illuminating discussion. In this

Le Guin in 2001 (photograph by Marion Wood Kolisch; from the dust jacket for The Other Wind)

story of a little girl, Myra, who is befriended by a coyote after she is the only survivor of a plane crash, Le Guin makes use of the Native American legends of Coyote as trickster but also explores her own concern with interspecies communication. Armbruster demonstrates that in this story Le Guin "renders the natural world in the form of speaking, active subjects, thus questioning the idea of impermeable boundaries between human and animal (especially the boundary that excludes the nonhuman from discourse)." Discussing the ways in which the Coyote of the story reflects the Coyote of Western Native American cultures, Armbruster notes that "True to this biological and legendary relationship with human culture, Le Guin's Coyote represents such an openness to interconnection, even when connecting means crossing hostile boundaries erected by human culture. As Myra figures out, 'That was Coyote's craziness, what they call her craziness. She wasn't afraid. She went between the two kinds of people, she crossed over.'"

Unlocking the Air and Other Stories appeared in 1996; a collection of Earthsea stories in 2001; and another collection of stories, *The Birthday of the World and Other Stories,* in 2002. Clearly, Le Guin continues to work actively in the short-story form.

Of her recent fiction, *The Telling,* a novel in the Hainish series, includes an interesting conjunction of Le Guin's themes and interests. Although critics in general have found *The Telling* less fully realized than some of her earlier novels, its spareness and its somewhat didactic approach do convey to readers how much her work is relevant to an "ecofeminist" approach. The main character is Sutty, a "Terran" of South Indian background, whose name is associated with "sati," the old practice of Indian widows being burned on the pyres of their dead husbands. This association is in contrast to Sutty's being a lesbian whose beloved partner was killed as a direct result of institutionalized homophobia. As an observer for the Ekumen on the planet Aka, Sutty observes the devastating result of a systematic destruction of all tradition and literature, which has led as well to an ecological imbalance and an entirely artificial mode of life: the dependence on packaged, artificial foods and the unavailability of natural foods are described, for instance. Some sly jokes are aimed at current U.S. products—for example, "The Corporation brand of akakafi was called Starbrew and was ubiquitous. Bittersweet, black, it included a remarkable mixture of alkaloids, stimulants, and depressants. Sutty loathed the taste, and it made her tongue furry...."

When Sutty travels to a remote, small city to expand her observations, she discovers a shop where herbal remedies are clandestinely available and associated with both the symbol of a tree and the forbidden religion known as "The Telling." The herbalist reluctantly shares his knowledge with Sutty:

> "The trunk of the tree," he said . . . "The branches and foliage of the tree, the crown of leaves." He indicated the five-lobed 'cloud' that rose above the trunk. "Also this is the body, you see, yoz." He touched his own hips and sides, patted his head with a certain leafy motion of the fingers, and smiled a little. "The body is the body of the world. The world's body is my body. So, then, the one makes two." . . . His fingers moved to the five lobes of foliage. "And the five bear the myriad, the leaves and flowers that die and return, return and die. The beings, creatures, stars. The being that can be told. But we don't see the roots. We cannot tell them."
>
> "The roots are in the ground . . . ?"
>
> "The mountain is the root."

Both tree and mountain are essential symbols of "The Telling," a fictional religion of harmony, balance, and nature, based again on Le Guin's own interest in Taoism. When, near the end of the novel, Sutty makes a long expedition to the hidden treasure of The Telling—a great, forbidden Library (the government has sought to destroy all books) hidden in a sacred mountain, Le

Guin's association of nature and word becomes clear once again.

Her interest in this association places her in the long history of writers who have found a text in nature or have employed the metaphor of "The Book of Nature." The most dramatic expression of this interest may be in her short story "The Author of the Acacia Seeds," the first story in *The Compass Rose,* which develops the conceit of a literary analysis of an infinitesimally small work of literature by an ant. "The messages are fragmentary, and the translation approximate and highly interpretative; but the text seems worthy of interest if only for its striking lack of resemblance to any other Ant texts known to us." What seems at first to be a mocking satire of both anthropology and literary history gradually becomes a touching cry for openness to the textuality of everything in the real world. The scholar who began by attempting to translate the passionate text of the "author of the Acacia Seeds"—". . . [I will] spend on dry seeds [my] soul's sweetness. . . . Touch this dry wood! [I] call! [I am] here!"—ends with a hopeful dream of understanding not only Ant but also Dolphin, Penguin, and Plant. The dream continues that perhaps someday there may "come that even bolder adventurer—the first geolinguist, who, ignoring the delicate, transient lyrics of the lichen, will read beneath it the still less communicative, still more passive, wholly atemporal, cold, volcanic poetry of the rocks: each one a word spoken, how long ago, by the earth itself, in the immense solitude, the immense community, of space."

Elizabeth Cummins remarks on the centrality of storytelling in Le Guin's work and how it relates to her environmental as well as cultural concerns:

A world's stories embody not only its current tensions, stresses, conflicts, and values but also its ability to dream of alternative ways of doing things, alternative political structures, environmental policies and values. In *Always Coming Home,* a novel which speaks with many narrative voices, Le Guin suggests that if American culture is embodied in its stories, then one way to change its headlong dash toward nuclear war and depletion of natural resources is to change the stories. If people can imagine an alternate world here on this planet, and imagine its inhabitants, then they have increased their chances of getting there.

Shortly after the attack on the World Trade Center on 11 September 2001, a book review in *The New York Times* (7 October 2001) made a similar point in a timely context. Reviewing *The Other Wind,* the fifth volume in the Earthsea series, along with other science-fiction works, Gerald Jonas remarked first on the relevance of science fiction to the current troubled times: "Looking closely at the books I had chosen to review for this column, I felt all the more certain of the importance of a genre rooted not in here-and-now reality but in untrammeled imagination—a literature free to stand apart from the specifics of today and speak about who we are and who we might be with daunting clarity." Writing specifically about *The Other Wind,* he praised the continuing accomplishment and relevance of Le Guin's vision:

The Earthsea saga, begun in 1968 as a series for young adults, has evolved into one of Le Guin's, and modern science fiction's, signature achievements . . . the islands of Earthsea are home to a magic as full of potential for good or ill as our science. Despite differences in history and outlook, the varied peoples of Earthsea must find ways to live together or die. At the age of 72, Le Guin has brought to bear on her youthful creation the hardheaded, cleareyed, ultimately optimistic view of human nature that she has forged during an extraordinarily productive and thoughtful career.

An example of how Le Guin's work has entered the canon of courses on nature literature is found in "News of the Land: A Course in Nature Writing in America," a 1990 master's thesis for the SUNY College of Environmental Science and Forestry, in which Catherine Landis features *Always Coming Home* as part of a course syllabus and remarks that "this work is less 'fantasy' than an imagining of the future based on paying, to the land, as close attention as the archaeologist of the past who listens for 'voices . . . in the streets of Troy.'" Several of Le Guin's novels have been included already in university courses on women and nature or environmental writing. Her work has begun, too, to be included in anthologies of literature about nature. From her unusual perspective as a science-fiction and speculative-fiction writer with strong concerns for the environment, Ursula K. Le Guin makes a significant contribution to environmental literature.

Interviews:
"Ursula K. Le Guin Interviewed by Jonathan Ward," *Algol,* 12 (Summer 1975): 6–10;

George Wickes and Louise Westling, "Dialogue with Ursula K. Le Guin," *Northwest Review,* 20, nos. 2–3 (1982): 147–159;

Jonathan White, "Coming Back from the Silence," *Whole Earth Review,* 85 (Spring 1995): 76–83;

William Walsh, "I Am a Woman Writer; I Am a Western Writer," *Kenyon Review,* 17 (Summer–Fall 1995): 192–205;

Sara Jameson, "Ursula K. Le Guin: A Galaxy of Books and Laurels," *Publishers Weekly,* 242 (25 September 1995): 32–33.

References:

John Algeo, "Magic Names: Onomastics in the Fantasies of Ursula K. Le Guin," *Names*, 30 (June 1982): 59–67;

Karla Armbruster, "'Buffalo Gals, Won't You Come Out Tonight': A Call for Boundary-Crossing in Ecofeminist Literary Criticism," in *Ecofeminist Literary Criticism: Theory, Interpretation, Pedagogy*, edited by Greta Gaard and Patrick D. Murphy (Urbana: University of Illinois Press, 1998), pp. 97–122;

Association for the Study of Literature and Environment, "The ASLE Collection of Syllabi in Literature and Environment" <http://www.asle.umn.edu/pubs/collect/collect.html>;

Brian Attebery, "The Beginning Place: Le Guin's Metafantasy," *Children's Literature*, 10 (1982): 113–123;

Soren Baggesen, "Utopian and Dystopian Pessimism: Le Guin's *The Word for World Is Forest* and Tiptree's 'We Who Stole the Dream,'" *Science-Fiction Studies*, 14 (March 1987): 34–43;

Douglas Barbour, "Wholeness and Balance in the Hainish Novels of Ursula K. Le Guin," *Science-Fiction Studies*, 1 (Spring 1974): 164–173;

Marlene S. Barr, ed., *Future Females: A Critical Anthology* (Bowling Green, Ohio: Bowling Green University Popular Press, 1981);

Barr and Nicholas D. Smith, eds., *Women and Utopia: Critical Interpretations* (Lanham, Md.: University Press of America, 1983);

Craig Barrow and Diana Barrow, "The Left Hand of Darkness: Feminism for Men," *Mosaic*, 20 (Winter 1987): 83–92;

James W. Bittner, *Approaches to the Fiction of Ursula K. Le Guin* (Ann Arbor: University of Michigan Research Press, 1984);

Bittner, "Chronosophy, Aesthetics, and Ethics in Le Guin's *The Dispossessed: An Ambiguous Utopia*," in *No Place Else: Explorations in Utopian and Dystopian Fiction*, edited by Eric S. Rabkin, Martin H. Greenberg, and Joseph D. Olander (Carbondale: Southern Illinois University Press, 1983), pp. 244–270;

Bittner, "Persuading Us to Rejoice and Teaching Us How to Praise: Le Guin's *Orsinian Tales*," *Science-Fiction Studies*, 5 (November 1978): 215–242;

Peter Brigg, "A 'Literary Anthropology' of the Hainish, Derived from the Tracings of the Species Guin," *Extrapolation*, 38 (Spring 1997): 15–24;

Barbara J. Bucknall, *Ursula K. Le Guin* (New York: Ungar, 1981);

Susanne Carter, "Variations on Vietnam: Women's Innovative Interpretations of the Vietnam War Experience," *Extrapolation*, 32 (Summer 1991): 170–183;

Thomas D. Clareson, ed., *Extrapolation*, special Le Guin issue, 21 (Fall 1980);

Anna Valdine Clemens, "Art, Myth and Ritual in Le Guin's *The Left Hand of Darkness*," *Canadian Review of American Studies*, 17 (Winter 1986): 423–436;

Robert Collins, "Fantasy and 'Forestructures': The Effect of Philosophical Climate upon Perceptions of the Fantastic," in *Bridges to Fantasy*, edited by Rabkin, George Edgar Slusser, and Robert Scholes (Carbondale: Southern Illinois University Press, 1982), pp. 108–120;

Elizabeth Cummins, *Understanding Ursula K. Le Guin* (Columbia: University of South Carolina Press, 1990);

Richard D. Erlich, "Ursula K. Le Guin and Arthur C. Clarke on Immanence, Transcendence, and Massacres," *Extrapolation*, 28 (Summer 1987): 105–129;

Anne Fadiman, "Ursula K. Le Guin: Voyager to the Inner Land," *Life*, 9 (April 1986): 23–25;

James P. Farrelly, "The Promised Land: Moses, Nearing, Skinner, Le Guin," *Journal of General Education*, 33 (Spring 1981): 15–23;

Robert Finch and John Elder, *The Norton Book of Nature Writing*, college edition (New York: Norton, 2002);

Carol Franko, "Acts of Attention at the Borderlands: Le Guin's *The Beginning Place* Revisited," *Extrapolation*, 36 (Winter 1996): 302–315;

Donald M. Hassler, "The Touching of Love and Death in Ursula Le Guin with Comparisons to Jane Austen," *University of Mississippi Studies in English*, 4 (1983): 168–177;

Linda Hogan, Deena Metzger, and Brenda Peterson, *Intimate Nature: The Bond between Women and Animals* (New York: Fawcett, 1998);

Keith N. Hull, "What Is Human? Ursula Le Guin and Science Fiction's Great Theme," *Modern Fiction Studies*, 32 (Spring 1986): 65–74;

David Ketterer, *New Worlds for Old: The Apocalyptic Imagination, Science Fiction and American Literature* (Bloomington: Indiana University Press, 1974);

Karl Kroeber, "Sisters and Science Fiction," *Little Magazine*, 10 (Spring–Summer 1976): 87–90;

David J. Lake, "Le Guin's Twofold Vision: Contrary Image Sets in *Left Hand of Darkness*," *Science-Fiction Studies*, 8 (July 1981): 156–164;

Holly Littlefield, "Unlearning Patriarchy: Ursula Le Guin's Feminist Consciousness in *The Tombs of Atuan* and *Tehanu*," *Extrapolation*, 36 (Fall 1995): 244–258;

164

Susan McLean, "The Beginning Place: An Interpretation," *Extrapolation,* 24 (Summer 1983): 130–142;

Walter E. Meyers, *Aliens and Linguistics: Language Study and Science Fiction* (Athens: University of Georgia Press, 1980);

Patrick D. Murphy, "Coyote Midwife in the Classroom: Introducing Literature with Feminist Dialogics," in *Practicing Theory in Introductory College Literature Courses,* edited by James M. Cahalan and David B. Downing (Urbana, Ill.: National Council of Teachers of English, 1991), pp. 161–176;

Murphy, *Literature, Nature and Other: Ecofeminist Critiques* (Albany: State University of New York Press, 1995);

Murphy, "The Non-Alibi of Alien Scapes: SF and Ecocriticism," in *Beyond Nature Writing,* edited by Armbruster and Kathleen R. Wallace (Charlottesville: University Press of Virginia, 2001), pp. 263–278;

Peter Nicholls, "Showing Children the Value of Death," *Foundation,* 5 (January 1974): 71–80;

Olander and Greenberg, eds., *Writers of the 21st Century Series: Ursula K. Le Guin* (New York: Taplinger, 1979);

Donald Palumbo, ed., *Erotic Universe: Sexuality and Fantastic Literature* (New York: Greenwood Press, 1986);

Suzanne Elizabeth Reid, *Presenting Ursula K. Le Guin* (New York: Twayne / London: Prentice Hall International, 1997);

Warren Rochelle, "The Story, Plato, and Ursula K. Le Guin," *Extrapolation,* 37 (Winter 1996): 316–329;

Robert Scholes, *Structural Fabulation: An Essay on the Future of Fiction* (Notre Dame, Ind.: University of Notre Dame Press, 1975);

Bernard Selinger, *Le Guin and Identity in Contemporary Fiction* (Ann Arbor: University of Michigan Research Press, 1988);

W. A. Senior, "Cultural Anthropology and Rituals of Exchange in Ursula K. Le Guin's 'Earthsea,'" *Mosaic,* 29 (December 1996): 100–112;

George Edgar Slusser, *The Farthest Shores of Ursula K. Le Guin* (San Bernardino, Cal.: Borgo Press, 1976);

Charlotte Spivack, "Only in Dying, Life: The Dynamics of Old Age in the Fiction of Ursula Le Guin," *Modern Language Studies,* 14 (Summer 1984): 43–53;

Spivack, *Ursula K. Le Guin* (Boston: Twayne, 1984);

Melissa Walker, *Reading the Environment* (New York: Norton, 1994);

Ian Watson, "Le Guin's *Lathe of Heaven* and the Role of Dick: The False Reality as Mediator," *Science-Fiction Studies,* 2 (March 1975): 67–75;

Kingsley Widmer, "The Dialectic of Utopianism: Le Guin's *The Dispossessed,*" *Liberal and Fine Arts Review,* 3 (January–July 1983): 1–11;

Donna Glee Williams, "The Moons of Le Guin and Heinlein," *Science-Fiction Studies,* 21 (July 1994): 164–172;

Susan Wood, "Discovering Worlds: The Fiction of Ursula K. Le Guin," in *Voices for the Future: Essays on Major Science Fiction Writers,* volume 2, edited by Clareson (Bowling Green, Ohio: Bowling Green University Popular Press, 1979), pp. 154–179;

J. R. Wytenbroek, "Always Coming Home: Pacifism and Anarchy in Le Guin's Latest Utopia," *Extrapolation,* 28 (Winter 1987): 330–339;

Marilyn Yalom, ed., *Women Writers of the West Coast: Speaking of Their Lives and Careers* (Santa Barbara, Cal.: Capra Press, 1983).

Papers:

Ursula K. Le Guin's manuscripts are at the University of Oregon Library.

Aldo Leopold
(11 January 1887 – 21 April 1948)

Deborah Fleming
Ashland University

BOOKS: *Game and Fish Handbook* (Albuquerque: United States Forest Service, 1915);

Report on a Game Survey of the North Central States, Made by Aldo Leopold for the Sporting Arms and Ammunitions Manufacturers' Institute under Direction of Its Committee on Restoration and Protection of Game (Madison, Wis.: Privately printed by the Democrat Printing Company, 1931);

Game Management (New York: Scribners, 1933);

A Sand County Almanac and Sketches Here and There, illustrated by Charles W. Schwartz (New York: Oxford University Press, 1949); republished as *A Sand County Almanac with Essays on Conservation from Round River* (New York: Ballantine, 1966);

Round River: From the Journals of Aldo Leopold, edited by Luna B. Leopold (New York: Oxford University Press, 1953);

A Sand County Almanac with Other Essays from Round River (New York: Oxford University Press, 1968);

Aldo Leopold's Wilderness: Selected Early Writings, edited by David E. Brown and Neil B. Carmony (Harrisburg, Pa.: Stackpole Books, 1990); republished as *Aldo Leopold's Southwest* (Albuquerque: University of New Mexico Press, 1995);

The River of the Mother of God and Other Essays, edited by Susan L. Flader and J. Baird Callicott (Madison: University of Wisconsin Press, 1991);

For the Health of the Land: Previously Unpublished Essays and Other Writings, edited by Callicott and Eric T. Freyfogle (Washington, D.C.: Island Press for Shearwater Books, 1999).

Edition: *A Sand County Almanac and Sketches Here and There,* introduction by Robert Finch (New York: Oxford University Press, 1987).

OTHER: *Carson Pine Cone* [newsletter of the Carson National Forest], includes contributions by Leopold (Tres Piedras, N.Mex., 1911–1914);

Game and Fish Handbook (Albuquerque: United States Forest Service, United States Department of Agriculture, D-3, 5 September 1915);

Aldo Leopold, 1946 (Leopold Collection, University of Wisconsin Archives)

Pine Cone (Albuquerque) (December 1915–July 1931)– nineteen issues edited by Leopold, and with contributions by Leopold.

Aldo Leopold–forester, naturalist, wildlife biologist, conservationist, writer, and environmental philosopher–is best known as the author of *A Sand County Almanac and Sketches Here and There* (1949), which includes the earliest articulation of the "land ethic" and the "ecological conscience," the idea that human beings, as citizens rather than masters of the land and biosphere, should treat the land with the same set of ethics and the same requirements of conscience with which they treat each other. Known also for his clear and analytical but also lyrical style, Leopold is heralded as a master of both scientific and poetic prose. Educated in forestry, author of the first textbook on game management, he also wrote more than 350 articles published in forestry and wildlife journals as well as many letters to colleagues and friends, book reviews, and papers on conservation of wildlife and land. Environmentalists compare Leopold with John Muir as a pioneer conservationist, with Henry David Thoreau as a writer of conservation philosophy, and with Rachel Carson as an educator of the public in conservation values. Born into a family of hunters, naturalists, and sportsmen, and having earned a master of science degree in forestry from Yale University in 1909, Leopold joined the United States Forest Service and went to work as crew chief in the Apache Forest in Arizona. He began his writing career, producing articles for the Forest Service newsletter known as the *Pine Cone*. He was promoted to deputy supervisor in the Carson National Forest in New Mexico. While in the Carson National Forest, Leopold's interests turned from forestry to game protection, carrying capacity of grazing lands, and recreational policy. Promoted to assistant district forester in 1919, he worked toward a policy of game protection and wilderness preservation in the Prescott National Forest and Gila Wilderness. In 1924 he became director of the Forest Products Laboratory in Madison, Wisconsin; the move from the Southwest to the upper Midwest was auspicious, since it brought him where the needs for conservation policy and public interest were strong. In 1924 he left the Forest Service to work on the privately funded *Report on a Game Survey of the North Central States, Made by Aldo Leopold for the Sporting Arms and Ammunition Manufacturers' Institute under Direction of Its Committee on Restoration and Protection of Game,* published in 1931. The election of Franklin Delano Roosevelt in 1932 brought an offer to work with the Civilian Conservation Corps (CCC); the next year he published the landmark *Game Management,* the first textbook of its kind, and received an offer from the University of Wisconsin to become its first and only Professor of Game Management, a position he held until his death in 1948. During his tenure as professor he created the new Division of Game Management, served on the President's Commission on Wildlife Restoration, toured central Europe in 1935 as a guest of the Oberlaender Trust (which funded a study of forestry methods there), served as adviser to the United Nations on conservation, and continued to write prolifically. He also investigated and helped to articulate the new scientific discipline of ecology, in which living things were looked at as part of an interrelated cycle of life. In 1935 he bought an abandoned farm of 120 acres in one of the "sand counties" of Wisconsin, where he and his family on weekend excursions planted thousands of trees and worked to restore the fertility of the land and the habitat for wildlife; his experiences on the farm furnished the setting for many of the essays in *A Sand County Almanac* and other articles published at the time. When he died fighting a brush fire on a neighbor's farm, he was one of the best-known conservationists of the time. *A Sand County Almanac,* published posthumously, initially had only modest sales, until the resurgence of interest in ecology in the 1960s made Leopold one of the most respected naturalists and philosophers of conservation ethics.

Rand Aldo Leopold (his first name was never used) was born on 11 January 1887 in Burlington, Iowa, the eldest of the four children of Carl Leopold and Clara Starker Leopold. Like so many pioneer fathers, Carl Leopold commemorated his son's arrival by planting an oak sapling in front of his house on Prospect Hill. Aldo was followed by Marie in 1888, Carl Jr. in 1892, and Frederic in 1895. The parents were first cousins (marriage between first cousins was not unusual on the frontier), and they were both descended from German immigrants recently arrived in the Middle West. Carl was the son of Charles Leopold of Hanover, whose family had ties to nobility; his mother was Thusneld Runge, whose family had come to America on the same passage. Charles pursued many vocations, including rope making, dairying, and sheep driving, the last taking him all over the West, including California, but none proved financially profitable. He passed on his roving spirit to his grandson Aldo. Aldo's mother, Clara, was the daughter of Charles Starker of Stuttgart and Marie Runge Starker, Thusneld Leopold's younger sister. Charles Starker possessed eclectic talents: by the time he was seventeen, he could design bridges and buildings, plant gardens, and paint scenes in watercolors. In America he was unable to use his engineering and aesthetic talents, but he found prosperity in the grocery business in Burlington, Iowa, a city growing with the westward expansion. Because of his success in business, he found himself able to devote more time to building his community—serving as alderman, designing the public square, and providing capital and credit to young businessmen. In the 1870s he persuaded three hundred families to move to Burlington: this influx endowed the city with a European character still apparent today. Charles Starker designed and built the Burlington Opera House, which Mark Twain described in a travel memoir five years before Aldo Leopold's birth. To his grandson, Charles Starker

Deputy Forest Supervisor Leopold, Forest Assistant Ira T. Yarnall, and Forest Supervisor Harry C. Hall at the headquarters of Carson National Forest, Tres Piedras, New Mexico, 1911 (photograph by Raymond Marsh; Leopold Collection, University of Wisconsin Archives)

seems to have bequeathed public-spiritedness and love of art and bird life.

Aldo grew up amid a prosperous extended family that included his maternal grandparents, his parents, and his siblings. His father, Carl, owned a successful furniture-making factory. The Starker estate boasted three hundred acres with gardens, an orchard, and two houses kept up partly by maids. The family spoke German at home, and all hands were engaged in the gardens: thus, Aldo gained a love for planting and watching things grow, and he learned about soils and erosion. His father was an avid hunter who was one of the earliest to realize that what had long been an activity that sustained families would soon become a sport. He realized that overhunting led to a decline in game populations, and by the time he was teaching his sons to hunt, he had developed a personal code of sportsmanship. Aldo later called his father a "pioneer sportsman." Aldo's hunting and naturalist interests, begun on his grandfather's estate, were nurtured at the family's summer holiday retreat, Les Cheneaux Island at the northern end of Lake Huron. Aldo also became a bird-watcher, beginning to record his observations in a disciplined way by 1902. A trip to Colorado and Yellowstone National Park in

1903 provided further material for his enthusiastically recorded observations of wildlife.

The trips to the island in Lake Huron yielded another boon: the headmaster of Lawrenceville Prep School in New Jersey met Aldo in 1901 and was so taken by his precociousness that he finally persuaded the boy's parents to send him east to school, although the Burlington schools were excellent by the standards of the day. Aldo spent his last year of high school in Lawrenceville, which had been preparing students for Ivy League colleges for ninety-four years. During this time, his interest in botany developed, although he wrote to his father that the instruction in English and history was inferior to that he had received in Burlington. Still, his experience prepared his way for Yale and gave him the opportunity to write the long, detailed, and informative letters that helped him to find his mature writing style.

In 1905 Aldo entered the Sheffield Scientific School at Yale, which offered a preparatory course of study for the Yale Forest School (then training the first generation of foresters for the nation). The university experience enabled him to combine his interests in society and the natural world, and he began writing letters in different styles and creating stories based on his experience, using himself as the protagonist. He attended lectures by such notables as Jacob Riis and Jack London, made friends in spite of his natural reserve and quietness, and developed a taste for fine clothes. His parents, in fact, encouraged him not to be too frugal and to indulge his tastes. He met Hamilton Drummond, who remained a lifelong friend, and, true to Yale tradition, he "adopted" a destitute local boy, Benjamin Jacobosky, whom Leopold taught to hunt and fish. In this relationship he learned how the less fortunate live. Usually a diligent student, he experienced a slump in his senior year during which he was placed on academic probation, but he worked his way out of it and graduated in 1908. His motto in the yearbook read "To hell with convention!"

Leopold entered Forest School at Yale in 1908 and received his master's degree the following year. In Leopold's short lifetime the emphasis in forestry in America had gone from the lumberjack's profession to the realization that the continent and its resources were in fact limited. The Forest Reserve Act, passed by Congress in 1891, gave the president of the United States authority to establish "forest preserves" under the auspices of the Department of the Interior. By the turn of the century, the emphasis shifted again to the scientific management of forest reserves, an emphasis dominated by the views of Gifford Pinchot, a forester educated at Yale and trained in Germany and France, who believed that forests should not be maintained as preserves but scientifically managed in order to produce a sustained yield of timber indefinitely. Regarded as the foremost exponent of this "utilitarian" view of forest management, Pinchot was able to put his ideas into practice when he was named chief of the U.S. Forest Service, newly created by President Theodore Roosevelt, who took office in 1901. Pinchot's family also donated funds to Yale to open its graduate program in forestry and land near Milford, Pennsylvania, for a forestry camp that all prospective foresters were required to attend.

Leopold received his master's degree and entered the U.S. Forest Service in 1909; his first assignment included surveying and drawing maps of the Apache National Forest in Arizona. On one surveying mission there, he embarked on the experience he later immortalized in "Thinking Like a Mountain" (written 1 April 1944; published in *A Sand County Almanac*): convinced at that time in his life that predator control was necessary to ensure good hunting, he shot a mother wolf and her cubs as she brought them over a mountain rimrock. He later described the "fierce green fire" dying in her eyes, the image that later became emblematic of his realization that all living things are interrelated. In the Apache National Forest he also saw the mountain Escudilla and

a great grizzly bear killed in the name of "progress," an experience he recorded in his essay "Escudilla."

At this time, too, Leopold met Maria Alvira Estella Bergere, born 24 August 1890 in Los Lunas, New Mexico, the daughter of one of the most prominent men in Santa Fe. Alfred M. Bergere, who had been born in Liverpool, England, of Franco-Italian parents, became a major political figure in Santa Fe and also brought classical music to New Mexico. Having been a prodigy before he left England, he turned his home in Santa Fe into a de facto recital hall. When he married the widow Eloisa Luna Otero, he allied himself with the wealthy and aristocratic Luna family, which boasted such ancestors as a young Spanish *capitano* who had defeated the Moors in 1091, Pope Benedict XIII of the Great Schism, a storied conquistador second in command to Coronado and first governor of Spain's Florida colony, two captains who served with Hernán Cortés, and Cortés's own wife. Leopold married Bergere on 9 October 1912, unwillingly stating the Catholic vows as her family required. The Leopolds moved into a modest house near Tres Piedras, overlooking the Rio Grande. Over the years they had two daughters and three sons: Aldo Starker (called Starker), born 22 October 1913; Luna Bergere, born 8 October 1915; Adelina (called Nina), born in August 1917; Aldo Carl (called Carl), born 18 December 1919; and Estella B. (called Estella Jr.), born 8 January 1927. Aldo and Estella Leopold's home life was a happy one, with husband and wife sharing each other's interests and Estella not only helping with Aldo's work but also, he realized, making it possible. Later, in 1921, Leopold's brother Carl married Estella Leopold's sister Dolores.

When disputes arose among sheepmen in the Jicarilla district, Leopold, who had been promoted to deputy supervisor of Carson National Forest in New Mexico, rode from Durango to investigate. For two weeks he rode alone except for staying one night with a member of the Apache tribe, finally returning to Tres Piedras, his body swollen and barely alive. He then took a train to Santa Fe, where a doctor diagnosed acute nephritis, also known as Bright's disease. Although his kidneys had failed, Leopold survived the initial attack but was forced to remain indoors and off the job. Always an enthusiastic and healthy outdoorsman, at the age of twenty-six he faced a lengthy convalescence and an uncertain future.

As usual, Leopold put his time to good use. He read widely during this period, the first time since his undergraduate days that he had been able to do so, wrote articles for the *Pine Cone* (the Forest Service bulletin), and rethought his approach to wilderness and forestry. In a telling letter to one of his supervisors, he articulated his view that the success of forestry work should not be measured in terms of reports or output but in terms of the effects on the forest. He also wrote that policy should guide daily tasks but not confine the minds of forester officers. Essentially, he formulated an early conservation ethic.

After more than a year on leave, Leopold was reinstated in the Forest Service, this time to the Office of Grazing. His supervisor, Arthur Ringland, wanted Leopold to work on publicity and game protection. Since at first his position involved office work, Leopold accepted, because he still could not walk far. Yet, changes were taking place. The Leopolds moved to Albuquerque on 4 October 1914 and returned to gardening. Leopold's father, Carl, died on the night of 22 December 1914. For nine months Leopold faced difficulties with his immediate supervisor, John Kerr, over differences in conservation philosophy: Leopold favored the approach the conservation movement as a whole was making—toward the protection of game; Kerr concentrated on the needs of stockmen. Still, Leopold's time in the Office of Grazing proved to be a valuable experience: his time in administration, combined with his field experience, made him a range manager as well as a forester; he had become aware of the idea of the carrying capacity of grazing lands; and he had proved to himself that he could work in difficult situations.

On 16 June 1915 Leopold became responsible for recreational policy in District Three, which included the Grand Canyon, and his first assignment was to investigate conditions there. Fifty years before, John Wesley Powell had embarked on his epic journey down the Colorado River. In 1903 President Roosevelt had visited the Grand Canyon and declared that it was to be preserved in its natural state. Leopold completed his *Game and Fish Handbook* in 1915, his first substantial written work on game conservation and the first the Forest Service ever issued; it won the praise not only of district personnel but also of the national office, and it caused officials there to press (unsuccessfully) for Leopold's transfer to Washington. He received a personal letter in 1916 from President Roosevelt congratulating him on his work on game protection. Leopold began writing a news bulletin for Albuquerque sportsmen, which he called *The Pine Cone,* borrowing his title from the old Forest Service newsletter to which he had contributed. He undertook, in 1916, a speaking tour on game protection, and in the same year he helped to found the New Mexico Game Protective Association, which envisioned three goals: enforcement of game-protection laws, establishment of game refuges, and control of predators. Although Leopold did not personally advocate the extermination of wolves, the NMGPA (New Mexico Game Protective Association)

did, and Leopold's writings reflected their policy rather than his own.

In 1916 the family moved into a larger house in Albuquerque, overlooking the Rio Grande, with grounds that gave them more room for gardening. Leopold organized new game-protection associations in Tucson and Payson, and enjoyed not only a national but an international reputation in the field. A recurrence of nephritis in September, which made him ineligible for the draft when the United States joined the war in Europe, also kept him at home or assigned to office duties. At this time, also, he learned carpentry and built a windmill and a house for chickens; he began to hunt again. Hunting, in fact, became a family activity by 1921. Leopold also increased his reading on wildlife, early exploration, philosophy, and literature. He read the Bible and works by Thomas Jefferson, John Stuart Mill, Thomas Carlyle, Samuel Butler, Victor Hugo, William James, Rudyard Kipling, and Epicurus, keeping a journal as always. These readings in turn inspired him to combine his interests in game protection with his interest in culture. One of his favorite sayings, which he had discovered in an article by Henry Seidel Corley, "The Undergraduate Background" (February 1915), in *Harper's* magazine, was that culture was "no mere affectation of knowledge, nor any power of glib speech, or idle command of the fopperies of art and literature, but, rather, an intelligent interest in the possibilities of living."

In 1917 Leopold accepted the position of secretary of the Chamber of Commerce of Albuquerque in order to increase his income and to continue his work in public relations. One of his missions, in which he proved himself the true grandson of Charles Starker, was to persuade businessmen that their city should take pride in and try to preserve its Old West and Spanish heritage, as Santa Fe had done. At the same time, he wrote and published articles that articulated his view of the interrelationship of wildlife and society and began to set the course for wildlife conservation in America. In January 1918 he published in *Outers Book–Recreation* his article "The Popular Wilderness Fallacy," in which he challenges the notion that a society must choose between wildlife and civilization.

The end of the war brought a resurgence in the activity of the Forest Service, and Leopold rejoined it in 1919 as Assistant District Forester in Charge of Operations. He now occupied the second most important position in the district, but his return, welcomed by the new generation of conservation foresters, was not looked upon with favor by the older generation, who thought Leopold had been promoted beyond his experience. Although Leopold was compassionate and sensitive, he could be smug as well. In spite of the objections to his appointment by his District Forester, Frank C. W. Pooler, and in spite of his receiving an offer to head a district in the northern Rockies and another offer to take charge of the seventy-four bird and game refuges of the nation, Leopold stayed in Albuquerque, determined to make good on the job he had been given. He wrote detailed and well-organized reports on the Apache and Sitgreaves National Forests and argued that foresters needed more individual responsibility in their jobs as well as encouragement to think independently and creatively.

Although *The Pine Cone* had to be discontinued in 1920, in November of the following year Leopold published in *Journal of Forestry* a seminal article, "The Wilderness and Its Place in Forest Recreation Policy," in which he discusses wilderness protection in national forests. It was the first formal discussion of the topic in the profession of forestry. Leopold was reacting to the National Park Service, which, charged with both protecting the national parks and opening them up to public use, was concentrating more energy on the latter responsibility. Leopold's article called for more preservation from a recreational standpoint. Wilderness preservation was already an issue in the East, but not in the West, which faced serious conservation issues. He states that his purpose is "to give definite form to the issue of wilderness conservation, and to suggest certain policies for meeting it, especially as applied to the Southwest." He also states that Gifford Pinchot's utilitarian policies had been good but had "already gone far enough to raise the question of whether the policy of development (construed in the narrow sense of industrial development) should continue to govern in absolutely every instance, or whether the principle of highest use does not itself demand that representative portions of some forests be preserved as wilderness." Leopold offers his definition of *wilderness:* "a continuous stretch of country preserved in its natural state, open to lawful hunting and fishing, big enough to absorb a two weeks' pack trip, and kept devoid of roads, artificial trails, cottages, or other works of man." Although always couching his arguments in utilitarian terms (from the recreational point of view), Leopold had departed not only from the Pinchot philosophy of conservation but also from the Roosevelt path of protection. Leopold knew as early as 1922 that concern for the land itself must govern conservation policy. Two reports written that year reflected his skill in organizing and presenting detailed material—one on the Prescott National Forest and one on the proposed Gila Wilderness Area in Arizona.

The Russian philosopher-mythic Peter Ouspensky's *Tertium Organum* (1916; translated into English, 1920), which tries to reconcile Western science with

Estella and Aldo Leopold on their wedding day, 9 October 1912 (Bradley Study Center, Aldo Leopold Reserve)

Eastern mysticism, and which Leopold had read by 1922, further propelled him in what became an articulation of the ecological conscience and the need for wilderness preservation. Ouspensky writes, "In organic nature where we see life it is easier to assume the existence of a psyche. But life belongs not alone to separate, individual organisms—anything indivisible is a living thing." Leopold intuited that the difference between this organic view of life and the mechanistic one provided by the Western sciences belonged to the realm of linguistics and so guided Western thinking on the subject. In a paper titled "Some Fundamentals of Conservation in the Southwest" (written in 1923), unpublished during his lifetime, Leopold ponders the question of whether the earth was created for human beings or whether human beings merely enjoyed the privilege of possessing it. Most religions and most sciences took the former view, but Leopold says that if this is the case, the earth existed long before human beings came along to take charge. Deferring his philosophical arguments until later, Leopold points out that "God started his show a good many million years before he had any men for audience—a sad waste of both actors and music" and that other cultures had lived in the Southwest prior to European occupation without inflicting irreparable damage on the earth.

Leopold's tenure in the Southwest came to a close in 1924, when he left the region for good to accept the position of Director of the Forest Products Laboratory in Madison, Wisconsin. That year he published an updated version of a 4 December 1922 public address that he had called "Erosion as a Menace to the Social and Economic Future of the Southwest." The revised article, published in *Sunset* magazine (May 1924), was titled "Pioneers and Gullies" and provided a metaphor for the effects of pioneering and settlement on fragile land. His years in the Southwest had taught him incontrovertibly that human beings must develop ways of living in harmony with, not against, the natural world.

Although he regarded himself as a "fish out of water" at the Forest Products Laboratory, Leopold found the move to Madison auspicious. Not overwhelming, his official duties left him time for writing. He had come to a place where public interest in conservation was strong. The Izaak Walton League was the most effective conservation organization in the country. Leopold and his family rediscovered the canoe country of upper Minnesota. They resided on the same street (Van Hise Avenue) as the historian Frederick Jackson Turner, who had retired from Harvard and returned to Madison to write. While Leopold does not appear to have had many professional encounters with Turner, Curt Meine, Leopold's biographer, speculates that Leopold enjoyed many backyard conversations. At any rate, Leopold's writing at that time in his life often reflects the influence of Turner.

During the years 1924 until 1928, Leopold published articles on game management, technical forestry, and wilderness. He became the foremost spokesman in the United States for the preservation of wild country. In October 1925 the *Journal of Land and Public Utility Economics* published "Wilderness as a Form of Land Use," which begins with Leopold's belief in the recreational value of wilderness but emphasizes also the cultural and historical values in preserving wilderness. "Wilderness as a form of land use," he writes, "is, of course, premised on a qualitative conception of progress. It is premised on the assumption that enlarging the range of individual experience is as important as enlarging the number of individuals; that the expansion of commerce is a means, not an end; that the environment of the American pioneers had values of its own, and was not merely a punishment which they endured in order that we might ride in motors." Although his article met with mostly positive response, Leopold was criticized for being "anti-road" and for advocating preservation only for the amusement of wealthy, misanthropic elites. This last charge disturbed him most, since one of his major concerns, which he articulated in a later article, was that without preservation the well-to-do would soon have a monopoly on wilderness.

In 1928 Leopold was forty-one, and advancement in the Forest Products Laboratory seemed remote. After receiving several job offers, he accepted a position as overseer of a national survey of game conditions to be funded by a group of industry representatives known as the Sporting Arms and Ammunitions Manufacturers' Institute, or SAAMI. On 26 June 1928 he left the Forest Service for good. His new job provided a large salary increase but no security: SAAMI could terminate the position whenever it became dissatisfied with the results. He kept the position, however, until 1932 and published his 1931 *Report on a Game Survey of the North Central States.* The same year Leopold founded, with farmers and businessmen hunters, the Riley Game Cooperative, both a hunting and a preservationist cooperative, which undertook to restock wildlife and provide winter feed. The same year, he attended in Labrador a landmark conference on natural cycles that brought together a remarkably diverse group of scientists, writers, legislators, and administrators. At the conference, Leopold met Charles Elton, whose book *Animal Ecology* (1927) Leopold had read by early 1931. The meeting with Elton sparked a friendship in which Elton's ecological and Leopold's conservation theories enhanced each other's thinking. Leopold had also gained the terminology to describe his view of the land.

The Great Depression years of 1931 and 1932 took their toll on the Leopold household as well as on the rest of the nation. Leopold's position with SAAMI came to a close. Still, Leopold and Estella managed to keep two sons in college and two maids busy. Leopold received an offer from Charles Scribner's Sons to publish *Game Management* (1933) if he would agree to certain revisions; he signed the agreement on 11 January 1932, his forty-fifth birthday. The book constituted the most comprehensive collection of information on wildlife conservation yet written, including explanations of population dynamics, game range, winter cover, and refuge patterns, but it also included management theory and technique, history, and Leopold's own philosophy of conservation. In 1931 Leopold received the Gold Medal Award from *Outdoor Life* and an intriguing letter from the scientist and naturalist Olaus Murie, a Biological Survey research worker in Jackson Hole, Wyoming, who wrote that predator control had been given too much emphasis, that predators were part of the environment, and that extermination could prove harmful. His ideas coincided with the direction in which Leopold was moving–toward belief in the coexistence of economic prosperity and the preservation of wilderness.

In 1933 Franklin Delano Roosevelt became president, and Leopold received an offer to assist in the CCC. Although he did not adhere to the tenets of the New Deal, Leopold accepted the position, and by the

Leopold on a research trip along the Rio Grande, 1918 (Leopold Collection, University of Wisconsin Archives)

end of April he was supervising erosion-control work in New Mexico in the old District Three of the Forest Service while Estella and the family remained in Madison. Impressed with the energy harnessed in the cause of conservation, Leopold remained skeptical that any one political strategy–public or private ownership– could suffice to answer all the problems of conservation. He became discouraged with groups on the same job working in opposition to each other because of poor organization by the supervisors, including himself, who had not foreseen the complexities of the grand new program.

In May 1933 Leopold delivered four major addresses in one week, including one at the Southwest division of the American Association for the Advancement of Science. Asked to present the keynote John Wesley Powell address, Leopold gave one of the major papers of his career, "The Conservation Ethic," in which he states that the real end of conservation philosophy is "a universal symbiosis with land, economic and esthetic, public and private." The paper revealed the culmination of years of the development of Leopold's philosophy of conservation and the beginning of his development of a philosophy of ecology.

During the same year, Leopold was offered and accepted the position that he kept until his death. The Wisconsin Alumni Research Foundation approved funds to support a game-management program within the University of Wisconsin. The grant was to last for a five-year trial period during which Leopold would be paid $8,000 per year to cover his salary and all expenses for the program, including travel costs. The program created a two-person department of game management made up of Leopold and his secretary. After evaluation at the end of the trial period, the program, if successful, would be funded by the state of Wisconsin. Leopold's duties included giving radio addresses on conservation, creating short courses for farmers, directing research at a new arboretum, teaching a graduate seminar on game management and technique, overseeing graduate-student progress, assisting in special conservation projects throughout the state, and conducting other extension work. Leopold accepted the position in July and was at work by the following autumn.

Leopold was a teacher of remarkable talents. Using the Socratic technique, he first framed the issues by asking many rhetorical questions, challenging students to use their own powers of reasoning to find answers before he provided the specifics. The true conservationist, he believed, was inspired not by fear but by curiosity. In keeping with this belief, he lectured in an informal tone quite different from his elegant prose. His graduate students thought so much of him that they found new quarters for him on the university campus–the former residence, then unused, of a dean–and moved the entire Game Management Division (books, furniture, laboratory equipment, and Leopold's personal possessions) into it. University officials protested, but to no avail. Shortly thereafter the division was funded for another year.

Leopold was no New Dealer; he had been a Progressive without a party affiliation since Theodore Roosevelt had left the Republicans. He could best be described as a Jeffersonian individualist, but he served in enough capacities in Franklin Roosevelt's administration to be called a veteran of New Deal politics. He had served in the Southwest with the CCC. In Wisconsin he advised the operations of the Soil Erosion Service, and he was appointed one of three members of the president's Committee on Wild Life Restoration, formed in January 1934 to coordinate the president's $25 million program to purchase submarginal agricultural lands for wildlife refuges. Although he did not oppose public ownership of land, Leopold believed that it was not the only solution to conservation problems. In "Conservation Economics," published in the *Journal of Forestry* in May 1934, he refers to erosion as "a leprosy of the land" that can be cured only by universal reformation of land use. The article explores in greater detail the social and economic problems of conservation that he had discussed the previous year in "Conservation Ethic." Leopold concludes that in taking over abused private land, the government is assuming the debt incurred by the private landowner, who should in fact be the one to make the reforms. "The thing to be prevented is destructive private land-use of any and all kinds," he writes. "The thing to be encouraged is the use of private land in such a way as to combine the public and private interest to the greatest possible degree."

During the severe drought year 1934, Leopold conducted research on quail and cosupervised a survey of marshlands for the Wisconsin Conservation Commission and the Biological Survey. In May an offer came to Leopold from Washington to replace Jay Darling in the Wild Life program of the Department of Agriculture. Darling had become frustrated over efforts to block the purchase of land for wildlife refuges. After much consultation and consideration—the position would have provided a much larger salary—Leopold decided to stay in Wisconsin, where he believed he could be of more help conducting research at the local level. The following month Leopold was named chairman of the twenty-member Committee on Wild Life of the National Research Council. Two members protested the appointment, stating that the committee needed a "broader perspective" than Leopold's. Game management at that time did not enjoy the status of more-classical fields, such as zoology; Leopold, how-

ever, remained chairman until 1936. Also in June, officials dedicated the Arboretum and Wild Life Refuge of the University of Wisconsin. In August, Leopold gave a coast-to-coast radio broadcast called "The Game Cycle," in which he warned of "biological eclipse." Two trips, in July and September, brought to Leopold's attention the sandhill crane, the great endangered bird that occupied the dunes of the sand counties. Although they were not game birds, their fate, Leopold could see, was connected to that of game birds; he understood the interconnection of all wildlife. Sighting the cranes inspired "Marshland Elegy," published in the October 1937 issue of *American Forests,* in which Leopold articulated the idea that wildlife was the living reminder of the environmental past of America. "Our appreciation of the crane," he writes, "grows with the slow unraveling of earthly history. . . . When we hear his call we hear no mere bird. He is the symbol of our untamable past, of that incredible sweep of millennia which underlies and conditions the daily affairs of birds and men."

In January 1935, one day after Leopold's forty-eighth birthday, he and a friend visited an abandoned farm in Sauk County, one of the "sand counties" of Wisconsin, which was near one of the boyhood homes of John Muir. The trail they followed had been a pioneer wagon route. The farmhouse had burned down; the only remaining building was a chicken coop, and its only occupant was a year's supply of manure that was to become the beginnings of the family garden. That coop eventually became "the shack," the dwelling place of the Leopold family on their weekend excursions to "the farm," 120 acres near the Wisconsin River.

The year 1935 proved busy for Leopold. He became one of the founding members of the Wilderness Society, a reflection of how the scope of his interests was expanding from game management to wildlife in all its forms—the biotic values of wilderness, the importance of predators to the issue of "carrying capacity," and the stability of land as organism. In August, Leopold, as a guest of the Oberlaender Trust, took the only overseas trip he ever made, to study with five others the forestry methods of central Europe, especially Germany. The group toured state forests in Saxony, Czechoslovakia, Bavaria, and Wurttemberg. Although impressed with the interest in conservation that he found there, Leopold felt repelled by the artificiality of the methods used, both in forestry and game management. What was missing, he wrote, was not only wilderness, but wildness. In a never-completed essay he notes that "monuments to wildness are an esthetic luxury which Germany, with its timber deficit and the evident land-hunger of its teeming millions, cannot afford." The forests he saw lacked "a certain exuber-

Leopold in the late 1930s (Aldo Leopold Foundation)

ance which arises from a rich variety of plants fighting with each other for a place in the sun. . . . I never realized before that the melodies of nature are music only when played against the undertones of evolutionary history." He also discovered the combination of nativism and nationalism that plagued conservation movements in those years in Germany. Leopold's letters and speeches late in the year reveal that his assumptions regarding conservation were changing. In a December lecture titled "Deer and Forestry in Germany" he states that "All land-uses and land-users are interdependent, and the forces which connect them follow channels still largely unknown." In a letter to the president of the National Rifle Association he protests the indiscriminate shooting of eagles in Alaska, which at that time paid bounties for killed eagles. "I would infinitely rather that [the author] shoot the vases off my mantelpiece than the eagles out of my Alaska. I have a part ownership in both." Also in December, Leopold responded to an editorial in the *Journal of Forestry* that called the Wilderness Society a "faddish cult." "The question of the 'highest use' of remaining wilderness is basically one of evaluating beauty," he writes in a 20 December 1935 letter to H. A. Smith, "in the broadest ecological sense of that word."

The harsh winter of 1935–1936 affected the quail population managed by Leopold and his student

Arthur Hawkins as much as unmanaged quail populations. The stability of Wisconsin's deer herd, as well as threatened species and predator populations, was also in question. Leopold began to realize that game management alone could not reestablish the equilibrium of the natural population that civilization had disrupted. During a speech at Beloit College in May of 1936 he warned his audience that the interdependence of the biotic community would not allow for the replacement of natural equilibria with artificial ones. The fundamental issue, he said, was the role of human beings in the equation.

In September, Leopold and his friend Ray Roark visited the Southwest for a two-week bow-and-arrow deer hunt in the wild interior of the Sierra Madre Occidental in northern Mexico. The area around the Rio Gavilan, a topographical and ecological counterpart to the areas around the Gila and the Blue Rivers, had not suffered the same devastation of its soil and wildlife because Apache and Mexican antipathy, as well as Pancho Villa's bandits, had kept human immigration in check; mountain lion and wolf populations, therefore, had not been reduced, and they in turn kept the numbers of game animals (especially deer and wild turkeys) abundant but not excessive. Leopold returned to the Sierra Madre the following year with his brother Starker. During these two trips, Leopold later recalled, he first realized that land was an organism, that all his life he had seen only "sick land," while here was a "biota still in perfect aboriginal health." The term "unspoiled wilderness" acquired a new meaning. "Song of the Gavilan," written years later and published in the July 1940 issue of the *Journal of Wildlife Management,* describes not only the music of the river but also the biosphere:

> This song of the waters is audible to every ear, but there is other music in these hills, but by no means audible to all. To hear even a few notes of it you must first live here for a long time, and you must know the speech of hills and rivers. Then on a still night, . . . sit quietly and listen for a wolf to howl, and think hard of everything you have seen and tried to understand. Then you may hear it—a vast pulsing harmony—its score inscribed on a thousand hills, its notes the lives and deaths of plants and animals, its rhythms spanning the seconds and centuries.

In the spring of 1938, *Bird-Lore* published Leopold's "Conservation Esthetic," in which he returns to the subject of outdoor recreation, stating that true outdoor recreation should not damage land or wildlife. Too much transportation ruins the resources the tourists travel to see. "Recreational development is a job," he writes, "not of building roads into lovely country, but of building receptivity into the still unlovely human mind." By the autumn of that year Leopold had ceased to sign himself as "Professor of Game Management," using instead "Professor of Wildlife Management." In November he delivered a lecture on "Economics, Philosophy, and the Land," in which he rejected the idea that esthetics and utility are separate. He began a series of more than thirty articles, published in *Wisconsin Agriculturalist and Farmer,* in which he provided farmers with information about wildlife conservation. Owning a farm added authority to his advice. In February 1939 he gave the talk called "The Farmer as a Conservationist," which was later published in *American Forests* (June 1939). In it he posits that the farmer is the primary person who can restore the biosphere. He describes conservation as a "state of harmony" between the land and the people.

On 1 February 1939, the Leopold family visited the "shack" only to find it vandalized, the furniture broken, and the honey and homemade jam ruined. They set about restoring the cabin, however, and in the process improved it with a wooden floor and whitewashed interior. Later that year Leopold was able to undertake another rescue, this time the brother of his Jewish friend Alfred Schottlaender, whom Leopold had met in Germany. Schottlaender had escaped from the Nazis to Kenya but asked Leopold's help in getting his brother

out of Germany. Although the U.S. State Department proved to be no help, an old friend from Lawrenceville found a job for the man in his South African company.

In the spring of 1939 Leopold made fundamental changes in his academic program. He no longer called it "Game Management" or even "Wildlife Management"; he now called the course "Wildlife Ecology." In requesting renewed funding, Leopold argued that three things were needed for successful restoration of wildlife: critical judgment of citizens, their enthusiasm for wildlife, and deeper understanding of the natural mechanisms. During all this activity he prepared the address called "A Biotic View of Land," which became his major essay to date on the importance of uniting the science of ecology with the practice of conservation. He delivered the address on 21 June 1939 in Milwaukee to a joint meeting of the Society of American Foresters and the Ecological Society of America. No one can say anymore, he argued, where utility ends or begins. The biosphere is so complex and interdependent that terms such as "useful" or "harmful" have become meaningless. "The only sure conclusion is that the biota as a whole is useful, and biota includes not only plants and animals, but soils and waters as well." He explains the idea of the "biotic pyramid" and the concepts, now generally accepted, of food webs, energy flow, trophic layers, and energy circuits. By early 1940 he continued working on these ideas in a manuscript called "Biotic Land Use," in which he defined the health of the land in terms of both stability and diversity.

Later that year Leopold spent three weeks in the Southwest studying for the Soil Conservation Service, reviewing wildlife conditions and in particular the status of rodent populations. In August 1940 he finished "Escudilla," a reminiscence of his days in the Apache National Forest and the death of its old grizzly bear. Together with "Song of the Gavilan," this essay marked a change in Leopold's style from the technical (but always entertaining) to the more lyrical quality of his later work.

When Bob and George Marshall of the Wilderness Society were accused in February 1941 by *The Saturday Evening Post* of Communist connections, Leopold responded with characteristic open-mindedness. Writing to another member of the Wilderness Society council, he expressed faith in the Marshalls' clear and sensible thinking and declared that the society need not be concerned about political labels.

At the same time, Leopold was in the process of articulating his views on wilderness as necessary to the study of land health, twenty years after his first article on the subject of preservation. In "Wilderness as a Land Laboratory" for *Living Wilderness* (July 1941) he argues that to preserve wilderness is necessary in order

Part of the Leopold family in 1940: Leopold, Nina, wife Estella, daughter Estella, Luna, Flick the dog, and Starker (Aldo Leopold Foundation)

to provide "a base-datum of normality, a picture of how healthy land maintains itself as an organism." From this point, Leopold broadened his belief that conservation was a moral issue, the social ramifications of ethical philosophy. In a lecture in March of 1941 he stated his conviction that a better living standard did not necessarily ensure higher ethics. It concludes, "There can be no doubt that a society rooted in the soil is more stable than one rooted in pavements. Stability seems to vary inversely to the mental distance from fields and woods."

Early in 1941 Leopold produced a new essay (published in *A Sand County Almanac* as "Clandeboye") on the birds of Clandeboye Marsh, and later that summer he took a three-week trip throughout the West in order to inspect the progress of the Cooperative Wildlife Research Units in Utah and Oregon. In Modoc National Forest in Oregon he noted the invasion of the range by an imported weed, cheat grass, which he describes later in his essay "Cheat Takes Over," published in *The Land* (Autumn 1941). Leopold also observed the deterioration of the land in almost every

area of the intermountain West. The deer herd was being bolstered while the predator population was being controlled. Hunting alone, Leopold knew, would be an insufficient method for keeping the deer population within the limits that the range could sustain. He recommended that the wildlife agencies also maintain predator populations large enough to prevent overpopulation by deer.

Throughout the year Leopold had been thinking of compiling essays in a book to be illustrated by Albert Hochbaum, one of his students. Toward the end of 1941 Leopold wrote two essays, the first works in which he drew on his experiences from his farm. One concerned the return of the geese in spring and the other, a banded chickadee (number 65287), the one that had spent the longest time at the shack. He found in December, however, that another bird deserved the title of longest chickadee resident when he discovered banded bird number 65290. He revised his essay accordingly. He also began work on an essay titled "Yet Come June," in which he investigates the relationship between the land and the cycles of civilization as well as the continuity of nature. The essay was never completed. Nonetheless, in early December he delivered to the Seventh Annual Midwest Wildlife Conference his address called "Wildlife in American Culture," in which he spoke about the capability of outdoor experiences to stimulate awareness of American history. Such experience was the best nationalism, he said; it reminded Americans of their dependence on the "soil-plant-animal-food chain." "We fancy that industry supports us," he said, "forgetting what supports industry." Wildlife patterns could offer insights into social problems, he postulated.

The day after the conference ended, the Japanese attacked Pearl Harbor, and Leopold's son Carl joined the marines. Both his other two sons took part in the war, but none so extensively as Carl. In 1944, when Carl was stationed in the South Pacific, secrecy of his mission was so imperative that he was not permitted to let his parents know his exact location. He did continue, however, to report in his letters his sightings of birds. From this information Leopold was able to pinpoint his son's location. Leopold's students, too, continued throughout the war to record bird life and to correspond with each other and with their professor concerning their observations.

The beginnings of the war inspired Leopold to write, in an essay titled "Land-Use and Democracy," published in *Audubon Magazine* (September–October 1942), that Adolf Hitler had been right that no democracy used its land decently. Leopold considers the individual's role in conservation and concludes that, while government programs are indispensable in preserving the land, the most important is the individual's role. Citizens who want to avoid undue government intervention must take up the responsibility for conservation themselves. "Culture is a state of awareness of the land's collective functioning," Leopold writes. "A culture premised on the destructive dominance of a single species can have but short duration."

The war also gave Leopold the subject for the essay called "Flambeau," published in *American Forests* (January 1943). During a canoe trip on that river in northern Wisconsin, Leopold met with two college boys who were also camping and canoeing on the river. This trip, Leopold surmises, afforded them both their first and last taste of freedom for a long time, between two regimented ways of life, the campus and the barracks. Wilderness travel gave them complete freedom to make mistakes, to learn the rewards and punishments of wise and foolish acts, which woodsmen face every day. He theorizes, "Perhaps every youth needs an occasional wilderness trip, in order to learn the meaning of this particular freedom."

The busy year of 1943 allowed Leopold little time to write, although he was still planning his collection of essays. He also envisioned a textbook that would "describe the workings of land by following the known history of a series of landscapes or communities" and in July managed to complete the introductory essay to the volume called "Land as a Circulatory System." The book, which was never completed, was to be called "Land Ecology." In September, Leopold composed an essay that became one of his favorites; it was drawn from his experiences of observing and recording wildlife at the shack. It was to be called "Great Possessions," the title he also chose for the proposed volume itself.

A Christmas trip to Burlington inspired a new essay, "Illinois Bus Ride," written on New Year's Day 1944, and a few days later he wrote an account called "The Green Lagoons" (published in *A Sand County Almanac*), about his and his brother's canoe trip on the Colorado River twenty-two years before. His observations include the ominous prophecy of a world without wilderness: "Man always kills the thing he loves, and so we pioneers have killed our wilderness. Some say we had to. Be that as it may, I am glad I shall never be young without wild country to be young in. Of what avail are forty freedoms without a blank spot on the map?" Correspondence with Hochbaum concerning these essays in fact led Leopold to probe more deeply his own convictions. Like many students, Hochbaum proved more teacher than pupil. Even as he noted the strong points of the writing, he criticized that Leopold never admitted his own part in the destruction of wilderness. Always able to receive criticism diplomatically, Leopold continued the correspondence and delved more deeply into his own conclusions. Throughout March, as he gathered data on deer and wolf populations, he must have meditated on Hochbaum's comments. On 1 April 1944 he brought together his experience of shooting the wolf on the Blue River rimrock, his observations of deer overgrazing in Colorado, and his work with the sportsmen of Wisconsin. The result was one of his best-known and most frequently anthologized essays, "Thinking Like a Mountain," in which he acknowledges and explains his part in the destruction of the wolf. He was young then, he says, and full of "trigger-itch," and he thought that eliminating wolves would create a hunter's paradise. As he watched the death of the old wolf he had shot, however, he realized that the mountain itself would not have agreed with his view.

The issue of deer overpopulation consumed much of Leopold's time during the war years. The herd in Wisconsin had overgrown its grazing range, and Leopold recommended a five-year program of herd

Leopold measuring pine trees on his property in Sauk County, Wisconsin, 1946 (photograph by R. McCabe; Leopold Collection, University of Wisconsin Archives)

reduction through hunting. In northern Wisconsin, however, a group called "Save Wisconsin's Deer," headed by Roy Jorgensen, argued that the problem in Wisconsin was too few, not too many, deer, and he ridiculed those people, including Leopold, who claimed that many deer needed to be eliminated in order to maintain the health of the forests. The public viewed the overabundance of deer as normal and called for reenacting a bounty on wolves. Leopold, who had opposed the bounty on the basis of the danger of extinction of the timber wolf, in 1943 changed his position, not because he wanted the wolf population to be lessened, but because he feared that increases in the coyote and wolf populations would severely trim the deer herd in northern Wisconsin. In an awkwardly worded explanation in the *Wisconsin Conservation Bulletin,* he admits that he recognizes and regrets his own part in exterminating wolves from part of both New Mexico and Wisconsin and states his conviction that human beings have no right to exterminate any species.

Leopold was in the midst of preparing an essay called "The Outlook for Farm Wildlife" when the war ended. He, Olaus Murie, and others in the Wilderness Society found themselves contemplating the function of the organization in a postwar world in which everyone seemed focused on the economy and rebuilding. An influx of new students provided one answer: having endured the destruction of war, they had become interested in wildlife preservation. In addition, people had begun to think internationally. During this time, one of Leopold's most influential correspondents, William Vogt, interested Leopold in studying the problems of conservation in Latin America, which were exacerbated by poverty, dictatorship, exploitation of resources, and the unyielding stand of the Catholic Church on birth control. That wildlife recognized no international boundaries provided a metaphor for the now-accepted truth that social problems, too, had become truly everyone's concern. Accordingly, in early 1948 Leopold agreed to serve as one of about forty advisers on the American panel of the International Scientific Conference on the Conservation and Utilization of Resources, to be sponsored by the United Nations Economic and Social Council in 1949 and 1950.

Leopold never served on this panel. In 1947, however, he gave one of his most effective lectures to the Conservation Committee of the Garden Club of America in Minneapolis. The speech, which became the basis for his essay "The Ecological Conscience," published in the *Bulletin of the Garden Club of America* (September 1947), states unequivocally that the responsibility for conservation rests with the individual and that the reason conservation had seen little progress at that point was that philosophy and ethics had heretofore been omitted from the conservation debate. "No one has ever told farmers that in land-use the good of the community may entail obligations over and above those dictated by self-interest," he asserted. Leopold employed four case histories—involving soil, wildlife, forests, and water—in order to demonstrate the truth of his conviction that "trying to improve the face of the land without improving ourselves" is futile.

Eye problems that began in 1947 resulted in a minor operation for Leopold in early 1948. He was sixty, his career at its zenith, his academic program solidly funded, and his work on his proposed new book moving forward. He attended a conference at the King Ranch in Texas, which he praised for its wildlife restoration. While there, he learned that his illustrator, Hochbaum, would be unable to supply the drawings for the new book; Hochbaum also noted in private that Leopold had aged tremendously since they had last met. Even without Hochbaum, however, Leopold moved forward on his project. He found a new illustrator, Charles W. Schwartz. In November of 1947 he wrote "Axe-in-Hand," on the moral implications of using tools and encouraging or destroying species. In this essay he defines conservation as "what a man thinks about while chopping, or while deciding what to chop. A conservationist is one who is humbly aware that with each stroke he is writing his signature on the face of the land." In January 1948 he wrote "Good Oak" (collected in *A Sand County Almanac*), in which he chronicles natural history as he and the "chief sawyer," Estella, cut through the rings of an eighty-year-old black oak tree felled by lightning. He begins, "There are two spiritual dangers in not owning a farm. One is the danger of supposing that breakfast comes from the grocery, and the other that heat comes from the furnace." The problems with the book, however, had increased. After approaching several publishers, some of whom remarked on the lack of unity of Leopold's collection, Luna Leopold contacted Oxford University Press, which became the publisher of the book. Using the working title "Great Possessions," Leopold divided the essays into three parts: "A Sauk County Almanac," essays about the shack, arranged chronologically over a year; "Sketches Here and There," essays about other parts of Wisconsin and the country;

and "The Upshot," his philosophical writings. The tone progresses from anecdotal observations of nature to an awareness of what has been lost; the final section provides the ethical underpinning for a philosophy of conservation. For this final section he uses "Conservation Esthetic" (1938) and "Wildlife in American Culture" (1941). In a new essay, "Wilderness," he summarizes a lifetime of ideas on that subject. He needed, however, a final essay to make his case for an ecological understanding of man's place in relation to the land (human beings as citizens of the land rather than masters of it) and the ethical obligations of conservation. His solution was to bring together—probably sometime in July 1947—"The Conservation Ethic" (1933), "A Biotic View of Land" (1939), and "The Ecological Conscience" (1947) into his best-known essay, "The Land Ethic."

On 14 April 1948 Leopold learned that Oxford University Press had decided to publish his book in 1949. He was also working on a proposal with Andrew Weaver, another professor at the University of Wisconsin, to acquire John Muir's boyhood farm for a state park. On 21 April he was at the shack ready for tree planting and bird counting. The wind rose, and a trash fire at Jim Ragan's neighboring farm developed into a brush fire. Leopold joined a dozen neighbors who tried to fight the fire by wetting the back of the flames. Estella wetted some of the plantations on their own land, which were endangered; Estella Jr. went to call the fire department. Just after beginning work, Leopold lay down on the grass near his beloved sand farm and died of a heart attack.

Leopold's children were left to finish his project. Luna retitled a few essays and part 1 of the manuscript from "A Sauk County Almanac" to "A Sand Country Almanac" and finally to "A Sand County Almanac," which also became the title for the collection itself. From the time of its publication, *A Sand County Almanac* received praise from conservationists and critics, including Joseph Wood Krutch. Luna edited excerpts from his father's hunting journals and unfinished essays, which Oxford published under the title *Round River: From the Journals of Aldo Leopold* (1953). This book brought criticism of Leopold's avidity as a hunter, even from so eminent a figure as Rachel Carson. By the late 1950s Leopold had become as important a figure in the conservation movement as Henry David Thoreau and John Muir. The 1966 republication of *A Sand County Almanac* in paperback, occurring after the publication of Carson's *Silent Spring* in 1962 and the passage of the Wilderness Act in 1964, made it one of the seminal works of the environmental movement. Leopold's essays are widely anthologized in texts on nature writing and ecological philosophy.

"A Sand County Almanac," the first part of the collection bearing that name, consists of twelve sections, one for each month, and represents a journal of a farm year. The essays are short, recounting single observations or incidents; as Robert Finch notes in his introduction, they are like lyric poems or fables. The series establishes clearly the narrative voice, which is both engaged and objective, humanistic and scientific, interested in the broad view and the minute detail, and appreciative and bemused. Through the voice the reader perceives the relationship between observer and observed, and the personality and the environment. "January Thaw," which is the whole of the January section, observes the "cycle of beginnings and ceasings which we call a year" and speculates anthropomorphically on the motives of animals, specifically the mouse, hawk, rabbit, and skunk, while "Good Oak" (February) states that "Man brings all things to the test of himself." The lightning-felled black oak that Leopold and his wife cut tells the history of the land as no library can and establishes the interaction of man and nature. Not only the man-man community may be dismembered, he says, but also the man-land community. The saw, wedge, and ax, he declares, are tools good for the oak and good for history. In "The Geese Return" (March) he begins: "One swallow does not make a summer, but one skein of geese, cleaving the murk of a March thaw, is the spring." He accounts for love in the goose world, as all live in pairs and lone geese are "bereaved survivors of the winter's shooting, searching in vain for their kin." Geese also tell of the interconnectedness of people and nature, nation and nation: "It is an irony of history that the great powers should have discovered the unity of nations at Cairo in 1943. The geese of the world have had that notion for a longer time, and each March they stake their lives on its essential truth."

The April section includes four parts: "Come High Water," "Draba," "Bur Oak," and "Sky Dance." In the first part, Leopold observes that a pile of lumber deposited by high water is "not only a collection of personalities, but an anthology of human strivings in upriver farms and forests. The autobiography of an old board is a kind of literature not yet taught on campuses, but any riverbank farm is a library where he who hammers or saws may read at will." "Draba" is a paean to the small, seemingly useless wildflower. "Bur Oak" declares that "he who owns a veteran bur oak . . . owns a historical library, and a reserved seat in the theater of evolution." "Sky Dance" is an ode to the mating dance of the woodcocks "enacted nightly on hundreds of farms."

The May section, "Back from the Argentine," is devoted to plovers and June to "The Alder Fork—A *Fishing Idyl*." July includes "Great Possessions" and

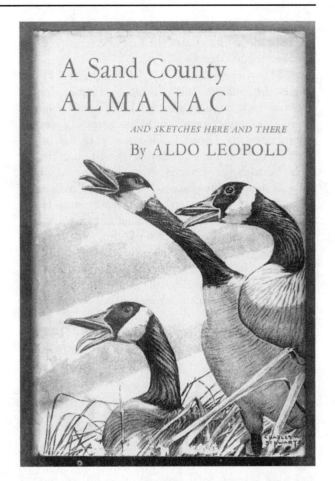

Dust jacket for Leopold's 1949 book, essays collected by his children after his death (Ken Lopez catalogue, 2000)

"Prairie Birthday." The first sustains the metaphor of land as a book. The second employs a more specific example in the discussion of Silphium, a prairie wildflower that can withstand grazing but not continuous mowing and thus thrives only in corners of fields where mowers cannot go. "Tell me of what plant-birthday a man takes notice, and I shall tell you a good deal about his vocation, his hobbies, his hay fever, and the general level of his ecological education," Leopold writes. Arguing that roads, grazing, and clear-farming destroy natural flora, Leopold states that "the backward farmer's eye is nearly twice as well fed as the eye of the university student or businessman."

"The Green Pasture" (August) continues the metaphor of the river as artist begun in "Come High Water." "The Choral Copse" (September) and "Smoky Gold," "Too Early," and "Red Lanterns" (October) describe the landscape of the farm in autumn. The November section includes "If I Were the Wind," "Axe-in-Hand," and "A Mighty Fortress," which again asserts the educational value of the land. "Every farm woodland," the essay begins, "in addition to yielding lumber, fuel, and posts, should provide its owner a liberal education. This crop of wisdom never fails, but it is not always harvested."

The year concludes with "Home Range," "Pines above the Snow," and "65290." "Home Range" declares the farm to be a textbook on animal ecology. "Pines above the Snow" includes Leopold's cryptic comment on the Creator: "God passed on his handiwork as early as the seventh day, but I notice He has since been rather noncommittal about its merits. I gather either that He spoke too soon, or that trees stand more looking upon than do fig leaves and firmaments." The last essay is the culmination of a chickadee-banding experiment, in which the author and his family had to be concerned with the direction of the wind, which the chickadee avoids. Leopold comments sardonically on the quality of classroom education: "Books on nature seldom mention wind; they are written behind stoves."

The second part of the book, "Sketches Here and There," includes six sections on different parts of the country. The narrative voice is less personal than in the first part and dwells on what is remembered and lost, not what is before the viewer. The purpose is to educate, however, not to condemn; humankind's ignorance, not its perverseness, brought about the losses. "Thinking Like a Mountain" is the seminal essay on the education of the self in the truths in conservation, and although Leopold can sound critical of human nature, he includes himself in the criticism. "Wisconsin" includes the essays called "Marshland Elegy," "The Sand Counties," "Odyssey," "On a Monument to the Pigeon," and "Flambeau." The first praises the sandhill crane and laments the destruction of its habitat. The second declares that although the sand counties have poor soil, they harbor beautiful wildflowers. "Odyssey" discusses the cycles of nature and demonstrates that every species has a place; when pigeons that ate wheat were killed off, cinch bugs proliferated, eating more wheat. Overplanting of wheat finally depleted the soil, which washed away, putting an end to wheat farming. "Flambeau" chronicles Leopold's encounter with the boys on the river and reaffirms the value of wilderness.

"Illinois Bus Ride" is the first essay in the next section, called "Illinois and Iowa"; it eulogizes the loss of the prairie and questions what is of value. "Red Legs Kicking," an account of a partridge-kill, is reminiscent of Thoreau's dictum that the value of hunting is to introduce a boy to the joys of wilderness. The section called "Arizona and New Mexico" draws from Leopold's days with the Forest Service and includes "On Top," "Thinking Like a Mountain," and "Escudilla." United by their mountain landscapes, the three

also make clear that in destroying the frontier in order to find safety, human beings have brought not only desecration of beauty but also a different threat—destruction of the land. "On Top" declares that a life entirely free from fear is a poor life. "Thinking Like a Mountain" argues that too much safety leads to danger of other sorts. "Escudilla" shows that a mountain devoid of its bear loses a great deal of its essence.

"Chihuahua and Sonora" includes three essays inspired by Leopold's Mexican trips—"Guacamaja," "The Green Lagoons," and "Song of the Gavilan"—all concerned with sensitivity to the mood of the land and lamenting that the wilderness has been all but destroyed. "Cheat Takes Over" ("Oregon and Utah") decries overgrazing and the result, an exotic species re-creating the landscape and crowding out indigenous species. In "Clandeboye" ("Manitoba"), Leopold complains of the narrowness of education that leaves out nature. "Education, I fear," he writes, "is learning to see one thing by going blind to another."

Part 3, "The Upshot," includes the four sections "Conservation Ethics," "Wildlife in American Culture," "Wilderness," and "The Land Ethic." In those sections Leopold adopts a more formal, analytical tone in order to describe the need for reform in people's relationship to the land. While not inundating the reader with facts, Leopold avoids abstraction by grounding his philosophical statements with details. His defining ethics in ecological terms and adopting an ethical approach toward mankind's relationship to land have become part of the philosophical underpinning of the environmental movement.

The success of *A Sand County Almanac* has led to the publication and republication of many of Leopold's other works. In 1990 Stackpole Books published *Aldo Leopold's Wilderness: Selected Early Writings,* a selection of Leopold's early essays on game restoration, game management, recreational use of wilderness, threatened species, and land health. In addition, Island Press in 1999 published *For the Health of the Land: Previously Unpublished Essays and Other Writings,* arranged, like Leopold's most famous book, into three parts: "Conserving Rural Wildlife," "A Landowner's Conservation Almanac," and "Conservation and Land Health." The second part follows the pattern of "A Sand County Almanac": the essays are arranged by season and represent a journal of a farm year. In addition, part 3 includes essays of a more philosophical character, such as "Biotic Land-Use" and "The Land-Health Concept and Conservation" (both previously unpublished). This book includes a variety of approaches to wildlife and land conservation, revealing the range of Leopold's talent as a writer of informative, entertaining, and elegant prose. It has much practical information on attracting birds and providing habitat. Also included is the charming and humorous "Helping Ourselves: Being the Adventures of a Farmer and a Sportsman Who Produced Their Own Shooting Ground," first published in 1938 in *Field and Stream,* which adopts a semiarcane diction (imitative in places of the King James Bible) in order to relate the adventures of the founders of the Riley Game Cooperative.

Aldo Leopold's reach has extended through his family as well as through his writings. All of his children became scientists and naturalists. Carl, who returned from the war, became a plant physiologist and pathologist at the Boyce Thompson Institute for Plant Research at Cornell University. Starker taught wildlife ecology at the University of California at Berkeley. Nina worked in wildlife studies in the United States and Africa, eventually maintaining a wildlife research center at the Leopold family farm in Wisconsin. Luna became a leading expert in the hydrology of river systems with the U.S. Geological Survey. Estella Jr. became a paleobotanist with the U.S. Geological Survey and finally head of the Quaternary Research Center at the University of Washington. Each can be seen as in some way continuing Leopold's work.

In Curt Meine's comprehensive biography he sums up Leopold's achievement:

> His influence on conservation in America remains pervasive. As a forester, he gave to the profession a standard of wise stewardship, a balance of the visionary and the pragmatic, that still stands. As a defender of wild lands, he framed his concern in terms that struck to the roots of the nation's historical and philosophical development; he helped make respect for wilderness a matter of national priority, and national pride. The science of wildlife ecology and the practice of wildlife management would have developed without him, but not with the same degree of integrity or sense of direction. As a teacher, he inspired hundreds of students to see and understand land, to study it rigorously, and to care for it. As a thinker, he gave the conservation movement philosophical definition. As a poet, he enriched the nation's bookshelf of nature writing.

Although quiet and unassuming, Leopold was tenacious in the pursuit of his goals for conservation. He mostly enjoyed hunting, bird-watching, and being out-

doors, but he also liked to dress well, to attend parties, to see movies, and to read books. Although he lived most of his life in towns and cities, he was deeply concerned with the ramifications of the intersection of agriculture and conservation.

Bibliography:
Curt Meine, *Aldo Leopold: His Life and Work* (Madison: University of Wisconsin Press, 1988), pp. 589–620.

Biography:
Curt Meine, *Aldo Leopold: His Life and Work* (Madison: University of Wisconsin Press, 1988).

References:
J. Baird Callicott, "Aldo Leopold on Education, as Educator, and His Land Ethic in the Context of Contemporary Environmental Education," in *In Defense of the Land Ethic: Essays in Environmental Philosophy* (Albany: State University of New York Press, 1989), pp. 223–238;

Callicott, "Hume's *Is/Ought* Dichotomy and the Relation of Ecology to Leopold's Land Ethic," in *In Defense of the Land Ethic: Essays in Environmental Philosophy* (Albany: State University of New York Press, 1989), pp. 117–128;

Callicott, "Leopold's Land Ethic," in *In Defense of the Land Ethic: Essays in Environmental Philosophy* (Albany: State University of New York Press, 1989), pp. 239–248;

Curt Meine and Richard L. Knight, eds., *The Essential Aldo Leopold: Quotations and Commentaries* (Madison: University of Wisconsin Press, 1999);

Dennis Ribbens, "The Making of *A Sand County Almanac,*" *Transactions of the Wisconsin Academy of Sciences, Arts and Letters,* 70 (1982): 3–12;

Thomas Tanner, ed., *Aldo Leopold: The Man and His Legacy* (Ankeny, Iowa: Soil Conservation Society of America, 1987).

Papers:
Many of Aldo Leopold's unpublished and uncollected works, including letters, journals, and manuscripts, are held by the University of Wisconsin, Madison.

Barry Lopez

(6 January 1945 –)

Susan M. Lucas
University of Nevada, Reno

See also the Lopez entry in *DLB 256: Twentieth-Century American Western Writers, Third Series.*

BOOKS: *Desert Notes: Reflections in the Eye of a Raven* (Kansas City, Kans.: Sheed, Andrews & McMeel, 1976);

Giving Birth to Thunder, Sleeping with His Daughter: Coyote Builds North America (Kansas City, Kans.: Sheed, Andrews & McMeel, 1977);

Of Wolves and Men (New York: Scribners, 1978; London: Dent, 1979);

River Notes: The Dance of Herons (Kansas City, Kans.: Andrews & McMeel, 1979);

Winter Count (New York: Scribners, 1981);

Arctic Dreams: Imagination and Desire in a Northern Landscape (New York: Scribners, 1986; London: Macmillan, 1986);

Crossing Open Ground (New York: Scribners, 1988; London: Macmillan, 1988);

Crow and Weasel, with illustrations by Tom Pohrt (San Francisco: North Point Press, 1990);

The Rediscovery of North America (Lexington: University Press of Kentucky, 1990);

Children in the Woods (Eugene, Ore.: Lone Goose Press, 1992);

Field Notes: The Grace Note of the Canyon Wren (New York: Knopf, 1994);

Lessons from the Wolverine, with illustrations by Pohrt (Athens: University of Georgia Press, 1997);

Apologia, with woodcuts by Robin Eschner (Eugene, Ore.: Lone Goose Press, 1997);

About This Life: Journeys on the Threshold of Memory (New York: Knopf, 1998; London: Harvill, 1998);

Letters of Heaven (Eugene: Knight Library Press, University of Oregon, 2000);

Light Action in the Caribbean (New York: Knopf, 2000).

Edition: *Desert Notes: Reflections in the Eye of a Raven and River Notes: The Dance of Herons* (New York: Avon, 1990).

RECORDINGS: *Winter Count,* read by Lopez, Columbia, Mo., American Audio Prose Library, 1985;

Barry Lopez: Coyote Stories, read by Lopez, Kansas City, Mo., New Letters on Air, 1986;

About This Life: Journeys on the Threshold of Memory, read by Lopez, Los Angeles, New Star Media, 1998;

River Notes: The Dance of Herons, read by Lopez, St. Paul: HighBridge, 1999;

Crossing Open Ground, read by Lopez, St. Paul, HighBridge, 2000;

Field Notes: The Grace Note of the Canyon Wren, read by Lopez, St. Paul, HighBridge, 2000;

Light Action in the Caribbean: Stories, read by Lopez, St. Paul, HighBridge, 2000.

OTHER: "Meeting Ed Abbey," in *Resist Much, Obey Little: Some Notes on Edward Abbey,* edited by James Hepworth and Gregory McNamee (Tucson: Harbinger House, 1985), pp. 67–70;

"Apologia," *Witness,* 3, no. 4 (Winter 1989): 75–79;

"Renegotiating the Contracts," in *This Incomperable Lande: A Book of American Nature Writing,* edited by Thomas J. Lyon (Boston: Houghton Mifflin, 1989), pp. 381–388;

Stephen A. Trimble, *The Sagebrush Ocean: A Natural History of the Great Basin,* introduction by Lopez (Reno: University of Nevada Press, 1989);

"The American Geographies," in *Finding Home: Writing on Nature and Culture from Orion Magazine,* edited by Peter Sauer (Boston: Beacon, 1992), pp. 116–132;

"A Staging of Snow Geese," in *Out of the Noösphere: Adventure, Sports, Travel, and the Environment: The Best of Outside Magazine,* edited by Mark Bryant and others (New York: Simon & Schuster, 1992), pp. 276–287;

Joseph Barbato and Lisa Weinerman, eds., *Heart of the Land: Essays on Last Great Places,* foreword by Lopez (New York: Pantheon, 1994);

"Looking in a Deeper Lair: A Tribute to Wallace Stegner," *Earth Island Journal* (Fall 1995): 34–35;

"Offshore: A Journey to the Weddell Sea," in *American Nature Writing,* selected by John A. Murray (San Francisco: Sierra Club, 1995), pp. 26–67;

Barry Lopez (photograph from the dust jacket for Field Notes, *1994)*

"The Stone Horse," in *The Nature Reader,* edited by Daniel Halpern and Dan Frank (Hopewell, N.J.: Ecco, 1996), pp. 204–213;

"Theft: A Memoir," in *The Woods Stretched for Miles: New Nature Writing from the South,* edited by John Lane and Gerald Thurmond (Athens: University of Georgia Press, 1999), pp. 195–202;

Heart of a Nation: Writers & Photographers Inspired by the American Landscape, introduction by Lopez (Washington, D.C.: National Geographic Society, 2000);

SELECTED PERIODICAL PUBLICATIONS– UNCOLLECTED: "Renegotiating the Contracts," *Parabola,* 8 (Spring 1983): corrected and reprinted in *This Incompareable Lande: A Book of American Nature Writing,* edited by Thomas J. Lyon (Boston: Houghton Mifflin, 1989);

"California Desert: A Wordly Wilderness," *National Geographic,* 171 (January 1987): 42–77;

"Landscapes Open and Closed," *Harper's,* 275 (July 1987): 51–58;

"A Chinese Garland," *North American Review,* 273 (September 1988): 41–42;

"Our Frail Planet in Cold, Clear View," *Harper's* (May 1989): 43–49;

"Discovering the Americas, Again," *New York Times,* 12 October 1990, p. A17;

"Benjamin Claire, North Dakota Tradesman, Writes to the President of the United States," *North American Reivew,* 277 (September/October 1992): 16–20;

"The Interior of North Dakota," *Paris Review,* 34 (Winter 1992): 134–144;

"Thomas Lowdermilk's Generosity," *American Short Fiction,* 12 (Winter 1993): 36–46;

"Reuben Mendoza Vega, Suzuki Professor of Early Caribbean History, University of Gainesville, Offers a History of the United States Based on Personal Experience," *Manoa,* 6 (Summer 1994): 43–49;

"Caring for the Woods," *Audubon,* 97 (March/April 1995): 58–60, 62–63;

"A Literature of Place," *Portland,* 16 (Summer 1997): 22–25;

"The Language of Animals," *Wild Earth,* 8 (Summer 1998): inside front cover, 2–6;

"The Naturalist," *Orion,* 20 (Fall 2001): 38–43;

"A Scary Abundance of Water," *L.A. Weekly,* 11 January 2002, pp. 26–34.

When talking about his work, Barry Lopez often speaks explicitly of the core issues that drive his prose. Words such as "dignity," "tolerance," "prejudice," and "service" infuse discussions of his literary philosophy and sense of storytelling. Such terms as these may seem tangential to the genre of nature writing, which is too often construed simply as either animal stories, landscape descriptions, or overwrought environmental rhetoric. Lopez's writing, however, challenges such reductive views of nature writing. In a 1985 interview with Trish Todd, Lopez said, "When you write about animals and landscape and wilderness, you write about what appears to be natural history. But my principal interest is in human beings and how we arrive at our ideas. My lifelong commitment is to some kind of elucidation of these ideas—what is prejudice, what is tolerance, and what does it mean to live a dignified life." By exploring these questions Lopez demonstrates how the life of a place, plant, or animal is bound up with the lives of humans. His writing reveals that humans' ideas are deeply rooted in their relationship to the environment and that where they live, work, and travel has everything to do with how they treat others.

In both his fiction and his nonfiction, Lopez takes readers into challenging territory; he constantly asks how humans can best live their lives, what they can learn from history, and what native cultures can teach humans today. For him, the writer's role is not simply to entertain, achieve brilliance, or develop an unwavering expertise. Rather, as he explains in a 1994 interview with Douglas Marx, the writer's job requires him or her "to be the one who recognizes the patterns that remind us of our obligations and our dreams." Working from an interdisciplinary approach, Lopez juxtaposes natural history with cultural history, fact with fiction, and scholarship with fieldwork to articulate a sense of hope and a concept of how to live a good life even in difficult circumstances.

The elder of two children, Barry Holstun Lopez was born in Port Chester, New York, on 6 January 1945. His biological father, John Edward Brennan, was a billboard advertising executive, and his mother, Mary Frances Holstun Brennan, worked in journalism. His brother, Dennis, was born in 1948, the same year his family relocated from Long Island Sound to the San Fernando Valley in California. In 1950 his parents divorced, leaving Barry and Dennis in their mother's care. The three of them remained in Resada, California, where Mary Brennan worked as a teacher and dressmaker to support them. Barry never saw his father again, but he, his mother, and his brother spent the next six years in the semirural valley of southern California.

The agricultural landscape of southern California provided endless possibilities for Lopez's boyhood adventures. In "A Voice," the introductory essay to *About This Life: Journeys on the Threshold of Memory* (1998), Lopez remembers playing among "fruit orchards and wisteria hedges, in horse pastures and haylofts, and around farming operations, truck gardens, and chicken ranches." He tells of bicycle rides on summer nights, the thrills of raising tumbler pigeons, and playing along the Los Angeles River channel before it was "floored and walled in concrete." Mary Brennan conscientiously broadened her sons' sense of California beyond the valley, taking them on weekend car trips to the surrounding deserts, nearby lakes, and coastal towns. In the foreword to *Heart of the Land: Essays on Last Great Places* (1994), he remembers that as a boy he pored over *Hammond's Illustrated Library World Atlas* (1949). He mapped out ambitious overland routes in the United States and journeys to more exotic locales that he planned to visit someday. This early interest in travel and fascination with place descriptions manifested itself much later in his own writings, and his experience living in both rural and urban landscapes proved to be crucial to his development as a writer.

When Barry was eleven, his mother married Adrian Bernard Lopez, who adopted Barry and his brother and became the father figure they had never truly had in John Brennan. "A Voice" recounts the new family's move from the "intensely physical landscape" of rural California to a world of privilege and a penthouse apartment in Manhattan. Lopez describes the move as "wrenching" and "bewildering" but also tells how well he adapted, indeed, "thrived in the city in spite of the change in landscape." In New York, Lopez attended a Jesuit preparatory school that stressed the arts and cultivated a skepticism of authoritative ways of knowing—two traits that still mark his thinking. He gained a first-class education, lettered in three varsity sports, and became the president of his senior class. Looking back, Lopez realizes how deeply each landscape shaped his sensibilities as a writer. In a 1994 interview with Alice Evans, he explained, "My emotional and metaphorical frameworks were set in my involvement with animals and the desert when I was a kid in California, and then at the age of 11 I got this sort of overlay, of school and intellection and reading and a formal exposure to the arts." Following high-school graduation, Lopez and fifteen of his classmates spent the summer traveling around Europe.

In the fall of 1962 Lopez continued his education at Notre Dame, and during this time he began practicing two habits that eventually led to his life as a writer: he kept a journal, and he continued to feed his wanderlust, taking long weekend road trips across the American landscape. By the time he graduated, he had visited every state with the exception of Oklahoma, Alaska, and Hawaii. During his sophomore and junior years at Notre Dame, he began writing stories. In "A Voice" he recalls his initial understanding of the "urge to write as a desire to describe what happened, what I saw, when I went outside." From reading such writers as Herman Melville, William Faulkner, Thomas Hardy, Willa Cather, and Ernest Hemingway, he developed a sense of story as "a powerful clarifying human invention" and of language as a tool for creating beauty and cultivating mystery. However, the effect of storytelling on an audience confirmed Lopez's desire to become a writer. In the same essay he recalls listening to Robert Fitzgerald read from his 1961 translation of *The Odyssey* and remembers how "the audience was galvanized in beauty by his presentation." At that moment Lopez decided, "Whatever Fitzgerald did in that hour, that's what I wanted to do."

Lopez's belief in story and faith in language that he was only realizing during his college years remains a prominent feature of his fiction and nonfiction. Lopez trusts the social function of story—that narrative can activate change and heal a world plagued by an overwhelming lack of intimacy and unprecedented environmental problems. Indeed, much of Lopez's work responds to a loss he perceives in Western culture, a failure to understand the power of language and the value of story. Talking with Kay Bonetti in 1988, he observed, "In our culture we throw language around all the time. We use it in the most indiscriminate and disrespectful ways. So, we've lost a little bit of what it means to prepare to tell a story, to use language. The language has a power to heal and to elevate and instill hope in the bleakest of circumstances, and we, both as readers and writers, should be more aware of that than we are sometimes."

In 1966 Lopez graduated cum laude from Notre Dame, and although he was certain that he wanted to be a writer, he remained unsure of the best way to pursue this goal. He was adamant about maintaining a sense of service through his work and seriously considered becoming a Trappist monk. At the abbey of Gethsemani in Kentucky, however, Lopez ultimately decided against monastic life. On 10 June 1967 he married Sandra Jean Landers (they divorced in 1999) and settled on teaching as a way for him to balance a life of writing and service. He returned to Notre Dame in 1967 to earn a master of arts in teaching and com-

pleted the degree the following year. In 1968 he and his wife moved west so that he could pursue a master of fine arts degree at the University of Oregon. Lopez spent only one semester in the program but remained at the university studying folklore with Professor Barre Toelken.

Lopez's relationship with Toelken proved life-changing for him. In "A Voice" Lopez describes Toelken as a "singular teacher" who "helped me frame the questions seething inside me then about how justice, education, and other Enlightenment ideals could be upheld against the depth of prejudice and the fields of ignorance I saw everywhere around me." Toelken introduced him to anthropological research, which became a hallmark of much of Lopez's research and writing. In Toelken's company, Lopez began to realize what his previous educational experiences lacked. Through Toelken, Lopez met an array of "insightful people from outside white, orthodox, middle-class culture," encounters that gave him a sense of the diverse voices that are "indispensable to our survival" on this planet—voices absent throughout his experience at Notre Dame.

In 1970 he and Sandy moved onto some land along the McKenzie River near Finn Rock, Oregon (where he currently lives). His life as a writer was beginning to take shape. At this time he was writing for *Popular Science,* contributing photographs and articles to magazines and newspapers, and working on his short stories. But six years passed before his first collection of fiction, *Desert Notes: Reflections in the Eye of the Raven* (1976), was finally published.

The first book in a trilogy, *Desert Notes* includes eleven stories that attest to the subtlety and mystery of arid landscapes. Lopez's interest in Native American cultures, skepticism of science, and practice of travel permeate these spare narratives. Literary critic Sherman Paul has observed, "Lopez's desert is not Edward Abbey's or Gary Nabhan's; it has other dimensions and is as much out of space and time as it is out of mind, a place of mystery, disorientation, and self-transformation, where one goes crazy and comes to oneself, though a certain craziness—despair of the world—is needed to go there in the first place. Fancy hardly covers what is found there." *Desert Notes* deliberately unsettles readers by intermingling extraordinary experiences with ordinary circumstances, an effect Lopez has used in all of his subsequent fiction collections.

Lopez treads the boundary linking imagination and science, beginning the book with a lengthy epigraph from Charles Darwin's *The Voyage of the Beagle* (1836) that contemplates the hold that arid landscapes have on the human mind. These stories explore the fascination of a land that "does not give easily" yet

Dust jacket for Lopez's first book (1976), eleven short stories
exploring the human fascination with arid landscapes
(Ken Lopez catalogue, 2000)

tion one has learned from what one can discern from personal experience in the desert. The narrator assures the reader: "I know what they tell you about the desert but you mustn't believe them."

Desert Notes evokes a sense of fieldwork through the title and the physical activity the stories often represent; however, the collection suggests an alternative kind of fieldwork, one that operates in contrast to the scientific, categorizing method of natural history. Many of the narrators are knowledgeable about these places but have become so through methods that defy logic and expediency. In "The Raven," for example, one learns about the raven via the knowledge of the crow, "who has left the desert." The narrator shares information he has gained from watching and even talking to the birds themselves. Told of the crow's penchant for tricks and compulsiveness, the narrator explains how the raven "will open his mouth as if to say something. Then he will look the other way and say nothing. Later, when you have forgotten, he will tell you he admires the crow." Learning anything of the desert or its inhabitants takes time—a sense of time unfathomable in a fast-paced, industrialized society. The narrator explains that "the only way to be sure what you have seen is a raven is to follow him until he dies of old age" and that if you want to know more you must "bury yourself in the desert" with only your eyes protruding, not blinking, and even then you must "Wait until a generation of ravens has passed away."

This vast country of alkaline desert, raven habitat, and intense sunlight poses physical, spiritual, and intellectual challenges for all who visit; and Lopez's stories suggest a land that is anything but empty. *Desert Notes* portrays an animated landscape with a sun that can strike one across the face and turn somersaults, with creeks that abandon their channels, and with air that flows like water. Lopez was only twenty-three years old when he wrote *Desert Notes,* and he told Evans that it is a "very innocent" book.

Before he published *Desert Notes,* Lopez had already written *Giving Birth to Thunder, Sleeping with His Daughter: Coyote Builds North America* (1977). This collection of Native American folktales was a direct result of his work with Toelken at the University of Oregon. In his conversation with Evans, Lopez explained, "When I discovered the trickster figure with him, I saw something that was tremendously exciting to me, a character who had been distorted by the process of tearing it out of an indigenous culture." *Giving Birth to Thunder, Sleeping with His Daughter* includes sixty-eight tales of Coyote's adventures drawn from many different Native American tribes. In the introduction Lopez explains that he hoped to suggest the "fullness of coyote's character," not just one side. An inherently contradictory

requires a traveler to spend time and still may yield nothing. The book conveys a sense of intimacy through an introduction that directly addresses the reader, as well as first-person narratives that recount desert trips and share observations. Other stories use an omniscient narrator who depicts characters' most private moments: a man's annual ritual journey in "The Hot Springs" and a woman's nude bath in the sun, air, and dust of the desert in "The Wind."

Stories such as "Desert Notes" and "The Raven" teach readers about particular places and their inhabitants through a kind of one-on-one tutorial. The narrator of "Desert Notes" explains his attempts to "get all these things about time and place straight. If we don't, we will only have passed on and have changed nothing." The story opens by beckoning the reader to follow: "I know you are tired. I am tired too. Will you walk along the edge of the desert with me? I would like to show you what lies before us." What emerges is a lesson in waiting, in trying to untangle the misinforma-

figure, Coyote emerges from these tales as both clever and foolish, heroic and cowardly, magical and sometimes even powerless.

The opening story, an adaptation from the Okanagon, "Coyote Keeps His Name," forecasts the complexity of this figure as he appears in the following tales. This story recounts Coyote's attempt to change his name to something more admirable than *Sinkalip* (trickster and imitator), to something more powerful and warrior-like, such as Grizzly Bear, Eagle, or Salmon. The Great Spirit has decided to rename all of the creatures at dawn the following morning; whoever arrives first can choose any name, so Coyote plans to stay awake all night to ensure himself first pick. Despite his best efforts, he falls asleep, and his wife, Mole, does not wake him for fear that a new name will take him away from her. Coyote arrives too late and must keep his name; however, the Great Spirit feels compassion for Coyote and assigns him the important job of assisting the New People. Coyote will teach them survival skills, and though he may never be free from foolishness, he receives a special power to change into anything and communicate with everything except water.

Other stories display Coyote's power to resuscitate others and even himself. He is often victim of his own temper. For example, in the Menomini adaptation "The Tree Holders" he loses a fresh meal to wolves, and in the Southern Ute tale "Coyote and Spider" he falls victim to his own gullibility when spiders easily dupe him out of a meal. The final narrative, "Coyote Finishes His Work," echoes the initial story by reminding readers of Coyote's paradoxical qualities; this Nez Percé tale relates how well Coyote completed the tasks the Old Man Above had assigned him. The Great Spirit descends to the earth to bring Coyote "back to the place he started," vowing that neither will return until a change on the earth requires their attention. The Great Spirit says, "Coyote will come along first, and when you see him you will know I am coming. . . . Earthmother will go back to her first shape and live as a mother among her children. Then things will be made right." The final line of the tale explains, "Now they are waiting for Coyote." Ending the book with this narrative articulates Lopez's sense of the importance of storytelling and the significance of bringing the figure of Coyote to the public's attention.

Giving Birth to Thunder, Sleeping with His Daughter received mixed reviews. In his biography of Lopez, Peter Wild reports a disparity between those who found these retellings uplifting and others who perceived them as insulting to Native Americans. Toelken's foreword to *Giving Birth to Thunder, Sleeping with His Daughter* defends Lopez's approach, arguing that it "does *not* pretend to be an 'Indian book.'"

Toelken supports Lopez's work, explaining that the "stories are retold in a way that is both faithful to native concepts of Coyote and how his stories should go, and phrased for an audience which reads without listening, for whom literature is studied and reflected upon, for whom Coyote is an imaginary but interesting protagonist." Though Lopez traveled in many of the places from which these tales emerged, he did not interview Native Americans to collect their stories; rather, *Giving Birth to Thunder, Sleeping with His Daughter* resulted from library research. Even so, this book should not be considered a work of scholarship, and Lopez emphasized this point in a 1986 interview with Jim Aton: "I made no pretension, I had no presumption of doing anything in a scholarly way. I just wanted the stories to come alive and to see them more widely circulated."

Lopez made more effective use of scholarship and fieldwork in his next book. *Of Wolves and Men* (1978) evolved from an assignment for *Smithsonian Magazine;* this book blends library research with field excursion to present a study of an animal created and vilified by Western culture. Indeed, *Of Wolves and Men* brought Lopez the critical acclaim that had so far eluded him with his fiction; Wild refers to *Of Wolves and Men* as "Barry Lopez's watershed." In 1979 *Of Wolves and Men* received the John Burroughs Medal for distinguished natural history writing, the Christopher Medal for humanitarian writing, and the Pacific Northwest Booksellers Award for excellence in nonfiction. The following year, it was nominated for an American Book Award and the National Book Award for General Nonfiction (paperback). *Of Wolves and Men* garnered praise from literary critics and professional biologists, firmly establishing Lopez in the field of natural history and nature writing.

Each of the four sections of the book presents the wolf from a different perspective. In the introduction Lopez says, "I have looked for a wolf different from that ordinarily given us in the course of learning about animals." This book does not simply represent information about this elusive animal in scientific terms but also incorporates knowledge, ranging from indigenous cultures to that of livestock owners, along with information about the wolf from European cultures. *Of Wolves and Men* includes photographs by John Bauguess and a variety of wolf images, including medieval manuscripts, paintings, woodcuts, and prints, from Western and Native American culture.

In the introduction Lopez reminds readers that despite all of the information he has compiled, "The truth is we know little about the wolf. What we know a good deal more about is what we imagine the wolf to be." Lopez opens part 1, "*Canis Lupus* Linnaeus," with a narrative composite of a wolf drawn from biological studies. He gives details of height, weight, eating and hunting habits, multiple species, and general life expectancy. Lopez explains how difficult survival is for these animals even without the threat of man. Having worked with biologists in the field, Lopez presents the complex social dynamics of the pack and humans' limited understanding of the wolf's sense of territory and relationships with other animals, such as caribou, moose, and ravens. He credits scientific inquiry and serious study of the wolf for bringing the animal "out of the darkness of superstition."

Though Lopez clearly values the empirical method of Western science, he turns to indigenous knowledge for a contrasting view of the wolf in part 2, "And a Cloud Passes Overhead." The Nunamiut Eskimo provide a "precise but open-ended" sense of wolves, insights that can only come from the cultural accumulation of knowledge in watching, hunting, and living with the animal for centuries. Lopez further explores Native American relationships with and observations of the wolf as well, specifically how these cultures identify with the animal as fellow hunters.

Part 3, "The Beast of Waste and Desolation," explores the motivations that led to the virtual extermination of the wolf in particular parts of the globe. Lopez draws from a variety of accounts that reveal the darker sides of human nature and the insecurity of Western humanity, which could never achieve the kind of strength and determinism it witnessed in the wolf. He also discusses the troubled relationship between humans and wolves in the United States, classifying it as an "American pogrom" against the creature.

The fourth section, "And a Wolf Shall Devour the Sun," traces the roots of Western prejudice against the wolf through cultural representations, ranging from ancient Greek myths to medieval manuscripts, folklore, and children's literature. Lopez emphasizes that the wolf of books is largely a product of imagination and is in no way representative of the complex creatures of muscle and bone that have survived the destructive campaigns against them. According to Todd, *Of Wolves and Men* exceeded the praise and sales of Lopez's previous books, selling more than two hundred thousand copies. Lopez told Bonetti that this book "made me very visible," pushing him into the spotlight as a public figure.

While he was writing *Of Wolves and Men,* Lopez was preparing another collection of fiction that came out the following year. *River Notes: The Dance of Herons* (1979) is the second book in a trilogy, and as with the first collection, these stories take place in one particular region, the Pacific Northwest. In a biographical essay, "Barry Lopez," ecocritic John Tallmadge says that he considers *River Notes* "Lopez's most challenging and

original book, the work of a master"; yet, Wild finds it less so, observing that "the intent is much the same: to report back to his audience of mystical experiences gained through the medium of nature." Like the stories of *Desert Notes,* these twelve stories are spare and convey a sense of intimacy with the reader; multiple narrators relay the startling details of living in this wet, harsh world along rivers.

River Notes begins at the convergence of a river with the Pacific Ocean and a narrator who is "worn out with waiting." In this introduction the narrator shares information learned from close observation and physical contact with the land, methods reminiscent of the habits of attention and patience that *Desert Notes* uses. The narrator never explicitly states what he waits and watches for on the coast, but he has the vision and intensity of one who has sojourned long in this place. He is "alert to the heartbeats of fish moving beyond the surf" and so intensely attuned to the elements that he can read any strip of sand with his fingertips or flawlessly imitate the sound of "sandpipers walking in the darkness at the edge of a spent wave." The introduction foreshadows themes of loss, alienation, and personal transformation throughout this collection as the stories move inland from the coast, along the banks of the river, and finally to its headwaters. *River Notes* is more somber in tone than *Desert Notes,* exploring the painful emotional and physical consequences for people who time and again fail to understand their relationship to place and each other. Still, the collection evolves into a message of hope, selflessness, and connection.

According to ecocritic William H. Rueckert, the pace of *River Notes* leads readers to realize their "need to have a deep extraverbal or nonverbal knowledge of nature that makes it possible to enter into a profound nondestructive relationship with all parts of it." In this wet world of overcast skies and violent rainstorms, the landscape can clearly devastate, but it can also heal. Stories such as "The Search for the Heron" and "The Shallows," for example, take readers into intimate contact with this varied, enigmatic world, playing out the narrator's desire to know it. While full comprehension remains impossible, readers can learn much from a single place.

"The Log Jam" explores the strained human history with a region, tracing the thirty-year accumulation of a jam that began in 1946 with the butt of a tree from a logging accident and continued until 1973 with the addition of the crown of a 447-year-old fir felled by termites. The interim years record other characters' stories associated with particular pieces of the growing jam. This multifaceted narrative culminates with a pair of osprey making a nest in the jam and living "as well as could be expected in that country." While the reader

Dust jacket for the book that won the 1979 John Burroughs Medal
(Collection of Tracy Simmons Bitonti)

understands that this narrative of "The Log Jam" has ended, the ongoing story of this landscape—this river-scape—has not. The jam functions as the perfect vehicle to tell the biography of the woods, representing the varying transformations of trees from timber and shelter to instruments of death and obstruction.

"The Rapids" also addresses the difficult conditions of living in this region. Set along the edge of the river, this story includes multiple voices as they respond to a rafting accident. Most prominent is the figure of a journalist, an outsider who in trying to obtain

the tragic details comes away from the experience with "a different slant" on the river. He begins to understand from a local man that the river is not to blame in such circumstances. But *River Notes* also includes stories of physical transformation that Tallmadge and Rueckert liken to magical realism. Many of these stories represent shape-shifting figures that move from animal to human realms without difficulty or surprise.

"The Falls" tells the story of a man the narrator knew on and off throughout his life; it is a narrative that "must" be told so that "you shouldn't think this man just threw his life away." The value of the man's story resides not in recalling his life as an itinerant worker but in his intimate relationship with nature–his ability to exchange places with his dog or "become the wind or a bird flying overhead." This shamanic figure is exactly opposite of the man in the "The Salmon," who in an attempt to represent these "anadromous fish" ultimately offends them with his giant sculpture of a male sockeye salmon. His work bears the trappings of intimacy, as it is composed of the river stones and informed by scientific, aesthetic, and empirical knowledge. This magnificent sculpture has taken four years to create and represents the fish exactly; once complete, however, the sculpture disrupts the seasonal migration of the salmon. Only then does the man realize the "assumption in his act, made the more grotesque by its perfection." "Drought" ends the collection with the story of one man's restorative gesture that not only halts the oncoming drought but also allows him to communicate and dance with the forest animals, who acknowledge his "completely selfless" act. Blue Heron tells him: "Before we could ask for rain there had to be someone to do something completely selfless, with no hope of success. You went after that fish, and then at the end you were trying to dance. A person cannot be afraid of being foolish. For everything, every gesture, is sacred." *River Notes* exemplifies Lopez's sense that one can live well and make personal changes that matter, even in the bleakest of circumstances.

What followed *River Notes,* Lopez told Evans, was "another kind of story" than the ones he had been writing for the trilogy. In 1981 he published *Winter Count,* nine stories organized around the Native American practice of marking the passage of time from one year to the next. In a prefatory note Lopez explains that this tradition of remembering and recording within some northern plains tribes allows for multiple winter counts to occur simultaneously and for each to be distinguished by the "personality of its keeper." Unlike the earlier collections, this one does not concentrate on one geographical region but represents landscapes ranging from the prairies of North Dakota and Nebraska to the mountains of Wyoming and deserts of Arizona. Lopez also depicts the urban landscapes of New York City and New Orleans, along with the exotic locales of the Caribbean, the Arctic, and northern Spain. As always, the places Lopez depicts function as more than simple backdrops for human events; they are the determining factors that bring people together or keep them apart.

The stories of *Winter Count* are longer and more fully developed than the ones of earlier collections, though the prose maintains Lopez's characteristic spare line and precision. The narrator of "The Woman Who Had Shells" speaks of "the uncanny accidents by which life is shaped," a phrase representative of most of these narratives. Many of the characters in *Winter Count* stumble upon meaningful experience when they least expect it. For example, the opening story, "Restoration," follows one man's surprising discovery of the history and significance of a tourist site in Killdeer, North Dakota, while "The Orrery" plays out several years of one man's perpetual return to a Sonoran desert valley he had first visited as a child with his father. The narratives do not explicitly instruct readers how to learn place or behave properly with strangers as in the *Notes* collections; instead, they convey the intimacy between people that is forged within certain landscapes. "Winter Herons" recalls the dissolution of one relationship despite one man's attempts to bring a woman from New York City into his world of vast Montana expanses.

Lopez's interest in Native American experience and culture, evident from the title, emerges in this collection more directly, with stories such as "Buffalo" and "The Location of the River." These two narratives portray the rupture between the myth time and storytelling of northern plains tribes with the rational view of natural history and Western scholarship. The need for a logical explanation fails the curious researcher, Benjamin Foster, in his effort to account for the disappearance of upper Niobrara River, and so, too, the narrator of "Buffalo," who tries to discover the cause of the animals' disappearance from the plains in 1845. Similarly, the story "Winter Count 1973: Geese, They Flew Over in a Storm" explores the gap between the Anglo perspective of certainty and logic and the Native American perspective that allows for diversity and multiple truths. This narrative follows teacher Roger Callahan to an academic conference in New Orleans. He is ambivalent about the benefits of such a meeting, having "long ago lost touch with the definitive, the awful distance of reason." This story intersperses a series of winter counts with Callahan's own as it unfolds in the sterile hotel environment during a storm.

Winter Count brought Lopez critical acclaim for his fiction. In the following years he continued working on his nonfiction as well, contributing articles about his travels to such magazines as *Harper's, Outside, Orion,* and *National Geographic.* He was also traveling periodically to the Arctic, researching what became his best-known work to date, *Arctic Dreams: Imagination and Desire in a Northern Landscape* (1986). In his interview with Evans, Lopez discussed the origin of this book, explaining that he had just completed *Of Wolves and Men* and had returned to the Brooks Range in Alaska when he realized, "Oh, I've missed something here. I've been looking at wolves so long I've missed these other things." With *Arctic Dreams* Lopez extends his inquiry beyond a single animal to explore the relationship between the physical details that characterize the Far North and the human perception of it. This book remains his longest, most ambitious work. With *Arctic Dreams* Lopez sealed his reputation as one of the most important contemporary natural history writers, winning the National Book Award for nonfiction the same year the book was published.

In a 1986 review for *The New York Times,* Edward Hoagland asserted that Lopez had come to his "full voice and confidence" as a writer with *Arctic Dreams.* Tallmadge characterizes the book as an "epic work" on the order of Dante's *The Divine Comedy* (written 1307?–1320?). In his biographical essay on Lopez, Tallmadge explains, "Like all epics it unfolds on a grand scale, moralizing the landscape, detailing feats of heroism, engaging the deepest spiritual, political, and historical questions, and propounding a view of the noblest possibilities for human life." *Arctic Dreams* blends natural history with cultural history and personal experience with scholarship in detailing this harsh but intriguing landscape. The book bears both his poetic sensibilities and his scholarly tendencies, including notes, maps, and appendixes, along with a bibliography and index to assist the reader in navigating the geographic and scientific information.

Arctic Dreams spans the area between the Bering Strait and Davis Strait, territory Lopez traversed in the company of Eskimo, marine ecologists, landscape painters, biologists, and men involved in the oil industry. In the prologue, "Pond's Bay, Baffin Island," he offers a cautionary tale beginning with the devastation brought to this area and its inhabitants by the British whaling industry during its heyday in 1823. Fewer than ten years later the waters were overfished, and Eskimo villages were ravaged by smallpox, diphtheria, and other diseases spread by European sailors. This brief history, according to Lopez, serves as a "microcosm" for the current level of exploration, industry, and commerce in the Arctic, that still threatens the ecosystem and the traditional Eskimo ways of life.

The nexus of these past and current concerns of the region informs the three major themes *Arctic Dreams* addresses: "the influence of the arctic landscape on the human imagination. How desire to put a landscape to use shapes our evaluation of it. And, confronted by an unknown landscape, what happens to our sense of wealth." In the nine chapters that follow, Lopez proceeds to investigate these issues. "Arktikós" sets the scene by describing the physical features of this remarkable ecosystem, explaining the unfamiliar movements of the sun, the makeup of the soil, and methods of various animal and plant adaptation over millennia in this environment. Each of the next three chapters focuses

on what Tallmadge refers to as "celebrity" animals of the region–the musk ox, polar bear, and narwhal. Chapter 5, "Migration: The Corridors of Breath," includes descriptions of other animals, attending to the patterns of movement so central for the survival of species in this climate; this chapter also considers the migrations of humans from their initial entry into this region more than thirty-five thousand years ago to Lopez's contemporary travels with the Eskimo.

"Ice and Light" examines the beauty and danger of icebergs and the phenomena that animate the arctic sky, such as solar and lunar rings, the aurora borealis (northern lights), and the fata morganas (mirages). This landscape poses particular challenges for painters and resists all human attempts to know it fully, whether through science, art, or physical experience. Lopez writes, "Whatever evaluation we finally make of a stretch of land, however, no matter how profound or accurate, we will find it inadequate. The land retains an identity of its own, still deeper and more subtle than we can know. Our obligation toward it becomes simple–to approach with an uncalculating mind, with an attitude of regard." His investigation of the limitations of human perception of place continues with the following chapter, "The Country of the Mind," in which he explores the multiple ways of knowing through language, mapping, and carefully walking and observing a place.

Chapters 8 and 9 survey the exploration of the area from its beginnings somewhere around 330–325 B.C. into the nineteenth and twentieth centuries. Still, by the end of his thorough inquiry into the Arctic, Lopez concedes, "There are simply no answers to some of the great pressing questions. You continue to live them out, making your life a worthy expression of a leaning into the light." Lopez ends the narrative with a literal leaning, bowing to the mystery of life that is this place.

In 1986 Lopez received an award from the American Academy of Arts and Letters for his overall body of work. The following year he received a Guggenheim Fellowship and the first of five National Science Foundation Grants. (The others came in 1988, 1991, and 1992, and 1999.) In 1988 he published *Crossing Open Ground,* a collection of essays that had all been published previously in magazines and journals dating from the late 1970s to the mid 1980s. The fourteen essays of *Crossing Open Ground* mostly recount Lopez's travels around the North American continent and out to its fringes. Familiar themes play out in these essays–such as the value and importance of storytelling, Lopez's efforts to come to terms with humans' troubled relationship with the natural world, and the privilege of witnessing the mysterious lives of animals.

Dust jacket for Lopez's 1981 book, nine short stories organized around the method by which Native Americans mark the passage of time (Richland County Public Library)

Many of the narratives for *Crossing Open Ground* are derived from his research and writing for *Arctic Dreams* but were not included in that book. For example, he muses on snow geese during a visit to Tule Lake in Northern California in "A Reflection of White Geese"; he sojourns among the Nunamiut in "Landscape and Narrative"; and he participates in a biological survey of the Beaufort Sea in "Borders" and in the killing of seals in "The Lives of Seals." In other essays, Lopez argues for wilderness preservation, as in "Gone Back into the Earth" and "Yukon-Charley: The Shape of Wilderness," while in "Grown Men" he explains the lessons he learned during college road trips and summers working in Wyoming and West Virginia.

"A Presentation of Whales" remains one of the most haunting narratives in *Crossing Open Ground*. This essay recounts the unprecedented stranding of forty-one sperm whales on the central Oregon coast in 1979, a scene that elicited "the worst and the best of human behavior." Similarly, the final essay of the collection, "The Passing Wisdom of Birds," explores the dark side of human nature in the figure of Hernán

Cortés, who set fire to the aviaries in Mexico City in 1520. Lopez explains that Cortés's act does not simply represent the "destructive madness that lies at the heart of imperialistic conquest; it is also a symbol of a long-term failure of Western civilization to recognize the intrinsic worth of the American landscape, and its potential value to human societies that have since come to be at odds with the natural world." Lopez articulates the "need to reexamine our experience in the New World" and outlines a method combining indigenous knowledge with natural history not only to overcome this colonial legacy but also to cultivate a reciprocal relationship with the land, a theme he revisited more fully three years later with the publication of *The Rediscovery of North America* (1990).

Lopez's next major work after *Crossing Open Ground* broadened his audience to include adolescent readers. Lopez wrote the text for the novella *Crow and Weasel* (1990), which artist Tom Pohrt illustrated. This coming-of-age narrative follows two young men on their journey "farther north than anyone had ever gone, farther north than their people's stories went." Crow and Weasel are part-animal and part-human figures. These two friends undertake a journey that begins with adolescent fantasies of distinguishing themselves but quickly evolves beyond mere personal gratification to include the history and significance of their larger community. Before they depart, Mountain Lion, a tribal elder, admonishes them to remember their people. He tells them, "you are runners. You are carrying our way of life with you, for everyone to see. Listen. Be strong. When you are tempted to give up, think of your relatives."

The journey unfolds over several months, during which Crow and Weasel must navigate through unknown lands, endure inclement weather, survive encounters with strangers, and learn to rely on one another. This allegory reflects some of Lopez's most important themes; among them are the necessity of travel for a critical understanding of the world and of one's home community, and the value of storytelling. Perhaps one of the most meaningful experiences Crow and Weasel have is the time they spend with Badger. She teaches them how to assemble stories "in a good pattern, to speak with a pleasing rhythm, and to call on all the details of memory." Both men find these skills helpful and learn that storytelling is much more than simply sharing information: it can enable one to survive. Badger urges them to remember that "The stories people tell have a way of taking care of them. . . . Sometimes a person needs a story more than food to stay alive. That is why we put these stories in each other's memory. This is how people care for themselves."

Lopez told Evans that *Crow and Weasel* is a narrative outside the Western tradition that usually represents unequal pairings between a handsome, moral character and his foil, or clownish companion. Lopez created both Crow and Weasel as strong characters who, he says, "discover that each has a strength, and that the only way they will survive is by being aware of these strengths and learning how to defer to each other." These characters defy the traditional Western narrative in another way: they do not set out to conquer the land and its inhabitants but instead set out to learn from it. Lopez explained, "And when they come home, they come home with the desire to take on a full and mature life in the village."

Lopez continues exploring the implications of storytelling for the community in his 1990 book-length essay, *The Rediscovery of North America*. In this narrative he challenges the popular account of the discovery of the New World by retelling the story of Christopher Columbus's landfall on the island of Samana Cay. Drawing on the eyewitness accounts from Bartolomé de las Casas, Lopez reports the horror that occurred during the Spanish "incursion" into the New World. He concedes that no one today can know the mind of Columbus and his men, "But we know that in those first few hours a process began we now call an incursion. In the name of distant and abstract powers, the Spanish began an appropriation of the place, a seizure of its people, its elements, whatever could be carried off."

The Rediscovery of North America examines the long shadow of the Columbian legacy; Lopez reads this history as the point of origin for man's alienation in the New World. He argues that this "incursion" initiated the unrelenting search for wealth in North America that remains at the heart of the environmental crisis. With *The Rediscovery of North America,* Lopez summons the fullest extent of the power of story in the hope of reversing the harmful fiction that "one is *due* wealth in North America." In this narrative he insists that this dreadful history may be overcome, that "this violent corruption needn't define us . . . we can take the measure of the horror and assert that we will not be bound by it. . . . But, five hundred years later, we intend to mean something else in the world." Lopez proceeds to outline a plan for moving beyond this medieval mind-set, beginning with cultivating a sense of home through the local knowledge of place.

The process Lopez articulates in *The Rediscovery of North America* follows what he demonstrated earlier in books such as *Of Wolves and Men* and *Arctic Dreams*. It involves the shift from constantly imposing one's expectation on the land and its inhabitants to learning how to propose one's ideas. He advocates research of

local archives and the importance of traveling with native guides. In addition, he asserts that one should take the time to walk and listen to the land. While *The Rediscovery of North America* displays some of Lopez's most vitriolic prose, it conveys a measured anger. Even in light of the tragic demise of the Guanahaní and other indigenous groups, as well as the gravity of the current environmental conditions, Lopez offers a message of hope. He emphasizes that people must believe in the possibility of change and in the human abilities to counteract the darker aspects of existence, that on the opposite side of gold, silver, individualism, and tyranny lie goodness and community.

Four years later Lopez finished the *Notes* trilogy with the collection *Field Notes: The Grace Note of the Canyon Wren* (1994). The stories of this collection, however, operate more like those of *Winter Count* than do the stories in the previous collections. *Field Notes* does not focus on a single place but instead includes twelve stories that take readers through a variety of landscapes—from the Mojave Desert and the Australian Outback to the rainy lushness of the Pacific Northwest and as far away as the stark lands of the Brooks Range in Alaska and northern Greenland. These narratives are not the compact two- and three-page stories of *Desert Notes* and *River Notes,* but are more substantial, with carefully drawn characters whose histories are bound up with place.

Readers will recognize familiar figures in these stories—those who can communicate with or are aided by animals, such as the narrator from the "Introduction: Within Birds' Hearing"; the researcher Edward Bowman in "Pearyland"; and the narrator of "Lessons from the Wolverine." Lopez returns to such issues regarding the pitfalls of rational thinking and how academic success can distance one from the immediacy of place and family. "Homecoming" focuses on the turning point for Dr. Wick Colter, a highly successful botanist, who realizes he has not only lost touch with his local landscapes but also with his wife and daughter. Many of these stories highlight characters' moments of recognition of the poverty in their own lives. "The Negro in the Kitchen" depicts an encounter between two men—a white man entrenched in routine and a black man completely open to the moment. The men serve as perfect counterparts: both are investment bankers; both are highly educated; and both have an abiding interest in the natural world. Yet, the black man's personal journey is what reminds the fastidious narrator of how he might better live his life.

Field Notes includes more female characters than any of Lopez's previous collections of fiction. "The Open Lot" depicts the quiet strength of paleontologist Jane Weddell, while "Empira's Tapestry" tells of the eccentric teacher and weaver Empira Larson and the mark she leaves on the small community of Idora. In "Conversation" Essie is the environmentally conscious voice in dialogue with her old friend Lewis, who has become a Missouri senator and holds the fate of the endangered ferruginous hawk in his hands. The final story, "The Runner," offers a glimpse of a brother's attempt to reconcile with his estranged sister, Mirara Graham. Gradually, from reading newspapers and talking with one of her acquaintances, he learns of her discoveries of ruins throughout the Grand Canyon. The narrator determines that what makes Mirara's connection with the canyon so remarkable is that "she's given herself away to the place," and it responds to her. Throughout *Field Notes* Lopez emphasizes the act of surrendering to a place or to another from which/whom one might gain greater self-knowledge, understand the importance of community, or catch a glimpse of the magnificence of nature.

In 1997 Lopez again teamed up with artist Pohrt to publish the story "Lessons from the Wolverine" (from *Field Notes*) as a separate volume. As in *Crow and Weasel* Pohrt's watercolors enliven Lopez's vivid prose; his paintings capture the delicate light of the Far North and the distinct markings of the wolverine. Less than a year later Lopez worked on a similar project with artist Robin Eschner. Together they published as a single volume his essay "Apologia," which was originally published in 1989 in an issue of the journal *Witness,* especially dedicated to new nature writing. Eschner's black-and-white woodcuts of animal tracks and human hands provide haunting illustrations for Lopez's powerful tale. This essay recounts Lopez's drive from Oregon to Indiana during which he stops to remove from the road the bodies of animals that have been hit by cars. Lopez clearly articulates the violent clash between the lives of animals and humans. The evidence of roadkill, for most, is an invisible cost of industrialized culture, but through his repeated act of respect, Lopez conveys his hope that humankind may become more mindful of its relationship with all that is not human.

"Apologia" also appears in the collection *About This Life: Journeys on the Threshold of Memory.* These essays are undoubtedly Lopez's most personal to date, and most of them were previously published in magazines. "A Voice," the introductory essay, maps his development as a writer; he recalls how different landscapes and mentors shaped his sense of language. Lopez also offers advice to aspiring young writers in this essay, giving them three directives: "Read. Find out what you truly believe. Get away from the familiar." *About This Life* includes many narratives documenting Lopez's own travels of one kind or another: diving in Bonaire, visiting friends in Japan, and exploring the implications of ecotourism during a trip to the Galápagos Islands.

In "Flight," an essay that first appeared in *Harper's* under another title, Lopez contemplates the absurdities of globalization, recounting his experience flying 110,000 nautical miles on 747 freighters and passenger planes. The essay conveys a mix of Lopez's awe at the engineering feat involved in the construction of these transcontinental airplanes and his continuous surprise with the contents of their cargo. The planes carry everything from cases of explosives to luxury cars and such oddities as bear testicles. Often the 747s transport live animals such as horses, dogs, and even an occasional tiger or killer whale.

Lopez shares many stories from his childhood in this collection: a series of vignettes in the essay "Death" and odd encounters from his college road trips in "Murder" and "Speed." In her review of the book, "*About This Life: Journeys on the Threshold of Memory,*" in *The Antioch Review* (1999), Carolyn Maddux rightly points out that "Lopez's prose is always more than natural history, exposition, autobiography." *About This Life* offers readers a larger sense of Lopez's personal experience and the evolution of his thinking.

In his return to fiction in *Light Action in the Caribbean* (2000), Lopez ostensibly maintains the direction of such earlier collections as *Winter Count* and *Field Notes,* specifically in story length and geographical range. Despite those similarities, this volume is decidedly different from his earlier fiction writing: it presents a much darker narrative line than any other. In "Doing What Comes Naturally," a review of *Light Action in the Caribbean* for *The New York Times Book Review* (10 December 2000), Robert Draper characterizes the author as having finally lost his patience with the state of contemporary American society. Draper writes that Lopez "betrays a purist's contempt for philistines that for most of his career he has kept in check." Readers may recognize figures such as the naive young man in "Stolen Horses," the gifted gardener in "Thomas Loudermilk's Generosity," and the Amerindian shaman of "Emory Bear Hands' Birds." But other stories, such as "Rubén Mendoza Vega, Suzuki Professor of Early Caribbean History, University of Florida at Gainesville, Offers a History of the United States Based on Personal Experience," "The Deaf Girl," and "Light Action in the Caribbean" offer a stark look at the emptiness that can fill one's life in the wake of denial.

"Rubén Mendoza Vega" portrays an out-of-touch scholar, a figure in Lopez's work who is always at odds with inexplicable or irrational events. This story, however, depicts an extremely recalcitrant man. Vega is an academic and a father who has lost his middle son to suicide. Embittered by the act in which he believes his

Dust jacket for the book that won the 1986 National Book Award for nonfiction
(Richland County Public Library)

son "repudiated his heritage," Vega fails to recognize his own shortcomings. The form of the story is unusual, told mostly as extensive footnotes to a single paragraph that must be the start of an academic paper; it also includes a detailed bibliography. The haunting narrative "The Deaf Girl" demonstrates a striking reversal of the deep experience that comes with age. This middle-aged narrator tells of his encounter with a young woman whose life has been shaped by tragic events. In realizing the depth of her awareness of violence and the injustice that often follows, he also realizes his helplessness and naiveté: "She was out there somewhere, way past where I had gone. She was walking in from some distant place, and I knew I had to get there."

The true departure point of Lopez's thinking and writing comes in the story that shares the title of the collection, "Light Action in the Caribbean." In his review Draper refers to this story as a "cautionary tale," but the level of violence makes this designation seem an understatement. In this narrative Libby Dalaria and her new boyfriend, David, travel to the fictitious San Carlos island together for a diving trip. They are icons of a vapid, consumer society. She worries about just the right underwear to pack, purchas-

ing matching fins for her scuba gear, and reading useless articles in fashion magazines. He sneaks "dope *in*to the Caribbean," talks incessantly on a cell phone, and constantly sells the virtues of the World Wide Web to Libby and the locals. Readers are hard-pressed to summon any compassion for these characters, even as they witness their graphic demise.

Still, despite this shift in storytelling, the collection maintains Lopez's sharp, clear prose and ends on a hopeful note. "The Mappist," the final story, tells of geographer Phillip Trevino's search to find Corlis Benefideo, an extraordinary mapmaker and writer. Trevino learns of Benefideo's meticulous and innovative maps that can account for "geology and hydrology, where water was . . . and the botany and biology, and the history of the place from Native American times." Benefideo's method, however, had caused him to leave the U.S. Coast and Geodetic Survey in Washington, and, as a former colleague tells Trevino, Benefideo "couldn't give up being comprehensive, you understand, and they just didn't know what to do with him."

This mapmaker is a figure who has resisted the shallow course of expediency and industrialization that has enveloped the United States. During their meeting Benefideo tells Trevino: "I've nothing against human passion, human longing. What I oppose is blind devotion to progress, and the venality of material wealth. If we're going to trade the priceless for the common, I want to know exactly what the terms are." While Lopez is not by any means Corlis Benefideo, the battle this character expresses between the colossal loss in quality of life and work to a more cost-effective process lies at the heart of this collection. Through these thirteen stories Lopez explores what the "terms" are in this devastating trade-off. *Light Action in the Caribbean,* then, maps the terms of loss, yet still posits a sense of hope and reminds readers, again through Benefideo, that "The world is a miracle, unfolding in the pitch dark."

During almost thirty years of writing both fiction and nonfiction, many patterns have emerged in Lopez's work. He never writes of just landscape or just people but constantly explores what they have to do with each other. While he may indeed be shifting more deliberately to focus on the darker elements of life, Lopez maintains the desire for sharing stories that help humans remember how to act, as well as how to recover their obligations to themselves and, more important, to their communities. Whatever the outcome of Barry Lopez's current projects, another collection of nonfiction and his first novel, they will probably pose difficult questions yet still point readers in the direction of healing. At the end of "A Voice" Lopez writes, "If I were asked what I want to accomplish as a writer, I would say it's to contribute to a literature of hope." Hope is the dominant pattern within Lopez's work; it is the impulse that drives humankind's survival and activates its ability to change.

Interviews:

Trish Todd, "Barry Lopez Recalls His *Arctic Dreams,*" *Publishers Weekly,* 228 (11 October 1985): 35–36;

Jim Aton, "An Interview with Barry Lopez," *Western American Literature,* 21, no. 1 (Spring 1986): 3–17;

Nicholas O'Connell, "Barry Lopez," in *At the Field's End: Interviews with Twenty Pacific Northwest Writers* (Seattle: Madrona, 1987), pp. 3–18;

Kay Bonetti, "An Interview with Barry Lopez," *Missouri Review,* 11, no. 3 (1988): 59–77;

Ken Margolis, "Paying Attention: An Interview with Barry Lopez," *Orion* (Summer 1990): 50–53;

Alice Evans, "Leaning into the Light: An Interview with Barry Lopez," *Poets and Writers Magazine,* 22, no. 2 (March/April 1994): 63–79;

Douglas Marx, "Barry Lopez: 'I Am a Writer Who Travels,'" *Publishers Weekly,* 241 (26 September 1994): 41–42;

Barry Lopez, Charles Wright, and Maxine Hong Kingston, "A Chinese Garland," *North American Review,* 273 (September/October 1998): 38–42;

Dan Philippon, "Ecologies of Love: An Interview with Barry Lopez," *Ruminator Review* (Winter 2002–2003): 22–25, 47–48.

Biographies:

Peter Wild, *Barry Lopez,* Boise State University Western Writers Series, no. 64 (Boise: Boise State University, 1984);

John Tallmadge, "Barry Lopez," in *American Nature Writers,* volume 1, edited by John Elder (New York: Scribners, 1996), pp. 549–568.

References:

"Ecology and the Human Imagination: Barry Lopez and Edward O. Wilson," *Writing Natural History: Dialogues with Authors,* edited by Edward Lueders (Salt Lake City: University of Utah Press, 1989), pp. 7–35;

Cheryll Glotfelty, "Barry Holstun Lopez," *Updating the Literary West* (Fort Worth: Texas Christian University Press, 1997);

Sherman Paul, "Making the Turn: Rereading Barry Lopez," in his *For Love of the World: Essays on Nature Writers* (Iowa City: University of Iowa Press, 1992), pp. 67–107;

William H. Rueckert, "Barry Lopez and the Search for a Dignified and Honorable Relationship with Nature," in *Earthly Words: Essays on Contemporary American Nature and Environmental Writers,* edited by John Cooley (Ann Arbor: University of Michigan Press, 1994), pp. 137–164;

Scott Slovic, "'A More Particularized Understanding': Seeking Qualitative Awareness in Barry Lopez's *Arctic Dreams,*" in his *Seeking Awareness in American Nature Writing: Henry Thoreau, Annie Dillard, Edward Abbey, Wendell Berry, Barry Lopez* (Salt Lake City: University of Utah Press, 1992), pp.137–166.

Papers:

The Southwest Collection / Special Collections Library at Texas Tech University in Lubbock, Texas, holds the papers of Barry Lopez as part of the James Sowell Family Collection in Literature, Community and the Natural World.

Peter Matthiessen

(22 May 1927 –   )

David Clippinger
Penn State University

See also the Matthiessen entries in *DLB 6: American Novelists Since World War II, Second Series,* and *DLB 173: American Novelists Since World War II, Fifth Series.*

BOOKS: *Race Rock* (New York: Harper, 1954; London: Secker & Warburg, 1955);

Partisans (New York: Viking, 1955; London: Secker & Warburg, 1956);

Wildlife in America (New York: Viking, 1959; London: Deutsch, 1960);

The Cloud Forest: A Chronicle of the South American Wilderness (New York: Viking, 1961; London: Deutsch, 1962);

Raditzer (New York: Viking, 1961; London: Heinemann, 1962);

Under the Mountain Wall: A Chronicle of Two Seasons in the Stone Age (New York: Viking, 1962; London: Heinemann, 1963);

At Play in the Fields of the Lord (New York: Random House, 1965; London: Heinemann, 1966);

The Shorebirds of North America, text by Matthiessen, illustrations by Robert Verity Clem, edited by Gardner D. Stout (New York: Viking, 1967); text by Matthiessen republished as *The Wind Birds,* drawings by Robert Gillmor (New York: Viking, 1973);

Oomingmak: The Expedition to the Musk Ox Island in the Bering Sea (New York: Hastings House, 1967);

Sal Si Puedes: César Chavez and the New American Revolution (New York: Random House, 1969; revised, 1973);

Blue Meridian: The Search for the Great White Shark (New York: Random House, 1971; London: Harvill, 1995);

Seal Pool (Garden City, N.Y.: Doubleday, 1972); republished as *The Great Auk Escape* (London: Angus & Robertson, 1974);

The Tree Where Man Was Born, with Eliot Porter's *The African Experience* (New York: Dutton, 1972; London: Collins, 1972);

Far Tortuga (New York: Random House, 1975);

Peter Matthiessen (photograph © Nancy Crampton; from the dust jacket for The Snow Leopard, *1978)*

The Snow Leopard (New York: Random House, 1978);

Sand Rivers (New York: Viking, 1981; London: Aurum, 1981);

In the Spirit of Crazy Horse (New York: Viking, 1983; London: Harvill, 1992);

Indian Country (New York: Viking, 1984; London: Collins Harvill, 1985);

Midnight Turning Gray (Bristol, R.I.: Ampersand, 1984);

Nine-Headed Dragon River: Zen Journals 1969–1982 (Boston: Shambhala, 1986; London: Collins Harvill, 1986);

Men's Lives (New York: Random House, 1986; London: Collins Harvill, 1988);

On the River Styx and Other Stories (New York: Random House, 1989; London: Collins Harvill, 1989);

Killing Mister Watson (New York: Random House, 1990; London: Collins Harvill, 1990);

African Silences (New York: Random House, 1991; London: Harvill, 1991);

Baikal: Sacred Sea of Siberia (San Francisco: Sierra Club, 1992; London: Thames & Hudson, 1992);

Shadows of Africa (New York: Abrams, 1992);

East of Lo Monthang: In the Land of Mustang (Boston: Shambhala, 1995);

Lost Man's River (New York: Random House, 1997; London: Harvill, 1998);

Bone by Bone (New York: Random House, 1999);

Tigers in the Snow (New York: North Point, 2000);

Birds of Heaven: Travels with Cranes (New York: North Point, 2001).

Collections: *Everglades: Selections from the Writings of Peter Matthiessen,* edited by Paul Brooks (San Francisco: Sierra Club, 1970);

The Peter Matthiessen Reader (New York: Vintage, 2000).

SELECTED PERIODICAL PUBLICATIONS–
UNCOLLECTED: "Sadie," *Atlantic Monthly,* 187 (January 1951): 55–58;

"The Fifth Day," *Atlantic Monthly,* 188 (September 1951): 60–63;

"Martin's Beach," *Botteghe Oscure,* 10 (1952): 310–318;

"The Tower of the Four Winds," *Cornhill,* 166 (Summer 1952): 143–149;

"A Replacement," *Paris Review,* 1 (February 1953): 46–56;

"Late in the Season," *New World Writing* (May 1953): 320–328;

"Lina," *Cornhill,* 169 (Fall 1956): 53–58;

"Traveling Man," *Harper's Bazaar,* 214 (February 1957): 57–65;

"The Wolves of Aguila," *Harper's Bazaar,* 27 (August 1958): 76–150;

"Annals of Crime," *New Yorker,* 34 (1 November 1958): 119–145;

"Midnight Turning Gray," *Saturday Evening Post,* 236 (28 September 1963): 56–67;

"A Reporter at Large: Sand and Wind and Waves," *New Yorker,* 41 (3 April 1965): 116–144;

"The Last Great Strand: Corkscrew Swamp Sanctuary," *Audubon,* 69 (March 1967): 64–71;

"The River-Eater," *Audubon,* 72 (March 1970): 52;

"Kipahulu: From Cinders to the Sea," *Audubon,* 72 (May 1970): 10–23;

"Lignumvitae–the Last Key," *Audubon,* 74 (January 1972): 20–31;

"In the Dragon Islands," *Audubon,* 75 (September 1973): 4–49;

"The Craft of Fiction in Far Tortuga," *Paris Review,* 15 (Winter 1974): 39–82;

"Happy Days," *Audubon,* 77 (November 1975): 64–95;

"A Track on the Beach," *Audubon,* 79 (March 1977): 68–106;

"Horse Latitudes," *Antaeus,* 29 (Spring 1978): 7–14;

"A Whale in Spring," *Westigan Review of Poetry,* 3 (1978): 38–39;

"Stop the GO Road," *Audubon,* 81 (January 1979): 48–65;

"My Turn: The Price of Tellico," *Newsweek,* 94 (17 December 1979): 21;

"How to Kill a Valley," *New York Review of Books,* 27 (7 February 1980): 31–36.

While Peter Matthiessen's publications include several well-received novels, his reputation as a writer rests largely on his nonfiction nature books, which passionately yet scientifically document the often uneasy balance between human existence and the survival of wildlife and their habitats. For Matthiessen, the natural landscape cannot be extracted from the human world: the two are inextricably interwoven, and his nonfiction prose renders in remarkable poetic detail how the sociopolitical bears upon the ecological, as well as how ecological balance is an issue with sociopolitical import. Perhaps the most significant theme that is sustained throughout his writing life is that the survival of all forms of wildlife and the conservation of natural habitats are the only means of ensuring the survival of humanity. Therefore, the human and the natural worlds are so tightly bound together that the human cannot exist without the sustenance of the natural world.

Matthiessen's environmental position can be traced to his upbringing and family life. Born in New York City on 22 May 1927 into an affluent family, he was the second of three children of Erard A. Matthiessen, an architect and a trustee of the National Audubon Society, and Elizabeth Carey Matthiessen. Matthiessen spent much of his childhood in the rural areas of New York State and Connecticut, where his interest in the natural world was sparked. After graduating from the Hotchkiss School, he served in the United States Navy at the close of World War II and then enrolled at Yale University, where he earned a B.A. in English while also studying zoology and ornithology. During his junior year at Yale (1948–1949), Matthiessen studied at

*Dust jacket for the book Matthiessen based on the journal he kept during a 250-mile
trek in the Himalayas (Richland County Public Library)*

the Sorbonne, University of Paris, an experience that solidified his desire to become a writer. After returning to the United States, he began to write short stories, one of which was awarded the *Atlantic* Prize in 1951, and after completing his college degree in 1950, Matthiessen taught creative writing at Yale for one year.

While teaching at Yale, he gained momentum as a writer, but that year marked an important change in his personal life as well. On 8 February 1951 he married Patricia Southgate, whose father was a diplomat. A few months after the wedding, the Matthiessens moved to Paris, where they were the heart of a group of American writers that included James Baldwin, William Styron, Terry Southern, and George Plimpton. With Harold Humes, Matthiessen cofounded *The Paris Review* in 1953, and Plimpton, Matthiessen's childhood friend, was designated the editor—hence, this group of young American writers became known as the *Paris Review* crowd. During this time in Paris, Matthiessen composed his first novel, *Race Rock* (1954). He also became a father; his son Lucas was born in 1953, and his daughter Sara in 1954.

The Matthiessens returned to the United States in 1954, where Peter's life in Long Island, New York, was split between working as a fisherman and the cap-

tain of a deep-sea-fishing charter boat for half the year and writing during the other half. His work as a fisherman barely provided a living, a circumstance that further weakened the Matthiessens' already troubled marriage. Yet, his experience as a fisherman later proved to be invaluable by providing insightful material for *Men's Lives* (1986), which explores the lives of Long Island fishermen. The marital tension, though, ultimately led to the couple's separation in 1956 and divorce in 1958.

According to the lore of Matthiessen's life, at the time of the separation in 1956 he packed up a convertible with only a collection of books, a shotgun, and a sleeping bag, with the intention of exploring the diverse landscape and wildlife of North America. His travels culminated in *Wildlife in America* (1959), which fostered the image of Matthiessen as a modern-day Henry David Thoreau. The book was met with critical acclaim and along with Rachel Carson's *Silent Spring* (1962),which was published three years after *Wildlife in America,* became a cornerstone of the environmental conservation movement. More important, the commercial success of the book allowed Matthiessen to devote all of his time to writing and to travel on expeditions throughout the world.

Wildlife in America also sketches the parameters of the philosophical, artistic, and political agendas that dominate his nonfiction prose. In brief, the book argues that conservation is the mark of "civilization" and not the "spoliation" that has been "confused with progress." Further, the work advances the position that "Forests, soil, water, and wildlife are mutually interdependent, and the ruin of one element will mean, in the end, the ruin of them all"—including humankind. In this respect, Matthiessen warns that mankind is, in fact, the "most dangerous" factor in the stability and survival of the ecosystem.

Matthiessen broadened his ecological worldview and skeptical portrayal of humankind in his next two books—*The Cloud Forest: A Chronicle of the South American Wilderness* (1961) and *Under the Mountain Wall: A Chronicle of Two Seasons in the Stone Age* (1962)—wherein man's "dangerous potential" is shown as not only a threat to the natural world but to indigenous people as well. These two texts, with their extended explorations of the cultures of the Amazon River in Peru (*The Cloud Forest*) and the Kurelu tribe of Western New Guinea (*Under the Mountain Wall*), bring into relief a predominant theme, which John L. Cobbs in *DLB 6* describes as the "tension between vulnerable innocence and corrupt civilization" as well as the "concern for fragile traditional cultures and natural ecologies in the onslaught of civilized destruction." As described in *Under the Mountain Wall*, "The Kurelu offered a unique chance, perhaps the last, to describe a lost culture in the terrible beauty of its pure estate . . . [before] the proud and war-like Kurelu will be no more than another backward people, crouched in the long shadow of the white man." The issue of colonialization is reinforced further by the stylistic and thematic parallels with Joseph Conrad and particularly *Heart of Darkness* (1902), significant influences for Matthiessen.

The narrative structure of *Under the Mountain Wall* also marks a signature element of Matthiessen's nonfiction prose: the process of composition is to keep an extended and sensuously detailed expedition journal that later is honed and shaped into the published text. The nonfiction, therefore, emerges out of a diaristic response to the immediacy of a situation. William Dowie emphasizes that the recurring thematic thrust of Matthiessen's work is the exploration of what it means "to be here"—whether that "here" is New York City, South America, Siberia, New Guinea, Paris, or Africa.

While the 1960s were a period of great activity that included many expeditions throughout the world and the composition of nonfiction and fiction, in 1960 Matthiessen settled in Sagaponack, Long Island, where he met Deborah Love, whom he married on 16 May 1963. In 1964, his son Alexander was born, and he adopted Deborah's daughter, Rue. Domestic life and a young family, though, did not prevent Matthiessen from continuing to travel—including extended trips to Nunivak Island in the Bering Sea in 1964, which he described in *Oomingmak: The Expedition to the Musk Ox Island in the Bering Sea* (1967); the Serengeti plain of East Africa, from which journey he wrote *The Tree Where Man Was Born* (1972); and an extensive around-the-globe adventure to capture the great white shark on film, upon which he based *Blue Meridian: The Search for the Great White Shark* (1971).

Yet, *The Shorebirds of North America* (1967), a work grounded in the immediate locale of Long Island, is perhaps the most significant text from the early 1960s. Whereas the travel books objectively document the character of a place, its culture, and its habitat, *The Shorebirds of North America* brings to the fore an element central to but often veiled by the seemingly "objective" style—that is, the question of personal subjectivity and how the individual (and his or her discovered "meaning") is implicated in the nexus of the world that he or she is observing. The natural world, in this respect, is perceived as a mirror that prompts introspective inquiry. This process, for example, is accentuated in the following passage: "As we contemplate that sanderling, there by the shining sea, one question leads inevitably to another, and all questions come full circle to the questioner, paused momentarily in his own journey under the sun and sky." No longer is the rumination upon ecology merely the survival of species, habitats, and civilizations: from *The Shorebirds of North America* onward, the contemplation of nature is cast in a more personal hue. In this respect, *The Shorebirds of North America* marks an important juncture in Matthiessen's nonfiction wherein the writing takes on a more "literary" quality: the diaristic journal notes are melded with his objective gaze and lyric style into graceful works that interrogate the human condition and the question of being.

Despite the graceful moments of *The Shorebirds of North America*, Matthiessen's mature literary style does not fully emerge until his 1972 *The Tree Where Man Was Born* and *The Snow Leopard* (1978), although the tension between high art and political activism is evident in many of the works of the 1960s. Matthiessen speaks of this tension when he acknowledges that when a particular piece of writing is in service of a specific political cause, its artistic potential is severely limited. An apt example of this tension is *Sal Si Puedes: César Chavez and the New American Revolution* (1969), which was composed after he spent time in San Jose, California, with Chavez, an activist working for reforms for migrant workers. Whereas the oppression between cultures is masked beneath ecological discussions in the earlier works, *Sal*

*Dust jacket for Matthiessen's 1983 book, a controversial defense of Leonard Peltier, who was found guilty of killing two
FBI agents during a gun battle at the Pine Ridge Reservation in South Dakota (Richland County Public Library)*

Si Puedes is a much more overtly political work; it sets
the stage for the highly politicized *In the Spirit of Crazy
Horse* (1983) and *Indian Country* (1984). Yet, the ecological still figures largely in these works: as described in
Sal Si Puedes, environmental factors directly affect
human society: "In a damaged human habitat, all problems merge. For example, noise, crowding, and smog
poisoning are notorious causes of human irritability;
that crowded ghettos explode first in the worst smog
areas of America is no coincidence at all." Consequently, the socio-economic revolution of Chavez is
blended with Matthiessen's own desire for an "evolution in our values" that aims "at an order of things that
treats man and his habitat with respect."

Around the time of the publication of *Sal Si Puedes*
in 1969, Matthiessen found validation of his socio-
environmental worldview in Zen Buddhism, with its
blending of mindfulness, compassion for all sentient
beings, and interdependence of all things—ideas that resonated quite strongly with Matthiessen. He could easily
have found those ideas in Native American spiritual
teachings as well, but as he noted in *Nine-Headed Dragon
River: Zen Journals 1969–1982* (1986), "If I had found
an American Indian teacher willing to work with me . . .
I might well have chosen a North American tradition

over an Asian one." Regardless, the appeal of Zen Buddhism had a more personal layer as well: his wife Deborah had become a Zen practitioner, and she introduced
Peter to Zen. Together they immersed themselves in its
practices, and as a result, their marriage, which had
been weakened by frequent travel and Peter's prolonged absences, was strengthened. But just as their
marriage was growing more intimate and vibrant, Deborah was found to have inoperable cancer, and in January of 1972, she died. This period of personal difficulty
was countered by some critical successes, including the
publication of what many regard as Mathiessen's masterpieces—*The Tree Where Man Was Born, The Snow Leopard,* and his novel *Far Tortuga* (1975). Moreover, both
The Tree Where Man Was Born and *The Snow Leopard*
were nominated for the National Book Award, and in
1979 *The Snow Leopard* was awarded the National Book
Award for contemporary thought; the paperback edition won the American Book Award in 1980.

The Tree Where Man Was Born revisits the Africa
that Matthiessen first encountered in *Under the Mountain
Wall,* and the work, published with sumptuous photographs by Eliot Porter, focuses on a recurring fascination with the sense of origins, innocence, and mystery.
The narrative style strives to match the honesty of Por-

ter's camera lens, thereby depicting with little emotion a pack of wild dogs killing a zebra foal and another pack surrounding and devouring a "docile" pregnant zebra mare. Similarly, the text documents human violence from an emotionally removed distance, thereby refusing to interpret the events; thus, the ebb and flow of everyday life is conveyed. Nevertheless, as rendered by the book, the violence portrayed in the animal world is an extension of the natural order of survival, whereas the murder humans visit upon each other and the poaching of animals reveal the greed and envy that are evidence of fundamental flaws in human character. Consequently, *The Tree Where Man Was Born* is a celebration of the mysterious origins of life on Earth, while simultaneously it is cast in a dark tone that captures human flaws and a natural order in which life hinges upon death.

The quest for origins and the central role of death in life is continued in *The Snow Leopard,* but the "objectivity" of style is overshadowed by an intimacy that is an extension of the personal nature of the work. One year after Deborah died, Matthiessen embarked on a 250-mile trek across the Himalayas with naturalist George Schaller. Matthiessen and Schaller hoped to find the elusive snow leopard, but Matthiessen also wished to visit an ancient Buddhist shrine on Crystal Mountain and to meet with its revered Lama of Shey. The book, presented as journal entries covering two months, documents the beauty and hardship of life in the mountains of Nepal and Tibet, but it is also a spiritual pilgrimage and an introspective dialogue that grapples with the tenets of Zen Buddhism—impermanence, egolessness, compassion, and death—in light of Matthiessen's grief over the death of his wife.

Perhaps more than his other nonfiction, *The Snow Leopard* demonstrates how the natural world bears on the spiritual by analyzing how objects in nature are unobfuscated signs of "being": "The secret of the mountains is that the mountains simply exist. . . . The mountains have no 'meaning,' they *are* meaning; the mountains *are* [Italics in the original]." To perceive the mountains as such yields an epiphany that refuses to elevate the human over the natural world. Moreover, the mountains signify how such secret "being" always remains beyond the inadequacies of human language and outside the parameters of human understanding. As noted in the book, "to try to capture what cannot be expressed" is meaningless. This recognition of being leads to an insight central to Zen practice, whereby one extends "acute awareness into ordinary moments, in the moment-by-moment experiencing of the lammergeier and the wolf, which . . . have no need for any secret of true being."

The inner journey of *The Snow Leopard* is representative of the essence of the oeuvre of Matthiessen's nonfiction—the deep respect and admiration for things as they are and not, in the capitalist notion, for the potential economic value inherent in a place, animal, or object. This lesson culminates, most poignantly, in the fact that despite evidence that a snow leopard is nearby and Matthiessen, for all of his efforts, never sees it, the "secret" being remains intact and thereby untainted by language. In this respect, the figure of the snow leopard is an apt symbol for the spiritual implications of all things as well as a subtle argument for conservationism as a means of maintaining the spiritual aspects of nature. Soon after receiving the National Book Award for *The Snow Leopard,* Matthiessen affirmed his spiritual affiliations with Zen Buddhism by having Tensugen-Sensei, a Soto-Zen teacher, officiate at his marriage to Tanzanian-born Maria Eckhart, an editor of *Condé Nast Traveler.* In 1981 Matthiessen was ordained as a Zen Priest in the Soto tradition, a step that eventually led to his Dharma transmission, which recognized him as a legitimate heir of the Soto-Zen tradition.

After the success of *The Snow Leopard,* Matthiessen again turned his attention to the sociopolitical—the incident at Pine Ridge Reservation in South Dakota in which two FBI agents and one member of the American Indian Movement (AIM) were killed during a shootout. In spite of a great deal of controversy, AIM activist Leonard Peltier was arrested and convicted, an occurrence that is the subject of Matthiessen's most controversial book, *In the Spirit of Crazy Horse* (1983). After the book was published, Matthiessen and his publisher were sued by an FBI agent and William Janklow (the governor of South Dakota) for libel in an amount totaling $49,000,000. (The libel suit was dismissed in 1989.) Despite its political agenda, *In the Spirit of Crazy Horse* does not radically depart from the trajectory of prior works, and its critique of the "underlying issues of history, racism, and economics"—in particular, Indian sovereignty claims—certainly are evident in earlier books. In a manner similar to that used in *The Snow Leopard, In the Spirit of Crazy Horse* traces how the environment is imbued with a spirituality and suggests that survival depends upon maintaining the spiritual resonances of humankind and place. Matthiessen quotes John Trudell, a Native American: "If we are to continue to survive, to endure, we must keep our spirit connection to our people who came before us; in this earth is where our power lies."

The next work, *Indian Country* (1984), which investigates the damming and flooding of the Cherokee River in the Tennessee Valley, an "unnatural inversion that forces man out of harmony with his surroundings," is a continuation of Matthiessen's interrogation of the relationship of ecology, place, spirituality, and human history. *Indian Country* draws upon the experience of Native Americans in order to foreground the concept of ecojustice. Specifically, *Indian Country* presents how economics and (white) money subsume spirituality and tradition, and in this way, the damming of the river and the subsequent flood fulfills a Cherokee prophecy that the white man would disturb "earth's natural balance, with calamitous consequences for mankind." While the theme of ecojustice informs much of Matthiessen's earlier socio-environmental work, it is a dominant theme in the more politically charged works published in the 1980s.

While the next work of nonfiction nature writing, *African Silences,* was first published in 1991, it is, in fact, a synthesis of previously published essays from several earlier journeys to Africa. The book offers a unified ecological position; that is, the survival of life on Earth is linked to the survival of every species—in the specific case of *African Silences,* the forest elephant: "The very survival of the bongo, okapi, and lowland gorilla, which browse on the new growth in elephant made gaps in the canopy, may depend on the survival of the forest elephant." Similarly, *Shadows of Africa* (1992)—a sumptuous coffee-table-sized book that includes Mary Frank's etchings of African wildlife—is a continuation of *African Silences:* it is a collection of refined journal entries from prior expeditions in Africa that carefully describes a range of animals and their habitats. The book largely gestures back to *The Tree Where Man Was Born* and more immediately to *African Silences* and even quotes liberally from both texts in the epilogue. Subsequently, both of these books have a retrospective character that largely revisits and reiterates the adventures and ideas documented earlier.

The book that follows—*Baikal: Sacred Sea of Siberia* (1992)—is more original in scope and content than earlier works, perhaps because it was the result of a foray into previously uncharted territory for Matthiessen. In 1990, at the urging of Paul Winter, a musician and environmentalist, Matthiessen traveled to Lake Baikal, the deepest and oldest freshwater lake in the world. Winter hoped that Matthiessen would use his writing to generate worldwide attention for the destruction of the ecosystem of that region. *Baikal* is a brief but beautiful book wherein Matthiessen's polished journal entries are juxtaposed with Boyd Norton's crisp, evocative photos in order to posit a compelling "defense" of Baikal against industrialization and the consequent destruction of the habitat. Many of Matthiessen's published works of the early 1990s—including *African Silences, Shadows of Africa,* and *Baikal*—share the common purpose that they were written "to help out certain groups," which, as Matthiessen acknowledges, com-

Matthiessen (photograph © 1991 Nancy Crampton; from the dust jacket for African Silences, *1991)*

promises the literary quality of the work, but he remarks that he had no "illusions about the literary quality of those books," since they were in the service of particular causes.

Matthiessen's research took a more spiritual and personal turn in 1992 when he returned to Nepal in order to visit the city of Lo Monthang and, in conjunction with the photographer Thomas Laird, to document a remote Buddhist culture that had not been visited by Westerners for thirty years. While *East of Lo Monthang: In the Land of Mustang* (1995) is primarily ethnographic in scope and reiterates Matthiessen's admiration for the ecological and spiritual Buddhist worldview first rendered in *The Snow Leopard,* the expeditions to Siberia in 1990 and Nepal in 1992 also offered an unusual opportunity to study the tigers and cranes of those regions. In 1996 Matthiessen returned to the Far East in order to complete his study of those animals, which formed the foundation for his two most recent works of nonfiction—*Tigers in the Snow* (2000) and *Birds of Heaven: Travels with Cranes* (2001). While *Tigers in the Snow* posits a familiar refrain—that the ecosystem is a delicate web in which the survival of the entire system depends upon the survival of all of the animals that inhabit it—the book makes another compelling argument for the preservation of tigers. He points out that the extinction of the tiger would drastically alter collective human consciousness. Subsequently, Matthiessen pairs his prose with Maurice Hornocker's color photographs of the tigers living in the Siberian Tiger Project as well as plates of Chinese, Korean, Persian, and Siberian works of art, in order to substantiate his claim that "Life would be less without the tiger." The text, in this regard, argues that the need for animals such as the tiger goes beyond the ecological and speaks to the animistic and mythic resonances between humanity and the natural world. Subsequently, when Matthiessen posits that the tiger has been called the "soul of India," he is suggesting that the tiger (as well as other animals) occupies a vital and necessary place in the human psyche as well as in the natural order of the ecosystem.

Birds of Heaven offers a parallel argument to *Tigers in the Snow* in that the future survival of cranes not only directly bears upon physical human survival, but also the act of saving the cranes becomes a necessary means of preserving and affirming those attributes that denote humanity—compassion, selflessness, memory, and imagination. While the books of the 1990s and into the present frequently celebrate environmentalists, *Birds of Heaven* exemplifies Matthiessen's ongoing admiration for the efforts of a range of international conservation groups, caretakers, game wardens, scientists, and naturalists, who study and preserve the ever-dwindling habitats of such animals as cranes. These individuals often are portrayed as more than conservationists: they are the keepers of human history and tradition upon whom Matthiessen places immense hope—a hope for ecological balance as well as for a cooperative global community working beyond nationalistic and sociopolitical boundaries for the good of the earth and for humanity as a whole. Subsequently, Matthiessen regards the transnational efforts of these individuals and groups as the most profound model for ecological harmony, peace, and the continued survival of humankind.

While many of the works that have been written over the last twelve years of Matthiessen's career continue to critique humanity's careless attitudes regarding the relationship of a habitat, its wildlife, human history, and spirituality, the underlying rhetorical argument is no longer that the natural order will survive if certain attitudes and political policies are changed; rather, survival depends upon a sustained and global effort to preserve nature. Subsequently, the later books move away from merely exposing the social and ecological problems that are endemic to a particular environment and move toward an argument for international environmental stewardship for the planet as a whole. In this regard, the early image of Matthiessen as a pioneer who exposed the political and environmental hubris of

human civilization has been replaced with that of the environmental shaman—a wise man who unveils the nexus in nature of the spiritual, historical, and human—and the environmental activist working to maintain the careful balance of the human and the natural world by bringing together a community of international naturalists. Regardless of these shifts in his image, Matthiessen's message remains the same throughout all of his nonfiction: without sustained and conscientious human effort, life is always imperiled.

Interviews:

Wendy Smith, "PW Interviews Peter Matthiessen," *Publishers Weekly,* 229 (9 May 1986): 240–241;

Kay Bonetti, "An Interview with Peter Matthiessen," *Missouri Review,* 12, no. 2 (1989): 109–124;

Paul Rea, "Causes and Creativity: An Interview with Peter Matthiessen," *Re Arts & Letters: A Liberal Arts Forum,* 15 (Fall 1989): 27–40;

Deborah Houy, "A Moment with Peter Matthiessen," *Buzzworm,* 5 (March 1993): 28.

Bibliography:

D. Nicholas, *Peter Matthiessen: A Bibliography: 1951–1979* (Canoga Park, Cal.: Orirana Press, 1979);

James Dean Young, "A Peter Matthiessen Checklist," *Critique,* 21, no. 2 (1979): 30–38;

William H. Roberson, *Peter Matthiessen: An Annotated Bibliography* (Jefferson, N.C. & London: McFarland, 2001).

References:

Henry Allen, "Quest for the Snow Leopard's Secret: And Other Journeys Into Meaning with Best-Selling Author Peter Matthiessen," *Washington Post,* 13 December 1978, pp. D1, D15;

Bruce Bawer, "Nature Boy: The Novels of Peter Matthiessen," *New Criterion,* 6 (June 1988): 32–40;

Peter Becker, "Zen and the Art of Peter Matthiessen," *M Inc.,* 8 (July 1991): 54;

Bert Bender, "*Far Tortuga* and American Sea Fiction since *Moby-Dick,*" *American Literature,* 56 (May 1984): 227–248;

Bender, *Sea-Brothers: The Tradition of American Sea Fiction from Moby-Dick to the Present* (Philadelphia: University of Pennsylvania Press, 1988);

John Cooley, "Matthiessen's Voyages on the River Styx: Deathly Waters, Endangered Peoples," in *Earthly Words: Essays on Contemporary American Nature and Environmental Writers,* edited by Cooley (Ann Arbor: University of Michigan Press, 1994);

Nicholas Dawidoff, "Earthbound in the Space Age: Peter Matthiessen Explores the Wild and the

Majestic," *Sports Illustrated,* 73 (3 December 1990): 119–124;

Marc Dolan, "The 'Wholeness' of the Whale: Melville, Matthiessen, and the Semiotics of Critical Revisionism," *Arizona Quarterly,* 48 (Fall 1992): 27–58;

William Dowie, *Peter Matthiessen* (Boston: Twayne, 1991);

Trip Gabriel, "The Nature of Peter Matthiessen," *New York Times Magazine* (10 June 1990): 30;

James P. Grove, "Pastoralism and Anti-Pastoralism in Peter Matthiessen's *Far Tortuga,*" *Critique,* 21, no. 2 (1979): 15–29;

Michael Heim, "The Mystic and the Myth: Thoughts on *The Snow Leopard,*" *Studia Mystica,* 4 (Summer 1981): 3–9;

Pico Iyer, "Laureate of the Wild," *Time,* 141 (11 January 1993): 42–44;

Richard F. Patteson, "*At Play in the Fields of the Lord:* The Imperialist Idea and the Discovery of the Self," *Critique,* 21, no. 2 (1979): 5–14;

Patteson, "Holistic Vision and Fictional Form in Peter Matthiessen's *Far Tortuga,*" *Bulletin of the Rocky Mountain Modern Language Association,* 37, nos. 1–2 (1983): 70–81;

George Plimpton, "The Craft of Fiction in *Far Tortuga,*" *Paris Review,* 15 (Winter 1974): 79–82;

Rebecca Raglon, "Fact and Fiction: The Development of Ecological Form in Peter Matthiessen's *Far Tortuga,*" *Critique,* 35 (Summer 1994): 245–259;

Michael Shnayerson, "Higher Matthiessen," *Vanity Fair,* 54 (December 1991): 114–132;

William Styron, *This Quiet Dust and Other Writings* (New York: Random House, 1982), pp. 249–252, 295–298;

W. Ross Winterowd, "Peter Matthiessen's Lyric Trek," in his *The Rhetoric of the 'Other' Literature* (Carbondale: Southern Illinois University Press, 1990), pp. 133–139.

Papers:
The Harry Ransom Humanities Research Center at the University of Texas at Austin holds some of Peter Matthiessen's papers.

John McPhee

(8 March 1931 –   )

Mark C. Long
Keene State College

See also the McPhee entry in *DLB 185: American Literary Journalists, 1945–1995, First Series.*

BOOKS: *A Sense of Where You Are: A Profile of William Warren Bradley* (New York: Farrar, Straus & Giroux, 1965);

The Headmaster: Frank L. Boyden of Deerfield (New York: Farrar, Straus & Giroux, 1966);

Oranges (New York: Farrar, Straus & Giroux, 1967);

The Pine Barrens (New York: Farrar, Straus & Giroux, 1968);

Levels of the Game (New York: Farrar, Straus & Giroux, 1969);

A Roomful of Hovings and Other Profiles (New York: Farrar, Straus & Giroux, 1969);

The Crofter and the Laird (New York: Farrar, Straus & Giroux, 1970);

Encounters with the Archdruid (New York: Farrar, Straus & Giroux, 1971);

Wimbledon: A Celebration, text by McPhee, photographs by Alfred Eisenstaedt (New York: Farrar, Straus & Giroux, 1972);

The Deltoid Pumpkin Seed (New York: Farrar, Straus & Giroux, 1973);

The Curve of Binding Energy (New York: Farrar, Straus & Giroux, 1974);

Pieces of the Frame (New York: Farrar, Straus & Giroux, 1975);

The Survival of the Bark Canoe (New York: Farrar, Straus & Giroux, 1975);

Coming into the Country (New York: Farrar, Straus & Giroux, 1977);

Giving Good Weight (New York: Farrar, Straus & Giroux, 1979);

Basin and Range (New York: Farrar, Straus & Giroux, 1981);

In Suspect Terrain (New York: Farrar, Straus & Giroux, 1983);

La Place de la Concorde Suisse (New York: Farrar, Straus & Giroux, 1984);

John McPhee (photograph by Nancy Crampton)

Table of Contents (New York: Farrar, Straus & Giroux, 1985);

Heirs of General Practice (New York: Farrar, Straus & Giroux, 1986);

Rising from the Plains (New York: Farrar, Straus & Giroux, 1986);

The Control of Nature (New York: Farrar, Straus & Giroux, 1989);

Looking for a Ship (New York: Farrar, Straus & Giroux, 1990);

Assembling California (New York: Farrar, Straus & Giroux, 1993);

The Ransom of Russian Art (New York: Farrar, Straus & Giroux, 1994);

Irons in the Fire (New York: Farrar, Straus & Giroux, 1997);

Annals of the Former World (New York: Farrar, Straus & Giroux, 1998);

The Founding Fish (New York: Farrar, Straus & Giroux, 2002).

Collections: *The John McPhee Reader,* edited by William L. Howarth (New York: Farrar, Straus & Giroux, 1976);

Outcroppings, text by John McPhee and photographs by Tom Hill, edited by Christopher Merrill (New York: Farrar, Straus & Giroux, 1988);

The Second John McPhee Reader, edited by Patricia Strachan, with an introduction by David Remnick (New York: Farrar, Straus & Giroux, 1996).

OTHER: *The Princeton Anthology: Favorite Pieces by the Ferris/McGraw Writers at Princeton University,* edited by McPhee and Carol Rigolot (Princeton, N.J.: Princeton University Press, 2001).

SELECTED PERIODICAL PUBLICATIONS–UNCOLLECTED: "Eucalyptus Trees," *Reporter* (19 October 1967): 36–39;

"Water War," *New Yorker* (26 April 1993): 120;

"Don't Scare Them Off," *Discover* (November 1993): 95;

"Other Snows," *New Yorker* (22 January 1996): 90;

"Silk Parachute," *New Yorker* (12 May 1997): 108;

"Swimming with Canoes," *New Yorker* (10 August 1998): 33;

"Farewell to the Archdruid," *Sierra* (January–February 2001): 8.

John McPhee's career as a writer began during the 1960s when American nature writing was infused with the social and political urgencies of late-twentieth-century environmentalism. The modern age of environmental activism, ushered in by such writers as Rachel Carson, widened public concern with environmental issues. McPhee has consistently been engaged with environmental issues although uninterested in environmental advocacy or activism. His regional imagination has raised provocative questions about the ways humans live and work in local environments, and his desire to understand technology and the sciences has enriched his readers' understanding of these human activities as having profoundly changed the way people understand the natural world.

McPhee's accuracy and sensitivity as a literary journalist have extended the genre of nature writing as a field of inquiry. His elegant prose moves the reader away from the ease of nature and human culture in the abstract. McPhee's uneasiness with abstractions about nature, his impatience with wholesale attacks on the human endeavor, and his reticence to take sides in environmental debate have unsettled many conservation-minded readers. At the same time, McPhee has earned respect among readers less satisfied with simple resolutions to determining the place of humankind in the natural world.

John Angus McPhee was born on 8 March 1931 in Princeton, New Jersey, the youngest of three children of Harry Roemer McPhee and Mary Ziegler McPhee. The McPhee family moved to Princeton from Iowa when McPhee's father, a doctor with expertise in sports medicine, joined the faculty and agreed to serve as the physician for the athletic programs of Princeton University. McPhee attended public school and, from the age of six, spent summers at a boys' camp, Keewaydin, on Lake Dunmore, south of Middlebury, Vermont. Following his graduation in 1948 from Princeton High School, McPhee spent one year at Deerfield Academy in Massachusetts before enrolling at Princeton University. He spent his sophomore and junior years in the creative-writing program, studying with R. P. Blackmur and Randall Jarrell. His senior thesis in English was a novel, "Skimmer Burns."

McPhee spent a postgraduate year in England, at Cambridge University, studying literature and, in his spare time, playing basketball. When he returned to the United States, he began writing for *Time* magazine. He also submitted articles to *The New Yorker* magazine, but his efforts were rebuffed until, in 1963, his "Basketball and Beefeaters" appeared. Two years later McPhee's profile of Bill Bradley, "A Sense of Where You Are," was published in *The New Yorker,* and McPhee began his current position as a staff writer for the magazine. In addition to emerging as one of the most talented writers of his generation, McPhee is a well-regarded teacher. Since 1975 he has taught a writing seminar, "The Literature of Fact," at Princeton University, where he is Ferris Professor of Journalism. He has inspired many of his talented students to continue on to successful careers as writers and editors.

McPhee's eclectic interests as a literary journalist can be traced to his childhood in the Northeast during the middle part of the twentieth century. In an unpublished 1986 interview with Norman Sims, McPhee observes, "If you make a list of all the work I've ever done, and put a little mark beside things that relate to activities and interests I had before I was twenty, you'd have a little mark beside well over ninety percent of the pieces of writing." His remarkable profiles of people include a preparatory-school headmaster, family doctors in Maine, a physicist, a builder of birch-bark canoes, and a collector of Soviet art. McPhee's immersion in sports led him to his first profiles of basketball star and Rhodes scholar Bill Bradley and, later, the world-class tennis players Arthur Ashe and Clark Graebner. McPhee's outdoor activities at Keewaydin–where his father worked during the summers as a physician—developed McPhee's appreciation for nature and sharpened his skills in the outdoors. "I grew up in a summer camp—Keewaydin—whose specialty was canoes and canoe travel," McPhee recalls in his essay "Swimming with Canoes." "We were in them every day wherever we were, in and out of Vermont. We were like crustaceans with our rib-and-planking exoskeletons, and to this day I do not feel complete or safe unless I am surrounded by the protective shape of a canoe."

William L. Howarth, editor of *The John McPhee Reader* (1976), suggests that Princeton—an affluent cultural enclave in New Jersey, a haven for scholars and people of varied origin—is "the epicenter" of McPhee's cartography. Critic James N. Stull, similarly, traces McPhee's pastoral vision of nature to his relatively stable suburban life. "While McPhee does write about some of the most pressing environmental concerns of his time," according to Stull, "when we consider his fondness for wilderness settings and timeless, out-of-the-way places, as well as the prototypical individuals who populate his world—individuals who are competent, trustworthy, and morally good—we enter a semi-idealized realm that reflects, more generally, McPhee the author's private vision of the world." Literary critic Thomas C. Bailey, however, makes the case that McPhee's "private vision" of the natural world has evolved away from an accepting pastoral engagement with the natural environment. In "John McPhee: The Making of a Meta-Naturalist" Bailey argues that since the late 1970s, McPhee "seems no longer so interested in nature as a timeless pastoral or as a peaceful Edenic world despoiled by humans." Rather, McPhee "proposes that time properly understood is almost incomprehensibly violent, that nature's system is inherently in conflict with human culture, and that as those systems collide, the puny ones devised by human intelligence are doomed to defeat."

"I've written about nature and it is terribly important to me," McPhee said in a 1993 interview with Michael Pearson. Indeed, many of McPhee's books are concerned with long-standing questions about preservation and human development. Yet, McPhee's interests are in people who have balanced their own concerns with those of the environment that sustains their activities. In the words of Pearson, McPhee is interested in "showing his readers the world through the people who live in it." Pearson, the author of the only book-length study of McPhee to date, concludes that it might be best to call McPhee a nature writer in spite of himself. David Remnick, in the introduction to *The Second John McPhee Reader* (1996), draws much the same conclusion. Over time, Remnick writes, McPhee "has become the most effective literary advocate for environmentalism." But he "does not preach, nor does he shout doomsday in a crowded room.

He tells stories—stories that, in the margins, fairly bark the most important ecological questions."

McPhee's first two books are about exceptional people: *A Sense of Where You Are: A Profile of William Warren Bradley* (1965) presents the life story of Bradley, and *The Headmaster: Frank L. Boyden of Deerfield* (1966) tells the story of the headmaster of Deerfield Academy. McPhee's third book, *Oranges* (1967), traces the human uses of citrus from its origins to the modern juice-concentrate industry in Florida. For the student of nature writing, *Oranges* is the first indication of McPhee's interest in the history of attempts to use nature to satisfy human desires and needs. A year later McPhee published the first of his books to take its place in the American tradition of nature writing. *The Pine Barrens* (1968) profiles the sparsely populated forest of south-central New Jersey, sandwiched between the coastline and Interstate 95, and situated in one of the most densely populated states in the union. The book moves back and forth between the history of the pine barrens and its present-day status as an unusual and threatened ecosystem. McPhee marvels at the astonishingly pure aquifer—"the equivalent of a lake seventy-five feet deep with a surface area of a thousand square miles"—and the forest on top of it, calling it "an incongruous place in space and time."

The natural history of the pine barrens, however, is not one of unspoiled or unchanging nature. For McPhee the importance of the place is its human history—its use as a smugglers' El Dorado; as a refuge for fleeing Tories during the American Revolution; as the primary source of iron for cannonballs used in the revolution as well as in the War of 1812; as the area used by the government to establish Brotherton, the first Indian reservation in North America; and as the area used by African Americans in their migrations north to escape slavery. McPhee travels with the people who live in the pine forest today—the "pineys," a "tolerant people with an attractive spirit of live and let live"—and focuses not only on their rugged individualism but also on their embrace of isolation.

For McPhee the spirit of a place is captured through the ongoing history and present activities of people living on the land. "The nonfiction writer," he insists in his interview with Sims, "is communicating about real people in real places." The first of many profiles of place and the self-sufficient people who give meaning to the land, *The Pine Barrens* anticipates McPhee's study of his ancestral homeland of Colonsay, a small island in the Hebrides off the west coast of Scotland, in *The Crofter and the Laird* (1970). *The Pine Barrens* is also a prototype for McPhee's ambitious regional profile of Alaska almost ten years later in *Coming into the Country* (1977). Imagining a region, for McPhee, is congruent with his ethic as a literary journalist—his commitment to arranging and presenting the facts as he sees them. He consistently teases out descriptions of the landscape through its cultural history, as well as through the experience of the people who live with the land. In *The Pine Barrens,* as well as in his subsequent books about place, McPhee registers the encroachment of human activity on unusual natural and human communities. When longtime pine-barren resident Fred Brown asked McPhee why he was in the area, though, he explained to his host only that "I was in the pines because I found it hard to believe that so much unbroken forest could still exist near the big Eastern cities, and I wanted to see it while it was still there."

McPhee's regional imagination is in this work a kind of stay against what writer Barry Lopez has called the increasingly "homogenized national geography" of America. In fact, McPhee ends *The Pine Barrens* with doubts that the current balance between people and the natural environment will last. "They seem to be headed slowly to extinction," he writes. "In retrospect, people may one day look back upon the final stages of the development of the great unbroken Eastern city and be able to say at what moment all remaining undeveloped land should have been considered no longer a potential asset to individuals but an asset of the society at large—perhaps a social necessity." Despite this mournful tone, the ecosystem of the pine barrens has maintained a tenuous hold. In 1979 the New Jersey Pineland Protection Act designated more than one million acres as a "preservation area" in which growth is monitored. These still-contested reserve lands on the periphery of the pine barrens surround a thousand-square-mile core of land that remains relatively untouched by the effects of development.

In the first of his essay collections, *A Roomful of Hovings and Other Profiles* (1969), McPhee includes a delightful meditation on the quintessentially American aspiration to live off the land. In "A Forager, a Profile of Euell Gibbons," first published in *The New Yorker,* McPhee joins the naturalist and author of *Stalking the Wild Asparagus* (1962) on a weeklong hike in central Pennsylvania. The profile recounts the less-public personal history of "the greatest living wild chef" and reveals the particular skills of a person who sees beyond the obvious. As McPhee writes, with evident admiration, Gibbons is able "to read the land as if it were a language." After six days of foraging, the two return from the woods no worse for wear. "We found that I had gained eight ounces," adds McPhee. "Gibbons had gained two pounds."

Two years later McPhee published a profile of David Brower, *Encounters with the Archdruid* (1971). Brower, the first Executive Director of the Sierra Club, a position he held from 1952 through 1964, and the founder of Friends of the Earth and the Earth Island Institute, was chosen to fulfill a plan that McPhee conceived following his experiment two years earlier with Arthur Ashe and

Clark Graebner in *Levels of the Game* (1969). When a profile of two people worked out, McPhee imagined a more difficult challenge. He conceived a narrative structure that would profile one person through that person's encounter with three other people. "I had no idea what the subject would be," McPhee admitted. He was, however, interested in the outdoors, and by the late 1960s the environmental movement was starting. So he traveled to Washington, D.C., to talk with people in conservation organizations and to the people they were fighting. Brower emerged as the ideal subject: he had enemies; he believed in his cause; and he had a reputation as a successful advocate for preservation of wild areas that was second to none. McPhee arranged three wilderness journeys with Brower and his "natural enemies": in Glacier Peak Wilderness of Washington State he traveled with Charles Park, a geologist and mineral engineer, "who believes that if copper were found under the White House, the White House should be moved"; on Cumberland Island, off the coast of Georgia, with Charles Fraser, a land developer who despite his own interest in the land regards preservationists such as Brower as druids, "religious figures who sacrifice people and worship trees"; and in Grand Canyon National Park, with Floyd Elgin Dominy, United States Commissioner of Reclamation, who, not unlike a beaver (to invoke Brower's metaphor for Dominy in *Encounters with the Archdruid*) cannot tolerate the sound of running water.

Throughout *Encounters with the Archdruid* McPhee highlights Brower's informed and principled stance as a preservationist of wild land. At one point in "A Mountain," the first essay, while debating the concept of wilderness with Park, Brower crystallizes the problem facing the conservation movement. The movement is consigned to deferring destruction of habitat, explains Brower. Permanent victories are not possible, and the vulnerability of wild areas requires constant vigilance on the part of those who wish to conserve land in a relatively undisturbed state. McPhee's admiration for Brower is evident, but Park, Fraser, and Dominy are cast as compelling figures as well. Allowing the choreographed drama to play itself out, McPhee refuses to take a side in each of the three environmental skirmishes. Rather than tell readers what to think, McPhee guides them to the difficult philosophical and political questions that underlie the modern environmental movement. Hence, *Encounters with the Archdruid* may appear to sponsor the wilderness ethic by profiling one of its most visible proponents. But McPhee is less interested in the truth of Brower's position than in situating him in the ongoing cultural debates over the use of natural resources, development, and the damming of rivers.

McPhee's next two books venture into the fields of science and technology. *The Deltoid Pumpkin Seed*

Dust jacket for McPhee's 1968 book, about the sparsely populated forestland between the coast and Interstate 95 in New Jersey (Bruccoli Clark Layman Archives)

(1973) is a story about the design and testing of a hybrid airplane and airship; *The Curve of Binding Energy* (1974) is a primer on nuclear energy and a profile of the theoretical physicist and bomb designer, Theodore Taylor. *Pieces of the Frame* (1975) collects eleven essays, three of which are of special interest to the student of McPhee as a nature writer—"Travels in Georgia," "Reading the River," and "Ranger." McPhee's first *New Yorker* profile of a woman, "Travels in Georgia," rambles over the back roads and waterways of the state with a field zoologist and activist from Atlanta, Carol Ruckdeschel. The essay ends with a canoe trip on the Chattahoochee River with the governor of Georgia, Jimmy Carter, who invites McPhee and his companions to the governor's mansion for lunch.

The Survival of the Bark Canoe (1975) begins as a profile of the birch-bark canoe builder, Henri Vaillancourt, of Greenville, New Hampshire. McPhee describes the expert craftsman in his workshop in Greenville and traces the history of the bark canoe—

from its distinctive native designs among the tribes of the Northeast, especially the Malecites in Maine and New Brunswick, to the uses of bark canoes in the north woods of Canada, most notably in the fur trade. The first part of the book, based in Vaillancourt's shop, follows the master craftsman as he gathers birch bark and builds canoes. McPhee discusses the range of *Betula papyrifera*—"variously called the white birch, the silver birch, the paper birch, the canoe birch"—and the concentration of the larger trees in the East. He recounts the preservation of the design of birch-bark canoes by Edwin Tappan Adney (1868–1950). Adney, who had built a bark canoe under the guidance of a Malecite craftsman, dedicated much of his life to recording the craft and tribal styles of bark canoes. The sketches were edited and published by Smithsonian curator Howard Chapelle in the 1964 book *The Bark Canoes and Skin Boats of North America.*

McPhee joins the master canoe builder on a 150-mile trek in the Penobscot and Allagash watershed of Maine. The canoe trip unfolds along two thematic lines. The first theme is a reflection on the idea of wilderness, which draws on passages from *The Maine Woods* (1864), Henry David Thoreau's account of his travels by canoe in the same watershed more than a hundred years before. "There is more to Maine," McPhee says with evident satisfaction, "than exists in the imagination." The second theme, a dramatic counterpoint to the first, is Vaillancourt's character as the qualified craftsperson who is singularly unqualified in the water and in the woods—indeed in the world of people. "The great beauty of the lake apparently means nothing to him," McPhee writes. "He has worked for two days to get to it, and now wants to rush across it and portage away from it in the dusk and dark." Hence, the Thoreauvian idyll of wilderness travel is, by the end of the book, no longer as simple as it might have seemed at the beginning.

Coming into the Country is a widely acclaimed classic in the tradition of American nature writing. First published in *The New Yorker* in eight parts, the book earned McPhee the 1977 Award in Literature from the American Academy of Arts and Letters. *Coming into the Country* is a masterful example of literary nonfiction organized around narrative and exposition, anecdote and fact. The complicated and captivating narrative weaves natural history and environmental politics with enduring profiles of people who have come to live in Alaska. The first of three essays, "The Encircled River," recounts two trips on the Salmon and Kobuk Rivers. McPhee joined a combined state and federal research team studying the possibility of designating the Salmon River (a tributary of the Kobuk River) a national wild river. McPhee travels with the group—Pat Pourchot of the Federal Bureau of Outdoor Recreation; John Kauffmann, a National Park Service planner; Bob Fedeler, a wildlife biologist with the Alaska Department of Fish and Game; and Stell Newman, from the National Park Service—in one Grumman canoe and two collapsible Klepper kayaks, a double and a single.

Coming into the Country is one of the few works by McPhee in which the subject is genuinely wild land. "In a lifetime of descending rivers, this was the clearest and the wildest river," McPhee writes, in awe at the sheer expansiveness of the territory. Here water flows "without the questionable benefit of names," and human time is not an especially relevant convention. For the Salmon River, McPhee explains, "the sixteenth century has not yet ended, nor the fifteenth, nor the fifth":

> The River flows, as it has since immemorial time, in balance with itself. The river and every rill that feeds it are in an unmodified natural state–opaque in flood, ordinarily clear, with levels that change within a closed cycle of the year and of the years. The river cycle is only one of many hundreds of cycles–biological and meteorological–that coincide and blend here in the absence of intruding artifice. Past to present, present reflecting past, the cycles compose this segment of the earth.

The river, described first as timeless, becomes almost mythical in its natural state. The representation of the wild land of Alaska as "in balance with itself," in a series of natural cycles "in the absence of intruding artifice," however, is only one part of the story of Alaska. The other part of the story is the human presence on the land. "The central paradox of Alaska is that it is as small as it is large–an immense landscape with so few people in it that language is stretched to call it a frontier let alone a state," observes McPhee. "The question now," he adds, "is what to do with the land."

Although the essay is organized around the rhythms of river travel and is set in the wildest place one can imagine, McPhee never moves far from the fate of the wild rivers and land of Alaska. The day-to-day travel down the river provides the setting for a political history of the state and the accompanying controversies that have shaped Alaskans' attitudes toward the land: the Alaska Purchase Treaty in 1867, the 1958 Alaska Statehood Act, and the 1971 Alaska Native Claims Settlement Act. The Trans-Alaska Pipeline project led to intensive lobbying of Congress by conservationists and resulted in eighty million acres of preserved parkland, wildlife refuge, and wild rivers.

Not surprisingly, then, the conversation on the river trip focuses on the various ways humans might choose to value the land. McPhee focuses on the regional history of human settlement and what he calls Alaskans' "wheel of attitudes toward the land." He

begins with the mobile lives of the Kobuk River people, who traditionally followed herds of caribou. The Native Claims Settlement Act, which allotted sixty thousand natives of the state $1 billion and forty million acres, however, forced the native people of Alaska to establish their lands as mostly contiguous with their villages. When a boundary is established around native lands, however, a difficult question arises: What if the caribou go somewhere else? Traditionally, the Kobuk peoples had held land in common. But in accepting the Native Claims Settlement Act they were agreeing to adopt what was for them the foreign concept of private property and ownership.

At other times in the essay, McPhee plays the role of Socrates in a double kayak. When longtime friend Kauffmann makes the preservationist case that the lands of Alaska comprise the last opportunity for the federal government to set aside wild land, McPhee intervenes. "In part to make him paddle harder, I said, 'Yes, but why do all you sneakerfaces, you ecocentrics, think you need so much of it?'" Having sparked an impassioned speech by Kauffmann on the need for federal oversight of the local land use with another question–"Why lock it up?"–McPhee senses the need to reward his interlocutor. He concedes Alaska offers one of a few precious moments in human history when people can actually make decisions to save the land in its natural state.

The second essay, "What They Were Hunting For," serves as a counterpoint to the first. McPhee joins the Capital Site Selection Committee, a group of nine members appointed by the governor of Alaska to study alternative sites to the present capital in the southeastern panhandle city of Juneau. As Bailey observes, the second essay juxtaposes "the urge of many Alaskans to preserve their environment, and the equally passionate desire of just as many Alaskans to develop it for all it's worth." McPhee shuttles back and forth between the present capital city, Juneau, and its northern sister cities, Anchorage and Fairbanks. He compares the perceptions of northern Alaska from the perspectives of Juneau and the northerner's view of the city to the south, working to characterize these geographical and attitudinal polarities as part of the provincial whole: "In Alaska, the conversation is Alaska. Alaskans, by and large, seem to know little and to say less about what is going on outside." Urban Alaska is rife with many human conflicts that are never far from the land, as in the case of the proposed capital relocation project.

"Coming into the Country" is the third and longest essay in the book. It was written during two visits to Alaska: the first during spring and summer of 1976 and the second in the winter of 1977. McPhee spent time in the towns of Eagle, Circle, and Central in the Upper

Yukon, northeast of Fairbanks. McPhee's attention is on the people in Alaska who live outside the urban centers of the state. "With a clannish sense of place characteristic of the bush," McPhee begins, "people in the region of the upper Yukon refer to their part of Alaska as 'the country.' A stranger appearing among them is said to have 'come into the country.'" McPhee traces the new arrivals, and he lingers with those who have chosen to stay.

The essay is a chronicle of the people whose comings and goings have shaped a human culture that endures despite the powers of wilderness and government. A decade or more brings deep seniority in Alaska. People arrive steadily, and people go. Some, of course, are only interested in a year or two of work at high wages, which they save and take back to the lower forty-eight states. Others, though, mean to adapt to Alaska, hoping to find a sense of frontier, a fresh and different kind of life. They come continually to Eagle and to Circle, the next settlement below Eagle down the Yukon. McPhee pieces and stitches these characters into an elaborate human quilt of tenacious miners, resourceful trappers, bush pilots, and refugees from the lower forty-eight who harbor a deep distrust of the federal government.

McPhee first introduces Donna Kneeland, an Alaskan native who, living for two years in an isolated cabin twenty miles from the nearest neighbor, has established a reputation for "her way with fur." Her companion, Dick Cook, runs traplines and serves as a kind of sage and mentor for the newcomers to the area. In conversation with Kneeland, McPhee notes his own attempts to make sense of Alaska. He compares his densely populated home state of New Jersey to the unpeopled reaches of Alaska. McPhee realizes how easy it is for people to come to Alaska with a highly romanticized view of the wilderness.

The latter part of the essay is an extended profile of the Gelvin family. When Stanley Gelvin was born in 1950, he sensed that he could live wherever he pleased; however, when Alaska became a state and oil was discovered, the era of homesteading ended. McPhee writes that when the reapportionment of Alaskan land took place, "the squares seemed to be moving as well as the checkers." Where McPhee then goes with the Gelvin story is not surprising. Reflecting on their claim far into the country that has disassembled a pretty little stream for gold, McPhee does not cast the Gelvins as destructors of a virgin landscape for perhaps a "peanut-butter jar filled with gold." He continues, "Am I disgusted? Manifestly not. Not from here, from now, from this perspective. I am too warmly, too subjectively caught up in what the Gelvins are doing. In the ecomilitia, bust me to private."

McPhee reasons that the mine is insignificant, "a cork on the sea." What is significant is the relationship between the father and the son:

Only an easygoing extremist would preserve every bit of the country. And extremists alone would exploit it all. Everyone else has to think the matter through—chose a point of tolerance, however much the point might tend to one side. For myself, I am closer to the preserving side—that is, the side that would preserve the Gelvins.

This penultimate vignette of the book reveals much about McPhee as a nature writer. He shows both a deep love for the land and an admiration for the people who inhabit it. He is unwilling to reduce the complex situation of the human use of land to a simple calculus. The point of tolerance is chosen according to the situation and the author's sympathy with the heroic struggles of other human beings. Decisions about the land and the people who must live with such decisions, McPhee suggests, must be made on the ground, with a sense of where you are.

The essays collected in *Table of Contents* (1985) represent the range of McPhee's environmental interests. "Under the Snow," "A Textbook Place for Bears," "Riding the Boom Extension," and "Minihydro" are all of particular interest to the student of nature writing. "North of the C.P. Line" is a clever profile of John Malcom McPhee, a game warden and pilot in northern Maine. Their common heritage and surname originating from a small island in the Hebrides leads to one of McPhee's most interesting biographical portraits. Critics have noted that at least explicitly, McPhee's essays are neither politically nor personally inclined; rather he most often reveals who he is, as James N. Stull observes, "by talking about others." "North of the C.P. Line" enacts this strategy. Author McPhee's honest and revealing admiration for John McPhee the game warden/pilot is uncharacteristically revealing: "From anecdote to anecdote, unself-consciously he poured forth his knowledge—of natural disasters and human intrusions, of isolated phenomena and recurrent events, of who was doing what to whom." McPhee concludes, "I remember a wistful feeling—it has not diminished—imagining the life that had produced that knowledge." The itinerant journalist wishes for the knowledge earned over a lifetime in the woods and the evident ease of living in the natural environment, and he concludes that "when I think of him, I invariably find myself wishing that I were [that] John McPhee." These words suggest some of the passion and longing that move this prolific and provocative writer to go back out into the field again and again.

An interest in technology and the earth sciences has been the most evident trend in McPhee's writing through the 1970s and 1980s. Both *Encounters with the Archdruid* and *The Curve of Binding Energy* were nominated for the National Book Award in the category of science; and *Annals of the Former World* (1998) received the 1999 Pulitzer Prize in general nonfiction. This shift in concern since *Coming into the Country* can be traced in McPhee's third collection of essays, *Giving Good Weight* (1979), which includes two pieces that explore the dilemmas played out between "environmentalists" and "intervenors." "The Atlantic Generating Station," set in his home state of New Jersey, describes the Public Service Electric and Gas Company engineer Richard Eckert and his idea to build an immense nuclear-power plant. Eckert, a New Jersey native, was employed to find sites and then build nuclear-power plants, and in 1971 his idea for the floating reactors was accepted by Public Service as feasible. The essay, which begins, literally, in Eckert's shower, follows the idea as it finds purchase and then gains momentum as a possible solution to the energy demands of New Jersey.

"The Keel of Lake Dickey" is, in the words of Pearson, "an example of what is best in McPhee's nature writing and at the same time a departure from his typical methods." The story chronicles a trip on St. John River in Maine, a river that runs free for two hundred miles until it crosses into New Brunswick, where it has been dammed. The debate over the fate of the St. John is, as McPhee puts it, written in delible ink. The idea of a dam at the confluence of the Allagash and St. John Rivers is tied to the dream of local power, although the proposed project would offer New England merely 1 percent of its electricity. McPhee concludes, "we throw away more power than Dickey Dam could ever give us, by ten times ten. We throw it away in kilowatt years. And anyone who would do that would throw away a river."

McPhee's interest in human attitudes toward the natural world is the subject of *The Control of Nature* (1989). The three essays are about people whose lives have come into direct conflict with the forces of nature. Whereas Rachel Carson says at the conclusion of *Silent Spring* (1962) that the "control of nature" is a phrase conceived in arrogance, "when it was supposed that nature exists for the convenience of man," McPhee seems to answer: be that as it may, such attitudes are not so easily overcome. The first story, "Atchafalaya," recounts the history and present state of the Mississippi River and its distributary, the Atchafalaya, which without human intervention would capture the water of the Mississippi. The United States Army Corps of Engineers in 1963 erected a dam at the Old River site, where the Mississippi's waters were likely, in time, to spill into the Atchafalaya. The problem, however, is that since 1860 the Atchafalaya had naturally been drawing more water from the Mississippi as the river sought the most direct course to the Gulf of Mexico.

McPhee begins by orienting the reader to the geography of the region. The points of orientation are natural (the river) and human (the parishes above New Orleans). McPhee describes the river, the navigation lock, and the people who live and work with the river. He quotes Mark Twain on river pilots and takes a ride with the Mississippi River Commission. While traveling on the river with the commission, McPhee pauses to recount the history of the Army Corps, and when the riverboat on which he is riding runs aground on a sandbar, he then recounts the history of the river control project. "Atchafalaya" serves as a parable, bringing up the larger questions about human attempts to manage the forces of nature.

McPhee's parable is not transparent—in part because of his controlled description and sharp, ironic commentary. One of the Army Corps employees feels that the river can be held back—that man can control nature, or at least he can try. Later, at the division headquarters of the corps, McPhee hears the same message, in this case from General Sands. "Man against nature. That's what life's all about." Past and present attempts to arrest the inevitable movement of the river, however, suggest that, in the end, nature will have its way.

In "Cooling the Lava," also, nature appears to have the upper hand. The story centers on a fissure that opened in 1973 on the small island of Heimaey, a community of five thousand people off the coast of Iceland. In five and a half months the eruption laid "a curtain of lava five hundred feet high and a mile long." The human strategy is to pour tens of millions of gallons of seawater on the lava in order to cool it and attempt to save the town. The resulting anomaly to the natural flow of lava raised the interesting question of whether the pumping had actually caused the lava to turn left and overrun the city. "The answer," McPhee writes, "lay somewhere on the spectrum between probably and yes." The conclusion that follows might apply to all three stories in the book, indeed any natural system altered by humans. "After the human contribution passed a level higher than trifling, the evolution of the new landscape could in no pure sense be natural. The event had lost its status as a simple act of God. In making war with nature, there was risk of loss in winning."

"Los Angeles Against the Mountains" begins with a breathtaking anecdote about the Genofile family, whose home was hit by a rock-and-mud debris flow in the winter of 1978. The creek beside the Genofiles' home is a component in the Los Angeles basin river system that has been tightly controlled by concrete. The paradox of human settlement in the steep, brush-covered hills has to do with the relative infrequency of exceptional flows, which course down the mountainside once every ten years or so. But they are

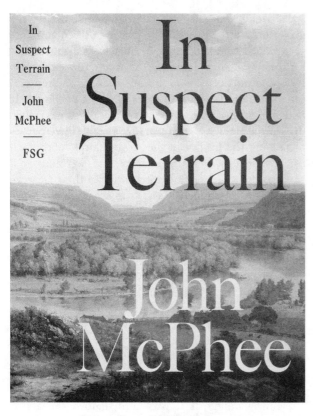

Dust jacket for McPhee's 1983 book, a geological portrait of the Appalachian Mountains (Richland County Public Library)

not frequent enough to deter people from building in the war zone. On the other hand, if looked at on the geologic time scale, the debris flows in the San Gabriel Mountains are constant.

During the 1980s and the 1990s McPhee was working on a series of books that have been collected together under the title *Annals of the Former World* (1998). *Annals of the Former World* compiles four previously published books: *Basin and Range* (1981), *In Suspect Terrain* (1983), *Rising from the Plains* (1986), and *Assembling California* (1993)—all "meshed, melded, and revised, in some places cut," McPhee explains in "A Narrative Table of Contents"—with a fifth book added, "Crossing the Craton." Viewing the natural world through more than 4.6 billion years of geologic time, *Annals of the Former World* provides the student of nature with one of the most interesting inquiries into the powers and the limits of human thinking about the natural world.

The omnibus edition comprises a geological cross section of North America at about the fortieth parallel; each book, built around an account of travels in the field with a geologist, sketches an overall picture of the science of geology. The geology books were conceived when McPhee asked Princeton geologist Ken Deffeyes if a blast-exposed face of a roadcut near New York City

might offer a slice of geologic history for a "Talk of the Town" piece for *The New Yorker*. McPhee suggested they journey north from roadcut to roadcut through the Adirondack Mountains in New York. Deffeyes responded that when studying the underlying structure of the North American continent, the geologist goes west, across the structure.

The controlling element of *Annals of the Former World* is the rise during the 1960s of the revolutionary and controversial theory of plate tectonics. McPhee began with the intention of presenting the science of geology and its practitioners to both the general reader and the practicing geologist. Each of McPhee's geology books has arrested the attention of these readers—but, as more than one reviewer has characterized it, by bogging them down in mind-numbing technical detail. The geological community, however, has embraced McPhee's contributions. McPhee was nominated as a fellow by the members of the Geological Society of America in 1986; in 1988 he was awarded the U.S. Geological Survey's John Wesley Powell Award for writing in the field of geology; and in 1992 he received the Association of Petroleum Geologists' Journalism Award. McPhee's writing about the field of geology led writer Wallace Stegner to describe McPhee in a *Los Angeles Times Book Review* article as "our best and liveliest writer about the earth and the earth sciences."

McPhee takes his title *Annals of the Former World* from a phrase in James Hutton's 1785 *Theory of the Earth*. Hutton's theory was that the earth's crust had been shaped over long periods of time. He believed, further, that these geological changes were knowable and predictable, dependent upon natural patterns of cause and effect. Hutton, the father of the modern science of geology, had at the same time proposed a novel and—to his contemporaries—incomprehensible sense of geological time. The uniformitarianism of Hutton supposed that the present could tell the story of the former world—a doctrine, McPhee adds, that opens the way to Charles Darwin, as "time is the first requirement of evolution."

Still, the first person to see the natural history of earth in a stream bank where the river had laid bare flat-lying sandstone and beds of schistus below it standing straight on end, "Hutton had no way of knowing that there were seventy million years just in the line that separated the two kinds of rock, and many millions more in the story of each formation—but he sensed something like it, sensed the awesome truth, and as he stood there staring at the riverbank he was seeing it for all mankind." This passage from *Basin and Range* recalls the moment when Hutton's observations of an angular unconformity in Scotland "helped to bring the history of the earth, as people had understood it, out of theological metaphor and into the perspectives of actual time." The theory of Noah's flood, and the subsequent scientific explanation—"neptunism," the idea of the aqueous origin of the visible world—went out the window with Hutton's observations. "Something had lifted the rock out of the sea and folded it up as mountains."

Basin and Range begins in medias res: "The poles of the earth have wandered. The equator has apparently moved. The continents, perched on their plates, are thought to be going in so many directions that it seems an act of almost pure hubris to assert that some landmark of our world is fixed." Beginning the journey of the *Annals of the Former World* requires the reader to accept immediately and irremediably the startling possibility that the present understanding of the human place in the natural world is severely limited. The problem, McPhee explains, is that humans are unable to make the leap to understanding themselves embedded in "deep time":

> The human consciousness may have begun to leap and boil some sunny day in the Pleistocene, but the race by and large has retained the essence of its animal sense of time. People think in five generations—two ahead, two behind—with heavy concentration on the one in the middle. Possibly that is tragic, and possibly there is no choice. The human mind may not have evolved enough to comprehend "deep time." It may only be able to measure it.

Even geologists, McPhee admits, question their abilities to "sense" the passage of millions of years. At the same time, geologists attest to the effects of thinking, for example, that a million years is the shortest unit of measure worth thinking about when one is confronted with geological problems. As one geologist put it to McPhee, a person tuned to the planet's timescale has a different kind of relationship with the earth.

Basin and Range moves from Utah to eastern California with Deffeyes and Karen Kleinsphen, at the time a recent Princeton graduate. *Basin and Range* is the primer on plate-tectonic theory. McPhee explains that during college he had learned the "Old Geology." Years later, in the 1960s, the field of the earth sciences was transformed by the theory of plate tectonics. However, McPhee mentions that he had read in the journal *Geology* that one in eight geologists does not accept the plate-tectonic theory. One of those people was Anita Harris of the United States Geological Survey—the scientist-protagonist of the second book in the series, *In Suspect Terrain* (1983).

In Suspect Terrain moves from the outwash plain of Brooklyn to Indiana and Ohio with Harris, whose biography, including her professional career, is the subject of part 1. The book actually begins with a reproduction of George Inness's 1859 painting *Delaware Water Gap*.

The painting serves as a synecdoche for the geological lessons of the Appalachian Mountains. "Tell me what made that scene," writes McPhee, "and you will tell me what made the eastern United States." The age of the river, McPhee finds, is about fifty million years; the rock in Water Gap four hundred million years; and the Taconic Mountains fifty million years before that. The timescale is unintelligible unless one is able to imagine an analogy between a hundred million years of geology and one human century. The capacity to extend human thinking about the natural world is limited by the ways in which humans measure space and time. The scale of human centuries is simply inadequate.

Extending human thinking about nature through analogy leads to stunningly simple questions. For example, what makes the mountains rise? One answer—using the dominant paradigm theory of modern geology—is the movement of plates. But for Anita Harris—"a geologist with few weaknesses, who is at home in igneous and metamorphic petrology no less than sedimentology"—the answer is less clear. Harris does not reject plate theory out of hand, McPhee explains with admiration. Plate-tectonic theory works with the idea that a continental landmass up against the eastern edge of North America produced the Appalachians, explains Harris. She counters that this theory may prove a sufficient account in part of the range, but in other cases the idea just does not hold up. The problem with any theoretical model, Harris goes on to explain, is oversimplification or overapplication—the tendency to fold geological anomalies into an inflexible human model.

McPhee contrasts the controversies over plate theory in the twentieth century with the nineteenth-century theory of continental glaciation (Louis Agassiz's *Epoque Glaciaire*). "Plate theory was constructed in ten years by people with hard data who were consciously and frankly waxing 'geopoetical,'" McPhee explains. The metaphysical leaps of the science give field geologists such as Harris pause. Her work in the Appalachians has shown her regional anomalies that do not fit the plate theory. This skepticism appeals to McPhee. Harris points out that the theory replaces a more subtle regional understanding of geology. She explains that accurate regional pictures are impossible when one simply extrapolates plate tectonics through geologic time. In this way, Harris—and McPhee—call attention to the implied nonscientific method, "If at first it doesn't fit, fit, fit again."

Rising from the Plains (1986) moves west to the Rocky Mountains in the company of field geologist David Love. *Rising from the Plains* is about Rocky Mountain geology and a geologist, but the book is also about the family of the geologist—in particular, Ethel Waxham, Love's mother, a Wellesley College graduate and a woman who, McPhee says, was "probably the most

Pages from the manuscript for McPhee's 2002 book, The Founding Fish
(Collection of John McPhee)

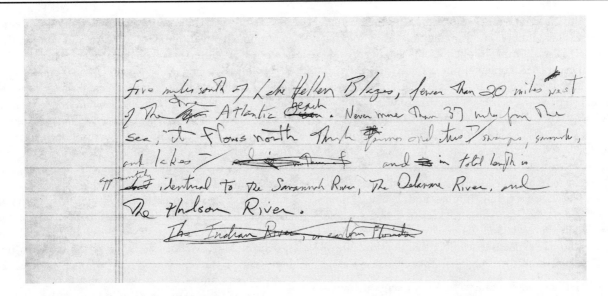

arresting personality I have encountered in my professional work." McPhee tells the story of Ethel Waxham's movement west through extensive quotations from her journals. (David Love's father, John Love, was a Scotsman whose uncle was environmentalist John Muir.)

From the Love ranch spread out over the geological center of Wyoming, McPhee continues his journey across the continent on Interstate 80, examining roadcuts. He is also drawn north and south by the diverse geology of the state. McPhee rambles through Jackson Hole and the Tetons, the Powder River Basin, the Wind River Basin, and the Laramie Range. He explores the geophysical hot spot of Yellowstone National Park and comparable sites in Hawaii, Bermuda, Iceland, Tristan da Cunha, and Mount Cameroon. At the same time, *Rising from the Plains* is true to its title. Shifting from human to geological time, McPhee again seeks language to describe the main event in the geological history of Wyoming, the Laramide Orogeny. He describes in detail the planing crustal sheets "piling up like shingles" and the radical movement of mountains. In half a billion years of history, the event takes place over a relatively brief geological time frame of ten million years. The next event is the subsequent burial and exhumation of the Rocky Mountains. Human time, once again, proves inadequate to the unstable and fluid dynamics of the natural world.

The book concludes with an extended profile of David Love. McPhee calls the sequence "an environmental montage of tensions between geological discovery and environmental preservation." McPhee first turns to Love, "the grand old man of Rocky Mountain geology," to trace changes in the life of a professional field geologist. Scientist, discoverer of resources, and vigorous environmentalist, Love carries within his experience the paradoxes of his culture. In the 1970s Love published

"Hydrocarbons in Thermal Areas, Northwestern Wyoming," which raised significant geophysical questions about oil deposits within Yellowstone Park. To environmentalists, Love's finding oil in Yellowstone raised a wider threat to preserved land. Most of the land in the wilderness areas of the United States had been preserved on the assumption that they were devoid of such nonrenewable resources. Love admits feeling some remorse over having been targeted as a traitor by such organizations as the Sierra Club. "My great-uncle John Muir founded the Sierra Club," Love explains.

Assembling California (1993) appeared thirteen years after *Basin and Range*. McPhee traveled with Eldridge Moores, an ophiolitologist (an expert on crustal-ocean rock) at the University of California, Davis. He is one of the "plate-tectonic boys" mentioned by Harris in *In Suspect Terrain*. *Assembling California* begins with McPhee and Deffeyes in San Francisco, after an automobile trip over the Sierra Nevada on Interstate 80, leaving the province of *Basin and Range*. *Assembling California* is a compilation of rambles with Moores. McPhee and Moores travel about the Sierra Nevada, west through the Central Valley, into the Coast Ranges, and up and down the major southeast running fault line of the San Andreas—with flashback trips with Moores to field-study sites in Cyprus and Greece, and his childhood home in Crown King, Arizona. McPhee's geological account of California is indebted to his periodic travels with Moores over a span of fifteen years.

Moores entered the field of geology when the theory of plate tectonics had begun to revolutionize the science. When McPhee began traveling with Moores in 1978, he drove "an oyster-gray Volkswagen bus with a sticker on its bumper that said 'Stop Continental Drift.'" According to present theory, explains McPhee, "the varied terranes and physiographic provinces that we now call California" are, geologically speaking, a relatively recent addition to the continent. The piecing together of California resulted from the twenty-odd lithospheric plates, continually in motion, and the tens of thousands of major earthquakes that are the incremental steps in the process. "After there was nothing," McPhee writes, "earthquakes brought things from far parts of the world to fashion California." Few people in the 1970s, however, "envisioned the western United States as a collection of lithospheric driftwood." Following McPhee—who is following Moores—is, once again, dependent upon relating human and geologic time. Moores describes the effort to keep the human (and emotional) timescale and the geologic timescale in the same mind. He explains to McPhee that the slow rate of geological processes has huge effects over many years.

McPhee returns to a piece of conventional environmental wisdom about the human place in the natural world that, he suggests, humans forget at their peril. Nature is more powerful and more permanent than humans are. Occasionally the human and geologic timescales coincide, McPhee explains, as in an earthquake felt by people, or when mining of any kind begins. *Assembling California* has two long set pieces that describe such moments: the first is an account of the California gold rush of the 1840s and 1850s, and the second is the 1989 Loma Prieta earthquake. McPhee also follows the conversation in the geological sciences through the 1970s, 1980s, and 1990s, and he chronicles the plate-tectonic narrative of the past 1.5 billion years. In reconstructing the narrative—which Moores admits is, after all, no more (or less) than a story—McPhee once again suspects that he is "following a science as it lurches forward from error to discovery and back to error." He then concludes with a caution to his readers. "In my effort to describe some of the early discoveries of plate tectonics I must also be preserving some of the early misconstructions."

The final and shortest of the five books in *Annals of the Former World,* McPhee explains, "describes Nebraska by visiting Colorado, because in Colorado you see the basement of Nebraska bent up into the air." "Crossing the Craton" focuses on the midcontinent with W. R. Van Schmus, a geochronologist at the University of Kansas. The interior craton is a relatively stable block of the earth's crust that has resisted change. The stable interior craton of North America spans from the Gulf of Mexico to the Arctic Ocean. The area is the domain of a scientist with an unparalleled understanding of the midcontinent below the sediments. As Van Schmus explains to McPhee, the rock of the craton includes a story. The problem for the geologist is to determine how to read the rocks.

However, interpreting rocks—reading deep time—is not possible with the naked eye. In addition to other methods of gathering geophysical data—measurements of varying magnetic fields, gravity anomalies, and well-drilling core samples from Precambrian rock—one method of connecting "various disjointed pieces of the Precambrian crust" is the use of radiometric dating techniques. Van Schmus reconstructs the history of rocks emerging from the mantle of the earth by measuring isotopes that belong to the elements samarium and neodymium. The field of geochronology seeks accurate and precise ages of rock to determine their history in the continental system. "You want to be accurate and precise," Van Schmus tells McPhee. In Precambrian geochronology, McPhee adds, "a window of two million years is an extremely narrow one. A date like 1746—plus or minus two—is very precise."

Annals of the Former World has the cumulative effect of unsettling human definitions of time and place, as well as human methods of knowing that they use to situate themselves in the world. For instance, awareness of geologic time leads to an understanding of the visible landscape as a momentary expression of the process of nature. An understanding of place through the language of the earth sciences may then lead humans to consider the relatively inconsequential place of the human endeavor. This consideration might lead, further, to a deepened awareness with respect to the ecosystems humans inhabit. It could even lead to a more contingent understanding of humanity's place in nature and, therefore, to a renewed context in which to think about the most difficult environmental issues humans face. *Annals of the Former World* might finally serve to renew in all a sense of awe and lead everyone to a greater respect for human limitations—and perhaps a more lasting feeling of reverence for nature.

Since completing the *Annals of the Former World,* McPhee has continued to publish essays of interest to the student of nature writing. The collection *Irons in the Fire* (1997) includes essays about a trip to a preserved tract of land in New Jersey, "In Virgin Forest"; a continuation of the author's geological musings, "The Gravel Page"; an account of the largest pile of scrap automobile tires in the world in the Central Valley of California, "Duty of Care"; and a meditation on the origins of the glacial erratic Plymouth Rock, "Travels of the Rock."

The Founding Fish (2002) chronicles McPhee's many years fishing for shad, mostly in the Delaware—a river that in its main stem runs 330 unfettered miles and offers the angler more range and variety of shad fishing than anywhere else on the continent. McPhee's first-hand knowledge of the American shad (he reports more than nine hundred and twenty-two hours on or in the river fishing) draws him to learn what there is to know about the schooling ocean fish with a range from the St. Johns River in Florida to the Labrador Sea. His interest leads him on fishing trips to the major shad rivers from Florida to Maritime Canada. On these trips he joins others with experience on the rivers and in the laboratories—from ichthyologists to a master maker of shad darts. He is challenged by the difficult art of filleting shad, and he revels in the pleasures of cooking shad and shad roe.

The book is a delightfully readable account of the science and history of the American shad. McPhee's account of the life cycle of this anadromous (literally "running up") fish is reminiscent of Rachel Carson's brief biography of the catadromous (literally "running down") eel in her 1941 book *Under the Sea Wind*. The difference is McPhee's engagement with Boyd Kynard, a fish behaviorist, Steve McCormich, a fish physiologist, and Willy Bemis, an anatomist, to name a few. The American shad have been surprisingly central in America's history as well. The "founding fish," it seems, was virtually everywhere in Colonial America. It was a subsistence resource and later a commercial asset for the native peoples living on the Pamunkey river in Virginia, for example. George Washington was a commercial shad fisherman—in 1771, he netted 7,760 American shad. Thomas Jefferson of Virginia was born in "Shadwell," in 1743, and was known to dine on shad.

The famine at Valley Forge in 1778, more notoriously, was alleviated by the annual run of Amerian shad, or so the story goes. For McPhee discovers, with the help of historian of Colonial America, Wayne Bodle, that "the emotive account of the nation-saving shad is a tale recommended by everything but sources." The legendary shad run that fed the starving soldiers at Valley Forge, in the words of Bodle, is little more than a "providentialist canard" that arises, again and again, despite the absence of textual and archeological evidence.

McPhee's account of the American shad develops through the twentieth century as an environmental history of its native Eastern rivers. With the exception of the two-hundred-mile stretch of the Delaware's shad fishery above Trenton, New Jersey, the major rivers of East Coast America are blocked by seventy-eight dams. McPhee writes that as he began to become aware of the historical migrations of the American shad, "and the extent to which they had been stifled, reduced, or absolutely cut off" by the damming of the rivers during the nineteenth century, he had trouble imagining the end-of-the-twentieth-century solution: get rid of the dams.

At Edwards Dam, in Augusta, Maine, for example, "ocean fish coming up river to spawn—such as Atlantic sturgeon, Atlantic Salmon, and American shad—had received essentially no consideration for sixteen decades." The dam at Augusta had stopped the shad from finding their way to the more ideal spawning grounds in the upper reaches of the river. In "Farewell to the Nineteenth Century" McPhee travels to the Kennebec to watch "the first big dam in a major river to be ordered out of existence by the federal government." The dams that had so unsettled Henry David Thoreau in *A Week on the Concord and Merrimack Rivers* ("Poor shad, where is thy redress?") are no longer so easily justified. By 1986 the Federal Energy Regulatory Commission was guided by an amended Federal Power Act to give more consideration to environmental factors when renewing licenses to operate dams. McPhee puts in play the arguments: on the one hand, the conservationists make the case for the ecological benefits of removing the dams; on the other hand, company spokespersons make the economic case for keeping the dams in place. In this case, as his title suggests, there is a reversal in the fortunes of the river and a restoration of a reach of one of the major watersheds of Maine. As McPhee puts it, "The Kennebec Rier, in Augusta, after a hundred and sixty-two years in the slammer, was walking."

Still, the 66,000 dams in the United States, the continued industrial and agricultural runoff, as well as other waste products in the waterways of the nation, present a daunting challenge to any anadromous fish that depends on clean, free-flowing rivers for its spawning cycle. Shad were once so plentiful, McPhee reports, that in 1875 near Palatka, Florida, "a single gill net caught 11,000." Similarly, on the Delaware River, commercial shad harvests had dropped from thousands of tons at the turn of the century to under forty thousand. In Lambertville, Fred Lewis netted about four thousand shad in 1939, about two hundred in 1945, and zero in 1953. The Clean Water Act of 1972 has subsequently had a dramatic effect on the fishery. Industrial outflows and other contributing sources were reduced and the shad fisheries returned. At the same time, McPhee notes that historically there have been rises and falls in the shad migrations that are difficult to trace to human activity or a single environmental change.

In the penultimate chapter, "Catch and Release," McPhee takes up his own question—"Why am I standing here doing this?"—as well as the history of attitudes toward killing fish. He quotes Robert Hughes, "that fishing is a jerk on one end of a line waiting for a jerk on the other," and the poet George Gordon, Lord Byron's remark, that "the art of angling [is] the cruelest, the coldest, and the stupidest of pretended sports," in an extended discussion of People for the Ethical Treatment of Animals (PETA) and what is known (and not known) about the physiology of fish.

McPhee is particularly interested in the claims on behalf of catch-and-release fishing. He suggests catch-and-release fishing "may be cruelty masquerading as political correctness" at the same time that he questions the grounding of their ethical appeals in the scientific understanding of the neurology of fish. Closer to home, McPhee's wife, Yolanda Whitman, compares catch-and-release fishing to "humane" bullfighting, in which the bull is not killed. Meat fishing is more like traditional bullfighting, she says. She then adds, "Fishing is crueler than hunting, in that your goal is to have the fish fight for its life. That's the 'fun.' Hunting, you're trying to kill a creature outright; fishing, you want to play with it." When McPhee protests, "That is not a fair description of your husband," she adds, "If you could just pull fish out of the water—boom—you wouldn't be a fisherman. Don't give me that, John."

To McPhee's ear, the chorus of advocates for catch-and-release fishing is too often sanctimonious about the practice. "At its best, it's the thrill of holding a beautiful animal in your hands for a moment, then watching it swim away. At its worst it is dire—an unintended failure." McPhee insists that there is no such thing as "no kill" fishing. And he makes his own position clear: "I fish for American shad because they are schooling fish that come into the rivers wild. They are not an endangered species. I catch to eat, and with that purpose am not troubled by killing."

As with his other books that explore the place of humankind in the natural world, *The Founding Fish* shows McPhee's anthropological interest in people living and working in the less visible landscape of our lives. In McPhee's view, nature is a place where people are. His accurate and sensitive attention to the multitude of ways humans live in nature will therefore broaden his readers' thinking about the place of humans in the natural world. And his regional imagination will serve as an indispensable repository of human attitudes toward the natural environment. For McPhee's essential lesson as a nature writer is that humankind's understanding of the natural world is something it must continue to shape as it broadens and deepens its inherently limited perspectives.

Interviews:

Edgar Allen Beem, "John McPhee on Maine: Conversation with the Archjournalist," *Maine Times,* 1 November 1985, pp. 14–16;

Douglas Vipond and Russell A. Hunt, "The Strange Case of the Queen-Post Truss: John McPhee on Writing and Reading," *College Composition and Communication* (May 1991): 200–210;

Michael Pearson, "Twenty Questions: A Conversation with John McPhee," *Creative Nonfiction,* 1 (Fall 1993): 76–87;

Jared Haynes, "The Size and Shape of the Canvas: An Interview with John McPhee," *Writing on the Edge,* 5 (Spring 1994): 109–125; 6 (Fall 1994): 108–125.

Bibliography:

Joanne K. Clark, "The Writings of John Angus McPhee: A Selected Bibliography," *Bulletin of Bibliography,* 38 (January–March 1981): 45–51.

References:

Thomas C. Bailey, "John McPhee: The Making of a Meta-Naturalist," in *Earthly Words: Essays on Contemporary American Nature and Environmental Writers,* edited by John Cooley (Ann Arbor: University of Michigan Press, 1994), pp. 195–213;

David Espey, "The Wilds of New Jersey: John McPhee as Travel Writer," in *Temperamental Journeys: Essays on the Modern Literature of Travel,* edited by Michael Kowalewski (Athens: University of Georgia Press, 1992), pp. 164–175;

Joan Hamilton, "An Encounter with John McPhee," *Sierra,* 75 (May/June 1990): 50–55, 92, 96;

Barbara Lounsberry, "John McPhee's Levels of the Earth," in *The Art of Fact: Contemporary Artists of Nonfiction* (Westport, Conn.: Greenwood Press, 1990), pp. 65–106;

Michael Pearson, "John McPhee," in *American Nature Writers,* edited by John Elder, volume 1 (New York: Scribners, 1996), pp. 583–598;

Pearson, *John McPhee* (New York: Twayne, 1997);

James N. Stull, "Self and the Performance of Others: The Pastoral Vision of John McPhee," in his *Literary Selves: Autobiography and Contemporary American Nonfiction* (Westport, Conn.: Greenwood Press, 1993), pp. 11–28.

John Muir

(21 April 1838 – 24 December 1914)

Terry Gifford
University of Leeds, U.K.

See also the Muir entry in *DLB 186: Nineteenth-Century American Western Writers.*

BOOKS: *The Mountains of California* (New York: Century, 1894; London: Unwin, 1894; enlarged, 1911);

Our National Parks (Boston & New York: Houghton, Mifflin, 1901; London: Gay & Bird, 1902?; enlarged, Boston & New York: Houghton Mifflin, 1909);

Let Everyone Help to Save the Famous Hetch-Hetchy Valley and Stop the Commercial Destruction Which Threatens Our National Parks (N.p., ca. 1909);

Stickeen (Boston & New York: Houghton Mifflin, 1909);

Edward Henry Harriman (Garden City, N.Y.: Doubleday, Page, 1911);

My First Summer in the Sierra (Boston & New York: Houghton Mifflin, 1911);

The Yosemite (New York: Century, 1912);

The Story of My Boyhood and Youth (Boston & New York: Houghton Mifflin, 1913);

Travels in Alaska (Boston & New York: Houghton Mifflin, 1915);

A Thousand Mile Walk to the Gulf (Boston & New York: Houghton Mifflin, 1916);

The Cruise of the Corwin: Journal of the Arctic Expedition of 1881 in Search of De Long and the Jeanette (Boston & New York: Houghton Mifflin, 1917);

Steep Trails, edited by William Frederick Badè (Boston: Houghton Mifflin, 1918);

John of the Mountains: The Unpublished Journals of John Muir, edited by Linnie Marsh Wolfe (Boston: Houghton Mifflin, 1938);

Studies in the Sierra, edited by William E. Colby (San Francisco: Sierra Club, 1950);

John Muir's Last Journey, South to the Amazon and East to Africa: Unpublished Journals and Selected Correspondence, edited by Michael P. Branch (Washington, D.C.: Island Press/Shearwater Books, 2001).

John Muir, circa 1890 (John Muir Papers, Holt-Atherton Special Collections, University of the Pacific Library; © 1984 Muir-Hanna Trust)

Editions and Collections: *The Writings of John Muir,* 10 volumes, Sierra edition, edited by Badè (Boston & New York: Houghton Mifflin, 1915–1924);

The Wilderness World of John Muir, edited by Edwin Way Teale (Boston: Houghton Mifflin, 1954);

John Muir: The Eight Wilderness-Discovery Books (Seattle: Mountaineers, 1992)—includes *The Story of My Boyhood and Youth, A Thousand Mile Walk to the Gulf, My First Summer in the Sierra, The Mountains of Cali-*

fornia, *Our National Parks, The Yosemite, Travels in Alaska,* and *Steep Trails;*
John Muir: His Life and Letters and Other Writings, edited by Terry Gifford (Seattle: Mountaineers, 1996).

OTHER: *Picturesque California and the Region West of the Rocky Mountains, from Alaska to Mexico,* 2 volumes, edited by Muir (San Francisco & New York: Dewing, 1888);
"Notes on the Pacific Coast Glaciers," in *Harriman Alaska Expedition,* edited by C. H. Merriam (New York: Doubleday, Page, 1901), I: 119–135.

On a May morning in 1903 two men pose for a photograph at Glacier Point, above Yosemite Valley in the heart of the Sierra Nevada of California. They have slept the night in the open and have woken under a blanket of four inches of snow. The man dressed in the knickers and neckerchief of an outdoorsman is the president of the United States, Theodore Roosevelt. He has requested a camping meeting with the famous wilderness sage, John Muir, who hopes to persuade the president to take jurisdiction for the valley itself away from the state of California and into the wider Yosemite National Park that Muir had been instrumental in creating in 1892. Characteristically, Muir used camping out as a form of lobbying on behalf of a landscape that he wished to see preserved for future generations to enjoy.

The notion of the national park system is credited to Muir, whose writings, in their mixture of the scientific and the lyrical, were ultimately dedicated to both informative and persuasive ends. Muir wanted his readers to appreciate the wonders of the American wilderness and then to join him in the fight for their preservation in a system of national parks that would provide sources of inner renewal for future generations. In the process Muir made important contributions to knowledge in botany, glaciology, and geomorphology—making links between them that anticipated what is now known as the science of ecology. He also, first as a diarist of Yosemite Valley and much later as a writer of books, brought urban audiences on both the East and West coasts in touch with the remarkable natural processes to be observed in wildness at a time when the American frontier had been declared closed. Muir's notion that the most distinctive wild landscapes should be protected from commercial exploitation as "parks" for the nation's future recreation has often been described as one of America's gifts to the world. The campaigning purpose of Muir's writing, together with his formation of the Sierra Club to endorse and monitor the new Yosemite National Park, has led to his being widely regarded as the founding father of the American conservation movement.

John Muir was a Scot who spoke with a Scottish accent all his life and later made some of his closest friends among the Scots of the San Francisco Bay Area. Born on 21 April 1838 in the coastal market town of Dunbar, forty kilometers east of Edinburgh, he was the third of seven children born to Anne and Daniel Muir before they moved to America when John was eleven years old. In those early years of playing on the seashore of the Firth of Forth and on the inland meadows, John developed a sense of adventure and wonder in the natural world. He learned to climb on the walls of Dunbar's fifteenth-century castle and devised, with his younger brother David, games of risk they called "scootchers." His father was a corn dealer, whose contributions to John's education were the Scots ballads and the Bible, the learning of the latter being encouraged by physical punishment. By the time the family left for America, Muir said that he had "about three fourths of the Old Testament and all of the New by heart and sore flesh." The biblical influence on his later writing style was as profound as his joyousness was a reaction against the misery of the method by which he learned it.

Daniel Muir gave up his fiddle and became increasingly puritanical, finding Dunbar's Calvinism not austere enough. He became a convert to the Disciples of Christ and was attracted to the primitive mode of living being advocated in America by the Disciples' Scottish immigrant leader, Alexander Campbell. John Muir later remembered his father announcing one evening, "We're gan to America the morn!" The prospects of exotic wildlife and adventures excited the young Muir. In fact, what faced him were years of hard labor under his tyrannical father's eye as they fought to establish a productive farm from the Wisconsin wilderness. The family settled among a Scottish farming community, and Muir's education was continued by the loan of books written by Sir Walter Scott, Robert Burns, and Scottish explorers such as Mungo Park. He had to read them surreptitiously by rising at one in the morning and retreating to the cellar, where he also had a workshop. There he made ingenious inventions, often connected to clocks—for example, a bed that would tip a sleeper onto the floor at the required time and a carousel of books for timed study. He eventually took these inventions to the state fair in Madison, where he learned that it was possible to attend lectures at the newly developed university.

Muir studied at the University of Wisconsin for two and a half years, taking courses in botany and geology. At the university he came under the influence of Ezra Carr, a professor who introduced Muir to the latest ideas in geology and taught him the essential discipline of reading a landscape. But it was Carr's wife,

Muir's sketch of the results of a rock slide in a side canyon of the Yosemite Valley, drawn in the journal he kept during his summer 1869 stay in the valley (John Muir Papers, Holt-Atherton Special Collections, University of the Pacific Library; © 1984 Muir-Hanna Trust)

Jeanne, who became the major influence on Muir's life through their mutual interest in botany. Jeanne Carr encouraged his writing, urged publication, and became a crucial correspondent and counselor, even finding Muir a wife later in his life. Muir left the university to evade the draft for the Civil War, which he felt was not his war. He botanized in Canada where, in a lonely sojourn in an icy swamp, he experienced an epiphany in the discovery of *Calypso borealis* that made him weep at its beauty and his meeting with it. While in Canada, Muir resolved to make a journey to South America and returned south to the United States. While Muir was working in a sawmill in Indianapolis to raise funds, a file slipped and entered his right eye. His other eye went blind in shock, and he was convinced that he had blinded himself in the accident. When he regained his sight, his vocation "to store my mind with the Lord's beauty" was resolved. He set out for the Amazon Basin on foot by the "wildest, leafiest, and least trodden way." Thus began what was recorded in the journal posthumously published as *A Thousand Mile Walk to the Gulf* (1916). Muir inscribed his small leather-bound journal of this journey "John Muir, Earth-planet, Universe," and, indeed, it was as much a journey that defined himself and his relationship with his planet as it was a journey through a largely inhabited natural universe. This journal represents the earliest extended writing by Muir that has been published. It established what became a feature of his journal writing: an interplay between scientific observation and philosophical reflection that could reexamine common assumptions. The result is a style that can celebrate an integrated vision of the natural world and the place of the human species within it. While the freshness of its vivid details derives from the excitement of being alert and on the move, its reflectiveness is that of a young man forging his own view of what is now called the ecosystem of "Earth-planet." *A Thousand Mile Walk to the Gulf* includes some remarkable reflections that break with many of the tenets of the culture of the times. "The world," he wrote, "we are told was made especially for man, a presumption not supported by all the facts." Muir's observations led not only to a rejection of the hubris of his species but also to a rejection of the image of a hard God of vengeance with which he had grown up. The living dynamics of the creation that Muir observed led him in the direction of a pantheistic view of the divinity of all aspects of Nature. Children, he wrote, should be taught to see that even death is "as beautiful as life" instead of as a subject to be avoided with mawkish fear: "Let children walk with Nature, let them see the beautiful blendings and communions of death and life . . . and they will learn that death is stingless indeed." For Muir all the interactive processes of nature could only lead to the view that "All is divine harmony." This view required some radical revisions of cultural attitudes toward certain aspects of nature.

The historian Roderick Nash has pointed out that in this journal Muir recorded the first claim made in America for the rights of nature. Muir reflected that alligators and snakes were not "fallen" creatures, as the Bible taught, but part of a "wisely planned" system that could be understood by analogy with the "balanced repulsion and attraction in the mineral kingdom." Muir saw human repulsion from snakes as a necessary defense but noted that they were "cared for" as part of "God's family." Two recurring debates about Muir's work can be located in this idea. One is the extent to which Muir was able to displace an anthropocentric focus in favor of an ecocentric one. Some commentators have regarded Muir's language as indulgently anthropocentric in its essential forms of celebration rather than objectively descriptive. The other is the extent to which Muir remained conventionally Christian in his revision of the Calvinist culture in which he was brought up. Did Muir ultimately become, in effect, fully pantheistic in his conception of a creator who is to be met by experiencing the divinity of every small natural thing? What has been recognized by many commentators is Muir's development of an ecological perspective through the deployment of analogy as a literary device that serves to communicate a scientific understanding. What for some readers is Muir's rather flowery language nevertheless becomes the means of communicating a profound vision of ecological parallels for others: predatory attractions and repulsions, for example, in which the human species plays a part, might be understood as the animal version of magnetic forces in minerals. In his protoecological understanding in the journal of *A Thousand Mile Walk to the Gulf* Muir comes to the conclusion that "There is not a fragment in all nature, for every relative fragment of one thing is a full harmonious unit in itself. All together form the one grand palimpsest of the world."

While Muir was recovering from a severe malarial fever in Florida, he remembered having seen a brochure advertising the marvels of Yosemite Valley in California and decided upon impulse to take a detour there before pushing on to the Amazon. Hence came a celebrated association of place and writer, who was developing a distinctive style only in small journals and in letters. Muir's publishing career actually evolved from the publication of his letters from Yosemite in the periodicals of the day, and many of his later books were drawn from his journal writing. The vivid, fresh quality of Muir's writing can be attributed to these earlier forms of writing that derive from total immersion in the Sierra Nevada Mountains of California.

Annie Wanda, Helen, Louie, and John Muir at their home in Martinez, California, 1901 (Bancroft Library, University of California, Berkeley)

Muir was thirty years old when he first walked from San Francisco through the sea of flowers in the Central Valley of California into the Sierra Mountains and arrived in the spectacular Yosemite Valley. Muir delighted in the giant sequoias of the Maraposa Grove before confronting the three-thousand-foot-high valley walls dominated by the protruding buttress of El Capitan on the north side and Bridal Veil Falls tumbling from the south rim. At the furthest end of the valley his eye was caught by a sliced granite dome that seemed to hang in the sky. This formation was then known as Tissiack, or South Dome, as well as the now familiar name Half Dome. The canyon that curled underneath it led up to Tenaya Lake and the region of Tuolumne Meadows. Muir's first visit to Yosemite Valley in 1868 cost $3.00 and lasted eight days. When he returned in the summer of 1869, he came as one of a party herding

sheep by the Mono Trail up to the summer grazing at Tuolumne Meadows. The botanist in Muir was ill at ease with his role in bringing these "hoofed locusts" through his fields of study, and he later fought to have them banned not only from Tuolumne Meadows but also from the whole Yosemite National Park.

The journal of this second trip into the Sierra was published three years before Muir died as *My First Summer in the Sierra* (1911). This book has come to be regarded as Muir's classic work. It conveys what Muir called "a glorious conversion" by which a landscape brings him into a "complete and wholesome" sense of himself and his role in life. Frederick Turner believes that Muir made few changes to the text of the original battered blue notebooks. But Michael P. Cohen has argued that the published book benefits from the mature man's vision forty years beyond the writing of the notebooks. As yet there are no scholarly editions of any of Muir's books with the exception of Ronald H. Limbaugh's work on the making of *Stickeen* (1909). *My First Summer in the Sierra* is an ecstatic diary of a naturalist and mountaineer who is also equally fascinated by his companions and the vagaries of a sheepherding journey into a sublime landscape. His sense of being at home in this environment was typically expressed by an interactive trope: "We are now in the mountains and they are in us." Muir had time to wander off for days on his own. He made the first ascent of Cathedral Peak and crossed over the Sierras by Bloody Canyon to Mono Lake. He closed his journal with a statement that has given the Sierras their popular designation: "I have crossed the Range of Light."

Muir returned that fall to find work at the hotel of James M. Hutchings, building a sawmill and producing timber for new cabins while writing lyrical letters about his exploring, observing, and note making. Indeed, in literary terms, the letters of this period are as important in their ideas, experiences, and literary skill as the later books. For the next decade Muir became the resident guide to the valley as his Madison friend Carr, who had now moved to Oakland, sent him a series of visitors, including novelist Thérèse Yelverton (whose 1872 novel *Zanita* painted an amusing portrait of "Kenmuir," the wild backwoodsman), Berkeley geologist Joseph Le Conte (who brought a group of his students to learn directly from the resident Sierra scientist), and elderly philosopher Ralph Waldo Emerson (who disappointed Muir by staying at a hotel instead of camping out with him). Carr was the person who first suggested to a reluctant Muir that he should write up his studies for publication. In October 1871 Muir found a living glacier that confirmed his observations that Yosemite Valley had been eroded by glaciation rather than caused by a single cataclysmic fall in the valley floor, as was the theory of the professionals of the California Geological Survey at the time. In December, Muir confounded the professionals with his evidence in "Yosemite Glaciers," published in the *New York Tribune* (5 December 1871). Although "Yosemite Glaciers" was a scientific article of devastating import, Muir began with the metaphor of finding a book in the mountains, the open pages of which, although "stained and torn," were easily readable. This metaphor was so convincingly sustained that it could have been read in a literal sense before its metaphorical power revealed itself. Indeed, the literary quality of all Muir's subsequent scientific writing served to celebrate his sense of the sublimity of creation through its deployment of heightened language.

Two further articles followed in the *New York Tribune,* and in 1872 Muir began a series of articles for *The Overland Monthly* culminating in what he thought of as his "Studies in the Sierra." These articles were not published as a book until the Sierra Club collected and reprinted them in 1950, although Muir worked on them continuously as though writing a book while staying with friends in Oakland during the winter and spring of 1873–1874. Muir's "Studies in the Sierra," with their diagrammatic detail of explanation and a literary lucidity, were his Sierra version of John Ruskin's explanation of the features of the Alps in volume four of *Modern Painters* (1843). Muir's text still stands out as one of the earliest and clearest studies of glaciation in America, and this series of articles made Muir famous. His command of his subject and the fluency of his style disguise the agonized reluctance with which Muir approached writing for publication. He preferred the immediacy of letter and journal writing, which could be undertaken outdoors. He wrote a famous letter to Jeanne Carr at midnight in early April 1871 from a rock shelf behind Yosemite Falls after a soaking from a sway inward by the waterfall. Perhaps the best introduction to Muir is the selection of letters with linking biographical commentary compiled by Muir's literary executor, William Frederick Badè, in *The Life and Letters of John Muir* (1924). This book was, in effect, the first biography of Muir; it also used fragments from Muir's unfinished second volume of autobiography. Out of print since its first publication, in 1996 it was republished in a volume that also includes "Studies in the Sierra" and the *New York Tribune* articles.

During the 1870s Muir moved between the city and Yosemite Valley more than he cared to admit in later life, when he accepted the image of wilderness hermit and sage. From his base in the valley he would take off to get to know the whole range with a blanket and with bread, tea, and notebook tied to his belt. Sometimes he would leave the blanket, and even a jacket, behind, then spend a night "dancing" on a summit to keep warm. His methods of study were eccentrically empirical. He said that he discovered the facts of glaciation by lying on the rocks as the ice had done. He climbed a tree to find out how much it "travelled" during a storm, writing in his journal, "We all travel the milky way together, trees and men; but it never occurred to me until this storm-day, while swinging in the wind, that trees are travellers in the ordinary sense." One day when his cabin began to vibrate, he rushed out crying "A noble earthquake!" and witnessed the collapse of a pinnacle called Eagle Rock, thus discovering that the talus at the foot of Yosemite's walls was actually caused by seismic activity rather than gradual erosion. He delighted in having experienced the dynamics of an avalanche from the inside and survived to write the breathless journal entry that became a chapter titled "A Ride on an Avalanche" in his 1912 book, *The Yosemite.*

Muir developed a persona in his writing about the natural world that was disarmingly naive, ecstatic, and simply praising of God's creation. This method later became a strategy for putting no pressure on the readers while actually drawing them into a conservationist concern for the landscape. It was a deft and deliberate tact that at once engaged the reader but offered a distance from the writer's eccentricities. The insights Muir brought to his readers were as easily consumed as they were profound. Concrete images provided metaphors for perceptions that were actually quite radical for their time. In *My First Summer in the Sierra* Muir wrote, "Contemplating the lace-like fabric of streams outspread over the mountains, we are reminded that everything is flowing–going somewhere, animals and so-called lifeless rocks as well as water." In this passage he was able to move from observation of the minerals carried by the smallest streams to engagement with the flowing of stars through the universe, which "pulsed on and on forever like blood globules in Nature's warm heart." Increasingly in his writing Muir used the word "Nature" instead of "God" or "the Creator."

At a time when, unknown to Muir, Ernst von Haechel (1834–1919) was introducing the term "Oekology" (1866), Muir was discovering the notion for himself in his own chains of observations and habits of thought. Muir later characterized himself as a "self-styled poetico-trampo-geologist-bot. and ornithnatural etc.!" To think of Muir as only a naturalist or a writer or a conservationist is certainly unsatisfactory. He persisted in calling himself a "mountaineer," by which he meant one who did all of these things in the mountain environment. Actually, modern mountaineering authorities have confirmed that he must also have been one of the leading technical American mountaineers of his day, in the conventional climbing sense, on the evidence of his recorded first ascents. Muir found himself at home in the mountains, and his periodical writing for largely urban audiences about his lifestyle in Yosemite Valley represented not only an adventurous backwoods life after the closure of the frontier but also a scientific one that was totally integrated with its mountainous field of study.

So Muir's awareness of the dynamics in nature led him to believe that even mountains were "going somewhere"–"mountains constantly walking," as Gary Snyder later put it. Muir's study of the mountain environment led him to a perception of integrated dynamic systems that anticipated the notion of "ecology." Characteristically, he expressed the idea in a folksy way that is as easily memorable as it is radically significant: "When we try to pick out anything by itself, we find it hitched to everything else in the universe." Cohen has

Muir in Sequoia National Park, 1902 (John Muir Papers, Holt-Atherton Special Collections, University of the Pacific Library; © 1984 Muir-Hanna Trust)

pointed out that Muir's studies in the mountains during the 1870s developed an ecological model of the Sierras "at least fifteen years before such models were introduced to scientific theory in the 1890s." Throughout his writings Muir was concerned to find natural systems of interlocking forces, so he had to use recurring key words such as "balance" and "harmony" to represent his protoecological awareness. His deliberate misreading of Ruskin during this period enabled him to position himself against the possibility that mountains could be the "foul . . . dead unorganised matter" he attributed as Ruskin's ultimate view. For Muir nothing could be "foul" in nature, no more than any creature, such as a snake, could be intrinsically evil. Even carnivores were in an ecological balance with each other. Muir's protoecological vision enabled him to celebrate even the death process, as he had done in his journal reflections on the human coyness about death during his walk to the Gulf of Mexico, so that he became able to recognize the largest and the smallest recycling processes in the natural world that was his home.

So much at home was Muir in his solo explorations of this mountainous environment that he rarely discovered that he had made a misjudgment of his ability to read the conditions in which he found himself. Mostly he learned how to adjust to sudden storms, for example, by observing the behavior of his "fellow mountaineers"–bears digging a snow-hole to wait out a snowstorm, squirrels hoarding resources, the water ouzel adapting itself to more than one element. A winter trip to Mount Shasta resulted in the essays that open the posthumous essay collection *Steep Trails* (1918). Among these is "Wild Wool," in which Muir argues that human culture is enriched by contact with wildness, written with a mode of address and a philosophy that has been compared with Henry David Thoreau's famous essay "Walking" (1862). But most significant was a journey through the Kings River sequoia belt that resulted in his first entry into conservation politics by way of the *Sacramento Daily Record-Union* and his 1876 essay "God's First Temples: How Shall We Preserve Our Forests?" The wasteful methods of destruction of the Sierra forests and their clearing for sheep pastures roused Muir to question whether the American government could control the exploitation of the natural resources that made America wonderfully distinctive. Muir played a crucial part in the debate until the end of his life, and his ideas have resonated beyond his death. At the moment he raised the question, he was invited to look further afield with the U.S. Coast and Geodetic Survey in Utah and Nevada and to send back reports for the San Francisco *Daily Evening Bulletin*. He found "monuments of fraud and ignorance" in the abandoned mineral mines that littered the desert landscapes. However, before he could develop his conservation agenda, he took on other agendas.

In 1879 he became engaged at the age of forty-one to the daughter of his friends the Strentzels of Martinez, California. Muir followed the engagement with his first six-month-long trip to Alaska. A year later, on 14 April 1880, he married Louie Wanda Strentzel before taking a second Alaska trip, to be followed by a third the following year. But thereafter for a decade Muir retreated from travel to build up the family fruit-farming business into which he had moved at his wife's family home in Martinez. This house became his home for the rest of his life and is now the John Muir Historical Site. Muir proved to be a good businessman and an enthusiastic agriculturalist. He eventually took over the whole acreage from his aging father-in-law, accumulating enough money to secure the future of his wife and two daughters, Annie Wanda (born 1881) and Helen Lillian (born 1886).

The role of Muir's wife in urging him to return to his writing during this period and eventually urging him to renew his conservation interests has been commented upon by biographers. Muir's disappearance for a decade from public view during the 1880s represented his own commitment to his family, but his wife encouraged brief summer camping trips to the mountains, writing to him that his staying away until he was rested was more important than "a few grapes more or less." In 1884 Louie Muir wrote to Muir during his visit to Oregon with William Keith that "the Alaska book and the Yosemite book, dear John, must be written." Since Muir had yet to face the writing of a book, his wife seems to have had more confidence in the potential impact of a book that Muir could write than he had himself. Ultimately, the first book he wrote was neither of these projects, since by then the conservation agenda required a different kind of book. Louie Muir encouraged her husband to meet the editor from the East who was on a trip to recruit Muir to write for *The Century Illustrated Monthly Magazine*. As a result of this meeting Louie Muir urged her husband to sell part of the ranch and lease out the rest so that he would be free to write, travel, and study into his old age. In 1887 Muir had undertaken to edit and contribute to an ambitious illustrated book titled *Picturesque California and the Region West of the Rocky Mountains, from Alaska to Mexico* (1888), which Muir thought of as "a big literary job." The publication of this work heralded his return to the business of making Americans aware of their landscape heritage.

Muir took the *Century* editor, Robert Underwood Johnson, camping in Yosemite Valley. By a campfire, the two hatched plans for the establishment of a Yosemite National Park. Johnson would lobby on the East Coast and Muir would provide the evidence in his eloquent prose. A two-part article addressed to the two hundred thousand subscribers of *The Century* was planned. The first part titled "The Treasures of Yosemite" drew attention to precisely what was under threat without protection, and the second part, titled "Features of the Proposed Yosemite National Park," suggested the boundaries proposed by Muir and Johnson. The latter article included a special section on what Muir called the "Tuolumne Yosemite," the Hetch Hetchy Valley. Not without a fight from the commercial lumber interests, the Yosemite bill was signed into law by President Benjamin Harrison in 1890, although the valley itself was still administered by the state of California, which leased it out for pig farms and orchards.

Although the notion of "a nation's park" had been proposed by George Catlin in 1832 to preserve the American Indian way of life on the Great Plains, the first national park was actually created in Yellowstone in 1872 in order to prevent the commercial exploitation by one company of the geyser called "Old Faithful." The significance of the Muir-Johnson 1890

Muir taking notes in Petrified Forest National Park, 1905–1906 (John Muir Papers, Holt-Atherton Special Collections, University of the Pacific Library; © 1984 Muir-Hanna Trust)

bill was the preservation of a landscape for the recreation and study of future generations. John Muir is credited with the national-park philosophy, as it is now internationally known, and regarded as the founder of the national-park movement. The cornerstone of Muir's concept was the democratic belief that if only the public could see for themselves the wonders of the American landscape, they would become voters for conservation. Some form of support group for the new Yosemite National Park was needed both to educate regular visitors in the need for conservation and to defend Yosemite Park from the threats that Muir perceived would inevitably come. Thus, in 1892 the Sierra Club was founded with Muir as its first president. Its dual purposes were to encourage both mountaineering and conservation, especially of the native forest reserves. That the Sierra Club has grown

into one of the most widespread lobbying conservation organizations in America is the result of a series of radical leaders who have taken their inspiration from Muir. His inheritance is thus both an internationally important mode of conservation and a national force for the practical participation in conservation by the American people. While debates continue about the directions these two institutions have taken since Muir's creation of them, the principles upon which they were founded are still widely regarded as fundamental: long-term responsibility for the land upon which we depend; "re-creation" through contact with wild nature that is also an education; state restraint on the commercial exploitation of resources; public involvement in local conservation issues; and the role of literary discourse as a means of unifying and exploring all these principles.

The Sierra Club needed a book that would open up the possibilities for its members' exploration of the new Yosemite National Park just as much as the park needed a guide for the increasing numbers of visitors from across the nation. That book was *The Mountains of California,* published in 1894 when Muir was fifty-six. It was his first book. Muir wrote to a friend, "You will say that I should have written it long ago; but I begrudged the time of my young mountain-climbing days." To his editor he wrote, "Six of the sixteen chapters are new, and the others nearly so, for I have worked hard on every one of them, leaning them against each other, adding lots of new stuff, and killing adjectives and adverbs of redundant growth." Muir went on to invite his editor to read the opening chapter: "In it I have ventured to drop into the poetry that I like, but have taken good care to place it between bluffs and buttresses of bald, glacial, geological facts."

The book opened with an overview of the Sierra Nevada range, in which that "poetry" was evident:

After ten years spent in the heart of it, rejoicing and wondering, bathing in its glorious floods of light, seeing the sunbursts of morning among the icy peaks, the noonday radiance on the trees and rocks and snow, the flush of the alpenglow, and a thousand dashing waterfalls with their marvellous abundance of irised spray, it still seems to be above all others the Range of Light, the most divinely beautiful of all the mountain chains I have ever seen.

In subsequent chapters Muir wove scientific recordings, vivid observations, and anecdotes of explorations and encounters in the range. He gave separate chapters to "The Water-Ouzel," "The Douglas Squirrel," "The Wild Sheep," and "The Bee-Pastures." Some of the material was taken from the journals that were later published as *My First Summer in the Sierra,* and some set pieces were anecdotes already shaped and published in periodicals.

The chapter titled "A Near View of the High Sierra," for example, was his already published account of becoming cragfast on the first ascent of Mount Rutter, which has become one of the classics of American mountaineering literature. Hammering ice off the holds with stones, high on the exposed rock face and beyond possibility of descent, Muir became unable to move. "My doom appeared fixed," he wrote.

I *must* fall. There would be a moment of bewilderment, and then a lifeless rumble down the one general precipice to the glacier below. When this final danger flashed upon me, I became nerve-shaken for the first time since setting foot on the mountains, and my mind seemed to fill with a stifling smoke. But this terrible eclipse lasted only a moment, when life blazed forth

with preternatural clearness. I seemed to become possessed of a new sense. The other self, bygone experiences, instinct, or Guardian Angel—call it what you will—came forward and assumed control. Then my trembling muscles became firm again, every rift and flaw in the rock was seen as through a microscope, and my limbs moved with a positiveness and precision with which I seemed to have nothing at all to do.

One of the twin purposes of the Sierra Club was the enjoyment of mountaineering, and for Muir a salutary chapter about tuning in to the rock faces by the calm application of "bygone experiences" was as important to the enjoyment of the Sierra as the scientific information of the other chapters of *The Mountains of California.*

Muir's studies had shown the importance of forests for water supply in California. In 1891 President Harrison had created the first national forest reserves, but pressure from timber interests required a survey of national priorities. Consequently, in 1896 Muir joined the Forestry Commission under the leadership of Charles S. Sargent, traveling from Nebraska to Wyoming, Montana, Washington, Oregon, and northern California. Everywhere the problems of timber theft were worse than anyone had been aware, leaving barren watersheds, eroding topsoils, and overgrazed foothills on both private and public land. But a conflict emerged between Muir and young Gifford Pinochet, the secretary of the commission, which was to represent a basic difference in notions of conservation in American culture. For Pinochet "the first principle of conservation is development." He believed in conserving resources for their "wise use" by ensuring that they were renewable. Muir wanted to keep some of the climax forests of the nation free from human intervention for their natural regeneration. This debate became a vibrant one when the commission sought to restrict the exploitation of the remaining great forests of America, which, although once stretching across the whole country, now only remained in the West. Therefore, Muir turned his writing skills to the service of these forests.

In a series of articles for Eastern journals such as *Harper's Weekly* and *The Atlantic Monthly,* Muir wrote with all his rhetorical power to draw attention to the crisis facing the greatest natural resource of America. By now Muir was a national figure who had been awarded an honorary degree from Harvard in 1896 and from his alma mater, the University of Wisconsin, the following year. He commanded a wide readership across the nation, and he addressed his readers with a national overview. Significantly, Muir wrote as though the new forest reserves were also national parks, speaking of both together in the first of his articles in 1897. When he came to realize that his second book needed to awaken the nation to the importance of national parks, he opened *Our National Parks* (1901) with the article "The Wild Parks and Forest Reservations of the West." Its first two sentences have become Muir's most famous and sum up his crucial argument most succinctly: "The tendency nowadays to wander in wildernesses is delightful to see. Thousands of tired, nerve-shaken, over-civilized people are beginning to find that going to the mountains is going home; that wildness is a necessity; that mountain parks and reservations are useful not only as fountains of timber and irrigating rivers, but as fountains of life."

Muir's argument was with American materialism and creation of wealth. The American people, he went on to argue, had lost their connection with their natural selves as they had with their natural environment: "Doing so much good and making so much money—or so little—they are no longer good for themselves." The self-destructiveness of a society alienated from nature is an argument that modern environmentalists borrow from Muir in contemporary debates about toxic waste and global warming. A true civilization, Muir implied, was not one that had lost its awareness of the fundamental source of its life and health. He did not discount the value and uses of timber. He had himself run a sawmill in Yosemite Valley using fallen wood. But the conservation of water sources should not be considered as somehow separate from the spiritual renewal of the American people. In a truly advanced civilization, Muir believed, these "fountains" of work, water, and wonder would flow from the same integrated source.

The essay with which Muir chose to conclude *Our National Parks* was an article he had published in *The Atlantic Monthly* in 1897. It was his most passionate defense of old-growth forests and represents, again, a shrewd line of argument on behalf of his adopted land. Muir began his conclusion to the essay with a sharp awareness of the position from which he made this intervention in American culture:

> The United States government has always been proud of the welcome it has extended to good men of every nation. . . . Let them be welcomed as nature welcomes them, to the woods as well as to the prairies and plains. . . . Mere destroyers, however, tree-killers, wool and mutton men, spreading death and confusion in the fairest groves and gardens ever planted—let the government hasten to cast them out and make an end of them. For . . . the axe and the saw are insanely busy, chips are flying thick as snowflakes, and every summer thousands of acres of priceless forests, with their underbrush, soil, springs, climate, scenery and religion, are vanishing away in clouds of smoke, while, except in the national parks, not one forest guard is employed.

Sweeping Back the Flood

Editorial cartoon ridiculing Muir's efforts to block the building of a dam in the Hetch-Hetchy Valley of Yosemite National Park to create a reservoir for the city of San Francisco (from the San Francisco Call, *circa 1909)*

From a broad appeal to the American spirit, to a criticism of the weak enforcement by the government of restraints upon that spirit, this was strong rhetoric and a risky intellectual strategy. But in his final paragraph Muir staked his argument on an appeal to religion and the state, on an instinct that religious family culture could influence national culture at this time in America. It was his personal test of the democracy to which he had committed himself.

> Any fool can destroy trees. They cannot run away. . . . Few that fell trees plant them; nor would planting avail much towards getting back anything like the noble primeval forests. During a man's life only saplings can be grown, in the place of old trees—tens of centuries old—that have been destroyed. It took more than three thousand years to make some of the trees in these Western woods—trees that are still standing in perfect strength and beauty, waving and singing in the mighty forests of the Sierra. Through all the wonderful, eventful centuries since Christ's time—and long before that—God has cared for these trees, saved them from drought, disease, avalanches and a thousand straining, levelling tempests and floods; but he cannot save them from fools—only Uncle Sam can do that.

Muir could remember that when he first crossed the Central Valley of California he had been walking through a continuous meadow of wildflowers. Now, he wrote, that has been "ploughed and pastured out of existence, gone forever." He believed that the fate of the forests would be the same, leaving ground like that in the Sierra "desolate and repulsive, like a face ravaged by disease." Even the wildest parts of the country, Muir argued, would eventually succumb to this ravaged state "unless awakening public opinion comes forward to stop it." Crucial to Muir's attempt to rally public opinion on behalf of remaining wild land was the notion that it would be of healing value to the human spirit in industrial America. He urged "business-tangled" Americans to visit the Bitter Root Reserve, for example, where, in a few minutes from the railway station at Belton, "you will find yourself in the midst of what you are sure to say is the best care-killing scenery on the continent." Ever the realist, Muir offered both practical advice as well as inspiration for the "re-creation" of the urban businessman and -woman. But simply looking at scenery was only the first natural and necessary step in the process of tuning in to nature. Muir knew that the deepest renewal would only come by the application of a discipline of attention exercising the whole mind and imagination: "When you are calm enough for discriminating observation, you will find the king of the larches, one of the best of the Western giants, beautiful, picturesque, and regal in port, easily the grandest of all the larches in the world." Such "discriminating observation" of nature, Muir went on to argue, can so renew the inner life of alienated urban "over-civilised" Americans as to actually prolong their lives: "Give a month at least to this precious reserve. The time will not be taken from the sum of your life. Instead of shortening, it will lengthen it and make you truly immortal." It was Muir's holistic vision that produced the rhetorical strategy of his writing. Tuning in to natural rhythms through relaxed observation would, Muir believed, lead to the saving of both the forests and the people, benefiting both nature and culture. Muir saw that, in his time, nature needed culture just as culture needed nature.

After the assassination of President William McKinley in 1901, a new president came into office, one who knew something of the healing power of nature from his own retreats at moments of personal crisis. Theodore Roosevelt was mountain climbing in the Adirondacks when McKinley died. President Roosevelt immediately announced that the most urgent problems confronting the nation were those concerning forests and water. When he requested a camping trip with John Muir in Yosemite Park, Muir's campaigning on behalf of forests was well known, but the issue of water was not yet on Muir's agenda. In fact, as early as 1901 Mayor James D. Phelan had begun moves to acquire rights to water within Yosemite National Park. He was convinced that the flooding of the Hetch Hetchy Valley would become necessary to ensure the need of the growing city for water. In February 1901 Congress quietly approved a bill to grant rights of way for water conduits through national parks in the public interest. The San Francisco earthquake and subsequent fires in 1906 brought the need for an improved water supply into public debate, and in 1908 Roosevelt's secretary of the interior, James R. Garfield, granted the city rights to Hetch Hetchy, although Garfield's successor later referred the matter to a commission. Muir and the Sierra Club faced a severe test of their ability to defend the integrity of the national park and the philosophy of conservation that underpinned it. For more than six years he was embattled in a bitter dispute with the city of San Francisco and the Pinochet philosophy of the "wise use" of resources in the public interest, even within a national park. Phelan accused Muir of considering Yosemite his private reserve and declared that Muir would "sacrifice his own family for the preservation of beauty." In 1908 California representative William Kent gifted a grove of redwoods to the nation that was to be named "Muir Woods." But in a late stage of the Hetch Hetchy debate, Kent described Muir as "a man entirely without social sense."

In 1912 Muir wrote to a friend, "Next month I mean to bring together a lot of Yosemite material into a handbook for travellers, which ought to have been written long ago. But the reason why it is needed now was [sic] that public opinion, based upon visits to Yosemite Valley, should raise its voice against the desecration of 'other Yosemites.'" As usual, Muir did not find the book-writing process easy, especially since his wife had died in 1905. "I'm in my old library den," he wrote, "the house desolate, nobody living in it save a hungry mouse or two." To another friend two years earlier he had written, "As for myself, I've been reading old musty, dusty Yosemite notes until I'm tired and blinky blind, trying to arrange them in lateral, medial, and terminal moraines on my den floor." *The Yosemite* (1912) takes the reader through Yosemite Valley—with information, anecdotes, and excursions—toward the threatened Hetch Hetchy. The final chapter begins: "Yosemite is so wonderful that we are apt to regard it as an exceptional creation, the only valley of its kind in the world; but Nature is not so poor as to have only one of anything." The chapter ends by pointing out that the plan to dam Hetch Hetchy is in the balance, still "under consideration" by the commission. Commentators have noted the reversion to an Old Testament language in the final sentences of *The Yosemite*:

*President William Howard Taft and Muir (standing in wagon, second from left and far right) during a 1909
tour of Yosemite National Park (John Muir Papers, Holt-Atherton Special Collections,
University of the Pacific Library; © 1984 Muir-Hanna Trust)*

"These temple destroyers, devotees of raging commercialism, seem to have a perfect contempt for Nature, and, instead of lifting their eyes to the God of the mountains, lift them to the Almighty Dollar. Dam Hetch Hetchy! As well dam for water tanks the people's cathedrals and churches, for no holier temple has ever been consecrated by the heart of man."

After writing these words, Muir set out on his long-planned trip to the Amazon. It has been the common practice to conclude the story of Muir's life with the suggestion that his death in 1914 was partly precipitated by the loss of the battle to save Hetch Hetchy in the previous year. But the recent publication of Muir's journals and correspondence from his eight-month trip to South America and Africa during 1911–1912 has prompted the view that he might have died as much fulfilled as frustrated. South America had been the ultimate goal of his walk to the Gulf of Mexico and remained "a dream long deferred." Muir had taken other trips abroad late in his life and was now being regarded as a world traveler as well as a champion of the Sierra. In 1893 he returned to Scotland before going on to observe glaciation in Europe. A decade later he set out with Sargent on a world tour that lasted from May 1903 to May 1904. This trip, which was primarily intended as a study of the trees of the world, took Muir through Russia to China, then on to India, where he saw the Himalayas before getting a boat to Egypt for the Pyramids. From there he went via Ceylon to Australia and New Zealand, making his way home through Malaysia, Japan, and Hawaii.

In August 1911 Muir wrote the final fiery sentences of *The Yosemite* in New York before boarding a ship bound for the Amazon. In South America, reporters followed him as an internationally famous wilderness sage and conservationist. Muir found the flora he had longed to see in the Amazon Basin and crossed the Andes into Chile before taking a ship to Cape Town, visiting Lake Victoria, the headwaters of the Nile, and returning home via the Suez Canal, Naples, and Gibraltar. He undertook this trip for the pleasure of personal study and not for the purpose of publications. In his maturity he had a wise sense of the priorities in his writing projects. Before leaving, Muir had listed all of the ten outstanding books he still wanted to write. In March 1911, while working on *The Yosemite,* he was correcting the proofs of *My First Summer in the Sierra* and also preparing a first volume of autobiography for his publisher. "I do not know what has got into me, making so many books at once," he wrote. "It is not natural."

In New York, Muir had arranged for the serial publication of *The Story of My Boyhood and Youth* (1913). The brutal honesty with which he described his school-ing in Scotland and his father's treatment of his eldest son as they made a farm out of the Wisconsin wilds shocked even members of his own family. What was intended as a first volume of autobiography took his life up to his "leaving one University for another, the Wisconsin University for the University of the Wilderness." This book might never have been written at all had Muir not been bullied into it by the railway tycoon, E. H. Harriman, with whom he had visited Alaska. In the summer of 1908 Harriman took Muir to his lodge on Klamath Lake, Oregon, and instructed his secretary to follow Muir on all his walks, taking dictated notes that Muir later reworked for the serial publication of *The Story of My Boyhood and Youth* in *The Atlantic Monthly,* 1912–1913.

In December 1913 the Senate passed the bill granting San Francisco the use of Hetch Hetchy. Two years earlier, as he set out for his circumnavigation of the world alone at the age of seventy-three, Muir had written in a letter to Betty Averell (2 March 1911) that he felt younger than he did during his first summer in the Sierra. "This, in part, is the reward of those who climb mountains and keep their noses outdoors," he said. At the news that his final conservation battle had been lost, Muir resolved to accept it stoically and put it behind him. In that year he was delighted and encouraged by the award of an honorary degree from the University of California at Berkeley. Yale had made a similar award two years before, and when Muir was in New York that year, the American Alpine Club held a dinner in his honor. Biographer Frederick Turner has said that toward the end of Muir's life, his image "had become as much a part of the national consciousness as the image of Buffalo Bill Cody." In the foggy winter of 1914 Muir caught the flu at home before he went to visit his daughter Helen and new grandson in the Mojave Desert at Daggart. His flu turned into pneumonia, and John Muir died in the California Hospital in Los Angeles on Christmas Eve 1914. The previous year he had written in his journal, "I only went out for a walk, and finally decided to stay out till sundown, for going out, I found, was really going in."

Muir had taken with him into the hospital the papers he was working on for a book of his Alaskan explorations. The almost completed manuscript of *Travels in Alaska* (1915) was brought to publication by Marion Randall Parsons, the widow of an old Sierra Club friend who was acting as his secretary. This book includes some of Muir's most remarkable mature thinking, embedded, as ever, in the detail of the three trips described in the book. Although Muir made two other journeys to Alaska, in 1881 and 1899, *Travels in Alaska* documents the three trips of 1879, 1880, and 1890. More than half the book is concerned with

Muir's first trip of 1879, which is also the subject of Samuel Hall Young's book *Alaska Days with John Muir* (1915). Muir traveled on a ship taking missionaries to convert the Inuit peoples around Fort Wrangell, whom Muir referred to as "Indians." The ship was met by the resident missionary, Samuel Hall Young, who befriended Muir and went with him on his botanical hikes. Finding himself on a mountain scramble, Young fell and dislocated both shoulders. Muir's rescue of Young became a famous story, which Muir retold in *Travels in Alaska* in order to counter a "miserable, sensational" version that had appeared. But for Muir the highlight of this section of the book was a canoe trip into Glacier Bay guided by the Indian chief Toyatte, whom Muir described as "a grand old Stickeen nobleman." Muir admired the way Toyatte was at one with his environment, not just surviving but doing so with a graceful dignity. The respect was returned as the Indians came to call Muir "the Ice Chief."

The 1880 trip became famous for the exploits of Young's little dog, which followed Muir on one glacier exploration. This story became so popular in Muir's retelling of it that he published it in 1909 as a book, *Stickeen*. Ronald Limbaugh's research into the making of this book is revealing in its philosophical dimensions. In *Travels in Alaska* Muir wrote of this dog: "He enlarged my life, extended its boundaries. I saw through him down into the depths of our common nature." Such humility combined with his deep sense of awe enabled Muir to listen attentively to the processes of nature among which he lived. Toward the end of the Alaska book he reflects upon the paradox of the huge destructive power of the glaciers as a creative force in sublime landscapes: "Out of all the cold darkness and glacial crushing and grinding comes this warm abounding beauty and life to teach us that what we in our faithless ignorance and fear call destruction is creation finer and finer." This image of a creative-destructive universe holds the core of Muir's vision of nature. In the late writing of *Travels in Alaska* Muir demonstrates a cosmic sense of nature that can surface in characteristically whimsical images. A dewdrop, for example, provides an image for a holistic sense of a dynamic universe: "When we contemplate the whole globe as one great dewdrop, striped and dotted with continents and islands, flying through space with other stars all singing and shining together as one, the whole universe appears as an infinite storm of beauty." Those final four words can act as a summary of Muir's notion of nature.

Muir's writing has greater significance than that of the founder of national parks and the American conservation movement. Located in a largely nineteenth-century prose discourse of scientific observation, philosophical reflection, and wilderness advocacy is a notion

Binding from Muir's 1911 book, based on the journal he kept during his 1869 trip to the Yosemite Valley (Ken Lopez catalogue, 2000)

of nature that anticipated modern ecology and harmonized nature and culture. Frederick Turner has written that Muir's "most significant American discovery had been a way to love the land and to extend that love to the society at large." Thinking of Muir's mentors, Emerson and Thoreau, Turner argued that Muir actually achieved what they were seeking: "In his own life he had reconciled the conflict between democratic individualism and participatory democracy." Muir's vision of nature included himself and his fellows. Muir the mountaineer only fell once in his life, when scrambling in the Sierra after a visit to the city. He knocked himself unconscious and woke on the brink of a drop into Tenaya Canyon. "That is what you get by intercourse with stupid town stairs and dead pavements," he recorded. Throughout his life Muir actually commuted between the city and the wild in the modern manner. He was also a successful horticultural businessman. But through the discipline of tuning in to the natural world, upon each return to it he could take risks in the mountains and trust his own judgment. In the modes of mountaineer, scientist, agriculturalist and writer, Muir demonstrated to the American people the possibility of an accommodation with the great American landscapes. He showed that an inner enlargement could be made by learning to be at home in the distinctively American natural environment. His essays and books remain popular because they are allegories of attuned ecological living.

John Muir could turn a lifestyle into a powerful and enduring social movement for his adopted country because he quickly developed a prose tool that was both accessible and flexible. Muir's stance as an innocent enthusiast helped engage his audience. He rarely explicitly philosophized in an abstract manner, although he could finally come to preaching when necessary. His skill was in combining a fluency of sentence structure with a deft use of concrete imagery that frequently became metaphor. To some modern tastes Muir's prose is too rich and too hyperbolic at times. He knew that he had to prune his adjectives and adverbs in redrafting his work for publication. Johnson and other editors, for example, urged him to reduce his use of the word *glorious*. But Muir's prose is always at the service of his home planet. His writings retain a significance and influence as mankind continues to search for a right relationship with nature. Muir's notion of civilization assumes a culture that continues that search. Muir's composure, his sense of himself with an inner nature attuned to external nature, is ultimately the basis for the power of his prose. Playfully, joyously, and with profound purpose, Muir used culture on behalf of reuniting culture and nature. His writings continue to have great influence.

Letters:

Letters to a Friend, Written to Mrs. Ezra S. Carr, 1866–1879 (Boston & New York: Houghton Mifflin, 1915);

William Frederick Badè, ed., *The Life and Letters of John Muir,* 2 volumes (Boston: Houghton Mifflin, 1924);

Terry Gifford, ed., *John Muir: His Life and Letters and Other Writings* (Seattle: Mountaineers, 1996);

Bonnie Johanna Gisel, ed., *Kindred Spirits and Related Spirits: The Letters of John Muir and Jeanne C. Carr* (Salt Lake City: University of Utah Press, 2001);

Michael P. Branch, ed., *John Muir's Last Journey, South to the Amazon and East to Africa: Unpublished Journals and Selected Correspondence* (Washington, D.C.: Island Press/Shearwater Books, 2001).

Bibliography:

William F. Kimes and Maymie B. Kimes, *John Muir: A Reading Bibliography* (Palo Alto, Cal.: Wrenden, 1977).

Biographies:

Linnie Marsh Wolfe, *Son of the Wilderness: The Life of John Muir* (New York: Knopf, 1945);

Stephen R. Fox, *The American Conservation Movement: John Muir and His Legacy* (Madison: University of Wisconsin Press, 1981);

Frederick Turner, *Rediscovering America: John Muir in His Time and Ours* (San Francisco: Sierra Club, 1985);

Thurman Wilkins, *John Muir: Apostle of Nature* (Norman: University of Oklahoma Press, 1996);

Steven Holmes, *The Young John Muir: An Environmental Biography* (Madison: University of Wisconsin Press, 1999).

References:

Michael P. Cohen, *The Pathless Way: John Muir and American Wilderness* (Madison: University of Wisconsin Press, 1984);

Ronald H. Limbaugh, *John Muir's "Stickeen" and the Lessons of Nature* (Fairbanks: University of Alaska Press, 1996);

Sally M. Miller, ed., *John Muir in Historical Perspective* (New York: Peter Lang, 1999);

Miller, ed., *John Muir: Life and Work* (Albuquerque: University of New Mexico Press, 1993);

Samuel Hall Young, *Alaska Days with John Muir* (New York: Fleming H. Revell, 1915).

Papers:

The major part of John Muir's papers is collected in the John Muir Papers, Holt-Atherton Special Collections, University of the Pacific Library, Stockton, California. These have been catalogued in the microform edition by Ronald H. Limbaugh and Kirsten E. Lewis, *The Guide and Index to the Microform Edition of the John Muir Papers, 1858–1957* (Alexandria, Va.: Chadwyck-Healey, 1986). The books from Muir's library, many of them annotated, are divided between the Holt-Atherton Library, University of the Pacific (broadly, the scientific books), and the Huntington Library, San Marino, California (broadly, the literary books).

Richard K. Nelson
(1 December 1941 –)

Shin Yamashiro
University of Nevada, Reno

BOOKS: *Literature Review of Eskimo Knowledge of the Sea Ice Environment* (Fort Wainwright, Alaska: Arctic Aeromedical Laboratory, 1966);

Alaskan Eskimo Exploitation of the Sea Ice Environment (Fort Wainwright, Alaska: Arctic Aeromedical Laboratory, 1966);

Hunters of the Northern Ice (Chicago & London: University of Chicago Press, 1969);

Hunters of the Northern Forest: Designs for Survival among the Alaskan Kutchin (Chicago & London: University of Chicago Press, 1973);

Kuuvangmiit: Contemporary Subsistence Living in the Latter Twentieth Century, by Nelson, Douglas D. Anderson, Wanni W. Anderson, Ray Bane, and Nita Sheldon (Washington, D.C.: National Park Service, 1978);

Tracks in the Wildland: A Portrayal of Koyukon and Nunamiut Subsistence, by Nelson, Kathleen H. Mautner, and G. Ray Bane, Occasional paper no. 9 (Fairbanks, Alaska: Anthropology and Historic Preservation, Cooperative Park Studies Unit, University of Alaska, Fairbanks, 1978);

Shadow of the Hunter: Stories of Eskimo Life (Chicago & London: University of Chicago Press, 1980);

Harvest of the Sea: Coastal Subsistence in Modern Wainwright: A Report for the North Slope Borough's Coastal Management Program (Barrow, Alaska: North Slope Borough, 1982);

Make Prayers to the Raven: A Koyukon View of the Northern Forest (Chicago: University of Chicago Press, 1983);

The Athabaskans: People of the Boreal Forest, edited by Terry P. Dickey and Mary Beth Smetzel (Fairbanks: University of Alaska Museum, 1983);

The Island Within (San Francisco: North Point Press, 1989);

Heart and Blood: Living with Deer in America (New York: Knopf, 1997).

PRODUCED SCRIPT: *Make Prayers to the Raven,* KUAC-TV, University of Alaska, Fairbanks, 1987.

Richard K. Nelson (photograph from the dust jacket for Shadow of the Hunter, *1980)*

OTHER: "Forest Resources in the Culture and Economy of Native Alaskans," in *North American Forest Lands at Latitudes North of 60 Degrees: Proceedings of a Symposium Held at the University of Alaska, Fairbanks, September 19, 20, 21 and 22, 1977* (Fairbanks: University of Alaska, Fairbanks, 1978), pp. 207–225;

"A Conservation Ethic and Environment: The Koyukon of Alaska," in *Resource Managers: North American and Australian Hunter-Gatherers,* edited by Eugene Hunn and Nancy Williams (Boulder, Colo.: Westview Press for the American Association for the Advancement of Science, 1982);

"A Mirror on Their Lives: Capturing the Human Experience," in *Sharing Alaska's Oral History: Proceedings of the Conference Held at the Captain Cook Hotel, Anchorage, Alaska, October 26 & 27, 1982,* edited by William Schneider (Fairbanks: University of Alaska Press, 1983), pp. 15–36;

Resource Use in a Small Alaskan City, Sitka, by George Gmelch and Sharon Bohn Gmelch, with the assistance of Nelson (Juneau: Alaska Department of Fish and Game, Division of Subsistence, 1984);

Interior Alaska: A Journey through Time, edited by Nelson and Jean Aigner (Alaska: Alaska Geographic Society, 1986);

"An Elder of the Tribe," in *Gary Snyder: Dimensions of a Life,* edited by Jon Halper (San Francisco: Sierra Club Books, 1991), pp. 344–351;

"A Letter from Richard Nelson," in *For Love of the World: Essays on Nature Writers,* by Sherman Paul (Iowa City: University of Iowa Press, 1992), pp. 163–176;

"Searching the Hunter's World," in *The Biophilia Hypothesis,* edited by Stephen R. Kellert and E. O. Wilson (Washington, D.C.: Island Press, 1993), pp. 201–228;

David Petersen, ed., *A Hunter's Heart: Honest Essays on Blood Sport,* introduction by Nelson (New York: Holt, 1996);

Jules Jette and Eliza Jones, *Koyukon Athabaskan Dictionary,* preface by Nelson (Fairbanks, Alaska: Alaska Native Language Center, University of Alaska Fairbanks, 2000).

SELECTED PERIODICAL PUBLICATIONS–
UNCOLLECTED: "Athabaskan Subsistence Adaptations in Alaska," *Senri Ethnological Studies,* 4 (1980): 205–232;

"Hunters and Animals in Native Land: Ancient Ways of the New Century," *Orion,* 8 (Spring 1989): 48–53;

"Alaska: A Glint in the Raven's Eye," *Wilderness,* 54 (Winter 1990): 20–21;

"The Embrace of Names," *Northern Lights,* 8 (1992): 18–19;

"Understanding Eskimo Science," *Audubon,* 95 (September/October 1993): 102–108;

"Contributor to The Place Where You Live," *Orion,* 14 (Spring 1995): 24;

"Forest Home," *Orion,* 16 (Summer 1997): 58–63;

"Beyond Understanding," *Orion,* 16 (Autumn 1997): 22–25;

"Patriots for the American Land," *Orion,* 4 (Winter 1999/2000): 3;

"Where the Sea Turns to Siku," *Sports Afield,* 223 (2000): 63–66.

Reviewing Richard K. Nelson's *Heart and Blood: Living with Deer in America* (1997) for *The New York Times Book Review* (30 November 1997), Robert Finch observed, "Nelson, more than any writer I know, has actually attempted to live out this Native American worldview." Having studied the lives of Arctic Eskimos and Native Americans in Alaska for about twenty-five years and written anthropological and ethnographic monographs, Nelson's nature writing has emerged from his scientific knowledge of their cultures and from his active participation in their lifeways, revealing his profound engagement with his subjects and his respect for their points of view.

Richard King Nelson was born on 1 December 1941 in Madison, Wisconsin, to Robert King Nelson, a state employee, and Florence Olson Nelson. In 1959 Richard Nelson enrolled at the University of Wisconsin, Madison, planning to major in zoology, but he soon found that he was more interested in a broad view of people and animals and how they relate to each other in the environment. Changing his major to anthropology, he started working with William Laughlin, a leading specialist on the Alaskan people and their culture, and took part in two summer research projects in Alaska. As he said in a 1983 interview with Michael A. Armstrong, Nelson had a "feeling that the way to learn about nature was through the traditions of native people, that their knowledge of nature was much greater and more profound than the knowledge I was getting from my zoology professors." After earning a B.S. in 1964, Nelson began work on a master's degree at Wisconsin, spending a year in 1964–1965 in the Alaskan village of Wainwright as a participant in a United States Air Force project. He learned Eskimo survival skills on the Arctic sea ice, living the native existence as closely as possible and recording what he learned for a military survival manual. The immediate results of his year in Alaska were two ethnographic studies, *Literature Review of Eskimo Knowledge of the Sea Ice Environment* and *Alaskan Eskimo Exploitation of the Sea Ice Environment,* both published in 1966. His experiences also led to his long-term engagement with the native cultures of Alaska.

The University of Chicago Press later gave Nelson the opportunity to consolidate his two reports into a single book, which was published as *Hunters of the Northern Ice* in 1969 and also served as his master's thesis. After earning an M.S. in anthropology at Wisconsin in 1968, Nelson entered a doctoral program at the University of California, Santa Barbara, earning a Ph.D. in anthropology in 1971. Based on Nelson's experiences during a year (1969) spent with the Kutchin Athabaskans in the forested interior of northern Alaska, Nelson's next book, *Hunters of the Northern Forest: Designs for Survival among the Alaskan Kutchin* (1973), also served as his doctoral dissertation. In both *Hunters of the Northern Ice* and *Hunters of the Northern Forest,* Nelson stresses the importance of "active"

*Dust jacket for the collection of short fiction Nelson has called his attempt "to give a more sensory account
of Eskimo people and their Arctic environment" (Richland County Public Library)*

or "full" participation, explaining that "the most 'competent' understanding comes through actual participation," as he says in the latter text. In practicing such "active" involvement, Nelson has learned not only about other cultures, but also, through comparison, about his own.

After receiving his Ph.D. in 1971, Nelson taught at the University of Hawaii, Honolulu (1971–1972); Memorial University of Newfoundland, St. Johns (1972–1973); the University of California, Santa Barbara (1978); and the University of California, Santa Cruz (1979). In 1973–1977 he was a research associate at the University of Alaska, Fairbanks. During the 1980s he was able to devote more of his time to writing and research while maintaining ties to the University of Alaska as an affiliate associate professor, and in the 1990s he was at the University of California, Davis, as a scholar in residence. Despite his achievements as a scholar, Nelson has never been comfortable in a university setting and prefers writing to teaching.

Shadow of the Hunter: Stories of Eskimo Life (1980), which he began in 1971 while still a graduate student at Santa Barbara, grew out of a desire to try a different approach to writing about nature and culture. As he told *Contemporary Authors,* he turned to fiction in an attempt "to give a more sensory account of Eskimo people and their Arctic environment, to present accurate information in a readable style, and to allow myself a chance for creative expression." In *Shadow of the Hunter* ten short stories named for the months of the Eskimo lunar calendar depict the Eskimos' ways of hunting and living in severe Arctic environments. Nelson's introduction explains that the book "does not claim to be *truth* in any absolute sense" because people and events are fictionalized. It is "only one person's view of Eskimo culture, and so its accuracy is always open to question" because "there are as many truths as there are observers."

While Nelson calls *Shadow of the Hunter* fiction, it is in fact a mixture of scientific discourse and literary expression, with clear and extensive documentation of his sources. Though *Shadow of the Hunter* is based on Nelson's scientific research, it focuses not merely on the facts of Eskimo culture but also on the emotions and experiences of people interacting with the environment.

Nelson on the island near his home in the Pacific Northwest where he kept the journals that were the basis for his 1989 book (photograph from the dust jacket for The Island Within)

While working on *Shadow of the Hunter*, Nelson continued to produce scholarly anthropological writings on Alaskan peoples and cultures. *Tracks in the Wildland: A Portrayal of Koyukon and Nunamiut Subsistence* (1978), *Harvest of the Sea: Coastal Subsistence in Modern Wainwright* (1982), and *The Athabaskans: People of the Boreal Forest* (1983) reveal Nelson's involvement in political efforts to protect the Alaskan environment and its native cultures. Nelson expressed political concerns as early as "The Death of Hunting" in his 1969 book, *Hunters of the Northern Ice*. In his scholarly writings of the late 1970s and early 1980s, he examined Native American lifeways in broad sociopolitical contexts, linking the disappearance of traditional Alaskan life with factors such as rapid population growth following the construction of the Alaska oil pipeline and increasing competition for a diminishing natural resource. Another contributing factor was the Alaska Native Claims Settlement Act (1971), which divided Alaskan lands among private owners, thus depriving native peoples of traditional tribal hunting grounds. Through scholarly writings on Alaska and its people and political efforts on their behalf, Nelson tries to preserve a culture that might otherwise be lost. Nelson's political activism has continued in later work such as *The Island Within* (1989) and *Heart and Blood* (1997).

Make Prayers to the Raven: A Koyukon View of the Northern Forest (1983) is based on Nelson's fieldwork among the Koyukon Athabaskan Indians, describing their traditional methods of surviving in the Alaskan environment and their beliefs about nature. It was the basis for a documentary television series, which aired in 1987. The book begins with Nelson's encounters with a raven–an omnipotent clown representing both genius and playfulness in the Koyukon belief system–and ends with Nelson's reflections on the raven. These personal, first-person narratives sandwich anthropological observations of the Koyukon and their natural environment. Nelson's introduction calls the book a "blend of empiricism and emotion" that represents "the whole reality." The thematically organized chapters resemble those of Nelson's scholarly books, but Nelson also includes his journal entries throughout the book to reveal his personal perspective on the material. The book is not a complete "blend of empiricism and emotion," because Nelson keeps his reflections separate from the Native American anecdotes he records and from his scientific data and observations. Even so, Nelson as narrator is ultimately a more visible presence in *Make Prayers to the Raven* than in his previous books, preparing readers for the personal perspective presented in his later books of nature writing.

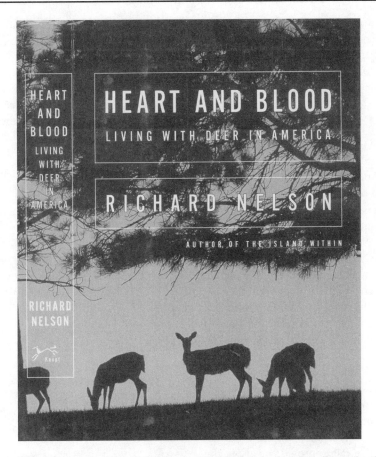

Dust jacket for Nelson's 1997 book, in which he defends hunting as an ecologically sound method
of maintaining a healthy deer population (Richland County Public Library)

The Island Within (1989) is a collection of essays based on Nelson's life on an unnamed island near his home in the Pacific Northwest, where he hunts, observes, and reflects on deer and other animals. He hopes "to acclaim the rewards of exploring the place in which a person lives rather than search afar, of becoming fully involved with the near-at-hand, and of nurturing a deeper relationship with home." Based on thousands of pages of Nelson's journal entries, the book is an account of his efforts to understand the island and his relationship to it. Nelson discusses his experiences hunting deer, the natural history of the island, his family, and the ways in which he has come to terms with the island. When he worked with the Eskimos and Athabaskans, Nelson depended on hunting as a primary source of food, practicing traditional Native American lifeways to survive. *The Island Within* depicts such methods. As a hunter who lives on the animals of the island, Nelson is so keenly absorbed in watching and stalking them that he seems to become like his prey:

I become absorbed in the process of moving quietly, staring ahead through the variegated leaves and branches. I feel the air against me, like a body of clear get-invisible flesh that fills the space inside the forest and covers the hard bones of rock underneath. . . . I move through them like a microorganism swimming inside a huge animal. I touch a spruce bough and sense it feeling me, as if it's becoming a nerve inside my own body, or inside the larger body [that] encompasses us.

Through his uses of first-person, present-tense narration in the style of a personal journal, Nelson creates a sense of immediacy and directness. The "larger body" is the island itself, and, crossing the boundary between humans and nonhuman nature, Nelson becomes part of the island and its ecological cycle. He has learned from his Native American teachers how to gain access to the animals' perspective, paying attention to their lifeways with reverence for other worldviews. As a predator he takes food from the island for his family, and, as a member of the ecological cycle of the island, he acknowledges that he is part of the food chain, not on top of it. *The Island*

Within is about Nelson's way of gaining a sense of place. Nelson encourages readers to think of the book not as a travel guide but as a "guide to nontravel," reminding them that they can nurture a deeper relationship with "the near-at-hand" through active involvement with their own places.

In *Heart and Blood* (1997) Nelson depicts deer not only as beautiful wild animals but also as occupiers of an ecological niche, showing readers how each individual who lives on agricultural products has a vested interest in the issues of hunting and controlling animal populations. Tracing his life from his youth—when he considered hunting "atavistic, arrogant, and immoral"—until he lived by hunting in Alaska, Nelson shows the process by which he concluded that hunting is the most environmentally effective way to maintain an ecologically sound relationship with the deer. With his dog, Nita, Nelson participates in the scenes he depicts, observing humans, animals, and natural phenomena and reflecting on the relationships between people and deer in this world. He talks to people such as farmers, scientists, ranchers, and animal-rights activists and writes more about what individuals can do to protect the environment. "The supermarket is an agent of our forgetfulness," he writes, suggesting that people tend to forget that human beings, especially dwellers in cities and suburbs, tend not to think about the animals that die to provide neatly packaged meat for grocery stores. He calls hunting a "biological process," a means by which to express respect for other living creatures and to be reminded of humankind's connectedness to them. Nelson does not avoid discussing the paradox of loving deer with deep compassion and, at the same time, stalking and killing them with a hunter's excitement. He considers ecologically sensitive, responsible hunting to be an effective way to practice conservation and a powerful way to create an awareness of the animals that die to feed humans.

Nelson has won the John Burroughs Medal (1991) for *The Island Within* and a Lifetime Achievement Award (1995) from the Lannan Foundation. Nature writer and ethnobotanist Gary Paul Nabhan has suggested that what distinguishes Nelson's writing from that of his contemporaries is its evocation of the senses through the recreation of the many sounds and scents of animals. Another nature writer, Rick Bass, admires Nelson's ways of telling stories through the eye of the hunter and the hunted, his methods of getting as close to a thing as pos-

sible in order "not so much to create metaphors as to uncover them" (*Orion*, Autumn 2000). Nelson has established a place in contemporary North American nature writing as a writer who treats his subjects with realism and compassion, writing about what he knows best and immersing himself in his subjects to the extent that readers can feel what he perceives through all his senses.

Interviews:

Michael A. Armstrong, "Richard Nelson: Man of Words and Waves," *We Alaskans* (10 July 1983): 8–11;

George Russell, "Ways of Knowing: An Interview with Richard Nelson," *Orion*, 9 (1990): 50–53;

Rob Baker and Ellen Draper, "Exploring the Near at Hand: An Interview with Richard Nelson," *Parabola*, 16 (Summer 1991): 38;

Richard Leviton, "The Island Within," *Yoga Journal*, 102 (1992): 50–73;

Jonathan White, "Life-Ways of the Hunter: Talking on the Water," in his *Conversations about Nature and Creativity* (San Francisco: Sierra Club Books, 1994);

Richard Nelson: In Conversation with Gary Nabhan, video, Lannan Foundation, 1998).

References:

Jerry Keir, "We All Share the Same Sky: Cultural Ecology in Four Contemporary American Nature Writers," M.A. thesis, Southwest Texas University, 1992;

Sherman Paul, "The Education of a Hunter: Reading Richard Nelson," in his *For Love of the World: Essays on Nature Writers* (Iowa City: University of Iowa Press, 1992), pp. 133–162;

Pete Sinclair, "Unbounded: Notes on the Life and World of Richard K. Nelson," *North Dakota Quarterly*, 59 (Spring 1991): 259–278;

John Tallmadge, "Richard K. Nelson," in *American Nature Writers*, 2 volumes, edited by John Elder (New York: Scribners, 1996), II: 683–696;

Katarzyna Tomkiewicz, "Gary Snyder, Barry Lopez, and Richard Nelson: Rituals of Appeasement," in her "Hunting and Fishing in Contemporary American Literature," dissertation, Michigan State University, 1994, pp. 97–136.

Sigurd F. Olson

(4 April 1899 – 13 January 1982)

Clayton T. Russell
Northland College

BOOKS: *The Singing Wilderness* (New York: Knopf, 1956);

Listening Point (New York: Knopf, 1958);

The Lonely Land (New York: Knopf, 1961);

Runes of the North (New York: Knopf, 1963);

Open Horizons (New York: Knopf, 1969);

The Hidden Forest, text by Olson, photographs by Les Blacklock (New York: Viking, 1969; Harmondsworth, U.K. & New York: Penguin, 1979; revised edition, Stillwater, Minn.: Voyageur Press, 1990);

Wilderness Days, text by Olson, photographs by J. Arnold Bolz (New York: Knopf, 1972);

Reflections from the North Country (New York: Knopf, 1976);

Of Time and Place (New York: Knopf, 1982);

Songs of the North, edited by Howard Frank Mosher (New York: Penguin, 1987);

The Collected Works of Sigurd F. Olson: The Early Writings, 1921–1934, edited by Mike Link (Stillwater, Minn.: Voyageur Press, 1988);

The Collected Works of Sigurd F. Olson: The College Years, 1935–1944, edited by Link (Stillwater, Minn.: Voyageur Press, 1990);

The Meaning of Wilderness: Essential Articles and Speeches, edited by David Backes (Minneapolis: University of Minnesota Press, 2001).

PRODUCED SCRIPT: *Wilderness Canoe Country,* motion picture, President's Quetico-Superior Committee, 1949.

SELECTED PERIODICAL PUBLICATIONS–
UNCOLLECTED: "Fishin' Jewelry," *Field and Stream* (November 1927);

"Snow Wings," *Boys' Life* (March 1928);

"A Wilderness Canoe Trip," *Sports Afield,* 83 (June 1929);

"Duck Heaven," *Outdoor Life,* 56 (October 1930);

"Confessions of a Duck Hunter," *Sports Afield* (October 1930);

Sigurd F. Olson, 1941 (Olson Family Collection)

"Stag Pants Galahads," *Sports Afield,* 84 (November 1930);

"The Poison Trail," *Sports Afield* (December 1930);

"Spring Fever," *Sports Afield,* 85 (April 1931);

"The Blue-Bills Are Coming!" *Sports Afield* (October 1931);

"Papette," *Sports Afield,* 87 (January and February 1932);

"Fortune at Lac La Croix," *Sports Afield* (September and October 1932);

"Trail's End," *Sports Afield,* 87 (October 1933);

"Roads or Planes in the Superior," *Minnesota Waltonian* (April 1934);

"A New Policy Needed for the Superior," *Minnesota Conservationist* (May 1934);

"Cruising in the Arrowhead," *Outdoors*, 2 (May 1934);

"The Evolution of a Canoe Country," *Minnesota Conservationist*, (May 1935);

"Canoeing The Superior-Quetico Canoe Country," *Northern Trails*, 1 (Summer 1935);

"Let's Go Exploring," *Field and Stream*, 42 (June 1937);

"Organization and Range of the Pack," *Ecology* (January 1938);

"Taking Us, Dad?" *Field and Stream*, 42 (January 1938);

"A Study in Predatory Relationship with Particular Reference to the Wolf," *Scientific Monthly* (April 1938);

"Wilderness Areas," *Sports Afield* (August 1938);

"Mallards Are Different," *Field and Stream*, 43 (November 1938);

"The Immortals of Argo," *Sports Afield*, 102 (July 1939);

"Mallards of Back Bay," *Sports Afield*, 102 (October 1939);

"Fireside Pictures," *Field and Stream*, 44 (March 1940);

"The Last Mallard," *Sports Afield* (November 1940);

"What! No Bass?" *Field and Stream*, 45 (January 1941);

"Wilderness Short Cuts," *Sports Afield Fishing Annual* (1942);

"War Comes to the Quetico," *Sports Afield* (February 1942);

"Wilderness Again on Trial," *Outdoor America* (May–June 1942);

"Quetico-Superior Wilderness International and Unique," *Living Wilderness* (December 1942);

"Packs and Paddles," *Sports Afield Fishing Annual* (1943);

"Gold in Them Hills," *Sports Afield*, 112 (July 1944);

"The Spring Hole," *Outdoor Life* (September 1944);

"I'm a Jump Shooter," *Sports Afield*, 112 (October 1944);

"Shift of Wind," *Sports Afield* (December 1944);

"Wilderness Manners," *Sports Afield* (May 1945);

"The Purist," *Conservation Volunteer* (May–June 1945);

"The Gremlins of Wind Bay," *Sports Afield* (November 1945);

"Spawning of Eelpout," *Conservation Volunteer* (January–February 1946);

"On Not Trimming Trees," *Conservation Volunteer* (March–April 1946);

"Canoeing for Sport," *Outdoorsman* (February 1948);

"Let's Finish What We Started," *Outdoor America* (February 1948);

"Moon Magic," *Sports Afield* (February 1948);

"Veterans Named," *Christian Science Monitor* (22 March 1948);

"Quetico-Superior Elegy," *Living Wilderness* (Spring 1948);

"Quetico-Superior Challenge," *Sports Afield*, 119 (May 1948);

"Wings Over the Wilderness," *American Forests*, 54 (June 1948);

"Voyageur's Return," *Nature Magazine*, 41 (June–July 1948);

"The Know-How in Camping," *Outdoorsman* (August 1948);

"Spawning of the Pike," *Conservation Volunteer* (January–February 1949);

"Battle for a Wilderness," *Forest and Outdoors* (March 1949);

"Frog Chorus," *Conservation Volunteer* (April 1949);

"Voyageurs' Country," *National Home Monthly* (October 1949);

"Swift as the Wild Goose Flies," *National Parks Magazine* (October–December 1949);

"A Victory for Wilderness!" *Outdoor America* (January 1950);

"Late Frontier Quetico-Superior," *American Heritage* (Spring 1950);

"Wilderness Victory," *National Parks Magazine* (April–June 1950);

"Orchids of the North," *North Country*, 1 (1951);

"Airplane Ban Goes into Effect," *Outdoor America* (January–February 1951);

"The Rainy Lake Pollution Problem," *Outdoor America* (November–December 1951);

"The Big Snow," *Gopher Historian* (January 1953);

"Voyageur's Country: The Story of the Quetico-Superior Country," *Wilson Bulletin* (March 1953);

"Conservation and Citizenship," *Gopher Historian* (April 1953);

"Airplanes to Wilderness," *Living Wilderness* (Spring 1953);

"Wilderness and the Flambeau," *Living Wilderness* (Spring 1953);

"Let's Take a Canoe Trip," *Recreation* (February 1954);

"The Challenge of Our National Parks," *National Parks Magazine* (April–June 1954);

"The Intangible Values in Nature Protection," *National Parks Magazine* (July–September 1954);

"Right Should Prevail," *Outdoor America* (July–August 1955);

"This Is No Little Bird Book," *Living Wilderness* (Winter–Spring 1955–1956);

"The Association's First Objective," *National Parks Magazine* (January–March 1956);

"A U.S. Comment," *American Forests* (February 1956);

"The Association's Second Objective," *National Parks Magazine* (April–June 1956);

"The Association's Third Objective," *National Parks Magazine* (July–September 1956);

"Outlaw Country," *True* (February 1957);

"Winning a Wilderness," *Naturalist* (Winter 1958);

Olson and Al Kennedy, the old miner who introduced him to the "canoe country"
straddling the United States-Canadian border (Olson Family Collection)

"Leisure Time: Man's Key to Self Realization–The Out-of-Doors," *Minnesota Journal of Education* (April 1958);

"The Quetico-Superior," *Outdoor America* (May 1958);

"Thanksgiving: More than a Holiday," *Outdoor America* (November 1958);

"Of Worms and Fishermen," *Outdoor America* (April 1959);

"Wilderness Manners," *Forest and Outdoors* (October 1959);

"Woodsmen's Skill for the Wild," *Living Wilderness* (Winter 1959–1960);

"Winning a Wilderness," *Outdoor America* (June 1960);

"Some New Books in Review: Portage into the Past," *Minnesota History* (March 1961);

"Explorers," *Naturalist* (Winter 1961);

"Six Decades of Progress," *American Forests* (October 1962);

"Sam Campbell, Philosopher of the Forest," *American Forests* (October 1962);

"Relics from the Rapids," *National Geographic* (September 1963);

"Wilderness Preservation," *Naturalist* (Winter 1964);

"Voyageur's Autumn," *Boys' Life* (November 1964);

"Minnesota's Proposed National Park," *Naturalist* (Spring 1965);

"Skindiving for Treasures of the Past," *Ford Times* (April 1965);

"Indiana Dunes Revisited," *Outdoor America* (January 1966);

"Natural Resource Readings: A Wilderness Bill of Rights," *Journal of Soil and Water Conservation* (March–April 1966);

"Wilderness Canoe Country: Minnesota's Greatest Recreational Asset," *Naturalist* (Spring 1967);

"A Certain Kind of Man," *Beaver* (Autumn 1968);

"A Tribute to F. L. Jaques," *Naturalist* (Spring 1970);

"Wilderness Challenge," *Living Wilderness* (Summer 1970);

"Wilderness Besieged: The Canoe Country of Minnesota," *Audubon* (July 1970);

"The Values of Voyageurs National Park," *Minnesota Conservation Volunteer* (May–June 1971);

"Alaska: Land of Scenic Grandeur," *Living Wilderness* (Winter 1971–1972);

"A Giant Step North," *Rotarian* (March 1974);

"Wild Islands of the Shield," *Naturalist* (Summer 1975);

"Caribou Creek," *Audubon* (March 1982);

"Lake Superior Speaks," *Horizons*, 6 (Spring 1984): 6–7.

Sigurd F. Olson is the author of nine books describing his adventures in nature and the spiritual

Sigurd, Elizabeth, and Robert Olson, circa 1930 (Olson Family Collection)

insights he gained there. He was one of the most effective and influential conservation leaders of the twentieth century. During his long career he received the highest award in nature writing, the John Burroughs Medal (1974), as well as the Founders Award from the Izaak Walton League of America (1963), the John Muir Award from the Sierra Club (1967), the Robert Marshall Award from the Wilderness Society (1981), and the Conservation Hall of Fame Award from the National Wildlife Federation (1991). According to Olson's biographer, David Backes, only "John Muir has received so much affectionate recognition in his lifetime as both a writer and environmental leader."

Sigurd Ferdinand Olson was born in the Humboldt Park neighborhood of Chicago on 4 April 1899, the second of the three sons of Lawrence J. (L. J.) and Ida May (Cederholm) Olson. In November 1906, when Sigurd Olson was seven, the family moved to Sister Bay, Wisconsin, where L. J. Olson became pastor of the Swedish Baptist Church. During his early years in Sister Bay, Sigurd Olson spent as much time as possible exploring farm fields, woods, swamps, and beaches along the shore of Lake Michigan. One day, after the family had been in Sister Bay for about a year, he followed the call of a foghorn to the end of an abandoned stone pier. Some fifty years later, in *The Singing Wilderness* (1956), he described the impact of this

adventure: "I was alone in a wild and lovely place, part at last of the wind and the water, part of the dark forest through which I had come, and of all the wild sounds and colors and feelings of the place I had found. That day I entered into a life of indescribable beauty and delight. There I believe I heard the singing wilderness for the first time."

In 1909 the Olson family moved west to the logging town of Prentice in north-central Wisconsin. Here Sigurd went fishing almost every day and also learned to hunt and trap, later referring to this period as his "Daniel Boone Days." The only member of his family who understood his love for the outdoors was his maternal grandmother, Anna Cederholm, who enjoyed listening to his tales of exploration and trout fishing and helped him cook the fish he caught. He referred to her fondly throughout his life as a "partner of the spirit."

In 1912 the family moved north to the Lake Superior port of Ashland, Wisconsin, where Olson's love of the outdoors continued. In Ashland he first demonstrated a talent for writing when in the fall of 1912, as a thirteen-year-old high-school freshman, he won first place and a $5.00 gold piece with an essay called "The Function of the Chamber of Commerce" in a school writing contest. He graduated from Ashland High School in 1916 and entered Northland College in Ashland that fall, enrolling in the agriculture program,

Olson (left) and U.S. Supreme Court Justice William O. Douglas (right) singing a song Olson wrote to publicize their fight to preserve the historic C. & O. Canal, which runs from Georgetown in Washington, D.C., into Maryland, 29 March 1954 (photograph by Abbie Rows, U.S. National Park Service)

which prepared students to transfer to the University of Wisconsin at Madison for their junior and senior years. During his two years at Northland, Olson met his future wife, Elizabeth Uhrenholdt, and learned his first lessons in conservation while working for her father, a respected farmer and conservationist, to clear a plot of marshy ground on the Uhrenholdts' farm.

Shortly before Olson graduated from the University of Wisconsin in June 1920, he got a job teaching animal husbandry, agricultural botany, and geology at high schools in the northern Minnesota mining towns of Nashwauk and Keewatin, where he spent nearly every weekend in the woods. During these rambles, an old miner, Al Kennedy, told him about the canoe country, a forested lake district straddling the border between Minnesota and the province of Ontario, Canada–Quetico Provincial Park in Canada and Superior National Forest in the United States. Olson took his first canoe trip in this Quetico-Superior region with four friends in early summer 1921. His first publication was an article about these wilderness travels, "Canoe Tourist Finds Joy of the Great Outdoors through the Vast Watered Wetland Wilderness of the North," published in the 31 July 1921 issue of the *Milwaukee Journal*.

Later that same summer, on 8 August, Olson married Elizabeth Uhrenholdt and took her on a three-week canoe trip. After this honeymoon, Olson returned to his teaching jobs in Nashwauk and Keewatin. In September 1922 he began graduate studies in geology at the University of Wisconsin, but the following February, having learned that his wife was pregnant with their first child, he returned to northern Minnesota to teach at Ely High School. Their first child, Sigurd Thorne Olson, was born on 15 September 1923. He was followed by Robert Keith Olson on 23 December 1925.

In summer 1923 Olson began the practice of supplementing his teaching income by guiding canoe trips for a company called Wilderness Outfitters, learning much about the canoe country from older guides. In 1926 he began teaching part-time at Ely Junior College while continuing to work at the high school. In 1929 he joined two other men in the purchase of an outfitting business, which they called Border Lakes Outfitting. As a guide and a teacher, he captivated listeners with his well-rounded naturalist's understanding of the area, his extensive knowledge of woodsman's lore, and his playfully romantic notions of the voyageurs, the fur trappers and traders who had worked the region in the eighteenth and nineteenth centuries. During the 1920s Olson also began selling stories to outdoorsmen's magazines, beginning with "Fishin' Jewelry" in the November 1927 issue of *Field and Stream*. In his journals he wrote often of his need to write, to share his appreciation of nature with a broader community and to achieve greater recognition.

In fall 1931 the Olsons moved to Champaign, Illinois, where Sigurd Olson began work on a master's degree in zoology at the University of Illinois. He earned his degree the following June with a thesis titled "The Life History of the Timber Wolf and the Coyote: A Study in Predatory Animal Control," based on firsthand research in Superior National Forest, the Minnesota portion of the wilderness area he knew best. Olson's thesis has been called the first scientific research ever done on the behavior of the wolf. In the course of writing it, Olson—who had earlier agreed with the U.S. Bureau of Biological Survey position that the wolf was a deadly predator and should be eradicated—developed a sympathetic understanding of the species. He called for designating the Superior National Forest as a sanctuary for carnivores such as wolves and coyotes—a radical idea at that time.

The Olsons returned to Ely in June of 1932. Having his master's degree, Olson was now primarily assigned teaching duties at the junior college. In 1936 he became dean of Ely Junior College. By that time he was gaining recognition as a conservation advocate. In fall 1937, to secure some isolation from the demands of job and family, Olson remodeled a single-car garage in his yard as a writing studio, which he called "the Shack," and immersed himself in a disciplined writing schedule.

One of the most important articles of this period was "Why Wilderness?" published in the September 1938 issue of *American Forests*. Written in the personal, lyrical style for which Olson became well known, this article contributed to the emerging wilderness debate. It was also the first place in which Olson used the term *racial memory* to describe his idea that the longing for wilderness experience has its roots in humankind's genetic makeup, that it is a product of its primitive heritage. "What we feel most deeply are those things which as a race we have been doing the longest," he asserted, "and the hunger men feel for the wilds and a roving life is natural evidence of the need of repeating a plan of existence that for untold centuries was common practice." This concept became central to Olson's support for wilderness preservation. In fall 1941 Olson began contributing to the syndicated newspaper column "America Out of Doors," becoming the sole author of the column by January 1942. The popular column gave him a broad national audience for his observations on nature and conservation. It was discontinued in 1944, after paper shortages during World War II caused newspapers to trim the size of their publications.

In the spring of 1947 Olson resigned his position at Ely Junior College to write full-time. Faced with a significant reduction in income, Olson began working in January 1948 as a conservationist for the Quetico-Superior Council, which had been formed by Ernest Oberholtzer in 1927 with the goal of developing a treaty between the United States and Canada for joint management of the entire Rainy Lake watershed, an area that includes Quetico Provincial Park and Superior National Forest. Olson's articles, speeches, and the script he wrote for *Wilderness Canoe Country* (1949), a movie produced by the President's Quetico-Superior Committee (an official U.S. government group created in 1934), as well as his work with Congress and various committees earned him national recognition as a leader in the conservation movement. His strongest statement in support of wilderness had been published as "We Need Wilderness" in the January–March 1946 issue of *National Parks* magazine, where he wrote:

> Wilderness to the people of America is a spiritual necessity, an antidote to the high pressure of modern life, a means of regaining serenity and equilibrium.
>
> I have found that people go to the wilderness for many things, but the most important of these is perspective. They may think they go for the fishing or the scenery or the companionship, but in reality it is something far deeper. They go to the wilderness for the good of their souls.

Olson's interest in wilderness preservation in the United States and Canada brought him together with Canadian nature writer Fred Bodsworth, who joined Olson and three other men in July 1950 on a two-week paddling trip in Quetico Park. Olson edited and commented on Bodsworth's article about the trip, which was published in the 15 May 1951 issue of the prestigious Canadian magazine *Maclean's*. The article was exactly the kind of "canoe public relations" for which Olson became well known and sparked Canadian interest in the fight to preserve the Quetico-Superior region. After reading about him in the article, Eric Morse, national director of the Association of Canadian Clubs, contacted Olson, and the two men collaborated on a series of highly publicized wilderness canoe trips that included prominent men from a variety of professions. For Olson these trips accomplished two things: his newfound Canadian friends became influential in advancing conservation efforts north of the border, and through the trips he made the closest friends of his lifetime. With Olson as their leader, the Voy-

The Voyageurs—Eric Morse, Elliott Rodger, Denis Coolican, Anthony Lovnik, Omond Solandt, and Sigurd
Olson—after a 1955 canoe trip on the Churchill River in Canada (Olson Family Collection)

ageurs, as the group became known, often followed historic fur-trade routes, and their travels were reported widely in the press.

The 1950s were extremely busy for Olson. He became vice president of the National Park Association in 1951 and president in 1953. In this position he became an advocate for the entire National Parks system while continuing his support of preserving the Quetico-Superior region. During his tenure as president, which continued until 1959, he took part in a successful campaign to prevent the building of a Colorado River dam that threatened the Dinosaur National Monument, supported a major funding initiative to restore and improve National Parks, and fought for legislation to establish a national wilderness preservation system. He also worked with U.S. Supreme Court Justice William O. Douglas on several high-profile conservation issues related to the National Parks System. All this work and extensive traveling came with a cost for Olson. He developed ulcers, insomnia, and a bothersome facial twitch. At the same time, however, he was given an opportunity for which he had been striving since early in his writing career. After hearing Olson deliver a 17

November 1954 speech on the Dinosaur National Monument, publisher Alfred A. Knopf invited Olson to offer a book to his firm. For nearly twenty years Olson had been trying unsuccessfully to interest publishers in a collection of his nature essays. The previous year, with the help and encouragement of his son Robert's wife, Yvonne Olson, he had revised a group of essays with that goal in mind. At Knopf's request he also wrote some new essays for the book.

The title for Olson's first book is a variation on the title of Donald Culross Peattie's book on John James Audubon, *Singing in the Wilderness* (1935). Published on 16 April 1956, Olson's *The Singing Wilderness* was an instant success. Among the many laudatory reviews in national publications was one in *The New York Herald Tribune Book Review* (29 April 1956), where well-known naturalist Roger Tory Peterson called *The Singing Wilderness* "unequivocally the best series of essays on the northwoods country I have ever read." The book also made the *New York Times* best-seller list. From the first paragraph of the introduction, *The Singing Wilderness* exhibits the same lyricism as Olson's earlier articles and speeches:

THE Singing Wilderness

By SIGURD F. OLSON

A vibrant book of discovery that re-creates the sights and sounds of the Quetico-Superior country and explores with deep insight the permanent values of a great wilderness area

ILLUSTRATED BY FRANCIS LEE JAQUES

Dust jacket for Olson's first book (1956), which Roger Tory Peterson called "unequivocally the best series of essays on the northwoods country I have ever read" (Richland County Public Library)

The singing wilderness has to do with the calling of the loons, northern lights and the great silences of a land lying northwest of Lake Superior. It is concerned with the simple joys, the timelessness and perspective found in a way of life that is close to the past.

Like nature guide Enos Mills and interpretive philosopher Freeman Tilden, Olson understood how to use his knowledge of natural processes to open people's hearts and minds to the deeply spiritual power of nature. Like later interpretive naturalists, Olson taught his readers that interaction with nature can be the appropriate remedy for the stress of modern life.

Four months after publication of *The Singing Wilderness,* the Wilderness Society elected Olson to their governing council. Later that same year, the Olsons purchased property on Burntside Lake, ten miles from Ely. In 1957 they had a one-room cabin moved to their lake property.

In his second book, *Listening Point,* published in September 1958, Olson used his lakeside retreat as a unifying device. Though not all the essays are set there, they are tied to that place in some way. The title was inspired by his daughter-in-law Yvonne Olson, who had been in the Middle East with Robert Olson, a U.S. Foreign Service officer. She noted similarities between diplomatic listening posts located around the world and Olson's land on Burntside Lake, where he went to absorb the colors, sights, and sounds of wilderness.

The theme of *Listening Point* is the need for balance between modern civilization and the natural world. David Backes has located "the heart" of the book in "The Whistle," which provides an insight into how Olson tried to achieve this balance. After hearing a train whistle in the distance from his lake property, he realized that the sound has

a deeper meaning than the train itself, one that encompasses man's inventive genius and all the realms of his exploring mind, a sound that was responsible for my own background and everything I knew and felt. . . . only because of its connotations and the contrasts that had been mine could I really appreciate the wilds and their importance to mankind. . . . Without that long lonesome wail and culture that had produced it, many things would not be mine—recordings of the world's finest music, books holding the philosophy, the dreams and hopes of all mankind, a car that took me swiftly to the point whenever I felt the need.

Olson suggests that everyone needs a listening point at which to "recapture some of the basic satisfactions and joys . . . renew the sense of mystery and wonder."

Olson's next book, *The Lonely Land* (1961), chronicles a five-hundred-mile canoe trip he and the other Voyageurs made down the Churchill River in Saskatchewan in 1955. The book celebrates the deep friendships forged by wilderness travel. The essays in *Runes of the North* (1963) reveal Olson's love for story, his understanding of the power of myth, and his inclination toward magic and mystery, as well as his sense of humor. Olson hoped this book would help his readers to have "touched something of man's ancient dream . . . and restored some sense of balance, wholeness and perspective." In "The Ross Light" Olson names the "last slanting rays of the setting sun" after *Saturday Evening Post* photographer Frank Ross and explains that he has long known such light rays were "magic," but "I was not fully aware of their significance and possibilities." Ross light, he continues, "does strange and wonderful things to all who see it and are sensitive to its meaning. No two ever see it alike, but this much is true, somewhere within it is a power that transfigures everything, even those who watch." Such passages suggest

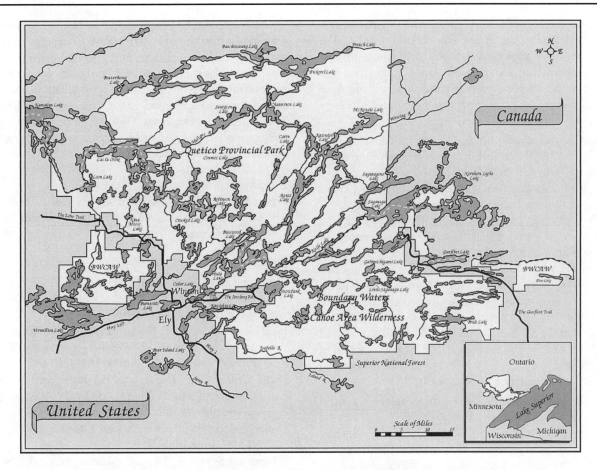

Map of "canoe country," including the Boundary Waters Canoe Area Wilderness Olson helped to preserve through his work on the Wilderness Act of 1964 (Cartography and Geographic Information Science Center, University of Wisconsin–Milwaukee)

the spirituality of Olson's communion with nature. He describes a similar moment of epiphany in "Jumping-Off Places," where he contends that anytime he encounters the unknown, he stands at a jumping-off place where "life and everything around me have special clarity and meaning."

In 1959 Olson resigned as president of the National Park Association and became a member of the National Park Service advisory board, remaining on the board until 1966. In 1962 he became a consultant on wilderness and National Park affairs to Secretary of the Interior Stewart Udall, and the following year he was elected vice president of the Wilderness Society. These and other conservation duties gave him less time to write, but his activism had positive results. The wilderness-preservation bill for which he had fought since 1956 finally passed as the Wilderness Act of 1964, which authorized the creation of a national system of wilderness preserves, including the parts of the Superior National Forest known as the Boundary Waters Canoe Area Wilderness. In 1965 he was a member of a task force that called for preserving almost

eighty million acres of land in Alaska. Because their report was politically controversial, their recommendation was not immediately followed, but their work lay behind the Alaska National Interest Lands and Conservation Act of 1980. In 1967 he helped to develop a master plan for managing Yellowstone National Park.

During the years 1965–1968, despite his busy schedule, he wrote an autobiography, *Open Horizons* (1969), in which he describes his adventures and spiritual encounters in the natural world. His message throughout the book is that intuition and a child's sense of wonder and hope can connect—in fact reconnect—the individual with the natural world and "the deep pools of racial memory." When this connection is regained, he believes, one can participate more fully in the natural world and help to create a meaningful future in which its wildness, beauty, and harmony are preserved.

In 1968 Olson was elected president of the Wilderness Society. That November he experienced a major heart attack during the opening dinner of the Wilderness Society Council meeting at Sanibel Island, Florida. He recovered after spending five weeks in Sarasota. During his presidency, Olson and the Wilderness Society helped to protect the Florida Everglades and to establish Voyageurs National Park in northern Minnesota west of the Boundary Waters Canoe Area, but they lost their fight to prevent construction of the Alaskan pipeline. Olson resigned as president in 1971, hoping to have more time for writing.

Chronologically arranged from spring to winter, *Wilderness Days* (1972) features photographs of the north country by J. Arnold Bolz with excerpts from Olson's first five books and new seasonal introductions. One of the most striking passages in the new sections occurs in the introduction for winter, where Olson describes the tension in the atmosphere prior to the first snowstorm of the season: "It may come on some quiet day in early November with a hush so deep and so profound it seems to press on everything. All living creatures feel it." In his epilogue Olson challenges his readers to consider the ultimate question: "what kind of world do we want?" He hopes that they will listen to Henry David Thoreau and pursue wildness, for in that choice "is hope for a world of beauty and meaning in which our spiritual roots will ever be nourished by love of the earth."

By 1973 Olson had given up most of his conservation work to start writing *Reflections from the North Country* (1976), his most philosophical work, which is admired by many readers. The essays in *Reflections from the North Country* express Olson's belief that values are eternal and help people to establish balance in their lives as they search for meaning in an increasingly complex world. Olson began his last book, *Of Time and Place* (1982), late in the summer of 1978, when he realized that "unless I am writing, I am not happy." The book is a series of anecdotes about his experiences.

Olson underwent surgery for colon cancer in December 1979. While the procedure was successful, he never regained his full strength. On 13 January 1982 he suffered a heart attack while snowshoeing near his home in Ely. A neighbor found him, face down in the snow, and called for an ambulance. Olson passed away soon after arriving at the hospital.

The next day Sigurd Thorne Olson went into his father's writing shack and found in the typewriter a piece of paper on which his father had typed:

> A new adventure is coming up
> And I am sure it will be
> A good one.

Olson wanted to be remembered as "a man of action who lived what he wrote." His writings express a spiritual sense of nature that so many wilderness travelers have felt and experienced, and his books continue to achieve one of his greatest joys, introducing people to the wilderness experience. In *Of Time and Place* Olson recalled some advice from Thoreau, noting that when one approaches the end of his days, it is comforting to look back and know that he has lived wisely.

Biography:
David Backes, *A Wilderness Within: The Life of Sigurd F. Olson* (Minneapolis & London: University of Minnesota Press, 1997).

References:
David Backes, "The Land beyond the Rim: Sigurd Olson's Wilderness Theology," *Forest and Conservation History,* 39 (April 1995): 56–65;

John Cooley, "Sigurd F. Olson: (1899–1982)," in *American Nature Writers,* 2 volumes, edited by John Elder (New York: Scribners, 1996), II: 697–709;

Frank Graham Jr., "Leave It to the Bourgeois: Sigurd Olson and His Wilderness Quest," *Audubon,* 82 (November 1980): 28–39;

Doug Hisson, "Wild about Sigurd Olson," *Isthmus,* 24 (11–17 June 1999): 8–9;

"Honoring Sigurd F. Olson," *Naturalist,* special Olson issue, 32 (Autumn 1981);

Omond Solandt, "Sigurd Olson: Mister Voyageur," *Che-Mum: The Newsletter of Canadian Wilderness Canoeing,* 69 (Summer 1992): 6–11;

Jim Dale Vickery, "Sigurd F. Olson: Visionary Voyageur," in his *Wilderness Visionaries: Leopold, Thoreau, Muir, Olson, Murie, Service, Marshall, Rutstrum* (Minocqua, Wis.: NorthWord Press, 1994), pp. 195–229;

A Voice for the Wilderness: Northland College Salutes Sigurd F. Olson (Ashland, Wis.: Sigurd Olson Environmental Institute, Northland College, 1999);

The Wilderness World of Sigurd F. Olson, video, Northwood, 1980.

Papers:
Many of Sigurd F. Olson's journals and letters, as well as other important documents, are located at the Minnesota Historical Society in St. Paul. A few items are located at the Sigurd Olson Environmental Institute at Northland College in Ashland, Wisconsin.

Donald Culross Peattie

(21 June 1898 – 16 November 1964)

Peter Friederici
Northern Arizona University

BOOKS: *Blown Leaves* (Chicago: Printed at the School of Education, Chicago University High School, 1916);

Bounty of Earth, by Peattie and Louise Redfield Peattie (New York & London: Appleton, 1926);

Cargoes and Harvests (New York & London: Appleton, 1926);

Up Country: A Story of the Vanguard, by Peattie and Louise Redfield Peattie (New York & London: Appleton, 1928);

Down Wind: Secrets of the Underwoods, by Peattie and Louise Redfield Peattie (New York & London: Appleton, 1929);

Flora of the Indiana Dunes: A Handbook of the Flowering Plants and Ferns of the Lake Michigan Coast of Indiana and of the Calumet District (Chicago: Field Museum of Natural History, 1930);

Vence: The Story of a Provencal Town Through 2000 Years (Nice: Imprimerie de l'Eclaireur de Nice, 1930); revised as *The Happy Kingdom: A Riviera Memoir,* by Peattie and Louise Redfield Peattie (London & Glasgow: Blackie, 1935); revised again as *Immortal Village* (Chicago: University of Chicago Press, 1945);

Port of Call (New York & London: Century, 1932); republished as *Karen's Loyalty* (London: Jarrolds, 1933);

Sons of the Martian (London & New York: Longmans, Green, 1932);

A Natural History of Pearson's Falls and Some of Its Human Associations (Tryon, N.C.: Tryon Garden Club, 1932); republished as *Pearson's Falls Glen: Its Story, Its Flora, Its Birds* (Tryon, N.C.: Tryon Garden Club, 1962);

The Bright Lexicon (New York: Putnam, 1934);

Trees You Want to Know (Racine, Wis.: Whitman, 1934);

An Almanac for Moderns (New York: Putnam, 1935; London: Allen & Unwin, 1936); republished in part as *Glory of the Earth* (Marazion, U.K.: Ark Press, 1960);

Donald Culross Peattie

Singing in the Wilderness: A Salute to John James Audubon (New York: Putnam, 1935; London: Allen & Unwin, 1936);

Green Laurels: The Lives and Achievements of the Great Naturalists (New York: Simon & Schuster, 1936; London: Harrap, 1937);

Old-Fashioned Garden Flowers (Chicago: Field Museum of Natural History, 1936);

A Book of Hours (New York: Putnam, 1937; London: Harrap, 1938);

A Child's Story of the World, From the Earliest Days to Our Own Time (New York: Junior Literary Guild/ Simon & Schuster, 1937); also published in six

255

parts as *The Story of the First Men, The Story of Ancient Civilization, The Story of the Middle Ages, The Story of the New Lands, The Story of America,* and *The Story of the Modern World from the French Revolution to Now* (New York: Grosset & Dunlap, 1937);

A Prairie Grove (New York: Simon & Schuster, 1938);

This Is Living: A View of Nature with Photographs, text by Peattie, photographs selected by Gordon Aymar (New York: Dodd, Mead, 1938);

Flowering Earth (New York: Putnam, 1939; London: Phoenix House, 1948);

The Road of a Naturalist (Boston: Houghton Mifflin, 1941; London: Hale, 1946);

Forward the Nation (New York: Putnam, 1942);

Journey into America (Boston: Houghton Mifflin, 1943);

The Declaration of Independence: A Story (Chicago: Parkinson, 1947);

American Heartwood (Boston: Houghton Mifflin, 1949);

A Cup of Sky, by Peattie and Noel Peattie (Boston: Houghton Mifflin, 1950);

A Natural History of Trees of Eastern and Central North America (Boston: Houghton Mifflin, 1950);

Sportsman's Country (Boston: Houghton Mifflin, 1952);

A Natural History of Western Trees (Boston: Houghton Mifflin, 1953);

Lives of Destiny, as told for the Reader's Digest (Boston: Houghton Mifflin, 1954);

Parade with Banners (Cleveland: World, 1957);

The Rainbow Book of Nature (Cleveland: World, 1957).

OTHER: *A Gathering of Birds: An Anthology of the Best Ornithological Prose,* edited by Peattie (New York: Dodd, Mead, 1939);

Audubon's America: The Narratives and Experiences of John James Audubon, edited by Peattie (Boston: Houghton Mifflin, 1940);

"Indian Days and the Coming of the White Man," "Men, Mountains and Trees," and "Blue Ridge Wild Flowers," in *The Great Smokies and the Blue Ridge,* American Mountain Series, edited by Roderick Peattie (New York: Vanguard, 1943), pp. 15–72; 152–171; 172–199;

"Father Serra's Rosary" and "Footsteps of Spring–A Wildflower Trail" in *Pacific Coast Ranges,* American Mountain Series, edited by Roderick Peattie (New York: Vanguard, 1946), pp. 1–22; 45–75;

David Brower, ed., *The Sierra Nevada: The Range of Light,* introduction by Peattie (New York: Vanguard, 1947).

SELECTED PERIODICAL PUBLICATIONS–
UNCOLLECTED:

"One Square Mile," *Natural History,* 40 (September 1937): 464–470;

"America's Don Quixote," *New York Times Magazine,* 2 June 1940, pp. 14–15, 21;

"The Business of Nature Writing," *Saturday Review of Literature,* 23 (5 April 1941): 3–4, 38–39.

Donald Culross Peattie became a popular American interpreter of nature in the mid 1930s, and over the next twenty years he created a large and impressive body of work, which has influenced naturalists and scientists as well as other nature writers. He celebrated the richness and diversity of the natural world and the human response to it, taking a broad view of nature and history in books that were often praised for their lyricism and sometimes condemned for their sentimentality. After his death most of his books passed into obscurity, but a few are still read and respected.

Born in Chicago on 21 June 1898, Peattie was the second child of a writing family. His father, Robert Burns Peattie, was a newspaperman, who in the course of his career worked in Chicago, Omaha, and New York. Often in poor health, Robert Peattie wrote vigorous unsigned editorials for a series of newspapers, and for many years he was the Chicago correspondent for *The New York Times.* Donald Peattie's mother, Elia Wilkinson Peattie, was the daughter of the publisher of the *Hyde Park* (Chicago) *Herald* and became the first woman reporter for *The Chicago Tribune.* Her short stories, poems, and essays appeared not only in *The Chicago Tribune* and other newspapers but also periodicals such as *The Atlantic Monthly, Harper's,* and *The Century;* she also published novels, travel writing, and other books. She continued her literary pursuits as the family resettled in Omaha, New York, and finally Chicago again. While raising her children–Roderick, Donald, Barbara (who died in childhood), and Edward–she reviewed books for the *Tribune.* Donald later attributed his regular work habits to his early and regular exposure to both books and daily journalism. Roderick Peattie also became a writer, producing several books during the course of his career as a professional geographer, while Edward Peattie became a businessman in New York.

The Peatties lived near the shore of Lake Michigan, some nine miles south of downtown Chicago, in a large house that had been built around 1880 by Elia Peattie's father. Set amid a partly undeveloped expanse of rolling sand dunes and black oak trees, it was a good childhood home for a budding naturalist.

During his childhood Donald Peattie took walking excursions to lake beaches, woodlands, the great sand dunes of Indiana, and the marshes and open waters of Lake Calumet. An avid reader and writer, he was a good student at Chicago University High School, writing and printing a chapbook of poems, *Blown Leaves*

(1916) during his fourth year in school and winning a competitive scholarship in English literature to the University of Chicago.

During his youth, Peattie came to know the Redfields, the descendants of a family that had settled in the Chicago area in the 1830s. Their ancestors included John Kennicott, a doctor, plant nurseryman, and farmer whose son Robert had been a prominent naturalist and one of the founders of the Chicago Academy of Sciences. The Redfields lived at the Grove, the original Kennicott homestead northwest of the city. It is now a nature preserve in the suburb of Glenview. The Grove–which encompassed a square mile of woodland, prairie, fields, and marshes–had once been the site of Native American camps and contributed to his interest in American history and natural history. Peattie's trips to the Grove to see his school friend Robert Redfield soon evolved into trips to visit Robert's sister Louise, who later became Peattie's wife.

Peattie remained at the University of Chicago for two years (1916–1918) before he moved with his family to New York. He worked briefly as a reader for the George H. Doran publishing house. Unhappy with this work, he went to the Bronx Botanical Garden one day in 1919 and there determined to become a professional nature writer. Convinced that a nature writer should have a rigorous scientific background, he resumed his university studies, enrolling at Harvard and graduating cum laude in 1922 with a degree in natural sciences. He also won a poetry prize that year and began publishing his first scientific papers on botany.

After graduation Peattie moved to Washington, D.C., and began working for the Office of Foreign Seed and Plant Introduction at the U.S. Department of Agriculture. He married Louise Redfield on 23 May 1923. His job as a government botanist took him to Miami, where he researched frost resistance in tropical plants. The job also provided him an opportunity to gather material for his first full-length nonfiction book, *Cargoes and Harvests* (1926), an exploration of how people have moved economically useful plants around the world. After completing the book in 1924, he resigned his job to devote himself full-time to writing. Soon thereafter he began writing a long-running column on nature, first for *The Washington Evening Star* and later for *The Chicago Daily News*. The column was well received–as well as a consistent source of income. As Peattie commented later in *The Road of a Naturalist* (1941), "It was an everyday world that I had to write of . . . transient as any newspaper work." Peattie's practice of celebrating suburban nature continued throughout his career. Much of his best writing profiles the wonders of nature that a careful observer can spot almost anyplace.

"I suspect it of being a classic"—*Mark Van Doren*

AN ALMANAC
FOR MODERNS
by Donald Culross Peattie

WITH DRAWINGS BY LYND WARD

"A curious and lovely book"—*The New Yorker*

Dust jacket for the 1935 book that established Peattie's reputation as a nature writer (Bruccoli Clark Layman Archives)

By 1928 Donald and Louise Redfield Peattie had written several books of fiction. *Up Country: A Story of the Vanguard* (1928) celebrates early American frontier life in a way that *The New York World* (18 March 1928) called "sincere enough, but not very important"; the *Saturday Review of Literature* (14 April 1928) labeled its ending "very bad melodrama." The Peatties next wrote a book of animal stories, *Down Wind: Secrets of the Underwoods* (1929), which the reviewer for *The New York Herald Tribune* (19 May 1929) compared favorably to the work of Gene Stratton-Porter and Ernest Thompson Seton. By then the Peatties had a son, Malcolm, and a daughter, Celia, and had decided to move to the French Riviera because, Peattie wrote later, they were "financially bogged . . . hungry for sunshine, and for some land where art is native and deep-rooted."

During their five-year stay in the French towns of Vence and Menton, Donald and Louise Peattie each wrote several novels and co-authored a history of the ancient provincial town of Vence (1930). Donald Peattie's novels received scattered good reviews. Herschel Brickell called *The Bright Lexicon* (1934), the story of a brilliant Russian émigré boy growing up as an expatriate in France during the 1920s, "one of the most distinguished pieces of fiction we have had this season" (*New York Evening Post,* 24 March 1934). But none of these works gained Peattie a wide reputation or much income. Louise Peattie's romantic fiction also received mixed reviews, and the family's living remained precarious. During their European sojourn their daughter, Celia, died, and Louise Peattie bore two more sons, Mark and Noel. In 1933 the family returned to the United States, having had to borrow the money for ship fare.

In the depths of the Depression, the two writers had few prospects. They settled at the Grove. Donald Peattie found freelance work writing an identification booklet titled *Trees You Want to Know* (1934). Louise Peattie worked on a lengthy novel about settlers at the Grove, *American Acres* (1936), which became one of her most successful books. Donald Peattie also began keeping a detailed daily journal of the workings of nature at the Grove. This discipline eventually resulted in three book-length manuscripts. Two, "A Catalogue of Spontaneous Flowering Plants at the Kennicott Grove" and "The Natural History of Kennicott's Grove," were never published. The third, *An Almanac for Moderns* (1935), became a critically acclaimed and commercially successful book that launched his public career as a nature writer.

An Almanac for Moderns received an award from the Limited Editions Club, which republished the book in 1938. Recognition for the book also helped Peattie to earn Guggenheim Fellowships in 1936 and 1937. The Peatties moved briefly to the mountains of North Carolina, an area Peattie had begun to explore as a child and the setting for much of his botanical fieldwork. In 1937 the family settled permanently in Santa Barbara, California.

An Almanac for Moderns freed Peattie to do exactly the kind of writing he wanted. During the second half of the 1930s, Peattie produced a flurry of books. He wrote historical works emphasizing human encounters with the natural world: *Singing in the Wilderness: A Salute to John James Audubon* (1935), *Green Laurels: The Lives and Achievements of the Great Naturalists* (1936), and *A Prairie Grove* (1938); nature writing: *A Book of Hours* (1937) and *Flowering Earth* (1939); children's history: *A Child's Story of the World, From the Earliest Days to Our Own Time* (1937), which was also published in six parts; and the text for a photography book: *This Is Living: A View of Nature with Photographs* (1938). He also edited *A Gathering of Birds:*

An Anthology of the Best Ornithological Prose (1939) and *Audubon's America: The Narratives and Experiences of John James Audubon* (1940). Mark Van Doren sardonically remarked in *North American Review* (Autumn 1937 / Winter 1937–1938) that readers would have no time to read Peattie's earlier books because he was turning out so many new ones. *A Prairie Grove* was serialized in *The Atlantic Monthly* (January–March 1938). *Flowering Earth* was named the best horticultural book of 1939 and earned Peattie an award from the Commonwealth Club of California. His books were translated into at least six different languages, and he became a regular columnist for *Bird Lore,* the predecessor to *Audubon* magazine. In 1941 he was elected a member of the National Institute of Arts and Letters, and in 1946 Harvard awarded him an honorary M.A. degree.

An Almanac for Moderns is a day-by-day celebration not just of Peattie's surroundings but of the natural world in general and of the efforts of humans to understand and explain it. In tightly written prose Peattie combined closely observed scenes from his own experience and tales of great naturalists of the past, with whom he had a lifelong fascination. The prose of *An Almanac for Moderns* is pithy, lyrical, and incisive; its structure is perfectly suited to Peattie's almost epigrammatic observations.

In *The New York Times* (28 April 1935), Anita Moffett called this style "distinguished and rising at times to an intense lyric beauty." Van Doren labeled *An Almanac for Moderns* "one of the best books I have ever read. I suspect it of being a classic" (*Books,* 14 April 1935). When the Limited Editions Club decided to republish *An Almanac for Moderns* in 1938, it called the volume the American book of the last three years most likely to become a classic.

Along with *A Prairie Grove* and *Forward the Nation* (1942), *Singing in the Wilderness* is one of Peattie's efforts to write fiction in which he could employ his skill at portraying the natural world. In these books the landscape generally becomes more real than any of the human characters. A fictionalized "salute" to John James Audubon, *Singing in the Wilderness* uses the techniques of fiction to profile the ornithologist-artist's life against the wilderness backdrop of early eastern North America. The results were mixed, and some reviewers found the novel unpleasantly sentimental. "Mr. Peattie's artifice does not match his nature writing," wrote Brooks Atkinson in *The New York Times* (22 September 1935). "His fiction style looks gaudy when it is set down in the midst of his glowing transcriptions of the outdoors."

The nonfiction book *Green Laurels: The Lives and Achievements of the Great Naturalists* fared better with reviewers. Peattie was at his best when conveying his own excitement about discovery, and these short vignettes on earlier scientists gave him ample opportunity to do so. In *Green Laurels,* as in *An Almanac for Moderns,* Peattie was able to pass on his enthusiasm to his readers. Clearly he had been studying the lives of his subjects for many years.

A Book of Hours is a sequence of twenty-four brief essays, one for each hour of the day. With its deft combination of close observation with well-informed philosophical speculations, it was widely viewed as a successor to *An Almanac for Moderns.* Here and elsewhere in his writing, Peattie was not shy about making philosophical inferences, including expressions of what some critics labeled pantheism. Such reflections combined with the lushness of his writing to give some critics pause. For example, Joseph Wood Krutch saw merit in the author's holistic viewpoint: "No pantheist ever had a completer sense of oneness with all created things"; yet, he also saw problems in Peattie's execution: "there is a tendency to the cultivation of the purple patch. . . . the author is obviously in need of a subject" (*The Nation,* 24 April 1937). Van Doren, however, was impressed. "Mr. Peattie is consumed by an interest in life which will not let him alone. . . . his achievement as a writer consists in having learned how to place his reader likewise in a large world—large, and at the same time swarming with detail. . . . Mr. Peattie gives me the impression of knowing how to talk about anything, and I am confident that he does, for I cannot imagine a subject in which he has not been interested" (*North American Review,* Autumn 1937 / Winter 1937–1938).

Flowering Earth gave Peattie another opportunity to showcase his lifetime of learning. The book may be described as a history of the world from the viewpoint of plants. Critics again had mixed reactions. They admired the breadth of Peattie's vision and erudition while on occasion chastising him for becoming too wrapped up in his subject matter. "The author approaches the plant world with the wide-eyed wonder of a boy who has just experienced the first thrill of collecting and identifying specimens," wrote J. H. Bradley in *The Boston Transcript* (23 December 1939).

The Road of a Naturalist includes some of Peattie's finest writing in its autobiographical story of a long road trip through the western United States. The book won a $2,500 prize from Houghton Mifflin, which published it as part of a new Life in America series. Excerpts appeared in *The Atlantic Monthly* (May 1941) and *Saturday Review of Literature* (5 July 1941). Peattie's recollections occur as a series of flashbacks, making for a sometimes confusing structure. The book is a paean to the wonders of American nature and society, which Peattie came to admire all the more as Europe sank into World War II. The book is Peattie's defense of the

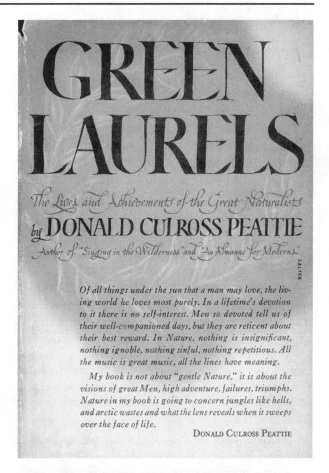

Dust jacket for Peattie's 1936 account of important discoveries in the natural sciences from the Middle Ages through the nineteenth century (Bruccoli Clark Layman Archives)

value of nature and nature study in a world consumed by war.

Peattie's book output slowed after he became a roving editor for *The Reader's Digest* in 1943, a position that allowed him many opportunities to travel and to write journalistic articles about nature, history, and travel. Having inherited from his parents the conviction that the journalist had a profound responsibility to the public, Peattie viewed it as his lifework to translate the insights of science into language that the public could understand and appreciate. While some of his work in this vein comes across as overdone—a charge made by some critics—the best of it is lyrical, even sublime. He also wrote for a wide array of periodicals other than *The Reader's Digest,* including *American Forests, The Atlantic Monthly, Good Housekeeping,* and *The Country Gentleman.* The books he published after the war were primarily collections of his magazine work, including *A Cup of Sky* (1950), which he co-authored with his seventeen-year-old son, Noel. *A Natural History of Trees of Eastern and*

Central North America (1950) and *A Natural History of Western Trees* (1953) are companion volumes that profile trees in a series of detailed and intimate portraits that combine natural and human history. These volumes of six hundred or more pages, each with hundreds of carefully drawn portraits of individual tree species, distilled knowledge he derived from his background as a botanist, his travels throughout the United States, and his extensive reading of the works of early naturalists and other literary travelers. These books confirmed Peattie's reputation as one of the most important popular interpreters of nature in North America, and they have never been out of print.

One might accurately state that Peattie was actively researching these books throughout his entire life. Robert Finch has called them "Peattie's great achievement," adding that "their most impressive quality is Peattie's ability to enter into an almost personal relationship with every tree he portrays. . . . Rarely has American nature had a celebrant as broadly knowledgeable and as infectiously enthusiastic as Donald Culross Peattie."

Peattie was unable to complete two companion volumes about trees of the American South and cultivated exotic trees in North America. He died at home of a heart attack on 16 November 1964. Louise Peattie died the next year.

Unlike similarly rhapsodic nature writers such as John Muir, who described nature as something removed from most human experience, Donald Culross Peattie celebrated human life as an integral part of nature. Though he appreciated wilderness and could write eloquently of such wild places as the great forests of the Appalachians or the Northwest, his vision might be called profoundly horticultural. That is, he did not see humans apart from nature. He hoped that, through observation and science, humans could learn from nature and could work with it to improve their lives. His vision of nature was pantheistic and holistic. Peattie, wrote Lewis Thomas, "writes from a central, obsessive hunch: that there is a connectedness among all living things."

References:

John Drury, *Old Chicago Houses* (Chicago: Bonanza, 1941), pp. 426–430;

Robert Finch, Introduction to *A Natural History of Trees of Eastern and Central North America* (Boston: Houghton Mifflin, 1991);

Peter Friederici, "Donald Culross Peattie: Remembering an Early Prophet in Chicago Wilderness," *Chicago Wilderness,* 4 (Fall 2000): 12–16;

Thomas J. Lyon, ed., *This Incomperable Lande: A Book of American Nature Writing* (Boston: Houghton Mifflin, 1989), pp. 269–276, 443–444, 472;

Lewis Thomas, Afterword to *An Almanac for Moderns* (Boston: Godine, 1980);

Mark Van Doren, "A New Naturalist," *North American Review,* 244 (Autumn 1937 / Winter 1937–38): 162–171;

Allison Bulsterbaum Wallace, "Phenology as Modernist Paradox in Donald Culross Peattie's An Almanac for Moderns," *ISLE: Interdisciplinary Studies in Literature and Environment,* 9 (Winter 2002): 83–90.

Papers:

Donald Culross Peattie's papers are housed at the University of California at Santa Barbara. Other notes and manuscripts are at the Grove in Glenview, Illinois.

Robert Michael Pyle

(19 July 1947 –   )

Robert Kuhlken
Central Washington University

BOOKS: *Watching Washington Butterflies: An Interpretive Guide to the State's 134 Species, Including Most of the Butterflies of Oregon, Idaho, and British Columbia* (Seattle: Seattle Audubon Society, 1974);

The Audubon Society Field Guide to North American Butterflies (New York: Knopf, 1981);

IUCN Invertebrate Red Data Book, by Pyle, Susan M. Wells, and N. Mark Collins (Cambridge: IUCN/ WWF Conservation Monitoring Centre, 1983);

A Field Guide to the Butterflies Coloring Book, by Pyle, Sarah Anne Hughes, and Roger Tory Peterson (Boston: Houghton Mifflin, 1983);

The Audubon Society Handbook for Butterfly Watchers (New York: Scribners, 1984); republished as *Handbook for Butterfly Watchers* (Boston: Houghton Mifflin, 1992);

Wintergreen: Rambles in a Ravaged Land (New York: Scribners, 1986); republished as *Wintergreen: Listening to the Land's Heart* (Boston: Houghton Mifflin, 1988); republished as *Wintergreen: Rambles in a Ravaged Land* (Seattle: Sasquatch Books, 2001);

Insects: A Peterson Field Guide Coloring Book, by Pyle and Kristin Kest (Boston: Houghton Mifflin, 1993);

The Thunder Tree: Lessons From an Urban Wildland (Boston: Houghton Mifflin, 1993);

Where Bigfoot Walks: Crossing the Dark Divide (Boston: Houghton Mifflin, 1995);

Chasing Monarchs: Migrating with the Butterflies of Passage (Boston: Houghton Mifflin, 1999);

Walking the High Ridge: Life As Field Trip (Minneapolis: Milkweed Editions, 2000);

The Butterflies of Cascadia: A Field Guide to All the Species of Washington, Oregon, and Surrounding Territories (Seattle: Seattle Audubon Society, 2002).

OTHER: "Union Bay: A Life-after-death Plant-in," in *Ecotactics: The Sierra Club Handbook for Environmental Activists* (New York: Pocket Books, 1969), pp. 106–111;

"Management of Nature Reserves," in *Conservation Biology: An Evolutionary-ecological Perspective,* edited by

Robert Michael Pyle (photograph by Thea Linnaea Pyle)

Michael E. Soulé and Bruce A. Wilcox (Sunderland, Mass.: Sinauer Associates, 1980), pp. 319–327;

"Urbanization and Endangered Insect Populations," in *Urban Entomology: Interdisciplinary Perspectives,* edited by G. W. Frankie and C. S. Kohler (New York: Praeger, 1983), pp. 367–394;

Mathew Tekulsky, *The Butterfly Garden,* introduction by Pyle (Boston: Harvard Common Press, 1985);

Ed Marquand, *Art of the Butterfly,* afterword by Pyle (San Francisco: Chronicle Books, 1990);

John Hinchliff, *The Distribution of the Butterflies of Washington,* foreword by Pyle (Corvallis: Oregon State University Bookstore, 1996);

"Secrets of the Talking Leaf," in *Facing the Lion: Writers on Life and Craft,* edited by Kurt Brown (Boston: Beacon, 1996), pp. 84–98;

The Enduring Forests, edited by Ruth Kirk and Charles Mauzy, foreword by Pyle (Seattle: Mountaineers, 1996);

James LeMonds, *South of Seattle: Notes on Life in the Northwest Woods,* foreword by Pyle (Missoula, Mont.: Mountain Press, 1997);

Jane Claire Dirks-Edmunds, *Not Just Trees: The Legacy of a Douglas-Fir Forest,* foreword by Pyle (Pullman: Washington State University Press, 1999);

Mary Paetzel, *Spirit of the Siskiyous: The Journals of a Mountain Naturalist,* preface by Pyle (Corvallis: Oregon State University Press, 1999);

Intricate Homeland: Collected Writings from the Klamath-Siskiyou, selected by Susan Cross, foreword by Pyle (Ashland, Ore.: Headwaters Press, 2000);

Nabokov's Butterflies, edited and annotated by Pyle and Brian Boyd, translated by Dmitri Nabokov (Boston: Beacon, 2000);

"Between Climb and Cloud: Nabokov among the Lepidopterists," foreword by Pyle, in *Nabokov's Butterflies* (Boston: Beacon, 2000), pp. 32–76;

"Field Notes from the Southwest," in *Getting Over the Color Green: Contemporary Environmental Literature of the Southwest,* edited by Scott Slovic (Tucson: University of Arizona Press, 2001), pp. 61–68;

John Muir's Last Journey, edited by Michael P. Branch, foreword by Pyle (Washington, D.C.: Island Press, 2001);

"Eden in a Vacant Lot: Special Places, Species, and Kids in the Neighborhood of Life," in *Children and Nature: Psychological, Sociocultural, and Evolutionary Investigations,* edited by Peter H. Kahn Jr., and Stephen R. Kellert (Cambridge, Mass.: MIT Press, 2002).

SELECTED PERIODICAL PUBLICATIONS–UNCOLLECTED: "Willapa Bay," *Audubon,* 72 (November/December 1970): 145;

"Can We Save Our Wild Places from Our 'Civilized' Public? National Parks in Jeopardy," *American West,* 9 (March 1972): 36–41;

"Silk Moth of the Railroad Yards," *Natural History,* 84 (May 1975): 43–51;

"Conservation of Lepidoptera in the United States," *Biological Conservation,* 9 (1976): 55–75;

"The Extinction of Experience," *Horticulture,* 56 (January 1978): 64–67;

"Particular Pleasures of Small Islands," *Pacific Search,* 13 (November 1979): 41–45;

"The Joy of Butterflying," *Audubon,* 86 (July/August 1984): 34–43;

"A Vision for Future Forestry," *High Country News,* 22 (19 November 1990): 29–30;

"Magdalena Alpine: Black Glider of the Rockies," *American Butterflies,* 1 (November 1993): 4–9;

"Receding from Grief," *Orion,* 13 (Winter 1994): 2–3;

"Parents Without Children: Confessions of a Favorite Uncle," *Orion,* 14 (Autumn 1995): 26–29;

"Elegy Written in a Country Farmyard," *Illahee,* 11 (Fall–Winter 1995): 124–129;

"Turning Fifty on Silver Star," *Orion Afield,* 2 (Summer 1998): 8;

"Resurrection Ecology: Bring Back the Xerces Blue!" *Wild Earth,* 39 (Fall 2000): 30;

"Las Monarcas: Butterflies on Thin Ice," *Orion,* 20 (Spring 2001): 16–25;

"The Rise and Fall of Natural History: How a Science Grew that Eclipsed Direct Experience," *Orion,* 20 (Autumn 2001): 16–23;

"Nightlife in Amsterdam," *Orion* (January–February 2003): 16–17.

Among the many practitioners of environmental writing in the United States today, Robert Michael Pyle stands apart. He is first and foremost an accomplished scientist, highly regarded as one of the world's leading experts on butterfly conservation. From this base of knowledge about the Lepidoptera, Pyle has acquired insight into the rest of the insects, birds, and practically all other fauna, along with having gained proficiencies in other disciplines, particularly botany and geography. Thus, he has arrived at an intimate understanding of the natural world through rigorous scholarship and systematic study of ecological science, not simply through an affection for nature writing nor from merely appreciative yet uncritical observation of the environment. Second, he is decidedly oriented to the outdoors, and his written statements are based on recorded field observations, not armchair musings or classroom rhetoric. In this regard, Pyle perpetuates a tradition established by the finest exemplars in the history of American nature writing–such as William Bartram, Aldo Leopold, and Rachel Carson–all of whose voices resonate more saliently now than during their lifetimes and who continue to exert profound influence. This insistence on actual, as opposed to virtual, appreciation of nature has been expressed most fluently in Pyle's notion of "the extinction of experience," first set forth in a 1978 article in the journal *Horticulture* and later amplified in his book *The Thunder Tree: Lessons from an Urban Wildland* (1993), which warns that the more humankind finds itself in the position of being insulated from direct encounters with and resultant knowledge of the natural environment, the less it will care about protecting and conserving the earth and all of its inhabitants. Thus, ignorance breeds indifference. Only through active education and strong efforts ensuring that humans always retain places in which to interact with the natural world will they have any chance of maintaining a harmonious relationship with the environment. Consequently, Pyle has dedicated his life to that end.

Pyle was born 19 July 1947, in Denver, Colorado, to Robert Harold Pyle, whose family hailed from Kentucky backwoods farm country, and Helen Lee Miller Pyle, whose family were Colorado ranchers. Pyle's three siblings included an older sister, Susan; an older brother, Tom; and a younger brother, Howard (Bud). While Pyle was still a young child, the family moved to what was then classified as suburban Denver, to the new tract housing development of Hoffman Heights in the mushrooming municipality of Aurora. Nearby was an important landscape feature that was for Pyle both introduction and perennial touchstone to the natural environment—the High Line Canal, an irrigation artery meandering by measured gradient from the foothills of the Rocky Mountains to the edge of the Great Plains. In *The Thunder Tree,* Pyle describes the canal and the pivotal role it played in developing his early awareness of nature, for along its twisting route he first encountered those lustrous flying beings that became his lifelong passion. When Pyle was eleven years old, he spied a large black-and-yellow swallowtail floating over him like an enchanting vision. It so captured his attention that it turned him away from collecting seashells, an activity that had engaged him since he was seven years old.

This earlier interest in shells was the first phase of the initiation into nature for Pyle, who much later fondly remembers those beginning efforts. Among the Pyle papers archived at the Allen Library of the University of Washington is a folder marked "Mollusc Papers, age 7–11" with this handwritten notation: "NB–very important file to me." Inside are loose sheets of lined notebook paper with various jottings copied from texts, cut and pasted *Mark Trail* panels from the Sunday newspaper comics, and pencil sketches of shells, each captioned with correct scientific nomenclature. Also included are price lists from mail-order shell dealers—the costly penalty for collecting molluscs in Colorado. Unlike his interest in shells, young Pyle's love of butterflies turned out to be no passing fad, for he had the chance to learn about nature through direct interaction

Dust jacket for Pyle's 1984 book, which advocates the preservation of butterfly species by observing them in their natural surroundings without collecting specimens (Richland County Public Library)

with native fauna. The same year he was captivated by the swallowtail he joined the Lepidopterists' Society, and the next year he applied to be a special assistant to the Curator for Spiders and Insects at the Denver Museum of Natural History. He quickly established ongoing correspondence with butterfly collectors around the world, trading specimens and comparing notes. Venturing afield, he learned to make proper records of occurrences and accounts of captures. Accompanied by his brother Tom, or just as often by his mother, Pyle combed the varied habitats provided by the canal and the small ranches and orchards it passed through, always seeking new species or learning a bit more about the old familiar ones. A friend or two might come along for the thrill of the chase but lost interest when Pyle made the careful scientific observations that he was already developing into a dedicated habit. An encounter also occurred one summer, while the family was vacationing at a cabin in Crested Butte, that solidified for Pyle his chosen field of study. He was out collecting with his net one day when he happened upon a group of people doing the same thing. They were renowned scientists Charles Remington and Paul Ehrlich with some of their students from the nearby Rocky Mountain Biological Laboratory. This meeting resulted in much encouragement and learning for Pyle, who later, while working on a doctorate at Yale University, conducted studies with Remington.

Tagged by literary critic Terrell Dixon as "an important early book," *The Thunder Tree* reveals a rite of passage from shy adolescent to budding naturalist. In his recollections Pyle ascribes an initial environmental awareness to his mother's penchant for gardening and his father's love of fly-fishing in the nearby mountain streams, although both parents represented a generation that had newly embraced the conveniences of urban life and was glad to be done finally with rural chores and the necessity of living close to nature. Pyle was never pushed but was nonetheless subtly encouraged by his parents in his steadfast pursuit of science. Upon his mother's death in 1967, he wrote most appreciatively of her support and of her own uncanny ability to find butterflies: "My finest memories of her consist of days in the field, when she constantly made unusual captures." Pyle's father had attended the University of Colorado and during World War II had served as a pharmacist's mate in the merchant marine. The elder Pyle later became a salesman for an office-supply firm, and though he enjoyed the outdoors, he never quite understood his second son's desire and determination to live close to the earth, often asking incredulously if he wanted to get back to the farm. Yet, he would drive Bobby and his older brother, Tom, to the museum or to places in the mountains where they could ramble while he fished. Pyle later remembered that "when my father took me fishing, I always drifted off with my butterfly net." Having read Charles Darwin at an early age, Pyle once announced that he was going to turn his bedroom into a laboratory, a statement that elicited a stern denunciation from his father. Yet, nobody protested when specimen jars piled up and the odor of chemical preservatives wafted through the house. However engagingly personal these anecdotes may be, the prologue of the book tells readers, "The ditch made the man, yet this is a memoir of a place, not a person." Within these leftover pockets of wild nature a curious child found solace, salvation, and freedom. At one point in the narrative Pyle describes the connection he made between wildlife occurrence and critical habitat when a marshy piece of ground that previously harbored an uncommon butterfly became the paved parking lot for the local Lutheran church. This revelation became a defining moment for the sensitive youth, a clarion call to become an ardent conservationist and champion of wild nature. Such early convictions later found an outlet in an environmental activism that began during his college days at the University of Washington and has persisted as a subtext throughout his writing.

Pyle attended Peoria Elementary School in Aurora, and although he did not earn straight A's, he was nevertheless an all-around good student. Teachers typically remarked on report cards that he was "capable of better work," but the need to share his sense of wonder at the world surfaced early in a propensity for show-and-tell; his third-grade teacher, Clara Haner, noted that "Bobby takes a lot of pleasure in bringing to school materials for our classes." He also participated in organized sports, first in wrestling and later in track and field. He once held his junior high school discus record and later recalled how this particular field event became a major passion. At Aurora's Central High he was involved in many extracurricular activities, including concert and marching band (drums), student council (class vice president), and biology club (president). During his final year he was president of the school's National Honor Society and was voted "Most Outstanding Senior Speaker." But the preeminent love for nature was there all along, and even before graduating from high school, he was accorded several scholarly honors: a National Science Foundation Award his junior year to attend the Jackson Laboratory Summer Science Studies Program in Bar Harbor, Maine, and a grant from the Colorado-Wyoming Academy of Sciences to study a butterfly known as the wood nymph. For that project his original research addressed complex questions of natural selection, speciation, and variation within a species. For Pyle, attending college was a foregone conclusion, and he knew all along that he wanted to pursue biology as an academic discipline. In his application to Colorado State University he wrote, "My lifelong choice for a career has been in the field of the biological sciences, and I not only intend to complete the four years of college in that major field, but also wish to work toward an eventual Ph.D." Applications to Princeton, Stanford, and the University of Washington included a statement of personal philosophy, in which he asserted, "My existence on earth is the result of combined biological and extraterritorial forces. . . . I believe I am *human* because of eons of evolution according to the laws of Mendel and Darwin."

In 1965 Pyle moved to Seattle, and over the next eight years he earned both a bachelor's and a master's degree from the University of Washington, where he not only played drums in the Husky marching band but quickly became a conservation activist, leading efforts to preserve wetlands and other remnants of wild nature around campus. He married high school sweetheart and fellow biology student JoAnne R. Clark on 30 July 1966. In his studies, stifled by the quantitative and theoretical constrictions of modern academic biology, he designed his own undergraduate curriculum, and in 1969 under the general studies program he received a degree in "Nature Perception and Protection." Coursework included electives taken from zoology, botany, geography, geology, and English; he particularly enjoyed taking a class from fiction writer Jack Cady. Pyle kept up his interest in Lepidoptera and taught butterfly biology to local students. During this time, Pyle's other two lifelong callings also began to assert themselves and compete for his time and effort–nature conservation and literary endeavors. He became a member of the university Conservation Council and traveled around the state to testify at hearings for proposed developments that threatened natural environments. He was involved in efforts to gain public support for the establishment of North Cascades National Park. Equally important, he was also writing. His notebooks from this period reveal a highly organized plan for completing several book-length projects as well as articles on a variety of topics, many of which have since come to fruition.

A Fulbright Fellowship in 1971 allowed Pyle to conduct research at England's Monks Wood Experimental Station, where he worked closely with John Heath, one of the people he has identified as an important mentor. While in Great Britain, Pyle founded the Xerces Society, an organization devoted to invertebrate conservation and named for an extinct butterfly species. In 1973 he and his wife, JoAnne, divorced amicably, and he married British botanist Sally Hughes on 7 June 1974. (His second marriage lasted a decade.) Back at the University of Washington, he completed his master's degree in nature interpretation in 1973 under the direction of outdoor recreation professor Grant Sharpe. Pyle's first book, *Watching Washington Butterflies: An Interpretive Guide to the State's 134 Species, Including Most of the Butterflies of Oregon, Idaho, and British Columbia* (1974), was published by the Seattle Audubon Society. Remarkably, all of the photographs were taken by the author, but even more significant, this butterfly field guide was the first to employ color photographs of the insects taken exclusively outdoors in their natural settings. In 1976 Pyle completed a Ph.D. in ecology under the direction of Remington at Yale University, where he also worked as a curator at the Peabody Museum. While at Yale, Pyle made contact with naturalist Edwin Way Teale, who resided nearby, and as a result of several meetings with Teale, Pyle resolved to pursue nature writing as a lifelong career. But there was other work to do, and for the next several years Pyle acted as a conservation consultant for a variety of projects

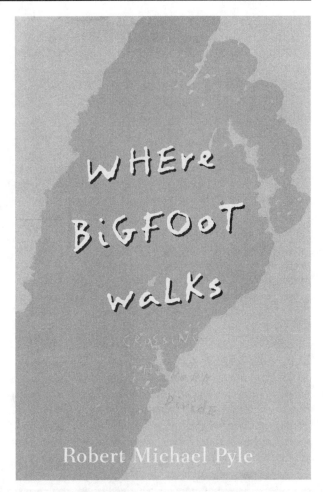

Dust jacket for Pyle's 1995 book, set in the forest near Mount St. Helens in the Pacific Northwest (Richland County Public Library)

around the world, including a memorable period in Papua New Guinea, advising local villagers who were raising in captivity the largest butterflies on earth, hence helping to protect wild populations of the species. At the insistence of Yale classmate Spencer Beebe, Pyle moved to Portland, Oregon, to begin working as the Northwest Land Steward for The Nature Conservancy. He also became a steady contributor of articles to *The Urban Naturalist,* published by the Portland Audubon Society.

In 1981 Pyle served as sole author for *The Audubon Society Field Guide to North American Butterflies,* a stunningly illustrated manual to identifying nearly seven hundred species of butterflies on the North American continent. Now in its fifteenth printing (2000), this book has become the standard reference work–giving the names for these beautiful insects, where they live at the scale of both range and habitat, and what their behavioral habits are. Far from being a dryly written catalogue, the brief descriptive passages that follow each species' template entry bear the characteristic knowledgeable phrasing of Pyle at his best, while the finely reproduced color portraits represent the efforts of more than a hundred different professional photographers. This book alone represents a remarkable scientific achievement and lends credence and authority to whatever other work Pyle has done.

During one of his area explorations, Pyle spotted an old farmhouse for sale that seemed like home to him in the rural hamlet of Gray's River, Washington. He subsequently purchased the place and has lived there since 1979. For Pyle this purchase represented a defining step, a deliberate migration, in the Thoreauvian sense, toward the requisite setting for confronting life's bare essentials and an attempt to see what effect it might have on the creative act of writing. A few years after moving to Swede Park, as he calls his Gray's River abode, he was joined by an old friend, silkscreen artist Thea Linnaea Peterson, whom he married on 19 October 1985.

From 1979–1982 he lived half-time in Cambridge, U.K., collaborating with other scientists to compile *IUCN Invertebrate Red Data Book,* aimed at providing baseline information for conservation efforts. His next book, *The Audubon Society Handbook for Butterfly Watchers* (1984), presents a deceptively straightforward primer on butterflies in their natural surroundings. Its nineteen chapters follow a logical sequence of topics, resembling one of those now ubiquitous FAQ (frequently asked questions) lists, beginning with the preliminary question "Why watch butterflies?" and ending with a pair of chapters outlining some favorite places for engaging in this activity in North America and abroad. In between are a series of lucid explanations covering scientific nomenclature and the organization of all butterflies into six major families; host plants and habitat requirements; how to conduct and record field observations; and the conservation of butterflies and their environments, including suggested pathways for educational activities. The ethical question of collecting versus watching is dealt with: collecting is allowed by the necessity for scientific investigation, as long as no harm is done to a species that may be threatened or on the decline. Pinning dead insects to a board as a hobby, Pyle suggests, is best replaced by the activity celebrated by the title of the manual. The chapter on butterfly behavior describes nectar sipping, mudding (most likely for salts), basking in the sun, and flying–evasive flight to avoid predation and a more lilting spiral for courtship. Pointing out these ethological aspects of his favorite creatures reveals Pyle's powers of observation and attention to detail. Out of such awareness come understanding and empathy. What renders the book truly inspirational is the author's insistence that anybody can

attain a similar bond with the natural world through patience and concentration. The chapter on rearing butterflies encourages the scientist in everyone and presents encouragement to become a close observer and recorder of natural phenomena. An underlying theme running through this book is how human beings might learn to share the world with these insects. Toward that end, special attention is given to the plants that butterflies require for nectaring and ovipositing (laying eggs) and to methods of tending these plants in a home butterfly garden. The epilogue to the book is a confession of finding serenity and tranquility in watching butterflies, "a kind of meditation" having the potential for profound effects on a society that seeks peace among its members.

With the publication of *Wintergreen: Rambles in a Ravaged Land* (1986), Pyle's work enters the realm of environmental literature, and his distinctive voice from then on commands a place in the genre of American nature writing. *Wintergreen* is at once an elegy and a celebration of the ravaged landscapes of Willapa Hills in southwest Washington. In the industrial view of the world, this place was doomed to exploitation. Wilder and more expansive terrain surrounding those ethereal snowcapped peaks just a crow's flight away have captured the attention of the nature preservationist's agenda, but even after logging has transformed this countryside, Pyle seeks communion with its indelible vitality. He speaks reverently of the rain-swollen rivers, the prolific vegetation, the surprisingly adaptable fauna, and the timber-dependent communities struggling to hang on in the wake of the pillaging of resources. A new message of conservation is set forth: understand and cherish local places. Received with widespread critical acclaim, the book prompted *Sierra* magazine writer Christopher Camuto to say that "The clear, complex topography of his language pays homage at every turn to the land he describes" and that "Pyle uses words with wit and care, as if they too were a resource not to be devalued by misuse." The book received the 1986 John Burroughs Medal for distinguished nature writing and the Pacific Northwest Booksellers Association Award. It also earned the author the first of his three Governor's Writers Awards.

In his 1993 book *The Thunder Tree,* Pyle again takes note of the everyday nature evident all around, especially its often surprising but redeeming presence amid urban and neglected lands. He shows the rewards of gaining special cognizance of "the secondhand lands, the hand-me-down habitats where you have to look hard to find something to love." The initiation process and blossoming fascination with natural phenomena come across well, but equally compelling is the way Pyle elucidates the intertwined context of Western water problems and patterns of explosive urban growth surrounding the natural corridor of the High Line Canal. Tim McNulty wrote in the *Seattle Times* (1 August 1993) that Pyle now "occupies an interesting niche among American nature writers: that of poet of damaged lands." In a review for *English Journal* (November 1994), James LeMonds declared that "the book is crafted with beauty and Pyle's gentle instruction about everything from cottonwoods to magpies to the politics of water . . . it is a fitting sequel to his previous effort, *Wintergreen*." In her assessment of these two books for the *Bloomsbury Review* (July/August 1994), Susan Tweit notes that "in both *Wintergreen* and *The Thunder Tree,* the earlier, more descriptive chapters are less moving than the later, more personal ones," and while avowing "there is plenty of power in Pyle's writing," she found that portions of *The Thunder Tree* proved "a difficult read–too much description, too much objectivity, too little personal engagement." Yet, this critique seems questionable for a work so self-consciously autobiographical.

In *Where Bigfoot Walks: Crossing the Dark Divide* (1995) Pyle returns to his adult home range and turns his attention not so much to the mythical creature of the title as to its alleged favored haunt and habitat–a forgotten corner of forest tucked in between the largest volcanoes of the Pacific Northwest. A prestigious Guggenheim Fellowship allowed him the time to conduct his research, and this book represents his findings. He dates his own interest in the fabled beast to a 1969 student excursion to Ape Cave, a large subterranean lava tube on the southern flanks of Mount St. Helens. Returning to the region twenty years later, he not only indulges in a focused exploration of cryptozoology but also offers a critique of Forest Service policy allowing off-road vehicle use and a timber-cutting regime that encourages erosion and loss of habitat. In searching for sign or spoor of Sasquatch, Pyle introduces his readers to the kind of debate that has become all too common in modern resource management circles, in which everyone has a stake in the decision, and the reality, the integrity, and the potential of the place simply fall off the map. In the context of nature writing, Pyle hits his stride in *Where Bigfoot Walks*. Plodding up and down footpaths with a heavy backpack full of provisions and empty notebooks to fill, or creeping dilatorily along rough logging roads in his venerable Honda Civic dubbed "Powdermilk," he stalks the shadowy primate and shares with his readers the adventure of simply being out there. But the book is more than just an amble through some woods that represent "the lair of creatures beyond our ken." Pyle envelops his story in a discussion of other legendary ape-like fauna around the world, such as Yeti of the

Pyle in the late 1990s (photograph by Thea Linnaea Pyle)

Himalayan Mountains. He tracks down and interviews the people who claim to have seen Bigfoot and those who intensely wish to, along with the scientists who continue to keep an open mind on the matter in light of evidence that points to the possibility of its existence. Perhaps dismissed as too regionalist, the book received positive but brief notice in the review sections of such periodicals as *The Atlantic Monthly* and *Western American Literature*. Closer to home, however, *Where Bigfoot Walks* was welcomed with more enthusiasm, and the *Seattle Post-Intelligencer* praised this "powerful meditation on man and nature and the importance of the unknown" as the latest offering from "one of the Northwest's most eloquent chroniclers of nature."

Chasing Monarchs: Migrating with the Butterflies of Passage (1999) is the story of a journey, or rather, two parallel journeys–one a remarkable insect migration and the other a quest more quotidian than quixotic, whereby Lepidoptery is combined with a road trip. The goal is to locate monarch butterflies and follow them south, netting and tagging them when the chance arises. Pyle has with him his beloved butterfly net

"Marsha," whose handle is composed of cottonwood from the High Line Canal. Ostensibly, the reason for chasing these creatures is to dispel what Pyle has termed "a major myth of American natural history: that all the monarchs west of the Rockies' crest migrate to California, only those east of the Rockies go to Mexico, and the two don't mix." But the book is also about place and the endlessly fascinating scenes that make up the American West. Along the way Pyle provides evocative descriptions of select sites as wildly distinct as Quitobaquito Springs in the Organ Pipe Cactus National Monument of Arizona, the riparian edges of the upper Columbia River in Canada, and a highway rest stop in the salt flats near the Utah-Nevada line. The animals he follows also lead readers onward, and Pyle manages to teach about them en route. The author knows that reading a travelogue is more fun than reading a scientific text, and he slips educational passages seamlessly into the narrative, as after tagging one of the few male monarchs encountered, he describes the way to tell the sexes apart in a one-paragraph anatomy lesson. Unlike Jack Kerouac, Pyle goes on the road with a specific purpose. Sleeping mainly in "Powdermilk" wherever night falls, he provides lessons in how to conduct field study by automobile: on the backseat is a "bulging book box" full of reference materials and published field guides. *Chasing Monarchs* earned for Pyle his third Governor's Writers Award, and while it received buoyant reviews from the literary press, popular periodicals delivered a more mixed reaction. Gregg Sapp, in *The Library Journal* (July 1999), wrote that the author "vividly conveys the lure of the butterflies, the quirky passions of those who study them, and the beauty and diversity of Western landscapes." Michiko Kakutani, reviewing the book for *The New York Times* (13 August 1999), on the other hand, complained of "windy, repetitious descriptions of vegetation and geologic formations that are of little interest to the lay reader," but stated that "by far the most absorbing portions of this book deal with Mr. Pyle's interaction with the monarchs (tagging and tracking them and watching them feed and navigate) and his musings on their history and their habits." Conversely, *USA Today* reviewer Jayne Clark, in the 17 November 1999 issue, praised the "often deft descriptions of the dusty Western locales few travelers see" but found the actual butterfly chase "tedious reading" and cautioned that "readers who are less than enraptured by the tenacious winged creatures probably won't make it as far as Mexico."

Among those people fully enraptured by butterflies was twentieth-century writer Vladimir Nabokov, who was also a lepidopterist. In 2000 Pyle collaborated with Nabokov biographer Brian Boyd to bring out a collection of Nabokov's letters and uncollected short pieces, *Nabokov's Butterflies,* for which Pyle prepared an informative preface. He expresses particular affinity for Nabokov's ability to navigate the world by straddling the realms of art and science, and he quotes the writer's deliberate aspiration toward such a stance: "Does there not exist a high ridge where the mountainside of 'scientific' knowledge joins the opposite slope of 'artistic' imagination?" Pyle's own next book takes its title from that rhetorical query. *Walking the High Ridge: Life As Field Trip* also appeared in 2000 and constitutes a thoughtful autobiographical and philosophical recollection of the manifold paths taken by Pyle, this scientist-writer whom David James Duncan labeled "triple-hatted" in deference to his efforts in literature, Lepidoptery, and conservation. The book also includes a brief biographical portrait of Pyle and a bibliographical compilation, both by University of Nevada professor Scott Slovic, founding president of the Association for the Study of Literature and the Environment (ASLE). In his 2002 book Pyle has actually returned to his first work, as the Seattle Audubon Society resurrects his long-out-of-print work on Washington butterflies in a greatly expanded and updated version, *The Butterflies of Cascadia: A Field Guide to All the Species of Washington, Oregon, and Surrounding Territories.*

Pyle has now written a dozen books, published several hundred articles, and received many accolades and honors, including a Fulbright Scholarship, a Guggenheim grant, many book awards, and the 1997 Distinguished Service Award from the Society for Conservation Biology. He has worked as a natural history educator and creative-writing instructor at institutions such as Utah State University, Evergreen State College, the North Cascades Institute, and Oregon's Sitka Center for Art and Ecology. For the past two decades he has been a steady contributor to *Orion* and a regular columnist for *Orion Afield* and is currently at work on another book that elucidates in greater detail the place he calls home. He is also nearing completion of a long-standing novel-in-progress titled "Magdalena Mountain." An undercurrent running throughout his work is the need to pay attention to the reality of nature everywhere. Pyle has long held that the world is composed of an arrangement of diverse and decidedly disparate places, and this awareness has informed his writing with an intense geographical disposition. An insistence on specificity of place in natural history found early expression in his 1976 dissertation for his doctorate at Yale University, "The Ecogeographical Basis for Lepidoptera Conservation." Pyle later explained, in *Handbook for Butterfly Watchers,* that "my own doctoral dissertation aimed to correlate butterfly distribution with that of nature reserves in Washington

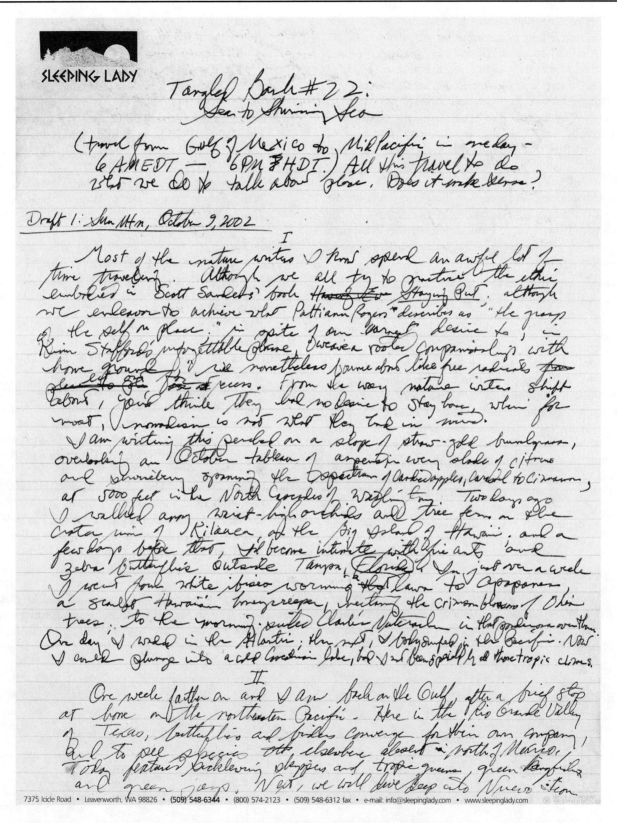

Manuscript page for Pyle's "The Tangled Bank No. 22, Sea to Shining Sea" for Orion *magazine*
(Collection of Robert Michael Pyle)

... by plotting 10,000 records of butterfly occurrences in the state." Using these data he was able to demonstrate critical spatial inconsistencies between "natural butterfly provinces" and the disproportionate allocation of nature reserves, thereby strengthening the impetus for more-rational conservation efforts. Elsewhere in *Handbook for Butterfly Watchers*, he explicitly states, "Biogeography is my own chief interest, and I find patterns of distribution fascinating in their own right." Although he often injects his narratives with lofty thoughts or flights of pure imagination, Pyle's writing remains rooted in detail and does not float away among the clouds of vague generalization. In *The Thunder Tree* he asserts, "When people connect with nature, it happens *somewhere*." This sense of place permeates Pyle's work, keeping it oriented.

Robert Michael Pyle has become a key contributor to the genre of American nature writing, and his work serves as an inspirational stimulus that coaxes and coaches readers into making connections with the environment. In a 1997 interview he asked, "Can creature or landscape act as guide, as a way beyond the vast wall of indifference and blunted sensibilities that we tend to carry around with us?" His impeccable scientific investigations into Lepidoptera have been the foundation for his own metamorphosis into a skilled literary stylist who has never lost his overwhelming sense of wonder and who wants to share that feeling of endless discovery. Simply by paying attention, being vigilant, and knowing where to look, he writes in *Handbook for Butterfly Watchers*, "you cannot help but gain a sense of the landscape, and in so doing, you will come to see the land through the eyes of butterflies."

Interviews:

Ray Kelleher, "'From a Distance, the Study of Butterflies Looks Like an Obsessive Pursuit of Nothing At All. On a Figurative Level, the Same Could Be Said of the Writing Life': An Interview with Robert Michael Pyle," *Poets & Writers*, 24 (March/April 1996): 54–61;

Casey Walker, "An Interview with Robert Michael Pyle," *Wild Duck Review*, 3 (February 1997): 23–26;

Erik Lundegaard, "Chasing Butterflies–Naturalist Robert Michael Pyle Is an Erudite Guide to Much More Than Monarchs," *Seattle Times*, 31 August 1999, p. E1;

Dave Howard, "Butterfly Chaser: Wahkiakum County Naturalist Works to Save Winged Beauties," *Grange News*, 91, no. 10 (December 2002): 6.

Bibliography:

Scott Slovic, "Bibliography of Robert Michael Pyle's Work," in Pyle, *Walking the High Ridge: Life As Field Trip* (Minneapolis: Milkweed Editions, 2000), pp. 147–185.

References:

Christopher Camuto, "The Wildness Not There," *Sierra* (May/June 1987): 83–86;

Terrell Dixon, "Inculcating Wildness: Ecocomposition, Nature Writing, and the Regreening of the American Suburb," in *The Nature of Cities: Ecocriticism and Urban Environments*, edited by Michael Bennett and David W. Teague (Tucson: University of Arizona Press, 1999), pp. 77–90;

David James Duncan, "Man of Two Minds," *Sierra*, 85 (September/October 2000): 52–57, 75–76;

Scott Slovic, "Robert Michael Pyle: A Portrait," in Pyle, *Walking the High Ridge: Life as a Field Trip* (Minneapolis: Milkweed Editions, 2000), pp. 119–146.

Papers:

Many of Robert Michael Pyle's personal and literary papers are held in Special Collections and Archives of Allen Library at the University of Washington, Seattle.

Theodore Roosevelt

(27 October 1858 – 6 January 1919)

Brian Adler
Valdosta State University

See also the Roosevelt entries in *DLB 47: American Historians, 1866–1912* and *DLB 186: Nineteenth-Century American Western Writers.*

BOOKS: *The Summer Birds of the Adirondacks in Franklin County, N.Y.,* by Roosevelt and H. D. Minot (Salem, Mass.: Privately printed, 1877);

Notes on Some Birds of Oyster Bay, Long Island (New York: Privately printed, 1879);

The Naval War of 1812; or, The History of the United States Navy during the Last War with Great Britain (New York: Putnam, 1882); republished as *The Naval Operations of the War between Great Britain and the United States* (Boston: Little, Brown, 1901; London: Sampson Low, Marston, 1901);

Hunting Trips of a Ranchman: Sketches of Sport on the Northern Cattle Plains (New York & London: Putnam, 1885; London: Kegan Paul, Trench, 1886);

Thomas Hart Benton (Boston: Houghton, Mifflin, 1886);

Essays on Practical Politics (New York & London: Putnam, 1888);

Gouverneur Morris (Boston & New York: Houghton, Mifflin, 1888);

Ranch Life and the Hunting-Trail (New York: Century, 1888; London: Unwin, 1888);

The Winning of the West: An Account of the Exploration and Settlement of Our Country from the Alleghenies to the Pacific, 4 volumes (New York: Putnam, 1889–1896);

New York (London & New York: Longmans, Green, 1891);

The Wilderness Hunter: An Account of the Big Game of the United States and Its Chase with Horse (New York: Putnam, 1893);

Hero Tales from American History, by Roosevelt and Henry Cabot Lodge (New York: Century, 1895);

American Ideals, and Other Essays, Social and Political (New York & London: Putnam, 1897);

The Rough Riders (New York: Scribners, 1899; London: Kegan Paul, Trench, Trübner, 1899);

Theodore Roosevelt in a photograph published on the cover of the 2 July 1904 issue of Harper's Weekly *(National Portrait Gallery, Washington, D.C.; gift of Joanna Sturm)*

Oliver Cromwell (New York: Scribners, 1900; London: Constable, 1900);

The Strenuous Life: Essays and Addresses (New York: Century, 1900; London: Richards, 1902);

California Addresses (San Francisco: California Promotion Committee, 1903);

Outdoor Pastimes of an American Hunter (limited edition, New York: Scribners, 1903; trade edition, New York: Scribners, 1905; London: Longmans, Green,

271

1905; enlarged edition, New York: Scribners, 1908);

Addresses and Presidential Messages of Theodore Roosevelt, 1902–1904 (New York & London: Putnam, 1904);

Good Hunting (New York & London: Harper, 1907);

Addresses and Papers, edited by Willis Fletcher Johnson (New York: Sun Dial, 1908);

The Deer Family, by Roosevelt, T. S. Van Dyke, D. G. Elliot, and A. J. Stone (New York: Grosset & Dunlap, 1908);

The Roosevelt Policy; Speeches, Letters and State Papers, Relating to Corporate Wealth and Closely Allied Topics, of Theodore Roosevelt (2 volumes, New York: Current Literature, 1908; enlarged edition, 3 volumes, edited by William Griffith, New York: Current Literature, 1919);

Outlook Editorials (New York: Outlook, 1909);

Stories of the Great West (New York: Century, 1909);

African Game Trails, An Account of the African Wanderings of an American Hunter-Naturalist (New York: Scribners, 1910; London: Murray, 1910);

African and European Addresses (New York & London: Putnam, 1910);

American Problems (New York: Outlook, 1910);

The New Nationalism (New York: Outlook, 1910);

The Conservation of Womanhood and Childhood (New York: Funk & Wagnalls, 1912);

Realizable Ideals (The Earl Lectures) (San Francisco: Whittaker & Ray-Wiggin, 1912);

Theodore Roosevelt: An Autobiography (New York: Macmillan, 1913);

Progressive Principles: Selections from Addresses Made during the Presidential Campaign of 1912, edited by Elmer H. Youngman (New York: Progressive National Service, 1913);

History as Literature, and Other Essays (New York: Scribners, 1913; London: Murray, 1914);

Life-Histories of African Game Animals, 2 volumes, by Roosevelt and Edmund Heller (New York: Scribners, 1914; London: Murray, 1915);

Through the Brazilian Wilderness (New York: Scribners, 1914; London: Murray, 1914);

America and the World War (New York: Scribners, 1915; London: Murray, 1915);

A Book-Lover's Holidays in the Open (New York: Scribners, 1916; London: Murray, 1916);

Fear God and Take Your Own Part (New York: Doran, 1916; London: Hodder & Stoughton, 1916);

Americanism and Preparedness. Speeches, July to November, 1916 (New York: Mail and Express Job Print, 1916);

The Foes of Our Own Household (New York: Doran, 1917);

National Strength and International Duty (Princeton, N.J.: Princeton University Press, 1917);

The Great Adventure: Present-Day Studies in American Nationalism (New York: Scribners, 1918; London: Murray, 1919);

Average Americans (New York & London: Putnam, 1919);

Newer Roosevelt Messages: Speeches, Letters, and Magazine Articles Dealing with the War, Before and After, and Other Vital Topics, edited by Griffith (New York: Current Literature, 1919);

America and Japan (Portland, Ore.: Wheelwright, 1920);

Roosevelt in the Kansas City Star: War-Time Editorials by Theodore Roosevelt (Boston & New York: Houghton Mifflin, 1921);

Campaigns and Controversies (New York: Scribners, 1926);

East of the Sun and West of the Moon, by Roosevelt and Kermit Roosevelt (New York & London: Scribners, 1926);

Literary Essays (New York: Scribners, 1926);

Social Justice and Popular Rule: Essays, Addresses, and Public Statements Relating to the Progressive Movement (New York: Scribners, 1926);

Theodore Roosevelt's Diaries of Boyhood and Youth (New York & London: Scribners, 1928);

Colonial Policies of the United States (Garden City, N.Y.: Doubleday, Doran, 1937);

The Hunting and Exploring Adventures of Theodore Roosevelt, edited by Donald Day (New York: Dial, 1955);

Memories of the American Frontier (New York: Westvaco, 1977);

Frontier Types. In Cowboy-Land (Palmer Lake, Colo.: Filter Press, 1988).

Editions and Collections: *The Works of Theodore Roosevelt,* 24 volumes, Memorial Edition (New York: Scribners, 1923–1926);

The Works of Theodore Roosevelt, 20 volumes, National Edition (New York: Scribners, 1926);

American Bears: Selections from the Writings of Theodore Roosevelt, edited by Paul Schullery (Boulder: Colorado Associated University Press, 1983).

OTHER: *American Big-Game Hunting,* edited by Roosevelt and George Bird Grinnell (New York: Forest and Stream, 1893)—includes essays by Roosevelt;

Hunting in Many Lands, edited by Roosevelt and Grinnell (New York: Forest and Stream, 1895)—includes essays by Roosevelt;

Trail and Camp-Fire, edited by Roosevelt and Grinnell (New York: Forest and Stream, 1897)—includes essays by Roosevelt;

Forest Preservation and National Prosperity: Portions of Addresses Delivered at the American Forest Congress,

January 2 to 6, 1905, by President Roosevelt, Ambassador Jusserand, Secretary Wilson, and Others (Washington, D.C.: Government Printing Office, 1905);

Lucy Warner Maynard, *Birds of Washington and Vicinity: Including Adjacent Parts of Maryland and Virginia* (Washington, D.C.: Woodward & Lothrop, 1909)—edition includes Roosevelt's "List of Birds Seen in the White House Grounds and About Washington during His Administration."

Theodore Roosevelt was a prolific author, the twenty-sixth president of the United States, the first American to win a Nobel Peace Prize, and the only United States president to be awarded a Congressional Medal of Honor. He was a rancher, a hunter, an heir to a sizable fortune, and the devoted father of five children. He is also responsible, through his writings and legislative actions, for helping to preserve more of the environment of the United States than any other individual. As one reads through Roosevelt's nature writings, one is compelled to notice his strong desire simultaneously to preserve the environment for the enjoyment of future generations and to learn all he can about the flora and fauna. At times Roosevelt treats the natural world harshly: the number of animals he killed in hunts is perhaps staggering. Following such a slaughter, however, he frequently comments on the supreme beauty of nature, revealing detailed knowledge that could have come about only through long study and unstinting devotion to nature.

Theodore Roosevelt, born 27 October 1858 in New York, New York, was the second of four children born to Theodore Roosevelt Sr. and Martha Bullock Roosevelt. Theodore Sr. came from a prominent social background and worked in the family hardware business. He was also a founder of the Metropolitan Museum of Art and the American Museum of Natural History. His wife was from a wealthy Southern slave-holding family.

Roosevelt's earliest nature writing dates to his first extant letter, written to his mother when he was nine. His mother was in Savannah, Georgia, visiting relatives. Roosevelt, from the family home, located at Broadway and Fourth Street in New York City, wrote on 28 April 1868, expressing astonishment at the number of flowers his mother received during her visit. He speaks of jumping with delight at her describing the sound of a mockingbird and requests that his mother bring to him some feathers if she can. He expresses sorrow that some trees have been cut down because of vandalism. Writing in the same letter to his sister Corinne, he describes in some detail the behavior of two mice in his possession, Lordy and Rosa.

This letter is a precursor of the writing of Roosevelt when he and his family embarked on a grand

Alice Hathaway Lee (whom Roosevelt married in 1880), Roosevelt, and Rose Saltonstall, Boston, 1879 (Theodore Roosevelt Collection, Harvard College Library)

tour of Europe in the spring of 1869. Roosevelt kept a journal throughout the trip, offering keen observations of the sights, with a special emphasis on nature. One reason for this trip was to improve the health of Theodore Jr., who suffered terribly from asthma. His attacks did not improve, so the tour was often punctuated with his great health crises, and he frequently recorded bad nights in his journal. On Easter Sunday, 17 April 1870, he recovered from an asthma attack and was able to comment on having walked through woods near Paris, where he describes seeing a 1,400-year-old tree and a 300-year-old tree.

Sometime in September 1870, after the Roosevelts had returned home to New York, Theodore Sr. spoke to his son, saying young Theodore must "make" his body if he hoped to rise above the sickly and asthmatic youthful condition that had to this point occupied his life and had to a large extent dominated his family's life. Theodore Jr. responded that he would make his body and immediately began a regime of exercises that included long, brisk walks out-of-doors and horseback riding.

He lived a rich life with nature early on. As a boy of two, he had associated the face of a fox with that of God, according to his sister. He filled notebooks with drawing after drawing of mice and birds, and he closely observed insects of all kinds, writing detailed descriptions in his notebooks. In his seventh or eighth year he came upon a dead seal in a Broadway fish market. He got as much information as he could about the seal, took detailed measurements, and offered to buy it for his Museum of Natural History (at this time, located conveniently in his bedroom, but given a great deal more space, up in the attic, in his family's new house). By the age of thirteen, Roosevelt had read works by Charles Darwin, John James Audubon, and Spencer Fullerton Baird (compiler of such works as the *Catalogue of North American Birds* [1858] and *North American Reptiles* [1853]). As part of the project to strengthen his son, the senior Roosevelt took the family to the Adirondacks in the summer of 1871, where Theodore Jr. took copious notes in his journal about the local fauna and flora. He clearly put his time in the woods to good use; the official records of the American Museum of Natural History note in the fall of 1871 the receipt of a sizable collection of natural specimens from Roosevelt, including the skull of a red squirrel and a bat.

Roosevelt's nature collection shortly expanded greatly when in the following year his father presented him with two things he had never had before—a gun and a pair of glasses. Roosevelt was almost fourteen before his family realized that his eyes were in need of augmentation, and with glasses Roosevelt could now truly see the world. He rapidly expanded his collection of specimens, engaging in a kind of systematic slaughter that he justified from the perspective of expanding his knowledge of the natural world. His hunting continued for many years, and indeed, shortly before he was to enter Harvard in 1875, he wrote to his sister Anna from the family's country retreat at Oyster Bay about his smelly room, full of his latest specimens (in this case the skins of six night herons). At about this time Roosevelt wrote a scientific essay titled "Blarina talpoides (Short-Tailed Shrew)," which describes in great detail the behavior of this ferocious but tiny animal.

By 1877 Roosevelt's collection of stuffed and mounted animals numbered in the hundreds, and he discussed with his father his future career. He told his father that he wanted to be a scientist, and with his father's somewhat lukewarm approval, he pursued, with even greater enthusiasm than before, scientific and naturalistic studies at Harvard. William James was Roosevelt's instructor in his sophomore course of comparative anatomy and physiology of vertebrates, and the young man spent a great deal of time in the Harvard Museum of Comparative Zoology, the curator of which was the son of Louis Agassiz. Unfortunately, by the time Roosevelt graduated from Harvard, having along the way been elected to Phi Beta Kappa, and finishing 21st out of a class of 171, he found himself to have grown quite alienated from his original plan to become a natural historian. As he states in his journal, "I had no more desire or ability to be a microscopist and section-cutter than to be a mathematician." In making this statement, Roosevelt was speaking more of changes within him than making any commentary on the supposed deficiencies of the Harvard curriculum, which, with such men as Nathaniel Southgate Shaler on the faculty of the natural history department, should have given Roosevelt much more than a view of the natural world through a microscope.

But other major changes had occurred in Roosevelt's life. In 1878 his father, known to the family as "Greatheart," had died, an event that greatly affected the closely knit Roosevelt family. It took Roosevelt many months to return to some semblance of normalcy after this event. At the same time, with his father's passing, Roosevelt came into a considerable amount of money, abruptly finding himself as a college junior with an annual income greater than that of the president of Harvard.

Having to assume responsibilities as the oldest male in the family after his father's death, Roosevelt clearly felt he had to do something other than to pursue the world of natural science. His father had spent the last year of his short life (dying at age forty-six) embroiled in a political battle that had sullied his otherwise unblemished reputation. Roosevelt's father died two months after a vicious and highly visible fight involving President Rutherford B. Hayes and the United States Senate on one side and Tammany Hall politicians on the other. Shortly thereafter Roosevelt began speaking more about politics as a profession.

In 1880 he graduated from Harvard and on 27 October married Alice Hathaway Lee, whom he had been courting for two years. As a married man and head of a family that included, in addition to his wife, his mother, two sisters, and a brother, Roosevelt joined various civic-minded organizations and began to study law at Columbia University. He was also becoming more actively involved in politics, winning a seat in the New York State Assembly in 1881. He continued to engage in travel, heading out West to the Dakota Territories in the summer of 1881 to hunt and to help improve his health. After such an excursion he returned to New York with the news that he had shot a buffalo and that he had purchased a cattle operation in the Badlands of the Dakota Territories. In his political career, he built for himself a reputation as a political reformer and continued to hold his assembly seat through four elections.

He had given up the study of law, but on the whole, by 1884, life seemed to be extremely good for him.

However, on Valentine's Day 1884, his life changed drastically. On that day he suffered two terrible blows: his mother, to whom he was devoted, died at the age of forty-three of typhoid fever, and a few hours later, his wife, Alice, died of Bright's disease, only two days after having given birth to their child, a girl soon to be named Alice. For Roosevelt, the answer to overcoming such severe emotional blows lay in devoting himself to his western cattle concerns, but before he did so, he exerted himself in the political realm in a significant way at the 1884 Republican National Convention, where he worked closely with politicians such as William McKinley and Henry Cabot Lodge.

After the convention, one newspaper reported in headline letters: "Roosevelt Takes to the Woods." Indeed, Roosevelt removed himself to his ranch, which he named Elkhorn, located thirty miles north of the nearest town, Medora, in the Dakota Territories (eventually becoming North Dakota), ten miles away from the closest neighbors. Altogether, Roosevelt spent a little more than thirteen months out West, spread over a three-year period (1883–1886). During this time he published *Hunting Trips of a Ranchman* (1885), a first-person account of his initial time out West. He had invested much time, money, and personal labor in ranching operations. On 4 July 1886 Roosevelt was asked to make the keynote address during Independence Day observances in Dickinson, Dakota Territories. In a revealing list he speaks of liking big things: "like all Americans, I like big things; big prairies, big forests and mountains, big wheat fields, railroads—and herds of cattle, too—big factories, steamboats, and everything else." Roosevelt talked about the responsibility Americans have to protect all that has been granted them—freedom, material prosperity, and as implied in this expansive catalogue of big things, the largest thing of all, the world of natural resources. For Roosevelt, there is nothing odd about combining mountains with factories. In his mind, both are important; both need protection and management; and both offer much to mankind.

After withdrawing from further ranching operations in 1886, Roosevelt returned more or less permanently to New York City. He ran for mayor in 1886 but lost. On 2 December 1886, he married Edith Carow.

In December 1887 Roosevelt—along with George Bird Grinnell, editor of *Field and Stream*—founded the Boone and Crockett Club. Roosevelt was the first president of the club (remaining president until 1894). This club became extremely influential with Congress in promulgating a message of conservation and environmental stewardship. Later members included Gifford Pinchot and William Tecumseh Sherman. Roosevelt and Grin-

Edith Carow in 1885, about the time of her engagement to Roosevelt (Theodore Roosevelt Collection, Harvard College Library)

nell edited three volumes of their own brand of nature writing: *American Big-Game Hunting* (1893), *Hunting in Many Lands* (1895), and *Trail and Camp-Fire* (1897), each of which included essays by Roosevelt. Through such publications and lobbying efforts the club played a significant role in encouraging Congress to pass the Forest Reserve Act (1891), which gave the president of the United States the authority to set aside without review any wooded or partially wooded land for the future benefit of the country, and the Park Protection Act (1894), which strengthened rules governing land set aside by the government. Roosevelt's organization (still extant and powerful) continues to publish works that fit squarely within Roosevelt's own perspective on ecological concerns and interaction with the land. In 1925, for example, Grinnell and Charles Sheldon published *Hunting and Conservation,* a collection of essays the basic premise of which Roosevelt would have supported.

During this time Roosevelt was publishing in *The Century Illustrated Monthly Magazine* essays on ranch life that were bound together and published as *Ranch Life and the Hunting-Trail* (1888). This book is a comprehensive treatment of Roosevelt's three years in the Dakota Territories. Chapters are detailed enough and written with such clarity that someone completely unfamiliar with ranching could use Roosevelt's book as a kind of instruction manual. *Ranch Life and the Hunting-Trail* conveys the harshness of life on the Great Plains but also something of the beauty. One theme is the tension between the law and order of civilized outposts and the lawlessness that can often be found on the frontier when individuals find themselves confronted with harsh nature and little else. Throughout the work, Roosevelt emphasizes the importance of the individual to bring meaning and order to this vast panorama: "Civilization seems as remote as if we were living in an age long past . . . it is the life of men who live in the open, who tend herds on horseback, who go armed and ready to guard their lives by their own powers, whose wants are very simple." In handling his herds, Roosevelt speaks of a sophisticated ecological principle that conservationists have only recently begun to take into account as they view various wildlife habitats, that of how much land each animal needs in order to survive. Roosevelt says that to an observer, the range may look empty, but that on the average, for cattle, twenty-five acres of ground are needed for each animal. Thus, to an "Eastern and unpracticed eye," the Plains may look empty and underutilized, but in reality, for the herd to remain healthy, an immense amount of land is needed to meet the true needs of the animals.

Roosevelt also speaks of a perspective that propelled him later in his conservation work. He writes that the way of life he experienced on the plains is doomed: "The great free ranches, with their barbarous, picturesque, and curiously fascinating surrounds, mark a primitive stage of existence as surely as do the great tracts of primeval forests." Roosevelt laments the passing of all that this way of life holds, not only for the loss of the benefits inherent in the activities themselves, but also because to future generations this type of living will be completely lost. Roosevelt feels "real sorrow that those who come after us are not to see, as we have seen, what is perhaps the pleasantest, healthiest and most exciting phase of American existence." Such a lament was the impetus for all of Roosevelt's future actions regarding the environment.

During the 1890s Roosevelt became increasingly visible and important in governmental affairs, progressing from city to state to national prominence, as well as cobbling together the Rough Riders and participating with such distinction in the Spanish-American War in 1898 that he was nominated for the Congressional Medal of Honor (which he received posthumously in 2001). Having risen to such prominence, Roosevelt ran for governor of New York in 1898 with the support of the powerful but corrupt politician Thomas Collier Platt. Platt thought he could control Governor Roosevelt, but when he discovered he could not, he encouraged Roosevelt to join William McKinley as his vice presidential running mate. Roosevelt became president upon the assassination of McKinley in 1901.

In April 1903 Roosevelt went on an extended camping trip. His camping companion in Yellowstone National Park was John Burroughs, and then in May, Roosevelt camped with John Muir in Yosemite National Park. During this camping trip the iconographic photograph of John Muir and Roosevelt standing on a peak in the High Sierras was taken. Two years after this expedition, Roosevelt combined his account of this trip with accounts of earlier hunting trips (published in *The Century* and other periodicals) into *Outdoor Pastimes of an American Hunter* (1903), a work that Roosevelt dedicated to Burroughs, addressing him as "Dear Oom John." Aside from the essays dealing with Burroughs and Muir, however, much of this work covers a level of carnage that Roosevelt engaged in as a hunter that will be difficult for contemporary readers to fathom. Indeed, on every page, through most of the volume, there are multiple accounts of wanton and indiscriminate killing. Old game, nursing mothers, mating animals, cubs—all are shot at by Roosevelt and his companions. The book is replete with photographs, many poignant ones of young, terrified bears in the tops of spindly trees trying to avoid the packs of dogs below, most ending up being shot—as Roosevelt gleefully expresses repeatedly—"through the heart." In spite of the carnage, throughout the book Roosevelt reveals his immense knowledge of mammalian behavior. In places, Roosevelt becomes lyrical in describing the natural world. In a kind of Wordsworthian reverie Roosevelt thinks back to his youth, when he killed his first deer. He speaks of that time in the woods of the Adirondacks as being enchanting, where "I had enjoyed everything; poling and paddling the boat, tramping through the woods, the cries of chickaree and chipmunk, of jay, woodpecker, chickadee, nuthatch, and cross-bill, which broke the forest stillness; and above all, the great reaches of somber woodland themselves."

Clearly, the ability to see into the heart of nature is what attracted men such as Burroughs and Muir to Roosevelt, in spite of his proclivity later in life to hunt excessively. Burroughs wrote his own version of the camping trip, *Camping and Tramping with Roosevelt* (1907), in which he perceptively states that Roosevelt's "instincts as a naturalist . . . lie back of all his hunting expeditions, and, in a large measure, I think, prompt them." Toward the end of *Outdoor Pastimes of an American Hunter,* Roosevelt himself says that hunting and the love of natural history should go together, and this entwined,

Roosevelt and John Muir on Overhanging Rock, Glacier Point, during a camping trip in Yosemite Park,
May 1903 (Theodore Roosevelt Collection, Harvard College Library)

if at times complexly tangled, relationship prompted much of Roosevelt's actions as president of the United States in terms of protecting the natural environment of the nation. Perhaps struck by the level of carnage in some of the earlier essays, Roosevelt ended his volume with the hope that "the days of mere wasteful, boastful slaughter are past, and that from now on the hunter will stand foremost in working for the preservation and perpetuation of the wild life, whether big or little."

During his seven-and-a-half-year presidential term (finishing the term of the assassinated McKinley and serving one full term of his own), Roosevelt did much to advance his agenda of protecting the environment in a way that enabled resources to be available for future generations. Roosevelt had developed this ecological philosophy on his own, but he also incorporated the perspectives of W. J. McGee, an environmental theorist of

the time who promulgated the concept of interrelated parts of the natural world acting harmoniously with the assistance of humanity.

In his *Theodore Roosevelt: An Autobiography* (1913), Roosevelt writes about his achievements in the realm of conservation. He describes a dysfunctional system of government when he became president, one in which all the forests belonging to the United States were held in one department, while all the foresters were in another entirely separate department, the Bureau of Forestry, headed by Pinchot. Roosevelt speaks of the trend toward consistently placing private interests above the public good. As a man who had spent considerable time in the harsh but delicate landscape of the West, Roosevelt could see that the prevailing attitude of the time was that the natural resources of the country were inexhaustible. At the same time, entirely absent was any sense that a connection existed between the health of the natural resources of the nation and its ability to weather crises. Roosevelt relates how in his first message to Congress, on 3 December 1901, he made clear the importance of this connection and also indicated the importance he ascribed to managing these resources, especially water and the forests. Under Roosevelt's leadership, Congress passed the Reclamation Act on 7 June 1902, which began his legislative agenda to keep the welfare of the natural environment strongly in the public eye. Roosevelt writes that the chief executive is "the steward of the public welfare," a principled stand that prompted him to withdraw millions of acres of land from the possibility of private ownership and potential exploitation and destruction.

Under Roosevelt the Inland Waterways Commission was formed in 1907, charged by the president to be attentive "to the value of our streams as great natural resources" and to come up with comprehensive, "progressive" plans that would protect, develop, and control these resources. In his autobiography Roosevelt further relates how in 1908 he invited all the state governors and other important officials to attend the first conference on natural resources ever held by a developed nation. The meeting was held at the White House on 13 May–15 May 1908 and resulted in the creation of the National Conservation Commission, headed by Pinchot and charged with taking an inventory of the entirety of the natural resources possessed by the United States. This report, when conveyed to Congress, prompted Roosevelt to declare it "one of the most fundamentally important documents ever laid before the American people." Roosevelt's actions spoke as loudly as his words did. By the time he left office, he had created 150 national forests, 51 federal bird reservations, 4 natural game preserves, 5 national parks, and 18 national monuments (including the Grand Canyon), increasing the land holdings of the government from 43,000,000 acres to more than 230,000,000 acres. Some of these holdings include the Muir Woods, Pinnacles National Monument, and Mount Olympus National Monument. Within a span of two days, Roosevelt succeeded in having the Grand Canyon declared a game preserve consisting of 1,500,000 acres (thus sparing it from development and mining interests) and having most of the District of Columbia (45 square miles) declared a national wildlife refuge.

After leaving office in 1909, Roosevelt continued to travel extensively and to write about his own method of contact with the natural world. A ten-month safari in Africa immediately upon his leaving the White House resulted in his writing *African Game Trails, An Account of the African Wanderings of an American Hunter- Naturalist* (1910), which overwhelms the reader with Roosevelt's

level of detailed knowledge of the flora and fauna he encountered, although it also reveals that a high body count of animals was still an endeavor that he found satisfying.

A change seemed to occur over the next few years, however, and in 1913, having accepted speaking engagements in Argentina and Brazil, Roosevelt decided to turn his return trip into one of extensive exploration of a part of the Amazon River basin that was virtually uncharted. The account of this expedition was published in 1914 as *Through the Brazilian Wilderness*. Roosevelt took along several naturalists from the American Museum of Natural History and wrote a remarkable account of an adventure that resulted in new rivers being discovered (including one named the Rio Kermit, after his son, who was part of the expedition), as well as in two members of the team losing their lives. Throughout, Roosevelt demonstrates his usual encyclopedic store of biological knowledge. His eye for detail is remarkable as he describes the many kinds of poisonous snakes that he encounters. Elements of the reformer and improver are evident in his accounts as he details the myriads of insects that plague the expedition, leading him to comment that of all the dangers he faced on this trip (including many encounters with piranhas), the "worst animal foes of man, indeed the only dangerous foes, are insects; and this is especially true in the tropics." Animals were shot on this trip, but in limited quantities (for Roosevelt, at least); they were taken for the most part only as specimens for the museums. Indeed, Roosevelt frequently speaks about shooting animals with a camera. On one occasion he comes upon a nest of the jabiru, located in a large fig tree on the edge of the jungle. The nest contains four young and their parents. Roosevelt leaves them unmolested but describes them thoroughly and says a "naturalist could with the utmost advantage spend six months" on just this one small part of the vast jungle that he and his group visited. Roosevelt is overwhelmed with the richness of animal life in the Amazon jungle, and he has both an intuitive and an educated sense of how much he is observing that is utterly new to science.

Passing through the undamaged and pure forests of the Amazon, he comments that extensive "observation in the field is what is now most needed. Most of this wonderful and harmless bird life should be protected by law; and the mammals should receive reasonable protection. The books most needed are those dealing with the life-histories of wild creatures." After six weeks in the rain forest, having suffered painful ant bites and clothing that never dried out, Roosevelt can still speak of the landscape in glowing terms: the "country was lovely. The wide river . . . wound among hills; the shower-freshened pacova-leaves stamped the peculiar look of the tropics on the whole landscape–it was like passing by water through a gigantic botanical garden." As they begin to encounter aspects of civilization in the outposts of native villages, Roosevelt's group begins to understand the kinds of discoveries they have made. He states that they have been on a river as big as the upper Rhine or Elbe, yet that did not appear on any map. As they end the expedition, Roosevelt comments on the desire he and the others have to return to their homes, with the land in full blossoming spring. Roosevelt's language is lyrical and vivid as he describes his "home country": "spring had now come, the wonderful northern spring of long glorious days, of brooding twilights, of cool delightful nights. Robin and bluebird, meadow-lark and song sparrow, were singing in the mornings at home; the maple-buds were red; windflowers and bloodroot were blooming while the last patches of snow still lingered."

At the end of this remarkable volume Roosevelt discusses the condition of scientific knowledge of the time and maps out where he thinks science needs to go in order to advance zoological and geographical knowledge, observing that his own accomplishments are all of a preliminary nature. He maintains that scientific knowledge must advance and should do so in a vehicle that combines analytical probity with clear prose. On this point Roosevelt is emphatic. He praises Darwin's *Voyage of the Beagle* (1839) as an exemplary work that advances knowledge in a revolutionary fashion while it can also be read as well-written travel literature. Roosevelt goes on to say that modern "scientists, like modern historians, and above all, scientific and historical educators, should ever keep in mind that clearness of speech and writing is essential to clearness of thought and that a simple, clear, and if possible, vivid style is vital to the production of the best work in either science or history. Darwin and Huxley are classics, and they would not have been if they had not written good English." In an element that harks back to his ranching writings of thirty years before, Roosevelt adds an appendix titled "The Outfit for Travelling in the South American Wilderness," in which he details, down to the level of appropriate underwear, what one should bring in order to go on such an expedition. This catalogue is fully within the tradition of American nature writing, harking back in its specificity to the number of nails Henry David Thoreau reports on using to build his cabin at Walden Pond.

Roosevelt's last large work focusing on the outdoors and nature is *A Book-Lover's Holidays in the Open* (1916). A collection of essays detailing expeditions and hunts in Canada and the United States, this work reiterates Roosevelt's major concerns regarding the preservation of nature and acknowledges the close and potentially uneasy connection between the modern and the natural worlds, "for the edges of the wilderness lie close beside the beaten roads of present

Roosevelt and his son Kermit with a Cape buffalo they shot during an African safari, circa 1909 (Edmund Heller Papers, Smithsonian Institution Archives)

travel." In a vivid catalogue Roosevelt describes various natural scenes that the traveler in the natural world may experience:

> He can see the red splendor of desert sunsets, and the unearthly glory of the afterglow on the battlements of desolate mountains. In sapphire gulfs of ocean he can visit islets, above which the wings of myriads of sea-fowl make a kind of shifting cuneiform script in the air. He can ride along the brink of the stupendous cliff-walled canyon, where eagles soar below him, and cougars make their lairs on the ledges and harry the big-horned sheep. He can journey through the northern forests, the home of the giant moose, the forests of fragrant and murmuring life in summer, the iron-bound and melancholy forests of winter.

As beautiful and as rich as the landscape was, Roosevelt was also keenly aware that it was a fragile ecosystem that required attentiveness and vigilance if it were to be preserved for future generations. He speaks about

> the public preserves. These by their very existence afford a certain measure of the extent to which democratic government can justify itself. If in a given com-

munity unchecked popular rule means unlimited waste and destruction of the natural resources–soil, fertility, water-power, forests, game, wild-life generally–which by right belong as much to subsequent generations as to the present generation, then it is sure proof that the present generation is not yet really fit for self-control, that it is not yet really fit to exercise the high and responsible privilege of a rule which shall be both by the people and for the people.

Roosevelt clearly believed that the health of the natural resources of the nation and the strength of democratic principles and institutions are linked.

Roosevelt spent the remainder of his life in furthering various causes, as he railed against President Woodrow Wilson and pushed for U.S. intervention in World War I. His health was failing; indeed, he had never fully recovered from his African and South American trips. A few months before he died, he suffered another heartbreak, with the death of his favorite son, Quentin, in the war. Theodore Roosevelt died in his sleep on 6 January 1919, of a massive heart attack. He was sixty.

Taken as a whole, Roosevelt's nature writings convey in a robust, if at times blood-soaked, fashion the importance of preserving the natural landscape as fully as possible. Management and usefulness were key concepts in terms of Roosevelt's perception of nature, but he was never blind to the beauty, majesty, and power that the natural world possesses.

Letters:

Theodore Roosevelt's Letters to His Children, edited by Joseph Bucklin Bishop (New York: Scribners, 1919);

Letters of Theodore Roosevelt, 8 volumes, edited by Elting E. Morrison (Cambridge, Mass.: Harvard University Press, 1951–1954).

Bibliographies:

Gilbert Black, *Theodore Roosevelt, 1858–1919: Chronology, Documents, Bibliographical Aids* (Dobbs Ferry, N.Y.: Oceana Publications, 1969);

Harvard University Library Theodore Roosevelt Collection: Dictionary Catalogue, and Shelflist, 5 volumes (Cambridge, Mass.: Harvard University Press, 1970);

The Theodore Roosevelt Collection: Manuscript Accession Records of the Houghton Library, 3 volumes (Cambridge, Mass.: Harvard University Press, 1979).

Biographies:

Edmund Morris, *The Rise of Theodore Roosevelt* (New York: Coward, McCann & Geoghegan, 1979);

David McCullough, *Mornings on Horseback* (New York: Simon & Schuster, 1981);

H. W. Brands, *TR: The Last Romantic* (New York: BasicBooks, 1997);

Morris, *Theodore Rex* (New York: Random House, 2001).

References:

John Burroughs, *Camping and Tramping with Roosevelt* (Boston: Houghton, Mifflin, 1907);

Paul Russell Cutright, *Theodore Roosevelt: The Making of a Conservationist* (Urbana: University of Illinois Press, 1985);

Cutright, *Theodore Roosevelt, the Naturalist* (New York: Harper, 1956);

Robert Dorman, *A Word for Nature: Four Pioneering Environmental Advocates, 1845–1913* (Chapel Hill: University of North Carolina Press, 1998);

Francis J. Henninger, "How Theodore Roosevelt Began the Salvation of the Earth," *University of Dayton Review,* 24 (Winter 1996–1997): 40–47;

Daniel G. Payne, *Voices in the Wilderness: American Nature Writing and Environmental Politics* (Hanover, N.H.: University Press of New England, 1996);

Daniel J. Philippon, "Representing 'Nature': American Nature Writers and the Growth of Environmental Organizations, 1885–1985," dissertation, University of Virginia, 1998.

Papers:

The Library of Congress has an extensive collection of materials by Theodore Roosevelt. An extremely comprehensive Theodore Roosevelt Collection is housed in Harvard's Widener and Houghton Libraries. Among the holdings are included Roosevelt's personal papers (25,000 items), books (12,000 volumes), photographs (11,000), political cartoons (4,000), and ephemera.

Leslie Marmon Silko

(5 March 1948 –)

Ellen L. Arnold
East Carolina University

See also the Silko entries in *DLB 143: American Novelists Since World War II, Third Series; DLB 175: Native American Writers of the United States;* and *DLB 256: Twentieth-Century American Western Writers, Third Series.*

BOOKS: *Laguna Woman: Poems* (Greenfield Center, N.Y.: Greenfield Review Press, 1974);

Ceremony (New York: Viking, 1977);

Storyteller (New York: Seaver, 1981);

Almanac of the Dead: A Novel (New York & London: Simon & Schuster, 1991);

Sacred Water: Narratives and Pictures (Tucson: Flood Plain Press, 1993);

Rain, by Silko and Lee Marmon (New York: Whitney Museum of American Art, 1996);

Yellow Woman and a Beauty of the Spirit: Essays on Native American Life Today (New York: Simon & Schuster, 1996);

Gardens in the Dunes (New York: Simon & Schuster, 1999).

OTHER: "The Man to Send Rain Clouds," "Yellow Woman," "Tony's Story," "Uncle Tony's Goat," "A Geronimo Story," "Bravura," and "From Humaweepi, the Warrior Priest," in *The Man to Send Rain Clouds: Contemporary Stories by American Indians,* edited by Kenneth Rosen (New York: Viking, 1974), pp. 3–8, 33–45, 69–78, 93–100, 128–144, 149–154, 161–168;

"Leslie Silko, Laguna Poet and Novelist," in *This Song Remembers: Self-Portraits of Native Americans in the Arts,* edited by Jane Katz (Boston: Houghton Mifflin, 1980), pp. 186–194;

"Language and Literature from a Pueblo Indian Perspective," in *English Literature: Opening Up the Canon,* edited by Leslie A. Fiedler and Houston A. Baker Jr. (Baltimore: Johns Hopkins University Press, 1981), pp. 54–72;

"Private Property," in *Earth Power Coming: Short Fiction in Native American Literature,* edited by Simon J. Ortiz (Tsaile, Ariz.: Navajo Community College Press, 1983), pp. 21–30;

Leslie Marmon Silko (photograph by Gus Nitsche)

"Replacing Confusion with Equity: Alternatives for Water Policy in the Colorado River Basin," by Silko, Helen M. Ingram, and Lawrence A. Scaff, in *A River Too Far: The Past and Future of the Arid West,* edited by Joseph Finkhouse and Mark Crawford (Reno: Nevada Humanities Commission, 1991), pp. 83–103;

"Foreword," in *Circle of Nations: Voices and Visions of American Indians,* edited by John Gattuso (Hillsboro, Ore.: Beyond Words, 1993).

SELECTED PERIODICAL PUBLICATIONS–
UNCOLLECTED: "An Old-Time Indian Attack Conducted in Two Parts," *Yardbird Reader,* 5 (1976): 77–84;

Silko and Lawrence J. Evers, "A Conversation with Frank Waters," in *Sun Tracks: An American Indian Literary Magazine,* 5 (1979): 61–68;

"Here's an Odd Artifact for the Fairy-Tale Shelf," review of *The Beet Queen* by Louise Erdrich, *Impact/Albuquerque Magazine* (7 October 1986): 10–11, and *SAIL,* 10 (Fall 1986): 178–184;

"Landscape, History, and the Pueblo Imagination," *Antaeus,* 51 (1986): 83–94;

"Introduction to a Book Titled *Blue Sevens, or Protect Yourself from Witchcraft While You Get Rich,*" *Conjunctions,* 34 (2000): 189–195.

Leslie Marmon Silko is one of the most important writers to emerge from the Native American Renaissance, a period of intense literary productivity by Native Americans that began with the 1968 publication of N. Scott Momaday's Pulitzer Prize–winning novel *House Made of Dawn.* When Silko's first novel, *Ceremony,* appeared in 1977, she had already established a reputation for her lyrical, tightly written short stories, many of which were anthologized in *The Man to Send Rain Clouds: Contemporary Stories by American Indians* (1974) and for her collection *Laguna Woman: Poems,* published the same year. *Ceremony,* the story of a World War II veteran's return home to Laguna Pueblo, was only the third novel by a Native American woman to be published in the United States. Since its publication, *Ceremony* has grown steadily in popularity and critical acclaim; considered a foundational text of Native American literature, it remains the work for which Silko is best known, and it has earned a solid place in the canon of American literature. *Ceremony* has received consideration as an example of American nature writing as well; in his influential 1995 book, *The Environmental Imagination: Thoreau, Nature Writing, and the Formation of American Culture,* Lawrence Buell declared *Ceremony* "one of the major works of contemporary American environmental fiction."

Ceremony was followed by *Storyteller* (1981), a multigenre autobiography; *The Delicacy and Strength of Lace: Letters between Leslie Marmon Silko and James Wright* (1986); the controversial apocalyptic novel *Almanac of the Dead* (1991); *Sacred Water: Narratives and Pictures* (1993), a handmade volume of prose poems and photographs; an essay collection, *Yellow Woman and a Beauty of the Spirit: Essays on Native American Life Today* (1996); and *Gardens in the Dunes* (1999), an historical novel. Currently, Silko is at work on a satirical novel with the working title "Blue Sevens, or Protect Yourself from Witchcraft While You Get Rich." The variety and breadth of Silko's writing have established her as one of the most creative and versatile of living American writers. Her work is widely known and respected in Europe

as well, where she is considered a major American author, rather than an ethnic writer, as she is most often categorized in the United States.

Leslie Marmon was born 5 March 1948 in Albuquerque, New Mexico, the first of three daughters of Leland (Lee) Marmon and Mary Virginia Lee Leslie. She grew up at Old Laguna, a Pueblo Indian reservation west of Albuquerque on the Rio Grande plateau, a high desert area inhabited by the Laguna people for at least one thousand years. Of mixed Laguna, Mexican, and Euramerican ancestry, Silko is a descendant of Robert G. Marmon; he and his brother, Walter, came to Laguna in the 1870s as government surveyors and traders, married Laguna women, and settled permanently. While the brothers both served as governors at Laguna and were instrumental in bringing outside influence to the community, the women of the family kept Pueblo traditions alive.

Silko grew up next door to her great-grandfather Robert's second wife, Marie Anaya, the Grandmother A'mooh of *Storyteller,* who, with Aunt Susie (Susie Reyes Marmon, wife of Silko's great-uncle) and Grandma Lillie (Francesca Stagner Marmon, her paternal grandmother), filled Silko's youth with ancient Laguna stories and encouraged her to keep the stories alive, a responsibility that later became an impetus and foundation of her writing. The old stories helped to shape Silko's identity, providing context to her relationships within the community and to the place that is Laguna, which she came to know intimately through a childhood spent wandering on foot and horseback through its sand hills and mesas.

Silko attended the Bureau of Indian Affairs school at Laguna through the fourth grade and then Manzano Day School, a private Catholic school in Albuquerque, where her parents took her to avoid putting her in an Indian boarding school. When she was in the fifth grade at Manzano, Silko first discovered the sense of empowerment that writing can provide. Given an assignment to make a story from a list of spelling words, she found she could re-create through writing that sense of being surrounded "with the voice of the storyteller telling you a story," with the comfort and security of home and family: "it's what's always kept me going all these years," Silko told interviewer Stephen Pett in 1992.

In 1969 Silko graduated Phi Beta Kappa from the University of New Mexico with a degree in English. That year her first important publication, the short story "The Man to Send Rain Clouds," appeared in *New Mexico Quarterly.* Inspired by her father's role in helping Laguna win back a piece of land from the state in the 1950s, Silko entered the Fellowship Program in American Indian Law at the University of New Mexico. In 1971 she received a National Endowment for the Arts Discover Grant; frustrated by a legal system she had come to feel would never achieve justice for Native Americans, Silko dropped out of law school and began to think of herself as a writer. She entered a graduate program in English at the University of New Mexico but left to teach at Navajo Community College. In 1973 she moved to Ketchikan, Alaska, where she wrote *Ceremony*. Returning to Laguna in 1976, she took a position at the University of New Mexico. Since 1978 Silko has made her home in Tucson, where she taught at the University of Arizona until 1981, when a five-year MacArthur Foundation Grant made it possible for her to write full-time. Married and divorced twice, Silko has two sons, Robert William Chapman, born in 1966, and Cazimir Silko, born in 1972. She and her first husband, Richard Chapman, were married in 1966 and divorced sometime after their separation in 1969; she and her second husband, John Silko, married in 1971 and later divorced.

Silko's rootedness in the desert landscape and the living oral tradition of Laguna provide the primary themes of her work—the identity of humans and land, the interconnectedness of all things, and the power of story to create and maintain relationship. These themes are evident in Silko's earliest writing. "The Man to Send Rain Clouds," based on an event at Laguna, centers on the death of Old Teofilo. Found dead at a sheep camp on an early spring morning by brothers-in-law Leon and Ken, Teofilo's body is prepared for burial in the traditional way by friends and family, with the understanding that his spirit will join the rain clouds and continue the cycles of death and rebirth by bringing rain to Laguna. Leon's wife, Louise, suggests that the Catholic priest might sprinkle holy water on the body to quench her Grandpa's thirst and to add an additional blessing to the ceremony. At first Father Paul refuses, distressed that he was not asked to administer last rites; sensing a lost opportunity, he changes his mind.

The gently ironic story encompasses a single day, from sunrise to sunset, and ends with a comforting sense of closure for the family: "now the old man would send them big thunderclouds for sure." But Father Paul leaves struggling to recover a memory that escapes him, failing to understanding how his act has transformed the holy water into the promise of August rain. The family's willingness to accept aspects of Catholic ritual that fit their sense of the wholeness of the world contrasts sharply with the priest's sense of failure to convert them. The story illustrates the close relationship between Laguna people and place and establishes another of the themes critics have found characteristic of Silko's work—the strength of a communal, inclusive worldview to incorporate and adapt the intrusions of the outside world for its own purposes, not only to survive but also to remain vital and creative.

"The Man to Send Rain Clouds" became the title story for Kenneth Rosen's 1974 anthology, *The Man to Send Rain Clouds: Contemporary Stories by American Indians,* the first book to bring Native American short fiction to the attention of the general public. That volume included six other short stories by Silko: "Yellow Woman," "Tony's Story," "Uncle Tony's Goat," "A Geronimo Story," "Bravura," and "From Humaweepi, the Warrior Priest." Of these, "Yellow Woman" is probably Silko's best-known short story. Considered by scholars to be foundational to Silko's writing, it became the subject of *"Yellow Woman": Leslie Marmon Silko* (1993), a casebook of critical essays edited by Melody Graulich.

"Yellow Woman" is a contemporary version of traditional Pueblo stories about Kochininako, or Yellow Woman, a mythological "everywoman," whose desire to escape the limitations of ordinary reality often results in her seduction or abduction by a powerful spirit man or animal. Frequently, she returns with gifts for the people, such as sources of food or water, twin boys who become heroes, or a new ceremony. Silko's telling of the story opens by the river at the boundary of the Pueblo, as the unnamed narrator awakens beside the strange man she met there the day before. The opening lines link the narrator's sexual awakening to a heightened awareness of the natural world: "My thigh clung to his with dampness, and I watched the sun rising up through the tamaracks and willows. The small brown water birds came to the river and hopped across the mud leaving brown scratches in the alkali-white crust." As Silko explains in an interview with Kim Barnes, "What's operating in those stories of Kochininako is this attraction, this passion, this connection between the human world and the animal and spirit worlds."

As the narrator follows the man (Silva) into the mountains, she begins to question the boundaries between reality and myth, wondering if she is the mythical Yellow Woman, whose stories her grandfather was so fond of telling, and Silva, the Ka'tsina, or mountain spirit. When she returns home from her stay in the mountains, she finds her mother telling her grandmother "how to fix the Jell-O" and her husband "playing with the baby." In the face of this everyday scene, she decides to tell them she was kidnapped by some Navajo; thus, she steps into her grandfather's role as storyteller, bringing back with her not only a reawakened spirituality but also a revitalization of the storytelling tradition, endangered by the encroachment of outside influences at the Pueblo.

This sense of intimate relationship between body and earth, place and spirit, is also present in Silko's

Silko's father, Lee H. Marmon, photographing the desert around Laguna, New Mexico
(Collection of Virginia L. Hampton)

other stories in this volume. "Tony's Story," based on an historical incident, recounts the killing of a racist state trooper by two Acoma Pueblo men who believe him to be a witch. His death relieves the drought that plagues the area, demonstrating the role of human respect and balance in maintaining the natural cycles of the earth. "Uncle Tony's Goat" is narrated by a seven-year-old who angers his Uncle Tony's prized billy goat by shooting toy arrows at his nannies and kids. The old goat charges and injures the child before running away. Uncle Tony and the child are both relieved that the goat escapes and does not have to be killed–Tony because of his pride in the goat's resourcefulness, the child out of a sense of guilt for mistreating the goats. Thus, the young narrator learns personal responsibility, respect for the animals, and the importance of their exchange with the human world.

A similar coming-of-age story, "A Geronimo Story," is narrated by Andy, a young man who accompanies his uncle Siteye, a scout with the Laguna Regulars, on a mission with the U.S. Cavalry to track the Apache leader Geronimo. As they travel toward Pie Town, where Geronimo is rumored to have camped, the reader becomes aware that the scouts know full well Geronimo is not there, that Siteye has brought his nephew along to experience the beautiful country south of Laguna. Andy comes to "know the trees and rocks all together with the mountains and sky and wildflowers," learns the careful attention to the distinctiveness of each rock and branch that will enable him to remember the trail. In contrast, Major Littlecock relies on the army's "sophisticated communications" rather than the deep knowledge of land and seasons that the Lagunas know govern Geronimo's movements. Critics have noted that the journey becomes Andy's initiation–not only into oneness with the land but also into knowledge of the racism of the white soldiers and of the potential for language to work reversals of power. Through the subtle resistance of language play, the Lagunas turn the course of events to their own purposes—using the trip to secure deer meat for the winter. That getting meat for the winter was probably their intention all along is suggested by Siteye's final ironic comment: "that was a long way to go for deer hunting."

"Bravura" is similarly structured on ironic reversals, poking gentle fun at a white college student eager to "get back to the land" and his Navajo friend who wishes to leave it. The blonde-bearded poet who calls himself Bravura travels to the Navajo reservation to experience "the simple life" but remains an outsider, while his friend, native to the place, remains in college and distances himself from his community. The experiences of both young men contrast to the education of the young narrator of "From Humaweepi, the Warrior Priest" (a selection from a longer work Silko never finished). This young man lives in the desert with his uncle, a traditional priest, and absorbs almost without realizing it "the songs and chants for all the seasons" and "the prayers for the trees and plants and animals." The nephew gradually takes on the role of the old man, learning "to take care of things," including the animal nature within himself, which must be nurtured and experienced before he can fully become part of the land. Considered immature examples of Silko's short story skills, "Bravura" and "From Humaweepi, the Warrior Priest" are the only stories in *The Man to Send Rain Clouds* that have not been republished.

In 1974 Silko also published *Laguna Woman,* her only book of poetry, for which she received the 1974 Chicago Review Award for Poetry and the 1977 Pushcart Prize. Silko's poetry has received relatively little critical attention in comparison to her fiction, though her poems reflect the same intimate connection to the Laguna oral tradition and landscape that characterizes all her work. A third important event of 1974 for Silko was the publication of the short story "Lullaby" in both the *Chicago Review* and the *Yardbird Reader*. Selected for *Best American Short Stories of 1975*, "Lullaby" is one of Silko's most-often republished stories, along with "The Man to Send Rain Clouds" and "Yellow Woman."

"Lullaby" is told through the memories of Ayah, an old Navajo woman who has lost her firstborn son to war, her two younger children to the U.S. government, and finally, her husband to poverty and alcoholism. In the closing scene of the story, Ayah and Chato, her husband, are caught by a snowstorm on their way home from the bar where Chato has spent his government check. As Ayah waits for the old man's death, she sings a lullaby that weaves her own bittersweet memories of

births and deaths into the ongoing story of creation, taking comfort that all life emerges from and returns to Earth: "The earth is your mother, / she holds you. / The sky is your father, / he protects you. / Sleep, / sleep. . . . / We are together always / We are together always / There never was a time / when this / was not so."

In 1976 Silko's essay "An Old-Time Indian Attack Conducted in Two Parts" appeared in *Yardbird Reader*. In it Silko attacks "white shamanism," the appropriation of Indian experience and point of view by Euramerican writers such as Gary Snyder. She points out that such artistic appropriation is based in the same imperialist assumptions as the theft of Native American land and resources that characterizes the European presence in the Americas, a theme that becomes an increasingly explicit focus of her work. In 1977 Silko published *Ceremony,* written during her two years in Alaska. Isolated in an unfamiliar place and dealing with a troubled marriage, physical illness, and continuous rainfall, Silko wrote to reconstruct the desert landscape of home and save her own sanity. The novel is at once a healing ceremony and an analysis of the effects of colonialism and world war on contemporary Native Americans. Above all, the novel is about the power of stories both to wound and to heal.

Ceremony tells the story of Tayo, a veteran of World War II who returns to Laguna suffering from "battle fatigue." Already an outcast from his community because of his mixed-blood status, he is tortured by guilt: he failed to bring his cousin Rocky home alive; his Uncle Josiah died while Tayo was gone; and Josiah's precious Mexican cattle, which Tayo was to help him breed, have wandered away. Moreover, Tayo has contributed to the drought at Laguna by cursing the heavy rain that tormented him and the dying Rocky in the Philippines. Tayo returns home culturally alienated and spiritually fragmented, racked by nightmares and flashbacks, crying, and vomiting.

Tayo's recovery is slow and painstaking. The army doctors, who encouraged him to think only of himself, failed to help him. The Scalp Ceremony, conducted by the traditional Kurena medicine man Ku'oosh to purify returning warriors, helps Tayo sleep and keep down some food, but the effort is not enough. "There are some things we can't cure like we used to," says Ku'oosh, "not since the white people came." A new kind of ceremony is required, and Tayo's family sends him to the Navajo medicine man Betonie, a mixed breed himself and especially qualified to treat problems associated with the white world. Betonie explains that "after the white people came, elements in this world began to shift; and it became necessary to create new ceremonies . . . things which don't shift and grow are dead things."

Marie Anaya, Silko's Grandmother A'mooh, who told ancient tales of Laguna (photograph by Lee H. Marmon)

Betonie confirms Tayo's sense that his "sickness was only part of something larger." In a poem positioned at the center of the novel, Betonie describes the origins of a terrible witchery loosed on the world in a contest of witches. A mysterious witch tells the story of the invention of the white-skinned people, who "grow away from the earth / then they grow away from the sun / then they grow away from the plants and animals. / They see no life / When they look / they see only objects. / The world is a dead thing for them." The story sets in motion a pattern of destruction, based in a rationalist worldview of objectification and alienation, made manifest in conquest, disease, famine, drought, and the poisoning of the land and culminating in the creation of the atomic bomb. The ceremonies of healing must encompass a changing reality, which now includes the possibility of nuclear annihilation.

Betonie blends elements of Navajo, Pueblo, Mexican, and Euramerican stories and ceremonies to restore Tayo to wholeness through a ritual reimmersion in the land and the sacred stories and beings that inhabit it. In a journey up the slopes of Mt. Taylor reminiscent of Yellow Woman's journey to the home of the mountain

Ka'tsina, Tayo enters mythological time and becomes part of the old stories. Tayo reawakens to sexuality, relationship, and generativity with Ts'eh, the female spirit of the mountain, and with her help he locates and frees Uncle Josiah's cattle.

On the final night of his ceremony, at the uranium mine outside Laguna, Tayo confronts the witchery as he witnesses his former army buddies torture his old friend Harley. Here, so near Los Alamos, where the bomb was created, and White Sands, where it was tested, Tayo understands: "there was no end to it; it knew no boundaries; and he had arrived at the point of convergence where the fate of all living things, and even the earth, had been laid." Tayo resists the impulse to participate in the violence, realizing that witchery cannot be destroyed; it must be held in balance by a respect for life and careful attention to the stories of creation that counter stories of destruction. Restored to relationship, Tayo is received by the Kurena medicine men, who recognize the events he recounts as a continuation of the old stories and a promise of renewal. As a mixed breed who has learned to negotiate both white and Indian worlds, Tayo has special powers to bring balance to the community, confirmed by the ending of the drought.

The initial response to *Ceremony* by reviewers and critics was overwhelmingly positive. A few reviewers compared the novel unfavorably to Silko's short stories, finding it overly convoluted and unfocused, but the novel has consistently been praised for the power and lyricism of its prose, its innovative nonlinear structure and use of oral forms, and its revitalization of Native American cultural presence. Papers presented at a conference seminar on *Ceremony* appeared as a special issue of *American Indian Quarterly* in 1979, and became a foundation of subsequent critical study of the novel. The novel has been reprinted several times, and the large body of scholarship regarding it continues to grow. Some critics have misread *Ceremony* as blaming Europeans for the evils of the world, but the novel is explicit on this point; as Betonie tells Tayo: "That is the trickery of the witchcraft. . . . They want us to believe all evil resides with white people. Then we will look no further to see what is really happening." Recent critics more often treat the novel as what James Ruppert terms a "mediational" text, one that locates the source of evil in separation itself and works to bridge the splits between Native American and Euramerican cultures, between humans and the earth.

Some feminist scholars criticized Silko for writing from a masculine point of view, but other critics—such as Paula Gunn Allen, Judith A. Antell, and Edith Swan—interpreted Tayo's recovery as a reconnection to a maternal earth and to his own feminine, nurturing aspects. Allen, who is also from Laguna, praised *Ceremony* as a strong feminist text, emerging as it does from a cultural context in which female power has always been revered. However, in a 1990 essay, "Special Problems in Teaching Leslie Marmon Silko's *Ceremony*," Allen raised a different issue, criticizing Silko for revealing secret clan stories in the novel. The allegation persisted, expanding into a rumor that Silko was banished from Laguna for this or other transgressions of secrecy. Robert M. Nelson argues that the stories Silko retold had been recorded in print by ethnographers before Silko's birth and that her use of them was more a "repatriation" than a violation of secrecy. In a 1998 interview with Ellen L. Arnold, Silko attempted to lay both notions to rest, stating that the stories were entrusted to her by her relatives specifically for the purpose of keeping them alive and that she has never been banished from Laguna. "Laguna is not like that," she said; "that's not the Pueblo way."

After the publication of *Ceremony*, Silko's interests turned toward the visual elements of narrative. In 1980 she made a movie, *Estoyehmuut and the Gunnadeyah (Arrowboy and the Destroyers)*, an adaptation of a traditional story; the video was intended to be part of a series on Laguna oral narratives that was never completed. In 1981 Silko published *Storyteller*, which brings many of her previously published stories and poems together with accounts of family history and photographs (many taken by her father, Lee Marmon, a professional photographer), carefully arranged to create a coherent whole. Originally termed a "collection," *Storyteller* is now more often considered autobiography; in Arnold Krupat's words, "Silko's developing relation to every kind of story becomes the story of her life." The relationships of materials in the book emphasize the continuity of oral and literary traditions and the power of story to shape experience, while the photographs evoke a sense of place that helps readers imagine themselves inside the stories.

Silko's short stories have received extensive critical attention, partly because of their reappearance in *Storyteller*, where their relationship to the other elements of the book added new possibilities for interpretation, and partly because of their frequent inclusion in anthologies of ethnic American, contemporary American, and women's fiction. Notable among the studies that consider the stories in relationship to the whole of *Storyteller* are those in Graulich's casebook *"Yellow Woman,"* Gregory Salyer's chapter on *Storyteller* in *Leslie Marmon Silko* (1997), and Helen Jaskoski's recent book *Leslie Marmon Silko: A Study of the Short Fiction* (1998).

Storyteller includes five stories from *The Man to Send Rain Clouds* plus "Storyteller," "Lullaby," and "Coyote Holds a Full House in his Hand." The first short story in the volume is "Storyteller," originally published in *Puerto del Sol* in 1975. Silko's only work set completely outside the Southwest, "Storyteller" was written during her stay in Alaska; like *Ceremony*, it explores the relationship between the interior landscapes of the characters and the exterior landscape. Opening and closing on a jail scene in which a young Inuit girl contemplates a sky that is freezing over, "Storyteller" centers on the unnamed narrator's coming of age: orphaned when her parents were killed by poisoned drink sold them by a dishonest storekeeper, the girl is raised by her grandmother and the grandmother's companion, an old storyteller. After learning how her parents died, she lures the current storeman—the one responsible for the deaths has long since disappeared—onto the frozen river, into which he falls and drowns. The girl's revenge hinges on the completion of the story, and she refuses her court-assigned lawyer's advice to say the death was an accident, insisting that "the story must be told as it is."

Interwoven with the girl's story are two other story lines. In one, the old storyteller recounts a hunter's stalking of a polar bear, which is simultaneously the story of his own death; when the bear turns on the hunter, the old storyteller dies. The third layer of story is the coming of a "final winter," Earth's retaliation for the abuse the Gussucks (Russians) have perpetrated in extracting oil from the frozen tundra and killing off all the game. In telling the story as it "must be told, without any lies," the narrator steps into the role of the deceased storyteller. The narrative lines merge to tell the story of the colonial devastation of native Alaskans, their land, and their culture, and their continuing survival through story. Though admired by critics for its dense complexity and the stark power of its descriptive language, "Storyteller" is not often considered in relation to the body of Silko's work as a whole, beyond its role in *Storyteller*.

The final short story in *Storyteller* is "Coyote Holds a Full House in his Hand" (first published in *Triquarterly* in 1980). Critical interpretations of *Storyteller* have divided the volume structurally and thematically in a variety of ways, but most point to the trickster humor that characterizes the final section. "Coyote Holds a Full House in his Hand" offers a satirical counterpoint to the heavy tone of "Storyteller," but the primary theme is the same—the power of story to shape reality. The main character, Sonny Boy, is a likable ne'er-do-well—lazy, alcoholic, and lecherous, with a penchant for playing tricks that often backfire on him but sometimes accomplish important purposes, characteristics that readily identify him with Coyote of Pueblo oral tradition. Within the framework of this cultural story pattern, the story highlights the stories of daily life, the ones people tell to create certain impressions of themselves or to "justify why things happened the way they did."

Coming from Laguna to court the Hopi widow, Mrs. Sekakaku, Sonny Boy finds the widow and her clan sisters distressed over the illness of a bedridden aunt and his dream of sleeping with the widow thwarted. Sonny Boy declares himself a medicine man and calls the women together for an impromptu ceremony that allows him to rub ashes on their plump thighs, which he has been lasciviously admiring. Ironically, his ceremony cures the aunt; as Sonny Boy strokes the women's flesh, he enters a vision, feeling "the little crevices and creases like a hawk feels canyons and arroyos while he is soaring." In the interrelationships of body, spirit, and nature, the moment is transformed. The story Sonny Boy is inventing takes on a life of its own, and through it old Aunt Mamie rises from her bed and walks without assistance to have her own thighs stroked; Sonny Boy "could tell by the feel she'd probably live a long time." Sonny Boy returns home to Laguna with photographs commemorating his success as both trickster and healer. The playfulness of this story and the importance of its position as the conclusion of the volume have led some critics to comment that the tragic elements of Silko's work are often overstressed, at the expense of a full appreciation of the healing role of humor.

In 1983 Silko's only uncollected short story, "Private Property," was included in *Earth Power Coming: Short Fiction in Native American Literature,* edited by Simon J. Ortiz. Silko's only short story told from multiple points of view, it explores the complex interaction of ideas about property and ownership in a small community at the intersection of cultural influences. The story focuses on sisters-in-law, Reyna and Etta; their nieces, Juanita and Ruthie; Ruthie's philandering husband; and Cheromiah, whose quest for his runaway horses, who do not know they are owned, frames the narrative. The "old ways" are spoken for by the family matriarch, who said "to share and love one another," and that "we only make use of these things as long as we are here. We don't own them." Etta is singled out by the community as representative of outside ways; she has returned to the Pueblo after years among whites and wants to fence her yard and plant trees to protect her privacy. Yet, all the characters are invested in possessions of various kinds (horses, fields, inheritances, husbands, flowers, the good opinions of others), and each struggles against the forces of nature (the desires for love, pleasure, and freedom) that constantly work against ownership, fences, and boundaries. This story has received little critical attention, but Jaskoski consid-

ers it a strong example of communal storytelling voice and "one of Silko's most successful efforts at comedy."

The themes and structures of Silko's fiction are illuminated by two of her essays that have been widely anthologized—"Language and Literature from a Pueblo Perspective," a talk delivered to the English Institute in 1979 and published in 1981; and "Landscape, History, and the Pueblo Imagination," an essay published in *Antaeus* in 1986 and republished many times in a longer version titled "Interior and Exterior Landscapes: The Pueblo Migration Stories." These essays describe the power of language, the web-like nature of Pueblo expression and thought, and the role of stories in Pueblo life—mythic stories, family stories, even gossip—as repositories of memory and identity, as means of maintaining the complex interrelationships that connect humans, geographical places, and the larger community of living things. In 1986 Silko's letters to James Wright were published by Wright's widow, Anne, as *The Delicacy and Strength of Lace.* Silko and Wright met in 1978 at a writer's workshop and corresponded until Wright's death in 1980, developing a warm friendship even though they met in person only twice. The letters offer further insight into Silko's life and work during this period of her life, especially the creation of *Storyteller.*

In 1981 Silko was awarded a prestigious MacArthur Foundation grant to complete her second novel, *Almanac of the Dead.* The book was not published until 1991, on the eve of the Columbus Quincentennial, auspicious timing for an epic retelling of the five-hundred-year history of the conquest of the Americas, the dispossession of its native peoples, and their continuing resistance. *Almanac of the Dead* shocked many readers with its apocalyptic ferocity, and reviews were mixed. Many reviewers considered it a radical tour de force; in a review published in *Bloomsbury Review* (April/May 1992), Annette Jaimes named it "the masterpiece" of the Columbian Encounter. Others found the novel brutal, angry, and disorganized; John Skow, writing for *Time* (9 December 1991), called it a "dull headache," and Alan Ryan's review in *USA Today* (21 January 1991) described it as "bad judgment and inadequate craft" without "novelistic merit." A decade of serious critical attention suggests, however, that *Almanac of the Dead* is a major achievement of twentieth-century American fiction.

More than seven hundred pages long, *Almanac of the Dead* weaves history, myth, prophecy, cultural analysis, and political diatribe with several strands of narrative involving more than seventy primary characters in an intricate web. Most of the action occurs in the present, but in this present the past is alive and often pushes into the future, leading many critics to observe that Time itself is possibly the most important character in the novel. The title of the novel refers to an invented

Laguna, the setting for most of Silko's stories (photograph by Lee H. Marmon)

fifth Mayan codex or almanac; like the four historical Mayan codices that survived the invasion of the Europeans and now reside in museums, Silko's almanac consists of fragments of narrative, drawings, calendrical records, and prophecy; smuggled north into the United States, the almanac was passed to Lecha and Zeta Cazador by their Yaqui grandmother.

Originally, the massive novel was a continuous narrative without chapter breaks, like *Ceremony,* but Silko's editor encouraged her to make it more accessible for readers, and Silko redesigned the novel to resemble the almanac that is its subject. The text is highly fragmented, composed of short, nonlinearly arranged chapters, whose interconnections are not evident until well into the book. A "Five Hundred Year Map," a drawing with text labels that appears inside the book cover, summarizes the historical and geographical scope of the novel, foretelling "the future of all the Americas . . . the disappearance of all things European" and "the return of all tribal lands."

The primary narrative line of *Almanac of the Dead* centers on the Cazador sisters, sixty-year-old twins who occupy a heavily fortified ranch outside Tucson, from which Zeta operates a profitable drug- and gun-smuggling operation. Lecha, a high-living, drug-addicted television-talk-show psychic, is engaged in translating and transcribing the fragments of the sacred almanac, assisted by Seese, a young Anglo drug addict who seeks Lecha's help to locate her missing baby, kidnapped by a sadistic pornographer. Also employed at the ranch as a gardener is a Laguna man named Sterling, who was banished from the Pueblo for revealing to a Hollywood film crew the location of a recently appeared sacred stone snake (perhaps contributing to rumors that Silko herself had been similarly banished). The geographical center of the novel is Tucson, which is (according to the map) "home to an assortment of speculators, confidence men, embezzlers, lawyers, judges, police and other criminals" as well as traffickers in drugs, pornography, and body parts; and thousands of homeless people who inhabit the streets and arroyos of the city.

A second center of action lies south of the border, in Tuxtla Guiterrez, Mexico, where twin brothers,

Tacho and El Feo, are organizing a People's Army to reclaim the land stolen by the European invaders. The first half of *Almanac of the Dead* weaves together the stories of these and many other characters, setting up a series of violent events that unfold in the last half of the book in a domino effect toward the destruction prophesied by the Almanac and by the appearance of the giant stone snake in Laguna. As the interconnections of the characters through drug and arms deals, real estate machinations, and conspiracies of all kinds begin to erupt in murders, raids, and bombings, simultaneously mystics, prophets, New Age healers, and revolutionaries gather at a "Holistic Healers Convention" in Tucson, and a nationwide computer linkup of technoterrorists, ecoguerillas, and survivalists arises. Meanwhile, the spirits of the ancestors shake the earth and whisper in the ears of crazed suicides and snipers, and the People's Army begins to move north. The novel ends on the verge of chaos, with the implication of a new age to follow this period of destruction.

Much more so than *Ceremony, Almanac of the Dead* has been misinterpreted by some critics as a vengeful attack on Western culture and an unfair stereotyping of Euramericans as depraved oppressors. Others have pointed out that *Almanac of the Dead* describes the return of the days of the "Death's Eye Dog" foretold by the Mayan calendars, a "male reign" characterized by the worship of violence; in the revisionist history of the novel, the blood lust of the Aztecs called the conquistadors to the Americas. Some critics suggest that *Almanac of the Dead* expands the witchery poem at the heart of *Ceremony,* acting as a cautionary tale about the ultimate effects of the failure to respect Earth and life. In fact, *Almanac of the Dead* goes far beyond cultural retribution to a much more positive vision. At the end of the novel, Sterling, like Tayo, returns to Laguna and reimmerses himself in a ceremonial relationship to the land. As he stands by the Jackpile uranium mine, scene of Tayo's confrontation with witchery and the site of the emergence of the sacred stone snake, Sterling muses, "humans had desecrated only themselves. . . . Burned and radioactive, with all humans dead, the earth would still be sacred." As Silko explains in interviews and essays, she intends the retaking of the Americas and the "end of all things European" as metaphors for a global spiritual awakening already under way that will reconnect humans to the earth.

Scholarly work on *Almanac of the Dead* was slow to appear and focused in the beginning on the portrayal in the novel of the brutality of capitalism and colonialism in the Americas; only recently has criticism begun to address the implications of Silko's vision of revolution, based in a commitment to life that transcends boundaries of race, class, gender, and nationality, and the trickster humor that infuses the novel and balances its harshness. In 1998 the journal *Studies in American Indian Literatures* devoted a special issue to the novel, and a collection of essays on Silko's work edited by Louise K. Barnett and James L. Thorson appeared in 1999, which features work on *Almanac of the Dead* as well. Critical study of the novel is just beginning, and already several scholars have named it one of the most important novels of the twentieth century.

In 1993 Silko published *Sacred Water,* a small volume of prose poems about water accompanied by her own photographs. First produced on Silko's copier and stapled by hand on her living room floor, the book was later published by Silko's own Flood Plain Press, which also reissued *Laguna Woman* in 1994. Silko continued her experimentation with combining text and photographs in "An Essay On Rocks," first published in 1995 and collected in *Yellow Woman and a Beauty of the Spirit* and in *Rain,* a collaboration with her photographer father, published by the Whitney Museum in 1996. *Yellow Woman and a Beauty of the Spirit* collected Silko's essays, including well-known ones such as "Interior and Exterior Landscapes" and "Language and Literature from a Pueblo Perspective" as well as many previously unpublished essays composed while she was working on *Almanac of the Dead* and *Sacred Water.* Included is a tribute to the Maya Zapatistas, whose uprising in Chiapas, Mexico, in 1994 brought *Almanac of the Dead* eerily to life. Silko also describes the depression and paranoia she felt during the ten years she devoted to *Almanac of the Dead* and the need for beauty and healing that motivated the work that followed.

Silko's third novel, *Gardens in the Dunes,* published in 1999, counters the destruction portrayed in *Almanac of the Dead* by exploring ways humans can restore their contiguity with the world and participate in the recovery of Earth from the devastation of colonial and capitalist greed. Set at the turn of the twentieth century and written in a style reminiscent of Henry James, *Gardens in the Dunes* focuses on Indigo, an eleven-year-old girl of the fictional Sand Lizard tribe, a disappearing Colorado River group who cultivated lush gardens in the dunes along the river before invaders drove them from their homes. Separated from her family when soldiers attack a Ghost Dance gathering, Indigo is sent to boarding school. She escapes and takes refuge with Hattie Palmer, a scholar whose depression over the rejection of her thesis on the roles of women in early Christianity pushes her into a marriage of convenience to botanist Edward Palmer. Heir to a wealthy Long Island family, Edward struggles to rebuild their diminishing fortune by pirating plants to feed the Victorian obsession with collecting, cataloguing, and controlling the natural world.

Dust jacket for Silko's 1996 book, which includes her account of the ten years she spent writing her controversial 1991 novel,
Almanac of the Dead *(Bruccoli Clark Layman Archives)*

On a summer tour of the grand homes and gardens of the East Coast and European family and friends, Hattie instructs Indigo in the pleasures of books, art, and travel, while Indigo's intense sensory pleasure in the natural world and her determination to return home inspire Hattie to reclaim her emotional independence and to help Indigo find her family. Indigo's journey and the trope of gardening allow Silko to contrast two dramatically different ways of living in and consuming the world. Like Palmer, the Sand Lizard people collect and hybridize plants to increase beauty and yield, but they care for plants in mutually sustaining ways that respect the interdependence of all forms of life and spirit. The extravagant gardens of the New England robber barons, transplanted and forced to bloom at obscene cost, epitomize the capitalist exploitation of the land and its native inhabitants that is also evident in the damming of the Colorado River, the burning of large areas of Brazilian jungle to insure that Victorian investors possess the only specimens of orchid species, and

Edward's theft of citron cuttings in an attempt to break Corsican monopoly of the citron trade.

Gardens in the Dunes, like *Almanac of the Dead,* exposes Western patriarchy's oppression of women, indigenous peoples, animals, and the earth, and explores ways the exploited and powerless can form alliances across artificial national and cultural boundaries. *Gardens in the Dunes,* however, foregrounds the reverent, life-giving practices of caretaking and inclusiveness characteristic of indigenous communities, and heals breaches between Euramerican and Native cultures by drawing parallels between the indigenous spiritual traditions of the Americas and those of pre-Christian Europe and Gnostic Christianity. Little critical work on *Gardens in the Dunes* has appeared to date, but the novel was widely and favorably reviewed. Some reviewers found the narrative sluggish or contrived, but most praised Silko's imaginative versatility, her carefully researched details, and the luminous, dream-like qualities of her prose. Silko is currently at work on a satirical novel modeled on a self-help book, a chapter of which appeared in 2000 as "Introduction to a Book Titled *Blue Sevens, or Protect Yourself from Witchcraft While You Get Rich.*" This short excerpt is narrated by a writer looking for a new profession and promises to be as much of a surprise in terms of genre bending and subject matter as her previous work.

Native American writers are just beginning to make their way into studies of American nature writing, which has until recently focused on Euramerican male writers in the tradition of Henry David Thoreau, John Muir, and Edward Abbey. Ecocritics such as Joni Adamson and Patrick D. Murphy suggest that Native American writers add crucial new dimensions to the study of representations of nature in literature. Salyer, author of the first book-length study of Silko's writing, observes that with her work "comes a new chapter in the imagination of land in American literature. No writer has given the land such prominence and voice." Silko's work challenges anthropocentric notions of a passive Earth that humans can destroy or "save" and offers instead a vision of a natural world that is alive, sentient, and inspirited at every level, an active agent in shaping the identities of individuals, their communities, and the realities they inhabit. Silko thus calls into question the separation of culture and nature that the pastoral tradition and much of contemporary environmentalism take for granted. For her, human beings and their technologies are "forces of nature," part of the ongoing cycles of destruction and re-creation of Earth; neither "civilization" nor technology upsets the balance of those cycles, but the concept of their separation, which allows humans to imagine the world a lifeless source of objects for their use and thus to become agents of destruction. Some of the most recent criticism of Silko's work takes approaches of ecofeminism and ecojustice, focusing on the connections she draws between the objectification and exploitation of women, people of color, and the earth, and on the possibilities of the new stories she tells in the intersections of nature and culture to heal human alienation and bring about social, racial, and environmental justice. What kind of influence Leslie Marmon Silko's work will have on this field of study remains to be seen.

Letters:

Anne Wright, ed., *The Delicacy and Strength of Lace: Letters between Leslie Marmon Silko and James Wright* (St. Paul, Minn.: Graywolf Press, 1986).

Interviews:

Donna Perry, "Leslie Marmon Silko," in *Backtalk: Women Writers Speak Out,* edited by Perry (New Brunswick, N.J.: Rutgers University Press, 1993), pp. 314–340;

Ellen L. Arnold, ed., *Conversations with Leslie Marmon Silko* (Jackson: University of Mississippi Press, 2000).

Bibliography:

William Dinome, "Laguna Woman: An Annotated Leslie Silko Bibliography," *American Indian Culture and Research Journal,* 21, no. 1 (1997): 207–280.

References:

Joni Adamson, *American Indian Literature, Environmental Justice, and Ecocriticism: The Middle Place* (Tucson: University of Arizona Press, 2001), pp. 128–179;

Paula Gunn Allen, "The Feminine Landscape of Leslie Marmon Silko's *Ceremony,*" in *Studies in American Indian Literature: Critical Essays and Course Designs,* edited by Allen (New York: Modern Language Association of America, 1983), pp. 127–133;

Allen, "The Psychological Landscape of *Ceremony,*" *American Indian Quarterly,* 5, no. 1 (1979): 7–12;

Allen, "Special Problems in Teaching Leslie Marmon Silko's *Ceremony,*" *American Indian Quarterly,* 14, no. 4 (1990): 379–386;

Judith A. Antell, "Momaday, Welch, and Silko: Expressing the Feminine Principle through Male Alienation," *American Indian Quarterly,* 12, no. 3 (1988): 213–220;

Ellen L. Arnold, "An Ear for the Story, an Eye for the Pattern: Rereading *Ceremony,*" *Modern Fiction Studies,* 45, no. 1 (1999): 69–92;

Louise K. Barnett and James L. Thorson, eds., *Leslie Marmon Silko: A Collection of Critical Essays* (Albuquerque: University of New Mexico Press, 1999);

Peter Beidler, "Animals and Theme in *Ceremony,*" *American Indian Quarterly,* 5, no. 1 (1979): 13–18;

Jennifer Brice, "Earth as Mother, Earth as Other in Novels by Silko and Hogan," *Critique,* 39, no. 2 (1998): 127–138;

Lawrence Buell, *The Environmental Imagination: Thoreau, Nature Writing, and the Formation of American Culture* (Cambridge: Belknap Press of Harvard University Press, 1995), pp. 285–296, 300–304;

Robin Cohen, "Landscape, Story, and Time as Elements of Reality in Silko's 'Yellow Woman,'" *Weber Studies,* 12, no. 3 (1995): 141–147;

Laura Coltelli, "Leslie Marmon Silko's *Sacred Water,*" *Studies in American Indian Literatures,* 8, no. 4 (1996): 21–29;

Reyes Garcia, "Senses of Place in *Ceremony,*" *MELUS,* 10, no. 4 (1983): 37–48;

Melody Graulich, ed., *"Yellow Woman": Leslie Marmon Silko* (New Brunswick, N.J.: Rutgers University Press, 1993);

Helen Jaskoski, *Leslie Marmon Silko: A Study of the Short Fiction* (New York: Twayne, 1998);

Jaskoski, "Thinking Woman's Children and the Bomb," *Explorations in Ethnic Studies,* 13, no. 2 (1990): 1–24;

Arnold Krupat, "The Dialogic of Silko's *Storyteller,*" in *Narrative Chance: Postmodern Discourse on Native American Indian Literature,* edited by Gerald Vizenor (Albuquerque: University of New Mexico Press, 1989), pp. 55–68;

Kenneth Lincoln, *Native American Renaissance* (Berkeley: University of California Press, 1983), pp. 233–250;

Carol Mitchell, "Ceremony as Ritual," *American Indian Quarterly,* 5, no. 1 (1979): 27–35;

David L. Moore, "Myth, History, and Identity in Silko and Young Bear: Postcolonial Praxis," in *New Voices in Native American Literary Criticism,* edited by Krupat (Washington: Smithsonian Institution Press, 1993), pp. 370–395;

Patrick D. Murphy, *Literature, Nature, and Other: Ecofeminist Critiques* (Albany: State University of New York Press, 1995);

Robert M. Nelson, *Place and Vision: The Function of Landscape in Native American Fiction* (New York: Peter Lang, 1993), pp. 11–39;

Christopher Norden, "Ecological Restoration as Post-Colonial Ritual of Community in Three Native American Novels," *Studies in American Indian Literatures,* 6, no. 4 (1994): 94–106;

Bridget O'Meara, "The Ecological Politics of Leslie Silko's *Almanac of the Dead,*" *Wicazo Sa Review,* 15, no. 2 (2000): 63–73;

Lisa Orr, "Theorizing the Earth: Feminist Approaches to Nature and Leslie Marmon Silko's *Ceremony,*" *American Indian Culture and Research Journal,* 18 (1994): 145–157;

Louis Owens, "The Very Essence of Our Lives: Leslie Silko's Webs of Identity," in his *Other Destinies: Understanding the American Indian Novel* (Norman: University of Oklahoma Press, 1992), pp. 168–191;

Karen Piper, "Police Zones: Territory and Identity in Leslie Marmon Silko's *Ceremony,*" *American Indian Quarterly,* 21, no. 3 (1998): 483–498;

Running on the Edge of the Rainbow: Laguna Stories and Poems, video, University of Arizona Radio-TV-Film Bureau, 1978;

A. LaVonne Brown Ruoff, "Ritual and Renewal: Keres Traditions in the Short Fiction of Leslie Silko," *MELUS,* 5, no. 4 (1978): 2–17;

James Ruppert, "No Boundaries, Only Transitions: *Ceremony,*" in his *Mediation in Contemporary Native American Fiction* (Norman: University of Oklahoma Press, 1995), pp. 74–91;

Gregory Salyer, *Leslie Marmon Silko* (New York: Twayne, 1997);

Matthias Schubnell, "Frozen Suns and Angry Bears: An Interpretation of Leslie Silko's 'Storyteller,'" *European Review of Native American Studies,* 1, no. 2 (1987): 21–25;

Lee Schweninger, "Writing Nature: Silko and Native Americans as Nature Writers," *MELUS,* 18, no. 2 (1993): 47–60;

Jana Sequoya, "How(!) Is an Indian? A Contest of Stories," in *New Voices in Native American Literary Criticism,* edited by Krupat (Washington, D.C.: Smithsonian Institution Press, 1993), pp. 453–473;

Patricia Clark Smith and Allen, "Earthly Relations, Carnal Knowledge: Southwestern American Indian Women Writers and Landscape," in *The Desert Is No Lady: Southwestern Landscapes in Women's Writing and Art,* edited by Vera Norwood and Janice Monk (New Haven: Yale University Press, 1987), pp. 174–196;

Rachel Stein, "Contested Ground: Nature, Narrative, and Native American Identity in Leslie Marmon Silko's *Ceremony* and *Almanac of the Dead,*" in her *Shifting the Ground: American Women Writers' Revisions of Nature, Gender, and Race* (Charlottesville: University Press of Virginia, 1997), pp. 114–144;

Edith Swan, "Feminine Perspectives at Laguna Pueblo: Silko's *Ceremony,*" *Tulsa Studies in Women's Literature,* 11, no. 2 (1992): 309–327;

Swan, "Healing Via the Sunwise Cycle in *Ceremony,*" *American Indian Quarterly,* 12, no. 4 (1988): 313–328;

Swan, "Laguna Symbolic Geography and Silko's *Ceremony,*" *American Indian Quarterly,* 12, no. 3 (1988): 229–249;

Shamoon Zamir, "Literature in a 'National Sacrifice Area': Leslie Silko's *Ceremony,*" in *New Voices in Native American Literary Criticism,* edited by Krupat (Washington, D.C.: Smithsonian Institution Press, 1993), pp. 386–415;

Papers:

Many of Leslie Marmon Silko's papers and manuscripts are at the Beinecke Library of Yale University.

Gary Snyder

(8 May 1930   )

James J. Donahue
University of Connecticut

See also the Snyder entries in *DLB 5: American Poets Since World War II; DLB 16: The Beats: Literary Bohemians in Postwar America; DLB 165: American Poets Since World War II, Fourth Series; DLB 212: Twentieth-Century American Western Writers, Second Series;* and *DLB 237: The Beats: A Documentary Volume.*

BOOKS: *Riprap* (Kyoto, Japan: Origin, 1959); enlarged as *Riprap & Cold Mountain Poems* (San Francisco: Four Seasons, 1965);

Myths & Texts (New York: Totem/Corinth, 1960);

Six Sections from Mountains and Rivers without End (San Francisco: Four Seasons, 1965); enlarged as *Six Sections from Mountains and Rivers without End Plus One* (San Francisco: Four Seasons, 1970);

A Range of Poems (London: Fulcrum Press, 1966);

Three Worlds, Three Realms, Six Roads (Marlboro, Vt.: Griffin, 1966);

The Back Country (London: Fulcrum Press, 1967; New York: New Directions, 1968);

The Blue Sky (London: Fulcrum Press, 1967; New York: New Directions, 1968);

Earth House Hold: Technical Notes & Queries for Fellow Dharma Revolutionaries (New York: New Directions, 1969; London: Cape, 1970);

Regarding Wave (Iowa City: Windhover Press, 1969; enlarged edition, New York: New Directions, 1970);

Manzanita (Bolinas, Cal.: Four Seasons, 1972);

The Fudo Trilogy (Berkeley: Shaman Drum, 1973);

Turtle Island (New York: New Directions, 1974; Boston & London: Shambhala, 1994);

The Old Ways: Six Essays (San Francisco: City Lights, 1977);

He Who Hunted Birds in His Father's Village: The Dimensions of a Haida Myth (Bolinas, Cal.: Grey Fox, 1979);

The Real Work: Interviews & Talks 1964–1979, edited by William Scott McLean (New York: New Directions, 1980);

True Night (North San Juan, Cal.: Bob Giorgio, 1980);

Axe Handles (San Francisco: North Point, 1983);

Passage through India (San Francisco: Grey Fox, 1983);

Good Wild Sacred (Madley, U.K.: Five Seasons, 1984);

The Fates of Rocks & Trees (San Francisco: James Linden, 1986);

Left Out in the Rain: New Poems 1947–1985 (San Francisco: North Point, 1986);

The Practice of the Wild (San Francisco: North Point, 1990);

No Nature: New and Selected Poems (New York: Pantheon, 1992);

North Pacific Lands & Waters: A Further Six Sections (Waldron Island, Wash.: Brooding Heron, 1993);

A Place in Space: Ethics, Aesthetics, and Watersheds, New and Selected Prose (Washington, D.C.: Counterpoint, 1995);

Mountains and Rivers without End (Washington, D.C.: Counterpoint, 1996);

Three on Community, by Snyder, Wendell Berry, and Carole Koda (Boise, Idaho: Limberlost Press, 1996)—includes Snyder's "Coming into the Watershed";

The Gary Snyder Reader (Washington, D.C.: Counterpoint, 1999);

Look Out: A Selection of Writings (New York: New Directions, 2002).

SELECTED PERIODICAL PUBLICATION–UNCOLLECTED: "A Young Mazama's Idea of a Mount Hood Climb," *Mazama,* 18 (1946): 56.

Gary Snyder is one of the most significant American environmental writers of the twentieth century and a central figure in American environmental activism. Through his intelligent and provocative writing, he has contributed to both a greater knowledge of and a greater respect for the natural world. Although Snyder is primarily regarded as an environmental poet, his prose pieces powerfully convey his ecological attitudes. Snyder's environmental philosophy is influenced by Western, Eastern, and Native American cultures and traditions. This accumulation of various sources has led to, as he describes his work in the "Author's Note" to

Gary Snyder, at Kitkitdizze, his home in the Sierra foothills, October 1997
(Collection of John Suiter)

The Gary Snyder Reader (1999), a "mix of ideas, images, meters, archetypes, and propositions" that represents the "deliberate life I put myself to, all in the spirit of quest, of making art, seeking knowledge, courting wisdom, and nourishing home place Dharma practice and community." This "deliberate life," as reflected in his works, makes Snyder one of the most complex and comprehensive nature writers.

Gary Sherman Snyder was born to Harold and Lois Wilkey Snyder on 8 May 1930 in San Francisco. Roughly a year and a half after Snyder's birth, his family moved to a farm north of Seattle, Washington. Snyder had roots in the Pacific Northwest through his father, a native of Washington State. His mother, from Texas, had roots in Kansas. During the early years of Snyder's life, his family maintained a sim-

ple working-class life on what he later calls in *The Practice of the Wild* (1990) "the Depression stump-farm." Deeply affected by the hard work of both his family and the local foresters, a respect for whom is often reflected in his poetry, Snyder came to understand the complex forces at play in environmental relations, an understanding that passes beyond simple land-use needs for human consumption and production. This understanding is reflected in both his writing and his political and environmental activism.

Snyder acquired an early love of reading, in part through the influence of his mother, also a writer. His childhood reading habits were also partly shaped by his weekly visits to University Library, a branch of the Seattle Public Library; he often read at least one book per day, if not more. His teenage years were marked by reading the works of John Muir and Robinson Jeffers, two environmental writers to whom critics have pointed as Snyder's literary progenitors. However, Snyder's early reading habits were almost as widely defined as those of his adult years, ranging from literary to anthropological readings, from essays to poetry, from both Anglo-American and Native American traditions.

In 1942 the Snyder family moved to a low-income housing facility in Portland, Oregon. When his parents' marriage ended shortly thereafter, Snyder and his younger sister, Anthea, stayed with their mother. During his high-school years, Snyder worked at a camp on Spirit Lake in Washington, and in 1945 he climbed Mount St. Helens with a climbing party from the local YMCA. He later joined the mountaineering club Mazamas and spent much of his free time exploring the various peaks in the Pacific Northwest. Snyder's love for mountains became a recurring theme in much of his writing, from his 1965 translation of Han-Shan's "Cold Mountain Poems" to his 1996 epic collection, *Mountains and Rivers without End*. The mountaineering side of Snyder was also immortalized in Jack Kerouac's *The Dharma Bums* (1958) in the character of Japhy Ryder.

Snyder contributed to the school paper while in high school, but his first professional publication was in 1946 in the self-titled journal of the Mazamas' organization. "A Young Mazama's Idea of a Mount Hood Climb" represents both Snyder's firsthand knowledge of mountaineering and his good-natured humor, two qualities that can be seen in his later essays on environmental issues. After cautioning his readers, presumably inexperienced and ill equipped for the task at hand, not to attempt to climb Mount Hood, Snyder then ends the piece by telling his readers "I'm climbing it again next week."

In 1947 Snyder graduated from Lincoln High School and enrolled at Reed College on a scholarship. At Reed College, Snyder set out on many of the paths that he has followed in his adult life. He published his first poems in the Reed College student publications *Janus* and *Gurgle*, and he met fellow poets Lew Welch and Philip Whalen, a lifelong friendship with whom is commemorated in the dedication for *The Gary Snyder Reader*. Snyder became seriously involved with anthropological and archaeological work, and in 1950 he worked on his first archaeological site at Fort Vancouver. Snyder's undergraduate thesis was published in 1979 as *He Who Hunted Birds in His Father's Village: The Dimensions of a Haida Myth* and is the most photocopied thesis in the history of Reed College.

At Reed College, Snyder also met Lloyd Reynolds, a professor with a passion for the art of calligraphy and the poetry of William Blake. During the summer between his sophomore and junior years, Snyder shipped out as a merchant seaman, an unlikely but significant strand found in much of his work and evidenced by many of his poems. All of these early influences—contemporary poetry, myth and anthropology, Asian art and culture, working-class labor—became intertwined in Snyder's later life and work.

In 1950, a year before finishing his undergraduate career with a dual major in literature and anthropology, Snyder married fellow Reed College student Alison Gass. After spending the summer following his graduation working as a member of an Oregon logging operation, he hitchhiked to Indiana University to begin his graduate study in anthropology. In 1952 Snyder left graduate school and divorced his wife; soon after, he moved to San Francisco, where he lived with his college friend Philip Whalen. Although Snyder excelled in his formal education, it was only one of the many complex forces that he incorporated into his life and work.

Snyder returned to graduate school in 1953, enrolling at the University of California at Berkeley to study oriental languages, where he studied for three years without taking a degree. In the same year Snyder was employed as a fire lookout on Sourdough Mountain and worked on *Myths & Texts* (1960), a work whose "success" he qualifies in the introduction. For Snyder, the inhabitants of Turtle Island, a Native American name for North America, are "a still rootless population of non-natives." The people do not know where their water comes from or the names of the plants in their area. In this respect, his work is only the starting point to what became a lifelong pursuit in his writing—an understanding of his place in the world. As such, his success with this volume is almost entirely personal.

Also in 1953, Snyder met Kenneth Rexroth, the poetic elder statesman who served as mentor for a group of writers who were known later as "The San Francisco Renaissance," a group including Snyder, Michael McClure, and City Lights publisher Lawrence Ferlinghetti. Although affiliated with and working in San Francisco, Snyder was able to leave the city every summer and work in the forests of the Pacific Slope. In 1952 he worked as a fire lookout on Crater Mountain in the Washington Cascades, an experience chronicled in his personal diary and later incorporated in his 1969 prose work *Earth House Hold: Technical Notes & Queries for Fellow Dharma Revolutionaries*. Although his alleged Communist sympathies were used to deny him employment in subsequent years, the experience of working the fire lookout became important in both his spiritual and aesthetic development.

In many examples from "Lookout's Journal" one can see the use of prose and poetry simultaneously. The juxtaposition of prose and poetry strengthens Sny-

Snyder on fire watch at Crater Mountain Lookout, August 1952
(photograph © Harold Vail)

der's personal, narrative approach to poetry and represents the world realistically. In the journal are also the first signs that Snyder would become a major prose stylist. This selection additionally shows evidence of the Eastern thought that infuses much of his later work after his study of Zen Buddhism, a spiritual aesthetic that complements his poetic practice in the shared values of sparse description and direct apprehension of the natural world.

Snyder's own life plays an important role in many of his works. His experiences as a member of a trail crew in Yosemite National Park in the summer of 1955 inspired the poetry that was later published in his first collection, *Riprap* (1959). He defines "riprap" at the start of his collection as "a cobble of stone laid on steep, slick rock to make a trail for horses in the mountains." In a real sense, Snyder traces a trail for his readers to follow, providing the necessary footing for his audience. This volume shows Snyder's interest in and concern for the places he visits, an early indication of a motif that dominates his later work in both poetry and prose—man's sense of place.

However, his interest did not remain solely the environment, ignoring those who inhabit it. Many poems show a similar concern for people as well as place; the environment is not simply a place, a backdrop against which people and animals live, but the totality of place, including its varied inhabitants. The

later enlargement of this book to include Snyder's translations of Han-Shan's "Cold Mountain Poems" (*Riprap & Cold Mountain Poems,* 1965), poems of a seventh-century Chinese hermit, is further evidence of the influence of Buddhism on both his environmental views and his writing.

Also included in the enlarged text is Snyder's translation of Lu Ch'iu-Yin's preface to Han-Shan's poems. Lu, governor of T'ai Prefecture, recounts his introduction to Han-Shan and his work. Lu writes that because Han-Shan's poetry affected him as much as his life on the mountain affected his own religious sensibilities, he ordered that Han-Shan's poems be collected from the "bamboo, wood, stones, and cliffs" they were composed on. By including this preface to Han-Shan's works, Snyder shows the reader that art and civics, poetry and politics, need not be separate. Snyder's lifelong activism for social and political causes is not anything new but rather a return to an older tradition.

In the fall of 1955 Snyder moved to Berkeley, where he met and became close with Allen Ginsberg, who had moved to California from New York City. Through Ginsberg, Snyder met and befriended Kerouac. In his novel of Zen philosophy and mountain-climbing experiences, Kerouac describes Snyder as "really sharp—he's really the wildest craziest sharpest cat we've ever met. . . . Japhy Ryder is a great new hero of American culture." Although certainly flattering, this

Snyder and Philip Whalen atop a peak east of States Lakes Basin in Kings' Canyon,
5 July 1965 (photograph by Drummond Hadley)

description by his friend and fellow poet and Zen practitioner was as damaging as it was helpful. It provided for Kerouac's readership a new type of counterculture hero, one who is in touch with the natural world and able to escape the demands of the city, but it also worked to define Snyder as a "Beat Poet," a label that had both positive and negative effects. Although certainly part of the 1950s Berkeley–San Francisco poetry scene, Snyder was more involved with the San Francisco poets than with the New York poets who later came to San Francisco. Although he shared many of the principles of Beat poetry, his own poetry was less concerned with the urban world of social ills than with an attention to nature and the political significance of man's interactions with it. However, Snyder's fame was certainly increased by his association with the Beat Movement, an association cemented by his participation in the 6 Gallery reading on 7 October 1955 in San Francisco, famous as the first public reading of Ginsberg's famous poem "Howl for Carl Solomon."

In 1956 Snyder left for Japan, where he entered a Buddhist monastery in Kyoto and practiced Zen meditation. Although he left the school shortly thereafter, working in the engine room of the oil tanker *Sappa Creek* for eight months in 1957, he never abandoned his Zen practice; the Zen philosophy is evident in many of his subsequent works. While abroad, he married Joanne Kyger in 1960, whom he divorced in 1965. In 1967 Snyder married Masa Uehara in a ceremony on the rim of an active volcano, and in 1968 Snyder returned to California with his wife, settling on land he purchased with Ginsberg and others. He called his house "Kitkitdizze," a local Native American word for a shrub known commonly in English as "Miner's Misery." The couple had two sons, Kai in 1968 and Gen in 1969, and were divorced in 1987.

While abroad, Snyder published many volumes of poetry. *Myths & Texts* was published in 1960; *Six Sections from Mountains and Rivers without End* was published in 1965 (a collection that was not published complete until 1996), along with a new edition of *Riprap,* which included his translations of Han-Shan's "Cold Mountain Poems." *A Range of Poems* appeared in 1966, and *The Back Country* (first published by a London publisher in 1967) was Snyder's first collection published by a major U.S. publisher, New Directions in New York, in 1968. In 1969 *Regarding Wave* was published in a limited edition by the Windhover Press, and later published in expanded form by New Directions in 1970.

Although all of the above works express Snyder's concern for the natural world, his prose collection *Earth House Hold* most clearly expresses his views on the environment. Beginning with a title that plays on the root meanings of the word *ecology,* the subtitle, *Technical Notes*

& *Queries for Fellow Dharma Revolutionaries,* explains that this work is meant not only for reading pleasure but also as a guide for those interested in a more sustainable living with the natural world. One reads, then, the opening piece, "Lookout's Journal," not only as a diary of Snyder's experiences but also as a guide for how best to live alone in the mountains. His entry for 9 July succinctly explains his belief: "one does not need universities and libraries / one need be alive to what is about." His statements "To Fellow Dharma Revolutionaries" are clearer in later sections of the book, such as "Why Tribe" and "Dharma Queries."

"Why Tribe" sets forth Snyder's understanding of the "new society now emerging within the industrial nations," "based in community houses, villages and ashrams; tribe-run farms or workshops or companies; large open families; pilgrimages and wanderings from center to center." In short, the goal of such a society is "to live simply, with few tools and minimal clothes, close to nature." "Dharma Queries" begins with "A Quick Review of the Present Yuga," in which he lists a few points of current concern for him, such as his critique of "Contemporary Science," which is "the knowledge that society and any given cultural outlook is arbitrary; and that the more we conquer nature the weaker we get." For Snyder, the goal is not to conquer but to live with nature, recognizing that "all of us carry within us caves; with animals and gods on the walls; a place of ritual and magic." "The Buddha as Son and Lover of the Goddess" and "The Real Old Goodspell" both express his Buddhist worldview. Although early in his career, the publication of *Earth House Hold* marked Snyder as a major force in environmental thought and was the first major synthesis of the many threads that have influenced the rest of his career: the environment, Eastern religions, a personal approach to subject matter, and a concern for the ways in which humans live their lives in and with the natural world.

These major issues were the central themes in *Turtle Island* (1974), which won the Pulitzer Prize in poetry in 1975. Included in his work of award-winning poetry were also his first major prose essays on environmental issues, including "Four Changes," his detailed analysis of population control, pollution, and consumption. This essay is noteworthy for its detailed analysis of important issues, as well as its style. In this essay, reprinted with a "Postscript" in *A Place in Space: Ethics, Asthetics, and Watersheds, New and Selected Prose* (1995), Snyder abandons his personal narrative style, characteristic of both his poetry and most of his later prose pieces, and adopts a more general, structured tone. This new form allows him to discuss environmental issues that reflect their importance to the world at large in a way that is not possible from the first-person perspective.

In each of the four sections—"Population," "Pollution," "Consumption," and "Transformation"—Snyder begins with a statement on the current condition and situation, states the necessary goals, and then provides the actions that must be taken (personal, community, and political) in order to achieve these goals. In his "Postscript" to the 1995 version, Snyder restates the importance of these changes because the "few remaining traditional people with place-based sustainable economies are driven into urban slums and cultural suicide." Clearly, for Snyder, environmental issues are inseparable from other social and economic issues, and environmental problems cannot be solved without a conscious effort toward reversing the destructive practices of humanity, specifically those humans who populate the cities.

Snyder's next published collection of essays, *The Old Ways* (1977), included pieces that, though less inflammatory in tone than "Four Changes," equally reflect his political and environmental interests, and the ways in which the various human concerns overlap. In "The Yogin and the Philosopher" Snyder discusses the shared work of the poet, philosopher, and yogin, all of whom stand "not too far behind the shaman." "The Politics of Ethnopoetics" is a more personal approach to the same issues raised in "Four Changes." His argument that "What we are witnessing in the world today is an unparalleled waterfall of destruction of a diversity of human cultures" is perhaps the most common theme of his environmental prose. In this essay he argues that the destruction of the environment is only one aspect of a wholesale attack on human culture, an attack also found in the nuclear arms race, fossil fuel consumption, and the loss of older traditions. "North Beach" is a short celebratory essay on a familiar gathering place for many West Coast counterculture participants, and "The Dharma Eye of D. A. Levy" is a short celebration of his friend and fellow Buddhist. In "Re-inhabitation" Snyder discusses the benefits to the efforts of "the tiny number of persons who come out of the industrial societies (having collected or squandered the fruits of 8000 years of civilization) and then start to turn back to the land, to place." Finally, in "The Incredible Survival of Coyote," Snyder discusses the Native American trickster figure Coyote and its survival in the contemporary American poetry of his peers. In all of these essays, Snyder develops the ways in which art and culture, poetry and place, and myth and ecology interrelate.

Snyder's interest in place and the ways in which humans act out their lives in relation to it is the central theme in his three major collections from the 1980s— *The Real Work: Interviews & Talks 1964–1979* (1980), *Axe*

Dust jacket for Snyder's 1967 collection of essays about his life in Japan, his trip to India, and his return to the United States (Bruccoli Clark Layman Archives)

Handles (1983) and *Left Out in the Rain: New Poems 1947–1985* (1986). In such interviews as "The Landscape of the Consciousness," "On Earth Geography," and "The *East West* Interview," Snyder works out many of the issues dealt with in his other essays. This collection of interviews, then, does not provide substantially new discussions of different material; rather, it offers a chance for the reader to see how these issues take shape in Snyder's mind before they enter into his more polished prose. By following his thought process through these interviews, the reader is better prepared to read his essays, which always range widely in scope.

Axe Handles and *Left Out in the Rain* represent the same issues and themes, techniques and foci, of his earlier poetry. Such poems from *Axe Handles* as "Axe Handles," "Fence Posts," and "The Canyon Wren" are personal approaches to universal themes, using Snyder's own immediate experience as a means to convey general truths. The poems in this volume collectively describe a simple life, while forcing the reader to

account for complex human truths. *Left Out in the Rain* also describes Snyder's life, though by different means. The volume is divided into eight sections, six of which focus on periods in Snyder's life. In this way, the reader is able to trace Snyder's path, both through the world and through his consciousness. Snyder takes this theme up in more-epic proportions in his most ambitious collection of poetry, *Mountains and Rivers without End* (1996).

Although Snyder had for many years played the role of teacher of ecology, poetry, Buddhism, and Native American traditions, he did not realize that role until the 1980s. In 1986 Snyder joined the faculty at the University of California at Davis, teaching courses in creative writing and poetry, and assisting in the construction of the Nature and Culture Program. In the years following his appointment to the faculty, Snyder has produced his two most significant prose collections and has since become recognized as one of the leading environmental theorists in America.

The Practice of the Wild (1990) was Snyder's first book-length prose analysis of environmental issues. Although composed of individual essays, the volume represents the culmination not only of nearly half a century of environmental thought and activism but also a lifetime of learning about and living among diverse cultures. In "Blue Mountains Constantly Walking," he writes of his "learning how different societies work out the details of subsistence and celebration in their different landscapes. The line between use and misuse, between objectification and celebration, is fine indeed." Snyder walks this fine line in his writing, an intense focus on the object without falling into objectification.

Rather than simply relate a Native American tale in "The Woman Who Married a Bear," he uses the story as a springboard for a celebration of the power of myth in human culture. The tale is a lament for a way of understanding the world lost to most industrialized people; however, this lament also rings with a note of hope, for humanity's understanding is what is lost, not the myth. Snyder ends the essay at the completion of the bear dance, noting that "The power songs of the handgame players continue without break." These traditions are still practiced, and Snyder's celebration of them is his effort at passing them on.

The rest of the essays in this collection continue Snyder's efforts at representing the complex ways in which man interacts with the world. "Tawny Grammar" explores the "nature" of language. "Ancient Forests of the Far West" is both a personal celebration of the wilderness of the Pacific Northwest in which he grew up and worked and a critique of the capitalist economies that work at destroying such wild lands. Snyder recalls a Buddhist teaching in his conclusion to

Gary Snyder with Kai

Dust jacket for the book that won the 1975 Pulitzer Prize in poetry and includes Snyder's
first essays on environmental issues (Bruccoli Clark Layman Archives)

"Survival and Sacrament," the final essay of the collection. Dong-shan is asked by a monk: "Is there a practice for people to follow?" The answer is clear: "When you become a real person, there is such a practice."

Although the implication is that most people have not become "real" persons because of their participation in destructive environmental practices, Snyder reminds his readers that the best way to live for the future, the best way to ensure that the environment and the human cultures that live in it survive, is by returning to the old teachings. In the past what has been left behind is the secret to the future.

Snyder's collection of essays *A Place in Space* is a culmination of a lifetime of environmental thought and practice. The anthology collects many of Snyder's earlier essays, such as "Energy Is Eternal Delight," "The Politics of Ethnopoetics," and "The Incredible Survival of Coyote," as well as previously unpublished works, such as "A Virus Runs Through It," a review of William S. Burroughs Jr.'s 1962 book *The Ticket That Exploded,* and essay versions of lectures. This volume also collects Snyder's more-recent essays, on topics ranging from environmental studies to an homage of

Walt Whitman, "Walt Whitman's Old 'New World,'" in which he remembers Whitman's "vibrant and inspiring hope for a world people yet to come, a society that would become the best on earth." In these essays Snyder laments the loss of the old ways, yet reminds his readers that there is still hope for the future.

One essay in particular addresses many of the important themes that run through Snyder's work. In "The Rediscovery of Turtle Island," Snyder discusses the pressing environmental issues facing both academics and activists in the twentieth century. In the first section, he calls for a "humanistic scholarship that embraces the nonhuman," which he would, "in a spirit of pagan play," call "panhumanism." The second section of the essay is a first-person account of a 1969 conference he attended, where he first heard North America referred to as "Turtle Island," and its subsequent importance to him and his work. The final section of the essay retells the Nisenan and Maidu creation myth, which he uses to emphasize the importance of older, native traditions to contemporary environmental activism.

Besides his work in prose, Snyder also published two collections of poetry in the 1990s, *No Nature* (1992)

and *Mountains and Rivers without End.* Similar to his two essay collections published in the 1990s, these volumes of poetry represent a lifetime of writing on nature. *No Nature* is a collection of new and selected poems, generously sampling from his earlier volumes and including more than a dozen new poems. *Mountains and Rivers without End* is more of a cohesive whole and is read as an epic poem as often as it is as a collection of individual pieces. Begun in 1956, *Mountains and Rivers without End* is a collection of poems written throughout Snyder's lifetime, from various environments throughout the world, representing a wide array of human cultures. From this volume, one can read the poetic development of one of the most significant American poets of the twentieth century. For this reason, the book became an instant American classic. Well-reviewed by professional critics, it also became the subject of a yearlong seminar at Stanford University, a rare achievement for any book and a distinctive honor for any writer.

Snyder's literary achievements were also celebrated by his being awarded two prestigious awards. In 1997 he was awarded the Bollingen Prize, the most distinguished poetry prize of the nation, as well as the John Hay Award for Nature Writing. Snyder's work was further celebrated by the release of *The Gary Snyder Reader.* This anthology collects not only most of Snyder's most significant poems and essays from each of his important volumes but also samples from his more hard-to-find works, such as *He Who Hunted Birds in His Father's Village* and *Passage through India* (1983). Also included in this anthology are selections from his letters, journals, and translations, as well as uncollected and new essays and poems.

Despite the publication of this comprehensive anthology, there are no signs that Snyder's career is over. In the 1990s Snyder began editing his journals, which stretch back almost half a century, and he continues to write. In 1991 he married Carole Koda, with whom he lives at Kitkitdizze, which he remodeled in 1997. He remains active in local environmental politics and has worked closely with the Bureau of Land Man-agement in protecting public lands. Gary Snyder continues to be one of the most important American writers and activists on behalf of the environment.

Bibliographies:

Katherine McNeil, *Gary Snyder: A Bibliography* (New York: Phoenix Bookshop, 1983);

Tom Lavazzi, "Gary Snyder: An International Checklist of Criticism," *Sagetrieb,* 12 (Spring 1993): 97–128.

Biographies:

David Kherdian, *A Biographical Sketch and a Descriptive Checklist of Gary Snyder* (Berkeley, Cal: Oyez, 1965);

Jon Halper, ed., *Gary Snyder: Dimensions of a Life* (San Francisco: Sierra Club, 1991).

References:

Ann Charters, ed., *Beat Down to Your Soul: What Was the Beat Generation?* (New York: Penguin, 2001), pp. 516–533;

Charters, ed., *The Portable Beat Reader* (New York: Penguin, 1992), pp. 289–306;

Charters, ed., *The Portable Sixties Reader* (New York: Penguin, 2003) pp. 560–565;

Jack Kerouac, *The Dharma Bums* (New York: Viking, 1958);

Patrick D. Murphy, *A Place for Wayfaring: The Poetry and Prose of Gary Snyder* (Corvallis: Oregon State University Press, 2000);

Murphy, *Understanding Gary Snyder* (Columbia: University of South Carolina Press, 1992).

Papers:

The Gary Snyder Collection, housed at the University of California, Davis, includes more than one hundred thousand items. A large collection including materials related to Snyder and his contemporaries is housed in the special collections of the University of California, San Diego.

Wallace Stegner

(18 February 1909 – 12 April 1993)

Jason G. Horn
Gordon College

See also the Stegner entries in *DLB 9: American Novelists, 1910–1945; DLB 206: Twentieth-Century American Western Writers, First Series;* and *DLB Yearbook: 1993.*

BOOKS: *Clarence Edward Dutton: An Appraisal* (Salt Lake City: University of Utah Press, 1935);

Remembering Laughter (Boston: Little, Brown, 1937; London: Heinemann, 1937);

The Potter's House (Muscatine, Iowa: Prairie Press, 1938);

On a Darkling Plain (New York: Harcourt, Brace, 1940);

Fire and Ice (New York: Duell, Sloan & Pearce, 1941);

Mormon Country (New York: Duell, Sloan & Pearce, 1942);

The Big Rock Candy Mountain (New York: Duell, Sloan & Pearce, 1943; London: Hammond, Hammond, 1950);

One Nation, by Stegner and the editors of *Look* (Boston: Houghton Mifflin, 1945);

Second Growth (Boston: Houghton Mifflin, 1947; London: Hammond, Hammond, 1948);

The Preacher and the Slave (Boston: Houghton Mifflin, 1950; London: Hammond, Hammond, 1951); republished as *Joe Hill: A Biographical Novel* (Garden City, N.Y.: Doubleday, 1969);

The Women on the Wall (Boston: Houghton Mifflin, 1950; London: Hammond, Hammond, 1952);

The Writer in America, with notes by M. Hiramatsu (Tokyo: Hokuseido Press, 1951; Folcroft, Pa.: Folcroft Press, 1969);

Beyond the Hundredth Meridian: John Wesley Powell and the Second Opening of the West (Boston: Houghton Mifflin, 1954);

The City of the Living, and Other Stories (Boston: Houghton Mifflin, 1956; London: Hammond, Hammond, 1957);

The Papers of Bernard DeVoto: A Description and Checklist of his Work (San Francisco: Taylor & Taylor, 1960);

A Shooting Star (New York: Viking, 1961; London: Heinemann, 1961);

Wallace Stegner (Collection of Mary Stegner)

Wolf Willow: A History, a Story, and a Memory of the Last Plains Frontier (New York: Viking, 1962; London: Heinemann, 1963);

The Gathering of Zion: The Story of the Mormon Trail (New York: McGraw-Hill, 1964; London: Eyre & Spottiswoode, 1966);

Teaching the Short Story, Davis Publications in English, no. 2 (Davis: Department of English, University of California, Davis, 1965);

All the Little Live Things (New York: Viking, 1967; London: Heinemann, 1968);

The Sound of Mountain Water (Garden City, N.Y.: Doubleday, 1969);

Angle of Repose (Garden City, N.Y.: Doubleday, 1971; London: Heinemann, 1971);

Discovery! The Search for Arabian Oil (Beirut: Middle East Export Press, 1971);

Variations on a Theme of Discontent (Logan: Utah State University Press, 1972);

Robert Frost and Bernard DeVoto (Stanford, Cal.: Associates of the Stanford University Libraries, 1974);

The Uneasy Chair: A Biography of Bernard DeVoto (Garden City, N.Y.: Doubleday, 1974);

The Spectator Bird (Franklin Center, Pa.: Franklin Library, 1976; Garden City, N.Y.: Doubleday, 1976; London: Prior, 1978);

Recapitulation, text by Stegner, photographs by Eliot Porter (Garden City, N.Y.: Doubleday, 1979);

American Places, by Wallace Stegner, Page Stegner, and Porter, edited by John Macrae III (New York: Dutton, 1981);

One Way to Spell Man (Garden City, N.Y.: Doubleday, 1982);

The American West as Living Space (Ann Arbor: University of Michigan Press, 1987);

Crossing to Safety (Franklin Center, Pa.: Franklin Library, 1987; New York: Random House, 1987);

The Collected Stories of Wallace Stegner (New York: Random House, 1990);

Where the Bluebird Sings to the Lemonade Springs (New York: Random House, 1992).

OTHER: *This Is Dinosaur: Echo Park Country and Its Magic Rivers,* edited by Stegner (New York: Knopf, 1955);

Selected American Prose, 1841–1900; The Realistic Movement, edited by Stegner (New York: Rinehart, 1958);

The Letters of Bernard DeVoto, edited by Stegner (Garden City, N.Y.: Doubleday, 1975).

Much of the literary landscape of Wallace Stegner's prose is the literal landscape of the Rocky Mountain region that extends roughly from Colorado over to Utah and into Nevada, up to Idaho, Wyoming, and Montana, and into parts of Canada. This area is "Stegner Country," and whether Stegner is writing about the American West directly in his essays or indirectly through his biographies, histories, novels, and short stories, he captures the reality of living within a land often obscured by myths and dreams. Stegner's realism delivers a sense of actual experience as it connects readers to the land and space known as the American West.

The Rocky Mountain West is not thematically connected to all of Stegner's works. Some are set in New England, while others shift away from the canyons, rivers, high plains, and even higher mountains of Stegner Country to tamer areas of California, as does *Angle of Repose* (1971), the novel that earned Stegner his 1972 Pulitzer Prize, and *The Spectator Bird* (1976), the book that brought him the National Book Award in 1977. While Stegner flourishes as a writer when developing his works against the western land of his adopted region, he evokes through all his essays, stories, histories, and novels a sense of place that defines the natural and human environment.

Stegner's own feel for the land and space of the American West springs from early childhood experiences that occurred during the travels of his family. George Stegner, Wallace's father, set the pace by keeping his family continually on the move. In many ways, Stegner's father embodied the rugged individualism and pioneer spirit that define one of Stegner's most memorable characters—Bo Mason, from the autobiographically informed *The Big Rock Candy Mountain* (1943). Like Bo, George Stegner doggedly chased his dreams across the western landscape in the hope of making the land itself his road to riches. Neither Bo Mason nor George Stegner, however, could bend the land to his will.

Stegner was not born in the West but in the Midwestern town of Lake Mills, Iowa, on 18 February 1909. George Stegner, his wife Hilda Paulson Stegner, and their first son, Cecil, lived in Grand Forks, North Dakota, but Hilda Stegner gave birth to Wallace while the family was visiting her mother's Iowa farm. After Wallace's birth, Hilda looked forward to a stable family life and to settling down in an equally stable community. She found little stability with husband George, however, whose ventures kept his family in transit. Neither North Dakota nor Iowa could contain the passions and dreams that drove George Stegner, but Alaska might. So George Stegner moved his family to Washington en route to the Alaskan frontier, where he believed a man might make his fortune in gold. After his Alaskan plans fell through, however, George left his wife and sons in Seattle to explore possibilities for a new life on the Canadian frontier. Abandoned by her husband, Hilda Stegner found surviving financially difficult and had to leave her boys in a Seattle orphanage for a short period before she moved back to Lake Mills, Iowa, to live with her parents. George Stegner sent for his family in 1914, and Hilda and the boys moved to the town that left a lasting impression on Wallace Stegner's personal outlook and on the substance and style of his work—East End, Saskatchewan.

At its best, East End offered a child a grand and spacious playground, and Stegner enjoyed the few years he lived in the Saskatchewan region. He recalls the freedom he shared with other boys as they romped with the cattle in the town, pulled tricks on railway workers, ate vegetables from the vine, and hunted the ever present gophers. Although Stegner made the best of his frontier freedom while his family wintered in town, the summer months on his family's homestead on the prairie, little more than an isolated outpost, proved to be much harsher and lonelier. Nonetheless, Stegner's father, much like an early American pioneer, persisted in his attempts to tame this wild country. He did not intend, however, to settle permanently into the land or the community; rather, as with his Alaskan dreams, he looked forward to making his fortune, this time in a commodity in high demand during the war years, wheat. Six years of Canadian winters, several of which brought poor wheat harvests, however, dampened George Stegner's dreams. With family in tow, he moved to Great Falls, Montana, where he began bootlegging whiskey. After just five months, he took his new career and his family to Salt Lake City, Utah. Salt Lake City became home for twelve-year-old Wallace as he grew through adolescence and into young adulthood.

Although not a major U.S. city in 1921, Salt Lake City provided young Wallace Stegner with more than enough of the social, cultural, and intellectual stimulus denied by his years on the Canadian frontier and the nomadic wandering of his father. He might even have owed his writing career to his father's move to Salt Lake City, where Wallace began his studies at the University of Utah. Stegner, only sixteen years old, settled into his undergraduate years with little fanfare and showed little immediate promise as a writer or scholar. As with many freshmen, he attended more to his social life than his studies, and as a member of the tennis team of the university, he devoted more of his time to sport than to scholarship. He was fortunate enough, however, to study under novelist Vardis Fisher in his English composition course. Fisher was a demanding teacher, a firm believer in the revision process, and though Stegner struggled to polish his compositions, he began to understand himself as a writer and continued with Fisher in advanced writing classes. Before Stegner graduated in 1930, he took his first fiction-writing course and served as editor and contributor to the university literary magazine, *Pen*. He was also hired as a freelance writer for *The Salt Lake Telegram*.

By his senior year, Stegner had made up his mind to take writing even more seriously, and he knew he wanted to pursue graduate studies in English. After he received his bachelor's degree in 1930, he accepted a teaching assistantship from the University of Iowa, where he entered a master's program in creative writing. Stegner found himself studying under the direction of Norman Foerster, a well-known critic and dedicated scholar of American literature.

Stegner continued at the University of Iowa despite financial problems brought on by the Great Depression and family deaths. During Stegner's first year at Iowa (1930) his brother, Cecil, died from complications suffered after a sudden attack of pneumonia, and in 1933 Stegner's mother died after a lengthy struggle with cancer. His father took his own life seven years later. His mother's death affected Stegner most, however, because she had given her family some sense of cohesion even while his father maneuvered them across prairies and mountains. In the months before her death, she continued to show the strength and determination that Stegner later recalled through many of his women characters, especially through his portrait of Elsa in *The Big Rock Candy Mountain*.

A year after his mother's death, on 1 September 1934, Stegner married Mary Stuart Page, a graduate student he had met at the University of Iowa. The marriage revitalized Stegner and rekindled his passion for teaching and writing that had faltered following his mother's death. Stegner accepted his first full-time teaching position at Augustana College in Rock Island, Illinois. He was, however, unwilling to accept fully the college's Lutheran doctrine and left after one year. After earning his doctorate from Iowa in 1935, he began teaching at the University of Utah.

While teaching at Utah, Stegner published a few short stories of little note in the *Salt Lake City Tribune;* he did, however, publish the more important "Saskatchewan Idyll" in the *Monterey Beacon* in June 1935, a piece that begins with recollection of childhood experiences crucial to the themes and settings of later and more significant work. In 1935 Stegner published his first book, a revision of his dissertation, on the western travels and geological findings of Clarence Edward Dutton. He especially admired Dutton, whose detailed accounts of western wilderness areas during the last decades of the nineteenth century played an influential role in the preservation of several national parks. While Stegner was not yet the committed conservationist he later became, as one who spent his boyhood on the Saskatchewan frontier, he was deeply moved by Dutton's literary descriptions of western landscapes and their natural markings.

On 31 January 1937 Stegner's only child, his son, Stuart Page, was born, and his first novel, *Remembering Laughter,* was published the same year. On the surface, the novel reveals a complex set of relations between a husband and a wife and the wife's younger sister. Finding little happiness in a passionless marriage with a wife whose coldness continually dampens the fires of desire, the husband finds himself drawn to the vitality of the younger sister. Stegner links that vital spirit to nature itself and the older sister's frigidity to social conven-

Stegner hunting near Fish Lake, Utah, circa 1929
(Collection of Mary Stegner)

tions. At the same time, he connects the husband's affair with the younger sister and the child who is born of it to a natural expression of human emotions. While Stegner's use of nature in his first novel serves as a vehicle for understanding human emotions, it also provides an early example of his ability to frame social demands within the reality of natural limits.

Having gained national recognition and a prize of $2,500 for his first novel, Stegner was disappointed when the University of Utah failed to promote him. Seeking more time to write and better treatment, he took an instructorship at the University of Wisconsin. Finding time to write was still difficult at Wisconsin; yet, Stegner found himself among colleagues who shared in and encouraged his creative efforts. Part of that encouragement led to Stegner's finding a place on the writing staff of the Bread Loaf Writers' Conference.

Not only did Stegner polish his own skills while discussing his craft at this highly acclaimed Vermont conference, but he also met some of the professional writers he admired most. Bernard DeVoto and Robert Frost were chief among these, and while Frost certainly inspired Stegner, DeVoto became his mentor and lifelong friend.

Stegner nurtured that friendship after leaving Wisconsin for a teaching fellowship at Harvard in 1939, where DeVoto also taught. At Harvard, Stegner began to develop a personal voice for his fiction. Whereas he had employed nature to illuminate characters in his first novel, in his next works his characters lacked that link to the environment that followed from any real sense of personal involvement. That personal voice finds little expression in *The Potter's House* (1938) and *Fire and Ice* (1941), but it surfaces as a realistic force in the experiences described in *On a Darkling Plain* (1940). In this novel Stegner recalls the Saskatchewan life and land he knew well to deepen and direct the mood. Whereas nature was associated with the life and energy of young love in his first novel, Stegner now portrays it in a harsher light. He draws his earliest portrait of a rugged individualist in his hero Edwin Vickers. Vickers moves to one of the remotest spots on the Saskatchewan prairie, where the landscape, as Stegner describes it, evokes the lonely isolation that stems from Vickers's attempt to break all social bonds. After a flu epidemic breaks out in a nearby village, Vickers leaves his secluded life to aid suffering villagers. He dies doing so, but Stegner suggests his life and death have gained some meaning by his responsible actions in the community. The lone individual rarely fares well in Stegner's fiction of the West, and in *On a Darkling Plain,* the romantic myth of individualism that Stegner thought detrimental to the Western environment is set in opposition to the spirit of cooperation he championed.

Stegner defended his case for cooperation even more effectively in two nonfiction books devoted to Mormon culture—*Mormon Country* (1942) and *The Gathering of Zion: The Story of the Mormon Trail* (1964). Stegner generally held the Mormons up as model pioneers. They came to settle in the Rocky Mountain West and not just to exploit its natural resources. The Mormons countered the general thrust of those caught up in westward migration, those who assumed that western lands could sustain the living habits they brought from the East, habits that relied heavily on water for farming, raising cattle, and maintaining gardens. Even many of those who accepted the aridity of the West attempted to farm, mine, and log it for a quick personal profit and then left it dry and dusty for future comers. The Mormons, as Stegner traces their history, were different.

Stegner published *Mormon Country* while he was teaching temporarily at Harvard, exchanging ideas with model historians and literary scholars such as F. O. Matthiessen, Perry Miller, and Howard Mumford Jones. Stegner's publisher suggested that he write a book about the culture and history of the area he knew best, Utah and the Salt Lake City region with its predominantly Mormon population. As he did with all his histories and biographies, Stegner thoroughly researched his subject matter and presented his findings with the same descriptive powers he brought to his fiction. Like DeVoto, another model for writing literary history, Stegner selectively presented the facts in a narrative form that allowed for a colorful portrayal of character and a heightening of dramatic tension.

Dividing *Mormon Country* into two sections, Stegner first considers Mormon life before turning to the briefer second section on non-Mormons ("Gentiles") in Mormon country. His portrait of the Mormon way of life and Mormons in general is mostly positive, though he sometimes casts a more critical eye on Mormon leaders. He draws a particularly harsh portrait of Brigham Young, who as a leader could wield his theocratic powers in unjust fashion and strong-arm his people into accepting his rule. Yet, Stegner's individual portraits of lesser-known Mormons shows them to be less concerned with power and more in tune with one another and their surroundings. They embody those characteristics Stegner himself thought necessary for preserving community and Western life.

Stegner's opening chapter centers on the cooperation and communal solidarity of Mormon villages and the nurturing value of the weekly "Ward" meetings that encourage social interaction—among Mormon youth in particular. He realistically treats the environment in which the Salt Lake region lies, deftly describing its treeless mountains, sagebrush valleys, and desert animal inhabitants. Stegner reveals how Mormons adjusted to desert aridity by fitting themselves to the land. The Gentiles, by contrast, emerge in Stegner's book as less respectful of the region, mostly as miners and members of cults far less connected to the land than the Mormons.

In *The Gathering of Zion,* Stegner is less concerned with Mormon settlement practices and more with their sense of determination and resilient spirit. In this work he covers twenty-two years of Mormon history, from 1846 to 1868, as he traces the Mormon trail from Nauvoo, Illinois, to the Salt Lake basin. Bringing his skills with fiction to bear on history, Stegner dramatically recreates the life of these self-proclaimed latter-day saints as they pressed on toward the West. At the same time, he specifically reveals the reality of the western landscape through which the Mormons traveled. This land

was not the mythical garden paradise of those proponents of western exploitation that Stegner came to despise but a land whose beauty masked the harsh features of its reality. As Stegner's chief biographer, Jackson J. Benson, explains, with *The Gathering of Zion* Stegner fully embodies his ability to deliver a "sense of place" as he deals "with people and their environment." While adjusting the reader's senses through exact description and personal commentary, Stegner evokes the feel of another time and place.

Following his first book on Mormon culture, Stegner returned to the novel in *The Big Rock Candy Mountain.* While not true autobiography, Stegner's signature book recalls his family's history through a mix of fiction and personal recollections. The book was never far from his mind while he was teaching at Harvard, and he had written many of its scenes for the short stories he had been publishing since 1940. Most of these stories, including the O. Henry Award–winning "Two Rivers," were about his childhood and incidents revolving around the Stegner family.

In *The Big Rock Candy Mountain,* Stegner recollects his family life through the experiences of the Mason family as it moves across the western region from North Dakota, up to Saskatchewan, and then down to Utah. Through his depiction of his father in Bo Mason, Stegner portrays the type of individualism that became the central target of his later essays. Bo, like Stegner's father, is a willful man whose attempts to conquer the land fail through his own ignorance of it. That land is the plot of Saskatchewan earth upon which Stegner's father attempted to grow wheat. Lacking enough water, however, Bo's farming venture fails. "Rain was the life in that country," Stegner's narrator points out, while Bo endlessly waits for a "good soaker." Ultimately, not enough rain falls to support Bo's repeated plantings, and he must pack up the family and leave this "God damned country." Bo is the schemer, the type Stegner called a "Boomer," one who hopes to "clean up" as he gambles all he and his family have on each new venture. As the Masons end up in Salt Lake City, Bo, more often than not illegally, is still chasing a fast fortune. He dies with his dreams worn out, "no Big Rock Candy Mountain, no lemonade springs, no cigarette trees, no little streams of alcohol, no handout bushes" left in sight.

Stegner again took a break from fiction after writing this wide-ranging novel and devoted two years to studying the plight of minorities across the United States. He published his research in a 1945 book co-authored with the editors of *Look* magazine, *One Nation.* Stegner's part in this book emphasizes the community spirit that was lacking in his fictional account of his family's history. For Stegner, commitment to cooper-

*Stegner with his wife, Mary, and their son, Page, in
Greensboro, Vermont, circa 1942 (Collection
of Mary Stegner)*

ation allows for individual expression within the fabric of a larger community.

After publishing *One Nation,* Stegner gained his own sense of community at Stanford College. Stanford had offered Stegner a full professorship in creative writing, and in 1945 he accepted, with the condition that he only be required to teach a half-time load. A partial teaching load was all Stegner needed to initiate and lead Stanford's writing program toward national recognition. It was also all he needed to become part of an academic community that allowed him to grow as a writer. He remained at Stanford until 1971, and while building the writing program, he wrote and published some of his more notable works, which eventually included several more O. Henry Award–winning stories and the Pulitzer Prize–winning *Angle of Repose.*

Two years after arriving at Stanford, Stegner published *Second Growth* (1947), a novel in which he returns to the problems of community life. He sets his narrative this time in a New England village. Stegner's home away from California was Greensboro, Vermont, and

he shaped the events and people in his new novel after his knowledge of his Vermont neighbors. Stegner's descriptive talent delivers the beauty of the New England countryside with the same precision and realistic detail one finds in his western settings. Like his use of nature in *Remembering Laughter,* Stegner develops a sharp contrast between the natural environment and the social restrictions found in New England village life. The "second growth" of young people in Stegner's New Hampshire town finds little room for cultural or spiritual expansion apart from their natural surroundings.

In 1950 Stegner published two books: a novel about the labor martyr Joe Hill, called *The Preacher and the Slave,* and his first short-story collection, *The Women on the Wall.* He had been producing an impressive list of short stories while conducting his workshops at Stanford, and he continued producing short fiction until 1962. Along with *The Women on the Wall,* Stegner published two other collections–*The City of the Living, and Other Stories* (1956) and *The Collected Stories of Wallace Stegner* (1990). In his final collection, he included some of the most significant stories from his earlier collections. He wrote fifty-eight short stories in all during the 1930s, 1940s, and 1950s, and many of them were absorbed into his novels, as Stegner explains in the foreword to his final collection. Like many of his novels, the stories form a type of "personal record," as Stegner puts it. "I lived them," he explains, and "because I have a tyrannous sense of place, they are laid in places I know well and written from my knowledge of people in those places." It is the "only earth" and "human experience" Stegner is sure he knows. In delivering that solid experience of place, in particular, Stegner portrays the earth as a force to be respected and admired.

The conception of nature as a central force is especially apparent in his Saskatchewan stories. The cold and barren landscape in "Bugle Song," first published in July 1938 in the *Virginia Quarterly Review,* functions as a harsh reminder of the demands of the Canadian frontier, even as it reveals the effects of its isolating conditions on one young child. The story revolves around a boy's cure for the prairie blues– gopher killing. To fill his empty days, he captures and feeds gophers to weasels, taking undue pleasure in watching the weasels' vicious attacks. Stegner had killed his share of gophers as a child, and his treatment of the boy's indifference to killing the creatures in this story points to his own regret as much as to the boy's cruelty. The wind that sears across the plains is relentless but proper to place; the boy's cruelty is just relentless. The same lack of respect for animal and human life thematically appears in "Pop Goes the Alley Cat," another

Saskatchewan piece published in the June 1940 issue of *Atlantic Monthly*.

In "Goin' to Town," published in 1940, Stegner tells the story of one boy's excitement about temporarily breaking the routine of his life on a Saskatchewan homestead to attend a festive day in a nearby town, but after their old Ford fails to start, even with the help of a team of horses, he resigns himself to remaining on the farm. Stegner frames the increasingly chaotic set of events that form the heart of the story between serene connections to the earth. Before his father's struggle with the car and horse, which hilariously depicts a failure to dominate machine or animal, the boy begins his day by tracking across the damp ground of his yard. "Feeling the cool mud under his toes," he "pressed" the earth, noticing how smoothly his foot fit into it. At the same time, he experiences a type of transcendence as he intimately bonds with sky and prairie. After the commotion of the day fades, the boy finds his morning footprint and realigns his foot within its outline. "As if he were performing some ritual for his life," he circles around the yard impressing himself into the earth, and Stegner leaves him intimately bound to the earth.

"Goin' to Town" is just one of the many stories that acknowledge one's relation to the earth as a healthy antidote to the daily commotion that separates people from place. Stegner's people are often depicted as out of place and disconnected from social and natural ties, especially in the case of the rugged and aggressive male character modeled after his father that Stegner presents as nature's antagonist in "Butcher's Bird," first published in *Harper's Magazine* in June 1941. The story focuses on a boy and his parents, and their visit to new neighbors on the Saskatchewan plain. The new neighbors are the Garfields, and Mr. Garfield brings some odd views about nature to the western plains. He hates "killing things" and intends to work with the land in planting trees and bushes that it will sustain. The boy's father hates Mr. Garfield, laughs at the respect Garfield shows plants and wildlife, and is only too happy to kill animals for fun. The story ends with mother and son pleading in vain for the life of a sparrow, pleas that the father ignores as he kills the bird for target practice. As Benson points out about this story, "The death of the bird suggests the antilife, antilove force of traditional male values and the American frontier belief that nature was created for man's use" and "abuse." Mr. Garfield and the boy stand with the mother, Stegner's representative woman and his usual guardian of nature.

While the natural environment may not always command center stage in his stories, when it does, Stegner stands with those who respect it and responsibly live within it. Little wonder that he wrote two books on

the Mormons, a group whose environmental consciousness has allowed them to flourish in a dry land; and not surprising, he wrote two major biographies on two men who echoed and nourished his own respect for the life and land in the western United States–John Wesley Powell and Bernard DeVoto. His story of Powell, in particular, reaffirms his own realistic assessment of land use in the West; for Powell's "understanding of the West was not built on a dream" inspired by a myth of plenitude or by the promises of political fortune hunters, and neither was Stegner's. Stegner's *Beyond the Hundredth Meridian: John Wesley Powell and the Second Opening of the West* (1954), in fact, counters, from start to finish, this mythical dream of the West as an earthly paradise.

Stegner opens Powell's biography by pitting Powell's perspective on Western settlement against that of William Gilpin, an experienced Western explorer and writer of books that promoted unlimited settlement of the West. The West was a garden waiting to be tilled, according to Gilpin, where the dirt was rich and the water flowed freely. Gilpin, according to Stegner, "could see through a glass eye so darkly that he denied geography, topography, meteorology, and the plain evidence of his senses." In his opening chapter, Stegner traces Powell's running of the Colorado River while exposing just how Gilpin's speculations about the river and its canyons fell short of the truth. In succeeding chapters, Stegner continues to show how Powell lifted the "layers of fable" that Gilpin had cast over the country beyond the 100th meridian, for "ignorance covered the geography of the region, its topography, landforms, drainage, and scenery."

Stegner focuses as well on Powell's attempt to sway congressional opinion about the use and homesteading of public lands. Powell's *Report on the Lands of the Arid Region of the United States . . .* (1878) showed that much of the land beyond the 100th meridian could sustain small homesteads but not large farms or major cattle ranches. Most of the region, as Powell's report pointed out, received less than the twenty inches of rainfall needed to support agriculture and would require irrigation. The report made its way through Congress but was compromised by those who, according to Stegner, would rather chase their visions than accept the facts. Overall, Stegner presents Powell as successful in his "fight against the dragons of error, backwardness, and unchecked exploitation" of the West and as one of the most influential figures in America in persuading Congress to protect and preserve public land.

Stegner put his political abilities to the test in a little book that he edited for the Sierra Club, *This Is Dinosaur: Echo Park Country and Its Magic Rivers* (1955). Sent to all members of Congress, the book succeeded, through its informative essays and photographs, in revealing the

Stegner in a field behind his home in Los Altos Hills, California, circa 1982
(Collection of Tim Davis)

natural beauty of Dinosaur National Monument and in thwarting plans to build dams that would destroy it. Stegner continued to write for the causes of the Sierra Club and for the sake of the environment in general. Some of his more influential letters to Congress and to commissions set up to review land use carried the day for the environmental causes he was increasingly supporting. One letter in particular so profoundly moved Stewart Udall, the interior secretary under John F. Kennedy, that Udall read it verbatim at a wilderness convention in the early 1960s. Stegner went on to serve as Udall's special assistant, and though the Wilderness Act was not passed until 1964, Stegner's letter provided its supporters with one of their most effective statements for the cause of preservation.

Stegner brings this "geography of hope" into his 1961 novel, *A Shooting Star*. The story centers on the relationship that develops between a mother and daughter after the daughter returns home from an unsuccessful attempt at marriage. Both the mother and the daughter grow as they confront their lives and personal weaknesses, but what brings most hope for the mother is her growing awareness of the environmental necessity to preserve and protect land from commercial exploitation. In many ways she fictionally argues the case Stegner was making more overtly through his Sierra Club publications.

More complex than *A Shooting Star*, Stegner's *Wolf Willow: A History, a Story, and a Memory of the Last Plains Frontier* (1962), published as Stegner was beginning service on the National Parks Advisory Board, makes a case for knowing as well as preserving the environment. While the mixing of narrative modes makes classifying this book in any one genre difficult, the work represents the integration of personal recollections with geographical and historical facts to conjure up the Saskatchewan region Stegner knew as a boy. "Human intrusions seem as abrupt as the elevators that leap out of the plain to announce every little hamlet and keep it memorable for a few miles," Stegner says as he describes the region of his childhood, and the town of East End, renamed White Mud for the book, is just one of the isolated villages on the Canadian high plains.

As with his Mormon books, Stegner's careful research informs the historical matter in *Wolf Willow*. He accounts for the early expeditions of Meriwether Lewis and George Rogers Clark that pointed the way for further exploration into the Saskatchewan region and records the many skirmishes between early settlers, plains Indians, and the Canadian government over rights to the land. He describes the "frontier code" adopted by those who first used the land for cattle ranching as "inhumane and limited" and taken from the "value system of a life more limited and cruder than in fact ours was." The cattle culture conceded its way of life to nature, however, after a series of catastrophic winters, especially the winter of 1906–1907, literally transformed the region from grazing ranges to small farm settlements.

Living a mobile existence in tune with the demands of nature and the land becomes a guiding theme of Stegner's later essays, and in *Wolf Willow* he reveals the harsh fate of those who fail to acknowledge the conditions of an environment. Within his history, Stegner includes two fictions about ranchers caught in the winter of 1906–1907 that dramatically recount the deathly cold. Only the wolves meet the challenge of winter; the men bent on bending the West to their will find that the winter "is nothing but unrelieved hardship, failure, death, gloom."

Stegner concludes this book with George Santayana's remark to those who fail to learn from history: they are doomed to repeat it. Stegner's own father was one of those repeaters: he was one who failed to acknowledge the viciousness of a Canadian winter; one who ignored the cycle of irregular droughts; and one who could not accept the "marginal nature of agriculture on the arid Plains." To do so would have denied all would-be pioneers their hope, Stegner points out, a false hope that is linked to the myth of the West as a garden paradise. While the dream of finding and farming the rich fields of the West might have held out through the states of Illinois and Iowa, it shifted into nightmarish proportions on the more "arid Plains furred with their curly grass and seared by blowing winds." Like an environmental prophet, Stegner suggests that the pioneer spirit no longer has a place in the land west of the 100th meridian, where modern-day explorers and settlers must responsibly and respectfully live within the limitations set and enforced by nature.

Stegner published *All the Little Live Things* in 1967 but was not able to capture fully the broad sense of place again until the publication of his *Angle of Repose* in 1971. Much like Stegner in his attempts to recollect the past through his fiction, the first-person narrator in *Angle of Repose,* Lyman Ward, finds himself engaged in reconstructing the life of his grandparents while simultaneously defining the shape of his own existence. Stegner's mix of fact and fancy works to support, once again, his sense of community, this time through the connection he builds between past and present through Ward's reading of his grandmother's letter. At the same time, Stegner's portrait of Ward's grandfather, as it emerges from the letters, reveals a type of transplanted Westerner that Stegner seems to value, an Easterner determined not to exploit the land but to settle into it.

Stegner continued to experiment with time and place in his novels *The Spectator Bird* (1976), *Recapitulation* (1979), and *Crossing to Safety* (1987), but with these novels, his focus shifts more and more toward an inner landscape, where his characters relive and re-create the past in an effort to understand the connections that secure human relations. The vivid descriptions of the land are still evident, especially in *Recapitulation,* which returns Bo Mason to Salt Lake City, but they seem to speak as much for nature as for any cause related to nature. Stegner's nonfiction prose offered a better venue for causes, and in *American Places,* a collection of essays and photographs Stegner published with his son, Page, and Eliot Porter in 1981, he repeatedly condemns the irresponsible treatment of the natural environment of America by those who continue to overdevelop and exploit it. Calling it an important work in the "literature of conservation," Benson describes *American Places* as Stegner's "jeremiad on what has gone wrong with the land and how destructive our attitudes toward it have been." At the same time, the book calls up vivid scenes from Vermont to Utah and across the Midwest and down the Mississippi River.

Two more important collections reveal Stegner at his best in employing his rhetorical powers of description for the praise and preservation of the western environment. *The Sound of Mountain Water* (1969) represents more than twenty years of Stegner's writing, and many of the essays account for the summer explorations the Stegners made into western deserts, canyons, and mountains after their move to California and Stanford. While his descriptions argue for a respectful treatment of a beautiful land, Stegner keeps his environmental aim clearly up front, introducing his book with a warning about the misuse of natural resources. At the same time, he reveals that the pri-

Stegner in his Los Altos Hills office, 1986 (Collection of Mary Stegner)

mary problem with that misuse comes from ignoring the aridity of the West. "The history of the West," he notes, "until recently has been a history of the importation of humid-land habits (and carelessness) into a dry land that will not tolerate them."

Stegner focuses even more on the dryness that generally defines the West beyond the 100th meridian in *Where the Bluebird Sings to the Lemonade Springs* (1992). The first two sections, in particular, recall the topic Stegner found central to the survival of the West–water. He introduces his book with a warning that the West must "accept the limitations imposed by aridity" before he provides a brief history of western migration and its successive waves of "pillages." In the opening three essays that make up the first section, Stegner recalls his boyhood on the Saskatchewan plains and the virtues of his mother; he offers a powerful polemic for conserving wilderness areas. He laments in "Crossing to Eden" that while the 1964 Wilderness Act protected wilderness areas, these areas are being trampled by too

many visitors. He finds salvation, however, that "deeper wilderness lies further back," where one finds "no roads, no RVs, or trail bikes" to "stink up that clean air."

Stegner devotes the second section mainly to the topic of aridity. Three of its essays were originally published in Stegner's 1987 publication of *The American West as Living Space*–"Living Dry," "Striking Rock," and "Variations on a Theme by Crevecoeur." Through these essays, in particular, Stegner attempts to construct an "environmental conscience" for his readers, arguing that the clearness of air and intensity of light in the West result from the aridity. Rather than attempting to alter the Western climate and landscape to fit Eastern expectations, he goes on, one should recognize the particular beauty of dry land and adjust to it. Aridity shapes western plants, animals, air, towns, and farming. With water a scarce commodity, Stegner pleads for limited growth and federal management of both water and land rights.

This final collection of essays was the last book that Wallace Stegner saw through to publication. While in Sante Fe, New Mexico, in 1993, Stegner and his wife were involved in an automobile accident; Stegner died on 12 April from complications related to the accident. Recalling his life and career in the concluding essay of *Where the Bluebird Sings to the Lemonade Springs,* Stegner remarks that "school and college do sandpaper the roughness of the frontier, but the frontier leaves its tracks." While Stegner further notes that his academic and literary career represent "progress, of a sort," he emphasizes that he is "still the person my first fifteen years made me."

The western landscape had impressed itself on Stegner's mind and left an influential trail across the literary terrain of his books. If followed, that trail brings one to Stegner's realistic view that the land must be respected if humanity is to have any hope of continuing to survive on it. That hope was nearly squelched, as Stegner points out in *American Places,* "in our ignorance and hunger and rapacity, in our dream of a better material life"; but it can find new life through recognizing an "affinity with" and "dependence on" the natural environment and an "obligation toward it as the indispensable source of everything we hope for." Wallace Stegner never tired of reminding his readers of this obligation through his rendering of the land in his major prose works, nor did he sacrifice his realistic vision for the myths he found so destructive.

Interviews:

Wallace Stegner and Richard W. Etulain, *Conversations with Wallace Stegner on Western History and Literature* (Salt Lake City: University of Utah Press, 1990);

James R. Hepworth, ed., *Stealing Glances: Three Interviews with Wallace Stegner* (Albuquerque: University of New Mexico Press, 1998).

Bibliography:

Nancy Colberg, *Wallace Stegner: A Descriptive Bibliography* (Lewiston, Idaho: Confluence Press, 1990).

References:

Anthony Arthur, *Critical Essays on Wallace Stegner* (Boston: G. K. Hall, 1982);

Jackson J. Benson, *Down by the Lemonade Springs: Essays on Wallace Stegner* (Reno: University of Nevada Press, 2001);

Benson, *Wallace Stegner: His Life and Work* (New York: Viking, 1996);

Benson, *Wallace Stegner: A Study of the Short Fiction* (New York: Twayne, 1998);

Charles E. Rankin, ed., *Wallace Stegner: Man and Writer* (Albuquerque: University of New Mexico Press, 1996);

Forrest G. Robinson and Margaret G. Robinson, *Wallace Stegner* (Boston: Twayne, 1977);

Page Stegner, ed., *Marking the Sparrow's Fall: Wallace Stegner's American West* (New York: Holt, 1998);

John L. Thomas, *A Country in the Mind: Wallace Stegner, Bernard DeVoto, History, and the American Land* (New York: Routledge, 2000).

Papers:

Manuscripts, research notes, and letters of Wallace Stegner are held in the Cecil H. Green Library, Department of Special Collections, Stanford University, Stanford, California, and at the University of Utah in the Special Collections Department in the J. Willard Marriot Library, Salt Lake City, Utah.

John Steinbeck

(27 February 1902 – 20 December 1968)

Jason G. Horn
Gordon College

See also the Steinbeck entries in *DLB 7: Twentieth-Century American Dramatists, DLB 9: American Novelists, 1910–1945,* and *DLB 212: Twentieth-Century American Western Writers, Second Series.*

BOOKS: *Cup of Gold: A Life of Sir Henry Morgan, Buccaneer, with Occasional Reference to History* (New York: McBride, 1929; London & Toronto: Heinemann, 1937);

The Pastures of Heaven (New York: Brewer, Warren & Putnam, 1932; London: Allan, 1933);

To a God Unknown (New York: Ballou, 1933; London: Heinemann, 1933);

Tortilla Flat (New York: Covici-Friede, 1935; London: Heinemann, 1935);

In Dubious Battle (New York: Covici-Friede, 1936; London & Toronto: Heinemann, 1936);

Of Mice and Men (New York: Covici-Friede, 1937; London: Heinemann, 1937);

Of Mice and Men: A Play in Three Acts (New York: Covici-Friede, 1937);

The Red Pony (New York: Covici-Friede, 1937; enlarged edition, New York: Viking, 1945; London: Heinemann, 1949);

Their Blood Is Strong (San Francisco: Simon J. Lubin Society, 1938);

The Long Valley (New York: Viking, 1938; London: Heinemann, 1939);

The Grapes of Wrath (New York: Viking, 1939; London: Heinemann, 1939);

Sea of Cortez: A Leisurely Journal of Travel and Research, by Steinbeck and Edward F. Ricketts (New York: Viking, 1941); republished with "About Ed Ricketts," by Steinbeck, as *The Log from the Sea of Cortez* (New York: Viking, 1951; London: Heinemann, 1958);

The Forgotten Village (New York: Viking, 1941);

Bombs Away: The Story of a Bomber Team (New York: Viking, 1942);

The Moon Is Down (New York: Viking, 1942; London: Heinemann, 1942);

John Steinbeck at his summer cottage in Pacific Grove, California, 1960 (Steinbeck Research Center, San Jose State University)

The Moon Is Down: A Play in Two Parts (New York: Dramatists Play Service, 1942; London: English Theatre Guild, 1943);

Cannery Row (New York: Viking, 1945; London & Toronto: Heinemann, 1945);

The Pearl (New York: Viking, 1947; London: Heinemann, 1948);

The Wayward Bus (New York: Viking, 1947; London: Heinemann, 1947);

A Russian Journal (New York: Viking, 1948; London: Heinemann, 1949);

Burning Bright: A Play in Story Form (New York: Viking, 1950; London: Heinemann, 1951);

Burning Bright: Play in Three Acts (New York: Dramatists Play Service, 1951);

East of Eden (New York: Viking, 1952; London: Heinemann, 1952);

Viva Zapata! (Rome: Edizioni Filmcritica, 1952); new screenplay edition of movie (New York: Viking, 1974);

Sweet Thursday (New York: Viking, 1954: London: Heinemann, 1954);

The Short Reign of Pippin IV: A Fabrication (New York: Viking, 1957; London: Heinemann, 1957);

Once There Was a War (New York: Viking, 1958; London: Heinemann, 1959);

The Winter of Our Discontent (New York: Viking, 1961; London: Heinemann, 1961);

Speech Accepting the Nobel Peace Prize for Literature (New York: Viking, 1962);

Travels with Charley: In Search of America (New York: Viking, 1962; London: Heinemann, 1962);

America and Americans (New York: Viking, 1966; London: Heinemann, 1966);

The Acts of King Arthur and His Noble Knights: From the Winchester Manuscript and Other Sources, edited by Chase Horton (New York: Farrar, Straus & Giroux, 1976; London: Heinemann, 1976);

The Uncollected Stories of John Steinbeck, edited by Kiyoshi Nakayama (Tokyo: Nan'un-do, 1986);

John Steinbeck on Writing, edited by Tetsumaro Hayashi, Steinbeck Essay Series, no. 2 (Muncie, Ind.: Steinbeck Research Institute, Ball State University, 1988);

Working Days: The Journals of The Grapes of Wrath, 1938–1941, edited by Robert DeMott (New York: Viking, 1989).

PLAY PRODUCTIONS: *Of Mice and Men,* New York, Music Box Theatre, 23 November 1937;

The Moon Is Down, New York, Martin Beck Theatre, 7 April 1942;

Burning Bright: A Play in Three Acts, New York, Broadhurst Theatre, 18 October 1950.

PRODUCED SCRIPTS: *The Forgotten Village,* motion picture, Pan American Films, 1941;

La Perla (The Pearl), motion picture, screenplay by Steinbeck, Jack Wagner, and Emilio Fernández, Aguila Films, 1948;

The Red Pony, motion picture, Republic, 1949;

Viva Zapata! motion picture, 20th Century-Fox, 1952.

John Steinbeck may not be known for his work as a nature writer, at least in the sense of Ralph Waldo Emerson, Henry David Thoreau, John Muir, or Annie Dillard, but much of his work develops characters in relation to their environment and implicitly argues for a clearer understanding of how humans might best live within the limits of their natural surroundings. He belongs to that group of twentieth-century writers that includes Wallace Stegner, Edward Abbey, and Terry Tempest Williams, all of whom were influenced by Steinbeck's ability to evoke artistically the American landscape as part of the human condition. To be human, for Steinbeck, was to be a part of the larger ecological scheme, to be a living being linked to all life and to the earth itself. In many of his novels, stories, and nonfiction pieces, Steinbeck challenges his readers not only to acknowledge this link but also to evaluate how well they exist within this thick web of connections.

Steinbeck's importance, to be sure, stems from much more than his ability to express an ecological perspective in his fiction and essays. He is best known for his narratives about those living outside mainstream America—migrant workers struggling to survive in California in *In Dubious Battle* (1936) or dust-bowl refugees of Oklahoma escaping to the promise of a better life in *The Grapes of Wrath* (1939). A few of his novels were made into award-winning plays; *Of Mice and Men* won the New York Drama Critics Circle Award in 1937. Even more novels and stories were turned into motion pictures; notably, his novel *The Pearl* (1947) was made into a movie in 1948, and *The Grapes of Wrath* in 1940.

Apart from his artistic endeavors, Steinbeck was a friend and "unofficial" adviser to President Franklin Delano Roosevelt and a close friend of President Lyndon Baines Johnson, who awarded him the Presidential Medal of Freedom in 1964. While critics were divided on the quality of Steinbeck's later work, he nonetheless received the Nobel Prize in literature in 1962, near the end of his literary career. In his Nobel Prize acceptance speech, Steinbeck pointed out that as a writer he felt bound to expose "our many grievous faults and failures" and to improve upon the "dark and dangerous dreams" behind the failures. Steinbeck, for one, knew about human failure and was willing to risk writing about the darker truths of the imagination.

John Ernst Steinbeck was born on 27 February 1902 in Salinas, California, an agricultural town that, along with the Salinas Valley and the nearby Pacific coast, provided him with the settings for most of his major works. Living in the Salinas Valley region for the first seventeen years of his life, Steinbeck acquired a rural sensibility that found its highest expression in his earliest works, such as *The Pastures of Heaven* (1932), *Of Mice and Men* (1937), and *The Grapes of Wrath* (1939), though he continued to draw his settings from the land of his youth even in later novels, such as

New Start
Big Writing

I.

To the red country and part of the grey country of Oklahoma, the last rain came gently and they did not cut the scarred earth. The plows crossed and recrossed the rivulet marks. The last rains lifted the corn quickly and scattered weed colonies and grass along the sides of the roads so that the grey country and the dark red country began to disappear under a green cover. In the last part of May the sky grew pale and the clouds that had hung in high puffs for so long in the spring were dissipated. The sun flared down on the growing corn day after day until a line of brown spread along the edge of each green bayonet. The clouds appeared and went away and in a while they did not try any more. The weeds grew darker green to protect themselves and they did not spread any more. The surface of the earth crusted, a thin hard crust, and as the sky became pale so the earth became pale, pink in the red country and white in the grey country. In the water cut gulleys, the earth dusted down in dry little streams. Gophers and ant lions started small avalanches. And as the sharp sun struck day after day the leaves of the young corn became less stiff and erect; they bent in a curve at first and then as the central ribs of strength grew weak, each leaf tilted downward. Then it was June and the sun shone more fiercely. The brown lines on the corn leaves widened and moved in on the central ribs. The weeds frayed and moved back toward their roots. The air was thin and the sky more pale and every day the earth paled. In the roads where the teams moved, where the wheels milled the ground and the hooves of the horses beat the ground, the dirt crust broke and the dust formed. Every moving thing lifted the dust into the air; a walking man lifted a cloud as high as his waist, and a wagon lifted the dust as high as the fence tops, and an automobile buried a cloud behind it. The dust was long in settling back again. When June was half gone, the big clouds moved up out of Texas and the gulf, high, heavy clouds, rain-heads. The men in the fields looked up at the clouds and sniffed at them and held wet fingers up to sense the wind. And the horses were nervous while the clouds were up. The rain heads dropped a little spattering rain and hurried on to some other country. Behind them the sky was pale again and the sun flared. In the dust there were drop craters where the rain had fallen, and there were clean splashes on the corn and that was all. A gentle wind followed the rain clouds, driving them on northward, a wind that caressed the drying corn softly. A day went by and the wind increased, steady, unbroken by gusts. The dust from the roads fluffed up and spread out and fell on the weeds beside the fields and fell into the fields a little way. Now the wind grew strong and hard, and worked at the rain crust in the corn fields. Little by little the sky was darkened by the mixing dust, and the wind felt over the earth, loosened the dust and carried it away. The wind was stronger. The rain crust broke and the dust lifted up out of the fields and drove grey plumes into the air like sluggish smoke. The corn threshed the air and made a dry rushing sound. The finest dust did not settle back to earth now but disappeared into the darkening sky. The wind grew stronger, whistled under stones, carried up straws and old leaves, and even little clods,

Page from the manuscript for The Grapes of Wrath *(1939), about a family forced to leave Oklahoma during the great dust storms of the 1930s (Albert and Shirley Small Special Collections Library, University of Virginia)*

East of Eden (1952) and *Sweet Thursday* (1954). Steinbeck knew the Pacific Coast region especially well, having combed its beaches and scaled its rocky cliffs throughout his boyhood, and while he eventually moved to and finished his life in New York City, he always considered the Pacific coast his home, his "seed center," as he once wrote to Bo Beskow (19 September 1948), where he could deeply embrace the "damp sea fog" and the "fine wind over the kelp on the rocks."

As a young man, Steinbeck did not entirely lose himself within the grasp of his surroundings. While he preferred retreating to the shores and steep cliffs that he knew as the coast of California, he succeeded in advancing his more formal education in high school. His essays were singled out for praise by his high-school English teachers, in particular, and despite his near death from pneumonia during his senior year, Steinbeck graduated in the spring of 1919 and began his college career at Stanford University the following fall.

Steinbeck attended Stanford until 1925, though he never earned a degree of any kind. He attended more to his social than his academic life, to parties, late-night card games, and hard drinking and to the various jobs he worked to pay for his schooling. His studies suffered as a result. His work, especially on many ranches in the Salinas Valley, served him better as a writer than did his academic career. As Steinbeck recalled for one of his interviews, his characters were often "composites" of ranch workers, and his settings were drawn directly from his work experiences.

When not working or wandering, Steinbeck sometimes became an intensely involved student, and as a member of the "English Club" at Stanford, he grew as a writer through the many hours he spent analyzing and discussing the works of contemporary authors. The one course that influenced his writing as much as any, however, was not a literary but a scientific one, a summer course in marine biology at Hopkins Marine Station. Monterey Bay and its marine life were used as classroom material, and Steinbeck's scientific interests grew. He began building toward an ecological perspective that recognized the common bonds between all life-forms.

His view of this ecological whole developed more fully under the influence of Edward F. Ricketts, the marine zoologist, nature writer, and scientific philosopher Steinbeck met in 1930. Before coming under the influence of Ricketts and long before collaborating with him on the writing and publication of *Sea of Cortez: A Leisurely Journal of Travel and Research* (1941), a scientifically based narrative on investigations into the marine life in the Gulf of California, Steinbeck made his name as a novelist. While the most direct expression of his ecological vision is to be found in *Sea of Cortez*, parts of his work before this experimental narrative reveal a growing awareness of connections between the land and the life-forms that inhabit it.

While a student, Steinbeck published short stories in the *Stanford Spectator,* and for a brief period, he worked as a journalist for the *New York American* on his initial attempt to earn a living as a writer in New York City. After being fired for his incompetent journalistic work and after having had a collection of short stories rejected by various publishers, Steinbeck returned to California in 1927. He settled in Lake Tahoe, where he became a cabin caretaker during the slower seasons of the resort town. The relative solitude allowed for sustained periods of thought and writing, and Steinbeck was able to finish what became his first published novel, *Cup of Gold: A Life of Sir Henry Morgan, Buccaneer, with Occasional Reference to History* (1929).

A somewhat derivative work, most closely related to James Stephen's *Crock of Gold* (1912), Steinbeck's fictive biography of seventeenth-century pirate Henry Morgan relates the story of Morgan's successful attempt to win fame, fortune, and a beautiful woman. At the height of his success, however, Morgan finds himself a lonely and empty man. Although a simplistic story, it brought Steinbeck some recognition. Though he became increasingly embarrassed by the mild success of the novel, he appreciated the royalties the book made, as he told a friend, because they brought some economic security and provided time for creating more-complex, and less popularly oriented, literary ventures.

One such work was his *To a God Unknown* (1933), a book he had begun to write soon after he met Carol Henning, his first wife, in 1928. Before finishing and publishing this work, a book most publishers found too philosophically weighty for popular tastes, Steinbeck published *The Pastures of Heaven* in 1932. Integrating a collection of short stories into the thematic unity of a novel, *The Pastures of Heaven* presents separate accounts of how people use and relate to the land—specifically to an imaginary, yet representative, California valley whose name undermines an illusory and environmentally dangerous myth of California as a land of plenty, an earthly paradise. While Steinbeck reveals how this myth encourages false expectations and rampant exploitation of the land, he also suggests how expectations and environmental perspectives might be altered by deliberate attempts to understand the life of the land. The book is "ultimately a testimony to the triumph of human nature as it learns to live in harmony with the land," as John H. Timmerman writes in "Steinbeck's Environmental Ethic: Humanity in Harmony with the Land" (collected *Steinbeck and the Environment* [1997]), and reveals how individuals can "learn their own quiet patterns of living with the land."

The ten chapters in *The Pastures of Heaven* pivot thematically around the main characters as they attempt to

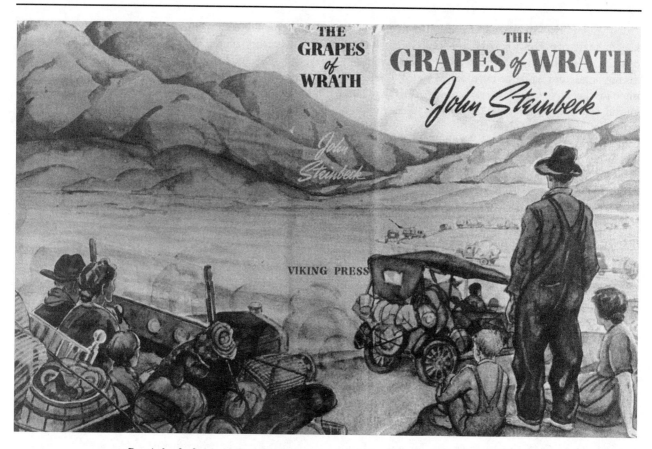

Dust jacket for Steinbeck's Depression-era novel, which depicts the human consequences of a major environmental disaster (Bruccoli Clark Layman Archives)

adjust to environmental conditions and change in relation to their attempts to develop the land. Some control its growth; some willfully organize it into shape; and some follow the land's natural bent and growth pattern. The land cannot be ignored, Steinbeck seems to say, without humans ignoring their own growth. In his epilogue, however, Steinbeck depicts a busload of "modern pilgrims" (in Timmerman's words), peering into the valley and wondering how they might use the land to their own advantage. None senses an intimate connection to the land or seriously considers how one might live in harmony with it. Steinbeck himself offers few answers, though one leaves the book with a sense that the land has much to teach those who are open to its lessons.

The full embrace of the land and the nature of existence find expression in *To a God Unknown*. With this book, Steinbeck, under the influence of Ricketts, combines fiction and philosophy in an attempt to deliver a view of how the ecosystem works. As Jay Parini succinctly says in his biography of Steinbeck, "Ricketts would bring to the surface and crystallize ideas that had been inchoate in Steinbeck." What Steinbeck admired most about Ricketts as a scientific investigator was his ability to observe nature while maintaining a sense of

how each part of it fits within a web of relations. This pursuit of interrelationships, Ricketts believed, could lead to one's "breaking through" to a wider realm of understanding, to an awareness of how all life, and all that exists, involves fragile connections. Steinbeck's abilities as a novelist, however, further complicated his attempt to present his and Ricketts's ideas in *To a God Unknown*.

In *To a God Unknown,* Steinbeck tells the story of Joseph Wayne and the land he embraces as a part of himself. After settling into a fertile California valley, Wayne first willfully attempts to dominate the land and ignore its natural cycles, which include droughts. While others move on after a particularly long drought, Wayne remains in his once fertile valley, confident that he can control its natural changes. He gradually accepts his part in the natural order and experiences a "breaking through" of sorts as he resigns himself to a larger controlling force. "There was this thing coming," he tells his understanding friend, Juanito, and "I felt it coming" and "creeping in on us" and "now it is nearly through." What Wayne learns is that he and the land are one. Having identified himself with the land, Joseph feels its dying pains as the drought takes its toll. Linking the dying land to himself, Joseph takes his own life, slicing his wrists while lying upon a dry rock. As he dies, the rains fall, and he realizes that he, the land, and now the rain are one. While the rain comes too late for Wayne's own recognition of the weather's cyclical patterns, Steinbeck's readers are left to ponder Wayne's sacrifice and their own place within nature's larger pattern.

Critics were slow to acknowledge the importance of Steinbeck's novel in environmental terms. The focus on the land was too entangled in the many symbolic layers and biblical allusions of the novel. Even Steinbeck's hero only clumsily recognizes his intimate connection to the environment after stubbornly attempting to force the dry earth to produce for him. Steinbeck, to be sure, was still developing his own ecological concepts, but his expression of cosmic wholeness in *To a God Unknown* points to the position he continued to draw for his characters in establishing their relation to their environment. Humans were a part of nature and not apart from it; and as a natural part of the environment, Steinbeck acknowledges with *To a God Unknown* that humans could be studied and portrayed in relation to their connection to, or disconnection from, natural surroundings. Steinbeck repeated this study and portrayal again and again in other works.

He did not find fame as a nature writer, however, and his writings did not emphasize his developing environmental ethic. Instead, he is most often remembered for his portrayal of working-class heroes and the downtrodden of American society. In *Tortilla Flat* (1935), Steinbeck tells the tragic tale of Danny and his friends, young Hispanics who live on Monterey's worst side and are unsuccessful in their quest for a better life. With *In Dubious Battle* (1936), Steinbeck began his exploration of the problems of the working class, specifically with the living and working conditions of Mexican migrant workers and with their treatment by both farm-labor organizers and corporate California farmers.

In *Of Mice and Men* (1937), Steinbeck portrays George Milton and Lennie Small as starting off in pursuit of rural happiness as they seek their own country paradise. George's last name offers the clue to the outcome of the novel, however, and both men lose their heavenly dream after Lennie accidentally kills an innocent woman, and George kills Lennie to save him from a mob's wrath. No plentiful pastures are to be found for George or Lennie, although in their vague longing to embrace the land as their own, they quietly expose Steinbeck's view that contentment lies with finding one's place within the larger natural scheme. Steinbeck clarifies this view somewhat in *The Red Pony* (1937), an initiation story that follows one boy's growing awareness of his place within the natural order. As the boy Jody matures, he learns that, like the pony he loses to seemingly cruel and indifferent acts of nature, the land itself is being lost to equally indif-

ferent acts of destruction. His knowledge leads to a compassionate recognition of needs other than his own, the needs of the land and of all living creatures.

These works, in general, through their focus on a chaotic set of social and natural relations, fail to offer the holistic vision that Steinbeck's hero realized at the conclusion of *To a God Unknown*. Steinbeck's characters in *Tortilla Flat* and *In Dubious Battle* stand outside the social flow of normal relations, for instance, while George and Lennie chase a harmonious existence that appears to be beyond the human reach. Only Jody and his grandfather in *The Red Pony* sense the fragility of all natural relationships. *The Red Pony* reveals, in fact, that modern society itself stands in the way of individuals achieving a larger understanding of ecological interdependence.

Steinbeck indicts not only society but also the political forces that govern it, forces that inhibit a wider understanding of one's place in the social and natural order. After Steinbeck took direct aim at such political powers in a short piece of nonfiction, his 1938 *Their Blood Is Strong*, he continued his literary assault in more-epic dimensions with the publication of *The Grapes of Wrath* in 1939. With this novel, Steinbeck brings to fruition his synthesis of fiction and philosophy, as he tells the story of the Joad family's hardships as it finds itself uprooted.

Leaving the Oklahoma dust bowl for the better life seemingly offered by California, the Joads, an even dozen of memorable characters, doggedly make their way toward the "land of plenty" through a series of tragic events. Family members die or desert the group on the journey, while those who make it nearly starve as they fend for themselves as poorly paid workers in fruit orchards and cotton fields. The situation is hopeless for the Joads, even though "Ma," who is the family's backbone, continues to hope for human kindness in the depth of the family's despair. Using the Joad family as his representatives, Steinbeck makes his points throughout the book about the plight of migrant workers in general by interweaving politically charged chapters of personal observations. The book stands as an indictment of the social and working conditions of migrant workers as much as it does as a tale of heroic suffering and perseverance.

Steinbeck's characters do have their moments of illumination, however, moments of realization that reflect those ideas about a natural unity that offer some type of salvation for suffering humanity. None are more enlightening than those visionary moments of insight that come to Jim Casy, the former preacher, labor organizer, and migrant martyr of *The Grapes of Wrath*. Breaking through traditional moralities and religious concepts, Casy preaches his own doctrine of natural harmony. Humans exist for Casy within a wider realm of being, and within that web of creation, all life is equally a significant unit of the whole. With Casy, however, Steinbeck takes his readers beyond the isolated insights and personal sacrifice of a Joseph Wayne; for Casy not only acknowledges the holiness of all creation through his understanding of natural unity but also sacrifices his life so that others might know the fullness of life's harmony and take their rightful place in its overall pattern.

Steinbeck carries this holistic view into the book that he and Ricketts published in 1941–*Sea of Cortez: A Leisurely Journal of Travel and Research*. As literary ecologists (though they would not have used this term) Ricketts and Steinbeck explored the Gulf of California in an effort to understand the interconnecting links between all living things. For nearly six weeks they explored the gulf, observing the marine life and collecting samples. The more scientifically minded Ricketts was responsible for the identification and classification of the marine life they collected, while Steinbeck provided the narrative for the voyage. The philosophies of both men intermingle as Steinbeck develops his story around a sense of the biological whole of the gulf; and as he narrates the life of the people and marine life that exist within the fragile habitat of the gulf, Steinbeck underscores the mixed blessings modern humanity has brought to the region. He records how indigenous gulf inhabitants cover their noses and mouths to avoid direct contact with white people and the contamination that springs from the evil poisons they bring with their industries. Steinbeck further notes that these poor and ragged Indians seem "so related to the seashore and the rocky hills and the loneliness that they are the things"; consequently, to know the country is to know them. They know when it will rain, as Steinbeck puts it, because they are the rain and all that surrounds them. This message of wholeness, which Steinbeck had been delivering at least since the writing of *To a God Unknown*, sets the tone for his narrative as he unravels the "complexity of the life pattern" in the gulf.

As Richard Astro writes in *John Steinbeck and Edward F. Ricketts* (1973), Steinbeck's narrative stands as a "celebration" of the "holistic world view" he shared with Ricketts. Steinbeck saw that humanity had drifted too far from its natural moorings by attempting to lift itself above and outside the larger environmental scheme. While other animals make "little impression of the world," as Steinbeck points out when reflecting on the evolution of species in the gulf, man has ravaged the world: "Its flora has been swept away and changed; its mountains torn down by man; its flat lands littered by the debris of his living." The problem, according to Steinbeck, is that modern humanity has so separated itself from the natural order by identifying with "external things" that it has become those things—"property, houses, money," and "concepts of power." Unless individuals begin to acknowledge their dependency on environmental conditions apart from their inventions and goods, Steinbeck warns, they face extinction at their own hands.

Steinbeck emphasizes this message in the concluding chapters of *The Sea of Cortez* in his reflections on the dredging operations of the Japanese fishing fleet. The monstrous dredge boats were scraping "every shrimp from the bottom" of the gulf as well as "every other living thing." The Mexican government, as Steinbeck observes, was allowing the Japanese sailors to destroy completely the food supply of the gulf. As Steinbeck points out, species thus decimated destroy the natural balance and the biological relationship necessary for its continuance. Even so, Steinbeck refrains from faulting the individuals involved, pointing out that they are caught up in a larger "destructive machine" that has ignored ecological concerns for profits. He saves his most bitter denouncement for his own country:

> We in the United States have done so much to destroy our own resources, our timber, our land, our fishes, that we should be taken as a horrible example and our methods avoided by any government and people enlightened enough to envision a continuing economy. With our own resources we have been prodigal, and our country will not soon lose the scars of our grasping.

In *The Sea of Cortez*, then, Steinbeck clearly takes an environmentalist stand as he leads his readers to an awareness of their connection to the earth and all the life that relies upon it. While Steinbeck rarely addressed environmental issues again with the same directness he brought to this narrative, he continued to offer his environmental message indirectly as he portrayed his fictional characters in relation to their surroundings.

Following *The Moon Is Down* (1942), his fictional study of human nature in relation to the demands of World War II, Steinbeck returned to his more typical California setting in *Cannery Row* (1945). In this story, Steinbeck portrays the attempt by social outcasts to live apart from the demands of society, on the Monterey beachfront. Characterizing "Doc," one of the main characters in the novel, as Steinbeck's most accurate rendition of Ricketts, Astro points out that Steinbeck questions the practical application of Ricketts's philosophy in "his clear-visioned evaluation of man's unsuccessful attempt to escape the realities of modern life." The experience of breaking through to underlying natural connections, as Steinbeck implies, can only be known within the primitive conditions of a Cannery Row, a refuge from respectable society and its consumptive embrace of its own artificial material world. Steinbeck's characters, however, neither seek nor experience the full illumination of a Joseph Wayne, whose depth of understanding caps *To a God Unknown*, and breaking through emerges more as a dream than a reality for modern individuals.

Captain Berry and Steinbeck aboard the Western Flyer *in 1940, while he and Edward Ricketts were studying marine life in the Gulf of California (Steinbeck Research Center, San Jose State University)*

In like manner, the characters in *The Wayward Bus* and *The Pearl,* both published in 1947, offer more of a study in human nature than in the relationships between the human and the natural, though Steinbeck does not completely ignore environmental concerns. In *The Pearl,* according to Kiyoshi Nakayama in "*The Pearl* in the *Sea of Cortez:* Steinbeck Use of Environment" (collected *Steinbook and the Environment*), Steinbeck thematically employs the environment of the Gulf of California as an opposing force to the commercial world that seeks to exploit it. Basing this novella on a folktale he had heard while exploring the gulf with Ricketts, Steinbeck tells how a poor inhabitant of the gulf region loses his natural connection to the sea, land, and people as greed enters into his life after he finds a large pearl. Kino, the poor villager from La Paz, pays a high price for his attempt to maintain possession of the pearl and the wealth it will bring: he murders those he believes intend to take the pearl and, in the end, flings the pearl back into the ocean as he rejects the life it offers. He returns to the simple life near the gulf, to the brush house and canoe he left behind. Steinbeck described his novella as a parable, and as such, it offers a simple story for the reader's edification: the farther Steinbeck's Indian villager moved from a harmonious existence within his environment, the more chaotic and inhuman became his life.

In his next three works, Steinbeck moved away from his environmental concerns and more toward political and moral ones. In *A Russian Journal* (1948), a collection of essays Steinbeck gleaned from his trip to Russia as a writer for the *New York Herald Tribune,* he intersperses descriptions of Russian farmers with biting comments about the power of the Soviet state. *Burning Bright: A Play in Story Form,* published in 1950, underscores the human capacity for love and the need for community. While the characters in *Burning Bright* may fail to carry the weight of Steinbeck's philosophy of communal humanity convincingly, as most critics point out, the characters in his 1952 *Viva Zapata!* his motion-picture script about the Mexican reformer who brought unity and power to his people, vividly embody that philosophy.

In 1952 Steinbeck also published *East of Eden,* the novel he had been sporadically writing for several years. With *East of Eden,* Steinbeck integrates historical reality with myth and romance, as he tries to mix "all forms, all methods" and "all approaches" into the book that offers his final full-length treatment of the nature of being human in the world. Steinbeck devoted nearly

Steinbeck receiving the Nobel Prize in literature,
10 December 1962 (Steinbeck Research
Center, San Jose State University)

only offer the hero as a sacrifice to a market-based society, as one who tragically fails in his virtuous struggle to transcend the grasp of American materialism.

Steinbeck had not completely lost faith in his ability as a writer to alter the actions and thoughts of his readers. He continued in his attempt to change the way Americans, in particular, viewed themselves in relation to their natural surroundings, especially in relation to the land. In 1962 he published a nonfiction work about his three-month journey around the United States in 1960 with his French poodle, Charley. *Travels with Charley: In Search of America* presents Steinbeck's observations on the people he met on his journey as well as his reflections on America itself—its natural, historical, and political landscape. The need for change rings throughout the chapters, especially for a change in the way Americans respond to their environment.

Steinbeck keeps the environment in the foreground in *Travels with Charley* by juxtaposing vivid descriptions of the land with detailed discussions of its exploitation. While beginning his trip up through the woods of New Hampshire, he notes the "foliage of the White Mountains" and describes the falling leaves "rolling in dusky clouds, and the conifers on the slopes" all "crusted in snow." Waking up weeks later in the trip to the chill of a Wisconsin morning, he recalls the "air . . . rich with butter-colored sunlight," this "land with richness," and the "fat cows and pigs gleaming against green" and "corn standing in little tents as corn should, and pumpkins all about." Still later in Montana, the state Steinbeck recalls most fondly, Steinbeck finds that the "calm of the mountains and the rolling grasslands had got into the inhabitants" and had made their towns "places to live in rather than nervous hives." This ecological contact, however, is a rarity in Steinbeck's experience of America.

Even in the early days of his journey, Steinbeck counters his brightest observations with dark and ominous thoughts. He warns how Americans threaten not only the beauty of the land with mounds of old "automobiles, machines," and "wrecks of houses," but their own lives as well by dumping deadly chemicals into rivers and lakes. Will there "come a time when we can no longer afford our wastefulness," Steinbeck wonders, "our chemical wastes in the rivers, metal wastes everywhere, and atomic wastes buried deep in the earth or sunk in the sea"? Will Americans continue to accept "traffic-choked streets, skies nested in smog, choking with the acids of industry," and a lifestyle carried forth by "the screech of rubber"? Many of the Americans Steinbeck mentions in his travels seem willing to accept such conditions, but Steinbeck is not. With an optimism that defies his dire observations and perhaps is based on the hope that his book might move his readers, Steinbeck prophesies that Americans will change their

five years to research of the historical parts of the book and even kept a journal of his work in progress, published in 1969 as *Journal of a Novel: The East of Eden Letters.* "The big novel" was a large-scale morality work, as Steinbeck told his editor, a "story of good and evil" and the imaginary history of one family's fall from grace and the real history of the Salinas Valley. While the novel may be oppressively stocked with symbols, as critics have noted, it nonetheless reveals an "ethics of human living" (in Timmerman's words again in his contribution to *Steinbeck and the Environment*) that springs from its characters' ability to live in harmony with all things, even apart from Edenic conditions. With *Sweet Thursday,* published in 1954, Steinbeck casts doubt on the possibility of finding such harmony as he tells the story of one man's unsuccessful struggle to exist significantly within a modern society that undermines connections of any kind. Seven years later in *The Winter of Our Discontent* (1961) Steinbeck denounces the emptiness of modern conditions that work to thwart natural connections. While doing so, however, he can

habits as the historical pendulum reverses itself and they seek escape from their polluted cities.

Steinbeck maintained that hope in light of his own belief in the human capacity to reform and his own reforming power as a writer. After warning his readers again in his *America and Americans,* published in 1966, that they were permitting the "reckless dumping of sewage and toxic wastes" and breathing the "filthy and dangerous" fumes coming from the "belching of uncontrolled products from combustion of coal, coke, oil, and gasoline," he relieves their consciences somewhat by drawing them as victims of a pervasive myth of unlimited resources and not as particularly responsible for their own polluting habits. Such a conclusion no doubt disturbed the more politically minded environmentalists that followed after Steinbeck, as Warren French notes in his his essay "How Green Was John Steinbeck?" (collected in *Steinbeck and the Environment*), but his hope for a "green" awakening, in which "we no longer believe that a man by owning a piece of America is free to outrage it," surely links Steinbeck's early efforts to the environmental activists who followed him.

John Steinbeck died 20 December 1968, a couple of years after the publication of *America and Americans.* Many believed that his best years were far behind him at the time of his death. For those who had continued to judge him only as a writer of Depression-era novels and as an artist of the working people, his greatness was summed up in the publication of *In Dubious Battle* and especially in *The Grapes of Wrath.* Steinbeck's reputation, however, is thriving as his views on humanity and its place within the natural environment are being reconsidered. Developed from his own scientific investigations and philosophical reflections, his holistic vision of life links all living creatures to the earth in an interconnecting web of associations. Ignoring these living connections brings death to many of Steinbeck's fictional characters, and Steinbeck attempts to enlighten his readers about the perils of upsetting the ecological balance and ravaging the environment. He wrote about what it meant for people to be cast from the land of plenty; he also wrote about the possibility of regaining paradise.

Letters:

Journal of a Novel: The East of Eden Letters (New York: Viking, 1969);

Elaine Steinbeck and Robert Wallsten, eds., *Steinbeck: A Life in Letters* (New York: Viking, 1975);

Thomas French, ed., *Steinbeck and Covici: The Story of a Friendship* (Middlebury, Vt.: P. S. Eriksson, 1979).

Bibliographies:

Tetsumaro Hayashi, *A New Steinbeck Bibliography, 1929–1971* (Metuchen, N.J.: Scarecrow Press, 1973);

Adrian H. Goldstone and John R. Payne, *John Steinbeck: A Bibliographical Catalogue of the Adrian H. Goldstone Collection* (Austin: University of Texas Humanities Research Center, 1974);

Robert B. Harmon, *Steinbeck Bibliographies: An Annotated Guide* (Metuchen, N.J.: Scarecrow Press, 1987);

Harmon, *John Steinbeck: An Annotated Guide to Biographical Sources* (Lanham, Md.: Scarecrow Press, 1996);

Michael J. Meyer, *The Hayashi Steinbeck Bibliography, 1982–1996* (Lanham, Md.: Scarecrow Press, 1998).

Biographies:

Richard O'Connor, *John Steinbeck* (New York: McGraw-Hill, 1970);

Nelson Valjean, *John Steinbeck: The Errant Knight: An Intimate Biography of His California Years* (San Francisco: Chronicle Books, 1975);

Thomas Kiernan, *The Intricate Music: A Biography of John Steinbeck* (Boston: Little, Brown, 1979);

Keith Ferrell, *John Steinbeck: The Voice of the Land* (New York: M. Evans, 1986);

Jay Parini, *John Steinbeck: A Biography* (New York: Holt, 1995);

Roy S. Simmonds, *John Steinbeck: The War Years, 1939–1945* (Lewisburg, Pa.: Bucknell University Press, 1996).

References:

Susan F. Beegle, Susan Shillinglaw, and Wesley N. Tiffney Jr., eds., *Steinbeck and the Environment: Interdisciplinary Approaches,* with a foreword by Elaine Steinbeck (Tuscaloosa: University of Alabama Press, 1997);

Harold Bloom, ed., *John Steinbeck* (New York: Chelsea House, 1987);

Robert DeMott, ed., *Working Days: The Journals of The Grapes of Wrath, 1938–1941* (New York: Viking, 1989);

John Ditsky, *John Steinbeck: Life, Work, and Criticism* (Fredericton, New Brunswick: York Press, 1985);

Louis Owens, *John Steinbeck's Re-Vision of America* (Athens: University of Georgia Press, 1985);

John Steinbeck IV and Nancy Steinbeck, *The Other Side of Eden: Life with John Steinbeck* (Amherst, N.Y.: Prometheus, 2001).

Papers:

John Steinbeck's correspondence and manuscript materials, as well as photographs and biographical matter, are located at Stanford University, the Bancroft Library of the University of California–Berkeley, Ball State University, the Preston Beyer Collection at Princeton University, the University of Texas at Austin, the University of Virginia, the Center for Steinbeck Studies at San Jose State University, and the Salinas Public Library in Salinas, California.

Edwin Way Teale

(2 June 1899 – 18 October 1980)

Thomas Potter

and

Roger Thompson
Virginia Military Institute

BOOKS: *The Book of Gliders* (New York: Dutton, 1930);
Grassroot Jungles: A Book of Insects (New York: Dodd, Mead, 1937; London: Putnam, 1938; revised edition, New York: Dodd, Mead, 1944; London: Hale, 1944); republished as *Exploring the Insect World* (New York: Grosset & Dunlap, 1953);
The Boys' Book of Insects: Interesting Facts about the Lives and Habits of the Common Insects, Together with Simple Instructions for Collecting, Rearing, and Studying Them (New York: Dutton, 1939); republished as *The Junior Book of Insects* (New York: Dutton, 1953);
The Boys' Book of Photography (New York: Dutton, 1939);
The Golden Throng: A Book About Bees (New York: Dodd, Mead, 1940; London: Hale, 1942); republished as *A Book About Bees* (New York: Dodd, Mead, 1959);
Byways to Adventure: A Guide to Nature Hobbies (New York: Dodd, Mead, 1942);
Near Horizons: The Story of an Insect Garden (New York: Dodd, Mead, 1942; London: Hale, 1947);
Dune Boy: The Early Years of a Naturalist (New York: Dodd, Mead, 1943; London: Hale, 1949);
Insect Life (New York: Boy Scouts of America, 1944);
The Lost Woods: Adventures of a Naturalist (New York: Dodd, Mead, 1945; London: Hale, 1952);
Days without Time: Adventures of a Naturalist (New York: Dodd, Mead, 1948);
North with the Spring: A Naturalist's Record of a 17,000-Mile Journey with the North American Spring (New York: Dodd, Mead, 1951; London: Eyre & Spottiswoode, 1954);
Circle of the Seasons: The Journal of a Naturalist's Year (New York: Dodd, Mead, 1953);
Insect Friends (New York: Dodd, Mead, 1955);
Autumn across America: A Naturalist's Record of a 20,000-Mile Journey through the North American Autumn (New York: Dodd, Mead, 1956); republished as *Autumn Journey: A Naturalist's Record of a 20,000-*

Edwin Way Teale (Thomas J. Dodd Research Center, University of Connecticut, Storrs)

Mile Journey through the North American Autumn (London: Eyre & Spottiswoode, 1957);
Journey into Summer: A Naturalist's Record of a 19,000-Mile Journey through the North American Summer (New York: Dodd, Mead, 1960);
The Lost Dog (New York: Dodd, Mead, 1961);
The Strange Lives of Familiar Insects (New York: Dodd, Mead, 1962);

Wandering through Winter: A Naturalist's Record of a 20,000-Mile Journey through the North American Winter (New York: Dodd, Mead, 1965);

Springtime in Britain: An 11,000 Mile Journey through the Natural History of Britain from Land's End to John O'Groats (New York: Dodd, Mead, 1970); republished as *Springtime in Britain: A Journey through the Land* (London: Cassell, 1971);

Photographs of American Nature (New York: Dodd, Mead, 1972);

A Naturalist Buys an Old Farm (New York: Dodd, Mead, 1974);

A Walk through the Year (New York: Dodd, Mead, 1978);

A Conscious Stillness: Two Naturalists on Thoreau's Rivers, by Teale and Ann Zwinger (New York: Harper & Row, 1982).

Collections: *Adventures in Nature: Selections from the Outdoor Writings of Edwin Way Teale* (New York: Dodd, Mead, 1959);

The American Seasons (New York: Dodd, Mead, 1976)—comprises chapters from *North with the Spring, Autumn across America, Journey into Summer,* and *Wandering through Winter.*

OTHER: Henry David Thoreau, *Walden: or Life in the Woods,* edited by Teale (New York: Dodd, Mead, 1946);

J. Henri Fabre, *The Insect World of J. Henri Fabre,* selected and edited by Teale (New York: Dodd, Mead, 1949);

W. H. Hudson, *Green Mansions,* introduction by Teale (New York: Dodd, Mead, 1949);

Green Treasury: A Journey through the World's Great Nature Writing, edited by Teale (New York: Dodd, Mead, 1952);

John Muir, *The Wilderness World of John Muir,* edited by Teale (Boston: Houghton Mifflin, 1955);

The Thoughts of Thoreau, edited by Teale (New York: Dodd, Mead, 1962);

Audubon's Wildlife, edited by Teale (New York: Viking, 1964; London: Thames & Hudson, 1965).

SELECTED PERIODICAL PUBLICATIONS—UNCOLLECTED: "Dinosaur of the Insect World: The Praying Mantis, Tyrant and Destroyer," *Travel,* 64 (February 1935);

"Gilbert White," *Audubon,* 47 (January 1945);

"DDT," *Nature Magazine,* 38 (March 1945);

"W. H. Hudson's Lost Years," by Teale and R. Gordon Wasson, *Saturday Review of Literature,* 30, no. 15 (12 April 1947);

"Fabre: The Explorer Who Stayed Home," *Coronet,* 29 (February 1951);

"John Burroughs: Disciple of Nature," *Coronet,* 31 (March 1952);

"Land Forever Wild," *Audubon,* 59 (May 1957);

"Henry Thoreau and the Realms of Time," *Thoreau Society Bulletin,* 64 (Summer 1958).

Edwin Way Teale can be credited with introducing nature writing to many Americans of the mid twentieth century. He appeared on television as spokesman for the environment and environmental writing, and he was known as a kind of neighborhood naturalist with a friendly manner and eagerness to teach people, especially children, about the natural world. His writings were widely admired, winning many awards. He also edited the popular *Green Treasury: A Journey through the World's Great Nature Writing* (1952), one of the first anthologies of the genre, and he was an accomplished nature photographer whose photographs appeared in a wide variety of books and magazines. His work has been translated into ten foreign languages and has been transcribed into Braille for the blind. He is frequently mentioned as an influence on many later nature writers.

The son of Oliver Cromwell Teale and Clara Louise (Way) Teale, Edwin Way Teale was born Edwin Alfred Teale in Joliet, Illinois, on 2 June 1899. His parents had moved there from Furnessville, Indiana, when his father took a job with the railroad. Young Teale spent school breaks and summers at Lone Oak Farm, his maternal grandparents' home in Furnessville, exploring the dune country of northern Indiana with his grandfather Edwin Way. Both Way and his wife, Jemima, encouraged their grandson's pursuit of the outdoors on and around their farm, the home in which his mother had been raised. Those experiences were the inspiration for Teale's book *Dune Boy: The Early Years of a Naturalist* (1943), which celebrates his adventures at Lone Oak Farm. During his time at the farm, Teale decided to become a nature writer, and there, when he was nine years old, he composed his first "book"—twenty-five short pieces he called "Tails of Lone Oak." When Teale was twelve, he changed his middle name from Alfred to Way, feeling that his given name was not sophisticated enough for his future profession as a famous author.

After completing high school in Joliet, Teale enrolled at the University of Illinois as a member of the Officer's Training Program during the latter stages of World War I. The war ended before Teale finished his first year there, and he transferred to Earlham College, a small Quaker liberal-arts school in Richmond, Indiana, where he lived with his uncle, the school president. Teale studied English literature and composition in preparation for a career in writing, but despite his

*Teale in his insect garden in Baldwin, New York (Thomas J. Dodd Research Center,
University of Connecticut, Storrs)*

dream of becoming a nature writer, he did not formally study any of the natural sciences at Earlham.

After Teale graduated from Earlham in 1922, he found a position on the faculty at Friends University in Wichita, Kansas. On 1 August 1923 he married Nellie Donovan, whom he had met at Earlham. She joined Teale at Friends University, where they both taught for one more year. Though both Earlham and Friends were Quaker schools, neither Teale nor Nellie Donovan had been raised in that denomination, Teale having been a Methodist and Donovan a Baptist.

In 1924 the Teales moved to New York City, where Teale enrolled in a master's program in English at Columbia University. During their two years in New York, David, their only child, was born in Joliet, where Nellie Teale had traveled to stay with her husband's parents during the delivery. It was a difficult birth, and the Teales learned that they would not be able to have more children. David Teale was killed in 1945, while fighting in Germany during World War II.

After earning his master's degree from Columbia in 1926, Teale became a ghostwriter for a syndicated inspirational columnist, Frank Crane. During this period the Teales lived for a short time in Los Angeles. When he received word that Crane had died while traveling in Europe, Teale found himself suddenly unemployed, and the family moved back to northern Indiana, the dune country of Teale's youth. Soon Teale left for New York City, where he rented a small apartment and began seeking employment with various magazines. In 1928 he was hired as a feature writer for *Popular Science Monthly,* where he worked until October 1941, when he resigned to pursue a career as a freelance writer and photographer. Annually for the rest of his life, Teale noted that date as his "Independence Day."

While at *Popular Science Monthly* Teale wrote his first book, *The Book of Gliders* (1930), published by E. P. Dutton. His second book, *Grassroot Jungles: A Book of Insects* (1937) was published by Dodd, Mead and Company, which after 1940 became his major publisher for the rest of his career. Teale's first two books are minor works. *Grassroot Jungles,* however, is more accomplished than his first effort and had some success in sales. A fascinating firsthand account, *Grassroot Jungles* comprises tales of the lives of insects related much in the manner of the great French entomologist, J. Henri Fabre, to whom Teale later dedicated one of his books. Each of Teale's chapters is the detailed story of a different insect, and the book is illustrated with 130 photographs taken by Teale. Teale also included commentary on current social issues. For example, when he wrote of the seventeen-year cicada, which spends the better part of its life underground, he opined, "From the viewpoint of an ordinary bug, our wars, elections, parades, mass meetings, headlines, and scientific discoveries are remote and unimportant. But to the seventeen-year cicada progress is a great tragedy. . . . woods are felled, highways made, subdivisions are laid out." In fact, *Grassroots Jungle* is in many ways an early confluence of Teale's most passionate interests: nature studies, insect collecting, writing, and photography. Following the publication of the book, in order to fulfill an agreement with Dutton, Teale wrote two more volumes for young readers, *The Boys' Book of Insects: Interesting Facts about the Lives and Habits of the Common Insects, Together with Simple Instructions for Collecting, Rearing, and Studying Them* and *The Boys' Book of Photography,* both published in 1939. These books were part of his lifelong project of showing young people the value of exploring nature without contributing to its destruction through hunting or capturing specimens.

During most of his years at *Popular Science Monthly* and until 1959, the Teales lived in the Long Island suburb of Baldwin, New York, a short train ride away from his office in New York City. As the years passed and he became increasingly disenchanted with his position at *Popular Science Monthly,* he began keeping a daybook in which he collected many of his thoughts as he traveled to the city. This small, unpublished work, which he titled "Street Thoughts," reveals a critical view of the world around him that is not apparent in Teale's published writings.

In 1940 Teale rented a small plot of land near his Baldwin home, which soon became well known as his "insect garden." He spent many hours there gathering details about the lives of insects for many magazine articles and several books. He also spent hours devising new techniques for photographing insects. The resulting photographs became an important source of revenue during his early years as a freelance writer. Many of his images appeared in textbooks, magazines, and encyclopedias. Information gathered in Teale's garden and photographs taken there are included in *The Golden Throng: A Book About Bees* (1940), *Byways to Adventure: A Guide to Nature Hobbies* (1942), and *Near Horizons: The Story of an Insect Garden* (1942). All three books were republished several times, and *Near Horizons* earned Teale the John Burroughs Medal in 1943.

The Golden Throng is a detailed study of the habitat and habits of bees with 85 photographs by Teale, including images of the birth and death of bees. The written text serves almost as a support for the photographs, describing and at times justifying the use of photography as a tool for gathering information. Teale considered photography a powerful alternative to other means of scientific observation because it allows the discovery of the insect's world without disrupting natural

Teale preparing to photograph a fly he had slowed down by refrigeration (Thomas J. Dodd Research Center, University of Connecticut, Storrs)

processes. *The Golden Throng,* however, is not just a scientific record of the life of bees; the work is a literary homage to the insect kingdom and includes fanciful dialogues between historical personages such as Samuel Johnson and James Boswell, observations from ancient writers such as Pliny the Elder, and colorful descriptions of the work of naturalists such as Karl von Frisch.

Thomas Dodd of Dodd, Mead and Company encouraged Teale to write *Near Horizons* after Teale showed him a large collection of insect photographs. More than 160 of them were included in the book, which was widely read and inspired many amateur and professional biologists. The book continues Teale's mission to give his readers a clear vision of the insect kingdom, and it displays again Teale's belief in the ability of photography to bridge the chasm between nature and humans.

Near Horizons is a record of Teale's insect garden, relating the story of where and how he created it. It includes accounts of wasps, cicadas, butterflies, crane flies, a praying mantis he named Dinah, and other insect adventurers. The garden was a haven for Teale, where he observed insects without disturbing their lives or raising the suspicion or concern of city folk. In the course of the book, the garden becomes a world of its own, with mountains, streams, forests, fields, and even burial grounds—a microcosm of the larger human world, with the behavior of insects providing lessons for humans. For example, a discussion on the power of insects such as ants to detect smells and follow their instincts ends with the suggestion that humans may be as finely tuned to odors as the ants but that people may have disavowed those connections in the name of science and progress. Odors such as the smell of "summer lawns," Teale argues, "are beyond the reach of the psychologist's IQ. They, like all the most important attributes of the human mind—courage, love, sincerity, devotion, imagination—are immeasurable." The ant, therefore, teaches Teale and his readers the value of the most basic senses. Each chapter of the book includes such lessons. A tale of exploration and discovery, *New Horizons* represents the transformation of the eighteenth-century explorer's natural-history tales about new lands into a twentieth-century nature writer's stories about miniature new lands found in previously "discovered" places. Teale spent many years studying and writing about the denizens of his insect garden, and many later stories about them were included in his books and magazine articles.

Soon after the success of *New Horizons,* Teale developed a routine that he followed for the rest of his career. He began work at 4:30 A.M. and continued until breakfast at 7:30 A.M. He then went back to his desk for the rest of the morning. Following lunch and a short break, he returned to his writing project until supper. In the evening Nellie Teale often read aloud his work, while he made notes for corrections and revisions. Over the years, as he carried on this routine, he also found time to go into the field to record his observations of natural events. He then stored them in large volumes titled "Nature Notes" and later extracted anecdotes for his books. This note taking and journal keeping is typical of many nature writers, among them Henry David Thoreau, Ralph Waldo Emerson, John Muir, and Annie Dillard.

The autobiographical *Dune Boy* describes the formative period in which Teale's maternal grandparents had a major influence on his decision to make nature writing his life's work. The book describes how he picked 250 quarts of strawberries to earn enough money to buy his first camera. As he completed the Sears, Roebuck order form, his grandfather chided him, "Better write large. Th' man may be deaf." Another humorous episode is Teale's account of his disappointing visit to a Chicago fur dealer who was not interested in purchasing the collection of mouse pelts Teale had prepared. Teale also included a favorite story of evenings spent on the front porch of the farmhouse while his grandmother read Miguel de Cervantes's *Don Quixote* (1605) to him and any neighbors who would listen.

Another episode in *Dune Boy* describes Teale's fascination with flight as he watched early airplane races around Lake Michigan. Inspired by those events, he designed and built his own glider, the Dragonette, using discarded farm implements. His grandfather stood by with a knowing suspicion of disaster as Teale made a short flight and crashed. Documenting a time, a place, and a way of life long past, the book depicts the natural spaces and nurturing environment from which Teale emerged as a writer.

In March 1945 Teale was working on a collection of semi-autobiographical essays titled *The Lost Woods: Adventures of a Naturalist* (1945) when he and Nellie Teale received word that their son, David, who had been serving in the U.S. Army since 1944, had become missing in action while on a nighttime reconnaissance patrol in Germany. After his disappearance, work on *The Lost Woods* helped Teale through this difficult time. Unlike his earlier descriptive works, *The Lost Woods* is reflective in style and tone. Once again Teale turned to his memories of Lone Oak Farm, writing of the woods through which he and his grandfather passed as they drove a wagon of farm produce to market in Michigan City, Indiana. Returning to those woods years later, he wrote in the title essay:

> For me, the Lost Woods became a starting point and a symbol. It was a symbol of all the veiled and fascinating secrets of the out-of-doors. It was the starting point of my absorption in the world of Nature. The image of that somber woods returned a thousand times in memory. It aroused in my mind an interest in the ways and mysteries of the wild world that a lifetime is not too long to satisfy.

Teale pursued such mysteries to the end of his life.

The nature essays in *The Lost Woods* illustrate Teale's growing interest in the power of nature to survive despite human intervention and in the pervasive influence of nature on human affairs. The essays—many of which had been published previously in periodicals such as *Audubon, Collier's,* and *Natural History*—cover such topics as undersea life, nature above New York City as viewed from the Empire State Building, reviews of well-known and not-so-well-known naturalists, and the mysteries of clouds. The book is illustrated by more than two hundred of Teale's photographs. Two of Teale's earliest lengthy appreciations of Thoreau, "On the Trail of Thoreau" and "Wildlife at Walden," are also included in the book. "On the Trail of Thoreau" describes Teale's retracing, exactly one hundred years later, of a trip on the Merrimack River taken by Thoreau and his brother, John, in 1839. A rumination on place, history, and nature, the essay illustrates the gen-

eral movement of the book as a whole, from natural space to human reflection.

The following year Teale edited a new edition of Thoreau's *Walden* (1854), with an introduction and interpretive remarks before each chapter, as well as 142 photographs "that would enable me to see for myself—through the eye of a camera—the places where Thoreau lived." Its combination of background information and photographs made Teale's edition popular. The introduction stresses Thoreau's pertinence to contemporary America, and the "interpretive remarks" often include descriptions of the current state of Walden Pond as well as historical depictions of it. Teale's Walden Pond is decidedly more connected to the world than Thoreau's.

During the 1940s Teale expanded his writing for magazines and natural-history journals, serving as a contributing editor for *Audubon* from 1942 to 1980. Many readers were introduced to Teale's writing through his work for this magazine. His "DDT" in the March 1945 issue of *Nature Magazine* is one of the earliest publications by an environmentalist that warned about the dangers of this insecticide, which was widely used from the 1940s through the 1960s to control mosquito populations. Teale cautioned against its use because he saw it as an indiscriminate killer, capable of wiping out wide stretches of wilderness. Teale's article preceded Rachel Carson's well-known warning, *Silent Spring* (1962), by more than fifteen years.

The semi-autobiographical *Days without Time: Adventures of a Naturalist* (1948) takes the reader into a world often overlooked by time-conscious moderns. Yet, Teale wrote, "there have been other days, days without time, days when I left watches and calendars behind and, in a small way, seceded from the World of the Clock. These were days of sun time and wind time." As in *The Lost Woods,* the essays in *Days without Time* cover a broad variety of topics, but all focus on the impact of nature in the human world. Unlike *Dune Boy, The Lost Woods* and *Days without Time* are increasingly metaphorical in style, as Teale describes a way of life in nature that he found more fulfilling than the rush of modern life.

In 1949 Teale edited works by two earlier naturalists: *The Insect World of J. Henri Fabre* and a new edition of W. H. Hudson's *Green Mansions* (1904), a romance novel set in South America, writing an introduction and interpretive comments for each book. In *The Insect World of J. Henri Fabre* Teale was particularly interested in expanding his audience's awareness of the animal kingdom, offering comments on how Fabre's work is relevant to American culture and science. Teale's goal of making the works of natural historians and nature writers available to the American public culminated in his editing of *Green Treasury* (1952). One of

Teale on a Florida beach near the start of the journey he described in his 1951 book, North with the Spring
(Thomas J. Dodd Research Center, University of Connecticut, Storrs)

the first nature-writing collections, this important anthology is organized in categories such as "Water," "The Seasons," and "The Life of the Earth: Reptiles." Teale included writings by well-known and obscure writers, from sacred and secular texts, and *Green Treasury* continues to be read by many environmentalists.

Soon after the publication of *Days Without Time*, the Teales began planning a major trip to document the coming of spring, for the first in a series of books about the seasons of the year in North America. Teale had developed a strong working and personal relationship with publisher Thomas Dodd, who advanced the funds that made the journey possible. For more than two years Teale researched, planned, and communicated with many people in preparation for a seventeen-thousand-mile journey from the Florida Everglades to Mount Washington in New Hampshire. As he traveled north, Teale recorded his many thoughts and observations in a series of spiral notebooks. At the end of each day he typed these notes onto pages that he later consulted as he wrote *North with the Spring: A Naturalist's Record of a 17,000-Mile Journey with the North American Spring* (1951). This book was followed by *Autumn across*

America: A Naturalist's Record of a 20,000-Mile Journey through the North American Autumn (1956), *Journey into Summer: A Naturalist's Record of a 19,000-Mile Journey through the North American Summer* (1960), and *Wandering through Winter: A Naturalist's Record of a 20,000-Mile Journey through the North American Winter* (1965). All four of these travel-nature narratives are illustrated with photographs Teale took on his journeys. For *Wandering through Winter*, Teale received a Pulitzer Prize for general nonfiction, becoming the first nature writer to win a Pulitzer Prize in this category. Each of the four books is dedicated to David Teale, "who traveled with us in our hearts."

As Teale prepared for the trip described in *North with the Spring*, he realized "that our dream was a universal one . . . leaving everyday responsibilities behind, drifting north with the spring." The Teales' journey carried them through familiar and unfamiliar parts of twenty-three states before they reached Mount Washington at the conclusion of their adventure. Teale's description of a shell island on the Gulf coast of Florida is a good example of his style: "So delicate, so beautiful, so fragile are these children of the sea that they, like snowflakes, seem to possess beauty for beauty's sake, beauty beyond needs of utility." At such moments he seems effortlessly to transport the reader to a new place and a new experience. With *North with the Spring* Teale became widely known as one of the great nature writers of his era.

For *Autumn across America* the Teales traveled twenty thousand miles across the northern half of the United States, from Monomy on Cape Cod in Massachusetts to Point Reyes, California, ending on the last day of the fall. Teale's photographs in this book include images as diverse as underwater seaweed and aerial views of marshes, documenting his travels across marshlands, the Continental Divide, and rain forests. Throughout this volume Teale interweaves narratives of his own explorations with stories of earlier naturalists. For instance, in the chapter "Warbler River," Teale documents development along the Au Sable River in Michigan while following the route of Norman Wood, a naturalist from the early twentieth century, intermingling Wood's discoveries with his own and answering some of Wood's questions with knowledge acquired from scientific literature published after Wood's voyage.

Journey into Summer describes the Teales' nineteen-thousand-mile journey from Lafayette Brook, near Franconia Notch in the White Mountains of New Hampshire (where *North with the Spring* ended), to Pike's Peak in Colorado. Like the first two books, *Journey into Summer* shows how the growth of the United States as an industrialized nation has affected its natural beauty. For instance, the final chapter moves from describing the natural wonders of the areas around Pike's Peak to a short history of the discovery of that well-known mountain and the subsequent rush to climb it. As a result, the peak is always crowded, the road leading to it is congested with traffic, and the parking lot at the summit is full of automobiles. At the peak Teale overheard two businessmen talking loudly about the social clubs to which they belonged as "the great spiritual experience of the mountains was passing them by. Unseen, unfelt, unappreciated, the beauty of the land unfolded around them." Such a "spiritual experience" was Teale's solution for a materialistic society. Speaking from a long transcendental tradition, Teale echoed his literary forebears in expressing the belief that a return to nature is necessary for spiritual rejuvenation.

Wandering through Winter ends, as was so often the case with Teale's writing, on a melancholy note: "To those of you who have journeyed so long, who have traversed the four seasons in our company, to all farewell. For here ends the story of our travels through the spring and summer and autumn and winter of the American Year." The volume is the last he dedicated to the memory of his son, and it also brings to an end the

last major journey Teale and his wife made together. The seasons series had taken more than fifteen years of planning, reading, exploring, and writing, and the four books are among Teale's most widely read works.

While working on the four-seasons series, Teale wrote other books as well. *Circle of the Seasons: The Journal of a Naturalist's Year* (1953) is a collection of nature observations that starts with the new calendar year and includes an entry for each day of the twelve-month cycle. Each entry is labeled with a theme and describes Teale's work for the day, often in his garden and neighboring natural spaces. The book concludes with the mixed sense of joy and melancholy common in much of his writing: "Last sunset, last twilight, last stars of December. And so this year comes to an end, a year rich in the small, everyday events of the earth, as all years are for those who find delight in simple things. There is in nature a timelessness, a sturdy, undeviating endurance. . . ."

In 1955 Teale published *Insect Friends,* a short book that includes many of his photographs. By this time Teale was appearing on many radio and television programs to talk about such creatures. He took a praying mantis on several live television programs and was a mystery guest on the popular television show *What's My Line.*

Editing *The Wilderness World of John Muir* in 1955, provided Teale yet another opportunity to educate readers about the rich history of American nature writing. Having already published new editions of Thoreau and Fabre, who are often considered nonconfrontational nature writers rather than activist environmentalists, Teale made a foray into environmentalism with *The Wilderness World of John Muir,* marking his own emergence as an environmental activist. As with his Thoreau and Fabre editions, Teale wrote an introduction and interpretive comments for each chapter of his Muir book. These comments are usually historical observations on Muir's action as an environmental pioneer, and Teale was careful to articulate Muir's role in the social agendas of his time. Teale ended his introduction by noting that Muir's accomplishments would be lost if his causes were not taken up by current writers and activists: "His finest monument is the wild beauty he called attention to and helped preserve—beauty, however, that is never entirely safe, beauty that needs as vigilant protection today and tomorrow as it needed yesterday." Teale became one of those vigilant protectors.

In 1959 Teale gathered selections from his earlier books in *Adventures in Nature.* During that same year the Teales made a major change in their lives. For a long while they had sought a place in the country where Teale could have solitude for writing but remain close to his publishers in New York City. After extensive research and exploration throughout Connecticut, they

*The Hampton, Connecticut, farmhouse the Teales bought in 1959 (Thomas
J. Dodd Research Center, University of Connecticut, Storrs)*

settled near Hampton, a small community in the eastern part of the state. There they found a farmhouse on one hundred acres of land with several brooks, large open fields, and woodlands. They named their haven Trail Wood and spent the rest of their productive lives there. In the garden of their new home Teale planted a cutting from his grandmother's pasture rose from the Lone Oak Farm.

At Trail Wood, in front of the large stone fireplace, the Teales spent evenings reading over and editing his manuscripts, or Nellie Teale read the literary classics aloud. They referred to those readings as their "fireside college," and over the years Nellie Teale kept a detailed list of all the books she read to her husband. She was also a great influence on his writing. If sentences in his manuscripts did not sound smooth when read aloud, she sent him back to the typewriter for revision.

In 1958 Teale was elected president of the Thoreau Society, an organization devoted to the study and dissemination of that writer's works. In preparation for editing *The Thoughts of Thoreau* (1962), Teale read

all Thoreau's works, including the two million words in his journals, and then selected excerpts from the works and organized them by topic with bibliographical references. The categories include thoughts, simplicity, books, friendship, science, poetry, society, and truth. This collection, which also includes a brief biographical sketch and an introduction by Teale, continues to be of value to scholars and other readers.

Also in 1962, Teale published *The Strange Lives of Familiar Insects,* which he dedicated to Fabre. Like most of Teale's work on insects, this book is an attempt to reach a wide readership about the need to understand and appreciate the insect world. In this book Teale describes how even the most common insects—such as the housefly, the cricket, or the ant—lead remarkable lives that offer lessons for humanity. The book is illustrated with more than twenty-five of Teale's insect photographs, many of which are close-ups showing the strange qualities of the insects.

When the announcement that Teale had won a Pulitzer Prize for *Wandering through Winter* was made in

Teale in his study at his farm in Hampton (Thomas J. Dodd
Research Center, University of Connecticut, Storrs)

early 1966, the Teales were visiting the home of novelist Thomas Hardy (1840–1928) in England, where Teale was gathering information for another springtime volume, *Springtime in Britain: An 11,000 Mile Journey through the Natural History of Britain from Land's End to John O'Groats* (1970). For some time he had wanted to explore the homeland of his father, who had immigrated to the United States from England as a young man. England was also the place where David Teale had been stationed just before he was killed in World War II. *Springtime in Britain* recounts an eleven-thousand-mile journey in Britain and reflects Teale's despair at the impact of industrialism on his ancestral home. The book, dedicated to his wife, was well received, though by the time of its publication the trope of describing nature through a long journey was well worn, and the book was not as successful as others. Even so, the volume was selected by the faculty and students of the University of Connecticut as the millionth volume of their library, a symbolic award that particularly pleased Teale.

As they continued to explore Trail Wood, often with visiting friends and naturalists, the Teales kept discovering new facts about this natural environment. Teale recorded this information in ledgers and used it as a resource for later books and magazine articles. By the early 1970s Teale was working on a book about Trail Wood, *A Naturalist Buys an Old Farm* (1974), which describes in great detail how they found their farm, explored it, and established trails on their land. He also

wrote about the many visitors, some famous, who had wandered the fields and forests with them, and he explained how he had a pond and writing cabin constructed so he could work in seclusion and observe nature. "Almost unconsciously," he wrote, "I take note of such small rustlings as the scurrying of a chipmunk, such snappings as that of a fly-catcher's bill . . . of goldfinches passing overhead."

Another product of Teale's new work environment was *A Walk through the Year* (1978), which, like *The Circle of Seasons,* is a daily recounting of nature observations. Unlike the earlier book, however, *A Walk through the Year* begins on the first day of spring, the vernal equinox, rather than at the start of the man-made calendar. Drawn from Teale's records of walks at Trail Wood, the daily entries are written in the first person, as though addressed directly to the reader.

Toward the end of his life Teale worked with Ann Zwinger on a book that was eventually published as *A Conscious Stillness: Two Naturalists on Thoreau's Rivers* (1982). They spent many hours researching and canoeing, together and separately, the Assebet, Sudbury, and Concord Rivers. Only the Assebet part was completed when Teale died in 1980. Zwinger used his notes to finalize the Sudbury portion, and the Concord part was never written. The book is written as a "conversation" in which the two naturalists share their observations of the natural world of Thoreau's New England, with alternating sections written by either Teale or Zwinger. The book includes historical information about the rivers and scientific information about particular places or animals, while never straying far from the personal observations that are typical of Teale and Zwinger. Zwinger later wrote the introduction for a 1998 edition of *A Naturalist Buys an Old Farm.*

During his long and productive life, Teale was a member of many natural-history organizations, including the Thoreau Society, the Explorers Club, the New York Academy of Sciences, the American Nature Study Society, the American Association for the Advancement of Science, the Brooklyn Entomological Society, the New York Entomological Society, the Linnaean Society, the American Ornithologists' Union, and the National Audubon Society. In addition to the 1966 Pulitzer Prize for *Wandering through Winter,* he won many other awards for his nature writing, including the Christopher Medal (1957), the Indiana Authors Day Award in nonfiction (1960), the Eva L. Gordon Award of the American Nature Study Society (1965), the Sarah Chapman Francis Medal of the Garden Club of America (1965), and the Conservation Medal of the New England Wildflower Society (1975). The award he appreciated most, however, was the John Burroughs Medal, which he won in 1943 for *Near Horizons.* Given each year to a person whose work is based on personal experience in the natural world, this award placed Teale in the elite group of writers such as William Beebe, Ernest Thompson Seton, Frank M. Chapman, Robert Cushman Murphy, and Arthur Cleveland Bent. Not long after receiving this award, Teale was invited to serve on the Burroughs Society award-selection committee and its board of directors. Teale's photographic work was exhibited at the Eastman House in Rochester, New York, and in the Audubon Gallery in New York City, and he was named an associate of the Royal Photographic Society of London. In addition to illustrating all his books, his photographs were published in magazines such as *Audubon, Life, Camera, Natural History, Nature, Outdoor Life, U.S. Camera,* and *Zoo Life*–as well as many textbooks and encyclopedias.

Teale died of cancer on 18 October 1980. Just before he died, the Teales donated Trail Wood to the Connecticut Audubon Society to be maintained as a nature sanctuary. Nellie Teale continued to live there until her death in 1993. Her death marked the transfor-

mation of Trail Wood into the Edwin Way Teale Memorial Sanctuary, which is managed by the Connecticut Audubon Society.

References:

Millard C. Davis, "Widened Horizons for the Dune Boy," *Conservationist,* 28 (April/May 1974): 10–13, 40;

Edward H. Dodd Jr., *Of Nature, Time and Teale: A Biographical Sketch of Edwin Way Teale* (New York: Dodd, Mead, 1960);

Frank Graham Jr., "The Last Naturalist," *Audubon,* 83 (January 1981): 8–10;

Walter Harding, "Edwin Way Teale," *Thoreau Society Bulletin,* no. 154 (Winter 1981): 6;

Harding, "Edwin Way Teale (1899–1980)," *Thoreau Society Bulletin,* no. 156 (Summer 1981): 4–5;

John P. McDonald, "Nature at Its Finest: The Edwin Way Teale Collection," *Harvest,* 15 (Fall 1987): 1–6;

David Stewart Miller, "An Unfinished Pilgrimage: Edwin Way Teale and American Nature Writing," dissertation, University of Minnesota, 1982;

Clell T. Peterson, "Inventorying God's Property: Edwin Way Teale," *American Book Collector,* 18, no. 9 (1968): 7–11;

Stan Tag, "Edwin Way Teale," in *American Nature Writers,* 2 volumes, edited by John Elder (New York: Scribners, 1996), II: 893–904;

Mary F. Tobin, "Nature Writers as Dissenting Moderns: Modernization and the Development of American Beliefs about Nature," dissertation, University of Maryland, College Park, 1981;

Edward Weeks, "The Peripatetic Reader: The Four Seasons," *Atlantic Monthly,* 216 (December 1965): 134–138.

Papers:

The bulk of Edwin Way Teale's papers, manuscripts, photographs, and memorabilia is housed in the Thomas J. Dodd Research Center at the University of Connecticut, Storrs. Most of his papers pertaining to Henry David Thoreau and the Thoreau Society are in the archives at the Concord Free Public Library in Massachusetts. Cornell University has some of Teale's letters.

Lewis Thomas

(25 November 1913 – 3 December 1993)

Ann Woodlief

Virginia Commonwealth University

BOOKS: *The Lives of a Cell: Notes of a Biology Watcher* (New York: Viking, 1974; Harmondsworth, U.K.: Penguin, 1978);

The Medusa and the Snail: More Notes of a Biology Watcher (New York: Viking, 1979; London: Allen Lane, 1980);

Research Frontiers in *Aging and Cancer: International Symposium for the 1980s* (Bethesda, Md.: United States Department of Health and Human Services, 1982);

The Youngest Science: Notes of a Medicine-Watcher (New York: Viking, 1983; Oxford: Oxford University Press, 1984);

Late Night Thoughts on Listening to Mahler's Ninth Symphony (New York: Viking, 1983; Oxford: Oxford University Press, 1984);

Could I Ask You Something? etchings by Alfonso Ossorio (New York: Library Fellows of the Whitney Museum of American Art, 1985);

The Lasker Awards: Four Decades of Scientific Medical Progress (New York: Raven Press, 1986);

Et Cetera Et Cetera: Notes of a Word Watcher (Boston: Little, Brown, 1990);

The Fragile Species (New York: Scribners, 1992).

Collection: *The Wonderful Mistake: Notes of a Biology Watcher* (Oxford: Oxford University Press, 1988)—comprises *The Lives of a Cell* and *The Medusa and the Snail.*

OTHER: *Rheumatic Fever: A Symposium Held at the University of Minnesota on November 29, 30, and December 1, 1951,* edited by Thomas (Minneapolis: University of Minnesota Press, 1952);

International Symposium on Injury, Inflammation and Immunity, edited by Thomas, Jonathan W. Uhr, and Lester Grant (Baltimore: Williams & Wilkins, 1964).

Few twentieth-century physicians bridged the gap between science and literature as well as Lewis Thomas, who spent most of his illustrious medical career as a researcher and administrator. The short essays he

Lewis Thomas (photograph by Jennifer Waddell; from the dust jacket for The Youngest Science, *1983)*

began writing "for fun" in 1971 established him as a serious author who combined his knowledge and insights into science, especially microbiology and immunology, with meditative reflections on nature and the human body in a style widely recognized as clear, graceful, and witty.

Lewis Thomas was born on 25 November 1913 in Flushing, New York, to Joseph Simon Thomas, a family physician and surgeon, and Grace Emma Peck Thomas, a nurse. Lewis Thomas was fascinated by his father's profession, and it became a baseline for his later understanding of the dramatic changes—not always good ones in his opinion—in the practice of medicine during the twentieth century. At fifteen he entered Princeton University, where he was an average student. While there he developed an interest in poetry and literary humor, writing much "good bad verse," as he described it in *The Youngest Science: Notes of a Medicine-Watcher* (1983), for *The Princeton Tiger.* These poems reveal his sense of humor about undergraduate life while exhibiting no particular interest in the natural world.

After earning a B.S. from Princeton in 1933, Thomas enrolled at Harvard Medical School. During the early 1930s medicine was becoming a clinical science, and antibiotics were soon to be developed. After graduating cum laude in 1937, Thomas served an internship at Boston City Hospital (1937–1939). During that time he supported himself by donating blood and publishing a dozen poems in *The Atlantic Monthly, Harper's Bazaar,* and *The Saturday Evening Post.* Most of these poems are about medical experiences, death, and war. Near the end of a residency in neurology at the Columbia Presbyterian Medical Center (1939–1941) he married Beryl Dawson, whom he later called his editorial collaborator, on 1 January 1941. Over the next eight years they had three daughters: Abigail, Judith, and Eliza.

Thomas began his medical career as a research fellow in neurology at the Thorndike Memorial Laboratories. In 1942 he was called for active service with the U.S. Naval Reserve as a medical researcher assigned to the Pacific. After World War II he went to Johns Hopkins University in Baltimore as an assistant professor to practice pediatrics and conduct research on rheumatic fever. His developing interest in immunological defense mechanisms became the basis of his later research. He later wrote a long essay on this subject, "On Disease," which was collected in *The Medusa and the Snail: More Notes of a Biology Watcher* (1979).

In 1948 Thomas became an associate professor at Tulane University, where he continued his research in microbiology and immunology. He became known for his creativity and ability to generate original hypotheses. In 1950 he moved to the University of Minnesota as professor of pediatrics and internal medicine and head of the pediatric-research laboratories at the University of Minnesota Heart Hospital, continuing his research on rheumatic fever. In 1954 he became head of the pathology department at New York University Medical School, where over the next fifteen years he helped to transform immunology into a clinical science and built unusually collaborative and interdisciplinary research teams. He was also director of medicine at New York University–Bellevue Medical Center (1959–1966). He became dean of the NYU Medical School in 1966. He moved to Yale University in 1969 to continue research in the pathogenesis of

mycoplasma diseases while serving as head of the pathology department (1969–1972) and dean of the School of Medicine (1972–1973).

In 1973 Thomas became president of the Sloan-Kettering Institute in New York, leading it to a position of international prominence in cancer research, treatment, and education. At a symposium held in his honor in 1982, Thomas was called "the father of modern immunology and experimental pathology."

In 1971, while Thomas was at Yale, his friend Dr. Franz Ingelfinger, editor of *The New England Journal of Medicine,* asked him to write a monthly column, "Notes of a Biology Watcher," of about one thousand words to fill one page of the journal. There was no pay for the column, but Ingelfinger promised there would also be no editing of Thomas's work. Thomas said he could not resist the opportunity.

At that point in his career, Thomas had written or cowritten more than two hundred scientific articles, and he was eager to try the informal essay, loosely modeled on the essays of sixteenth-century French writer Michel Eyquem de Montaigne. As he later wrote in *The Youngest Science,* Thomas welcomed the opportunity to break away from the "relentlessly flat style required for absolute unambiguity in every word" of scientific writing. His method for composing his essays was to work late at night, writing quickly, without outline and usually shortly after the deadline. He gradually developed a personal and engaging style, covering a range of subjects, both scientific and nonscientific. Like much other nature writing, Thomas's essays mix personal meditation and a vision of the integral connectedness of man and the universe with natural facts, but Thomas's facts generally relate to the human body rather than wilderness or landscape.

In 1974 Viking Press published *The Lives of a Cell: Notes of a Biology Watcher,* twenty-nine of the first thirty essays, exactly as they had appeared in *The New England Journal of Medicine.* This collection gives readers the opportunity to see the development of his essay style and voice. The first, the title essay, which has often been republished in anthologies as a model of literary prose, sets the tone and establishes the recurring themes of his essays. It draws an analogy between the workings of the cell and the workings of the earth and its organisms, including man. Thomas calls the earth "the toughest membrane imaginable in the universe, opaque to probability, impermeable to death" and man "the delicate part, transient and vulnerable as cilia," "embedded in nature" and not the master of the earth that he pictures himself to be. Human beings are not separate entities so much as interdependent beings, sharing cells with separate creatures such the mitochondria. He concludes that the earth cannot be called an organism because of its invisible complexities; yet, it can be compared to a single cell.

Many of Thomas's essays in *The Lives of a Cell* and later books elaborate on this idea of interconnectedness, employing clear explanations of Thomas's scientific and medical insights. He teaches readers not only about microbiology but also about how scientific discoveries in that field can illumine their understanding of an earth in which all beings work collaboratively and interdependently toward what he hopes will be a better world. Thus, the often sentimentalized idea of the essential unity of living things becomes compelling in Thomas's essays because he draws on his intimate understanding of cellular biology and immunology for metaphors to express human and cosmic realities, both physical and social. The essays express his fascination with technological developments in medicine, along with his worry that basic research may consequently be getting too little attention. Other subjects, which reappear in later essays, include meditations on aging and dying and on human paranoia about germs.

The Lives of a Cell includes essays on many other topics as well. Thomas contemplates the possibilities of extraterrestrial life as he thinks about space exploration. He compares the activity in termite nests to what happens at medical conventions, which are managed much less efficiently and collaboratively than the insect colonies. He considers how humans might communicate through their pheromones. Music, one of Thomas's major interests, is the basis for an essay on sounds in nature and a quantitative model of thermodynamic theory. Another favorite subject is the value of admitting to ignorance before acting precipitously. Thomas proposes that before humankind starts anything drastic to alter the environment, such as nuclear warfare, people should determine to understand fully the workings of a single form of life. In "An Ernest Proposal" his candidate for this single life form, which would be studied for at least ten years, is a protozoan in the digestive tract of Australian termites, a model of collaboration from which humans need to learn.

In *The Lives of a Cell* Thomas frequently turns to classical music and language, especially the etymology of words, to find analogies for order and the evolution of ideas. He believes that "rhythmic sounds might be the recapitulation of something else—an earliest memory, a score for the transformation of inanimate random matter in chaos into the improbably ordered dance of living forms" ("The Music of This Sphere"). Likewise, words such as *stigmergy* (from Greek for "to incite to work")—the process termite nestbuilding—fascinate him because of their "deeply seated, immutable

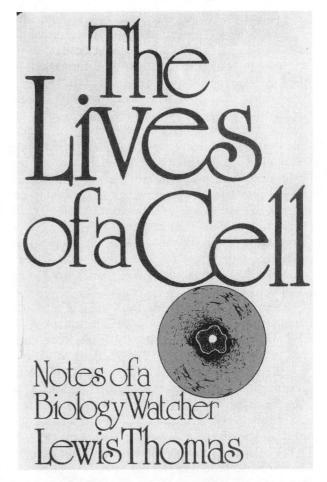

Dust jacket for Thomas's first book (1974), twenty-nine of the first thirty essays he wrote for his column in The New England Journal of Medicine *(Richland County Public Library)*

meaning, often hidden, which is the genotype" ("Living Language").

The final essay in *The Lives of a Cell,* "The World's Biggest Membrane," returns to the premise that all living things are interconnected. Looking at photographs of the earth taken from space, Thomas observes, "Aloft, floating free beneath the moist, gleaming membrane of bright blue sky, is the rising earth, the only exuberant thing in this part of the cosmos." He then compares the atmosphere to the membrane of a cell: "To stay alive, you have to be able to hold out against equilibrium, maintain imbalance, bank against entropy, and you can only transact this business with membranes in our kind of world." He develops this analogy as he describes the evolution of the sky, as "far and away the grandest product of collaboration in all of nature." As in most of his essays, such generalities come to life for the reader because Thomas can base them in clearly described scientific facts.

Thomas wrote the essays in *The Lives of a Cell* for a general scientific audience, including precise scientific details and reference notes at the end of each essay. Even so, the essays are also literary, almost poetic in their use of metaphor and image. Although Thomas's voice is apparent in his first book, he had not fully developed the distinct persona and voice of his later essays. He had, however, established the loose, almost intuitive, but focused, organization that typifies his essays. Perhaps the best description of Thomas's prose style came from poet Howard Nemerov, who commented that Thomas's essays are "organized on a sort of musical contrapuntal model, something like a passacaglia with melodic variations played over a more or less constant progression in the ground." An idea that might baffle the reader on a first reading, said Nemerov, would come up again with "new angles" and "new applications."

The Lives of a Cell was well received, and has been republished several times; within five years of first publication it had been translated into eleven languages and sold more than 250,000 copies. American reviewers were enthusiastic, with Joyce Carol Oates praising Thomas's "effortless, beautiful style" (*The New York Times Book Review,* 26 May 1974). Like many other reviewers, she lauded his ability for uniting scientific information with a larger vision of man's place in nature. Reviewers particularly noted Thomas's wisdom and optimism. John Updike balked at Thomas's "altruistic view of nature" yet applauded his "shimmering vision of hope" (*The New Yorker,* 15 July 1974). The book was awarded the National Book Award for arts and letters in 1975, having been nominated in both that category and in sciences.

The Medusa and the Snail: More Notes of a Biology Watcher (1979), a second collection of twenty-nine essays from Thomas's column in *The New England Journal of Medicine,* won the American Book Award for science and the Christopher Award in 1980. In that year Thomas, who had come to realize that most of the readers of his essays were nonscientists, moved his monthly column from *The New England Journal of Medicine* to *Discover* magazine.

The Medusa and the Snail includes more personal anecdotes and a more compelling authorial persona than *The Lives of a Cell*. By 1979 Thomas had been reading the essays of Montaigne for the previous eight years and had become increasing comfortable with the essay form. In *The Medusa and the Snail* Thomas addresses his readers as friends in a conversation, not as scientific colleagues, and there are no reference notes at the ends of essays. Yet, these essays are not about Thomas as a person. His topics are generally based in science and cover subjects of broad and current interest. Speaking with a friendly but reserved voice of common sense and gentle humor, he fits Ralph Waldo Emerson's description of the ideal scholar as "Man thinking."

The title essay is a meditation on uniqueness and "selfness," as he wrestles with the symbiotic relationship that has developed between the nudibranch (a common sea slug) and the medusa (a form of jelly fish), sustaining the life of each creature. He concludes his reflections in bewilderment: "I cannot get my mind to stay still and think it through." Indeed, the restless mind that cannot reach rational conclusions as it plays with the possibilities and wonders of nature and their human analogies is what gives his essays their special character.

In "The Tucson Zoo" a brief sense of intense, nonscientific connection with beavers and otters leads Thomas to think about the possibility of being genetically endowed with altruism. He then questions whether ants, working as a "single huge creature," can think; if so, what sort of thoughts might they have and would such an event make a single ant's hair "stand on end"? Thomas repeatedly explores this paradox: the coexistence of individuality and symbiotic unity in nature. "The Tucson Zoo" also has the typically intuitive structure of Thomas's essays. The reader never knows exactly where a Thomas essay might lead, as his mind jumps to resemblances and comparisons. As he says in "On Thinking about Thinking," "the effort we make to explain to ourselves how our brains work" can be best understood through music, especially the fugues of Johann Sebastian Bach.

Thomas took delight in mistakes and ignorance, suspecting that the secret of life, especially in evolution, is related to blunder and imperfection. In an essay on cloning he notes that a world in which organisms reproduced themselves identically would eliminate "new, natural, spontaneous, random, chancy children." He advises with humor, optimism, and wisdom: "Look for ways to get mutations more quickly, new variety, different songs. Fiddle around, if you must fiddle, but never with ways to keep things the same, no matter whom, not even yourself. Heaven, somewhere ahead, has got to be a change." As he asserts in "To Err Is Human," mistakes and random errors, even in computers, are the basis for human progress.

Medicine and medical education are the topics of four essays in *The Medusa and the Snail*. Thomas was always alert to hazards and unrealistic expectations of medical science, including human hubris. The most technical essay in the volume is "On Disease," which presents Thomas's favorite theory of disease as more of a flawed response by the body's immune system than an invasion of foreign pathogens.

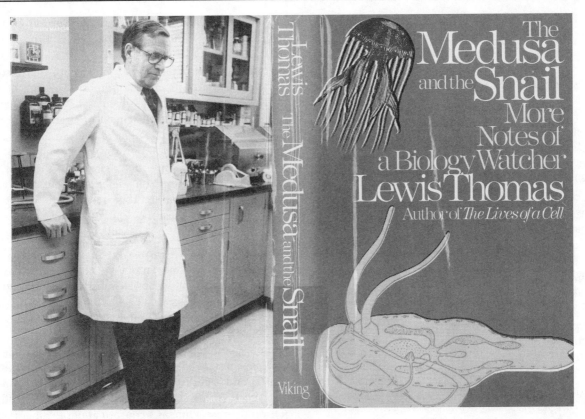

Dust jacket for Thomas's second book (1979), in which the symbiotic relationship between a jellyfish and
a sea slug serves as a metaphor for the interconnectedness of all living beings
(Richland County Public Library)

In "Why Montaigne Is Not a Bore" Thomas acknowledged his debt to the French writer. Many of the characteristics that Thomas appreciates in Montaigne's writing may also be found in Thomas's own essays, especially their conversational tone and their optimism. Like Montaigne, Thomas is at times both moralist and humorist. Yet, Thomas disagrees that "the nearest and most engrossing item in all of Nature is Montaigne." For Thomas the fascination lies in nature and man's inescapable, symbiotic connection with it, even at the cellular level. Thomas concludes, however, that "if Montaigne is an ordinary man, then what an encouragement, what a piece of work is, after all, an ordinary man! You cannot help but hope." As E. O. Wilson declared on the dust jacket of Thomas's book, "if Montaigne had possessed a knowledge of twentieth-century biology, he would have been Lewis Thomas."

The Youngest Science: Notes of a Medicine-Watcher (1983) is the autobiography of a man exploring his relationship to science, medicine, and language. This book reveals Thomas as a remarkable human being, knowledgeable in many areas, humane and generous,

articulate and at times poetic, with a gentle sense of humor and inbred optimism. His personal and professional evolution are presented modestly in this book, which places the origins of his literary voice more in his life and training than in any specifically literary source.

Unlike Montaigne, Thomas does not probe inner dramas of his own psyche as he reminisces about his life. *The Youngest Science* expresses his constant amazement at how much he was able to learn from his own ignorance and questions, and how lucky he was. Having personally witnessed modern medical history from the front lines of change, he teaches his readers much about the development and problems of modern medicine. He begins with affectionate descriptions of his parents—his father of necessity practicing medicine more as art than science and his mother as her husband's unpaid nurse in a family enterprise that took much time but brought in little money. As he describes his own progression through the field of medicine, Thomas focuses primarily on his research and the dramatic therapeutic changes that have come from basic research.

In the final chapter of *The Youngest Science* Thomas discusses his essays, primarily describing how he began the "habit" of writing them. After briefly noting favorable reviews and letters, he addresses criticisms from other scientists. He pleads guilty to optimism even as he writes about the "bad dreams" of modern life. He is drawn to the Gaia thesis, which he defines in a later essay as the idea that the earth is a "living, self-regulating being" and concludes that "the conjoined life of the planet not only comprises a sort of organism but succeeds in regulating itself, maintaining stability in the relative composition of the constituents of its atmosphere and waters, achieving something like the homeostasis familiar to students of conventional complex organisms, man himself for example." Alluding to the incurably optimistic Dr. Pangloss in Voltaire's *Candide* (1759), Thomas admits that his perspective may be Panglossian, but he insists, "This is in real life the best of all *possible* worlds, provided you give italics to that word *possible*." He goes on, however, to say, "I am not so optimistic about us. . . . I would not lay heavy odds on our survival unless we begin maturing some."

This darker analysis of the human condition underlies another book Thomas published in 1983, *Late Night Thoughts on Listening to Mahler's Ninth Symphony*. The twenty-four essays collected in this book were first published in *Discover, The New York Review of Books,* and *The New England Journal of Medicine* during the early 1980s. More political and more somber than Thomas's earlier essays, these essays confront the threat of nuclear holocaust and the diversion of funding for scientific research into "Star Wars" defenses. Largely abandoning his tone of learned geniality, Thomas expresses his anger about the possibility of nuclear war and about divisive nationalism, which is "probably the most stupefying example of biological error since the age of the great reptiles, wrong at every turn, but always felicitating itself loudly." He is also indignant about the billions of dollars going to developing thermonuclear missiles and to military-oriented research in general rather than to true scientific research.

The final, title essay in *Late Night Thoughts on Listening to Mahler's Ninth Symphony* returns to a subject that Thomas addressed throughout his writings: death as a natural process. "Death in the Open" in *The Lives of a Cell* defines as a "natural marvel" the fact that "All of the life of the earth dies, all of the time, in the same volume as the new life that dazzles us each morning, each spring." He urges his readers not to think of death as catastrophe but as part of a cycle: "Everything that comes alive seems to be in trade for something that dies, cell for cell. There might be some comfort in the recognition of synchrony, in the formation that we all go down together, in the best of company." Yet, he was

not thinking about the total, mass destruction of man and nature. In "Late Night Thoughts on Listening to Mahler's Ninth Symphony" he reveals that even music, so often a source of pleasure and analogies, fails to comfort him as he contemplates the possible death of the earth. Mahler's Ninth Symphony, in which he once heard "an open acknowledgment of death and at the same time a quiet celebration of the tranquillity connected to the process," now brings to mind "death everywhere, the dying of everything, the end of humanity." He now sees only images of bombs destroying beloved places. He can abide the thought of his own death much better than the death of nature.

The other essays in *Late Night Thoughts on Listening to Mahler's Ninth Symphony* remind readers of Thomas's stance as a moralist, although he rarely expressed his moral values as directly as he did in this book. The first essay, "The Unforgettable Fire," sets the tone as he thinks about so-called acceptable nuclear damage and two Japanese books on the atomic bombings of Hiroshima and Nagasaki, *Unforgettable Fire: Pictures Drawn by Atomic Bomb Survivors* (1977) and *Hiroshima and Nagasaki: The Physical, Medical and Social Effects of the Atomic Bombings* (1981). Other essays express Thomas's concern about the increasing connections of government and the military to technology, science, and medicine—which, he believed, violate the necessary symbiotic links between humans and nature. "Altruism" insists that biological altruism is a necessity, for without acknowledging "family ties and, with them, the obligations," humanity will pay the heaviest of prices: "If we do it wrong, scattering pollutants, clouding the atmosphere with too much carbon dioxide, extinguishing the thin carapace of ozone, burning up the forests, dropping the bombs, rampaging at large through nature as though we owned the place, there will be a lot of paying back to do and, at the end, nothing to pay back with."

Thomas had not lost his fascination with the workings of nature and what they show humankind about themselves, but his optimism had been tested. As he looked into an uncertain future, he concluded that he was grateful that he was not young. Like many nature writers, he became increasingly cynical about how humans define and treat nature.

In 1985 Thomas published a slim volume of fourteen poems—*Could I Ask You Something?*—in a limited edition illustrated with original etchings by Alfonso Ossorio. Thomas called the book a combination of "Surrealism and biology." These free-verse poems are lyrical meditations in a first-person voice, rephrasing ideas from his essays. Although too discursive to be great poetry, the poems do show what Andrew J.

Angyal has called Thomas's "unbounded aesthetic appreciation of the beauty and vitality of life."

Et Cetera Et Cetera: Notes of a Word Watcher (1990) is an exploration of language; only one of the essays in this volume had been previously published. These essays are the results of his twenty-year fascination with language and etymology, an passion evidently shared with his wife, Beryl Thomas, to whom he credits many of the ideas in the essays. Thomas's fascination with etymology is reminiscent of Henry David Thoreau's; both are convinced that the history of a word is still buried in its meaning. Unlike Thoreau, however, Thomas sees analogies between the evolution of such definitions and the development of living cells, which carry the biochemical traces of their microbial forebears, the symbiont mitochondria—an idea developed later in "The Art and Craft of Memoir" in *The Fragile Species* (1992). As Thomas says in the introduction to *Et Cetera Et Cetera,* "the earliest, antique feeling of certain roots persists, whether consciously perceived or not, inside some words, vibrating there alive, carrying the old significance into the depths of each new generation of cognates emerging in any language. Some words [like cells] contain genetic markers." The short essays in *Et Cetera Et Cetera* are written not by a linguist but by someone who collects dictionaries of etymology and finds strange connections in words. The essays often take unexpected directions. For example, "Testament, Third Party, Gaia etc.," begins with a reflection on being unable to remember information stored in his brain, a topic inspired by a visit to his lawyer about his will. In the word *testament* he finds *testis,* or *witness,* which reminds him of his own witness that "the earth is a living organism, of greater size but probably no more complexity than any other attested biological organism, including our own human cells." This thought leads to a discussion of the Gaia hypothesis, which he declares is "a central, plain fact of life." He considers how language and human society are part of the reproduction of Gaia, an argument that brings him back to the crucial role of language and the root *bheu* (being), which becomes "*phuein,* to bring forth and make grow, becoming *phusis,* live nature itself, then *phutos,* as plant" and eventually *physics, future, bondage,* and *tree.* He then traces *gen* (to give birth) to *pregnant, nature, kin, kindness, gentle, generation,* and at the end of a long list, *generous.*

Thomas's habitual optimism is tinged by the disorder that he acknowledges in the world—*threat,* or "a crowd or crush of people." He asserts that humans need time to grow up and learn. As usual he ends with a question: "If the earth is what I think it is, an immense being, intact and coherent, does it have a mind? If it

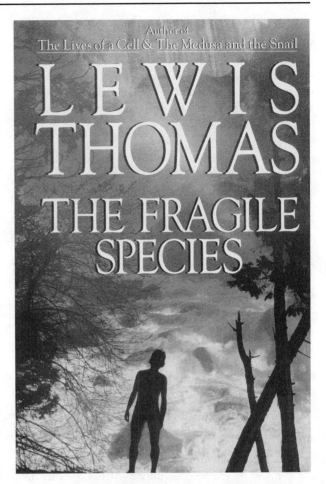

Dust jacket for Thomas's 1992 book, in which he reiterated his belief that "the most inventive and novel of all schemes in nature . . . is symbiosis, which is simply cooperative behavior carried to its extreme" (Richland County Public Library)

does, what is it thinking?" He suggests that there must be "a mind at work, adrift somewhere around or over or within the mass," not a Presence in charge, but "an immense collective thought, spread everywhere, unconcerned with the details." What does such a mind do? "It contemplates, that's what it does, is my answer." He concludes with his typical wit: "if It has a preoccupation with any part of Itself in particular, this would likely be, as Haldane once remarked, all the various and multitudinous beetles." Thomas repeated this passage at the conclusion of his next book.

The Fragile Species, Thomas's final book, collects the best of his unpublished essays and talks from 1984 to 1992. These essays are culminations of the different medical, scientific, and social ideas he examined through his literary career, seen from the final years of his long and productive life. He begins by reflecting on changes in medical science and education and with pleas for curriculum changes that take medical ignorance into account. He also asks for further basic medical research.

The first of the four sections in *The Fragile Species* ends with "The Life in the Mind," an essay that continues his reflections on the human brain as part of nature's machinery and his questions about the place of human consciousness:

> Why should there be something, instead of nothing? How do you organize a life, or a society, in accordance with physical laws that forbid purpose, causality, morality, and progress, especially when you have to do so with brains that stand alive with these very notions? Where's the fun in it?

These questions lead into a long discussion of pleasure as essential to humanity, even to nature; "Pleasure in being alive ought to exist as a special, independent, autonomous sense."

The second section deals with issues such as AIDS, drug abuse, the problem of aging, and the obligation—both moral and biological—for modern, industrialized societies to see that citizens of impoverished nations have the opportunity for longer life spans and better health.

The third section includes "random forays." "Comprehending My Cat Jeoffry" follows Lewis's hunches as he asks three questions, "what do we collectively mean by the word 'nature'?" "what does nature think about itself, and incidentally about us?" and "what lies at the center, for us and all the rest of nature to have our attention focused on, or is there indeed a center?" As usual, bacteria become major actors in his scenario, as well as the mating of crickets, the navigation of bats, the question of his cat's consciousness, the Fibonacci series of numbers, and scientific ignorance. His delight in mysteries and patterns had not diminished over time.

The final section presents three lectures that could be described as valedictory; "Cooperation," "Communication," and "Connections" express his major lifelong concerns. The theme of all three speeches, he announces in the first, is that "the driving force in nature, on this kind of planet with this sort of biosphere, is cooperation," and "the most inventive and novel of all schemes in nature, and perhaps the most significant in determining the great landmark events in evolution, is symbiosis, which is simply cooperative behavior carried to its extreme." Having noted that his view may be idiosyncratic and may involve haranguing as much as informing, he talks about amoebas that became dependent on invading bacterial pathogens, stromatolites (sedimentary fossils formed from layers of blue-green algae) and primordial bacteria as the beginning of life, termites as a

living paradigm of symbiosis, altruism, and a computer game based on models of cooperation. He ends with a characteristic quip: "Now I am all for the computers, and I hope the word gets around quickly."

"Communication" revisits Thomas's thoughts on the gift and evolution of human language and how it must have begun in children. He also considers the language of mathematics as best expressing new realities of the world, and especially the language of poetry, with its roots in childhood. "Connections" returns to Thomas's concern about the dangers of nationalism and the need for some "powerful steadying cohesive force" for human society to enhance "the comity of nations," which must be—Thomas insists—basic science. He is encouraged to find other people thinking about Earth as a living organism, a creature whose cells include humankind, with a "vast wiring diagram that maintains the interconnectedness and interdependence of all its numberless parts, and the ultimate product of the life: more and more information." He ends with the question he posed in the first essay: does Earth have a mind? Thomas concludes by repeating the point he made in *Et Cetera Et Cetera:* that such a mind must be able to contemplate and may be more preoccupied with beetles than human beings.

Perhaps the most remarkable essay in *The Fragile Species* is "The Art and Craft of Memoir," an "autobiography" of the cell and evolution, from microorganism to human, powered by the mitochondrial symbionts in each cell, "a condominium run by trustees." He exults in the idea that the earth is one living organism. As usual, Thomas touches on many subjects, concluding that he takes "an optimistic, Panglossian view, and I am quick to say that I could be all wrong." He ends with a personal, "cheerful footnote": "next time you feel a cold coming on, reflect on the possibility that you may be giving a small boost to evolution."

Lewis Thomas died on 3 December 1993 of Waldenstrom's disease, a rare lymphoma-like cancer. During a life of remarkable accomplishment, he had won many awards for his scientific and administrative work, including two that were named for him, the Lewis Thomas Award for Communications from the American College of Physicians (1986) and the Lewis Thomas Prize from Rockefeller University (1993). He was elected to the American Academy of Arts and Sciences in 1961 and the National Academy of Science in 1972. In 1986 the Lewis Thomas Laboratory at Princeton was dedicated. He received twenty honorary degrees in science, law, letters, and music. Models for modern, scientifically based nature prose writings, his essays are at once philosophical, scientific, and personal, revealing the good humor, skepticism, optimism, and faith of a renaissance man who never stopped learning about and taking delight in the mysteries of the natural world.

Interviews:

Jeremy Bernstein, "Lewis Thomas: Life of a Biology Watcher," in his *Experiencing Science: Profiles in Discovery* (New York: Basic Books, 1978), pp. 163–201;

David Hellerstein, "The Muse of Medicine," *Esquire,* 101 (March 1984): 72–77;

Peggy Langstaff, "A strong voice on a fragile subject: Lewis Thomas and the world we share," *Bookpage* (April 1992) <http://www.bookpage.com/BPinterviews/thomas492.html>.

References:

Chris Anderson, "Error, Ambiguity, and the Peripheral: Teaching Lewis Thomas," in *Literary Nonfiction: Theory, Criticism, Pedagogy,* edited by Anderson (Carbondale: Southern Illinois University Press, 1989), pp. 315–332;

Andrew J. Angyal, *Lewis Thomas* (Boston: Twayne, 1989);

Barbara Lounsberry, "Lewis Thomas and the Revival of Nineteenth Century Literary Tradition," *Markham Review,* 13 (Fall 1983/Winter 1984): 7–10;

Howard Nemerov, "Lewis Thomas, Montaigne, and Human Happiness," in his *New and Selected Essays* (Carbondale: Southern Illinois University Press, 1985), pp. 223–231;

Mary Ellen Pitts, "Undermining the Authority of Science: Epistemological Symbiosis in Loren Eiseley and Lewis Thomas," *Rendezvous,* 25 (Fall 1989): 83–90;

Steven Weiland, "'A Tune Beyond Us, Yet Ourselves': Medical Science and Lewis Thomas," in his *Intellectual Craftsmen: Ways and Works in American Scholarship 1935–1990* (New Brunswick, N.J.: Transaction, 1991), pp. 189–204;

Fred D. White, "Science, Discourse, and Authorial Responsibility," *San Jose Studies,* 10 (Winter 1984): 25–38.

Papers:

The Lewis Thomas Papers, 1941–1992, are at the Princeton University Library.

Terry Tempest Williams

(8 September 1955 –   )

Melissa A. Goldthwaite
Saint Joseph's University

See also the Williams entry in *DLB 206: Twentieth-Century American Western Writers, First Series.*

BOOKS: *The Secret Language of Snow,* by Williams and Ted Major (San Francisco: Sierra Club/Pantheon, 1984);

Pieces of White Shell: A Journey to Navajoland (New York: Scribners, 1984);

Between Cattails (New York: Scribners, 1985);

Coyote's Canyon (Salt Lake City: Peregrine Smith, 1989);

Earthly Messengers (Salt Lake City: Western Slope, 1989);

Refuge: An Unnatural History of Family and Place (New York: Pantheon, 1991);

An Unspoken Hunger: Stories from the Field (New York: Pantheon, 1994);

Desert Quartet: An Erotic Landscape (New York: Pantheon, 1995);

Leap (New York: Pantheon, 2000);

Red: Passion and Patience in the Desert (New York: Pantheon, 2001).

PRODUCED SCRIPT: *A Desert Sea,* television, written and narrated by Williams, KUED (Salt Lake City), 1993.

RECORDINGS: *Coyote's Canyon: A Collection of Stories,* read by Williams, NorthWord Audio Press, 1990;

Refuge: An Unnatural History of Family and Place, read by Williams, NorthWord Audio Press, 1994;

An Unspoken Hunger: Stories from the Field, read by Williams, NorthWord Audio Press, 1994;

Refuge: Passages from the Book, read by Williams, Wind over the Earth, 2002.

OTHER: David B. Madsen, *Exploring the Fremont,* foreword by Williams (Salt Lake City: Utah Museum of Natural History, 1989);

"A Full Moon in May," in *Wendell Berry,* edited by Paul Merchant (Lewiston, Idaho: Confluence, 1991), pp. 61–67;

Terry Tempest Williams (photograph from the dust jacket for Refuge, *1991)*

Rick Reese, *Greater Yellowstone: The National Park and Adjacent Wildlands,* volume 6, foreword by Williams (Helena, Mont.: Farcountry Press, 1991);

The Owl in Monument Canyon, and Other Stories from Indian Country, edited by Jackson Clark, foreword by Williams (Salt Lake City: University of Utah, 1993);

T. H. Watkins, *Stone Time, Southern Utah: A Portrait and a Meditation,* preface by Williams (Weehawken, N.J.: Clear Light, 1994);

Harvey Lloyd, *Sacred Lands of the Southwest: Aerial Photographs,* introduction by Williams (New York: Montacelli Press, 1995);

Atomic Ghost: Poets Respond to the Nuclear Age, edited by John Bradley, introduction by Williams (Minneapolis: Coffeehouse Press, 1995);

Great and Peculiar Beauty: A Utah Centennial Reader, edited by Williams and Thomas J. Lyon (Salt Lake City: Gibbs Smith, 1995);

Utah: A Centennial Celebration, foreword by Williams, photographs by Tom Till, text by Brooke Williams (Englewood, Colo.: Westcliffe, 1995);

"Book of Mormon and Isaiah," in *Communion: Contemporary Writers Reveal the Bible in Their Lives,* edited by David Rosenberg (New York: Anchor Books, 1996), pp. 357–366;

Testimony: Writers in Defense of the Wilderness, compiled by Williams and Stephen Trimble (Minneapolis: Milkweed Editions, 1996);

Mary Austin, *Land of Little Rain,* introduction by Williams (New York: Penguin, 1997);

Margaret E. Murie, *Two in the Far North,* foreword by Williams (Seattle: Alaska Northwest Books, 1997);

Katie Lee, *All My Rivers Are Gone: A Journey of Discovery Through Glen Canyon,* introduction by Williams (Boulder: Johnson Books, 1998);

New Genesis: A Mormon Reader on Land and Community, edited by Williams, William B. Smart, and Gibbs M. Smith (Salt Lake City: Gibbs Smith, 1998);

In Response to Place: Photographs from the Nature Conservancy's Last Great Places, foreword by Williams (Boston: Bulfinch Press/Little, Brown, 2001);

Patriotism and the American Land, by Williams, Richard Nelson, and Barry Lopez (Great Barrington, Mass.: Orion Society, 2002);

Wallace Stegner, *Crossing to Safety,* introduction by Williams (New York: Modern Library, 2002).

SELECTED PERIODICAL PUBLICATIONS–
UNCOLLECTED: "Elements of Love," *New England Review,* 16, nos. 1–4 (Winter–Fall 1994): 5–7, 69–70, 97–98, 105–106;

"A Cry for Wilderness," *National Parks* (November/December 1995): 24–29;

"On Hemingway and His Influence," *Hemingway Review,* 18, no. 2 (1999): 115–132.

In several interviews, Terry Tempest Williams has said that she writes out of her own biases of gender, geography, and culture–as a Mormon woman from the Great Basin and Colorado Plateau of Utah. Just as the borders between the genres she writes in are fluid, her works show little separation in nature, gender, and spirituality or in the connective threads of story, experi-

ence, community, art, and activism. She writes of a need for the natural world that is physical, spiritual, and artistic. As a fifth-generation Mormon, moreover, Williams concentrates on living a spiritual life rather than a religious one, choosing to value individual vision and experience as she pushes against the patriarchal nature of the Church of Jesus Christ of Latter-day Saints and focuses instead on the importance of family, story, and place–the parts of her spiritual heritage that sustain her and come through in her writing.

Williams writes partly for a Mormon audience and hopes that members of the church will understand through her religious inquiry the importance of respectfully questioning aspects of the theology and positions taken by the General Authorities in the name of "free agency." Though she wishes to have a voice in Mormon culture, her work has received the most scholarly attention from readers of American nature writing, students and scholars of literature and the environment, and those interested in women's studies and women's health. Her activism also has targeted another audience–politicians. She has testified twice before the United States Congress, and copies of both *Testimony: Writers in Defense of the Wilderness* (1996) and *Red: Passion and Patience in the Desert* (2001) were distributed to members of Congress.

Terry Lynn Tempest–the first of the four children of Diane Dixon Tempest and John Henry Tempest III–was born in Corona, California, on 8 September 1955. She was reared in Salt Lake City and has lived all her life in Utah. Williams describes her father, a pipe contractor and a conservative, as the quintessential Marlboro man without the cigarette–a rugged individual with firm opinions. Despite their political differences, Williams is also quick to point out her father's connection to land–that he works outside, along with his sons and other family members, digging in the earth.

Williams's connections to family, the land, and her Mormon spiritual roots are the basic elements of her writing. She credits her maternal grandparents, Lettie Romney and Donald "Sanky" Dixon, with demonstrating a path of individual freedom within orthodoxy and the land for giving her a voice. Williams also writes and speaks with great affection of her paternal grandparents, John Henry "Jack" Tempest Jr. and Kathryn Blackett "Mimi" Tempest, who listened to and interpreted Williams's dreams; gave Williams her first bird guide, Roger Tory Peterson's *Field Guide to Western Birds* (1941); went bird-watching at Bear River with her; catalogued shells with her; danced with her; and showed her the value of an independent mind and conscience, especially in spiritual matters. Williams listened especially to Mimi, whom she portrays in her writing as a storyteller and spiritual mentor.

After receiving her early education in Salt Lake City, Williams attended the University of Utah, where she earned her bachelor's degree in English in 1979 and a master's degree in environmental education in 1984. While working on these degrees, she also attended the Teton Science School in Jackson Hole, Wyoming, during the summers of 1974, 1975, and 1976. In 1979 she was hired as curator of education at the Utah Museum of Natural History, a job she held until 1986, when she became naturalist-in-residence at the museum, a position that provided her more time to spend on her writing and with her mother, who was suffering from cancer. Williams held that position until 1996, when she left to devote her time more fully to writing and activism.

While she was a student at the University of Utah in 1974 and working part-time in a Salt Lake City bookstore, Terry Tempest met Brooke Williams, a direct descendant of Brigham Young, and the two married on 2 June 1975, when Williams was nineteen years old. Brooke Williams became an environmental consultant and writer; he is the author of *Halflives: Reconciling Work and Wildness* (1999) and essays published in *Utah: A Centennial Celebration* (1995). In 1998 the couple moved from their home in Emigration Canyon, just outside Salt Lake City, to Castle Valley, Utah, near Moab and Arches National Park. In a 1995 interview with Scott London, when she was living in Emigration Canyon, Williams reflected on her connection to that place on the Mormon trail where Brigham Young and the early Mormon pioneers traveled in 1847. Of the place she came to live, "on the Colorado plateau where canyon walls rise upward like praying hands," she has said, "That place is holy to me." In *Red,* Williams reflects on this move and questions, "Am I running or am I returning to the place where my animal body resides?" Regardless of her answer, the power of the natural world emerges early in her writing.

The Secret Language of Snow (1984), Williams's first book, won the Children's Science Book Award (from the New York Academy of Science) in 1984. Written with Ted Major (founder of the Teton Science School) and illustrated by Jennifer Dewey, this book for children combines science, story, and myth to explore snow through the vocabulary of the Inuit people of northwestern Alaska. Divided into twelve chapters—the first two providing context, the next ten exploring the Kobuk people's language of snow—each section includes poetry, description, story, and activities. In language understandable to children, Williams and Major discuss the scientific studies of Russian naturalist A. N. Formozov and Canadian biologist William Pruitt, but they focus their attention on the Kobuk people's words for snow,

encouraging a new way of seeing by teaching a vocabulary grounded in a particular place and culture.

In this book, the many questions Williams asks invoke a sense of wonder. When discussing *annui* (falling snow) she asks, "Where does it come from? How is it made?" and follows these questions with both scientific explanation and metaphor: "Snow is a white serpent with many heads." This mix of science and metaphor, activity and story, pervades the work, exploring *api* (snow on the ground), *kanik* (rime), *siqoqtoaq* (sun crust), and six other incarnations of snow in a similar fashion. Even in her earliest published book, the themes and hallmarks that later came to define Williams's work are evident. *The Secret Language of Snow* demonstrates her interest in the ways human understanding of the world is shaped by language; the book also shows her curiosity, her respect for cultures that differ from but inform her own, and her belief in the power of story.

These themes are evident in her second book, which, like *The Secret Language of Snow,* was shaped by her interaction with place, children, and a culture that differed from but held similarities to her own. Of this second book, *Pieces of White Shell: A Journey to Navajoland* (1984), Williams writes, "This book is a journey into one culture, Navajo, and back out again to my own, Mormon." Though many of the stories take place far from her family home in Salt Lake City, Williams dedicates *Pieces of White Shell* to her family. Whether Williams is tracking deer with her father, speaking with two Navajo children on a bus about the importance of grandparents, or remembering Christmas ornaments, the significance of her family and culture is clear. For this book she received a 1985 Southwest Book Award from the Border Regional Library Association.

Pieces of White Shell was born of the question "What stories do we tell that evoke a sense of place?" The stories Williams tells come from her experiences teaching—and learning from—children on a Navajo reservation, from Native American mythology, from books, from her own family, and from her work as a curator at the Utah Museum of Natural History. She often tells these stories through reference to natural objects as reflected by her choice of such chapter titles as "A Sprig of Sage," "Rocks, Sand, and Seeds," "Turquoise, Obsidian, and Coral," "Yucca," and "Wool." At times her stories come through the voices of others, often the children, and sometimes through other published versions.

Most often the chapters are organized in a cyclical fashion, ending where they begin. For example, "Yucca" begins with the sound of chanting and the image of a basket "coiled: around and around and around and around. It was striped with persimmon." Ten pages

Dust jacket for Williams's 2000 book, in which she uses Hieronymus Bosch's triptych The Garden of Delights *(circa 1500) as a means to explore her faith and to present her hope for environmental renewal (Richland County Public Library)*

later, the chapter ends with the chanting of the same words and the image of the coiled basket striped with persimmon. Williams draws attention to the dominant images through her use of repetition, objects on which she meditates (such as those mentioned in the chapter titles), personification, and detailed description. Such conventions show Williams as someone who observes and listens closely.

Between Cattails (1985), another children's book, also demonstrates close attention to detail and sensory images. In verse, Williams describes a life-filled marsh—the sound of red-winged blackbirds singing, the sight of great blue herons fishing or of a muskrat building a home. She writes with clarity about a particular wetland ecosystem of cattails, teal, mollusks, weasels, and western grebes and the partnership of life and death, preying and preyed upon. Williams acts as tour guide, leading her reader on a scientific and lyrical walk through the marsh, and—as in her other work—she is attentive to the stories these natural relatives tell; she says that "To save these stories / we must treat the marsh / tenderly." Williams closes *Between Cattails* with the sound of red-winged blackbirds singing, a sound

she recalls later in *Refuge: An Unnatural History of Family and Place* (1991) while walking in the Bear River Migratory Bird Refuge.

In *Coyote's Canyon* (1989), readers are invited to see some of the places about which Williams writes, not only through her words but also through John Telford's stunning photographs. The same question that prompted her to write *Pieces of White Shell*—"What stories do we tell that evoke a sense of place?"—was the impetus for *Coyote's Canyon*. In "The Coyote Clan," the opening piece, Williams points to southern Utah as "Coyote's Country . . . where nothing is as it appears." The same trickster quality applies to Williams's prose, which takes on the same chameleon nature as the red-rock canyons. Williams writes story-essays in this volume—beautiful pieces that reside in a genre somewhere between nonfiction and myth.

Williams writes metaphorically of a "Coyote Clan—hundreds, maybe even thousands, of individuals who are quietly subversive on behalf of the land," and she populates her story-essays with examples of such individuals: Navajo children who chant their way from fear to joy; a woman who temporarily leaves her family to return to a canyon of her childhood, where she can be alone with herself and the healing earth; an archaeologist from Boulder, Utah, who buries poems and pictographs, piquing the townspeople's curiosity about Anasazi culture; six friends who take a ladder from a museum to restore it to its rightful place in the desert; a woman who dances in the desert; and a couple, grounded in place, who trace their own genealogies. Williams internalizes myths and stories, making them her own and passing them on to readers.

She acknowledges what many writers of memoir and personal essays understand, that what is most personal is also universal. In her best-known, most critically acclaimed memoir, *Refuge,* Williams chronicles her mother's diagnosis and eventual death from ovarian cancer, events that parallel the rise of the Great Salt Lake and eventual flooding of the Bear River Migratory Bird Refuge. Dedicated to her mother, *Refuge* demonstrates Williams's struggle with the question "How do we find refuge in the midst of change?" She asks this question of her grandmother Mimi, whose death from cancer she also recounts in *Refuge.*

In the face of the threat of losing her mother to cancer, Williams wrote, "I could not separate the Bird Refuge from my family. Devastation respects no boundaries. The landscape of my childhood and the landscape of my family, the two things I had always regarded as bedrock, were now subject to change." Williams writes about the changes in her mother's body after rounds of chemotherapy; about the changes in her own feelings, perceptions, and responses to death; about the changes in the places and people she loves. She feels that if she can learn to love death, she can find refuge in change.

Refuge, a book about loss and healing, embraces a sense of perpetual change and questioning of orthodoxy. Williams recounts an experience of her grandmother Mimi, who, after expelling a cancerous tumor, thought, "Finally, I am rid of the orthodoxy." Williams also includes her mother's wish that the women in her family might someday be able to stand in the circle to give a blessing, a position in the Mormon faith that is reserved for men. And Williams brings other tenets of Mormonism into question, calling for a mother body to balance out the Godhead, affirming her own belief that "the Holy Ghost is female," and proclaiming, "Dogma doesn't hold me. Wildness does." *Refuge* is a book about the consequences of blind obedience.

Williams names each chapter of *Refuge* for a bird and charts the water level of the Great Salt Lake. The book is filled with a remarkable precision throughout: dates, names, numbers, the scientific and common names of birds, and other specifics. Details also figure prominently in the widely anthologized epilogue, "The

Clan of One-Breasted Women," in which Williams ties her mother's death—and the deaths of many women in her family—to nuclear fallout, poisoning by radiation from aboveground atomic testing in Nevada from the 1950s until the early 1960s. Through the deaths of the women in her family, Williams learned to question authority, both religious and governmental. This sense of questioning authority is especially evident in the conclusion of the epilogue for the paperback version of *Refuge.* In the hardcover version, when Williams describes her arrest for an act of civil disobedience at a Nevada test site, she comments, the officer "did not find my scars." The paperback version omits this line and instead details what the officer did find:

> She found my pen and a pad of paper tucked inside my left boot.
> "And these?" she asked sternly.
> "Weapons," I replied.

The paperback conclusion shows Williams as a fighter rather than a victim, demonstrating her commitment to writing as activism.

One of the central questions of *An Unspoken Hunger: Stories from the Field* (1994) is, "Am I an activist or an artist?" Williams's answer is that she is both. Yet, she recognizes the tensions between the two, reconciling those tensions with a commitment to stay home, to write and fight for the land she loves. The essays are not all set in Utah—one takes place in the Serengeti Plains of Africa; another in Amarillo, Texas; one in Sitka, Alaska; one in New York City; another in Wyoming. Despite the various settings, though, Williams always makes reference to her home, the emotional and psychic lens through which she sees the rest of the world.

Dedicated to her nieces—Callie, Sara, and Diane, daughters of Ann and Steve Tempest—*An Unspoken Hunger* shows the influence of several members of Williams's family. In "The Architecture of a Soul" she writes of cataloguing shells with her grandmother Mimi; she points to shells as her inheritance and acknowledges that when she holds *Melongena corona* to her ear, she hears not only "the ocean's voice, but the whisperings of [her] beloved teacher." In "The Village Watchman," Williams writes of her Uncle Alan, who "reminds me of what it means to live and love with a broken heart; how nothing is sacred, how everything is sacred." Finally, in "A Patriot's Journal" Williams provides a complicated picture of her uncle, Senator Richard Tempest, a conservative Mormon Republican, who accompanied his daughter and Williams to a protest at a Nevada test site and said, "It was my generation who started this nuclear madness. Maybe it's up to my generation to stop it." Through portraits of family members and mentors, Williams demonstrates the multifaceted nature of inheritance.

This collection of eighteen essays also explores the questions "How do we engage in community?" and "How does a poetics of place translate into a politics of place?" A book about mentors, *An Unspoken Hunger* pays tribute to both people and places. In this volume Williams includes "A Eulogy for Edward Abbey"; an essay showing Georgia O'Keefe as trickster; a profile of writer and environmental activist Mardy Murie; and a piece dedicated to Wendell Berry. In describing the mentoring power of place, Williams describes Yellowstone National Park as a "Pansexual landscape," sees Africa through a beginner's eyes, and meets "Stone Creek Woman" on a trip down the Colorado River. Though some nature writers have been accused of not writing enough about people, Williams shows the interconnectedness of people and place, demonstrating the powerful mentoring force of both. Through lists, images, dreams, and a full range of feeling and response, Williams contemplates a hunger that cannot be satisfied by the material world and a politics fueled by places in need of preservation.

Dedicated to her husband, Brooke, *Desert Quartet: An Erotic Landscape* (1995) explores the question from *Red:* "If a sense of place can give rise to a politics of place, where might an erotics of place lead?" and also asks, "How might we make love to the land?" Accompanied by the paintings and drawings of Mary Frank, this short book is a poetic meditation on the four primal elements—Earth, Water, Fire, and Air. A different form of *Desert Quartet* was published a year earlier as "Elements of Love," sans the artwork, in four issues of the *New England Review.* Like the pieces in *Coyote's Canyon,* the differing versions of the story-essays in *Desert Quartet* demonstrate the fluid nature of genre in Williams's work. In "Elements of Love" the point of view shifts. While "Earth" is written from the first-person perspective, as it is for *Desert Quartet,* "Water" and "Fire" are written in third person. "Water" is about a man, and "Fire" is about a woman. The earlier version of "Air," though it also includes a first-person perspective, is more inclusive: the experience of "Air" is not solitary; "we" are present. The effect of *Desert Quartet,* which reads more as autobiographical essays rather than short stories, is in some ways more intimate and perhaps more feminist, but it moves away from the universality that "Elements of Love" suggests. Still, both versions, rhythmic and risky, powerfully enact an erotics of place, showing Williams's deep physical and emotional love for the Colorado Plateau.

In 1993 Williams, who was healing from the deaths of her mother and grandmother, traveled with her husband to Madrid, Spain. In the Prado Museum, she found Hieronymus Bosch's painting *El jardin de las delicias* (The Garden of Delights, circa 1500). She was familiar with "Paradise" and "Hell," two of the three panels of Bosch's triptych; her grandmother had hung prints of these panels over the bed Williams slept in when she visited. Williams had not, however, known that the middle panel, "The Garden of Earthly Delights," existed. She writes of seeing the middle panel for the first time:

> So little is hidden in the center panel, why was it hidden from me?
> The body.
> The body of the triptych.
> My body.

Leap (2000) was written out of Williams's experience of traveling in the landscape of Bosch's painting for seven years. She dedicates *Leap* to the men in her family: her father, John Henry Tempest III; her brothers, Stephen Dixon Tempest, Daniel Dixon Tempest, and William Henry Tempest; and her husband, Brooke Williams. In *Leap,* she explores the questions "What do I believe? At what cost?"

Divided into four sections, *Leap* functions as an interpretation of Bosch's painting, an investigation of faith and orthodoxy, an account of environmental destruction, a celebration of earthly delights, and a hope for spiritual and environmental renewal. The first section, "Paradise," takes readers into the left panel of Bosch's painting and into Williams's memories of childhood and her early understanding of the Mormon faith and her own beliefs. The second section, "Hell," includes disturbing newspaper clippings, descriptions of disease and environmental destruction, disconnection, dislocation, and pain. In a 2000 interview, while speaking of the section on "Hell," Williams points to the questions that guided her writing: "What does it mean to stand inside darkness? What does it mean to allow yourself to travel through Hell?" Section 3, "Earthly Delights," the longest section of the book, focuses on the center panel. This section is marked by dream, imagination, desire, color, vivid description, a sense of both connection with and disconnection from her spiritual roots, and Williams's claim that the "marriage between Heaven and Hell is Earth." In the final section, "Restoration," Williams describes the literal restoration of the painting and how its restorers see the process as spiritual. Restoration becomes a metaphor for Williams's own spiritual seeking and for her return home to Utah, to Paradox Basin, to a desert where she plants a garden.

Stylistically innovative, stream-of-consciousness, almost obsessive, this book defies generic categoriza-

For as far as I can see, the canyon country of southern Utah extends in all directions. No compass can orient me here, only a pledge to love and walk the terrifying distances before me. What I fear and desire most in this world is passion. I fear it because it promises to be spontaneous, out of my control, unnamed, beyond my reasonable self. I desire it because passion has color, like the landscape before me. It is not pale. It is not neutral. It reveals the backside of the heart.

—*from* RED

RED
PASSION AND PATIENCE IN THE DESERT
TERRY TEMPEST WILLIAMS

ISBN 0-375-42077-0 NATURE
52300

Dust jacket for Williams's 2001 book, in which she discusses her move to the Colorado plateau, a place she calls "holy to me" (Richland County Public Library)

tion; it includes fragments, lists, questions, labyrinthine sentences (some, hundreds of words long), one-sentence paragraphs, metaphors, similes, a poem in the shape of a DNA molecule, a print of a mushroom spore, song lyrics, and newspaper clippings. Williams moves from painting to memory to diatribe to historical fact, forsaking clear transitions for the power of association. Carefully researched, *Leap* also includes forty-seven pages of discursive notes and a long bibliography, as well as acknowledgments that help the reader trace Williams's influences. Through her writing and imagination, Williams enters into Bosch's painting, even into the mythology the painting suggests and revises; in doing so, she argues that there is no separation between internal and external landscapes.

Though Williams's other books were dedicated to members of her family, she writes her most recent book, *Red: Passion and Patience in the Desert,* for "The Coyote Clan and America's Redrock Wilderness." Without the artwork, *Red* includes the full texts of both *Coyote's Canyon* and *Desert Quartet,* as well as an introduction—"Homework"—that ties together the various texts, which were written over a period of more than a decade, and brings the political situation that informs her writing to the forefront. This book also includes a

section of newer essays (many previously published in literary journals) and a series of appendices—America's Redrock Wilderness Act, a map of America's Redrock Wilderness, a citizen's proposal, and a list of supporting organizations—that provide further context and information for political action.

In this book, Williams asks, "How are we to find our way toward conversation?" Her answer to this question is through story, but she does not stop there. She questions story: "How do the stories we tell about ourselves in relationship to place shape our perceptions of place?" In reflecting on the stories she will tell, Williams considers how she might speak a language that opens minds rather than closes them, remaining credible as she speaks from a place of love on behalf of the land she loves.

Like Williams's previous books, *Red* comprises a variety of genres and forms: stories, essays, poetry, journal entries, testimony, lists, song lyrics, and a letter about why she writes. She also pays tribute to mentors Aldo Leopold and Mary Hunter Austin. The themes remain the same, including the complicated intersections of family, religious heritage, and environmental commitment. And another theme emerges—slowness, patience. "To Be Taken" intertwines these themes in an especially powerful way. In this essay about "the slow art of revolutionary patience," Williams discusses her father's anger over the temporary shutdown of the Tempest family construction business because of the Endangered Species Act; she also tells of learning that her father and uncle had their own pet tortoise as children. She includes scientific information on the tortoise and reflects on its mythic significance. She writes of her relationship with her father, of her own choice not to have children (a choice unacceptable to some Mormon leaders), of speaking to the desert tortoise, of patiently waiting for answers. This essay, like many of her others, is organized associationally and includes many layers of meaning. *Red* was released into a changed world on 11 September 2001, and Williams spent much of her book tour listening to her audience, hearing their stories of pain and loss even as she called for "Wild Mercy," telling audiences from Oregon to New York, "Wilderness lives by . . . grace. Wild mercy is in our hands."

Throughout her life and career, Terry Tempest Williams has consistently demonstrated a passion for language, for questions, and for the land and people she loves. She writes out of that sense of love and passion, believing as she writes at the end of *Red*, "One day, this landscape will take the language out of me." The passion has led her to a commitment to home and local community. She is on the advisory boards of several environmental organizations and especially involved with the Southern Utah Wilderness Alliance, an organization committed to seeing the Redrock Wilderness Act (2001) passed. Whether she is fighting against the opening of southern Utah lands to commercial development, questioning the patriarchal nature of some tenets of Mormonism, or pushing the bounds of genre and traditional grammar, Williams's writing confronts both political and religious orthodoxy.

Interviews:

Edward Lueders, "Landscape, People, and Place: Robert Finch and Terry Tempest Williams," in *Writing Natural History: Dialogues with Authors: Barry Lopez and Edward O. Wilson, Robert Finch and Terry Tempest Williams, Gary Paul Nabhan and Ann Zwinger, Paul Brooks and Edward Lueders,* edited by Lueders (Salt Lake City: University of Utah Press, 1989), pp. 37–65;

David Petersen, "Memory Is the Only Way Home: A Conversational Interview with Terry Tempest Williams," *Bloomsbury Review,* 11 (December 1991): 8–9;

Mickey Pearlman, *Listen to Their Voices: Twenty Interviews with Women Who Write* (Boston & New York: Houghton Mifflin, 1993), pp. 121–133;

Scott London, "The Politics of Place: An Interview with Terry Tempest Williams," *Insight & Outlook* <http://www.scottlondon.com/insight/scripts/ttw.html>;

Ona Siporin, "Terry Tempest Williams and Ona Siporin: A Conversation," *Western American Literature,* 31, no. 2 (1996): 99–113;

Jocelyn Bartkevicius and Mary Hussman, "A Conversation with Terry Tempest Williams," *Iowa Review,* 27 (Spring 1997): 1–23;

Susie Caldwell, "Lighting the Match," *Whole Terrain* (2000–2001): 48–51;

David Thomas Sumner, "Testimony, Refuge, and a Sense of Place–A Conversation with Terry Tempest Williams," *Weber Studies,* 19, no. 3 (Spring/Summer 2002).

References:

Karla Armbruster, "Rewriting a Genealogy with the Earth: Women and Nature in the Works of Terry Tempest Williams," *Southwestern American Literature,* 22 (1995): 209–220;

Catherine S. Blake, "Mormon Author Draws Inspiration from Land and Life," *Los Angeles Times,* 9 December 2001, p. B11;

Laura L. Bush, "Terry Tempest Williams's *Refuge:* Sentimentality and Separation," *Dialogue: A Journal of Mormon Thought,* 28 (Fall 1995): 147–160;

Cassandra Kircher, "Rethinking Dichotomies in Terry Tempest Williams's *Refuge,*" *Interdisciplinary Studies in Literature and Environment,* 3, no. 1 (Summer 1996): 97–113;

Susan Reed and Cathy Free, "Friend of the Earth," *People,* 46 (15 July 1996): 145–149.

Papers:

Terry Tempest Williams's papers are currently housed at the University of Utah, Salt Lake City.

Ann Zwinger

(12 March 1925 –   )

Susan M. Lucas
University of Nevada at Reno

BOOKS: *Beyond the Aspen Grove* (New York: Random House, 1970);

Land above the Trees: A Guide to American Alpine Tundra, by Zwinger and Beatrice E. Willard, preface by Willard (New York: Harper & Row, 1972);

Run, River, Run: A Naturalist's Journey Down One of the Great Rivers of the West (New York: Harper & Row, 1975);

Wind in the Rock: The Canyonlands of Southeastern Utah (New York: Harper & Row, 1978);

A Conscious Stillness: Two Naturalists on Thoreau's Rivers, by Zwinger and Edwin Way Teale (New York: Harper & Row, 1982);

A Desert Country near the Sea: A Natural History of the Cape Region of Baja California (New York: Harper & Row, 1983);

Colorado II, text and drawings by Zwinger, photographs by David Muench (Portland, Ore.: Graphic Arts Center, 1987);

The Mysterious Lands: An Award-Winning Naturalist Explores the Four Great Deserts of the Southwest (New York: Dutton, 1989);

Utah, text by Zwinger, photographs by Muench (Portland, Ore.: Graphic Arts Center, 1990);

Aspen: Blazon of the High Country, text by Zwinger, photographs by Barbara Sparks (Salt Lake City: Peregrine Smith, 1991);

Downcanyon: A Naturalist Explores the Colorado River through the Grand Canyon (Tucson: University of Arizona Press, 1995);

Yosemite: Valley of Thunder, text by Zwinger, photographs by Kathleen N. Cook (San Francisco: HarperCollins, 1996);

The Nearsighted Naturalist (Tucson: University of Arizona Press, 1998);

Shaped by Wind and Water: Reflections of a Naturalist, Credo Series (Minneapolis: Milkweed, 2000).

Edition: *Beyond the Aspen Grove,* with a new preface by Zwinger (Tucson: University of Arizona Press, 1988).

Ann Zwinger (from the dust jacket for Downcanyon, *1995)*

PRODUCED SCRIPTS: "Visions of Nature: Ann Zwinger," television, Channel 6 (Denver), 1994;

Interview and reading by Zwinger from *Downcanyon,* radio, *Eco-Talk,* National Public Radio, 12 January 1996;

Reading by Zwinger from *Downcanyon,* radio, *The Environment Show,* National Public Radio, 16 April 1996.

RECORDINGS: *The Mysterious Lands,* read by Zwinger, NorthWord Audio, 1993;

Run, River, Run, read by Zwinger, NorthWord Audio, 1993;

Upcanyon, Downriver: A Naturalist's Journeys, read by Zwinger, NorthWord Audio, 1993.

OTHER: Cynthia Bennet, *Lightfall and Time,* introduction by Zwinger (Flagstaff, Ariz.: Grand Canyon Natural History Association & Northland, 1986);

Joseph Wood Krutch, *The Forgotten Peninsula,* introduction by Zwinger (Tucson: University of Arizona Press, 1986);

John Xántus, *John Xántus: The Fort Tejon Letters, 1857–1859,* edited by Zwinger (Tucson: University of Arizona Press, 1986);

Xántus, *Xántus: The Letters of John Xántus to Spencer Fullerton Baird from San Francisco and Cabo San Lucas, 1859–1861,* edited by Zwinger, Baja California Travel Series (Los Angeles: Dawson's Book Shop, 1986);

Cathy Johnson, *The Local Wilderness: Observing Neighborhood Nature through an Artist's Eye,* introduction by Zwinger (New York: Prentice Hall, 1987);

Rachel Carson, *The Sea Around Us,* introduction by Zwinger (New York: Oxford University Press, 1989);

"Of Red-Tailed Hawks and Black-Tailed Gnatcatchers," *The Norton Book of Nature Writing,* edited by Robert Finch and John Elder (New York: Norton, 1990), pp. 642–653;

Janet LeCompte, *Pueblo, Hardscrabble, Greenhorn,* introduction by Zwinger (Norman: University of Oklahoma Press, 1990);

"A Rinse in the River," in *Sisters of the Earth,* edited by Lorraine Anderson (New York: Vintage, 1991), pp. 47–49;

"Waking Up to Eternity," in *The Desert Reader,* edited by Peter Wild (Salt Lake City: University of Utah Press, 1991), pp. 206–215;

Robert C. Euler and Frank Tikalsky, *The Grand Canyon: Intimate Views,* introduction by Zwinger (Tucson: University of Arizona Press, 1992);

Fred Hirschmann, *America,* introduction by Zwinger (Portland, Ore.: Graphic Arts Center, 1994);

"Space and Place," in *Open Spaces, City Places,* edited by Judy Nolte Temple (Tucson: University of Arizona Press, 1994), pp. 61–69;

Writing the Western Landscape: Mary Austin and John Muir, edited by Zwinger (Boston: Beacon, 1994);

Women in Wilderness: Writings and Photographs, edited by Zwinger and Susan Zwinger (San Diego: Harcourt Brace, 1995);

Elizabeth Ferber and others, *The Walker's Companion,* introduction by Zwinger (New York: Nature Company/Time-Life Books, 1995);

"Thighbone of a Mouse," in *Testimony: Writers of the West Speak On Behalf of Utah Wilderness,* compiled by Stephen Trimble and Terry Tempest Williams (Minneapolis: Milkweed, 1995), pp. 32–33;

David Peterson, *The Nearby Faraway,* introduction by Zwinger (Boulder, Colo.: Johnson Books, 1997);

Tom Wessels, *Reading the Forested Landscape,* foreword by Zwinger (Woodstock, Vt.: Countryman, 1997);

Edwin Way Teale, *A Naturalist Buys an Old Farm,* introduction by Zwinger (Storrs: University of Connecticut Press, 1998);

David Muench, *Portrait of Utah,* essay by Zwinger (Portland, Ore.: Graphic Arts Center, 1999);

Clare Walker Leslie, John Tallmadge, and Tom Wessels, *Into the Field: A Guide to Locally Focused Teaching,* Nature Literacy Series 3, foreword by Zwinger (Great Barrington, Mass.: Orion Society, 1999);

Gordon Miller, ed., *Traces of Amphibians: A Collection of Classic Natural History,* epilogue by Zwinger (Washington, D.C.: Island, 2000);

Anthony E. Cook, *Fall Colors across North America,* essay by Zwinger (Portland, Ore.: Graphic Arts Center, 2001).

SELECTED PERIODICAL PUBLICATION–UNCOLLECTED: "A Naturalist's Legacy of Caring," *Whole Terrain* (1999/2000): 10–14.

In 1970 *Vogue* profiled several notable Coloradans, including Ann Zwinger, an unknown nature writer who had just published her first book, *Beyond the Aspen Grove* (1970). In a black-and-white photograph, Zwinger smiles among Canadian reed grass near the lake at "Constant Friendship," the forty acres she and her family own in the mountains of Colorado. The reviewer describes *Beyond the Aspen Grove* as "a discriminating, attracting book–part nature study, part adventure, all Colorado love song" and portrays the author as artist and writer, wife and mother, and Easterner turned Western conservationist. The energetic figure of Zwinger that emerges from this biographical sketch characterizes her career; at the time of this interview she was already completing a second book and was planning "to write, from experience, a cookbook for woodstoves." Two years later Zwinger and Beatrice E. Willard published *Land above the Trees: A Guide to American Alpine Tundra* (1972), but she has never produced the cookbook for woodstoves. Instead, Zwinger has gone on to publish more than a dozen books of natural history and many

Zwinger in a canyon of the Grand Gulch Plateau (photograph by John Running; from the dust jacket for Wind in the Rock, *1978)*

thought" until her friend later explained Rodell's stature in the publishing industry. Zwinger decided to contact Rodell and, at the age of forty-three, began a process that ultimately changed her life.

Zwinger's transformation from housewife to naturalist may seem an unlikely manifestation. Her life followed a circuitous route from art history to natural history; yet, the origins of her appreciation for nature and attention to detail are evident from childhood. Born 12 March 1925 in Muncie, Indiana, Ann Haymond grew up along the north bank of the White River. In her essay "Remembering Indiana" from *The Nearsighted Naturalist* (1998), she describes her father, William Thomas Haymond, as "a successful and very well-loved attorney" who "preferred to raise his children in a peaceful countryside" far from the chaos in a big city. Though her mother, Helen Louise Glass Haymond, was primarily a housewife, she also painted china professionally and, according to Scott Slovic, "passed along her love of the arts to her daughters." Ann had an older sister, Jane, born in 1910, who died in 1938 of heart complications resulting from a childhood illness.

Zwinger credits both of her parents with instilling in her certain sensibilities and skills that distinguish her work. In the preface to *Beyond the Aspen Grove,* Zwinger traces her talent as an illustrator to her mother, who ensured that she have drawing lessons, and she traces the dedication to her profession and love of detail to her father's "meticulous mind." Zwinger's mother played a primary role in introducing the younger of her two daughters to the natural world. In "Remembering Indiana" Zwinger recalls watching her mother cultivate gardens and accompanying her on canoeing excursions to watch the sunset or the building up of an oncoming storm.

Both Ann and her sister enjoyed the privilege of higher education. Jane studied music at the University of Michigan and later at the Cincinnati Conservatory of Music, while Ann went on to study art history at Wellesley College from 1942 to 1946. Graduating with honors, she returned to her home state and began pursuing an M.A. in art history at Indiana University. During this time she had her first child, Susan, in 1947. Though the marriage did not last, she finished her degree in 1950 and moved with her daughter to Massachusetts to teach art history at Smith College.

The following year Ann met the man who would become her second husband, United States Air Force pilot Captain Herman H. Zwinger. After a brief courtship, he spent a year stationed in Saudi Arabia, and she remained in the United States, working toward a doctorate in art history at Radcliffe College. The two married on 18 June 1952 after Herman Zwinger returned, and they soon moved to West Palm Beach, Florida, for his next post. Though Zwinger finished her residence

articles, making her one of the most prolific contemporary American nature writers.

Zwinger's entrance into the field of nature writing did not result from a lifelong goal. In *Shaped by Wind and Water: Reflections of a Naturalist* (2000), Zwinger admits, "I came to my current relationship with the natural world purely by chance." She has told this story many times in interviews and essays. In the spring of 1967 she agreed to help a friend entertain a visitor by driving them to Constant Friendship; she was unaware, however, that she was spending the day with Rachel Carson's close friend and literary executor, Marie Rodell. As a housewife, Zwinger had no plans to secure a book contract, much less launch a career in nature writing. During the tour, Zwinger explained what she could about the environment, sharing the sketches and botanical notes she had been making to learn the area. Zwinger recalls that "Marie asked out of the blue, 'Why don't you write a book on Colorado ecology?'" Zwinger ignored the suggestion as "too outrageous a

requirements for a Ph.D., the move afforded her no opportunities to complete her doctoral thesis. The next eight years brought the births of two more children—Jane in 1954 and Sara in 1956—and three major moves.

After living in Florida, Arkansas, and Kansas City, the Zwingers settled in Colorado Springs in 1960 for Herman Zwinger's final post. Throughout the challenges of moving and motherhood, Ann remained intellectually active and a strong presence in the lives of her daughters. According to Slovic, Zwinger led discussions in art history for the American Association of University Women in Florida, volunteered with the local Girl Scouts in Arkansas, and taught adult education classes at the University of Kansas City and art at the Benet Hill Academy in Colorado. In 1963 the Zwingers purchased forty acres in the Colorado Rocky Mountains that became a retreat for the family and the literal foundation of Zwinger's career as a nature writer. She describes and celebrates this landscape in *Beyond the Aspen Grove*.

Concerned with the particulars of place, *Beyond the Aspen Grove* recounts the Zwingers' discovery and exploration of the mountain retreat her eldest daughter named Constant Friendship. Rather than follow a traditional seasonal arrangement in her narrative, Zwinger describes the land according to its physical features. Chapter 1 recalls the family's search for this place, while the other chapters provide detailed examinations of the lake, streams, meadows, and forests. Zwinger serves as guide and incorporates brief anecdotes of her family enjoying themselves at Constant Friendship, but the focus of the book remains on the natural world. Weaving together personal observation with research, Zwinger shows the relationships among the varieties of plant, animal, and insect species that populate this montane ecosystem.

With this book Zwinger established patterns that came to characterize her work—an unobtrusive narrator, a combination of research and fieldwork, and a measured environmentalism. *Beyond the Aspen Grove* includes a glossary, index, selected references, and her own illustrations of flora and fauna. In his biographical essay of Zwinger in *American Nature Writers* (1996), Peter Wild observes that Zwinger's "first book clearly bears signs of a writing voice searching for its tenor as well as indications of its mature potential." Zwinger's ability to explain scientific information to the layperson was evident from the beginning, and this didactic approach has remained a strong element throughout her work.

Beyond the Aspen Grove brought Zwinger into the field of nature writing and into the acquaintance of Beatrice E. Willard, who checked the ecological information of the book. Together they published *Land above the Trees: A Guide to American Alpine Tundra* (1972). In the preface Willard describes the audience for this scientific book as the "interested novice." *Land above the Trees* takes readers to seven alpine tundra sites in the continental United States, revealing the breadth of life and activity that occurs above the timberline. Though even less personal than her first book, *Land above the Trees* portrays Zwinger in the field, researching and reporting on species, habitat, and the environmental significance of alpine ecosystems. Zwinger's illustrations supplement the text.

Zwinger honed her skills as a researcher and writer with these first two books and presented a more sophisticated style in *Run, River, Run: A Naturalist's Journey Down One of the Great Rivers of the West* (1975). Zwinger follows all 730 miles of the Green River from its source in the Wind River Range of Wyoming, through Utah, and on to its confluence with the Colorado River. The narrative is geographically continuous, although her experience of the Green River was not; in the first chapter, Zwinger explains that the weather makes a trip from one end to the other "impossible." Nevertheless, Zwinger has "been on every inch of the River at least once." She has walked its banks, driven alongside, flown overhead with her husband, and canoed and rafted its challenging waters. *Run, River, Run* paints a portrait of the natural and human history of the Green River with detailed personal observations, insights from previous explorers and inhabitants, and anecdotes of her own adventures.

For *Run, River, Run* Zwinger received the John Burroughs Memorial Association Award and the Friends of American Writers Award for nonfiction in 1976. These accolades brought her recognition, enlarging her circle of friends and colleagues to include such renowned figures as Edward Abbey and Edwin Way Teale. For Zwinger, *Run, River, Run* remains an important work. In an interview with Stephen Trimble, she refers to the experience of research and writing the book as a "real passage" in her evolution as a naturalist and solitary traveler. Her confidence with outdoor excursions plays out in her next book, *Wind in the Rock: The Canyonlands of Southeastern Utah* (1978). Culminating with a solo backpack on Honaker Trail, the book depicts five other hikes that Zwinger takes with various companions, ranging from trail guides to her daughters Susan and Sara.

Zwinger's formula is consistent throughout these books: she functions as guide, taking readers through the natural and cultural history of the region and constantly showing them how to look at the landscape. *Wind in the Rock* strikes more of a balance between scientific information and Zwinger's personal experience than do her earlier books; this book also offers what is perhaps her most explicit argument for wilderness preservation in all of her writing. *Wind in the Rock* celebrates the rigors of walking the canyon lands and glorifies the freedom that comes with wilderness travel. Never one to hide the challenges of backpacking or the discomfort

Dust jacket for Zwinger's 1975 book, which describes the 730 miles of the Green River from its source to its confluence with the Colorado River (Richland County Public Library)

that can accompany camping, Zwinger wears her bug bites, bruised shins, sunburn, and swollen extremities as badges of honor. In the introduction, she reflects upon the salutary effects of traveling in the canyon lands, writing "I feel ablaze with life. I suspect that the canyons give me an intensified sense of living partly because I not only face the basics of living and survival, but carry them on my back. And in my head. And this intense personal responsibility gives me an overwhelming sense of freedom I know nowhere else."

Shifting her attention from western to eastern landscapes, Zwinger began a book with Edwin Way Teale, examining the Sudbury, Assabet, and Concord Rivers in Massachusetts—three waterways that were important in the life and writing of Henry David Thoreau. Zwinger and Teale planned a three-part structure for the book that modeled the flow of the rivers: since the Sudbury and Assabet merge to form the Concord, each writer intended to explore one of the first two rivers; then together they would write the Concord section. In the preface Zwinger writes, "Before Edwin's death, we had canoed or walked most of each other's rivers at one time or another, together or separately, and had canoed the part of the Concord we wished to cover." Teale died in 1980 before the book was finished, leaving Zwinger to complete the project with the help of Teale's wife, Nellie. Though the Concord sec-

tion was never written, *A Conscious Stillness: Two Naturalists on Thoreau's Rivers* (1982) offers intimate accounts of both the Sudbury and the Assabet Rivers. The new structure presents both Zwinger's and Teale's observations of each river within every chapter, alternating between the easterner's and the westerner's impressions from canoeing the waters, walking the banks, researching local histories, and talking with residents.

The same year *A Conscious Stillness* was published, Zwinger began the first of two terms as president of the Thoreau Society. Still, Zwinger insists that she is no Thoreauvian and explains in an interview with Paul Rea that the book is not a tribute to Thoreau. Rather, *A Conscious Stillness* demonstrates how one learns place, and if there is a tribute in the book, it is Zwinger's preface, in which she remembers her friendship with Teale and his contribution to natural history. For this self-taught naturalist, collaborating with one of the major figures of twentieth-century natural history validated her work and confirmed her status in the field.

Zwinger conceptualizes natural history as a way of recording home, not just place. In interviews and essays she often comments on her ability to find a sense of comfort anywhere she travels by reading the details of the landscape. Her next book, *A Desert Country near the Sea: A Natural History of the Cape Region of Baja California* (1983), serves Zwinger's sense of home in multiple ways. Baja

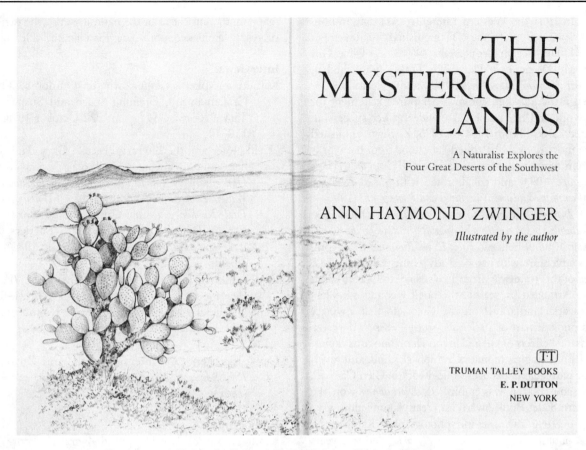

THE
MYSTERIOUS
LANDS

A Naturalist Explores the
Four Great Deserts of the Southwest

ANN HAYMOND ZWINGER

Illustrated by the author

T·T
TRUMAN TALLEY BOOKS
E. P. DUTTON
NEW YORK

*Frontispiece and title page for Zwinger's 1989 description of life in the Chihuahuan, Sonoran,
Mojave, and Great Basin Deserts (Richland County Public Library)*

becomes familiar as she plots the relationships among species and terrain, but this arid seascape also holds special significance for her family. In the introduction, Zwinger recalls their initial journey to the cape in 1970 as an effort to resist "the mania of Christmas and its pressures" in favor of family time. Zwinger's husband and daughters figure more prominently than usual in this narrative as they are integral to her sense of this coastal region.

A Desert Country near the Sea draws from years of sojourning in this landscape that others such as Joseph Wood Krutch and John Steinbeck also found infinitely fascinating. Zwinger's Baja includes many perspectives, ranging from those of her family and previous travelers to those of native inhabitants. This book includes Herman Zwinger's photographs and her sketches, along with other evidence of her research in notes and a list of plants, birds, mammals, reptiles, and amphibians. Ever the scholar, her work on Baja introduced her to the life and writings of John Xántus, a Hungarian immigrant, who was perhaps the most important species collector in the Baja area. She went on to edit two volumes of his correspondence, both of which appeared in 1986—*John Xántus: The Fort Tejon Letters, 1857–1859* and *Xántus: The*

Letters of John Xántus to Spencer Fullerton Baird from San Francisco and Cabo San Lucas, 1859–1861.

Zwinger remained busy throughout the 1980s, writing articles for the magazines *Audubon, Antaeus,* and *Orion;* her calendar was full with public lectures and readings as well as honorary teaching positions at schools around the country. In 1987 Zwinger and David Muench published *Colorado II,* a large-format book showcasing his photographs and her writing; in 1990 they teamed up again to publish *Utah.*

With *The Mysterious Lands: An Award-Winning Naturalist Explores the Four Great Deserts of the Southwest* (1989), Zwinger adds to the work of Krutch, Abbey, and Mary Austin in challenging the notion of the desert as a lifeless, uninteresting place. This ambitious project provides detailed renderings of the Chihuahuan, Sonoran, Mojave, and Great Basin Deserts. *The Mysterious Lands* represents Zwinger as an established naturalist, taking solo trips as well as companion journeys into this harsh territory. She travels with her husband, her daughter Susan, and also with other prominent naturalists and nature writers, such as Gary Paul Nabhan, Charles Bowden, and Terry Tempest Williams.

In 1991 the Western Literature Association honored Zwinger with the Distinguished Achievement Award. Her acceptance speech, "What's a Nice Girl Like Me Doing in a Place like This?" (published in *Western American Literature* in 1992 and collected in *The Nearsighted Naturalist*), conveys her pure excitement for fieldwork and her perpetual wonder at her successful, belated career. From 1994 to 1995, Zwinger published three more books. She edited selections from the works of John Muir and Mary Austin for *Writing the Western Landscape* (1994) and collaborated with Susan Zwinger on *Women in Wilderness: Writings and Photographs* (1995).

Zwinger returned to riverscapes with *Downcanyon: A Naturalist Explores the Colorado River through the Grand Canyon* (1995). Similar to *Run, River, Run,* this work combines adventure with nature study as she travels all 278.5 miles of this waterway from Lee's Ferry to Grand Wash Fault. Arranged by season, the book recounts six years of research and travel on the Colorado that Zwinger undertook as part of a scientific study to assess the environmental effects of Glen Canyon Dam. She runs rapids, counts bald eagles, monitors humpback chub, and revels in the particular challenges of fieldwork in Glen Canyon. The same year it was published, *Downcanyon* won the Western States Book Award for creative nonfiction.

In 1996 Zwinger and photographer Kathleen N. Cook published *Yosemite: Valley of Thunder,* and two years later Zwinger came out with *The Nearsighted Naturalist* (1998), a collection of essays from more than two decades of writing. Composed mostly of previously published essays from magazines, this collection traces Zwinger's ever-widening sense of home from Indiana, to Colorado, to Baja, and to as far away as the Yellow River in China.

Throughout her career, Zwinger has always focused more on nature than on her own personal experience in her writing, but *Shaped by Wind and Water: Reflections of a Naturalist* (2000) finds her exploring "the rivers of the mind," territory she believes to be "much more dangerous than being pummeled by rapids or actual rivers." *Shaped by Wind and Water* reiterates many of the same claims she made in earlier essays and interviews regarding her sense of home, the value of natural history, and the importance of drawing to her observations and writing. The biographical information she shares, combined with Slovic's thoughtful profile of her, offers a deeper, more personal look into Zwinger's life and work.

In "A Naturalist's Legacy of Caring," Zwinger explains that "more than anything I hope to leave trails by which every person can find a binding relationship to the natural world." Ann Zwinger's legacy grows out of her infinite curiosity to know the world and her willingness to share her findings with others. Hers is a voice linking the scientific with the lay community. In writing natural history Zwinger teaches readers how to see. By mapping the intricacies of the natural world, she demonstrates the limitless opportunities for a lifetime of learning.

Interviews:

Katherine Millett, "Ann Zwinger Outdoors: Quiet Craftsmanship, Creating Space and Suspending Time," *Colorado Springs Sun,* 22 October 1978, pp. 1, 8–10;

"Field Notes and the Literary Process: Gary Paul Nabhan and Ann Zwinger," in *Writing Natural History: Dialogues with Authors: Barry Lopez and Edward O. Wilson, Robert Finch and Terry Tempest Williams, Gary Paul Nabhan and Ann Zwinger, Paul Brooks and Edward Lueders,* edited by Edward Lueders (Salt Lake City: University of Utah Press, 1989), pp. 70–90;

Paul Rea, "An Interview with Ann Zwinger," *Western American Literature,* 24, no. 1 (May 1989): 21–36;

Gene Birkhead, "National Book Award Nominee 'Surprised,'" *Colorado Springs Sun,* 5 April 1993, pp. 11–12;

Cassie Kircher, "An Interview with Ann Zwinger," *ISLE: Interdisciplinary Studies in Literature and Environment,* 1, no. 2 (Fall 1993): 123–132.

Bibliography:

"Bibliography of Ann Haymond Zwinger's Work," in *Shaped by Wind and Water: Reflections of a Naturalist,* by Ann Zwinger (Minneapolis: Milkweed, 2000), pp. 113–152.

Biography:

Peter Wild, *Ann Zwinger* (Boise: Boise State University Press, 1993).

References:

"Catch Colorado," *Vogue,* 156, no. 9 (November 1970): 124;

Scott Slovic, "Ann Haymond Zwinger: A Portrait," in *Shaped by Wind and Water: Reflections of a Naturalist,* by Ann Zwinger (Minneapolis: Milkweed, 2000), pp. 87–111;

Stephen Trimble, "The Naturalist's Trance," *Words from the Land: Encounters with Natural History Writing,* edited by Trimble (Salt Lake City: Peregrine Smith, 1989), pp. 2–29;

Peter Wild, "Ann Zwinger," in *American Nature Writers,* edited by John Elder, volume 2 (New York: Scribners, 1996), pp. 989–1001.

Papers:

Ann Zwinger has donated all of her papers to the Tutt Library at Colorado College, where she has conducted research and taught for many years.

Checklist of Further Readings

Adams, Agatha Boyd. *Nature Writers in the United States*. Chapel Hill, N.C.: University of North Carolina Press, 1944.

Adams, Cass, ed. *The Soul Unearthed: Celebrating Wildness and Personal Renewal through Nature*. New York: Putnam, 1996.

Adamson, Joni. *American Indian Literature, Environmental Justice, and Ecocriticism*. Tucson: University of Arizona Press, 2001.

Albanese, Catherine. *Nature Religion in America: From the Algonkian Indians to the New Age*. Chicago: University of Chicago Press, 1990.

Allister, Mark. *Refiguring the Map of Sorrow: Nature Writing and Autobiography*. Charlottesville: University Press of Virginia, 2001.

Armbruster, Karla, and Kathleen Wallace, eds. *Beyond Nature Writing: Expanding the Boundaries of Ecocriticism*. Charlottesville: University Press of Virginia, 2001.

Ballowe, James. "Loving the World: Nature Writers/Writing," *North Dakota Quarterly*, 60 (Summer 1992): 72–79.

Bateson, Gregory. *Mind and Nature: A Necessary Unity*. New York: Bantam, 1979.

Belsey, Catherine. *Critical Practice*. London: Methuen, 1980.

Bennett, Michael, and David Teague, eds. *The Nature of Cities: Ecocriticism and Urban Environments*. Tucson: University of Arizona Press, 1999.

Bercovitch, Sacvan. *The American Jeremiad*. Madison: University of Wisconsin Press, 1978.

Bercovitch. *The Puritan Origins of the American Self*. New Haven: Yale University Press, 1975.

Bercovitch, ed. *The Cambridge History of American Literature*, 4 volumes. Cambridge: Cambridge University Press, 1994–2002.

Bigwood, Carol. *Earth Muse: Feminism, Nature, and Art*. Philadelphia: Temple University Press, 1993.

Bramwell, Anna. *Ecology in the Twentieth Century: A History*. New Haven: Yale University Press, 1989.

Branch, Michael P., Rochelle Johnson, Daniel Patterson, and Scott Slovic, eds. *Reading the Earth: New Directions in the Study of Literature and the Environment*. Moscow: University of Idaho Press, 1999.

Brooks, Paul. *Speaking for Nature: How Literary Naturalists from Henry Thoreau to Rachel Carson Have Shaped America*. San Francisco: Sierra Club, 1980.

Brooks, Van Wyck. *The Flowering of New England, 1815–1865*. New York: Dutton, 1936.

Bryant, Paul T. "Nature as Picture/Nature as Milieu," *CEA-Critic,* 54, no. 1 (Fall 1991): 22–34.

Buell, Lawrence. "The Ecocritical Insurgency," *New Literary History,* 30, no. 3 (Summer 1999): 699–712.

Buell. "Environment and the Literary Landscape," *Chronicle of Higher Education,* 47, no. 38 (1 June 2001): B15.

Buell. *The Environmental Imagination: Thoreau, Nature Writing, and the Formation of American Culture.* Cambridge, Mass.: Harvard University Press, 1995.

Buell. *New England Literary Culture from Revolution through Renaissance.* New York: Cambridge University Press, 1986.

Buell. *Writing for an Endangered World: Literature, Culture, and the Environment in the U.S. and Beyond.* Cambridge, Mass.: Harvard University Press, 2001.

Burton, Katherine. *Paradise Planters: The Story of Brook Farm.* London: Longmans, Green, 1939.

Callicott, J. Baird. "Hume's Is/Ought Dichotomy and the Relation of Ecology to Leopold's Land Ethic," *Environmental Ethics,* 4 (1982): 163–174.

Callicott and Roger T. Ames, eds. *Nature in Asian Traditions of Thought.* Albany: State University of New York Press, 1989.

Cartmill, Matt. *A View to a Death in the Morning: Hunting and Nature through History.* Cambridge, Mass.: Harvard University Press, 1993.

Cason, Jacqueline J. "Nature Writer as Storyteller: The Nature Essay as a Literary Genre," *CEA-Critic,* 54, no. 1 (Fall 1991): 12–18.

Clemmons, Linda M. "'Nature Was Her Lady's Book': Ladies' Magazines, American Indians, and Gender, 1820–1859," *American Periodicals,* 5 (1995): 40–58.

Clough, Wilson O. *The Necessary Earth; Nature and Solitude in American Literature.* Austin: University of Texas Press, 1964.

Coates, Peter. *Nature: Western Attitudes since Ancient Times.* Berkeley: University of California Press, 1998.

Conlogue, William. *Working the Garden: American Writers and the Industrialization of Agriculture.* Chapel Hill: University of North Carolina Press, 2001.

Cooley, John, ed. *Earthly Words: Essays on Contemporary American Nature and Environmental Writers.* Ann Arbor: University of Michigan Press, 1994.

Cotgrove, Stephen. *Catastrophe or Cornucopia.* Chicester, U.K.: John Wiley, 1982.

Cowley, Malcolm. "Naturalism in American Literature," reprinted in *Evolutionary Thought in America,* edited by Stow Persons. New York: George Braziller, 1956.

Cronon, William. "A Place for Stories: Nature, History, and Narrative," *Journal of American History* (1992): 1346–1347.

Cronon, ed. *Nature Writings.* New York: Library of America, 1997.

Daniels, Stephen. *Fields of Vision: Landscape Imagery and National Identity in England and the United States.* Princeton, N.J.: Princeton University Press, 1993.

Dean, John. "The Uses of Wilderness in American Science Fiction," *Science Fiction Studies,* 9, no. 1 (March 1982): 68–81.

Denall, Bill, and George Sessions. *Deep Ecology.* Salt Lake City: Gibbs Smith, 1985.

Dixon, Melvin. *Ride Out the Wilderness: Geography and Identity in Afro-American Literature.* Urbana: University of Illinois Press, 1987.

Dunsmore, Roger. "Earth's Mind," *Studies in American Indian Literature,* 10 (Fall 1986): 187–202.

Edwards, Thomas S., and Elizabeth A. DeWolfe, eds. *Such News of the Land: U. S. Women Nature Writers.* Hanover, N.H.: University Press of New England, 2001.

Ekrich, Arthur A. Jr. *Man and Nature in America.* New York: Columbia University Press, 1963.

Elder, John, ed. *American Nature Writers,* 2 volumes. New York: Scribners, 1996.

Elgin, Don D. *The Comedy of the Fantastic: Ecological Perspectives on the Fantasy Novel.* Westport, Conn.: Greenwood Press, 1985.

Elgin. "What is Literary Ecology?" *Humanities in the South: Newsletter of the Southern Humanities Council,* 57 (Spring 1983): 7–9.

Elliot, Emory, ed. *Columbia Literary History of the United States.* New York: Columbia University Press, 1988.

Finch, Robert, and Elder, eds. *The Norton Book of Nature Writing.* New York: Norton, 1990.

Fitter, Chris. *Poetry, Space, Landscape: Toward a New Theory.* New York: Cambridge University Press, 1995.

Foerster, Norman. *Nature in American Literature: Studies in the Modern View of Nature.* New York: Russell & Russell, 1923.

Foster, Edward Halsey. *The Civilized Wilderness: Backgrounds to American Romantic Literature, 1817–1860.* New York: Free Press, 1875.

Fowles, John. "Seeing Nature Whole," *Harper's,* 259 (November 1979): 66.

Francis, Richard. *Transcendental Utopias: Individual and Community at Brook Farm, Fruitlands, and Walden.* Ithaca, N.Y.: Cornell University Press, 1997.

Franklin, Wayne. *Discoverers, Explorers, Settlers: The Diligent Writers of Early America.* Chicago: University of Chicago Press, 1979.

Franklin and Michael Steiner. *Mapping American Culture.* Iowa City: University of Iowa Press, 1992.

Fritzell, Peter. *Nature Writing and America: Essays upon a Cultural Type.* Ames: Iowa State University Press, 1990.

Frothingham, Octavius Brooks. *Transcendentalism in New England: A History.* New York: Putnam, 1876.

Fussell, Edwin. *Frontier: American Literature and the American West.* Princeton, N.J.: Princeton University Press, 1965.

Gangewere, Robert J., ed. *The Exploited Eden: Literature on the American Environment.* New York: Harper & Row, 1972.

Glotfelty, Cheryll, and Harold Fromm, eds. *The Ecocriticism Reader: Landmarks in Literary Ecology.* Athens: University of Georgia Press, 1996.

Hall, Dewey W. "From Edwards to Emerson: A Study of the Teleology of Nature," in *Early Protestantism and American Culture,* edited by Michael Schuldiner. Lewiston, N.Y.: Edwin Mellen Press, 1995.

Halprin, Lawrence. "Nature into Landscape into Art," in *Landscape in America,* edited by George F. Thompson and Charles E. Little. Austin: University of Texas Press, 1995, pp. 241–250.

Harris, Wendell V. "Toward an Ecological Criticism: Contextual Versus Unconditional Literary Theory," *College English,* 48, no. 2 (February 1986): 116–131.

Hazard, L. L. *The Frontier in American Literature.* Chicago: Cornwell, 1927.

Henley, Don, and Dave Marsh, eds. *Heaven Is Under Our Feet.* New York: Berkley, 1991.

Hicks, Philip Marshal. *The Development of the Natural History Essay in American Literature.* Philadelphia: University of Pennsylvania Press, 1924.

Hilbert, Betsy, ed. "The Literature of Nature," *CEA-Critic,* 54, no. 1 (Fall 1991): 1–3.

Hitt, Christopher. "Toward an Ecological Sublime," *New Literary History,* 30, no. 3 (Summer 1999): 603–623.

Hodder, Alan. *Emerson's Rhetoric of Revelation: Nature, the Reader, and the Apocalypse Within.* University Park: Pennsylvania State University Press, 1989.

Hodder. *Thoreau's Ecstatic Witness.* New Haven: Yale University Press, 2001.

Hoffman, Michael J. *The Subversive Vision: American Romanticism in Literature.* Port Washington, N.Y.: Kennikat Press, 1972.

Hogan, Linda, and Brenda Peterson, eds. *The Sweet Breathing of Plants: Women Writing on the Green World.* New York: North Point Press, 2001.

Howarth, William. "Ego or Eco Criticism? Looking for Common Ground," in *Reading the Earth: New Directions in the Study of Literature and Environment,* edited by Branch and others. Moscow: University of Idaho Press, 1998, pp. 3–8.

Howarth. "Imagined Territory: The Writing of Wetlands," *New Literary History,* 30, no. 3 (Summer 1999): 509–539.

Howarth. "Literature of Place, Environmental Writers," *Isle,* 1, no. 1 (Spring 1993): 167–178.

Howarth. "Thoreau and the Cultural Construction of Nature," *Isle,* 2, no. 1 (Spring 1994): 85–89.

Huth, Hans. *Nature and the American: Three Centuries of Changing Attitudes.* Berkeley: University of California Press, 1957.

Hyde, Anne Farrar. *An American Vision: Far Western Landscape and National Culture, 1820 1920.* New York: New York University Press, 1990.

Kastner, Joseph. *A Species of Eternity.* New York: Knopf, 1977.

Katz, Eric. *Nature as Subject: Human Obligation and Natural Community.* Lanham, Md.: Rowman & Littlefield, 1997.

Keith, W. J. *The Poetry of Nature: Rural Perspectives in Poetry from Wordsworth to the Present.* Toronto: University of Toronto Press, 1980.

Kerridge, Richard, and Neil Sammells, eds. *Writing the Environment: Ecocriticism and Literature.* London: Zed, 1998.

Killingworth, M. Jimmie, and Jacqueline S. Palmer. *Ecospeak: Rhetoric and Environmental Politics in America*. Carbondale: Southern Illinois University Press, 1992.

Kollin, Susan. *Nature's State: Imagining Alaska and the Last Frontier*. Chapel Hill: University of North Carolina Press, 2001.

Kolodny, Annette. *The Land before Her: Fantasy and Experience of the American Frontiers, 1630–1860*. Chapel Hill: University of North Carolina Press, 1984.

Kolodny. *The Lay of the Land: Metaphor as Experience and History in American Life and Letters*. Chapel Hill: University of North Carolina Press, 1975.

Kroeber, Karl. *Ecological Literary Criticism: Romantic Imagining and the Biology of Mind*. New York: Columbia University Press, 1994.

Krutch, Joseph Wood, ed. *Great American Nature Writing*. New York: Sloane, 1950.

Langbaum, Robert. "The New Nature Poetry," in his *The Modern Spirit: Essays on the Continuity of Nineteenth- and Twentieth-Century Literature*. New York: Oxford University Press, 1970.

Lewis, R. W. B. *The American Adam: Innocence, Tragedy, and Tradition in the Nineteenth Century*. Chicago: University of Chicago Press, 1955.

Love, Glen A. "Ecocriticism and Science: Toward Consilience?" *New Literary History*, 30, no. 3 (Summer 1999): 561–576.

Love. "Revaluing Nature: Toward an Ecological Criticism," *Western American Literature*, 25 (1990): 201–215.

Low, Anthony. *The Georgic Revolution*. Princeton, N.J.: Princeton University Press, 1985.

Luke, Timothy W. "On Environmentality: Geo-Power and Eco-Knowledge in the Discourses of Contemporary Environmentalism," *Cultural Critique*, 31 (Fall 1995): 57–81.

Lutwack, Leonard. *The Role of Place in Literature*. Syracuse: Syracuse University Press, 1984.

Lyon, Thomas J. *This Incomperable Lande: A Book of American Nature Writing*. Boston: Houghton Mifflin, 1989.

Malamud, Randy. *Reading Zoos: Representations of Animals and Captivity*. New York: New York University Press, 1998.

Marx, Leo. *The Machine in the Garden: Technology and the Pastoral Ideal in America*. New York: Oxford University Press, 1964.

Matthiessen, F. O. *American Renaissance: Art and Expression in the Age of Emerson and Whitman*. New York: Oxford University Press, 1941.

Mazel, David. *American Literary Environmentalism*. Athens: University of Georgia Press, 2000.

Mazel, ed. *A Century of Early Ecocriticism*. Athens: University of Georgia Press, 2001.

McKusick, James. *Green Writing: Romanticism and Ecology*. New York: St. Martin's Press, 2000.

Meeker, Joseph W. *The Comedy of Survival: Studies in Literary Ecology*. New York: Scribners, 1972.

Mendelson, Donna. "'Transparent Overlay Maps': Layers of Place Knowledge in Human Geography and Ecocriticism," *Interdisciplinary Literary Studies,* 1, no. 1 (Fall 1999): 81–96.

Merchant, Carolyn. *The Columbia Guide to American Environmental History.* New York: Columbia University Press, 2002.

Miller, Perry. *Nature's Nation.* Cambridge, Mass.: Harvard University Press, 1967.

Mumford, Lewis. *The Golden Day. A Study in American Experience and Culture.* New York: Boni & Liveright, 1926.

Murphy, Patrick D. *Farther Afield in the Study of Nature-Oriented Literature.* Charlottesville: University Press of Virginia, 2000.

Murphy. *Literature, Nature, and Other: Ecofeminist Critiques.* Albany: State University of New York Press, 1995.

Murphy, ed. *Literature of Nature: An International Sourcebook.* Chicago: Dearborn, 1998.

Naess, Arne. "The Shallow and the Deep, Long-Range Ecology Movement: A Summary," *Inquiry,* 16 (1973): 95–100.

Nash, Roderick. *The Rights of Nature: A History of Environmental Ethics.* Madison: University of Wisconsin Press, 1989.

Nash. *Wilderness and the American Mind.* New Haven, Conn.: Yale University Press, 1967.

Newman, Lance. "The Politics of Ecocriticism," *Review,* 20 (1998): 59–72.

Newton, L. H., and C. K. Dillingham. *Watersheds: Classic Cases in Environmental Ethics.* Belmont, Cal.: Wadsworth, 1994.

Norwood, Vera. *Made from This Earth: American Women and Nature.* Chapel Hill: University of North Carolina Press, 1993.

Novak, Barbara. *Nature and Culture: American Landscape and Painting, 1825–1875,* revised edition. New York: Oxford University Press, 1995.

Oelschlaeger, Max. *The Idea of Wilderness from Prehistory to the Age of Ecology.* New Haven, Conn.: Yale University Press, 1991.

O'Grady, John P. *Pilgrims to the Wild: Everett Ruess, Henry David Thoreau, John Muir, Clarence King, Mary Austin.* Salt Lake City: University of Utah Press, 1993.

Parrington, Vernon Lewis. *The Romantic Revolution in America, 1800–1860.* New York: Harcourt, Brace, 1927.

Pattee, Fred Lewis. *The First Century of American Literature, 1770–1870.* New York: Appleton-Century, 1935.

Paul, Sherman. *For the Love of the World: Essays on Nature Writers.* Iowa City: University of Iowa Press, 1992.

Payne, Daniel G. *Voices in the Wilderness: American Nature Writing and Environmental Politics.* Hanover, N.H.: University Press of New England, 1996.

Persons, Stow. *American Minds: A History of Ideas.* New York: Holt, 1958.

Phillips, Dana. "Ecocriticism, Literary Theory, and the Truth of Ecology," *New Literary History,* 30, no. 3 (Summer 1999): 577–602.

Pojman, Louis P., ed. *Environmental Ethics: Readings in Theory and Application,* second edition. Belmont, Cal.: Wadsworth, 1998.

Regis, Pamela. *Describing Early America: Bartram, Jefferson, Crevecoeur, and the Rhetoric of Natural History*. De Kalb: Northern Illinois University Press, 1992.

Richardson, Robert D. Jr. *Myth and Literature in the American Renaissance*. Bloomington: Indiana University Press, 1978.

Rosenthal, Bernard. *City of Nature: Journeys to Nature in the Age of American Romanticism*. Newark: University of Delaware Press, 1980.

Ross, Carolyn. *Writing Nature: An Ecological Reader for Writers*. New York: St. Martin's Press, 1995.

Ross-Bryant, Lynn. "The Self in Nature: Four American Autobiographies," *Soundings*, 80, no. 1 (Spring 1997): 83–104.

Ryden, Kent C. "Landscape with Figures: Nature, Folk Culture, and the Human Ecology of American Environmental Writing," *Isle*, 4, no. 1 (Spring 1997): 1–28.

Ryden. *Mapping the Invisible Landscape: Folklore, Writing, and the Sense of Place*. Iowa City: University of Iowa Press, 1993.

Schama, Simon. *Landscape and Memory*. New York: Knopf, 1995.

Schmitt, Peter J. *Back to Nature: The Arcadian Myth in Urban America*. New York: Oxford University Press, 1969.

Schweighauser, Charles A. "'Know Thyself' Study Nature: The Contemporary Scientist's Dilemma," in *The Delegated Intellect: Emersonian Essays on Literature, Science, and Art in Honor of Don Gifford*, edited by Donald E. Morse. New York: Peter Lang, 1995, pp. 109–124.

Schweninger, Lee. "Writing Nature: Silko and Native Americans as Nature Writers," *MELUS*, 18, no. 2 (1993): 47–60.

Sears, John F. *Sacred Places: American Tourist Attractions in the Nineteenth Century*. New York: Oxford University Press, 1989.

Serafin, Steven R., ed. *Encyclopedia of American Literature*. New York: Continuum, 1999.

Shepard, Paul. *Man in the Landscape: A Historic View of the Esthetics of Nature*. New York: Ballantine, 1967.

Shi, David. *The Simple Life: Plain Living and High Thinking in American Culture*. New York: Oxford University Press, 1985.

Sibum, Heinz O. "The Bookkeeper of Nature: Benjamin Franklin's Electrical Research and the Development of Experimental Natural Philosophy in the Eighteenth Century," in *Reappraising Benjamin Franklin: A Bicentennial Perspective*, edited by J. A. Leo Lemay. Newark: University of Delaware Press, 1993, pp. 221–242.

Slovic. "Nature Writing and Environmental Psychology: The Interiority of Outdoor Experience," in *The Ecocriticism Reader: Landmarks in Literary Ecology*, edited by Glotfelty and Harold Fromm. Athens: University of Georgia Press, 1996, pp. 351–370.

Slovic. *Seeking Awareness in American Nature Writing: Henry Thoreau, Annie Dillard, Edward Abbey, Wendell Berry, Barry Lopez*. Salt Lake City: University of Utah Press, 1992.

Slovic, ed. *Getting over the Color Green: Contemporary Environmental Literature of the Southwest*. Tucson: University of Arizona Press, 2001.

Smith, Henry Nash. *Virgin Land: The American West as Symbol and Myth*. New York: Vintage, 1957.

Smithline, Arnold. *Natural Religion in American Literature*. New Haven, Conn.: College and University Press, 1966.

Soule, Michael E., ed. *Reinventing Nature?: Responses to Postmodern Deconstruction.* Washington, D.C.: Island Press, 1995.

Spiller, Robert E. *The Cycle of American Literature.* New York: Macmillan, 1956.

Spiller, and others. *Literary History of the United States,* 2 volumes, fourth edition, revised. New York: Macmillan, 1974.

Spirn, Anne Whiston. *The Granite Garden: Urban Nature and Human Design.* New York: Basic Books, 1984.

Spirn. *The Language of Landscape.* New Haven, Conn.: Yale University Press, 1998.

St. Armand, Barton L. "The Book of Nature and American Nature Writing: Codex, Index, Contexts, Prospects," *Isle,* 4, no. 1 (Spring 1997): 29–42.

Stewart, Frank. *A Natural History of Nature Writing.* Washington, D.C.: Island Press for Shearwater Books, 1995.

Sweet, Timothy. *American Georgics: Economy and Environment in Early American Literature, 1580–1864.* Philadelphia: University of Pennsylvania Press, 2002.

Tallmadge, John, and Henry Harrington, eds. *Reading under the Sign of Nature: New Essays in Ecocriticism.* Salt Lake City: University of Utah Press, 2000.

Taplin, Kim. *Tongues in Trees: Studies in Literature and Ecology.* Bideford, U.K.: Green Books, 1996.

Teague, David W. *The Southwest in American Literature and Art: The Rise of a Desert Aesthetic.* Tucson: University of Arizona Press, 1997.

Thacker, Robert. *The Great Prairie Fact and Literary Imagination.* Albuquerque: University of New Mexico Press, 1989.

Tichi, Cecelia. *New World, New Earth: Environmental Reform in American Literature from the Puritans through Whitman.* New Haven, Conn.: Yale University Press, 1979.

Tidwell, Paul L. "Academic Campfire Stories: Thoreau, Ecocriticism, and the Fetishism of Nature," *Isle,* 2, no. 1 (Spring 1994): 53–64.

Tuan, Yi-fu. *Topophilia: A Study of Environmental Perception, Attitudes, and Values.* New York: Columbia University Press, 1990.

Tucker, Herbert F. "Ecocriticism," *New Literary History,* 30, no. 3 (Summer 1999).

Turner, Frederick. *Spirit of Place: The Making of an American Literary Landscape.* San Francisco: Sierra Club, 1989.

Ulman, H. Lewis. "Seeing, Believing, Being, and Acting: Ethics and Self-Representation in Ecocriticism and Nature Writing," in *Reading the Earth: New Directions in the Study of Literature and Environment,* edited by Branch and others. Moscow: University of Idaho Press, 1998, pp. 225–233.

Vogel, Steven. *Against Nature: The Concept of Nature in Critical Theory.* New York: State University of New York Press, 1996.

Wall, Derek, ed. *Green History: A Reader in Environmental Literature, Philosophy and Politics.* London & New York: Routledge, 1994.

Walls, Laura Dassow. *Seeing New Worlds: Henry David Thoreau and Nineteenth-Century Natural Science.* Madison: University of Wisconsin Press, 1995.

Wendell, Barrett. *A Literary History of America*. New York: Scribners, 1900.

West, Michael. *Transcendental Wordplay: America's Romantic Punsters & the Search for the Language of Nature*. Athens: Ohio University Press, 2000.

Westbrook, Perry D. *A Literary History of New England*. Bethlehem, Pa.: Lehigh University Press, 1988.

Westling, Louise H. *The Green Breast of the New World: Landscape, Gender, and American Fiction*. Athens: University of Georgia Press, 1998.

White, Morton. *Science and Sentiment in America*. New York: Oxford University Press, 1972.

Wilson, Alexander. *The Culture of Nature: North American Landscape from Disney to the Exxon Valdez*. New York: Between the Lines, 2001.

Wilson, David Schofield. *In the Presence of Nature*. Amherst: University of Massachusetts Press, 1978.

Wilson, Edward O. *Biophilia*. Cambridge, Mass.: Harvard University Press, 1986.

Wilson, Eric. *Romantic Turbulence: Chaos, Ecology, and American Space*. New York: St. Martin's Press, 2000.

Worster, Donald. *Nature's Economy: A History of Ecological Ideas*. Cambridge: Cambridge University Press, 1977.

Contributors

Brian Adler . . . . *Valdosta State University*

Ellen L. Arnold . . . .*East Carolina University*

Benay Blend . . . . *Albuquerque, New Mexico*

Kathleen A. Boardman . . . .*University of Nevada, Reno*

Marie Bongiovanni . . . .*Lebanon Valley College*

David Clippinger . . . .*Penn State University*

James J. Donahue . . . . *University of Connecticut*

Deborah Fleming . . . . *Ashland University*

Peter Friederici . . . . *Northern Arizona University*

Terry Gifford . . . . *University of Leeds, U.K.*

Melissa A. Goldthwaite . . . . *Saint Joseph's University*

George Hart . . . . *California State University, Long Beach*

Jen Hill . . . .*University of Nevada, Reno*

Jason G. Horn . . . . *Gordon College*

Richard Hunt . . . . *Kirkwood Community College*

Gary Kroll . . . . *Plattsburgh State University*

Robert Kuhlken . . . . *Central Washington University*

Mark C. Long . . . . *Keene State College*

Susan M. Lucas . . . .*University of Nevada, Reno*

Bryan L. Moore . . . .*Arkansas State University*

Paul N. Pavich . . . . *Fort Lewis College*

Daniel G. Payne . . . . *State University of New York at Oneonta*

Thomas Potter . . . .*Martinsville, Indiana*

Bernard Quetchenbach . . . .*Florida Southern College*

Clayton T. Russell . . . . *Northland College*

Roger Thompson . . . . *Virginia Military Institute*

Charlotte Zoe Walker . . . . *State University of New York, Oneonta*

Mary L. Warner . . . . *Western Carolina University*

James Perrin Warren . . . . *Washington and Lee University*

Ann Woodlief . . . .*Virginia Commonwealth University*

Shin Yamashiro . . . .*University of Nevada, Reno*

Cumulative Index

Dictionary of Literary Biography, Volumes 1-275
Dictionary of Literary Biography Yearbook, 1980-2001
Dictionary of Literary Biography Documentary Series, Volumes 1-19
Concise Dictionary of American Literary Biography, Volumes 1-7
Concise Dictionary of British Literary Biography, Volumes 1-8
Concise Dictionary of World Literary Biography, Volumes 1-4

Cumulative Index

DLB before number: *Dictionary of Literary Biography,* Volumes 1-275
Y before number: *Dictionary of Literary Biography Yearbook,* 1980-2001
DS before number: *Dictionary of Literary Biography Documentary Series,* Volumes 1-19
CDALB before number: *Concise Dictionary of American Literary Biography,* Volumes 1-7
CDBLB before number: *Concise Dictionary of British Literary Biography,* Volumes 1-8
CDWLB before number: *Concise Dictionary of World Literary Biography,* Volumes 1-4

Cumulative Index

DLB 275

Gildersleeve, Basil 1831-1924 . . . . DLB-71

Giles of Rome circa 1243-1316 . . . . DLB-115

Giles, Henry 1809-1882 . . . . DLB-64

Gilfillan, George 1813-1878 . . . . DLB-144

Gill, Eric 1882-1940 . . . . DLB-98

Gill, Sarah Prince 1728-1771 . . . . DLB-200

Gill, William F., Company DLB-49

Gillespie, A. Lincoln, Jr. 1895-1950 . . . . DLB-4

Gillespie, Haven 1883-1975 . . . . DLB-265

Gilliam, Florence ?-? DLB-4

Gilliatt, Penelope 1932-1993 . . . . DLB-14

Gillott, Jacky 1939-1980 . . . . DLB-14

Gilman, Caroline H. 1794-1888 . . . . DLB-3, 73

Gilman, Charlotte Perkins 1860-1935 . . . DLB-221

Gilman, W. and J. [publishing house] DLB-49

Gilmer, Elizabeth Meriwether 1861-1951 . . DLB-29

Gilmer, Francis Walker 1790-1826 . . . . DLB-37

Gilmore, Mary 1865-1962 . . . . DLB-260

Gilroy, Frank D. 1925- DLB-7

Gimferrer, Pere (Pedro) 1945- DLB-134

Gingrich, Arnold 1903-1976 . . . . DLB-137

Ginsberg, Allen
1926-1997 . . . . DLB-5, 16, 169, 237; CDALB-1

Ginzburg, Natalia 1916-1991 . . . . DLB-177

Ginzkey, Franz Karl 1871-1963 . . . . DLB-81

Gioia, Dana 1950- DLB-120

Giono, Jean 1895-1970 . . . . DLB-72

Giotti, Virgilio 1885-1957 . . . . DLB-114

Giovanni, Nikki 1943- . . . DLB-5, 41; CDALB-7

Gipson, Lawrence Henry 1880-1971 . . . . . DLB-17

Girard, Rodolphe 1879-1956 . . . . DLB-92

Giraudoux, Jean 1882-1944 . . . . DLB-65

Gissing, George 1857-1903 . . . . . DLB-18, 135, 184

The Place of Realism in Fiction (1895) DLB-18

Giudici, Giovanni 1924- DLB-128

Giuliani, Alfredo 1924- DLB-128

Glackens, William J. 1870-1938 . . . . DLB-188

Gladkov, Fedor Vasil'evich 1883-1958 . . . DLB-272

Gladstone, William Ewart
1809-1898 . . . . DLB-57, 184

Glaeser, Ernst 1902-1963 . . . . DLB-69

Glancy, Diane 1941- DLB-175

Glanvill, Joseph 1636-1680 . . . . DLB-252

Glanville, Brian 1931- DLB-15, 139

Glapthorne, Henry 1610-1643? DLB-58

Glasgow, Ellen 1873-1945 . . . . DLB-9, 12

Glasier, Katharine Bruce 1867-1950 . . . . . DLB-190

Glaspell, Susan 1876-1948 . . . . . . DLB-7, 9, 78, 228

Glass, Montague 1877-1934 . . . . DLB-11

Glassco, John 1909-1981 . . . . DLB-68

Glauser, Friedrich 1896-1938 . . . . DLB-56

F. Gleason's Publishing Hall DLB-49

Gleim, Johann Wilhelm Ludwig
1719-1803 . . . . DLB-97

Glendinning, Victoria 1937- DLB-155

The Cult of Biography
Excerpts from the Second Folio Debate:
"Biographies are generally a disease of
English Literature" Y-86

Glidden, Frederick Dilley (Luke Short)
1908-1975 . . . . DLB-256

Glinka, Fedor Nikolaevich 1786-1880 . . . . DLB-205

Glover, Keith 1966- DLB-249

Glover, Richard 1712-1785 . . . . DLB-95

Glück, Louise 1943- DLB-5

Glyn, Elinor 1864-1943 . . . . DLB-153

Gnedich, Nikolai Ivanovich 1784-1833 . . . DLB-205

Gobineau, Joseph-Arthur de
1816-1882 . . . . DLB-123

Godber, John 1956- DLB-233

Godbout, Jacques 1933- DLB-53

Goddard, Morrill 1865-1937 . . . . DLB-25

Goddard, William 1740-1817 . . . . DLB-43

Godden, Rumer 1907-1998 . . . . DLB-161

Godey, Louis A. 1804-1878 . . . . DLB-73

Godey and McMichael DLB-49

Godfrey, Dave 1938- DLB-60

Godfrey, Thomas 1736-1763 . . . . DLB-31

Godine, David R., Publisher DLB-46

Godkin, E. L. 1831-1902 . . . . DLB-79

Godolphin, Sidney 1610-1643 . . . . DLB-126

Godwin, Gail 1937- DLB-6, 234

Godwin, M. J., and Company DLB-154

Godwin, Mary Jane Clairmont
1766-1841 . . . . DLB-163

Godwin, Parke 1816-1904 . . . . . . DLB-3, 64, 250

Godwin, William 1756-1836 . . . . . . DLB-39, 104,
. . . . 142, 158, 163, 262; CDBLB-3

Preface to *St. Leon* (1799) DLB-39

Goering, Reinhard 1887-1936 . . . . DLB-118

Goes, Albrecht 1908- DLB-69

Goethe, Johann Wolfgang von
1749-1832 . . . . DLB-94; CDWLB-2

Goetz, Curt 1888-1960 . . . . DLB-124

Goffe, Thomas circa 1592-1629 . . . . DLB-58

Goffstein, M. B. 1940- DLB-61

Gogarty, Oliver St. John 1878-1957 . . . DLB-15, 19

Gogol, Nikolai Vasil'evich 1809-1852 . . . DLB-198

Goines, Donald 1937-1974 . . . . DLB-33

Gold, Herbert 1924- DLB-2; Y-81

Gold, Michael 1893-1967 . . . . DLB-9, 28

Goldbarth, Albert 1948- DLB-120

Goldberg, Dick 1947- DLB-7

Golden Cockerel Press DLB-112

Golding, Arthur 1536-1606 . . . . DLB-136

Golding, Louis 1895-1958 . . . . DLB-195

Golding, William 1911-1993
. . . . DLB-15, 100, 255; Y-83; CDBLB-7

Goldman, Emma 1869-1940 . . . . DLB-221

Goldman, William 1931- DLB-44

Goldring, Douglas 1887-1960 . . . . DLB-197

Goldsmith, Oliver 1730?-1774
. . . . DLB-39, 89, 104, 109, 142; CDBLB-2

Goldsmith, Oliver 1794-1861 . . . . DLB-99

Goldsmith Publishing Company DLB-46

Goldstein, Richard 1944- DLB-185

Gollancz, Sir Israel 1864-1930 . . . . DLB-201

Gollancz, Victor, Limited DLB-112

Gomberville, Marin LeRoy de
1600?-1674 . . . . DLB-268

Gombrowicz, Witold
1904-1969 . . . . DLB-215; CDWLB-4

Gómez-Quiñones, Juan 1942- DLB-122

Gomme, Laurence James
[publishing house] DLB-46

Goncharov, Ivan Aleksandrovich
1812-1891 . . . . DLB-238

Goncourt, Edmond de 1822-1896 . . . . . . DLB-123

Goncourt, Jules de 1830-1870 . . . . DLB-123

Gonzales, Rodolfo "Corky" 1928- DLB-122

González, Angel 1925- DLB-108

Gonzalez, Genaro 1949- DLB-122

Gonzalez, Ray 1952- DLB-122

Gonzales-Berry, Erlinda 1942- DLB-209

"Chicano Language" DLB-82

González de Mireles, Jovita
1899-1983 . . . . DLB-122

González-T., César A. 1931- DLB-82

Goodbye, Gutenberg? A Lecture at the
New York Public Library,
18 April 1995, by Donald Lamm Y-95

Goodis, David 1917-1967 . . . . DLB-226

Goodison, Lorna 1947- DLB-157

Goodman, Allegra 1967- DLB-244

Goodman, Paul 1911-1972 . . . . DLB-130, 246

The Goodman Theatre DLB-7

Goodrich, Frances 1891-1984 and
Hackett, Albert 1900-1995 . . . . DLB-26

Goodrich, Samuel Griswold
1793-1860 . . . . DLB-1, 42, 73, 243

Goodrich, S. G. [publishing house] DLB-49

Goodspeed, C. E., and Company DLB-49

Goodwin, Stephen 1943- Y-82

Googe, Barnabe 1540-1594 . . . . DLB-132

Gookin, Daniel 1612-1687 . . . . DLB-24

Goran, Lester 1928- DLB-244

Gordimer, Nadine 1923- DLB-225; Y-91

Gordon, Adam Lindsay 1833-1870 . . . . . DLB-230

Gordon, Caroline
1895-1981 . . . . DLB-4, 9, 102; DS-17; Y-81

Gordon, Charles F. (see OyamO)

Gordon, Giles 1940- DLB-14, 139, 207

Gordon, Helen Cameron, Lady Russell
1867-1949 . . . . DLB-195

Gordon, Lyndall 1941- DLB-155

Gordon, Mack 1904-1959 . . . . DLB-265

Gordon, Mary 1949- DLB-6; Y-81

Gordone, Charles 1925-1995 . . . . DLB-7

Gore, Catherine 1800-1861 . . . . DLB-116

K

M

ISBN 0-7876-6019-1

90000